D1134593

OXFORD–WARBURG STUDIES

General Editors

DENYS HAY *and* J. B. TRAPP

OXFORD–WARBURG STUDIES

———

JOSEPH SCALIGER

A Study in the History
of Classical Scholarship

ANTHONY GRAFTON

I

Textual Criticism
and Exegesis

CLARENDON PRESS · OXFORD
1983

Oxford University Press, Walton Street, Oxford OX2 6DP

London Glasgow New York Toronto
Delhi Bombay Calcutta Madras Karachi
Kuala Lumpur Singapore Hong Kong Tokyo
Nairobi Dar es Salaam Cape Town
Melbourne Auckland
and associated companies in
Beirut Berlin Ibadan Mexico City Nicosia

Oxford is a trade mark of Oxford University Press

Published in the United States by
Oxford University Press, New York

British Library Cataloguing in Publication Data
Grafton, Anthony
Joseph Scaliger: a study in the history of
classical scholarship. – (Oxford – Warburg studies)
1: Textual criticism and exegesis
1. Scaliger, Joseph   2. Classicists – Biography
I. Title
938'.0072024   PA85.R/
√ ISBN 0-19-814850-X

Library of Congress Cataloging in Publication Data
Grafton, Anthony.
Joseph Scaliger: a study in the history of
classical scholarship.
(Oxford – Warburg studies)
Includes bibliographical references and index.
Contents: 1. Textual criticism and exegesis.
1. Scaliger, Joseph Juste, 1540–1609.   2. Clas-
sicists – France – Biography.   3. Humanists – France
– Biography.   I. Title.   II. Series.
PA85.S3G7 1983   938'.0072024   82–14451
ISBN 0-19-814850-X

Set by Hope Services, Abingdon
Printed in Great Britain
at the University Press, Oxford
by Eric Buckley
Printer to the University

**To
My Parents**

Preface

This volume is the first half of an intellectual biography of Joseph Scaliger. In it I describe his early work as an editor of and commentator on classical texts. I set that work into the wider context of classical scholarship in his time. I also try to interpret the major changes that Scaliger's work underwent as responses to pressures exerted by his social situation and emotional life. This complex of purposes may help to explain my choice of documents for analysis and topics for discussion. In order to reconstruct the origins and development of Scaliger's editions, I have given much space to those of his working materials — notes, collations, *libri annotati*, and the like — that survive. In order to evaluate his techniques and results critically, but without lapsing into unhistorical severity or uncritical historicism, I have spent as much space as possible on contemporary and near-contemporary reactions to his work — above all on the perceptive and witty marginalia with which Isaac Casaubon adorned his copies of several of Scaliger's editions. In order to read Scaliger's works historically, I have spent a very large amount of space on those of his predecessors and contemporaries, seeking to locate the precedents on which he drew and to identify the really novel elements of his own work. And in order to re-create, so far as is relevant, the flavour of his daily life and the character of the circles to which he belonged, I have quoted often from his and others' letters and from his matchless table-talk, the *Scaligerana*.

The nature of my subject-matter, which falls in a no-man's land between classics and history, has also affected the book. To make it accessible to historians I have identified some texts and people that will be familiar to any classicist; to make it accessible to classicists I have included a variety of facts that will be equally familiar to historians. I hope that specialists will be willing to skip over those passages that are clearly not to their address.

To make room for what seemed these essential kinds of material, I have had to omit others. I have provided only a limited sample of the material that could be assembled to re-create the vicissitudes of Scaliger's life, properties, and friendships; to include it *in toto* would have been to overwhelm my real topic. I have provided no bibliography of Scaliger's works, since one is readily available in the classical biography of him by Bernays. And I have provided no bibliography of secondary literature, since the works cited in the notes are so diverse that a list of them would serve no purpose, and good introductions to the historiography of scholarship are available elsewhere.[1] I will, on the other hand, provide a list of all manuscripts and *libri annotati* discussed here in the second volume of this work. And I hope that, in general, the gains derived from my decisions outweigh the losses.

Two further points need to be made. The first is minor. In spelling the proper names of the people mentioned here, I have followed the illustrious precedent set by Mark Pattison, and inconsistently used both vernacular and Latin forms, choosing whichever seemed most familiar to the largest number of readers. I hope that this practice will not offend too many readers, and that most will agree with me that it is the most convenient way to deal with a difficult problem.

The second is more important. I wish to stress that my treatments of Scaliger's predecessors in Chapters I to III make no claim to completeness or finality. Professor Perosa and his pupils are now revolutionizing our knowledge of Poliziano; L. Cesarini Martinelli promises to do the same for Vettori; and several scholars in both France and England are giving new form and definition to the great but misty figure of Dorat. My chapters are based on independent reading of the sources, and I have tried to take account of the secondary literature as well.[2] But I offer them merely as the backdrop necessary if I am to portray Scaliger himself in the round.

In eight years of work on Scaliger I have run up many debts. I can repay none of them, of course; but it is a pleasure to acknowledge them here.

Several agencies and universities gave generous financial support. Grants from the United States — United Kingdom Educational Commission and the Danforth Foundation enabled me to begin work in England and the Netherlands during 1973 to 1974. Grants from the History Department of Cornell University made possible the purchase of essential photocopies and microfilms during 1974 to 1975. A grant from the Princeton University Committee on Research in the Humanities and Social Sciences and a supplement to it from the American Philosophical Society supported a summer's exploration of manuscript collections in 1976. A term's leave from Princeton and a Grant-in-Aid from the American Council of Learned Societies allowed me to spend most of 1977 completing my research in England and on the Continent. Two final grants from the Princeton Committee on Research paid for the preparation of the final typescript and helped to defray the cost of publication.

A great many American and European librarians permitted me to explore the treasures in their custody, provided me with microfilms and photocopies, and called my attention to important documents which I should otherwise have missed. It was an exceptional case when I entered one library, on my second day of work there, to find every printed book or manuscript in the collection that had any bearing on Scaliger already piled up before my chair. But in general I cannot praise highly enough the sympathy, energy, and competence with which my too frequent requests were answered. In America I have had generous help from the Regenstein Library of the University of Chicago, the Olin Library of Cornell University, the Firestone Library of Princeton University, the Central Branch of the New York Public Library, the Folger Shakespeare Library, and the Walters Art Gallery. In Europe I have had help from the Amsterdam University Library; the Bayerische Staatsbibliothek, Munich; the Biblioteca Ambrosiana, Milan; the Bibliothèque de l'Institut, Paris; the Bibliothèque Royale Albert I, Brussels; the Bodleian Library, Oxford; the Burgerbibliothek, Bern; the Cambridge University Library; Eton College Library; and the libraries of the University of London and of University College London. But I am grateful above all to four libraries and their staffs: the Bibliothèque Nationale, Paris, where much of the colour and lively detail that I have been able to deploy was found lurking in the manuscripts of the Collection Dupuy and the *libri annotati* of the Réserve des Imprimés; the Leiden University Library, where Scaliger's private papers and the largest single collection of his own books were made available in the most pleasant of working conditions; the Warburg Institute of the University of London, where I found the ideal working collection of primary and secondary sources, open stacks, and generous help of every kind; and, last and above all, the British Library. This book is a report on years of swimming across small corners of the vast oceans of early printed books housed there. No thanks I can offer would come close to repaying the endless courtesy and efficiency of the British Library's staff.

The *Journal of the Warburg and Courtauld Institutes* gave me an ideal forum for early statements of some findings. A first version of Chapter VI appeared in volume xxxviii (1975), one of Chapter I in volume xl (1977). I am grateful to the editors for permission to reprint my articles here in amended form; to G. Pigman for correcting an error in the second one; and to G. Pete and D. Coppini, whose sympathetic reviews of the same article helped me greatly in revising it.

Teachers and colleagues of extraordinary learning and generosity formed me in my craft. I am grateful to Hanna Gray for her advice and encouragement at a very early stage; to Letizia Panizza, Sarah Hutton, D. P. Walker, and J. J. John for advice on a number of points of detail; to P. Tuynman and his staff at the Instituut voor Neofilologie en voor Neolatijn, Amsterdam, especially F. F. Blok, for much invaluable information; to M. D. Reeve for bringing several crucial documents and problems to my attention; to S. Timpanaro for the example of his work and the stimulus of his criticism; to C. B. Schmitt and Jill Kraye for their constant help and working companionship in London, and to Hans Aarsleff, Glenn Most, David Quint, and J. E. G. Zetzel for theirs in Princeton; to Father K. Jorgensen, S. J., who humanely helped to check the final typescript of a book about an inveterate enemy of his order. I am indebted beyond hope of redemption to Eric Cochrane, most conscientious of supervisors, who expended superhuman efforts in trying to clarify my naturally muddy prose; to J. B. Trapp, most patient of editors, who offered that perfect combination of encouragement, criticism, and forbearance that all authors hope for and hardly any find; and to A. D. Momigliano, who welcomed me as his pupil in London and has ever since lavished advice, help, and criticism upon me with his accustomed learning and generosity. Above all, I stand indebted to the three scholars on whose counsel I have leaned for eight years as heavily as Hope on her anchor. Carlotta Dionisotti took time from an overloaded schedule to introduce me to the history of classical scholarship in the Renaissance, and has annotated every draft of this book with meticulous care and miraculous speed. Henk Jan de Jonge welcomed me to his *patria* and his home in Leiden, checked my transcripts of documents, confirmed and challenged my interpretations of Scaliger's work — and gave me at all times a living example of that high philology that I had thought dead with Scaliger himself. Noel Swerdlow first suggested Scaliger as a dissertation topic and has patiently argued with me over every stage by which the dissertation grew into a book. To their criticism this book owes what solid contents it possesses; to their friendship I owe much of the pleasure that my research has brought me.

Finally I owe a vast debt to Joseph Scaliger himself. He has given me years of frustration and amusement, led me to dozens of texts and problems which I would not otherwise have explored, and offered me a tortuous but fascinating path into the complex, cluttered mental world of the sixteenth century.

Parturiunt montes — these words spring irresistibly to mind as I consider the greatness of what I have received and the littleness of what I have given in return. I could wish that this book were worthier of its subject and my teachers; but I could not have had a better subject or better help in pursuing it. And that is a great blessing in itself.

Princeton,
New Jersey
31 October 1982

---

1.   For an extensive list of materials about or relevant to Scaliger, see A. Grafton and H. J. de Jonge, *Joseph Scaliger. A Bibliography 1852-1982* (The Hague, 1982).

2.   The present book was completed in draft in 1979 and substantially revised in early 1981. I have only been able to take systematic account of work that reached Princeton by June 1981.

Contents

Abbreviations

I. Works by Scaliger

Autobiography   *Autobiography of Joseph Scaliger with Autobiographical Selections from his Letters, his Testament and the Funeral Orations by Daniel Heinsius and Dominicus Baudius*, tr. G.W. Robinson (Cambridge, Mass., 1927)

Epistolae   J. J. Scaliger, *Epistolae omnes quae reperiri potuerunt, nunc primum collectae ac editae*, ed. D. Heinsius (Leiden, 1627)

Lettres françaises   J. J. Scaliger, *Lettres françaises inédites*, ed. P. Tamizey de Larroque (Paris and Agen, 1879)

Scaligerana I   *Prima Scaligerana*, in *Scaligerana, Thuana, Perroniana, Pithoeana, et Colomesiana*, ed. P. Desmaizeaux, II (Amsterdam, 1740)

Scaligerana II   *Secunda Scaligerana*, ibid.

II. Secondary Works and Journals

AIV   *Atti dell'Istituto Veneto di Scienze, Lettere ed Arti*, Classe di scienze morali, lettere [ed arti]

Bernays, *Scaliger*   J. Bernays, *Joseph Justus Scaliger* (Berlin, 1855)

BHR   *Bibliothèque d'humanisme et Renaissance*

BIHBR   *Bulletin de l'Institut Historique belge de Rome*

CTC   *Catalogus translationum et commentariorum* (Washington, D.C., 1960–)

DSB   *Dictionary of Scientific Biography* (New York, 1970–80)

IMU   *Italia Medioevale e Umanistica*

JWCI   *Journal of the Warburg and Courtauld Institutes*

Rec. Soc. Agen   *Recueil des travaux de la Société d'agriculture, sciences, et arts d'Agen*

RhM   *Rheinisches Museum für Philologie*

Marginal glosses at the ends of block quotations indicate that the original texts are in the Appendices, pp. 342–52 below.

Introduction

It is not easy to meet the great scholars of the later sixteenth century on terms of intimacy. The grave and enigmatic faces that stare out from the pages of Meursius's *Athenae Batavae* and de Bry's *Icones Virorum Doctorum* inspire respect rather than affection. And the immense Latin books that their owners spent their lives in writing are more likely to inspire horror than respect. These swollen and prodigious volumes, running to hundreds of pages and studded with interminable quotations in Greek and Hebrew, were around 1600 the staple of Europe's intellectual life. The best publishers in Paris and Frankfurt competed to print them.[1] Their authors were the arbiters of European culture. Such men dominated the universities of the Protestant North and served rulers as different as Philip II of Spain and Maurice of Nassau. It is hard to imagine a culture more alien to that of the later twentieth century. How is the cultural historian to bridge the gap?

The path of least resistance and most advantage seems to be that recommended by Professor Gombrich: to concentrate on a dominant and innovative individual.[2] In the case of the later sixteenth century, the identity of the most remarkable scholar is not in doubt. Even in that age of polymaths, Joseph Scaliger stood out for the breadth and depth of his learning and the extravagant originality of his thought. The church-historian of Counter-Reformation Rome, Cesare Baronio, could hardly have been farther removed in space, culture, or loyalties from the Protestant philologist Isaac Casaubon, who wrote a devastating critique of his work. Yet the two of them agreed that Scaliger was the greatest scholar of their time.

Scaliger is appropriate for another reason as well. Alone among the scholars of the period, he has been studied with care by someone far better qualified to understand his world than any modern scholar could hope to be.[3] Jacob Bernays wrote Scaliger's biography in 1855; it will never be replaced.

Bernays could follow and evaluate Scaliger's work in both Semitic and classical philology, for he was the son and pupil of a great rabbi, Chacham Isaak Bernays, and the disciple of a great philologist, Friedrich Ritschl. Moreover, he had the orthodox Jew's interest in the history of scholarly debate, and by applying his rabbinical habit of mind to secular philology, he gained an unrivalled knowledge of the European context of Scaliger's thought. He read Scaliger with an enviable eye for biographical and psychological detail. He established the canon of Scaliger's works — many of them scattered in ephemeral publications — so well that almost nothing can be added to his information. And he clothed his findings in an eloquent and emotional prose that makes his *Joseph Justus Scaliger* a minor classic of nineteenth-century German literature.

But Bernays's biography was not completely successful, for he had more in mind than an objective account of Scaliger's life and work. In Scaliger he found not only a great scholar but a personal master, the first man to apply a single philological method to both classical and Near Eastern sources. Moreover, he had the German Jew's traditional distrust for the culture of Southern Europe, and this prejudice led him to underestimate the work of Scaliger's French and Italian contemporaries. His combination of biases resulted in a general thesis that the evidence does not support: namely, that Scaliger single-handedly changed the traditional, amateurish humanistic method of classical studies into a professional philology like that of nineteenth-century Germany. At best, Scaliger's contemporaries had given him materials to work upon; at worst, they had blindly opposed his methods. Bernays criticized Scaliger only for knowing less Hebrew than a well-educated orthodox Jew, and Scaliger himself had conceded that point. Brilliant though it is, then, Bernays's Scaliger — as its most intelligent critic, Moritz Haupt, pointed out — is panegyric as well as history.[4]

Scaliger worked for the most part in two well-established fields of study: classical philology and historical chronology. In each he drew heavily on the works of predecessors and rivals. In each, his innovations consisted less in the invention of wholly new methods — though he was inventive — than in the combination of methods that had normally been employed separately and in the enrichment of one discipline with ideas and approaches drawn from others. His intellectual biography, then, is less a story of creation from scratch than one of creative adaptation.

But the fact that Scaliger's work was not entirely original does not make him less interesting. Indeed, in some ways it makes him an even more appropriate centre for an investigation into the classical culture of his time. The reason for this lies in the nature of his personal ambition. One element in Bernays's portrait was clearly accurate. Scaliger did set out to establish new standards of inference and argument in his two special studies. Scaliger himself stated this ambition more than once, and his contemporaries also saw it as his aim. For instance, Gian Vincenzo Pinelli of Padua, a well-informed and independent man, remarked that Scaliger had set out to become 'the universal Critic' — *Aristarco di tutti.*[5] And he begged his correspondents in Paris, Claude Dupuy and Jacopo Corbinelli, to obtain for him a statement of Scaliger's views on the nature of philology and the duties of the critic.[6]

What Bernays did not take into account, however, is equally important. Both classical philology and historical chronology became disciplines during the sixteenth century. In one sense, to be sure, both fields had existed since ancient times. *Emendatio* and *enarratio* of texts had been the job of the teacher of grammar, the basic arts subject, since Alexandrian times.[7] Chronology, also invented by Alexandrians, had been especially cultivated by the Fathers of the Church, both as a tool for instructing converts and as a polemical device for refuting the insinuations of pagans about the novelty of Judaism and Christianity.[8] But neither field had been a discipline in itself. Neither was practised by a well-defined body of men who were paid chiefly for doing so. Neither possessed a well-developed technical vocabulary. Neither operated in terms of a clearly defined notion of intellectual property — that is, in neither was it established practice for the creator of an innovation in method to be praised and rewarded for having done so.[9] In neither did practitioners agree about the goals they were pursuing. Most important, in neither was there any clear notion of what constituted proper method in the analysis of ancient sources.

Between 1450 and 1600 this situation changed. The revival of classical education made the correction and interpretation of literary texts a more urgent task than it had been for a millennium. Humanists began to argue that the art of correcting and explicating texts must become a university discipline, as solidly established and as well paid as the rest.[10] And as the humanists won their point about university posts, controversies began to spring up about the aims and nature of these studies. How did one know which words in a text were corrupt and needed correction? How could one decide which points ought to be explained or discussed?

In chronology, related conditions gave rise to similar results. The Reformation and the controversies it entailed made many technical points of Jewish and early Christian history into matters of immediate interest to a wide public. At the same time, the discovery of the New World and renewed contact with the East presented intellectuals with unprecedented problems. They had to reconcile authoritative accounts of man's history with new facts that these could not accommodate. Chronology too became a university discipline, in both Protestant and Catholic universities.

Growing interest and institutional support did not produce straightforward progress in these two fields. In both, innovations in method were devised that proved to be of permanent value, once the smoke and noise had died down. But these innovations succeeded or failed for reasons that had more to do with the national and religious allegiances of their authors than with their intrinsic merits. Italians' bright ideas found little response among French Huguenots, and vice versa. Some of the most solid innovations found almost no acceptance. In both studies, schools grew up, the members of which regarded one another's work with automatic antipathy — even when, as sometimes happened, they shared interests or assumptions.

When Scaliger took positions about the methods of these studies, then, he was taking part in widespread and heated public debates. Rather than weaving the seamless cloth of new method that Bernays described, he looked over the whole tapestry of competing contemporary schools, cut out the sections that attracted him, and stitched them up in new combinations. And it is just this fact that endows his work with its broadest historical interest. In so far as each of his mature works is a response to one or more schools within a discipline and, often, to other disciplines as well, it can only be understood in the light of the work of those schools. By setting Scaliger's works in context, we shall be able to retrace not only the contours of his intellectual development but the wider lines of allegiance among his contemporaries and predecessors. To this extent, Scaliger's works are very literally a key to the classical culture of his time.

The organization of this biography is intended to take advantage of these facts. The present volume deals with Scaliger's work in textual criticism and exegesis, which occupied most of his attention for the first half of his career. It begins with three chapters on the condition of the field from 1450 to 1560, reconstructs his early life and education, and follows the changes that his methods and interests underwent. A second volume will deal with his work on chronology, which became his speciality during the second half of his career. It too will begin with chapters on the state of the art and then set the history of Scaliger's work into that wider context. The two parts of the biography, then, will tell three stories: that of Scaliger's life and those of the studies that he practised. Scaliger himself unifies them; for it will become clear that his technical innovations in widely diverse fields of scholarship were intimately connected with his emotional life.

One problem must still be dealt with. Probably no one would take serious exception to the objectives I have stated here. But the method that I have employed in carrying them out may seem to need defence. For this book does not deal, for the most part, with ideas about the nature of classical studies or general programmes for their advancement. The states of the two arts studied here and Scaliger's contributions to them are established by a series of detailed case-studies in the activities of scholars: how they interpreted specific ancient sources, how they argued on behalf of their interpretations. In short, the book proceeds by reconstructing a series of episodes, each of which involved technical solutions for technical scholarly problems.

In Germany or Italy, there would be no need to defend this method. The history of scholarship is there accepted as a normal field of historical inquiry and practised by eminent intellectual historians. But in England and the United States, both historians and classicists tend to regard such studies as exercises in antiquarianism. Old scholarship is for them dead scholarship; to rake up the embers of dead philological controversies seems to them tedious and unprofitable. After all, the technicalities of classical studies are not now of much concern to many people, or even to many intellectuals. The history of classical studies is *a fortiori* even less interesting.

It is not my purpose to investigate the deeper reasons for this situation, or to inquire why what is done at the École Pratique des Hautes Études is studied avidly by so many who pay no attention at all to the Scuola Normale Superiore di Pisa. But it is necessary to point out that the widely-held notions that I have outlined are both unexamined and misleading. In fact, neither Scaliger nor his world is comprehensible except in terms of the sort of episode studied here.

In the first place, Scaliger himself had little life outside the life of his mind, and the life of his mind was spent on the details of his work. He had little aptitude for or interest in generalizations. An accurate intellectual biography of Scaliger must be the story of what he thought about technical problems.

But there is more to it than that. The debates on philological and chronological method that Scaliger took part in can be understood only by studying a great many individual episodes. For the classical scholars and chronologists of the sixteenth century had one great problem when it came to argument about first principles: they could not, for the most part, talk about method in general terms. There was no tradition of general debate about method in either study; there was no literary genre in which it could be cast and no vocabulary in which it could be framed.

In so far as there was a natural place for discussing method, it was the prefatory letter or letters with which most Renaissance books begin. But the preface was inadequate, for two reasons at least. First, prefaces — even the more technical prefaces *ad lectorem* — were letters, and therefore governed by the rhetorical conventions of the art of letter-writing. These forbade too much discussion of technical problems as boring and inelegant. Humanists who discussed points of method in prefaces generally apologized for doing so and made their statements as brief as possible; often they simply did not raise such points. Second, prefaces were usually intended as advertisements for the author; hence they tended to omit any reference to those predecessors to whom he was most indebted. As a result, prefaces often mislead the student who wishes to establish the background and aims of a philological work. These two conditions do not always prevent prefaces from being revealing, as we shall see. But because of them, no history that relies on prefaces alone can possibly be adequate.[11]

For more general discussions than prefaces allowed, there were no precedents of any use. When Scaliger himself tried to define the duties of the critic, the only ancient theorist he could find to draw upon was the sceptical philosopher Sextus Empiricus, who had tried to show that the grammarians of his time had no criterion for telling truth from falsehood in interpreting texts, and that their art was accordingly devoid of any foundation. This was not terribly helpful. All that Scaliger could use from Sextus' work was a very general description of the branches of the art of grammar. Hence he never managed to define in a systematic and detailed way the methods and presuppositions of a good critic.[12] Renaissance treatises on philological method were far less penetrating and systematic than contemporary works on method in philosophy, law, or the physical sciences. And that is why histories that rely solely on general statements about the arts of criticism or chronology are also inherently inadequate.[13]

If scholars did not argue well in general terms, they none the less held and used sophisticated principles. But these must often be inferred from their practice and, more often, the practices they attacked. Moreover, even their attacks on others cannot always be understood immediately. Renaissance critics shared with their audiences a literary education that had made all of them responsive to verbal detail and retentive in memory to a degree that now seems inconceivable. They also shared assumptions about the nature of effective argument, assumptions drawn from the tradition of rhetoric rather than that of strict philosophy. They could attack an opponent's method by subtler and less substantial means than would now be possible: sometimes by attacking the opponent's character, sometimes by omitting a reference to an opponent in a place where praise might be expected, sometimes by attacking the opponent's master or friends. Even a phrase that now seems perfectly innocuous could be an insult. Even the choice of a literary genre or a title could amount to a programmatic statement. The debates were real enough; now and then the issues flicker into glaring light for a few sentences of an unusually frank preface. But for the most part, the lines of battle — and even the armies to which combatants belonged — can be reconstructed only by an archaeological approach. One must sink many shafts through the rubble of sixteenth-century technical literature to locate the few firm strata where personal allegiance and joint intellectual aims combined to produce schools.[14]

It is precisely in this regard that the study of highly controverted episodes can be of help. For taking a position on a technical point about which earlier scholars had fallen out was one of the most forceful ways of declaring one's intellectual allegiance. Certain technical problems can serve as litmus-paper

I Angelo Poliziano and the Reorientation of Philology

A book about the history of classical scholarship is in some measure a study of solutions to puzzles posed by texts. It may appropriately begin with a puzzle posed by certain modern texts. Historians of Renaissance culture, especially in America, have traditionally argued that Lorenzo Valla was the founder of professional classical scholarship. Valla, they maintain, was the first humanist to break away from the methods traditionally employed in the correction and interpretation of texts by teachers of grammar and rhetoric. He devised a historical approach to the study of language, literary texts, and political and religious institutions. Building on this monumental foundation, he created methods of textual and historical criticism which his successors had only to refine and apply, without changing them in any fundamental way. And it was to him above all that the great scholars of sixteenth-century France, Germany, and the Low Countries looked back as to a model and a guide.[1]

The puzzle here is simple. Most sixteenth-century scholars do not refer frequently to Valla's work as a classical scholar. Erasmus owed Valla a special debt. He had learned from Valla both the methodical approach to Latin prose style and the philological approach to the New Testament that led to some of his most original and influential works. Yet Erasmus did not regard Valla as the model for his own work on pagan texts. For exemplary work in philology he looked back not to Valla's Italy but to that of the generation just before his own: the Italy of Angelo Poliziano, Ermolao Barbaro, and the elder Filippo Beroaldo. Erasmus arrived in Italy too late to know these men, as he regretted until he died.[2] But he knew their works intimately, and he imitated them in trying to master and integrate into Latin culture the whole range of classical Greek sources. They had set the standards by which his own work and that of his contemporaries must be judged. When he wished to compliment Budé, Erasmus said that he had surpassed Barbaro and Poliziano; when he wished to praise the young Ulrich Zasius and, later still, the young Boniface Amerbach, it was to Poliziano that he compared them.[3] And if he used Poliziano's *Miscellanea* as an example of the sort of work that was written to win fame through eloquence, and so lacked the simplicity that Erasmus's work on the New Testament required, it was from the *Miscellanea* that he took the motto for his famous seal, with all its range of moral and religious resonance: TERMINVS CONCEDO NVLLI.[4]

The humanists of the generations after Erasmus's were even more inclined to see Poliziano's work as crucially important. He, not Valla, was the earliest humanist whose prose style and philological acumen were still taken seriously at the end of the sixteenth century. When Justus Lipsius recommended models for imitation in writing letters, Poliziano was the only modern whom he mentioned.[5] And Julius Caesar Scaliger said of Poliziano that he had been the first 'who dared to raise his nose in the air on behalf of good letters'.[6] Why is there so striking a contradiction between the views of modern scholars and those of the men they set out to discuss?

It is not hard to see why modern scholars have lavished such praise on Valla. His moral and intellectual independence make him a vastly attractive figure in general. His interest in the nature and development of language fits neatly into the preoccupations of many contemporary intellectuals, especially in the English-speaking world. And his brilliantly successful exploits in the higher criticism — above all, his exposés of the Donation of Constantine and the *corpus Dionysiacum* — have won him a matchless notoriety. Poliziano and his contemporaries are far less attractive. Less engaged than Valla in the great theological and moral controversies of their time, they concentrated on the most difficult and recherché classical texts and published their results in a frighteningly austere and technical form, at least from the standpoint of most twentieth-century readers. It is not surprising, then, that they have sometimes been dismissed as merely competent practitioners of a craft that Valla had invented.[7] These judgements are misguided. Valla's excellent moral and intellectual qualities are not *per se* sufficient grounds to consider him the first professional philologist. And a thorough study of the context within which Valla worked, as well as of the technical methods of Poliziano and their context, will serve to show that in the field of classical philology Valla was not so important historically as has often been believed.

To be sure, Valla was a very original philologist, as is not surprising in the one fifteenth-century humanist with a first-class mind. His extraordinary knowledge of Latin usage and Roman history made him an unrivalled critic of the text of Livy; for the books of the third decade, preserved in very corrupt form by the manuscripts, he devised a very large number of conjectural emendations that still appear in the texts of modern editions.[8] More important, he knew how to recreate the history of a text methodically as well as to divine individual corrections. Silvia Rizzo has shown how thoroughly Valla understood the causes of scribal error.[9] Alessandro Perosa has shown that in the last years of his life, when he was preparing the second recension of his notes on the New Testament, Valla had grasped all the complexity of the textual history of the New Testament and had realized the necessity of collating manuscripts in full and reporting their readings with precision.[10] Yet Valla founded no school. Few followers applied these insights to classical texts; the works in which Valla displayed them most clearly were at first unread. Even if he was, in a sense, the first professional philologist, he did not make philology into a profession. For in the environment in which he worked, the correction and explication of classical texts were not central activities in intellectual life. Both practical and cultural factors prevented Valla's purely philological work from attaining wide diffusion or exercising immediate effects.

The humanists of the period 1400–1460 wished above all to revive classical Latin culture.[11] In pursuit of this goal they hunted down, corrected, and copied manuscripts of previously little-known texts. They translated Greek works that filled gaps in the Latin culture of their time — above all, works of history, geography, and moral philosophy. They wrote their own treatises on grammar, usage, and style, ranging in size and originality from Guarino's various brief textbooks to Valla's *Elegantiae* and Tortelli's *De orthographia*, in which independent learning and acute criticism were combined to produce grammatical works more sophisticated and comprehensive than those the ancients themselves had compiled.[12] They applied the factual and stylistic knowledge they had acquired in writing letters, dialogues, polemical pamphlets, and histories of their cities, and even of all Italy.

The emendation and interpretation of particular texts naturally held a relatively minor place in this panoply of interests. Commentaries were written, but for the most part only on texts that could be used in teaching rhetoric: Cicero's speeches on the one hand, the manuals of Quintilian and the *auctor ad Herennium* on the other.[13] The commentators aimed to produce not independent works of scholarship but simple guides to the texts; they were interested not in technical problems of exegesis but in showing their students how to grasp the rhetorical structure that an author had employed. And, like most arts teachers throughout history, they did not make any pretence of originality. Where possible, they borrowed the matter and even the words of their comments directly from ancient and twelfth-century commentaries on the same texts. So long as exegesis was carried on for strictly pedagogical ends, it could not be affected by Valla's methodological insights.

When the early humanists addressed themselves to specific scholarly problems, they did so in a social context highly charged with personal and intellectual rivalry. The humanists tended to emend their texts in semi-public sessions — the circles that met in both Florence and Naples during the 1430s and 1440s to discuss critical problems in Livy are famous. Membership of these groups was a path to fame and patronage. But these were won less by solidity of results than by eloquent delivery and facility in argument. And in any case, such gatherings did not confine their discussions to questions of fact or interpretation. In 1450, for example, Valla and George of Trebizond held a day-long disputation about a remarkable topic, which had much exercised Livy: had Alexander the Great chanced to have a battle with the Romans, who would have won?[14] In this context, the emendation and interpretation of texts were not independent activities. They formed part of the humanist's arsenal of techniques for public disputation. Philology was very literally the handmaiden of rhetoric, and it served not so much to promote the advancement of knowledge as to discredit particular humanists in the eyes of a circumscribed audience of patrons and other humanists. It is no accident that Valla's *Emendationes* were published as one part of a much larger polemical work against his detractors.[15]

Even when the humanists got down to the discussion of a specific passage, it was inevitable that conjectural emendation would attract much of their energy. The elegant restoration of sense to corrupt passages was the field where talent and intellect could make themselves most apparent. Mere explication of difficulties or collation of manuscripts could never create so strong an impression of effortless ingenuity. This was the field where Valla first distinguished himself among his contemporaries; and as we have seen, he did work of lasting value in it. But Valla's concentration on conjectural emendation limited the range and influence of his achievement. Conjectural emendation is a matter of talent.[16] It can be practised with great success by scholars who have neither a strong intellect nor a historical understanding of the texts they correct, so long as they have a good knowledge of the language and a knack for solving puzzles. Knacks, however, cannot be explained or taught. They obviously cannot become the basis for professional training and practice. And in any case, conjectural emendation can solve only a limited number of textual problems. Brilliant though they were, Valla's Livian conjectures were a purely personal achievement. There was no generally applicable method that underlay them and that could be passed on to disciples or grasped by readers.

Purely technical factors limited the influence of Valla's work even more. On the one hand, the range of materials available to Valla and his contemporaries was necessarily narrow, given the difficulties of travel and the instability of libraries. Only a lucky chance gave Valla access to Petrarch's codex of Livy. In his day, the great public libraries did not yet exist. Extensive collation of manuscripts was wildly difficult. Moreover, in a world of manuscripts, the role of collation was at best problematic. There was no uniform base text against which collations could be made. And even when a manuscript had been collated against an older one, there was no way to publish the variants except by having them copied, and so introducing fresh errors and confusions into the text.[17]

On the other hand, the conditions of publication also served to inhibit the diffusion of new ideas or methods. In 1446 to 1447 Valla put Panormita and Fazio to shame before Alfonso of Naples by demolishing the corrections they had rashly entered in decade III of the Codex Regius of Livy. But in 1448 he left Naples for Rome, and his adversaries simply removed the third decade from the manuscript and substituted a new one whose text did not contain the corrections Valla had shown to be unsound.[18] In an age of manuscripts there could be no proof of what had happened, and readers had no way of knowing on whose side truth stood. Indeed, Valla's own emendations in the Harleian Livy were lost to sight until modern editors of Livy began to examine them. And even his *Emendationes*, highly polemical and intended for publication, did not find readers in Valla's time, but only 'at the height of the Cinquecento, because they were then printed . . . ' — in short, when a new generation, schooled by others in philological method, was ready to greet in Valla a forerunner — but not a master.[19]

After the middle of the century, however, three momentous changes took place in the context and character of humanism. In the first place, humanistically-educated princes and prelates began to assemble manuscripts into more or less accessible collections — above all, the new library of the Vatican and the Medicean public library of San Marco in Florence. Most classical manuscripts did not find secure homes at once: the Medicean Virgil and the Codex Bembinus of Terence led remarkably active lives of travel until far into the sixteenth century. Moreover, even the richest collections did not always attract scholarly attention. But in Florence and Rome at least, rich and relatively stable lodes of material now offered themselves up to the spade of anyone lucky enough to be given permission to dig them.[20]

In the second place, the invention of printing made possible a new level of precision in textual scholarship. Perhaps the texts that appeared in the *editiones principes* of Giovanni Andrea de Bussi and others were corrupt. Certainly they had the misfortune of being reproduced uncritically, and so turned into a permanent vulgate with an unjustified air of authority.[21] But at least there were now some hundreds of copies of any work that happened to be printed. Humanists all over Italy could now have access to generally uniform copies of most classical texts, and, within a few years, of commentaries on many of them as well. Falsification became harder, though by no means impossible. More important, a rudimentary standardization of references became possible. A printed text provided a standard for collation: and a collation in the margins of one printed book could be transferred to those of another with relative speed and accuracy. Above all, the very existence of standardized texts ensured that the same critical problems would attract the attention of humanists all over Italy at the same time. Far more humanists than could have crowded into one of Alfonso's *ore del libro* could now engage in collective debate on specific technical points.

Most important of all, a change had taken place in the direction of many humanists' scholarly work.[22] Thanks to the heroic work of the early humanists, one could now master Latin grammar and rhetoric with relatively little expense of time and effort — often after only a few years in a grammar school or university arts course. And as these studies lost their challenge, they also lost something of the absorbing interest that they had held for the pioneers of humanist education.

At the same time, a new generation of humanists appeared. The new men were born in the 1430s and 1440s. Domizio Calderini, Giulio Pomponio Leto, Giorgio Merula, Niccolò Perotti, Giovanni Sulpizio, and their like formed the crest of the mid-century *nouvelle vague*. Like other groups of impatient young intellectuals — like Poggio Bracciolini and Niccolò Niccoli fifty years before — they assimilated what their elders had to offer and thereafter took it for granted. Simple prose texts interested them less than Latin poetry — especially the works of the satirists, studded as they were with allusions and obscurities. When they studied prose at all, they preferred the elder Pliny's *Natural History*, as difficult as the verse of the satirists and more rewarding to the student. Unlike their predecessors, they came to maturity in a world in which such recondite interests could be pursued with ease. They grew up accustomed to the existence of humanist schools and arts faculties, in which they expected to find jobs as lecturers. They were also accustomed to the existence of the printing-press, and expected to serve the printers, not without remuneration, as editors of texts. Their students could be expected to attain a high level of linguistic proficiency quite soon. Given this situation, it is not surprising that the line-by-line commentary soon became the dominant form of humanist literature — the form by which reputations were lost and won. For it was by writing and publishing commentaries that the men of the new generation could best demonstrate their independence from the work of their immediate predecessors, while at the same time winning their colleagues' attention and serving the needs of their students, who shared their interest in poetry and Pliny.

Considered as a literary form, the detailed commentary had a number of advantages. In the first place, it was itself the revival of an ancient genre. There were many ancient or old line-by-line commentaries on standard authors: Servius on Virgil, Donatus on Terence, Porphyrio and Pseudo-Acro on Horace, the old scholia on Juvenal and Persius, the twelfth-century commentaries on Cicero. These works provided the starting-point for the earliest humanist commentaries on the works they dealt with; often the humanists did little more than repeat what their ancient predecessors had said, merely taking care to conceal the extent of their indebtedness. The first humanist commentary on Virgil, that by Pomponio Leto, relied very heavily on an interpolated text of Servius; Gaspare de' Tirimbocchi, the first humanist commentator on the *Ibis*, relied equally heavily on the extant scholia.[23] Where there was no ancient or pseudo-ancient commentary, there was sometimes a later one of similar form and method — for example, the twelfth-century commentary by 'Alanus' on the *ad Herennium*, which Guarino sedulously pillaged for his lectures.[24] Moreover, even for those commenting on texts that were not adorned with ancient scholia, the ancient commentaries provided an obvious model for style and method, one that was both readily accessible and at the same time satisfactorily different from the style of the late medieval classicizing friars.[25]

This style had other advantages as well. Line-by-line commentaries inevitably bulk as large as or larger than the texts they deal with. The commentator, in other words, was expected to fill a large amount of space. His audience expected him to turn any suitable word or phrase into the occasion for an extended digression: into the etymology of a word, into the formation of compounds from it, into its shades of meaning; most often, perhaps, into the justification in terms of formal rhetoric for its appearance in the passage in question. Many digressions departed even farther from the text, into mythological, geographical, antiquarian, and even scientific matters. A commentary on almost any ancient author could thus become an introduction to classical literature, history, and culture. In short, the commentary was a highly flexible instrument of instruction. Here too the humanists were following their ancient models. Servius, in particular, used the medium of a commentary on Virgil to impart quantities of information on almost every conceivable subject.[26]

Finally, this style was attractive to students. Since the commentator felt obliged to gloss every word that might present a difficulty, he generally made his text accessible even to students of mean intelligence or poor preparation. At the same time, the student who could write quickly enough to keep up with his teacher ended up with an invaluable possession. When he himself went out to teach, he could simply base his lectures on those of his teacher and so avoid the trouble of independent preparation. It is hardly surprising that students came to demand lectures of this kind; what student would not have his teacher do all the work? As M. Filetico, an unwilling practitioner of this style of commentary, wrote: 'At that time [*c.* 1468–73] certain very learned men had made the young accustomed not to want to listen to anything unless they added a definition on almost every word. . . . I therefore had to follow their customs.'[27] The style was long-lived. Poliziano himself employed various forms of it in his lectures, adapting the content of the excursuses to the needs of his hearers.[28] Its most preposterous result did not appear until 1489 — namely, Perotti's *Cornucopiae*, in which a thousand folio columns served to elucidate one book of Martial.

But the style had disadvantages as well as advantages. It forced the commentator to deal with every problem, the boringly simple as well as the interestingly complex. It also forced him to waste time and pages on the donkey-work of listing synonyms — which is all that thousands of the humanists' short glosses amount to.[29] Worst of all, in a period of intense literary competition the commentary made it impossible for its author to shine. For the most noticeable aspect of all the humanists' commentaries is their similarity to one another. Especially in their printed form, the so-called 'modus modernus', the commentaries are nearly indistinguishable. Waves of notes printed in minute type break on all sides of a small island of text set in large roman.[30] Even numerous digressions into one's field of expertise could not make one commentary distinctively superior to its fellows, for they were hidden by the mass of trivial glosses.

In the mid-1470s several humanists became aware of the drawbacks of the exhaustive commentary and began to move away from it. In 1475, for example, Domizio Calderini wrote: 'hereafter, I shall not be much concerned with commentaries'. Rather, he explained, he would concentrate on translation from the Greek and on another work,

which we have entitled 'Observations', in three books, of which the first contains explications of three hundred passages from Pliny; the second whatever we have noted as omitted by others in [explicating] the poets; the third what we have gathered and observed in Cicero, Quintilian, Livy, and all other prose writers.[31]

The pattern that Calderini sketched became the normal one. Instead of continuing to work through every detail of entire texts, he and others began to produce selective treatments of what they described as difficult and interesting passages — books, in short, written by and for scholars; books composed with publication in mind rather than by-products of teaching. Most of these works took one of two forms. The majority of them consisted of brief sets of annotations on one text. Calderini published an 'Explication of certain particularly difficult passages in Propertius'; Filippo Beroaldo brought out a short collection of 'Annotations against Servius'; more than half a dozen others wrote short treatises on selected passages in Pliny.[32] Others were miscellanies of short chapters, modelled above all on the *Noctes Atticae* of Aulus Gellius. Such works represented an effort to break away entirely from the commentary, tied as it was to a single text. Calderini himself published one, in the shape of a few selections 'ex tertio libro Observationum'; Beroaldo's first major piece of work was his more or less miscellaneous *Annotationes centum*.

It would be wrong to draw too sharp a distinction between the two new sorts of publication. Calderini's *Observationes* were less a methodological departure than an advertisement for himself, in which he quoted from his own commentaries at length and with relish.[33] And even though Beroaldo's preface contained a modish apology for the selective and disorderly character of his *Annotationes*, the work itself was little more than a collection of short treatises, each dealing with several passages in a text; author followed author in a most logical and orderly succession.[34] Even though the genres were not very clearly defined, the works that fell within them bore unmistakable marks of family resemblance. They were short, specialized, and polemical. Many of them were written by humanists at the very beginnings of their careers. And like other manifestoes by intellectuals, before and since, they were intended above all to win reputations for their authors as rapidly as possible — generally at the expense of the reputations of others.

Beroaldo, for example, began his literary career with his *Annotationes contra Servium*. Here he set out, not weighed down as yet by any great baggage of learning, to win a reputation by the simple expedient of abusing the best ancient commentator on Virgil. Some of his points were well worth making. His knowledge of Latin usage, already solid and independent, enabled him to prove that some of the fine lexical distinctions Servius laid down were not supported by the practices of Latin writers.[35] By drawing on Greek historians and geographers, especially Strabo, he was able to correct Servius on a fair number of miscellaneous points of fact.[36] But much of what Beroaldo had to say was neither original nor enlightening. Often, following Macrobius, he rebuked Servius for failing to recognize Virgil's allusions to esoteric philosophical doctrines: Servius should have known that Virgil was an expert in all forms of *remotior doctrina*. And he could have drawn the material for such explications from the same philosophical sources on which Macrobius had drawn. The duty of a good commentator was to include as many interpretations as possible of the work with which he was concerned; this Servius had failed to do.[37] It is hard to feel much sympathy for a man who criticizes Servius for being too concise. Yet Beroaldo's tactics had a certain logic. By showing where Servius had gone wrong, he could prove that he himself understood perfectly the duties of the commentator. But he could do so without burying the pearls of his — and Macrobius' — cleverness in the mudbank of a full-scale commentary.

Others, less discreet than Beroaldo, aimed their guns at the vulnerable living rather than the honoured dead. Giorgio Merula had won his reputation in the 1470s by attacking Domizio Calderini and Francesco Filelfo. In 1481 to 1482 he himself received a vicious broadside from Cornelio Vitelli, who set himself to avenge both Calderini and Martial for Merula's mistreatment of them. He accused Merula of committing wholesale plagiarism, corrupting the texts he set out to correct, and killing Filelfo by his vicious mistreatment of him. Merula, he quipped — and the joke is no unfair indicator of the intellectual qualities of such debates — should really have been named Merdula. And Vitelli was in turn answered by a student of Merula, as well as by Ermolao Barbaro, whose refusal to discuss Vitelli's objections to Merula was in itself an imposing rebuttal.[38] Often these critics were competing for the support of a limited number of local patrons, which made their quarrels hot and frequent.

At first reading, these works reveal few virtues to accompany their obvious vices. Their repugnant moral defects compete with their amateurish scholarship for the reader's disapproval. If their literary form is new, the philological methods employed in them are often old indeed. For their authors were still, for the most part, employed as teachers, and their monographs bear the stamp of their profession. Their methods were formed not in the study but in the lecture-hall. They never acquired the habit of full or precise quotation from their sources, for such precision was impossible to attain if they were to lecture comprehensively on the wide variety of topics that their texts suggested. In particular, they seldom quoted Greek extensively, as Greek would have been unintelligible to most of their students and unmanageable for most printers. Instead, they usually provided vague paraphrases, together with imprecise indications of sources. Worse still, like their ancient exemplars, they often invented explanations by back-formation from the texts they claimed to be elucidating: 'misinformation is often elicited from the text by aid of unjustified inferences.'[39]

When the members of this generation turned from the commentary to the collection of precise *Annotationes*, they did abandon one bad habit which had characterized their lectures. They no longer set out two alternative solutions of a given problem without choosing between them — a maddening habit which had characterized the classroom lecture since the Hellenistic period.[40] Indeed, the whole point of their new genre was to show off their ability at solving problems once and for all. Unfortunately, they did not abandon their other habits of sloppy, inaccurate citation and unjustified back-formation. Perotti, who tried to be honest, abbreviated the names of the authors he cited even when the resulting forms were ambiguous — for example, 'Lu.'. Moreover, he usually failed to inform his readers whether the verses he cited came to him at first or second hand, though often he was citing not a line from an extant work but a fragment preserved by Festus or Nonius Marcellus, and sometimes he was citing verses from standard works at second hand.[41] Calderini, as Dunston and Timpanaro have shown, knew Plautus only at second hand, though his words suggest first-hand knowledge.[42] Many of Perotti's contemporaries were dishonest as well as sloppy. Pomponio Leto gave out in his lectures that he had a complete text of Ennius. Calderini falsified his notes on Martial to refute a justified attack by Perotti. Worse, he invented a Roman writer, Marius Rusticus, from whom he claimed to derive disquieting information about the youth of Suetonius.[43]

It would be wrong to dismiss these works as unimportant. Their authors were unscrupulous, but by no means ignorant; and they often found that providing some of the new interpretations or information that they promised was an effective polemical tactic. Beroaldo's suggestions, though less methodically worked out than Poliziano's, were often highly plausible. Others also arrived at novel and valid results. Thus, when Merula decided to rebut Calderini's criticisms of his commentary on Ovid's *Epistula* XV of the *Heroides*, *Sappho Phaoni*, he did not confine himself to arguing that some of Calderini's interpretations were as implausible as they were clever. He also used recondite information to show that Ovid had modelled the Latin style of his poem on the Greek style of Sappho, who is represented as the speaker in the poem. At 39–40 Sappho says:

> Si nisi quae facie poterit te digna videri
> > Nulla futura tua est: nulla futura tua est
> ('If save for her whose face is quite divine
> > No woman shall be thine, no woman shall be thine').

The identical clauses of line 40 were not among Ovid's normal stylistic devices. Merula showed why he had repeated himself:

I shall add a point here drawn from the most recherché Greek learning. Ovid used that repetition not so much for emphasis as because by repeating the same words he could represent Sappho's style. According to Demetrius of Phalerum, she tried to make her poems graceful by *anadiplosis* [reduplication]. For in his treatment of the method of attaining grace, he wrote that 'The graces of speech which are produced by figures are obvious and frequent in Sappho: for example, *anadiplosis*, where the bride says to her maidenhood:
παρθενία παρθενία ποῖ μὲ λιποῦσα οἴχῃ
('Maidenhood, maidenhood, where are you going as you leave me?')
And her maidenhood answers her with the same figure:
οὐκέτι ἥξω πρὸς σέ, οὐκέτι ἥξω
('I shall not come again to thee; I shall not come.')' (*On Style* §140).[44]

Here and in other cases the gladiators of these paper contests made observations that modern scholars still consider valid, or at least take seriously.

In a more general sense, too, these treatises represented something new and vital: they were the first technical philological treatises since Antiquity. Here was a literary genre that made it possible for the humanists to engage in and publish the results of minute research. The existence of this literature proved a vital precondition for the rise of something like a profession of classical philologists. Like the scholarly journals of more recent times, it provided a convenient and inexpensive forum for widespread, technical debates about problems of both fact and method. Only two things were lacking: a literary form entirely divorced from dependence on specific texts and a set of standards by which the value of individual theses could be assessed. In 1489, Poliziano's *Miscellanea* provided both.

Poliziano was following some well-trodden paths. Like all his contemporaries, he was bent on making a reputation. Like them, he went about this self-imposed task above all by directing fierce polemics against his predecessors. Merula, Calderini, and other representatives of what he called *semidocta sedulitas*, he hammered without mercy. His disdain for competitors in scholarship was equalled in fervour only by his tail-wagging eagerness to praise his patron, Lorenzo de' Medici. These similarities, though important, are less striking than the differences. In scope, method, and results, the *Miscellanea* was a brilliantly original work, which fully deserved to exert widespread influence.

In the first place, the *Miscellanea* provided a novel and extremely versatile form for presenting philological material. Unlike his predecessors, Poliziano set out deliberately to imitate one ancient work, the *Noctes Atticae* of Gellius.[45] This work had several features which no humanist had so far thought to resurrect. It was entirely miscellaneous in character; by imitating it, Poliziano was able to break completely with the commentary tradition while still following a good ancient model. Moreover, it was laid out in an elegant and useful fashion. Each chapter was set off from the others and provided with a summary title; and a list of all the chapters occurred at the beginning of the work. Strange as it may seem, Poliziano's predecessors knew but failed to imitate these practices. By doing so, Poliziano made his work much easier to consult; and his creative imitation of Gellius soon found its own imitators among humanists, as the form he had re-created became the normal one.

Second, and more important, Poliziano took over from Gellius and greatly elaborated a new set of rules for judging his own and others' attempts to correct and explicate texts. He placed a new emphasis on the quality and quantity of his sources. From the preface onwards he attacked his predecessors' methods and treated his own as exemplary. He took great pains to state that he had cited only genuine works by genuine ancient authors.

But lest those men who are ill employed with leisure think that we have drawn [our conclusions] . . . from the dregs, and that we have not leapt across the boundaries of the grammarians, we have at the outset followed Pliny's example. We have put at the beginning the names of the authors — but only ancient and honourable ones — by whom these [conclusions] are justified, and from whom we have borrowed. But [we have not put down] the names of those whom others have only cited, while their works have disappeared, but those whose treasures we ourselves have handled, through whose writings we have wandered.[46]

Poliziano was hardly the first to claim that his researches had brought to light fascinating new material long hidden in rare sources. Calderini, for example, had this to say of his commentary on the *Ibis*: 'Ovid's work is full of anger and obscurity. As for me, I have gathered into the present short work, either from the Greeks Apollodorus, Lycophron, Pausanias, Strabo, Apollonius and his scholiast, and other writers, or from the Latins, whatever seemed relevant to its explication.' Poliziano turned Calderini's boasts into an indictment:

Domizio expounded Ovid's *Ibis*. He began by saying that he wrote matter drawn from Apollodorus, Lycophron, Pausanias, Strabo, Apollonius, and other Greeks, and Latins as well. In that commentary he invents many vain and ridiculous things, and makes them up extemporaneously and at his own convenience. By doing so he proves either that he has completely lost his mind, or that, as someone says, there was so great a distance between his mind and his tongue that his mind could not restrain his tongue.[47]

He backed up this tirade by dissecting Calderini's work on one line. Calderini had taken *Ibis* 569 as reading

Utque loquax in equo est elisus guttur Agenor

('And as the talkative Agenor was strangled in the horse').

'As the result of a fall from a horse', he explained, 'Agenor's hand became stuck in his mouth and he perished.'[48] This explanation, Poliziano insisted, was Calderini's own invention. In fact, the line must be emended to read

Utque loquax in equo est elisus guttur acerno

('And as the talkative one was strangled in the maple-wood horse').

Citing passages from true sources, Homer and Tryphiodorus, Poliziano explained the line as an allusion to the death of Anticlus, one of the Greeks who had entered Troy in the Trojan horse, whom Odysseus had strangled to prevent him from revealing their presence prematurely.[49] The moral of the episode was clear.

As one would expect, given the polemical tendencies we have seen in action, there was nothing new in accusing one's predecessors of inventing sources. Calderini had done the same. In his commentary on Quintilian, Valla had referred to an oration of Cicero *Pro Scauro*. 'Indeed', wrote Calderini:

I have read in Valerius Maximus and Pedianus that the case of Scaurus was tried in Cicero's presence. But I have never read that Cicero delivered the oration on his behalf from which Lorenzo claims that he drew these words. Nor do I believe that it exists. And I am afraid that Lorenzo recited these words following some ignoble grammarian, rather than having read them anywhere in Cicero.[50]

So much Poliziano might have said. The difference lies in two things: in the truthfulness of the attacks, and even more in their consistency with the attacker's actual practices. Calderini's attack was not in fact justified, for Valla had taken his quotation from the *Pro Scauro* from a fairly reliable source: Isidore's *Etymologiae*. Moreover, the commentary of Asconius Pedianus — which Calderini himself cited — clearly indicates that Cicero delivered a speech *Pro Scauro*. More important, Calderini's attack on Valla was inconsistent with his own practice. In the very next section of the *Observationes* he enthusiastically retailed what he had read about Simonides 'in a Greek writer' — 'apud Graecum scriptorem'.[51] One whose own references were so slipshod had no business correcting other people's footnotes — and can hardly have been upholding a personal ideal of full, clear, and accurate citation.

Poliziano normally used the principles by which he judged others. He identified the sources he drew on with elaborate, almost finicking precision. Even when he quoted a text at second hand, he generally pointed out that he was doing so and identified the intermediary source. In I.91, for example, he quoted some verses of the comic poet Eupolis, and wrote: 'We did not draw these verses of the poet Eupolis from the original source, since his works have been lost. We derived them partly from a remarkably accurate commentator on the rhetor Aristides, partly from a letter of the younger Pliny.'[52] Poliziano's attacks on the practices of his predecessors, then, were traditional only in form. They stemmed not only from a desire to gain a reputation and to destroy those of others, but also from a genuine desire to reform the current method of citation.

Poliziano's habits in drawing inferences from sources were as novel as his precision in identifying them. He compared and evaluated them in a consistently historical way — that is, by establishing their relationships to one another before he drew inferences from them. His sources presented him with various kinds of problem, some of which were fairly trivial. For example, he not uncommonly encountered ancient sources that contradicted one another about historical or mythological details. The solution in such cases was usually obvious. It was only natural to follow the most authoritative source, in most cases also the oldest. That was just what he did when, for example, he preferred Homer's testimony about the ages of Achilles and Patroclus to those of Aeschylus and Statius.[53]

So far there is nothing new here. Petrarch had encountered contradictions in his ancient sources while compiling his *De viris illustribus*. Salutati and Bruni had uncovered discrepancies in the ancient histories of republican Rome. Flavio Biondo had found ancient authors contradicting one another about the functions of certain ancient buildings.[54] All had found it possible to resolve such contradictions, by assuming that the more authoritative source, or the one which was itself based on more authoritative sources, was correct. The divergent accounts in other texts must have resulted either from scribal errors, in which case they could be emended, or from simple slips on the part of the less authoritative writer, due to bias or bad memory.[55]

Poliziano saw that even a group of sources that agreed posed a further problem. Given three sources A, B, and C, all of which agreed on a given point; if B and C depended entirely on A for their information, should they be considered to add any weight to A's testimony? Poliziano insisted that they should not. In other words, even a group of concordant sources must be investigated, and those which were entirely derived from others must be identified and eliminated from consideration. Such an investigation was best carried out by arranging the sources genealogically, and then paying attention only to the source from which the others were derived.

Poliziano stated this principle in *Miscellanea* I. 39, while explaining a riddle. In *Epistola* XIV.74 Ausonius had employed the expression 'Cadmi nigellas filias' — 'little black daughters of Cadmus'. Poliziano explained that it referred to the letters of the alphabet: 'For Cadmus was the first to bring letters into Greece from Phoenicia'.[56] Since the Latin letters were directly derived from the Greek, Ausonius could refer to them too as 'daughters of Cadmus'. Poliziano cited Herodotus as his authority for stating that Cadmus had imported the alphabet. He admitted that other ancient writers had said the same. But he argued that all of them were simply repeating what Herodotus had said. Since their testimony was entirely derivative, it must be ignored:

I omit Pliny and very many others, who say that Cadmus brought them into Greece. For since these different men recalled indiscriminately what they had read in Herodotus, I think it enough to have restored these matters to his authority. For in my opinion the testimonies of the ancients should not so much be counted up, as weighed.[57]

It is easy to show how original Poliziano's thinking is here. Beroaldo discussed the same riddle from Ausonius in *cap.* 99 of the *Annotationes*. He solved it in the same way, also citing his sources:

He [Ausonius] calls the letters 'daughters of Cadmus' because Cadmus is said to have been the inventor of letters. In Book vii of the *Natural History* Pliny says that he brought sixteen letters from Phoenicia into Greece. Therefore the ancient Greeks called the letters Phoenician, according to Herodotus in Book v. The same writer says that he saw 'Cadmean letters', very similar to Ionian letters, incised on certain tripods in the temple of Apollo. Furthermore, Cornelius Tacitus avers that Cadmus was the author of letters, while the Greek peoples were still uncultured.[58]

Beroaldo does not investigate the dependence or independence of his sources. Pliny is evidently as reliable as Herodotus, and Herodotus no more reliable than Tacitus. Since all agree on the main point in question, he cites them all. Other accounts he omits, not because they are derivative but because they seem to him irrelevant.

What Poliziano has done is to view the problem of the reliability of sources from a new direction. For him, the object is no longer, as it was for Beroaldo, simply to amass evidence, but to discriminate, to reduce the number of witnesses that the scholar need take into account. We know now that Poliziano's argument was not completely sound. Herodotus was not the sole source for later traditions about the origins of the Greek alphabet, and even so late a writer as Tacitus may preserve useful information not transmitted by older sources. In some sense, then, Beroaldo was 'correct' to draw eclectically on a wide range of texts. But this is one of the many cases in the history of scholarship in which it is deceptive to pay too much attention to the validity in modern terms of particular arguments. If Beroaldo was 'correct', it was for the wrong reasons. He cited Tacitus not because he had grounds for doing so but because he knew no better. Poliziano, on the other hand, was attacking the evidence with a novel tool. Given the texts available to him, he had no reason not to conclude that Herodotus was the sole source on whom later writers had drawn. Considered in its context, Poliziano's over-zealous application of a new and valid method is far more important historically than the 'correct' results on which Beroaldo blundered. In Poliziano's hands, systematic source-criticism led to a transformation in the central methods of classical philology.[59]

Poliziano's best-known application of his principles was in textual criticism.[60] Here too he strove to arrive at the independent sources from which later ones were wholly derived. When he found what seemed to him to be corruptions in recent manuscripts or printed versions of classical writings, he did not try to emend them by conjecture. He went back to the oldest sources — that is, to the oldest manuscripts. He recognized that they were not free from errors. But he insisted that they were the closest extant approximation to what the ancient authors had really written. The newer texts — notably the printed ones — were removed from antiquity by more stages of copying, and any apparently correct readings they contained were merely the result of conjectural emendation. Such alluring but historically unjustifiable readings offered the textual critic less of value than did the errors of the old manuscripts, for they at least 'preserve some fairly clear traces of the true reading which we must restore. Dishonest scribes have expunged these completely from the new texts'.[61]

Poliziano employed this method throughout the *Miscellanea*. In the vulgate text of Virgil, for example, he found *Aeneid* VIII. 402 in a metrically impossible form: 'Quod fieri ferro, liquidove potestur electro'. He consulted the Codex Romanus, and, as he wrote: 'in that volume, which is in the inner library of the Vatican, which is remarkably old, and written in capitals, you will find not 'potestur' but 'potest', a word more commonly used.'[62] Again, in the vulgate text of Suetonius he was troubled by a meaningless clause in *Claudius* 34: 'si aut ornatum, aut pegma, vel quid tale aliud parum cessisset'. In what he called the 'veri integrique codices', however, he found not 'aut ornatum' but 'automaton', a reading which made perfect sense: Claudius made his stage carpenters fight in the arena 'if a stage machine, or trap, or something else of the sort failed to work'. Poliziano took care to identify the codices on whose testimony he relied:

Look at the Bologna manuscript from the library of St Dominic, or another at Florence from the library of St Mark . . . ; both are old. But there is another older than either, which we ourselves now have at home . . . you will find this latter reading in all of them.[63]

To get a clear impression of the number and accuracy of Poliziano's citations of manuscripts, there is no better way than to read the collection of material in Silvia Rizzo, *Il lessico filologico degli umanisti.*[64]

This new method could not have been more in contrast with the practices of Poliziano's predecessors. Beroaldo, for example, relied almost exclusively on conjecture. Even when he cited manuscripts he identified them only in vague terms.[65] Here, for example, is how he gives the manuscript readings of a line in Juvenal:

The verse is to be read as follows:
   Turgida nec prodest condita pyxide Lyde
[*Sat.* II. 141]. There 'condita' is in the ablative and is connected with 'pyxide.' Quite recently I found that verse written thus in a very old manuscript. And some time ago Angelo Poliziano . . . told me that he had noted the passage written that way in a manuscript of unimpeachable trustworthiness.[66]

Here is how Poliziano described the latter manuscript:

We found the same reading [*cacoethes* (*Sat.* VII. 52)] in an old manuscript written in Lombardic script, which Francesco Gaddi . . . made available to me for study. But that [other] verse is also as follows in this codex:
   Turgida nec prodest condita pyxide Lyde.[67]

Poliziano's description includes the name of the manuscript's owner and a classification of its script. Beroaldo's citation — which is, if anything, unusually precise for him — gives neither.

The old manuscripts were usually more trustworthy than the new merely because they were older, and therefore fewer stages of transmission intervened between them and the author. Poliziano was able to analyse some textual traditions in a more complex and more decisive way. He applied his genealogical method of source-criticism to the manuscripts of certain texts and proved that one of them was the parent of the rest. In such cases, he argued, the parent must be the sole source used in establishing the text.

One case, as Timpanaro has shown, was that of Cicero's *Familiares.*[68] Poliziano had at his disposal in the library of St Mark the ninth-century Vercelli manuscript (Laur. 49,9 = M) and a fourteenth-century manuscript which he wrongly believed might have been written by Petrarch (Laur. 49,7 = P). He also consulted an unspecified number of more recent texts. In *Miscellanea* I.25 he argued that the fourteenth-century manuscript, in which a gathering had been transposed because of an error in binding, was the parent of all the more recent manuscripts, since the same transposition occurred in all of them, without any evidence of physical damage to account for it. He also asserted, without giving the evidence, that the fourteenth-century manuscript was itself a copy of the ninth-century one. He concluded that since the ninth-century manuscript was the source of all the others, it alone should be employed in correcting the text of the *Familiares*. As he wrote:

I have obtained a very old volume of Cicero's *Epistolae Familiares* . . . and another one copied from it, as some think, by the hand of Francesco Petrarca. There is much evidence, which I shall now omit, that the one is copied from the other. But the latter manuscript . . . was bound in such a way by a careless bookbinder that we can see from the numbers [of the gatherings] that one gathering has clearly been transposed. Now the book is in the public library of the Medici family. From this one, then, so far as I can tell, are derived all the extant manuscripts of these letters, as if from a spring and fountainhead. And all of them have the text in that ridiculous and confused order which I must now put into proper form and, as it were, restore.[69]

A second case was that of Justinian's *Digest* or *Pandects*. Here Poliziano used a different method to identify one manuscript as the parent of the rest. He received permission through his patron, Lorenzo, to collate the famous Florentine manuscript of the *Digest*. Certain erasures and additions in the preface, he thought, must have been made 'by an author, and one thinking, and composing, rather than by a scribe and copyist'.[70] He inferred from these signs that this must be the very manuscript which Justinian's commissioners first wrote. If the Florentine manuscript was the author's copy, it must be the archetype. Consequently, all texts of the *Digest* ought to be emended in accordance with the text of the Florentine manuscript. In *Miscellanea* I.41, for example, he replaced the vulgate reading 'diffusum' with 'diffisum', the reading of the Florentine manuscript, in *D*. II. xi. 2(3): 'Et ideo etiam lex xii. tabularum, si iudex vel alteruter ex litigatoribus morbo sontico impediatur, iubet diem iudicii esse diffisum'. The passage thus made perfect sense: the Law of the Twelve Tables orders that, if the judge or either of the litigants is prevented by illness from attending court, the day of the trial is to be 'postponed' (*diffisum*).[71] Again, in I.78 Poliziano examined the reading of the Florentine manuscript at *D*. I. xvi. 12: 'Legatus

mandata sibi iurisdictione iudicis dandi ius habet' — 'A deputy
on whom jurisdiction has been conferred has the right to appoint
judges' (tr. S. P. Scott). Here some of the vulgate manuscripts read
'ius non habet.' Both readings could be supported by parallels
from other parts of the *Corpus iuris*, and Accursius had discussed
both readings and the juristic problems each of them posed.[72]
For Poliziano, however, the passage presented no problem. If
the reading of the archetype made grammatical and juristic
sense, it must be right. Divergent readings in later codices could
by definition be nothing but alterations introduced by scribes
or jurists. As he put it: 'in those Florentine Pandects, which,
indeed, we believe to be the original ones, there is no negative at
all. Therefore the Florentine jurisconsult Accursius, who also
had a faulty codex, torments himself — I might almost say
wretchedly.'[73] In this case elimination of *codices descripti* apparently leads to the elimination of medieval legal science. There
was nothing new in attacking medieval jurists — Valla and Beroaldo had done the same.[74] But the method underlying the attack
was unprecedented.

Here Poliziano was both imitating and improving on his
literary model. Gellius frequently consulted older manuscripts
in order to correct errors in newer ones. Thus, he defended a
reading in Cicero's fifth Verrine in part because he had found it
so written in 'a copy of unimpeachable fidelity, because it was
the result of Tiro's careful scholarship'.[75] Again, he argued that
scribes had replaced the unfamiliar archaic genitive 'facies' with
the later form 'faciei' in a work by Claudius Quadrigarius. In the
oldest manuscripts, he said, he had found the old reading 'facies';
in certain 'corrupt manuscripts', on the other hand, he had
found 'facies' erased and 'faciei' written in.[76] But Gellius had
not cited his evidence with Poliziano's precision, or evaluated it
with Poliziano's discernment.

From Petrarch on, humanists had also sought out and copied
or collated old manuscripts. Some had even studied manuscript genealogy. Guarino's friend Giovanni Lamola, for example,
set out in 1428 to collate the codex of Cicero's rhetorical
works which had been discovered seven years before in the
cathedral archive at Lodi. This contained complete texts of
Cicero's *De oratore* and *Orator*, previously known only in mutilated form, and of his *Brutus*, hitherto unknown.[77] All these
works were fundamental for the rhetorical teaching of the
humanists. Consequently, the discovery attracted attention im-

mediately: Poggio Bracciolini, then in England, knew of it within a year.[78] Many copies of the new texts were soon in circulation. But as the Lodi manuscript was written in what the humanists called 'Lombardic script' — that is, an unfamiliar minuscule — they found it hard to read and made their copies not from the original but from other humanists' copies. As a result both of inevitable mistakes in transcription and of equally inevitable attempts at conjectural emendation, the texts in circulation soon became extremely corrupt.[79] Lamola declared that it was necessary to return to the original source. He wrote to Guarino that he had 'restored the whole work according to the earlier text'.[80] He knew that the Lodi manuscript was very ancient from its unusual script: he described it as 'summae quidem venerationis et antiquitatis non vulgaris effigies'. More important, its discovery had created a sensation only a few years before, and no other complete manuscript of the works it contained had been discovered. Therefore, Lamola, like every other humanist of his time, knew that the Lodi manuscript must be the archetype: 'from that accurate exemplar they copied the text which is now commonly accepted'.[81] He decided that any attempt to emend the text must be based on a collation of this manuscript. He even maintained that the errors in the Lodi manuscript required preservation and study. For even the errors of so old a manuscript were preferable to the conjectures of later scribes: 'I also took care [he wrote] to represent everything in accord with the old [manuscript] down to the smallest dot, even where it contained certain old absurdities. For I'd rather be absurd with that old manuscript than be wise with these diligent fellows.'[82]

Similarly, Giorgio Merula pointed out in his edition of Plautus (1472) that all the extant manuscripts of twelve of Plautus' comedies were descended from one parent: 'There was only one manuscript, from which, as if from an archetype, all the extant manuscripts are derived.'[83] The archetype to which he referred was the eleventh-century Orsini Plautus (Vat. lat. 3870), brought to Rome in 1429 by Nicholas of Cusa.[84] Like the Lodi manuscript, it had created a sensation among the humanists, for twelve of the sixteen plays which it contained had previously been unknown.[85] Hence, it too was widely known to be the source from which the rest had come. Merula could not collate it himself and had to content himself with reconstructing its readings by collating copies.[86] Though he failed to act on his knowledge of the textual tradition, Merula too understood that the manuscripts of one text could be arranged genealogically, and that the text should be based on the parent if it were extant and identifiable.

Both Lamola and Merula, then, had noticed that all the manuscripts of some works were descended from one parent. Both had agreed that in such cases the text should be based on the parent. And one of them, Lamola, had made a full collation of the parent, recording even its errors.

Poliziano, however, showed how to examine a group of manuscripts and discover their interrelations. He taught that such an examination could sometimes identify an archetype which was not commonly recognized as such. He maintained that even where the genealogy of the manuscripts could not be established, 'conjectural emendation must start from the earliest recoverable stage of the tradition.'[87] Moreover, he backed up his statements about the history of texts with precise identifications and evaluations of the manuscripts which he used. His consistently methodical approach to the recension of manuscripts went far beyond the isolated insights of Lamola and Merula.

Poliziano also employed collateral forms of evidence to support or modify that of manuscripts. In particular, he followed Tortelli in recognizing that inscriptions provided the most reliable evidence of ancient orthographical practices. Tortelli had collected inscriptions to prove that the Latin name of Rome should be spelt 'Roma', rather than 'Rhoma'.[88] Poliziano used inscriptions as well as the Florentine Pandects and the Codex Romanus of Virgil to show that the proper spelling of the poet's name was Vergilius.[89] What was new in Poliziano's work was not that he employed inscriptions but the manner in which he did so. For he used them as critically as he did manuscripts. He took care to show that he had studied the most up-to-date sylloge of inscriptions, which the highly proficient epigrapher Fra Giovanni Giocondo had presented to Lorenzo. And he followed Giocondo in making an explicit distinction between inscriptions he had inspected and those which he knew only at second hand.[90] In short, he showed that the most sophisticated epigraphic techniques of his time could be joined with his palaeographical expertise and applied to the solution of technical philological problems.

The historical approach to source-criticism was applicable to literary works themselves as well as to manuscripts. Poliziano knew that the Latin poets, whose works were his primary interest, had drawn heavily on Greek sources in a variety of ways. And he showed that only a critic who had mastered Greek literature could hope to deal competently with Latin.

Poliziano realized, first of all, that the comparative study of Latin and Greek was yet another tool for the textual critic — to be applied where the manuscripts afforded no help. In *Miscellanea* I.27, for example, he explained some puzzling lines in Cicero, *Fam.* VII. vi. 1. He recognized that they were lines of verse and, more important, that they were a translation of a passage from Euripides' *Medea* (214 ff.). He knew that Ennius had written a Latin adaptation of the *Medea*, and he rightly argued that the lines must be a quotation from Ennius' work.[91] In this case, knowledge of Cicero's Greek source enabled Poliziano to set out as verse lines that would otherwise have remained corrupt and incomprehensible. As a by-product he was able to reconstruct a forgotten chapter of early Roman literary history.

Elsewhere, recourse to Greek sources enabled him to defend Latin forms of Greek words, which others had wrongly held to be corrupt: for example, 'crepidas . . . carbatinas' in Catullus 98.4 and 'Oarion' (for Orion) in 66.94.[92] His neatest application of this method was at 66.48. Catullus himself had explained that poem 66 was a translation of Callimachus' *The Lock of Berenice*. This was lost. Poliziano found one line from it quoted in an ancient scholium: χαλύβων ὡς ἀπόλοιτο γένος. He realized that it corresponded to line 48 of the Latin: 'Iupiter ut caelitum omne genus pereat.' And he also realized that 'caelitum', which made little sense in that context, must be a scribal corruption of the unfamiliar word 'Chalybon', which Catullus had simply transliterated. So emended, the Latin became perfectly clear: Berenice's lock, wishing to be back on Berenice's head, prays that the race of Chalybes — a people famous for making metal tools, including the scissors that had cut the lock — may perish.[93] Poliziano had had predecessors in the use of Greek texts to correct Latin ones — notably his Florentine rival, Bartolomeo della Fonte.[94] But in erudition and virtuosity he was matchless.

Yet the most striking effects of his comparative method were not in textual criticism but in exegesis. For he insisted that proper exegesis of Latin writers must begin from the identification of the Greek sources they had drawn upon for both language and content. In I.26, for example, he pointed out that Ovid, *Fasti*, I. 357–8 was adapted from an epigram in the Greek Anthology

(*AP* IX. 75). Ovid had translated the Greek 'as literally as possible' — 'quam potuit ad unguem' — but he had still failed to capture all the nuances of the original: 'The Latin poet did not even touch that — if I may so call it — transmarine charm.'[95] Juxtaposition of details gave rise to some sweeping critical judgements. Quintilian had characterized Ovid's style as 'lascivus' — 'abundant', 'Asiatic'. Poliziano argued, on the basis of his comparison, that Ovid was unable to equal his Greek model not from lack of ability, but because the Latin language itself ran counter to his special stylistic gifts: 'This is the fault of the [Latin] language, not so much because it is lacking in words as because it allows less freedom for verbal play.'[96]

Elsewhere Poliziano was able to connect the study of verbal borrowings to that of intellectual ones. Tacitly following Landino, he showed that Persius had modelled his fourth satire on Plato's *First Alcibiades*. Persius had drawn the entire philosophical message of his poem from the dialogue: 'it is clear that Persius . . . drew from it the discussions which Socrates there holds with Alcibiades about the just and unjust, and about self-knowledge.'[97] Indeed, Poliziano said, the words 'Tecum habita', with which Persius' poem ended, were a good summary of the dialogue as well. 'When he says "tecum habita", doesn't he seem to have understood the meaning of that dialogue clearly — if indeed, as the commentator Proclus affirms, Plato here had in mind precisely that Delphic writing which admonishes every man to know himself?'[98] At the same time, he was able to point out that Persius had alluded directly to individual lines in the dialogue.[99] Persius is an extremely obscure and allusive poet. Medieval readers, at a loss to understand the satires, had invented wild explanations for them. Persius was said to be attacking 'leccatores' — gossips, gluttons, bishops and abbots who failed to live up to their vows.[100] Only after Poliziano's explanation appeared could Persius' poem begin to be read as its author had intended.

Poliziano was hardly the first to point out that Latin poetry was heavily dependent upon Greek models. Latin poets themselves generally claimed to be not the first to write a particular kind of poetry, but the first to introduce a particular Greek style or verse-form into Latin.[101] Moreover, Gellius had regularly compared passages from Latin poetry with the Greek originals from which they had been adapted, and had drawn broad conclusions from the exercise:

Whenever striking expressions are to be translated and imitated from Greek poems, it is said that we should not always strive to render every single word with literal exactness. For many things lose their charm if they are translated too forcibly — as it were, unwillingly and reluctantly. Virgil therefore showed skill and good judgement in omitting some things and rendering others when he was dealing with passages of Homer or Hesiod or Apollonius or Parthenius or Callimachus or Theocritus or some other poet.[102]

Similar information and arguments appeared in other works — for example, the *Saturnalia* of Macrobius, where Virgil and Homer are compared at length, and the commentaries of Servius.[103]

These texts, in turn, attracted the attention of medieval and Renaissance scholars before Poliziano. Richard de Bury, Bishop of Durham in the fourteenth century, had read his Gellius and Macrobius.[104] In consequence, it is not surprising to find him asking, in his *Philobiblon*,

What would Virgil, the chief poet among the Latins, have achieved, if he had not despoiled Theocritus, Lucretius, and Homer, and had not ploughed with their heifer? What, unless again and again he had read somewhat of Parthenius and Pindar, whose eloquence he could by no means imitate?[105]

It was a commonplace among humanist teachers in the fifteenth century that only those who had a sound knowledge of Greek literature could properly understand Latin.[106]

Calderini, moreover, had given detailed attention and much effort to the comparative study of Greek and Latin. In his brief commentary on Propertius, for example, he arrived several times at novel and interesting results.[107] He pointed out that Propertius I.20 is to some extent modelled on Theocritus XIII: 'In this passage his particular aim is to imitate and adapt Theocritus, on the story of Hylas'.[108] And his wide reading in Greek scholiasts, geographers, and historians enabled him to unravel a number of Propertius' mythological and geographical allusions. For instance, he rightly interpreted the phrase 'Theseae bracchia longa viae' in Propertius III. xxi. 24: 'He means the long walls, which were called μακρὰ τείχη in Greek. They ran from the city [of Athens] up to the Piraeus; a careful account is to be found in Thucydides.'[109] He also noticed that Propertius often used variant forms of well-known myths. Thus, in I. xiii. 21 Propertius described the river-god Enipeus as Thessalian. Calderini rightly pointed out that other ancient writers located Enipeus not in Thessaly, but in Elis.[110]

Despite its qualities, this commentary reveals the gulf that separated even Calderini from Poliziano. In IV. i. 64, Propertius calls himself 'the Roman Callimachus'.[111] The phrase is not so simple as it appears; when a Roman poet claims a particular Greek poet as his model, he may mean that he has derived his subject or his metre from the Greek, but he may also mean simply that he is as innovative, learned, and subtle as the Greek had been. Calderini, however, took Propertius at his word, assuming that Propertius must have written direct adaptations from Callimachus: '[Propertius] calls himself the Roman Callimachus. For he sets out Callimachus, a Greek poet, in Latin verse.'[112] And he applied this interpretation at least once in a most unfortunate way. In I. ii. 1 Propertius calls his mistress Cynthia 'vita' − 'my life'. 'The word', wrote Calderini, 'is drawn from Callimachus, who is Propertius' chief model. For he too, while flattering his mistress, calls her by the Greek word [for life (i.e., ζωή)] .'[113]

Calderini's arguments clearly found acceptance, for Beroaldo repeated them − without acknowledgement − in his own commentary on Propertius, which first appeared in 1487. He too argued that Propertius had taken Callimachus as his 'archetypon'. And he too described Propertius' use of 'vita' in I. ii. 1 as done in imitation of Callimachus.[114]

The notes of Calderini and Beroaldo stimulated Poliziano to produce a splendid rebuttal in *Miscellanea* I.80, where he raised an overstated, but none the less crushing objection to both Calderini's general interpretation and his reading of I. ii. 1 − namely, that there was not one shred of evidence that Callimachus had written any love poetry at all, much less a love poem in which ζωή was used as an endearment:

> I find it astonishing that Domizio and some others after him . . . dare to write that Propertius says this or that in imitation of Callimachus. For beyond a few hymns nothing at all remains to us of that poet, and certainly there is nothing at all that treats of love.[115]

Poliziano certainly had the best in the exchange. There is little reason to think that Calderini had found evidence to back up his theory. As a commentator on Juvenal, Calderini knew from *Sat.* VI. 195 that ζωή was sometimes used as an endearment. As to the notion that Callimachus had used the word in that sense, it was probably a clever guess.[116] Poliziano's rebuttal is even more significant when read in the light of the chapter in which it occurred. There he not only attacked Calderini, but gave an elegant demonstration of how to use Greek poetry to illustrate Propertius. In IV. ix. 57–8 Propertius alludes to the myth of Tiresias' encounter with Pallas while she was bathing.[117] To illustrate this Poliziano published, along with much other material, the *editio princeps* of Callimachus' entire poem on the Bath of Pallas, which he also translated word for word.[118] The Alexandrian poets, in other words, could be used to illuminate Propertius' mythological allusions. But they could not be used to explicate the verbal details of his poems. In *Miscellanea* I. 80 Poliziano showed that he understood the limitations as well as the virtues of the comparative method in exegesis. He understood that different Latin poets had used their Greek sources in different ways, and that the exegete must take these differences in poetic method into account when making his comparisons.[119] For all Calderini's reading in Greek prose texts and sensitivity to the nuances of Latin poetry, he could not rival Poliziano in the methodical application of source-criticism or in the systematic comparison of Greek and Latin poetry. Yet he was the most sophisticated of Poliziano's predecessors. In exegesis as in textual criticism, then, Poliziano's methodological innovations marked nothing less than a revolution.

Modern scholars still begin the study of Latin poems by looking for possible Greek sources and models. To be sure, when they find a model they compare it with the Latin in a far more detailed manner than Poliziano did. We want to know not only that Ennius translated Euripides, and that in doing so he made alterations, but also what specific changes he made, and what purpose they were meant to serve.[120] But it would be unhistorical to reproach Poliziano for not carrying his comparisons far enough. After all, he took them almost as far as had his model Gellius. Rather, Poliziano's work on the comparative method should be seen in the same perspective as his work on manuscripts: it is the lineal ancestor of the methods that are still employed.

Poliziano's thoroughness in the study of Greek sources paid off in novel results of other kinds. He mastered not only the whole body of Greek literary texts, but also the huge mass of scholarly material that had grown up among and around them since Hellenistic times, and above all the scholia on such Hellenistic poets as Aratus and Apollonius of Rhodes. By drawing on this material, he was sometimes able to move from the comparison of Latin and Greek to the partial reconstruction of lost

Greek works. In I.24 he discussed the myth of Theseus' encounter with Hecale. Beroaldo had already pointed out, drawing on testimonies in both Latin and Greek texts, that Callimachus had written a poem about Hecale. But Poliziano was able to go much farther. He found in a scholium on Callimachus what is still the only information about the exact nature of the poem and the reasons why Callimachus wrote it:

> Where Callimachus says, in his *Hymn to Apollo*: 'Envy whispered in Apollo's ear, I do not love the poet whose song is not as vast as the ocean' — the scholiast writes more or less as follows: 'Here he attacks those who mocked him for being unable to write a large poem. That is why he was forced to write the *Hecale*.'[121]

Here too, none of Poliziano's rivals could match either his mastery of recondite materials or his use of them to recreate what had seemed irrevocably lost.

Poliziano's detailed improvements to the art of criticism, finally, stood out all the more because he consistently used them as arguments in favour of an ambitious programme for the refinement of the *studia humanitatis*. He made new claims for the status of the critic and his importance for those studies. The competent critic must be more than a mere technician. Like Varro, he must have mastered not only Latin and Greek, but law, medicine, and dialectic — in short, all the disciplines, and philosophy above all.[122] Such a critic, Poliziano showed by precept and example, need not confine his talents to rhetorical and poetic texts. After all, the ancient philosophers as well as the poets were known only through imperfectly transmitted texts. Some of the most puzzling antinomies these presented were really corruptions, which the philosophers' logic could not resolve — but which the philologist's tools could readily eliminate.

Ioannes Argyropoulos, a philosopher of high repute in the Florence of the 1450s and '60s, had criticized Cicero for saying (*Tusc.* I. x. 22) that Aristotle's term for 'mind' was ἐνδελέχεια (continuous motion). Aristotle had denied motion to the mind, and the manuscripts of his *De anima* gave the philosophically more satisfactory term ἐντελέχεια (perfection.)[123] In the very first chapter of the *Miscellanea* Poliziano contested this view. The manuscripts of Aristotle, he pointed out, were notoriously corrupt, and Strabo's account of their vicissitudes above and below ground showed that they had first been published in an inaccurate and interpolated form. Moreover, he asked: 'Is it not possible that Cicero himself saw the archetype of Aristotle's works, which were published in his time?'[124] In that case, his testimony would carry more weight than that of Byzantine manuscripts. Study of the history of texts could thus be a powerful reinforcement for the many humanists who, like Poliziano himself and his friend Ermolao Barbaro, hoped to wrest the discipline of philosophy from the control of the scholastic professionals.[125]

Even more important, Poliziano showed that the critic's tasks included creation as well as study. His prose and poetry ranged from brief epigrams in Greek and Latin through longer translations of Greek texts to the extended prolusions in prose and verse with which he began his university lecture courses.[126] Into these works he fitted with the delicacy of a jeweller his linguistic, prosodic, mythological, and even text-critical discoveries. His preface to Alberti's *De re aedificatoria*, to take a simple example, announced four years before the *Miscellanea* that he had reworked the text of Suetonius *Claudius* 34:

Ita perscrutatus antiquitatis vestigia est, ut omnem veterum architectandi rationem et deprehenderit et in exemplum revocaverit, sic ut non solum machinas et *pegmata automataque* permulta, sed formas quoque aedificiorum admirabilis excogitaverit.[127]

And his poems, naturally, were crammed with every sort of learned allusion. Such Alexandrian refinement of allusion and imitation was just what Poliziano's audience expected from these splendid formal exercises.[128] Codro Urceo of Bologna not only urged Poliziano to publish the Greek epigrams of which he had been sent a sample, but also analysed in detail Poliziano's adaptation of particularly elegant metrical practices from the best ancient authors — for example, his habit of composing hexameter verses from a large number of short words *scatentibus dactylis*, after the manner of the first line of the *Odyssey*.[129]

To the intimate connection between his scholarship and his style Poliziano repeatedly called attention. In *Miscellanea* I.17 he wrote:

In Seneca's tragedy entitled *Hercules furens* the following *senariolus* occurs:
  Sublimis altas luna concipiat feras.
But the old manuscript in the public library of the Medici reads *alias*, not *altas*, as in the common text. [The emended text reads: 'The lofty moon may bring forth more wild beasts.'] You will not easily find the sense of this passage anywhere except in Achilles, an author whom Firmicus Maternus both cites and praises in his *Mathesis*. While discussing the moon

in his commentary on Aratus, he says: 'It is also inhabited, and has rivers and everything else found on earth, and they tell the story that the Nemean lion fell from it'. . . . Whence I [wrote] in the *Nutricia*:
Nemeaeaque tesqua
Lunigenam mentita feram [568–9].[130]

Here Poliziano took his own place with aplomb in the poetic genealogy that his scholarly researches had established. Just as Seneca had displayed his knowledge of Greek myth, so Poliziano — appropriately describing Pindar — invokes at once the Greek myth and the Latin allusion to it, and by doing so links his own poetic method with that of the ancients. Moreover, his translations from the Greek — especially the version of the *Lavacra Palladis* that he printed in the *Miscellanea* — also enabled him to combine accurate philology with poetic originality. Poliziano's letters became models of Neo-Latin prose.[131] His poems were considered classical enough to be the subject of university courses.[132] His translations set the standard for all others for a century and more.[133] It is not surprising, then, that his success as a stylist did much to help his technical methods and standards impose themselves.

Poliziano was more than a scholar trying to set new standards for the selection, citation, and interpretation of sources. Like Calderini and the rest, he was a writer and teacher who needed financial support and public acclaim. He had to show that his brand of scholarship deserved the protection of Lorenzo, the most discriminating of patrons, and the applause of Florentines, the most critical of audiences. His self-conscious adoption of a new standard of accuracy and precision enabled him to do just that. His constant references to rare materials both enriched his work and enabled him to give thanks in public to the noble friends who had made them available to him. In particular, he could thank Lorenzo, who 'in his service to scholars condescended' even to arrange access to manuscripts, coins, and inscriptions.[134] Some of Poliziano's distinctive technical innovations — in particular, his efforts to identify parent manuscripts — also amounted to elegant new forms of flattery.

Poliziano's environment exerted pressure on his scholarship at other levels as well. By treating the study of antiquity as irrelevant to civic life and by insisting that only a tiny élite could study the ancient world with adequate rigour, he set himself apart from the earlier tradition of classical studies in Florence. Earlier Florentine scholars, men such as Leonardo Bruni and

Donato Acciaiuoli, had studied the ancient world in order to become better men and citizens. They wanted to recover the experience of classical republicanism in order to build a sound republic in their own time. Poliziano evidently believed that one must study the ancient world for its own sake, and the exhaustive preparation which he demanded left little time for good citizenship.[135] Moreover, when he set ancient works back into their full historical context he eliminated whatever contemporary relevance they might have had. It was by misreading the satires of Persius that early medieval clerics had made them useful. Poliziano's historical reading clearly showed that the satires were not concerned with any problem contemporary with him. The use that one could make of Latin poetry, analysed by his methods, was purely literary: as sources to be drawn on and models to be imitated in one's own artificial, allusive verse — verse of just the sort that a cultivated élite of patrons would enjoy. As we have seen, that was precisely the practical application that Poliziano made of the new tools he forged.[136] In short, by eliminating moral interpretations and contemporary applications from classical studies, Poliziano made them an object for Medici patronage as decorative, harmless, and sophisticated as the elegant nonsense of the Neo-Platonists.

Poliziano's general intellectual environment did as much as his social and political milieu to shape his work. He belonged to a whole generation of humanists who turned — in Rome and Venice as well as in Florence — from the oration to the emendation, from an audience of eager young citizens to a reading public of crabbed, jealous scholars.[137] Like Calderini, Merula, and the rest, Poliziano was possessed by the need to excel the competition. Accordingly, his work sometimes resembled theirs in tone as much as it differed in substance. And because Poliziano started from so polemical a stance, the course he followed in argument sometimes wavered from the straight path that his principles laid down. He did not always confine himself to fair comment or treat his adversaries with as much attention as the ancient sources. Sometimes Calderini really had discovered in classical texts the facts that Poliziano accused him of inventing. For example, the material about rhinoceroses with two horns which Poliziano dismissed as error and confusion, Calderini had found in Pausanias and rightly applied to Martial.[138] Sometimes Calderini had seen the sense in passages which Poliziano treated as corrupt: for instance, his explanation of Martial's *Atlas cum*

compare gibbo (VI. lxxvii. 7) — which Poliziano wanted to
emend to *Atlas cum compare mulo* — as referring to a camel (a
'hump-backed beast').[139] Sometimes, too, Poliziano scrutinized
his own conjectures less harshly than those of others — for
example, his argument that Statius had married Lucan's widow,
Polla Argentaria, which he stuck to for more than a decade
despite the textual evidence that Statius' wife was named
Claudia.[140] These errors and exaggerations did not hinder Poliziano from devising more solid, original, and ingenious critical
methods than anyone else of his generation. But they did infuse
his prose with an acid and unpleasant tone.

Poliziano knew that his scholarly writing struck readers he
respected as too polemical. Iacopo Antiquario, after reading the
Miscellanea, wrote to praise its content and deplore its style:
'Domizio did what he could for literature.'[141] Poliziano conceded nothing: 'I show Domizio to students as I would a pitfall
to travellers.'[142] He made it clear that he saw scholarship not as
an ancient grammarian like Donatus had, as a collaborative,
cumulative enterprise, but rather as the poets of the Roman
Golden Age had seen their art: as a field for personal triumphs
over predecessors and rivals. Why write at all unless to criticize
what others have written?

My action is supported by prominent examples, unless one thinks Horace
an insignificant author — Horace, who slaughters Ennius, Plautus, Lucilius,
Dossennus, and that whole troop of ancient poets all at once, though the
people opposed him. What? Does Aulus Gellius not also attack Seneca
with great freedom of speech? . . . Do all the schools of philosophers not
cross swords above all with their predecessors?[143]

Poliziano saw the bitter, eristic style of the *Miscellanea* as an
essential component of the scholarship he wanted to produce.
That in turn meant not only that he would commit some errors
as serious as those he exposed, but also that he would inspire re-
buttals as fierce as any of his own. And that meant that his
complex of new methods would not be adopted as a whole.

Naturally some of Poliziano's results were accepted. Reading
the editions of the *Familiares* that appeared after 1489, he con-
gratulated himself: 'My restoration, so to speak, has now been
accepted, so far as I can see. Texts are printed everywhere in the
form which I had prescribed from the old manuscripts.'[144] Many
of the letters that the *Miscellanea* elicited were favourable.
Young men took the book apart so that several could read

different gatherings at the same time; old men were overwhelmed by its wealth of new material.[145]

As might have been expected from its tone and standpoint, the *Miscellanea* also generated anger and abuse. Michael Marullus, Poliziano's rival in both scholarship and poetry, ridiculed in biting epigrams his exaggerated claims of novelty, his obstinate refusal to accept perfectly plausible vulgate readings, and his strained efforts to interpret standard texts in novel ways.[146] Merula attacked the *Miscellanea* point by point, claiming that much of Poliziano's new material was stolen from himself and others.[147] Others, less engaged, criticized Poliziano even more obtusely. Why, they asked, should so able a poet waste his time in blowing dust from old manuscripts when much more legible new ones were available, neatly written in humanistic script?[148] Poliziano's burning rhetoric seemed as forced and curious to such readers as his technical arguments.

External factors joined with these internal ones to divert scholars from the path Poliziano had blazed. The political upheaval that Italy suffered in the 1490s created a sense of new needs and new men to fill them. The terrible years 1493 to 1494 brought the French into Italy, drove the Medici from Florence, and killed off Poliziano and Barbaro. No one had time after 1494 for the precision work that these had specialized in. Readers wanted encyclopaedias, like the *Commentarii urbani* of Raffaele Maffei, who reduced the whole corpus of Greek works on history and geography into an orderly, accessible, and fairly compact form, and plain texts like those of Aldo Manuzio, who saw the creation of a new philology as a task less pressing than that of providing the raw materials from which a new civilization could be built.[149] Italian Latinists turned away from the experimental and eclectic prose of Poliziano's generation to a new ideal of pure imitation of Cicero. And even Poliziano's disciples did not carry on their master's enterprise. Jacopo Modesti da Prato, who had collated manuscripts with Poliziano, published no learned works of his own. Pietro Crinito, who did publish, deliberately rejected Poliziano's methods in order to build a distinctive monument of his own, the mistitled *De honesta disciplina.*[150]

Editors and commentators did not revive Poliziano's full complex of methods for many years. And when they did so, they employed it in contexts and for purposes that would not have been to his liking. For their choices of methods and topics

II Poliziano's Followers in Italy
1500–1560

Poliziano's method of manuscript recension was first taken up by
two younger contemporaries: Pietro Bembo and Giano Parrasio.
At the age of twenty-one, in 1491, Bembo helped Poliziano to
collate his family's splendid manuscript of Terence. This meeting
was decisive for Bembo; after it he devoted himself for many
years to classical studies.[1] Around 1505 he set out to employ
the principles he had learned at Poliziano's side by recording the
readings of his two finest manuscripts in his *De Virgilii Culice et
Terentii fabulis Liber*. This is a dialogue between Pomponio
Leto and Ermolao Barbaro, supposedly overheard and repeated
to Bembo by his friend Tommaso Inghirami. Leto recites the
entire *Culex*, as preserved in a codex of the *Appendix Virgiliana*
which he describes as his own; he pauses from time to time in
order to exclaim about the superiority of his manuscript's text.
Barbaro repays him for this kindness by reciting a series of
readings from *his* codex of Terence, the physical condition of
which he describes in some detail. Barbaro is rather more attentive to details than Leto: he quotes the title of the *argumenta*
that occur before the plays in order to prove that Terence did
not write them, and he even quotes two of the manuscript's
marginal scholia. But both characters delve with evident pleasure
into the minutiae of Latin orthography, citing inscriptions as
well as manuscripts.[2]

Unfortunately, the work's idiosyncrasies went far towards
ensuring that it would exercise little influence. The pretence
that the manuscripts in question had belonged to Leto and
Barbaro, rather than to the Bembo family, could create little
save confusion. The literary device of a dialogue in which both
characters are quoting from memory is rather strained — and
has occasionally deceived later readers. Bembo's reports of the
readings of the manuscripts were careless and inaccurate, even

on important points.[3] Moreover, Bembo himself turned for many years to different and more original pursuits; he did not publish the dialogue until 1530. Accordingly, his work did not contribute to the diffusion of Poliziano's methods.

Parrasio accomplished even less of substance. A clever poet and interpreter of poetic texts, he had also grasped Poliziano's technical principles. Like Poliziano, he was a notable hunter of manuscripts, who made purchases literally everywhere in Italy and extracted or copied many important manuscripts, including the best one of Charisius, from the great monastic library at Bobbio.[4] He clearly understood Poliziano's ideas about systematic recension, some of which he reiterated in his correspondence. Like Poliziano, he insisted that textual criticism be based on the reliable testimony of old manuscripts — 'antiquorum codicum fides'. 'Anyone of sound mind', he declared, would prefer the readings of such manuscripts to the corruptions and interpolations that filled the 'vulgati codices'.[5] He reviled scribes and printers for altering their texts arbitrarily. And he even understood that manuscripts could be evaluated only after their genealogy had been established. For instance, he argued that his manuscript of Ammianus Marcellinus was of value because it had been copied 'from a manuscript of great antiquity'.[6] And he pointed out that his manuscript of the Livian *Periochae* had the merit of being descended from Petrarch's copy of the work.[7]

A number of circumstances combined to prevent Parrasio from applying these admirable principles in his own editorial work. Even for a humanist, he led an unusually rackety life. When he was not caught up in a feud, he was chronically ill.[8] His manuscripts suffered terribly from the many removals that his hot temper forced him to make. The Italian wars that Poliziano did not live to see continually disrupted his studies. And one may legitimately doubt his dedication to the near-absolute honesty that Poliziano's method required. He himself admitted that as a young man he had helped Pomponio Leto with a notorious forgery: pseudo-Fenestella on Roman antiquities.[9] At all events, his published editions and commentaries reveal little or no effort at a systematic exploitation of the manuscript evidence. Even the publication of his codex of Charisius was left to a pupil, who published only a transcript of a transcript of the Bobbio codex.[10]

If Bembo and Parrasio did not produce major critical works, they contributed to the preservation and dissemination of

Poliziano's method. Both were influential members of the great circle of humanists that formed and flourished in the Rome of Leo X. And the members of this circle produced the first efforts to apply Poliziano's teachings to the criticism of entire texts.

Not even Lorenzo had assembled so dazzling an *équipe* as did Leo. In his Curia gathered Sadoleto, Inghirami, Bembo, Parrasio, Angelo Colocci, the younger Filippo Beroaldo, Andrea Navagero, and Baldesar Castiglione, as well as the many other talented poets and humanists whose names Sadoleto recalled with melancholy pleasure in a famous letter, and whose deaths Pierio Valeriano described in grisly detail in the terrible *De literatorum infelicitate*.[11] There was plenty of new material for these men to exercise their talents upon. Leo X sent agents to search systematically through the monastic libraries of Northern Europe and extract their best classical manuscripts. For these he was willing to pay top prices both in cash and in indulgences.[12] There were private collectors to compete with him: Bembo, Parrasio, and the learned but half-crazed Colocci, who rivalled Leo in generosity as well as in bibliomania.[13]

Moreover, in this ambience the study and imitation of classical authors were fashionable and well-rewarded activities. Bembo and his associates earned their posts in the Curia because they could write Ciceronian prose extempore and compose Propertian elegies on demand. In their meetings in Heinrich Goritz's revived Roman academy and in Colocci's Orti Sallustiani, they expended much energy and wit in arguing about the merits of their favourite authors and on the criticism and elucidation of particular passages. In the retinue of a Medici pope, himself a former pupil of Poliziano's, it was inevitable that this combination of patronage, material, and intellect would bear fruit in new attempts to put Poliziano's ideas into practice.

The first to do so was Beroaldo. Skulduggery of the well-known kind had brought the only manuscript of Tacitus' *Annales* I-VI to Rome from Corvey. This Beroaldo published in 1515. He imitated Poliziano in a number of ways. His work began with an effusive prefatory letter in which he praised Leo for following the tradition established by Lorenzo and assembling rare manuscripts for the use of scholars.[14] He also claimed to have reproduced what was indeed a codex of exceptional importance with exceptional care. Where he found errors in the manuscript too serious to correct, he 'left them as they were, placing asterisks at the inner margin to show that the codex was faulty'.[15] He retained in his text a number of the manuscript's unusual spellings, which he listed for the reader's convenience at the end of his few critical notes on the text.[16] To give the reader absolute confidence in the reliability of his text, he collated the printed sheets with the manuscript and filled a final leaf with corrections — after which appeared, as a final fillip, an offer of 'premia non mediocria' for anyone who brought the Pope further manuscripts of unpublished works.[17]

Beroaldo did not publish a simple transcript of the Corvey manuscript. He pointed out that it contained a good ·many obvious errors and added that, after consulting with 'learned men', he had silently corrected many of them.[18] Strictly speaking, then, the reader could not be absolutely sure that any given word — except the corruptions marked with asterisks — was actually the manuscript reading. But there was common sense in much of what Beroaldo did. Many of his corrections were so clearly plausible that they retain a place in the text or apparatus of the most recent critical edition.[19] In most respects, then, if not in every detail, Beroaldo's Tacitus was quite an impressive publication of new manuscript material.

Pierio Valeriano applied Poliziano's teachings in the most coherent and original fashion. Valeriano's intellectual roots lay in the Italian humanism of Poliziano's time. He had studied Greek with his uncle, the traveller and humanist Fra Urbano Bolzani, who had served as tutor to Giovanni de' Medici. He had also studied with Sabellico — who, indeed, had been responsible for Valeriano's change of name, from the ordinary Pietro to Pierio: 'child of the Muses'.[20] In Rome Valeriano knew all the Curial humanists; he was especially close to Parrasio, who encouraged him to do what he himself had never done — to complete a large-scale work on textual criticism.[21] Valeriano did indeed compile and publish a systematic collation of several manuscripts of Virgil, which he published in 1521.

In his preface, Valeriano argued that the printed texts of Virgil had to be corrected against the oldest extant manuscripts. He set out to provide not a new edition but new evidence with which future editors could improve the printed vulgate. He carefully identified the manuscripts that he had collated and listed the standard names by which he would refer to them:

Before we approach the subject itself, it seems advisable first to give the names by which we refer to certain especially important manuscripts. They are: Codex Romanus, which is undoubtedly the oldest. We call it

Roman because its script is very similar to that of the Romans — that is, to that which we see everywhere . . . in old inscriptions on marble slabs or brass tablets, and in coins. It is kept with great care in the inner sanctuary of the Vatican library and is written in letters of almost a finger's breadth. Another, which is in small letters and is quite old in its own right, will be called Oblongus from the form of the pages. There is also a Codex Mediceus among the correct ones.[22]

App. II

Valeriano rightly refused to arrange his Virgil manuscripts genealogically, for not even the Codex Romanus could be singled out as the parent of the rest; indeed, it contained a large number of obvious errors at points where other manuscripts had superior readings:

We did not think that we should attach to any single copy so much weight that, if anything good appeared in the others, we should reject them. In fact all of them, if you examine them carefully, are uniformly full of corruptions and errors. From the comparison . . . of several, however, we arrive at truer or at least more probable results.[23]

App. II

If he could not employ the elimination principle, Valeriano nevertheless emulated Poliziano in other ways. He regularly mentioned the owner or location of the manuscripts he cited, and he gave clear if summary indications of their age and script. If he disagreed with Poliziano on the spelling of Virgil's name, he recognized that he had to argue the case on Poliziano's grounds and he discussed the same evidence, using the same techniques.[24]

Even more carefully than Poliziano, he recorded every detail of the manuscript evidence. His note on *Aeneid* XII, 78-9, is typical in its precision:

Teucrum arma quiescant/ et Rutulum nostro dirimatur sanguine bellum. In the Codex Romanus, in the Vatican Oblongus, in the Porcian manuscript, and in many other old ones the reading is *Teucrum arma quiescant et Rutuli.* The variation is not inelegant. In the Mediceus the last syllable has been falsified by a second hand, since it is clear that it originally read *Rutuli.* As to the fact that the vulgate texts read *dirimatur,* . . . in all these old ones I have found the reading *dirimamus.*[25]

Moreover, and most important, the whole form of Valeriano's work showed how clearly he had grasped one of Poliziano's central insights. For the *Castigationes* appeared without a text of Virgil; they are merely a set of critical annotations. As we have seen, it was not uncommon to publish commentaries that dealt mostly with text-critical matters. Poliziano's friendly rival Ermolao Barbaro had published a masterly work on the text of the elder Pliny's *Natural History* — the *Castigationes Plinianae*, which had appeared without text in 1492 to 1493, and which probably provided Valeriano with his own title. Barbaro had not attempted to publish exhaustive or precise collations of the manuscripts of Pliny, for he not unreasonably believed that it was more important to assemble the Greek sources on which Pliny had drawn and correct the Latin text against them. Valeriano was the first to publish a text-critical commentary that centred on recording and assessing the readings of the manuscripts. By doing so, he created something like a critical apparatus in the modern sense. And by printing an *apparatus editorum in usum*, he showed that he had grasped Poliziano's insight into the difference between collation and emendation. Like Poliziano, he understood that all the manuscript evidence must be collected and recorded before a critical text could be established. Moreover, by declining to furnish a text, he avoided digging a pit for himself like the one into which Beroaldo fell. Since he was not trying to provide his readers with a readable Virgil, he did not have to correct interesting manuscript readings and, by doing so, conceal them from his readers.

Naturally, Valeriano's notions of completeness and precision were different from ours. One tiny sounding will suggest some of his limitations. Virgil's Fourth Eclogue is sixty-three lines long. In his notes on it Valeriano explicitly mentioned seventeen readings from Romanus, and one more which he attributed to all the oldest texts.[26] He also quoted the Eclogue's title from Romanus, 'Saeculi novi interpraetatio', though he regularized the last word to 'interpretatio'.[27] His accuracy was quite good; sixteen of his seventeen readings were exactly correct, and his one slight imprecision was of no importance.[28] So far so good. However, he also quoted 'patris' in line 17 as being 'in some very old manuscripts', and he remarked that 'Terras' in line 51 was 'much more splendid' than the singular 'Terram'.[29] In neither case could his reader know that these were the readings of Romanus. Moreover, the reader had no way of knowing that four readings Valeriano attributed to 'several old manuscripts' were not to be found in Romanus.[30] Worst of all, Valeriano omitted a good many other readings, some no odder than those he chose to record.[31] In short, his notes hardly amount to a complete record of the readings of Romanus.

It would be unjust to criticize Valeriano for producing collations less accurately than a twentieth-century editor armed with microfilm reader and Cappelli. After all, he did publish — to extrapolate from our sample — several hundred readings from Romanus, many good, and enough bad ones to prove his thesis that Romanus was not by itself a sufficient basis for a critical text. He had also devised a simple and effective literary form for recording and publishing collations.

Sadly, this most sophisticated product of the textual scholarship of Leo's Rome was also the last. Poliziano had been interested in much besides the collation of manuscripts. He had shared the weakness of his generation for Egyptian gods and hieroglyphs.[32] So had Urbano Bolzani, who had even visited Egypt to pursue his researches and had included a discussion of the hieroglyphic significance of the eye in his — evidently rather idiosyncratic — lectures on Pindar.[33] Valeriano inherited this interest, as did many of his friends in the Roman group. They urged him to explain to them the deeper meanings of the gems in their collections and the monuments they saw while on their *fêtes champêtres.*[34] At the same time, Giles of Viterbo and other reformers were calling for a new style of classical studies, one which would be of moral and religious help to the ordinary educated Christian.[35] Here hieroglyphs were splendidly apposite, since they could be made to reveal, in elegantly crystallized form, whatever their interpreters wished — including the central tenets of Christianity. So Valeriano dedicated himself to decades of research, which ended with the publication of his monumental *Hieroglyphica* in 1556. Even here the old Adam of the textual scholar reappears from time to time. Valeriano cites a Vatican manuscript of Horapollo as well as a Latin Dioscorides in 'Lombardic script' which he had also cited in the *Castigationes.*[36] He even records a reading from the Florentine Pandects in order to correct a corrupt passage in the vulgate text of the *Digest.*[37] But the character of his interests had clearly shifted. Once embarked on his journey across the *mare magnum* of ancient symbols, Valeriano could hardly paddle back to the dry beach of Latin textual criticism. He wrote no sequel to the *Castigationes.* And the sack of Rome in 1527 destroyed the world in which the *Castigationes* had originated. The Curial humanists scattered: some subsided gently into literary retirement, others returned to their neglected benefices or dedicated themselves to reforming the Church from within its Roman heart. Colocci and a few others hung grimly on in Rome, picking up the pieces of their sculptures and reassembling the remnants of their libraries. But for the moment, there could be little effort to continue the work of Beroaldo and Parrasio.[38]

Ironically, the political crisis that scattered the Roman group also led to the creation of a new tradition of textual scholarship in Florence, where Poliziano's principles were next revived. The man chiefly responsible, Pier Vettori, could never have chosen classical scholarship as a calling if the destruction of the independent Italian political system had not forced him out of public life.

It is not entirely clear why Vettori set out to imitate Poliziano. A member of one of Florence's most influential families, he took part in the meetings in the Rucellai Gardens during the early 1520s, where young patricians planned to overthrow the Medici and restore the old oligarchical republic. When the 1527 crisis led to the expulsion of the Medici, he took an active part in the new republican regime. We have the speech that he delivered to the militia in 1529, in which he proved with a wealth of historical examples that a sound citizen army was 'la conservation del viver civile'.[39] His friend Jacopo da Diacceto, who helped him to collate classical manuscripts, was executed for his part in the anti-Medicean conspiracy of 1522.[40] The aristocratic republicanism of these young patricians harked back to the Florentine humanist tradition of a century before. It is thus difficult to see why they were interested in reviving the philology of Poliziano, closely identified as it had been with Medicean predominance and pro-Medici propaganda.

Part of their inspiration may simply have come from Poliziano's impressive literary heritage, much of it preserved in Florentine collections. It is clear that they had access to some of the many printed books in the margins of which he had entered his collations of manuscripts. He had regularly appended to his collations short but pungent subscriptions in which he identified, dated, and evaluated the manuscripts. He usually explained the circumstances of consultation and gave the date when the work was completed. Sometimes, he took the opportunity to single out one manuscript as the parent of the rest or to make forceful summary statements of his critical principles. 'I, Angelo Poliziano', he wrote in one:

collated these books on farming by Cato and Varro with a very old manuscript from the library of St Mark in Florence, in such a way that I copied even what seemed to be largely corrupt. For I have decided on the following method of correcting new texts: not to add anything of my own arbitrarily, and not to omit anything that I found in older exemplars. Had earlier scribes chosen this method, they would certainly not have left so much trouble and labour for those who came after them. Therefore, wherever I have applied my own judgement, I have nevertheless left some traces of the original reading, thus leaving freedom of judgement to all. Farewell, reader, and think well of this work of mine. At Florence, in the Church of St Paul, on the very day of the Bacchanalia, 1482.[41]

That Vettori and Diacceto learned from these books is obvious from the subscription that they entered in their own copy of Varro *De lingua latina*:

Pier Vettori and Jacopo da Diacceto collated [this book] with an old manuscript written in Lombardic script from the library of St Mark, with so much diligence, or rather peevish attention to detail, that we copied here even the corrupt passages in the [manuscript]. 14 April 1521.[42]

The evidence now available does not tell us whether Vettori and Diacceto had any help in learning to imitate Poliziano. Both knew Jacopo Modesti da Prato, who had been Poliziano's student and friend, and he might have taught them.[43] It is just as likely that they mastered Poliziano's method on their own. However it happened, Vettori at once took Poliziano's teachings to heart. And unlike any of Poliziano's other disciples, he proved able to embody them in many editions and to impart them to a wide circle of colleagues and disciples. More adaptable than his close friends and life-long correspondents, Donato Giannotti and Bartolomeo Cavalcanti, he came to terms with the restored Medicean regime that took the place of his defeated republic. He returned to the city as soon as possible after its fall in 1530. Obviously the Medici could not give him political office. But he was a grandee and therefore worth conciliation. To give him academic preferment was a most logical way to provide him with a respectable but safe position in the new order. And Vettori's own interests and training led him to adopt a style of scholarly work that made him an ideal candidate, just as Poliziano had been, for Medicean patronage. It is not surprising, then, that by 1538 he had won a professorship in the Florentine Studio, and that he was able to use this position — along with his own social prominence — both to gain disciples and to obtain access to more and more manuscripts of unpublished or badly edited texts.

Vettori early decided that his mission was to complete what he regarded as Poliziano's unfinished life-work. Poliziano's annotated books, he argued, were the *disjecta membra* of a great enterprise. They were the first step toward the production of critical editions of and commentaries on the major ancient authors. But Poliziano's early death had prevented the completion of these works:

Since he was diligent and accurate he took the greatest delight in this collation of books, and rightly believed that good authors could thus be cleansed of many blemishes. Therefore, he carefully noted down in printed books whatever he had found in original manuscripts. If he had lived longer and had been able to complete what he intended, his labour and assiduity would have brought great profit to students of literature and would have freed from very great trouble many men who have worked since his time on this necessary task of correcting books. But all these things now lie unfinished and incomplete. For he rarely showed what he thought; [he] only copied the readings of old manuscripts accurately into these texts. In my opinion he was awaiting a more convenient time at which he could make a ripe judgement about these matters. But death surprised him, and he could not complete what he had planned. His books were scattered at his death, and though there were many of them, [only] a few can be found.[44]

Vettori was not quite right about Poliziano's intentions. Poliziano had indeed promised to publish a full commentary on the *Digest*.[45] Some of his university lectures amounted to full commentaries on texts, including both manuscript evidence and Greek parallels. He apparently set out to write a text-critical commentary on Suetonius.[46] But he nowhere said that he intended to edit all, or even a large number, of the major ancient writers. When Poliziano spoke of his new 'emendandi novos codices institutum', he was referring not to a method of preparing texts for publication but to a method of correcting the printed texts in his own possession. He was saying merely that, where earlier humanists had entered conjectures in their personal copies of classical texts, he would enter only the variants he found in manuscripts. Vettori's error was scholarship's gain, for he tried to execute what he thought to have been Poliziano's plans.

Vettori, in fact, imitated Poliziano's method in a rather one-sided way. He looked up to Poliziano above all as an accurate student of manuscripts, and it was manuscript studies that he emphasized in his own works. As we shall see, though he understood Poliziano's exegetical method perfectly well, his applications of it were less original and distinctive than his use of manuscripts.

The one-sidedness of Vettori's method is already apparent in his first major piece of work, the edition of Cicero which he carried out in the 1530s. He did not intend his notes to this edition to be a full commentary. Rather, he intended them to be almost entirely concerned with textual criticism. He called them 'castigationum explicationes' — that is, explanations of the more significant instances where his text deviated either from the printed vulgate or from the best manuscripts. His debt to Poliziano is particularly evident in his notes on the *Familiares*, since he could there draw on Poliziano's account of the textual tradition and base his own text on the manuscript which Poliziano had shown to be the archetype.

From these notes it is clear that Vettori was less interested in emending the text than in using the best manuscripts to expunge other critics' emendations. 'We did not intend', he admitted, 'to castigate or emend the accepted texts of Cicero, but by the use of the original exemplars to expel and erase the rash and value-less conjectures of certain rash men.'[47] According to Vettori, the oldest or least interpolated manuscript was the best source for the text, and applications of this principle filled most of his notes. In a note on *Familiares* IX. 16, for instance, he wrote:

Tum enim cum rem habebas quaestiunculis te faciebam attentiorem] : The very old Medicean codex alone preserves the correct reading. For the manuscript that seems to have been copied from it (which they say was written by the hand of Francesco Petrarca) has degenerated, as happens, from that correctness. *Sic omnia fatis in peius ruere*, as the prudent poet says. For it reads QVAESTIVNCVLIS, from which, we think, came the vulgate reading. The more correct manuscript still preserves QVAESTICVLIS, which is very appropriate to this point.[48]

Vettori did not always insist that the reading of the Medicean manuscript replace that of the vulgate texts. In a note on XVI. 11, for example, he admitted that he had followed the 'modern grammarians' in rejecting one reading given by his manuscript. But he still recorded it in his note, remarking rather defensively that 'We did not dare to accept so new and, from our point of view, so peculiar a combination of words. But we still do not think that we deserve blame for not being reluctant to mention this matter, whatever its value.'[49] In other words, even the errors found in the oldest manuscript must be recorded. A new in-scription might reveal that apparent corruptions were really genuine but unusual words.[50] Even where Vettori had to follow the vulgate texts, he still hoped that his oldest manuscript might prove to be correct. And for the most part he followed his manuscript very faithfully, even to the point of using such spellings as *relicum, vementer, dest,* and *benest.*[51]

Vettori defined the duties of the critic largely in terms of his use of manuscripts. The duties, he said, were arduous, and the preparation needed to assume them was long and trying: 'Not just anyone can deal with old manuscripts'.[52] The critic must compare the spellings and abbreviations found in his own manuscripts with those of the oldest extant manuscripts and of inscriptions.[53] He must observe the habits of scribes in order to be able to diagnose the probable causes of their errors.[54] He must master the whole vocabulary of classical Latin in order to recognize the vestiges of unusual words — words which ignorant scribes had wrongly thought to be corrupt and had tried to correct.[55] The critic who fulfilled all these requirements could restore a text to its original state, so that its author spoke again in 'the dialect which was used in [his] time, . . . and not in one adjusted to the rules and custom of later men'.[56]

What the critic must not do, on the other hand, was to engage in arbitrary attempts at conjectural emendation. Vettori did not deny that valid conjectures could be made, and he ventured some of his own. But far more often he sharply criticized those who dared to make emendations 'wilfully, and by conjecture, rather than with the aid of old and incorrupt manuscripts'.[57] When he made conjectures, he tried to follow the *ductus litterarum*, preferring to change only one letter. He described this method as one of 'departing moderately from the old reading', and he repeatedly drew attention to its advantages.[58]

Vettori was well aware of the value of Greek sources for the elucidation of Latin ones. In a note on *Familiares* VIII. 11, for example, he followed Poliziano in criticizing those who 'delete immediately what they do not understand by wit alone. . . . For', he continued: 'they ought to bear in mind . . . that many things which are now hidden will soon be illuminated, since every day new authors — Greek ones especially — are dug up from the shades.'[59] Greek historians were particularly useful, since they described some aspects of Roman civilization better than the Romans had: 'They wrote for foreigners, who did not know Roman customs, [and] they [thus] dealt carefully and in detail with matters which the Latin writers had omitted as being of common knowledge.'[60] He spent much more time, nevertheless, on discussing manuscript readings than on citing passages of Greek — or, indeed, on explaining what Cicero had said.

Later, even Vettori realized that he should have devoted more effort to explaining the text. In his *Posteriores castigationes* of 1541, he sought not only to reply to the attacks of Paolo Manuzio but also to correct what he now saw as the defects of his Cicero edition. He promised explicitly to explain 'obscuriores aliquos locos' which he had failed to discuss in his earlier notes.[61] He explained many passages, and he sometimes employed Greek material — particularly passages from historians — in doing so. But Vettori's tastes and principles hampered him at every turn. He still gave more space to manuscript readings than to explaining them. Again and again he returned to the praise of his two Florentine manuscripts: 'these two are so authoritative in my opinion . . . that I trust their testimony more than that of all the rest.'[62]

This weak attempt to try harder at exegesis satisfied no one. The unlearned found nothing novel or compelling in Vettori's continuous reference to manuscript readings. 'I went to find that blessed Bishop', wrote Giannotti after the *Posteriores castigationes* reached Rome.

He said to me that . . . so far as he had read, he found it very good, and he would find it even better if you did not trust so much in your old texts, which were corrupt even before Cicero's time; and the same must be said of the others that survived the Gothic and Lombardic destruction. All in all he means that you rely too heavily on old texts. And that is all he has to say, which I do not take more seriously than I have to, because — between ourselves — I find him a great pedant.

Even the competent wanted more comment and illustration than Vettori was willing to provide. Giannotti suggested that Vettori might enlarge the book 'by explaining many things that you correct and do not explain; for you would please those who are not very learned, and scholars will never think that you explain too· much'.[63] Such were the trials of a man of too much principle.

Vettori's editions of Greek texts resembled his editions of Latin works, for here too his emphasis lay somewhat more on the discovery and publication of new material than on the literary interpretation of texts that were already well known. In the mid-1540s two younger Florentines, Girolamo Mei and Bartolomeo Barbadori, collated manuscripts of the Greek tragedians under Vettori's direction. The first fruit of their efforts was the *Electra* of Euripides, which they discovered and passed on to Vettori. He published the *editio princeps* of the play in 1545.[64]

Barbadori and Mei also discovered a very important manuscript of Aeschylus: Laur. 31. 8, which contained the full text of the *Agamemnon* (the other manuscripts gave only a few hundred lines of the play). Using this codex, they were able to distinguish between the *Agamemnon* and the *Choephori*, which had previously been conflated into a continuous and highly corrupt text. During the 1550s, Vettori assembled the results of their efforts in a new edition of Aeschylus and used the new information they had provided to elucidate Aristotle's *Poetics*.[65] Vettori, then, had achieved quite striking results. He had dramatically improved the texts of major Greek and Latin writers, and he had also begun to build up a school. Both Barbadori and Mei continued for decades to pursue the studies into which Vettori had initiated them. As late as the 1580s Mei was still corresponding with Vettori about Greek manuscripts in the Vatican.[66] It is also a famous story that in 1560 Barbadori finished copying a manuscript of Plutarch while at Padua, in the company of Michael Sophianus, Gian Vincenzo Pinelli, and that remarkable bluestocking of easy morals, Λουκρήτιον ἡ ἑταῖρα.[67]

In one important respect, however, Vettori did not act on all the implications of his own insights in these early works. On the one hand, he saw the printed vulgate of the texts he edited as inaccurate and derivative and set out to correct it against the text of the manuscripts. But at the same time he tended to respect the vulgate in practice. Thus, his *Castigationum explicationes* were designed to explain not his departures from the best manuscripts but his departures from the printed vulgate — even though he regarded the vulgate text of the *Familiares*, at least, as wholly derivative from that of his manuscripts. Similarly, for his 1548 edition of Aristotle's *Rhetoric*, he collated the oldest manuscript (A) and used it to revise the orthography of the text quite radically. But even in this case he sometimes hesitated or refused to alter the readings of the Aldine edition in passages where those of A — or his own conjectures — were clearly better.[68]

To the modern student these attitudes seem mutually contradictory. If the text should follow the best manuscripts, then departures from them, not from the vulgate, need justification. But to criticize Vettori on such grounds is to some extent unfair. When considered in context, his attitudes have some measure of consistency. What he detested above all was the practice of making emendations in a text without indicating that they had been made or identifying the sources that justified them. By doing so, editors made it impossible for their readers to know the sources of their text. This problem had hindered Vettori from the start of his career. While editing Cicero he realized that Cratander's 1528 Basel edition had drawn upon valuable manuscripts. But Cratander's imprecision in citing them made it hard for Vettori to use his material with full confidence.[69] To some extent, it may have seemed to Vettori that even a vulgate provided some sort of fixed starting-point for collation and discussion. To alter it arbitrarily was merely to throw matters into confusion. And even a limited amount of material from manuscripts, presented in the notes to an avowedly corrected vulgate, might be of more use to the reader than a cleverly corrected text the sources of which were not made clear. To this extent, Vettori's respect for the *lectio recepta* may have been the result of principle rather than superstition.

Vettori did not fail to apply the exegetical side of Poliziano's method. Even in the Cicero edition he called readers' attention to the Greek sources from which the philosophical works — notably the *Tusculan Disputations* — were drawn.[70] And his twenty-five books of *Variae lectiones*, which appeared in 1553, were a sustained set of exercises in comparative exegesis. Vettori's account of the work's origin sounds strikingly like Poliziano: he wrote that while reading Latin authors, he had come across 'a good many things which, it seemed, were either translated from Greek writers, or could receive much benefit and illumination from them'.[71] The form of his work, which dealt with subjects in a completely random order while describing the contents of each chapter in a detailed heading, clearly recalled that of the *Miscellanea*.[72] So did its frequent references to Vettori's benefactors and friends.[73] So, most important, did its contents.

Throughout the *Variae lectiones* Vettori followed up Poliziano's innovation of matching Latin dramatic fragments with their Greek sources. He suggested a good many identifications of his own.[74] And in XX. 13 he took a fresh look at the Ennius fragment that Poliziano had spotted in *Familiares* VII. 6. He pointed out that Ennius had evidently departed from his model Euripides when he described Medea's hands as 'coated with gypsum', 'for there is nothing in Euripides . . . that shows Medea's hands or any part of her body to have been dyed any colour at all'.[75] He plausibly explained the gypsum as a cosmetic used to simulate beauty of complexion.[76] And he accurately linked Ennius' infidelity to the normal practice of Roman adaptors of Greek works: 'We must not be surprised that Ennius added this. For it was the custom of the ancient poets to add certain things and omit others when translating Greek plays.'[77] To move from matching Latin fragments and Greek originals to pointing out differences between them was to refine Poliziano's method — was, indeed, to return to the full sophistication of Gellius' approach. But to treat in detail the same case that Poliziano had, while accepting his results in their main lines, was also to admit a methodological debt — as a hostile reader acknowledged when he attacked Poliziano's and Vettori's arguments simultaneously.[78] And elsewhere Vettori openly admitted that he was following Poliziano — for example, in pointing out an error on Cicero's part in citing Homer.[79]

Above all, as he said, Vettori investigated the ways in which Latin writers had drawn everything from single turns of phrase to complex philosophical theses from the Greeks. He had almost as good an eye as Poliziano for interesting points of syntax and diction, and he was very widely read. Hence he often showed considerable insight in his analyses of the cultivated and allusive prose and poetry of the late Republic and early Empire. 'The Latin poets', he wrote in X. 22:

> often used new idioms, completely unknown to the Romans. . . . Those who systematically studied Greek writers were especially apt to make this sort of departure from the norm. For as a result of their long occupation with that language, they tended to imitate even the turns of phrase that were peculiar to that nation, and to put words together in a fashion very different from the ordinary one of their fellow-countrymen. One who pays careful attention to this point will find that Horace often did this. For it is clear from a number of kinds of evidence that he had great affection for that language and derived his knowledge of Greek thought from Greek writers. To omit other cases, he is clearly doing this when he says in the *Ars poetica*:
>
> > *Invitum qui servat idem facit occidenti*
> > ('He who saves someone against his will does
> > the same as he who kills him.' (467))
>
> For the Latins do not say *idem illi* when they wish to say *idem quod ille* [the same as he (who) . . .]. But the Greeks always say ταυτὸν ἐκείνῳ [the same as he (who) . . .]; it is the only expression they use. There is no need to give examples for so clear a point. Lucretius also used this expression and imported it from Greek into Latin . . .[80]

App. II

The passage is typical both in its verbosity and in the accuracy of the glimpse it gives into Horace's study. The excellence of the observation is guaranteed by the fact that the greatest of sixteenth-century Horace commentators, Denys Lambin, repeated it in his note on the line.[81] It was by no means the only one of Vettori's insights to establish itself in that way.[82]

Vettori also tried to imitate Poliziano by using his scholarship for literary ends. It served to adorn the prose style of his exercises in formal rhetoric and to embellish the inscriptions that he composed for public pageants.[83] It also served literary ends when he turned his attention to formal literary theory. For he was able to use his critical and exegetical skills to make available in a newly accurate and accessible form the great ancient literary manuals, Aristotle's *Rhetoric* and *Poetics*.[84] He also advised Bartolomeo Cavalcanti in detail on the composition of his vernacular rhetoric, thus greatly enhancing the rigour and scholarship of the body of Italian-language literary theory.[85]

Yet Vettori's literary and exegetical scholarship never imposed itself as firmly as his textual criticism. For in this field his applications of Poliziano's principles were less original and less fruitful than they had been in editorial work *tout court*. The comparative exegesis of the *Variae lectiones*, as we have seen, moulded itself all too firmly to Poliziano's last. And even in his work on the *Poetics* Vettori was not so much breaking new ground as using slightly sharper implements. When he discussed the question of which arts can be considered imitative in Aristotle's sense of the word, or tried to identify the inconsistency in Iphigeneia's behaviour singled out in *Poetics* 1454 a 28-32, he was following furrows that previous commentators had already ploughed.[86] Moreover, his exegetical labours produced far less than Poliziano's had in the realm of literature. Vettori's special pride was not a rich and splendid vein of poetry but a stately and orotund brand of prose. And that had less and less appeal to readers already bored by the perfectly Ciceronian prose and Virgilian verse of Bembo's generation.[87]

Finally, Vettori simply had less talent for literary exegesis than for historical and philological criticism. In the *Ars poetica* Horace recommends that the poet devote himself to the study of *exemplaria Graeca*:

> At nostri proavi Plautinos et numeros et
> Laudavere sales, nimium patienter utrumque,
> Ne dicam stulte, mirati...

('But our forefathers praised the metre and the humour of Plautus, admiring both too patiently, not to say foolishly.' (270-2))

'This', Vettori commented in the *Variae lectiones*:

is inappropriate to his low condition, and to the son of a freedman. Had he spoken thus he would have been ridiculed and rightly criticized by everyone. But there is a great discrepancy between [this statement] and his cast of mind. For he always emphatically called attention to and admitted his low birth. The reading should therefore follow that of the manuscripts, *At vestri proavi*. For he was addressing himself to men of an old and noble family [scil. the Pisones].[88]

Here Vettori's unease with the vulgate text was well founded; his report of the manuscript readings, though imprecise, was accurate; and his appreciation of Horace's social context — not surprising in an editor of Cicero — was acute. But his argument, in its concentration on a brief passage rather than its context, left out one crucial consideration. If Horace was too modest to boast about his ancestors, would he have ventured to criticize the judgement of the Pisones' *proavi*? Any interpretation of the line must resolve this question. It was not hard for a sensitive critic to do so. As an anonymous sixteenth-century reader of Vettori commented in his copy of the *Variae lectiones*:

What if when the poet referred to his *proavi* he did not mean his direct ancestors, but in general all those who preceded him by many generations or centuries, mingling himself with the other Romans; and by *proavi* [might he have meant] all the old Romans, whom both poets and other elegant writers often referred to in that way? We still use that idiom frequently.[89]

The point is this: the only way to account for Horace's criticism of the *proavi* is to realize that the poem as a whole was not written only for the Pisones, to whom Horace addressed himself, but really for all cultured Romans, or at least all Roman writers. Only when seen in that light does Horace's criticism become inoffensive.[90] It was just this literary understanding of Horace's work that Vettori lacked. True, both Lambin and Richard Bentley accepted Vettori's argument and repeated it in their own works.[91] But the episode none the less reveals a certain insensitivity on his part as a reader of poetry — a tendency to concentrate on details at the expense of seeing works whole and to overemphasize historical and philological methods at the expense of literary ones. Perhaps Vettori was right to give his best efforts to textual criticism.

As time went on, moreover, Vettori seems to have turned his attention more and more to critical problems. In particular, he became increasingly aware of the methodological inconsistencies in his earlier editions and tried to remedy them. For his associates in Florence and Rome began to publish works that reflected Poliziano's ideas even more clearly than Vettori's own editions. He responded to their work by changing his own style of editing.

Vettori's Florentine associates specialized in legal studies. The doyen of the group, and the man responsible for its chief original discovery, was Lelio Torelli, the legal adviser to Cosimo I. But the Spanish lawyer Antonio Agustín first won public attention for their work. These men applied Poliziano's genealogical method to the manuscripts of the *Digest*. Poliziano had believed that the Florentine manuscript was an official copy drawn up by Justinian's commissioners, and hence by definition the parent of the rest. He had not, however, examined the vulgate manuscripts in order to see if they contained common errors clearly deriving from the Florentine manuscript. Torelli made such an examination. And Agustín published Torelli's findings — along with some of his own — in his *Emendationes et opiniones* of 1543. The antepenultimate and penultimate leaves of the Florentine manuscript, Torelli discovered, had long ago been mistakenly transposed by a binder. The resulting transposition in the text, which fell in the title *De diversis regulis juris antiqui*, also occurred in all the vulgate manuscripts. It was therefore obvious, Agustín argued, that the Florentine manuscript was the archetype and that it alone should be used to establish the text of the *Digest*:

> From this it is clear that all the scribes followed the Pisan scribe's error. I venture to deny that any text of the *Digest* exists in which the same error does not occur. From these facts we may conclude that all the other manuscripts were copied from the Florentine. If this is true, as I have shown that it is, then all copies must be emended in accordance with the text of that manuscript.[92]

Or, as he put it elsewhere: 'Since these errors are in all texts, they show that all the texts have the same origin. Since this is the case, let us admit that the other manuscripts must be emended in accordance with the text of this one.'[93]

Agustín did not confine himself to Poliziano's method of using transpositions to establish a genealogy. He showed that the lack of word-divisions and punctuation in the Florentine manuscript had engendered errors in the vulgate text, thereby providing further confirmation for his account of the manuscript tradition.[94] He also refined Poliziano's dating and description of the Florentine manuscript. Agreeing that it had been written in

Greece, not in Italy, he pointed out that 'the scribes in many
places used abbreviations of numbers and words', a practice
which Justinian had prohibited. Consequently, it must not have
been an official copy, but rather one written for private use
— probably, Agustín thought, a few years after Justinian's
death.[95] He keyed his new readings to the most recent and the
most readily available version of the vulgate text: Gregory Haloander's 1529 edition of the *Digest*. And he carefully explained
how every correction should be entered in that edition. Since,
he explained, 'many copies [of Haloander's text] are readily
available in every library, it will be easy for all to use our emendations.'[96]

Agustín later drifted away from manuscript studies. Inscriptions and coins, he came to believe, were more trustworthy
witnesses than manuscripts to Roman history and orthography.
Even the oldest Latin manuscripts then available dated only
from the late Empire, whereas there were plenty of material
remains from the Republican period.[97] But Torelli remained
faithful to Vettori's method. In 1553, after years of preparation,
he and his son Francesco published an edition of the Florentine
manuscript. In their prefaces, they argued yet again that
the Florentine manuscript was the archetype and that literal
reproduction was the only editorial method suitable to so
decisive a textual witness: 'First of all, let it be known that in
no matter of any moment have we departed even slightly from
the testimony of that [manuscript], so that, so far as possible,
its appearance should be truly represented.'[98] In fact, the edition
was not merely a facsimile, for the Torelli introduced word- and
sentence-divisions and corrected what they took to be obvious
errors. Vettori also helped by conjecturally emending several
passages in Greek.[99] But in most respects it reproduced the
manuscript closely. The Torelli employed a variety of typographical conventions, which they carefully explained, in order
to preserve the manuscript's idiosyncrasies without incon-
veniencing the reader. When a letter was capitalized in the
middle or the end of a word, for example, it indicated that
either a double or a different letter was called for. Thus the
reader, encountering *adIcere*, knew both that the manuscript
read *adicere* and that it should be taken as reading *adiicere*.[100]
The edition even retained variant spellings from the original
whenever both forms could be justified by the evidence of other
very old manuscripts or of inscriptions: 'What we found written

in different ways in that volume — if, to be sure, it was correct — we likewise set down in different ways. Hence you will find *Compraehendere* and *Comprehendere, Extare* and *Exstare, Plebiscitum* and *Plebisscitum.*'[101] Even more than Agustín's monograph, the Torelli's edition and prefaces made Vettori's methods known to a wide European public.

At the same time, Vettori gradually began to build up firm connections with a group of like-minded scholars in Rome. Cavalcanti and Giannotti helped to make his name and work familiar. In the 1540s Angelo Colocci wrote to him to discuss orthographical and epigraphical problems and to ask for information about manuscripts in the collection of the Medici.[102] Marcello Cervini helped Vettori to obtain collations of Roman manuscripts and matrices of good Greek type.[103] And the best biblical and patristic scholars in Rome, Guglielmo Sirleto and Latino Latini, were deeply sympathetic to Vettori's editorial principles and hoped to join him in applying them to patristic texts and even, so Sirleto hoped, to the Bible itself.[104]

Most important, from the early 1550s Vettori corresponded with Gabriele Faerno, a scriptor in the Vatican library.[105] Faerno was the only one of the Romans who was Vettori's match — or perhaps more than his match — as a classical scholar. Faerno rivalled Vettori in mastery of the classics of Latin prose, especially Cicero and Livy. Unlike Vettori, he was also a brilliant student of Latin verse. He was himself a successful Neo-Latin poet. His hundred Aesopic fables in Latin verse, illustrated by Pirro Ligorio, were reprinted as late as the eighteenth century. Not unnaturally, he concentrated much of his scholarly activity on Roman poetry. In particular, he made a special study of the metres and manuscript tradition of Terence, subjects that Vettori had treated only in passing.[106]

If Faerno's interests differed somewhat from Vettori's, his critical methods — or at least so his contemporaries believed — did not. Latini, for example, was convinced that Faerno would employ conjectural emendation only as a last resort. 'In Livy', he wrote to his Flemish friend Andreas Masius: 'I wouldn't want you to conceive the idea that he is either so bold or so self-satisfied as to change or add anything without the authority of old manuscripts, except where they are most obviously corrupt.'[107] Faerno's palaeographical skill aroused wonder even in his enemies. 'Faerno', recalled Marc-Antoine Muret in a sarcastic but revealing note of 1570:

was remarkable in this study. As stable-boys pronounce on the age of horses after examining their teeth, so he judged the age of old books by inspecting their paper, [and] he did not hesitate to say: 'This one is ten, or twenty, or thirty years older than that one.' Nor did he say that he 'thought so', but he spoke as firmly and authoritatively as if he himself had been present when all of them were written.[108]

Some of Faerno's works confirm the estimate of his contemporaries that he was a whole-hearted follower of Vettori. In a letter that Francesco Robortello published without his knowledge in 1557, Faerno dissected Carlo Sigonio's corrections of Livy. Sigonio, he admitted, was brilliant and learned, but he was no critic, did not know how to evaluate manuscripts, and made too many arbitrary emendations. He erred, Faerno said: 'not . . . for want of wit, for he has a fine mind, but partly because he hit on bad manuscripts, partly because he did not know how much to rely on conjecture in correcting authors'.[109] On the other hand, Faerno singled out for praise those of Sigonio's corrections 'where the conjecture changes only one letter'.[110] That is exactly what Vettori would have said, though he would no doubt have taken longer to do so.

Faerno's edition of Terence, which he was preparing during the 1550s, also followed Vettori's principles.[111] The several earlier Terence commentaries had all been imitations of the ancient one by Donatus. They had all imitated their model in going to great lengths to extract moral precepts and rhetorical principles from the plays — and in doing relatively little towards correcting the text. Faerno broke with this tradition. His pithy notes, most of which ran to only a few lines, were concerned with two subjects above all: metrical analysis and textual criticism.[112] And the text-critical notes clearly resembled Vettori's in their concentration on manuscript evidence. Faerno collated one ninth- and one tenth-century manuscript from the Vatican as well as the Codex Bembinus, and he set down their readings with a meticulous accuracy reminiscent of Valeriano. At times he even recorded details about the scholia in the Bembinus and about the changes made in it by a second hand.[113] He reviewed his collations time and time again, writing to Vettori for information about Poliziano's collation of the Bembinus, then in Vettori's hands, where he was unsure about his own accuracy.[114] His collations were as comprehensive as they were precise. The Codex Bembinus ends at *Adelphi* 914. In his notes on these 914 lines alone, Faerno gave more than two hundred readings from the Bembinus; only fourteen were incorrect.[115] Moreover, most of Faerno's deviations were minute, involving only the expansion of words elided in the manuscript or the silent correction of obvious errors. Even his most serious mistakes consisted for the most part in changing only one letter (Faerno *ordine*: MS *ordinem*; Faerno *amat*: MS *amet*).[116] In short, he was at least as able as Vettori at collating manuscripts and publishing their readings.

It is not surprising, then, that Vettori and Faerno took to one another. Some of Faerno's letters to Vettori are preserved in the British Library. The topics they treat are technical, and Vettori must have found Faerno's views on them highly sympathetic. Faerno described in great codicological and palaeographical detail the manuscript of Cicero's *Philippics* and other speeches that he had just discovered (Vatican Basilicanus H 25).[117] He thanked Vettori for the loan of a Terence manuscript, the critical importance of which he emphasized, and he sent him materials for his own work in progress.[118] And he expressed the greatest admiration for Poliziano's prowess in collating manuscripts.[119]

Encouraged by the achievements of Agustín and Torelli and by the sympathy of Faerno, Vettori reconsidered his own approach to textual criticism. He slowly lost his earlier respect for the vulgate and began to maintain that a good editor could not be content with reprinting it in an improved form. Rather, he should attempt to produce as his final text the closest possible approximation to that of the best manuscripts. If one of them could be singled out as the parent of the rest, it should serve as the basis of the edition, even if the vulgate or later manuscripts seemed on occasion to offer better readings.

In 1557 to 1558 Vettori began to put these new principles into practice. He prepared a new edition of the *Familiares*, the preface to which was clearly intended to serve as a programmatic statement. In it he repeated and confirmed Poliziano's analysis of the textual tradition. He explained that he had collated as many manuscripts of the *Familiares* as he could lay his hands on: 'Many honourable and learned men can bear witness to this, who came to visit me during this period. For they found me surrounded on all sides by copies of these letters, all lying open.'[120] All was to no avail. Every manuscript he could find contained errors that proved it was descended from the Vercelli codex. He had therefore set out to reproduce the manuscript as accurately as possible, preserving even its errors, and employing its own inconsistent orthography. This seemed to him the only possible way to provide all the information that future editors would need and to rid the text of all attempts at emendation.[121] He took care to draw attention to the parallel case of the *Digest* and to Torelli's transcript of the Florentina; indeed, he said that his own new edition was an attempt to imitate Torelli.[122] And he also claimed to be acting with the advice and support of Faerno.[123] 'Habes igitur optime lector', he concluded, 'simulacrum quoddam optimi exemplaris, magna sedulitate fabricatum.'

This preface was a remarkable piece of propaganda. Vettori presented himself as the head of a school of like-minded men; he represented himself, Torelli, and Faerno as engaged in a common enterprise and on the look-out for recruits to the cause. Any reader would believe that Torelli and Faerno agreed with Vettori's notions about the editor's task. This was not in fact true. To be sure, Faerno had advised Vettori to follow his manuscript's orthography;[124] and he was, as Vettori said, 'planning to publish both the plays of Terence and the *Philippics* of Cicero, which he has collated with very old manuscripts'.[125] In fact, it was precisely during the time that Vettori was preparing his second edition of the *Familiares* that it became clear that he and Faerno were not agreed on editorial technique.

As soon as Vettori sent him the first printed sheets of his text, Faerno expressed reservations. Pointing out that the later manuscripts sometimes gave better readings than those of the Vercelli codex, he urged Vettori to accept them despite their lack of manuscript authority: 'It is clear that often even the best manuscripts can lead us astray. Therefore, we must not always trust them. In fact, sometimes even a very recent copy, so long as it is a manuscript, contains the truth where the old manuscripts are in error.'[126]

Moreover, Vettori's description of Faerno's plans for the *Philippics* was also somewhat misleading. For he knew very well that Faerno did not mean to found his text of the speeches solely on the new manuscript he had discovered. It is clear that Vettori urged Faerno to publish a simple transcript of the Basilicanus. In April 1558, Faerno explained precisely why he could not do so. In the first place, he rightly pointed out that the manuscript contained an unusually large number of gross errors that there was no reason to preserve: 'It was written by someone who understood nothing, . . . And remarkable errors appear in it even in passages where the other manuscripts and the vulgate are correct.'[127] Moreover, even where the manuscript contained better readings than the rest: 'it does not always have the precisely correct reading, but often only traces from which one can reconstruct the correct reading with a bit of judgement.'[128] In short, simply to reproduce the manuscript 'saria un corrumperle et non correggerle, et si faria gridar tutto il mondo'. He promised only to record those readings that were better than the vulgate's and to explain, where necessary, his reasons for trying to improve on them.[129]

When Faerno readied the *Philippics* for the press, he added a prefatory letter to Vettori in which he repeated his earlier arguments and added a new and potent one. He pointed out that certain readings in his manuscript served to bear out conjectures that both he himself and Vettori had previously proposed. If these conjectures were valid, it was logical to assume that others could also be so — could be, as it were, the readings of a still better manuscript that happened now to be lost. And it was illogical to refrain from venturing conjectures in order to present the reader with the incomprehensible text of the codex.[130] Faerno, in short, declared in formal public Latin as well as the Italian of his private letters that he could not accept Vettori's new principles in their full rigour.

By 1558, then, Faerno had decided that Vettori's principles were over-simplified. He seems to have realized that a strict genealogical ordering could only be imposed on certain textual traditions — for example, that of the *Familiares*. And he insisted that even where one manuscript could be identified as the parent, the editor could not merely reproduce it warts and all. That Vettori tried to paper over these differences in his preface makes clear how strongly he wished to appear as the head of a united school.

In fact, however, no split developed. For Faerno was a loyal friend as well as an independent thinker.[131] And just in the period that he was working on the *Philippics* and arguing with Vettori, a new school of critics centred in France began to challenge Vettori. Its members concentrated on the literary side of Poliziano's method — above all on the comparative study of Latin and Greek. They did not find the work of Vettori and his associates worthless, but they did regard it as one-sided and, to some extent, misdirected. And to represent them in Italy there came the brilliant and unscrupulous Muret, who transformed the methods of the new school into a programme for attacking the work of Vettori and his allies. Faerno was willing to disagree with Vettori in a principled manner but not to see him attacked unfairly by men he regarded as incompetent. The two men joined in a concerted attempt to repel these impudent boarders from beyond the Alps. And it is the rise of the new school and the struggles it occasioned that provide the immediate context for Joseph Scaliger's earliest works.

III Poliziano's Legacy in France
1500–1570

Poliziano's comparative approach to Greek and Latin found competent imitators sooner than his systematic recension of manuscripts. In the first place, his friendly rival Barbaro saw the possibilities of the method employed in the *Miscellanea* and applied it more systematically than had Poliziano himself. His *Castigationes Plinianae* lacked the stylistic flair and the literary relevance of the *Miscellanea*. Nevertheless they derived a certain rhetorical force from the overwhelming learning that Barbaro displayed. His dry notes, which often deployed three, four, or five references to Greek texts in order to support the change of one letter in a place-name, proved beyond doubt that classical Latin science and philosophy needed both illustration and correction from the deeper resources of the Greeks.[1]

To a limited extent, Poliziano's ideas imposed themselves even upon men of rather different interests. Aldo Manuzio did not adopt Poliziano's method of textual criticism. But he imitated him in using Greek sources to elucidate allusions and metrical practices in Horace.[2] The later works of Beroaldo — especially his Apuleius commentary — rested on a vast accumulation of Greek sources and parallels, and may well have represented his attempt to meet the standards that Poliziano had set.[3] Even Girolamo Avanzio, who set out to prove that Poliziano's attacks on Calderini had been vicious and unfounded, had to accept some of Poliziano's text-critical applications of Greek sources.[4]

The real heirs to Poliziano's comparative method were the Northerners of Erasmus's generation. They had again to fight the battle — long won in Italy — against those who maintained that Latin culture needed no enrichment from Greek. Erasmus's *Adagia* were a sustained exercise in the comparative method. Erasmus consistently tried to show that Latin and Greek culture formed an indissoluble unity — for example, that the proverbs that crystallized the moral wisdom of the ancients had existed in both languages in related forms. He admitted that both his method and his material owed much to Poliziano — for instance, that his comparison of Greek and Latin epigrams on the goddess Occasio was based on *Miscellanea* I. 49.[5]

Guillaume Budé's work was closer than Erasmus's to Poliziano's variety of scholarship. Accordingly, he made even heavier use of Poliziano's methods, though his explicit references to Poliziano were for the most part severely critical. He attacked him for everything from plagiarism to bad handwriting.[6] Yet the very acidity of Budé's remarks no doubt revealed his uneasy awareness of his debt. In his first great work, the *Annotationes in XXIV primos Pandectarum libros*, largely a demonstration of the debt of Latin culture to Greek, he used his knowledge of Greek literature to identify the sources on which Roman jurists had drawn. He thus showed that the doctrine of equity was derived from Aristotle, bolstering his argument with a wealth of quotations from the Greek text.[7]

What Budé did for the sources of Roman ideas, he did with far more power and original learning for the sources of Latin style in his *Commentarii linguae graecae* of 1529. This immense work began as a survey of Greek legal terminology, but it ended as a general, non-alphabetical lexicon of both Latin and Greek usage. It was the first book to provide for students of Greek what Lorenzo Valla's *Elegantiae* had provided for students of Latin: a guide to the language in which all the rules were drawn from the practices of ancient authors and illustrated with appropriate examples.[8] At the same time, the *Commentarii* were also a polemic in favour of Poliziano's comparative study of Greek and Latin style. 'The best part of the copiousness of Latin', proclaimed Budé, 'is derived from the famous treasures of the Greeks.'[9] That this treasure had become available to Latins had been largely the work of Cicero, who 'desired above all to translate the elegance of Greek writers and the forcefulness [*vim*] of Greek words into the Roman language'.[10] He had used many Greek words 'as if they were clearly Latin',[11] bringing over Greek turns of phrase:

Aristotle in the third book of the [*Nicomachean*] *Ethics*: πότερον δὲ ἀπὸ ποτέρου καλεῖται, οὐδὲν πρὸς τὰ νῦν διαφέρει. ['Which is named after which makes no difference at present.'] Cicero imitated this in the *Pro Milone*: 'Uter utri insidias fecerit.'[12]

Indeed, he had appropriated devices wholesale from Demosthenes. Budé went on to show that the other Latin authors of the Golden Age — notably Livy — had also imitated the Greeks.[13] Having amassed the details of the Romans' borrowings, he was able to show that this study was not an end in itself, but rather a means to a literary end: in order to learn how to write like Cicero, one must learn to adapt Greek words and phrases as he did. He insisted that modern writers had the same rights: 'When Cicero imported that *copia* from Greece to Italy, he did not withdraw the right to trade.'[14]

Budé did more than leave written directions for the study of Greek and Latin. He also collaborated in the founding of the royal lectureships in classical languages that ultimately became the Collège de France. Thus he ensured that in Paris, at any rate, Greek would continue to be taught, and that his knowledge of Greek and his comparative method would be passed on by his disciple, Jacques Toussain, who became the first *lecteur du roi* in Greek.[15] Toussain knew Poliziano's method intimately, for he had supplied Latin translations for all the Greek passages in the 1518 to 1519 Badius edition of Poliziano's *Opera*. In his teaching he seems to have applied it consistently. The array of parallel passages that he assembled in his lectures on Proclus' *Sphaera*, and that has been used to characterize his methods, in fact proves little.[16] An earlier commentator, Ioannes Stoeffler, had assembled a much richer stock of parallels, and Toussain may well have been following the normal teacher's practice of looting his predecessor.[17] Of his lectures on Hermogenes we know only that they included a translation of the text.[18] One source, however, gives an inkling of his approach to problems of exegesis and imitation.

In 1526 Toussain published a commentary on Budé's letters, compiled, so he said, from Budé's own explanations.[19] He approached the text much as Poliziano and Budé approached the classics — with both eyes open for sources, parallels, and echoes. In a letter to Thomas More, Toussain found a characteristic Latinization of a Greek idiom:

Mirum quantum me totum. Mirum quantum is used in place of *maxime*. Livy, Book I: *Mirum quantum illi viro haec nuncianti fides fuerit* ['That man received remarkable credence when he announced these things' (I. xvi. 8)]. This is also drawn from the Greeks, who say θαυμαστὸν ὅσον and θαυμάσιον ἡλίκον. Demosthenes: ταῦτα δὲ θαυμάσια ἡλίκα καὶ συμφέρουντ' ἐδόκει τῇ πόλει ['These things seemed remarkable and useful to the city' (XIX. 24).][20]

Where Budé wrote to Vives of an 'Iliad of troubles', Toussain similarly showed that he was employing a Greek turn of thought: 'This comes from a Greek proverb: ἰλιὰς κακῶν. Demosthenes: καὶ κακῶν ἰλιὰς περιειστήκει θηβαίους ['And the Thebans were surrounded by an Iliad of evils' (XIX. 148)]. This proverb is derived from the great size of the poem.'[21] Here and elsewhere the connection between comparative exegesis and stylistic originality — if not elegance — was made as clear as in the *Miscellanea*. Presumably, Toussain's lectures on Budé's Greek letters followed a similar pattern.

In Paris, moreover, a new literary milieu was forming that proved receptive to the teaching of the *lecteurs du roi*. In the house of Lazare de Baïf on the Rue des Fossés Saint Victor and in the nearby Collège de Boncourt, men gathered in the hope of bringing about a revival in French literature through the creative adaptation of classical models.[22] Baïf was well qualified to aid and protect this movement. A former pupil of Janus Lascaris and a correspondent of Erasmus, he had written some of the earliest specialized antiquarian works of the sixteenth century. In them he had shown a predilection for studying Greek and Latin sources side by side and a sharp eye for the details of Roman practice in translating from Greek.[23] No wonder that he hoped to enrich the French language by following Roman example and borrowing from the Greeks. He gathered around him a group of poets, including his son Jean-Antoine, and scholars, including Jean Dorat, tutor to his son; and they set about transforming French into a polished literary language that would be the match of Latin or Italian.

These men had competitors. In 1540 the Benedictine Joachim Perion published two editions in which classical Latin texts — Cicero's *Timaeus* and the Latin *Aratea* — confronted on facing pages the Greek originals from which they had been translated.[24] Poliziano's ideas seem to have prompted him to do so. In the notes to the *Aratea* he explicitly referred to Poliziano's habit of drawing on Aratus in his own Latin verse.[25] His notes on both books compared the facing texts in detail, if somewhat mechanically.[26]

What is more, Perion transformed the general awareness of Rome's literary debt to Greece into a controversial literary programme. He decided that Cicero had been the ideal translator of the Greek classics. Dissatisfied with the un-Ciceronian translations from Aristotle that dominated university teaching and philosophical research, he set out, between 1540 and 1553, to replace them with a series of new Ciceronian translations, which he defended at length in a polemical treatise *De optimo genere interpretandi*.[27] Perion's innovations threatened the foundations of the university curriculum, and aroused sharp criticisms from French and Italian philosophers. At the same time, the crudity of his stylistic views — above all, his notion that the elaborate periodic style of Cicero was the best Latin equivalent for the dry Greek of Aristotle's treatises — irritated philologists like Vettori.[28]

Accordingly, the Parisian scholars faced two problems: they had both to establish their own programme and to show its superiority to Perion's. This double motivation is clearly revealed by Denys Lambin's letters. On the one hand, Lambin believed in and worked towards the literary revival of French. In 1552, two of Etienne Jodelle's tragedies on classical subjects were performed before Henri II at the Collège de Boncourt. Lambin's letter of congratulation to the principal of the college is revealing:

I was particularly pleased by the section of your letter [that was] about comedies and tragedies in French. I am always glad to see that our language — which other nations claim to be barbarous and impoverished — can accept, adapt, and express the charms and graces of the ancient poets. In this the Italians boasted that they were better than we. But I am sure that they will soon see that they are dealing with combative and powerful opponents.[29]

At the same time, he was pained by the damage that Perion's work had done to the reputation of the French. Here, for example, is his comment on Perion's translation of the *Nicomachean Ethics*:

I take my oath to you that Perion has made so many gross errors in this useful and attractive work of Aristotle that it makes me ashamed for our country when I am abroad. For in Italy I often heard the complaints of excellent scholars who said that Perion's works have nothing save a sort of empty stylistic elegance.[30]

This combination of motives — the desire to renew and win court favour for French literature and the will to rival the Italians in the field of Greek scholarship — became the dominant characteristic of French scholars around the middle of the century.

The leading Parisian scholar of the 1540s and '50s was Jean Dorat. At Baïf's house he was a splendid private tutor. As head of the Collège de Coqueret he inspired Ronsard to throw himself into an ascetic regime of full-time Greek studies. As *lecteur du roi* he became *the* teacher of Greek in Paris, and students flocked to him from the Netherlands and even Italy as well as from the French provinces.[31]

It is not easy to reconstruct Dorat's teaching with precision. He was prodigal with his time when it came to writing liminary verses for the books of others. But as a minor nobleman himself, and a fashionable teacher of young noblemen, he seems to have felt it beneath him to unite the materials that he gathered for lectures into a full commentary on a text, or even to publish a set of *Variae lectiones*. Accordingly, our evidence about his methods is fragmentary. Traditional anecdotes help us a little. Students' notes on some of his lectures survive. Some of his pupils published emendations and interpretations that they attributed explicitly to him. And some of his own poems give us some inkling of his own views on the task of the critic. A few conjectures will allow us to wire these *membra disiecta* together into a reasonably coherent form.

First, the anecdotes. According to Claude Binet's life of Ronsard, Dorat 'par un artifice nouveau luy apprenoit la langue Latine par la Grecque'.[32] Dorat also told Ronsard that he would some day be the Homer of France and translated Aeschylus' *Prometheus Bound* into French for him. 'And this', says Binet: 'in turn inspired Ronsard to translate Aristophanes' *Plutus* into French and have it performed in public at the Collège de Coqueret. It was the first French comedy played in France.'[33] What the 'artifice nouveau' was we cannot say. But these stories at least suggest that Dorat's teaching involved continual attention to parallels between Latin and Greek, and that his central aim was the enrichment of French poetry.

Students' notes bring us a little closer to Dorat's classroom. They reveal the tactics one might expect on the part of a six-teenth-century Greek teacher who wanted to do more than drill his pupils in the elements. Dorat offered a mélange of elementary glosses and paraphrases, more elaborate explanations drawn from the Greek scholia and a wide range of other sources, and still more refined allegories intended to reveal his deftness at pro-viding a usable antiquity.[34] Here he is lecturing on *Odyssey* X:

$\phi\iota\lambda\epsilon\hat{\iota}\nu$ means not only to love, but to receive someone in a friendly, loving, liberal, and generous way.
$\pi\acute{\epsilon}\mu\pi\epsilon\iota\nu$ however means not only to send away, but to accompany the person who is leaving, to furnish him with provisions for the trip, and, so to speak, give him journey-money.

By the skin of an ox we can understand the last sail of a ship. When this is properly set, sailors can use any wind and sail, or even make against an opposing wind. Ulysses can signify the citizen who looks towards his fatherland, that is, towards civil felicity; for they who stay in their fatherland are thought happy . . . And he desires to have saved his companions, that is, to keep his fellow citizens in duty and justice, but the winds blow against him. Thus many things prevent us from reaching our goal.[35]

Dorat's lectures were not all inspired. His skill in Latin textual criticism was apparently not great. His literary criticism could also be fairly leaden; it did not take a master of Greek scholarship to say that 'Of Pindar's odes, the longest are the best.'[36] And his elaborate moral and physical allegories, however appealing to the young Ronsard, seemed silly to more independent listeners.[37] Yet most of his students were enchanted. Dorat chose his texts cleverly. Homer, Hesiod, Pindar, and Theocritus illustrated the Latins any modern poet had to master. The *Sibylline Oracles* and the *Orphic Hymns* gave off a fashionable tang of natural magic. And others — Aeschylus above all — revealed literary possibilities not offered by the tired favourites of the Latin curriculum.[38]

Moreover, Dorat's advanced teaching — which may have been carried on in informal, quasi-seminars rather than in formal lectures — provided a sophisticated introduction to the whole body of Greek poetry. His vast knowledge of both the texts themselves and the scholiasts and grammarians enabled him to illuminate a wide range of dark corners in the literary history of Greece. One problem Dorat identified and solved was that posed by the abrupt beginning of Hesiod's poem on the shield of Hercules:

ἢ οἵη προλιποῦσα δόμους ικαὶ πατρίδα γαῖαν
ἤλυθεν ἐς Θήβας
'Or like the woman who, leaving her home and fatherland,
came to Thebes'.[39]

He knew from Pausanias that Hesiod had written a number of poems comparing famous women. And he knew from the scholia on Pindar that they all began with the words ἢ οἵη ('or like the woman who'). Accordingly, they had been called the ἠοῖαι. 'The extant *Shield of Hercules*', he concluded, 'is a fragment of those poems. It consists of one of the comparisons of which the whole work was composed. Therefore it begins, like the others, with 'Or like the woman who'.[40] In a society that treated ancient poetry as something to be read, marked, inwardly digested, and outwardly adapted, Dorat offered an incomparably detailed and critical introduction to the sources. The young poet who had studied with him was equipped with the best possible training. He could reconstruct and employ just the sort of mythological and literary details that the cultivated audience and patrons of the time wanted. No wonder then that Dorat attracted so many pupils.

Finally, Dorat's own poetry contains some fairly straightforward statements on the nature of ancient literature:

> Homer, Musaeus, Orpheus, all were thieves,
>   And Hesiod, who stole Achilles' shield,
> And gave what had been his to Hercules.
>   Both he and Homer, too, were glad to wield
> The Sibyls' verses as their own. Don't think
>   Because the Greeks have always been great liars
> That Latin poets did not also wink
>   At stealing from the great Greek versifiers.
> For Ennius, the first of their array,
>   Made out of Homer's works his chosen prey.[41]

These bald statements clearly licensed modern writers to practise similar thefts. No doubt such views also came up in Dorat's teaching, to form the link between the texts that he explained and those that he helped his pupils to write. In short, it seems that Dorat's teaching represented a revival of Poliziano's entire programme for the study of poetry. Detailed comparative study of the ancients provided the foundations for new compositions, as imitative and allusive as their models.

The first effects of Dorat's teaching appeared in the form of new poems. As early as 1549, Du Bellay summarized Dorat's views in his *Deffence et illustration de la langue françoise*.[42] And by 1550, Dorat himself and Ronsard had published Pindaric odes, in Latin and French respectively. In 1552 appeared Ronsard's *Amours*, so crammed with allusions that their public needed a commentary in order to follow them.[43] In so far as the poetry of the Pléiade exploited new classical models, it clearly showed the impact of Dorat's teaching. As a well-informed witness wrote in 1552:

Those who wished to be considered poets in our vernacular for a long time wrote pieces fit to please women with time on their hands, not to hold the attention of scholars. I think that Pierre Ronsard, who had devoted himself to studies under the supervision of that most learned man Jean Dorat, and had worked through the writings of the ancient poets in both languages with his guidance, was the first who set out to adorn his writings with those foreign riches. Jean Antoine de Baïf, Ioachim du Bellay, and many others followed his example. They made so much progress so quickly, that total success seems now to have been achieved, or will be achieved soon.[44]

Developments in the vernacular were soon matched in the Latin culture of the humanists. During the 1550s, technical works began to present the programme and the results of the new French philology to a European public.

In 1554, for instance, Henri Estienne published the *editio princeps* of the *Anacreontea*. Splendidly printed in large and elegant type, made notorious in advance by careful leaks of information to Pier Vettori and others, the edition was something of a manifesto.[45] Estienne proved that Horace had drawn upon the poems, and went on to discuss Horace's techniques of borrowing and adaptation in general:

Horace also borrowed something from Pindar — for example, this beginning of an ode:

> *Quem virum aut heroa lyra vel acri*
> *Tibia sumis celebrare Clio?*

For Pindar wrote, similarly:

> Ἀναξιφόρμιγγες ὕμνοι Τίνα θεὸν τίν᾽ ἥρωα
> Τίνα δ᾽ἄνδρα κελαδήσομεν;

In sum, Horace borrows without attempt at concealment from the poets I have mentioned and others. But he changes these borrowings, wishing them to seem original with him, into such different forms that their authors could scarcely recognize them as their own. And this is the honourable form of theft. The Greeks have shown us by their own precedent that it is not wrong to steal from an ancient writer. A great many of their thefts are recorded. Homer stole a good deal from Orpheus and Musaeus. In turn, almost all later poets stole much more from Homer. Take the tragic poets: Euripides stole in quantity not only from Homer but also from those who came after Homer's time. Sophocles in turn stole a great deal from Euripides. Nor did the comic poets keep their hands off the work of others.[46]   App. III

He explicitly declared that the practice of the ancients should serve as a model for his contemporaries: 'These points are worth our notice, so that we may learn to imitate the ancients skilfully and to take advantage of anything we find in them, but in such a way that it seems not borrowed but our creation.'[47] He added a partial Latin translation to his Greek text so that the poems — short, charming, and easily imitated — would be useful to poets as well as scholars. Even before the edition appeared, Estienne had given Ronsard access to some of its contents; for Ronsard drew on the *Anacreontea* in his *Amours* of 1552. He greeted the publication of the full text not only with a great toast to Estienne himself but also with further imitations of the new poems it contained.[48]

Throughout the 1550s and 1560s a stream of publications by French scholars drove home the same set of points. In 1549, Jean Brodeau published a commentary on the Greek Anthology — one of the best training-grounds for small-scale poetry.[49] His *Miscellanea* of 1555 deliberately challenged comparison not only with Poliziano, but with Vettori and Alciato as well. In particular, he criticized Vettori's errors in discussing Cicero's use of Greek sources.[50] Estienne and Adrien Turnèbe flooded the book fairs with new Greek texts; France and French-speaking Basel and Geneva began to dominate the world of classical publishing. And Turnèbe exhaustively reconstructed the Greek sources of Cicero's *De legibus*, which, he showed, was based less on Plato's dialogues than on the lost works of Greek Stoics.[51]

More than anyone else, however, Denys Lambin transformed the new programme into the reality of full-scale works. The son of a family of locksmiths in Montreuil, he was the social inferior of minor noblemen like Dorat and Turnèbe. Because he was a clever scholar and a stylish writer of Latin, he won preferment by his wits in the entourage of the Cardinal de Tournon and, later, as a *lecteur du roi*.[52] His intellectual gifts were not accompanied by adequate social graces. From his point of view, this lack was particularly unfortunate, for his 'schoolmasterish ill-manners'[53] tended to irritate the gentlemen among whom he lived and on whom he depended for advice, preferment, and loans of manuscripts. From our point of view it is helpful. For it led him to state explicitly and to demonstrate at enormous length points that his betters dealt with less directly or fully. Accordingly, his works enable us to identify securely both the virtues and the vices of the French exegetical manner.

In his editions of Horace, for example, Lambin applied the comparative method on a heroic scale. Not all his results and observations were original. Readers of Estienne and Brodeau would not have been surprised to learn that Horace's *Nunc est bibendum* was borrowed from Alcaeus.[54] And when Lambin pointed out that 'insanientem sapientiam' (*Odes* I. xxxiv. 2) was 'a graceful expression, after the model of the Greeks, who often use this figure', many would have recognized that he was only repeating, with some new examples, an observation of Vettori's.[55] Indeed, even the borrowings that Lambin expressly acknowledged as such must run to many dozens. Moreover, the effort to elucidate the sources of single words and expressions often blinded him, as it had blinded Vettori, to wider problems of context and interpretation. Yet for all its imperfections the Horace was a great book. Lambin disassembled with all a locksmith's patience and attention to detail the delicate workings of Horace's syntax and diction. No modern critic had ever studied with so much thoroughness and method the language of an ancient poet.

One example will reveal some of Lambin's characteristic strengths and weaknesses. In *Odes* I. xxii Horace begins full of high sentence: *Integer vitae, scelerisque purus*, the man of upright life and free from crime needs no arrows or javelins to defend himself. This maxim Horace supports with personal experience: a wolf, encountering Horace as he wandered unarmed through the Sabine wood, singing of Lalage, ran away without harming him. He will always continue, he concludes, whatever wild and inhospitable lands he may wander through, to love Lalage 'who laughs sweetly, who speaks sweetly'. The poem's movement is neatly symmetrical. On the one hand, Horace's ending mocks his beginning, since he turns from sonorous moralizing to love; on the other hand, the beginning gives a higher meaning to the close, since it shows that love and the lover are themselves of high moral worth.[56]

Lambin's notes say nothing of this play of thought. He moves from word to word, heaping up verbal parallels. The man who is free from crime, he remarks, is the man with clean hands; then he quotes a good many passages that mention men whose hands are or are not clean.[57] He explains points of geography and historical references: 'Horace says "Moorish javelins" because the Moors were excellent javelin-hurlers.'[58] He gravely explains that 'the voyagers of our and our fathers' times' have proved that the torrid zone, which Horace describes as uninhabitable, is really 'temperate and habitable'.[59] One is reminded of the young Scaliger's well-known harsh verdict: 'commentariorum mole laborat.'[60]

Such criticisms miss the point. What Lambin lacked in literary sensibility he made up for in virtues perhaps more valuable to a commentator: an ability to pick out interesting details for analysis and an honest desire to instruct his readers in Horace's techniques. His learning is for the most part unborrowed, and especially on points of diction and syntax his collections of evidence were well-defined and illuminating. Few scholars would

not have learned from his characteristically systematic illustration
of the adverbial accusatives in the last lines of *Odes* I. xxii:

DVLCE RIDENTEM.] So Catullus to Lesbia: *identidem te Spectat et
audit Dulce ridentem, misero quod omneis Eripit sensus mihi* [51. 3-6].
This, to be sure, Sappho had said in Greek (for Catullus translated it from
her for his own use): γελώσας ἱμερόεν ['laughing charmingly']. Catullus
also: *illa quam videtis Turpe incedere* [42. 7-8]. Homer, *Od.* XIV [465]:
καὶ θ'ἁπαλὸν γελάσαι ['and to laugh softly']; and Pindar, in *Pyth.* IX [38]
χλιαρὸν γελάσαις ['smiling softly']. And Apollonius, *Argon.* III [1009]:
Νεκτάρεον μείδησε ['she smiled sweetly']. The following lines of Horace
are similar: *Odes* II. xii *me voluit dicere lucidum Fulgenteis oculos*; and
II. xix *turbidum Laetatur*. And *epist. ad Iul. Flor.* II: *Canet indoctum,
sed dulce bibenti*. And *Odes* III. 27: *Perfidum ridens Venus*. But *canet
indoctum, sed dulce bibenti* can be said to be different, since *canere* is
normally joined with the accusative, and is in the active voice.[61]

Many similar notes reveal Lambin's virtues: patience, accuracy,
close acquaintance with his author's habits and sources. No
wonder that in the riper wisdom of his sixties Scaliger described
the Horace as 'outstanding'[62] — a judgement that should not be
forgotten when his earlier, negative one is cited. If Dorat had
drafted the plans of the French method, Lambin built the walls
and laid on the roof.

Lambin also tried to show that there was a clear connection
between this style of exegesis and the new French literature. In
Ars poetica 136-52 Horace advises the poet to begin his work in
as simple and unadorned a way as possible. As an example he
paraphrases the beginning of the *Odyssey*. Lambin commented:

DIC MIHI MVSA VIRVM] The *Odyssey* begins Ἄνδρα μοι ἔννεπε μοῦσα
πολύτροπον etc. It pleases me to make this passage the occasion for sel-
ecting some lines from the *Franciade* — the French poem by Pierre Ronsard,
poeta regius, which is clearly comparable to Homer's *Iliad* and Virgil's
Aeneid — and setting them out for the readers of my commentary in a
Latin version by that splendid scholar Jean Dorat, *poeta regius*. Thus
foreign nations may realize what great talents our France produces and at
what a high level liberal studies flourish here.[63]

Two passages followed, with French and Latin texts in parallel
columns. It would have been hard to make bolder claims for the
merits of French culture. By including them Lambin managed
to give the immense and reliable tool he forged a strong polemical
edge.

The French, in short, had revived both Poliziano's exegetical
method and his claim that it should help to produce great poetry.
Their claims were taken seriously. At home Dorat and Ronsard

served as court poets, receiving ample fees for their part in providing the programmes, based on recondite Greek sources, for
royal entries and court festivals.[64]

Even abroad alert young men wished to imitate them. In 1562
Simon Wirt of Prague — he called himself Proxenus when writing
Latin — began a long journey to the universities of France. He
had already published some volumes of Neo-Latin verse. In
France he hoped to find guidance at a high level: both new
models to imitate and, if possible, master-classes in Greek and
Latin verse composition. In Paris early in 1564, he eagerly
recorded in his diary the academic gossip about Dorat:

> Louis Cospeau came to our inn. I gave him my epithalamium to show to
> Dorat, so that he may judge it. After lunch I had bought the poems of
> Michel de l'Hôpital and Joachim du Bellay. I will buy even more works of
> the French poets if I can. Cospeau told me — what N. Maignan told me in
> more detail on another occasion — that no one in Europe is more learned
> than Jean Dorat in explicating and understanding the Greek poets. Ronsard
> owes everything to Dorat. The other professors, one and all, run to consult
> him if a problem crops up in Greek.[65]

Even scholars whose origins were less provincial than Wirt's had
to admit the pre-eminence of French scholarship and poetry. In
1585, for example, Bonaventura Vulcanius wrote to Theodore
Canter:

> The Ronsard that you asked for is finally on its way to you . . . In the
> meantime I have spent my leisure hours for some weeks reading it with
> great pleasure and profit. I was delighted by his accurate and very success-
> ful imitation of both Greek and Latin poets, so delighted that if my age
> and white hairs did not prevent it, I would try to set forth a similar example
> for our countrymen as well. For our language is not so sterile or barbarous
> that it cannot allow for just as much flexibility in syntax and grace . . . [66]

In Vulcanius's longing to create a refined Flemish literature on
the French model we see him acceding to all the claims that
Lambin and his countrymen had advanced.

The French were interested in textual criticism as well as
comparative exegesis. But their text-critical methods were not
drawn, even at several removes, from those of Poliziano. They
were great believers in conjectural emendation. Dorat, in particular, had a gift for conjecture. Thanks to long practice in
close reading and composition of Latin and Greek verse, he
could often re-create by imaginative sympathy what an ancient
poet must have written at points where neither the vulgate text
nor the manuscripts offered a plausible reading. Muret records
one strikingly simple divination:

I remember that Jean Dorat, a great scholar and my close friend, once corrected a line from Callimachus' hymn to Apollo in the same way [by altering the word-divisions]. The vulgate reading is:

Οὐδ᾽ ὁ χορὸς τὸν Φοῖβον ἐφ᾽ ἓν μόνον ἦμαρ ἀείσει
Ἔστι γὰρ εὔυμνός τις · ἂν οὔρεα Φοῖβον ἀείδει   [*Hymni* II. 30-1].

This should read as follows, as the learned gentleman whom I mentioned pointed out:

Ἔστι γὰρ εὔυμνος · τίς ἂν οὐ ῥέα Φοῖβον ἀείδοι;

['For he is a splendid subject for praise. Who would not find it easy to sing of Phoebus?']. For the poet is saying that no one is so crude and illiterate that he does not find it very easy to praise Apollo. For he has so many praiseworthy attributes that no one — not even the most ineloquent — who decides to celebrate him can be at a loss for something to say.[67]

Dexterity of this order not unreasonably convinced other French scholars of the value of conjectures. Here is what Henri Estienne found to say about the same passage in his *Corpus poetarum* of 1566:

Εστι γὰρ] Whenever I recall this verse I am forced to recall Jean Dorat, who has displayed great cleverness both in emending many other passages in the poets and especially in this one. For the vulgate reading was

ἔστι γὰρ εὔϋμνος τις, ἂν᾽ οὔρεα Φοῖβον ἀείδει,

and the normal interpretation, which involved slight changes in the Greek, was: 'For Phoebus is easily praised [or abounds in praise]; who sings of Phoebus in the mountains?' Dorat smelled out the fact that the verse contained some further hidden corruption, since he saw that it could not yield any sense that was even apparently appropriate to the passage. And he asserted that ἀν᾽ οὔρεα [in or through the mountains] must be changed to ἂν οὐ ῥέα [(who) would not easily . . . ?]. This emendation found such great approval among scholars that their coryphaeus, Adrien Turnèbe — even though he had previously followed both the vulgate reading and the interpretation that fitted it, while interpreting this passage in public — afterwards was not ashamed to confess, also in public, that both reading and interpretation had been wrong, and that he completely agreed with Jean Dorat.[68]

App. III

Estienne went on to say that he had found a manuscript reading that supported Dorat's conjecture, but the passage chiefly reveals his and others' enthusiasm for just the sort of simple, drastic remedy that Vettori and his followers most disliked. The case we have examined was by no means exceptional. To the text of Aeschylus' *Agamemnon* alone Dorat contributed twenty-seven conjectural emendations that are still accepted or taken seriously.[69] His friends and students competed to take down the suggestions that he threw off in such an easy, aristocratic way. No wonder that such men came to see divinatory emendation as the quintessence of the critic's art.

The French also consulted manuscripts energetically. Learned collectors like Henri de Mesmes and Aimar de Ranconnet and humanists like Pierre Daniel and Jacques Cujas eagerly bought up the treasures that the Wars of Religion shook loose from monasteries throughout France. They saw it as a duty to make their acquisitions available to scholars or to publish them themselves. And some French scholars — notably Lambin — also did research in the great Italian libraries. As a result, French scholars were able during the 1550s and '60s to publish both first editions of new texts and the readings of new manuscripts of standard authors.[70]

What the French did not do, for the most part, was to cite, evaluate, and report on their manuscripts in the manner that the Italians thought proper. They were disinclined to be informative about the documentary sources of their texts; at times, indeed, they were downright deceptive about the owners or locations of manuscripts. Their records of variant readings were incomplete and imprecise. They introduced conjectures into their texts without saying that they had done so.

Turnèbe's editions, for example, were neatly — though not, of course, deliberately — calculated to irritate Vettori. In the preface to his Aeschylus of 1552, he admitted that he had consulted only one manuscript, and that the 'splendid old copy' had contained only three plays.[71] He gave no critical notes. And his three-page list of variants was headed 'those which read differently in some copies' — there was no further indication of the sources from which they were drawn.[72] But he nevertheless claimed to have 'restored a good many passages to full health', using variants recorded in the old scholia and, where necessary, conjectures dictated by the sense.[73] Unfortunately, he did not indicate the changes he had introduced; hence the reader could not know for certain the source of any given reading.

Again, when preparing his 1553 edition of Sophocles, Turnèbe happened on a manuscript that had been corrected by the Byzantine scholar Demetrius Triclinius. For Vettori, signs of deliberate alteration meant that a manuscript did not represent accurately the exemplar from which it had been copied. It should therefore be ignored by critics.[74] For Turnèbe, however, Triclinius's emendations only made the manuscript that much more useful: 'We obtained a manuscript which has been very well emended and polished by the critical signs, stichographies, explanatory notes and corrections of Demetrius Triclinius.'[75]

Worse, from Vettori's point of view, Turnèbe did not reproduce his manuscript faithfully. He edited eclectically, introducing readings from the 1502 Aldine edition and his own conjectures, without indicating the sources of the corrections he accepted in the text or the variants he recorded in the margins.[76]

Even those French or French-trained scholars who enjoyed close relations with Vettori's school and shared its members' interest in manuscripts did not master his method. Lambin, for example, spent eleven years in Italy.[77] He collated a good many manuscripts of Lucretius and Horace there. He knew Faerno well enough to borrow manuscripts from him.[78] And yet he too used his manuscript evidence unsystematically throughout his career. He made no attempt to arrange his nine Horace manuscripts in genealogical order, to distinguish consistently among them on grounds of age, or to eliminate even the newest of them as unlikely to contain significant information.[79] His reports of their readings were inconsistent and irregular; and sometimes he gave incomplete reports of variants even though he knew that the word or line in question presented textual problems.[80]

Even more striking is the case of Henri Estienne. While in Italy in the early 1550s, he made so deep an impression as a scholar-printer that Vettori entrusted his edition of Aeschylus to him for publication.[81] The tragi-comedy that ensued shows how far Estienne was from grasping Vettori's ideas. Vettori, as usual, had prepared a conservative edition — based on what he took to be the best manuscript: Laur. 32.9. The attractive variants of a Triclinian manuscript he rejected as the results of mere conjecture.[82] But Estienne did not print what Vettori gave him. While he was putting the work through the press, he tells us, a friend happened to come to see him.

'What method', he asked, 'did you employ in printing the text, given this great variety of readings? Did you set out to follow one manuscript consistently, or did you make a choice of some kind [among the readings] ?' I replied that I trusted Vettori's manuscript more than any other, but that I had not followed it with the absolute consistency of one who had sworn to uphold its readings. He replied: 'Then it is your duty not merely to print the variant readings by themselves, but to explain your rationale at the same time.'[83]

So Estienne equipped his text with a critical appendix. And there he made it absolutely clear that his *ratio consilii* had little in common with Vettori's. He openly admitted that while he had followed Vettori's manuscript in most instances, he believed that 'in some cases it would be rash and senseless not to trust the other manuscripts'.[84] Even where he had rejected the readings of the Medicean manuscript, he had 'preserved them to be set down at the end of the book. That is, I did what I thought Vettori himself would have done had he been here.'[85] But he nowhere tried to advance the only argument that might have justified such changes in Vettori's eyes: namely, that other manuscripts besides the Medicean were independent witnesses to the textual tradition. Sense rather than *Überlieferungsge-schichte* governed Estienne's choice of readings; and that was just the habit of mind that Vettori wished to stamp out. Nor did Estienne improve his position by suggesting that one good reading had probably been in Vettori's manuscript, and that Vettori had simply missed it when making his collation.[86] The Aeschylus that appeared in 1557 was more readable than the one Vettori had projected; but he can hardly have derived much pleasure from that fact.[87]

If Lambin, Turnèbe, and Estienne lacked a rigorous critical method, they did not act as they did out of frivolity or ignorance. They saw classical texts as valuable for their literary and philo-sophical content. In so far as textual criticism could help to recover that content or make its textual embodiment more accessible to readers, they practised it. In so far as conjectural emendation seemed to them a stimulating, useful, and even elegant pursuit, one that displayed their talents without com-mitting them to drudgery, they pursued it for its own sake. But they did not see any reason to go to Vettori's lengths or to take the complex and tedious measures he called for. To them exegesis was a more pressing task, as it served a clear educational and cultural purpose. Their position was just as reasonable — and, for that matter, unreasonable — as Vettori's.[88]

Only one French scholar of this generation fully understood the Italians' critical method; and he rejected it. Jacques Cujas studied the textual tradition of the *Digest*. He collated manu-scripts and mastered the works of Poliziano, Agustín, Vettori, and the Torelli,[89] concluding that they were wrong to claim that the Florentine manuscript was the archetype. He admitted that it was the oldest, and regretted all his life that Cosimo de' Medici had refused to lend it to him when he was at Turin.[90] He used the Torelli's edition of it to reconstruct archaic words and names of jurisconsults that appeared in corrupt forms in the vulgate.[91] But he insisted that meaning must take precedence even over the Florentine manuscript: 'Though I know how authoritative this manuscript is in everyone's eyes, I myself attribute more weight to legal principles than to any manuscript. For nothing is more easily corrupted than they are.'[92] And he also insisted that the Florentine manuscript was not the sole source of the rest:

Admittedly, many insist vehemently that now that the Florentine Pandects have been published, nothing more is needed for the restoration of the Pandects. I encourage all students to obtain nevertheless as many other manuscripts of the Pandects as possible, and to examine and consider their readings with good judgment. For I do not think that we should believe those who claim that all the other manuscripts are descended from the Florentine.[93]

Cujas's arguments, prominently stated at the beginning of his great series of *Observationes*, presented a challenge to Italian methods rather than an alternative set of interests. And his brilliant teaching ensured that a large and malleable public of students learned his views.

By the mid-1550s, then, French scholars had developed Poliziano's methods in as one-sided a fashion as had Vettori. Scholarly disagreements alone might not have led to open conflict. Lambin, after all, found the Italians friendlier than his fellow-countrymen, despite their different interests. But, as we have seen, a certain cultural nationalism was always one of the roots from which French scholarship grew. Professional ambitions and personal animosities soon combined to transform nationalism into imperialism, and so to transform moderate disagreement into an emotionally charged conflict of the kind formerly provoked by Poliziano.

The root of the conflict was an old personal feud. Aldo Manuzio's son Paolo, who had taken over the family business and become a scholar in his own right during the 1530s, had always disliked Vettori. He shared his father's wish to publish usable texts; Vettori's conservative editorial policies stood in the way. He felt that commentators should concentrate on historical and literary background rather than textual criticism: his own model was the eminently practical Roman commentator on Cicero, Asconius Pedianus.[94] Most important, he was 'in setta' with Ubaldino Bandinelli, a rival of Vettori both as a Ciceronian scholar and as a humanist seeking preferment.[95] This combination of motives impelled him to attack Vettori on all fronts in his 1540 scholia on the *Familiares* and *Epistolae ad Atticum*. He argued that Vettori had been wrong to single out two manuscripts of the *Familiares* as the only ones of value; an eclectic approach would yield better results.[96] Vettori's collations were less complete than he had claimed, for he had sometimes identified as the reading of 'all the old codices' what was only that of the Medicei. Of his conjectures, some were too conservative, dictated by the *ductus literarum* rather than the sense. The better ones he had plagiarized from Bandinelli, Pierre Danès, and others.[97]

Like the pamphlets of the 1480s and '90s, Manuzio's *Scholia* argued as much *ad hominem* as *ad rem*. He pretended that he had had help from Vettori's friends in gaining access to manuscripts. And he referred to Vettori himself merely as 'Florentini'. Florentines — especially Florentine patricians — were not the men to miss or to forgive such tactics. Cavalcanti wrote acidly to Vettori of 'Manuzio's spiteful turns of phrase, his failure to mention you by name, his attribution of your work to the Florentine nation as a whole'. Cavalcanti and Giannotti did not think that a gentleman of Vettori's rank should waste his time refuting 'a pedant and a spiteful man'.[98] But Cavalcanti collated new manuscripts on his behalf and both men regularly offered criticism as Vettori sent drafts and descriptions of his reply. The result, the *Posteriores castigationes* of 1541, was a long and intemperate pamphlet that exposed many errors on Manuzio's part but failed to silence him.

Manuzio continued to cherish his desire to dishonour Vettori. In 1533 providence — in the form of a charge of sodomy that forced Marc-Antoine Muret to flee from France to Italy — gave Manuzio just the coadjutor he needed. Muret was one of the cleverest members of the French school. A man of clear vision and no scruple, he was out to make a name in what he saw as a corrupt world.[99] In Manuzio he found a loyal friend and able editor. Together they set out to introduce French philology into Italy and to destroy Vettori.

Muret's Catullus of 1554 attacked Vettori both explicitly and through Poliziano. He accused Poliziano of deliberate deceit in quoting and discussing manuscript evidence. And he gleefully quoted Michael Marullus's epigrams against Poliziano, which accused him of immorality as well as bad scholarship.[100] Egged on by Manuzio, he then produced editions of Terence, Propertius, and Tibullus, all of them characterized by resort to conjectural emendation and by an emphasis on comparison with Greek sources.[101] And in 1558 the attack became direct. Five years before, as we saw, Vettori had published twenty-five books of

Variae lectiones, designed as his contribution to comparative exegesis. Muret now published a work with the same title on the same subject, one chiefly designed to show that he, and French scholars in general, were far better than Vettori at the central pursuits of the critic. The best way to grasp the scope and force of Muret's attack is simply to watch him at work:

The greater a scholar's literary authority, the greater must be his care not to let slip any remark about which his knowledge is uncertain. For when men of little or no repute do this sort of thing, the damage is not serious. We need not fear that anyone will follow them. But with regard to the other sort, the more valuable each of them is, the greater the danger when he errs. But desire for novelty moves man's spirit. Sometimes, allured by its outward attractiveness, and paying too little heed to what is set before it, it embraces empty vanities in place of solid truths. Now I would not wish to refer to Pier Vettori save as to a man of consummate learning. No other course of action would be proper. For I am accustomed not only to confess but even to proclaim that I have derived more benefit from his efforts than from those of any other man of our time. But now and again I am compelled — and I mean no offence in saying this — to wish that he would show a little more diligence and accuracy. For what is to be made of his recent statement that Euripides has Helen's mother Leda transformed into a lioness?[102] For in the very tragedy from which he believed that he had elicited that marvellous metamorphosis, it is often stated that Leda strangled herself with a noose, out of sorrow at her daughter's shame. For there are these lines at the very outset:

Helen: We are undone. Is Thestia's daughter still alive?
Teucer: Do you mean Leda? She is quite dead.
Helen: It was not the shame of Helen that killed her?
Teucer: They say so. She fitted her noble neck to the noose
           [*Helen* 133-6].

Therefore Helen herself, while recounting her misfortunes a little while later, speaks as follows of her mother's death:

Λήδα δ' ἐν ἀγχόναις
Θάνατον ἔλαβεν αἰσχύ-
νας ἐμᾶς ὑπ' ἀλγέων.

['Leda chose death by strangling out of grief for my shame.' (200-2)]

For I think that should be the reading. And the chorus, mourning:

Your mother is dead [219].

But even a blind man could see that the passage that [Vettori] took as referring to Leda is to be taken as referring to Callisto [375-80].

What is to be made of his proposal, unsupported by any certain evidence, to read *actionibus* in *De oratore* I [101]? There our compatriot Douaren has since shown that the reading must be *cretionibus*.[103]

And there are more things of that kind in the *Variae lectiones* than I would wish. For I want only to defend his reputation. But it seems wrong to conceal what he said in Book I about *theriaca* [an antidote for poison], since it could lead someone to err. For he says that it was apparently once the custom to drink *theriaca*. Therefore it must have been more liquid, for it is now made rather thick and saturated with matter in suspension. This he infers from the words of Varro, as given by Nonius, from his book on the education of children: *Vel maxime illic didici, et sitienti, theriacam, mulsum; esurienti, panem cibarium, siligineum; et exercitato somnum suavem* ['I learned there that to the thirsty man *theriaca* seems like mead; to the hungry man, black bread seems like wheaten; to the man who has taken exercise, sleep seems sweet' *(apud* Non. 88 M.)] [104] Now as I live I cannot sufficiently express my surprise that a man of Vettori's quality said this. First of all, where had he found even one word about that liquid *theriaca*? For every rogue and quack doctor knows what our *theriaca* is like, and in my view it is the same as that of the ancients. Then since it is clear that Varro is there setting common and plebeian foods in opposition to elegant and sumptuous ones, I would like to know whom he could have hoped to convince that poor and unimportant men were once as accustomed to drink *theriaca* — that is, a bitter and unpleasant drink — as to eat black bread. . . . For if he wanted some bitter medicine to oppose to mead, he should by the same token have opposed to wheat bread not black bread, but purging agaric or colocynth.

As for me, I retain the opinion that I held about that passage from Varro before Vettori published his *Variae lectiones.* And I shall now reveal it in order that competition may determine which opinion is the truer one. I think, then, that this should be the reading: *Vel maxime illic didici, sitienti videri acam mulsum, esurienti panem cibarium siligineum, et exercitato somnum suavem* ['I learned there that to the thirsty man water seems like mead . . .']. For I suspect that incompetent scribes turned the two words *sitienti videri* into *sitienti teri.* But *acam* is the archaic spelling for *aquam,* as *loci* for *loqui, coad* for *quoad, cotidie* for *quotidie.* This then is what Varro says: that he learned there that to the thirsty man water seems like mead. Anyone who does not like this conjecture is free to suggest a better one. Certainly anything would be better than choking down that liquid *theriaca.* But I would suspect that when Varro wrote this he had in mind this passage from the first book of Xenophon's *Cyropaedia:* 'If someone thinks either that they take no pleasure in eating when they have only bitter-cress on their bread, or that they take no pleasure in drinking when they drink water, let him recall with what relish a hungry man eats barley-cake and bread, and with what relish a thirsty man drinks water.' [105]   App. III

The attack is undeniably impressive. Muret catches Vettori making mistakes in each of his special fields: misinterpreting a Greek tragedy; refusing to emend, and therefore misinterpreting, a fragment of Republican Latin; missing the Greek source of both the content and the language of the Latin fragment. The points of attack were chosen with care; taken together they amounted to a blow at every one of the pillars on which Vettori's authority rested. The style was chosen with equal niceness. By adopting a tone rounded and oracular, even a little pompous, Muret manages to present himself, rather than Vettori, as the guardian of responsible criticism, while portraying Vettori as a flighty and irresponsible man who did not think his arguments through. In a sense, Muret is turning Vettori's own philological vocabulary against him — save that now it is French exegesis and conjectures rather than Italian-style collation of manuscripts that is shown to be the centre of the art of criticism.

At first Manuzio and Muret hoped to isolate Vettori. Manuzio even tried to induce Faerno to join with Muret in producing a revision of the latter's Terence. But the tactic failed.[106] Faerno was disgusted by Muret's supine indifference to manuscript evidence and his incompetence as a metrist. 'One Muret', he wrote to Vettori, 'has completely ruined Terence.'[107] He took a high tone in his reply to Manuzio, refusing his request and explaining its absurdity at length. He suggested rather tactlessly that Muret was a talented man who should find a trade other than textual criticism.[108] And he urged Manuzio to cease publishing works like Muret's, which would destroy the great tradition of his press.[109] As to Muret's *Variae lectiones*, he wrote to Vettori that he had picked the book up in a shop and thrown it down in disgust after reading one chapter.[110] He sturdily set out to dedicate his edition of the *Philippics* to Vettori, thus showing in public that his personal loyalty was unaffected by disagreement on method.[111]

Manuzio and Muret reacted by declaring Faerno an enemy as well. In 1560 Muret apparently made conciliatory noises. 'He speaks of you very honourably', wrote Giannotti to Vettori, 'and I am sure that if he were to publish his *Variae lectiones* now, he would be more measured in what he writes about you.'[112] This was clearly nothing but a feint. When Faerno died in 1562, Manuzio wrote triumphantly to Muret about what seemed to both of them splendid news. In 1561 Muret had managed to get access to the Basilicanus of the *Philippics*. And while in France in 1562 he completed an edition of the text, obviously designed to steal Faerno's thunder; in fact the editions both came out in 1563.[113]

During the 1560s, moreover, Manuzio even managed to plant an agent in Vettori's stronghold. Giovanni Battista Titi collated the Florentine manuscripts of the *Familiares* against Vettori's edition, looking especially for tacit deviations from the manuscript readings of the sort Vettori had condemned in theory: 'I have collected the readings that Vettori seems to have rejected without sufficient reason, especially considering that he claims to have followed consistently the authoritative testimony of that codex.'[114] Titi advanced an ingenious and attractive palaeo-graphical argument in one letter: that the Vercelli MS might have been copied from a manuscript in 'Lombardic' script:

I have often wondered whether the Mediceus and other similar manuscripts might have been copied from Lombardic manuscripts by scribes who knew some Latin but found that script very difficult, especially because of the large number of abbreviations. Among other things, the appearance in these manuscripts — the Mediceus, the Vatican Caesar, and others — of the Lombardic *r* provides evidence for my theory. . . . Otherwise I would find it impossible to account for the large number of errors in these manuscripts. For there are fewer both in the majuscule manuscripts written before the Lombards and in the Lombard manuscripts themselves.[115]

He cleverly pointed out that Vettori's editorial practices were actually in accord with Faerno's theories rather than his own.[116] But his main interest was clearly less to advance scholarship than to denigrate Vettori. If Vettori came to know of what he was doing, Titi cautioned Manuzio: 'he will complain, and call on the Gods, and ask men to bear witness that I have deserted him and gone over to your side.'[117] Both tone and content here reveal the seriousness of the split between Vettori and Manuzio; even contemporaries saw the matter as one of party lines and conspiracies.

During the same period three more French works, none so polemical as Muret's, served to widen and confirm the split between the two schools. In 1564 Henri Estienne published the *Fragmenta veterum poetarum Latinorum* that his father had collected while compiling his great Latin dictionary.[118] We have seen that matching Latin dramatic fragments with Roman authors and Greek sources was a favourite study of the Italians. In one book the Estienne revolutionized the field. In place of the traditional piecemeal identifications Robert found secure homes for dozens of verses, while Henri provided many of the Latin passages' Greek sources and brief notes on historical and philological problems — for example, the question, already raised by Vettori, of whether Ennius' *Medea* and *Medea exul* were two different works (Vettori held that they were; Estienne was not sure).[119]

Not surprisingly, the collection sparked even more interest in archaic Latin among French scholars. Fruterius wrote to Willem Canter that:

I have just read — and I am sure that you did too — the fragments [collected] by Henri Estienne, or rather his father. I know that Dorat is working on them, and I am aware that Turnèbe also did so in the second volume of the *Adversaria*, which is still in the press and will, so they say, certainly appear soon. And unless I'm wrong, I too have made some contribution, and perhaps a large one.[120]

It must have gravelled Italian scholars that any future work in this formerly Italian field would have to begin from a French collection of the evidence. Aldo Manuzio the Younger, for example, manufactured an opportunity in his commentary on the *Ars poetica* to publish a collection of testimonia on Accius 'in order to show that I long ago thought of editing the fragments of the poets'. He claimed that the fruits of his *vigiliae* in this field would be far richer than those of the Estienne.[121]

Turnèbe's *Adversaria* of 1564 to 1565, though sprawling and half-ruinous, also presented a challenge to Vettori. Turnèbe took every opportunity to praise the achievements of French scholars from Budé — some of whose manuscript notes he published (as Vettori had Poliziano's) — down to his own contemporaries Muret, Lambin, and Buchanan.[122] He insisted that 'even though it is often dangerous and chancy to rely on one's conjectures while dealing with authors, in many affairs we nevertheless rely on conjecture alone.'[123] He joked, a little insensitively, that he had advanced one conjecture 'nulla tot editionum et mysticorum librorum verecundia ductus'.[124] And he treated Vettori as an honest but rather simple scholar who had kindly supplied the raw material from which Turnèbe could cleverly spin conjectures.[125] Vettori had indeed suggested that the variants he recorded might be used in such a way,[126] but did not enjoy being taken quite so literally. In his second set of *Variae lectiones*, which appeared in 1568, his irritation was quite open: 'I wish that [Turnèbe], who was clearly learned and well read, had not been so eager to emend absolutely everything. He would have done better both for us and for his own reputation.'[127]

Paradoxically, Lambin aggressively challenged Italian pre-eminence in textual criticism. His four-volume folio Cicero of 1566 was clearly designed to supplant Vettori's edition of the 1530s as the standard text of the Latin classic *par excellence*. Even the format and typography amounted in their grandeur to a polemical statement. Lambin's notes went even farther. His title, *Emendationum rationes*, recalled Vettori's *Castigationum explicationes* even while departing from it. In method he proclaimed his independence. He agreed that Vettori's manuscript of the *Familiares* was far superior to the rest, but not that it was the only valid witness. 'Vettori followed his manuscripts', he wrote at *Fam.* VII. 20; 'we followed ours — that is, those of de Mesmes.'[128] French manuscripts, then, were just as valuable as Italian ones. Furthermore, Lambin explicitly claimed the right to emend the text by conjecture 'even though all the manuscripts contradict me'.[129] And it must have seemed a deliberate insult when he treated Muret and Faerno as equally reliable witnesses to the Basilicanus's readings in the *Philippics*.[130] He did not make any attempt to argue directly against Vettori's views on the history of texts — to show, that is, that his manuscripts of the *Familiares* were not descended from the Medicei. Indeed, he probably did not understand Vettori's principles in detail. But his general assertions of the importance of conjecture and his denigration of Vettori's manuscripts were an attack in themselves, all the more shattering for the friendliness with which Vettori and his school had treated Lambin in his Italian days.

True, even in the period around 1570 there was no absolute social break between members of what had become two schools. Vettori's Roman friend Fulvio Orsini, who distrusted French scholars deeply, depended for patronage on the same great Roman churchmen who supported Muret; open quarrel would have embarrassed them and might have put a stop to their support. Hence the anomaly that Orsini and Muret evidently spent some time together at the watering-places of the literati, such as the Este villa at Tivoli. Indeed, Orsini joined Muret in helping the clever young Flemish Latinist Lipsius while he was in Rome from 1569 to 1571.[131]

The intellectual split grew none the less. In 1570 Muret published a new edition of the Terence which included double-edged compliments about Faerno's minute and pedantic palaeographical skills and severe strictures on his character.[132] In 1576 he still felt strongly enough to fill the margins of Vettori's new commentary on Aristotle's *Politics* with remarks about 'seniles ineptiae'.[133]

Muret's tactical skills and the comparative inaccessibility of Vettori's method combined to give Muret the victory, so far as numbers of recruits were concerned. Vettori and his allies made a strong impression on one French-trained scholar, the Portuguese Achilles Statius. He learned from them to collate manuscripts in great detail, to take a generally conservative position as a critic, and to revere Poliziano.[134] In his editions of Catullus and Tibullus he presented careful collations of large numbers of manuscripts — eight of Catullus — along with an impressive collection of Greek parallels. But he never quite mastered the notion that manuscripts must be assessed for age and independence; though he collated R, one of the three fourteenth-century manuscripts of Catullus, he did not notice that it was older and more independent than the other manuscripts at his disposal.[135] He made no attempt at a genealogical approach to his evidence. Yet he, and the learned but somewhat thick-witted Orsini, were Vettori's only recruits.[136] When Curzio Pichena, some years later, published his careful collations of Tacitus manuscripts, he was inspired not by the tradition of Vettori but by the suggestion of an English visitor, 'Dutch' Richard Thomson of Clare Hall, Cambridge.[137]

Muret, on the other hand, exerted more and more influence as time went on. His advocacy of the masters of Silver Latin prose, Seneca and Tacitus, made him attractive to a younger generation tired of Vettori's Ciceronian orthodoxy.[138] Both in Italy and, even more, in France he began to gain disciples who shared his interests and methods, not uncritically but none the less with enthusiasm.[139]

What is important for our purposes is his impact in France. The 1560s saw the rise of a new intellectual generation to maturity. Its members included Pierre Daniel, Claude Dupuy, Pierre Pithou, Florent Chrestien, Alphonse Delbene, and Joseph Scaliger; allies from the Low Countries whose training and sympathies were largely French included Janus Dousa, Lucas Fruterius, Willem and Theodore Canter. These men had in one respect a broader training than the generation before. Most of them came from the new *noblesse de robe* — a tribute in itself to the success that Dorat and Lambin had had in making their studies fashionable.[140] All were interested in the law. Many therefore decided to combine the literary training available in Paris with a spell of legal studies under Cujas in Valence or Bourges. They thus combined classical humanism with the best of provincial antiquarianism; none of their elders could match them in breadth of skills and interests.[141]

Not surprisingly, they were especially fascinated by archaic Latin literature and law on the one hand and archaizing later Latin on the other. They studied the fragments of early Latin laws and plays that their elders had collected. Several of them embellished the Estienne's *Fragmenta* of the early Latin poets with critical marginalia as soon as it appeared. At the same time, they studied the poetry, the technical grammatical works, and the legal texts of late Antiquity. The world that had produced the free republic of Franco-Gallia on the one hand and the *Corpus Iuris* on the other had for them the compulsive attraction of a reflection in a mirror. In the life of the ancient provincial aristocrats and the work of the late imperial civil service they saw a culture like their own, one that combined extravagant literary erudition with a serious commitment to political life. If some of them detested Tribonian as a 'terrible simplificateur', they all shared a taste for the rococo rhetoric and inkhorn vocabulary of later Roman writers — and for the treasures of learning embedded in such repellent settings as Servius' commentary on Virgil and the old scholia on Persius.[142]

To understand the literary works of late Antiquity, these men needed the training in Greek and in comparative exegesis that the older literary masters could give. Scattered but revealing bits of evidence show that they learned not only from Dorat, who taught many of them, but from Muret — both through personal contact and by reading his works. Some of them inherited his belief in the superiority of his method to Vettori's and in the inevitability of conflict between French and Italian methods. Sometimes the belief was even strengthened by journeys in Italy and meetings with Vettori and his allies.

The first piece of evidence comes from Dorat's pupil Fruterius. His copy of Muret's 1558 edition of Catullus, Tibullus, and Propertius is preserved in Leiden; and his marginalia reveal that he read both texts and commentaries exactly as Muret had intended.[143] He gave much attention to textual criticism, recording his own and Dorat's conjectures as well as variants from Statius' apparatus to Catullus.[144] He tried to explain difficult allusions and rare words.[145] And he worked through Muret's discussions of Greek sources and parallels with care and enthusiasm. Muret had taken over two Greek parallels that Poliziano had discovered for Catullus 66. Fruterius corrected Muret's Greek quotations against Poliziano's. He gave references to the relevant chapter numbers in the *Miscellanea*.[146] And he evidently worked back and forth between text and notes, studying the Latin in the light of the Greek. On 66.48, Muret suggested that the corresponding line from Callimachus should be emended to read

Ζεῦ πάτερ, ὡς Χαλύβων πᾶν ἀπόλοιτο γένος.[147]

Fruterius evidently agreed; for he entered the line, so emended, at the appropriate point in the margin of the text proper. He also entered parallels of his own discovery, some better chosen than others. At 115.6 ('Usque ad Hyperboreos') he wrote: 'VI Epigram. ἄχρις ὑπερβορέων'.[148] At Tibullus II.i.87 ('Iam nox iungit equos, currumque sequuntur') he entered 'Euripid. ὦ νὺξ μέλαινα χρυσέων ἄστρων τροφέ'.[149] And at Propertius II.x.6 he even supplied a parallel from one of Poliziano's Greek epigrams, itself translated from a Latin original.[150] Finally, he noticed and relished Muret's attacks on Poliziano: 'Poliziano was a lover of boys', he wrote at one point, to elucidate Marullus's epigrams against him.[151] Other notes confirm his interest in Muret's implied and explicit polemics.[152] Fruterius was by no means an uncritical follower. He urged Lambin to incorporate the central feature of Italian method into his Lucretius commentary:

> I very much want to ask and receive one favour from you: namely, that you always mention in your commentaries the reading of the old manuscript, whether it is sound or, to use Plautus' word, unsound, or even obscure and incomprehensible. The result will be that everyone will be grateful for your accuracy. Moreover, you will give scholars the opportunity to try to elicit the full and correct reading from the corrupt one. The excellent Vettori, with his high standard of accuracy, does this, and quite rightly.[153]

But it is clear from his reading of Muret that he accepted for the most part the methods and presuppositions of his French masters, and took their side in the French-Italian split.

The case of Claude Dupuy is even more revealing. Like Lambin, he spent time in Italy — an extended *Wanderjahr* in 1570 to 1571. Like Lambin, he made friends there. Vettori and Orsini welcomed him warmly and spoke well of him after his departure.[154] So did Manuzio and Muret.[155] All these found the time to instruct this clever and well-born young jurist in their working methods. Latini used the manuscript reading of a passage in Columella to show how Turnèbe had gone wrong in trying to defend what was really a corruption.[156] Orsini showed him that Manuzio had been wrong to emend the transmitted text of a passage in Nepos.[157] Vettori gave him a characteristic glimpse of his workshop, which Dupuy described:

> Cicero, *ad Att.* XII.4, writes as follows on Cato: 'Quin etiam si a sententiis eius dictis, si ab omni voluntate, consiliisque quae de Republica habuit, recedam, ψευδῶςque velim gravitatem constantiamque eius laudare.' Pier Vettori corrects ψευδῶς to ψιλῶς. He was aided by the manuscript written by Petrarch, which reads ψειλως. He showed me that this sort of

error is common in that manuscript, giving several examples. Cicero opposes τὸ ψιλόν to *ornatum*.[158]

Dupuy himself, after working through Faerno's edition of the *Philippics*, collated the Basilicanus and used it to refute one of Muret's conjectures.[159]

Exposure did not lead to contagion. Dupuy remained loyal to French methods. He consulted Muret on points of Roman law and spent his last day in Rome copying down Muret's conjectural emendations to Tacitus (admittedly, even Orsini was interested enough in them to ask for a copy).[160] He filled the margins of his copy of Vettori's *Variae lectiones* with detailed and apparently approving summaries of Muret's attacks.[161] Most revealing of all is a letter he wrote to Delbene, who was contemplating an *iter Italicum* in order to master humanist jurisprudence:

I will not lead you to expect great things of the Italian scholars — [that is] that you will slake your thirst by meeting and listening to them. Italy, to which other nations owe the Renaissance of letters, now has no juris-consults; none, at least, [who profess] that genuine Roman law that has found defenders among us. . . . . In the other disciplines you will find only five or six who are very good.[162]

Despite Delbene's family connections with Vettori's school (he was related to Cavalcanti), when he came to Italy he seems to have found Dupuy's predictions not unjustified.[163] At all events, he took especial pleasure in his meeting with the Francophile Manuzio, who spoke with him at length about French scholars, praising Dorat unreservedly.[164]

A final piece of evidence comes from Jacques-Auguste de Thou, who travelled in Italy from 1572 to 1574. In Florence, Vettori showed him the great libraries. Like a good jurist, de Thou examined the Florentine Pandects and noticed the trans-posed leaves that appeared in the last title. He decided that Agustín had probably been correct about the transmission of the text. But he also remembered Cujas's criticisms of the Tor-elli's edition. Though he was well received by Vettori and Sig-onio, he remained fiercely loyal to his French masters and friends, and angrily resented the slurs that he heard against his new but close friend Scaliger.[165]

This generation was Scaliger's. As we shall see, his training and interests followed the same pattern as theirs. He shared their consciousness of the division between French and Italian methods. Like them, he fully understood both programmes; like them, he preferred at first the one that he had been trained to follow.

But neither Scaliger's character nor his external circumstances permitted him to refrain from publishing for many years, as most of the others did. Accordingly, he was brought up more sharply than they against the dilemmas posed by French-Italian rivalry. How could someone who understood the Italians' principles edit texts without applying them? How could someone apply French or Italian principles without falling into a posture exaggerated to serve polemical ends? Was there any hope of reviving Poliziano's programme for a unified philological method? The story of Scaliger's early life is in large part the story of his responses to these questions.

IV Young Scaliger

In the lively and arrogant autobiography that he published in 1594, Jospeh Scaliger emphasized the fact that he had received little formal education. It is true that in 1552, at the age of twelve, he had entered one of the finest schools in France, the Collège de Guyenne at Bordeaux. Despite the high standards and tough competition of the Collège, which had numbered Montaigne among its students and Buchanan and Muret among its teachers, he had greatly impressed his tutors there with his ability 'to grasp immediately whatever he hears' and to write Latin themes extempore.[1] But he had had to leave the Collège after only three years because of an outbreak of plague, and he had therefore learned only 'the rudiments of Latin' there.[2]

To some extent, however, he did not really need formal education. For he was able to study with his father, Julius Caesar Scaliger, one of the most prolific and wide-ranging scholars of the sixteenth century, whose most notorious literary work was the attack on the *Ciceronianus* of Erasmus by which he first made a literary reputation.[3] He also commented on and translated botanical works by Aristotle and Theophrastus and engaged in a lively and abstruse philosophical controversy with Girolamo Cardano. His *De causis latinae linguae* of 1540 was one of the most influential and original of sixteenth-century works on Latin grammatical theory, a popular subject. He was thus well qualified to serve as tutor to his gifted son, and to teach Joseph composition: '[My father] . . . required from me daily a short declamation. I chose my own subject, seeking it in some prose narrative. This exercise, and the daily use of the pen, accustomed me to write in Latin.'[4] He also acted as his father's secretary, taking down verses so that he 'imbibed some savour of the art of poetry'. Here too his progress was swift. His father was amazed by his precocious originality: 'Sometimes he would lead me aside and ask me whence I drew those ideas and embellishments. I answered him truly, that they were mine, and original.'[5] By the age of sixteen he had become proficient enough to write a Latin tragedy on the myth of *Oedipus*; so far as is known, the work does not survive.

Joseph's father tried to form his son's personality as well as his mind. He impressed upon Joseph the fact that he was a nobleman — indeed, a great aristocrat, a della Scala. As it happened, he was lying.[6] Joseph believed him, and the belief did much to form his character. Julius, paradoxically, also cautioned him again and again always to tell the truth.[7] He insisted that a della Scala must always be intellectually as well as personally independent. 'Neither I nor my father', said Joseph, 'ever wrote anything which had to our knowledge been written or said by anyone else.'[8]

Julius Caesar's death in 1558 put an end to this curious regime. Joseph's reaction was both heartfelt and paradoxical. On the one hand, he became deeply — in our terms, clinically — depressed. His bowels, previously efficient, ceased to work for two and a half weeks, and he suffered from chronic constipation and strange dreams for the rest of his life.[9] Yet at the same time the death freed him. Julius Caesar had believed that classical Latin literature was absolutely superior to Greek; like the older generation of Italian scholars whom he had known as a young man, he saw mastery of Latin composition as the scholar's most valuable skill. This view no doubt explains why he did not teach his most talented son any Greek. Joseph was fascinated by Greek culture; 'those who do not know Greek', he had decided, 'know nothing at all.'[10] His independence, though bought at a high emotional price, enabled him to fulfil a cherished and thwarted resolve.

He went to Paris and tried to find a teacher. For two months he attended Turnèbe's public lectures; but he discovered that he did not know enough Greek to follow them. He therefore set out to learn on his own:

I secluded myself . . . in my study, and, shut in that grinding-mill, sought to learn, self-taught, what I had not been able to acquire from others. Beginning with a mere smattering of the Greek conjugations, I procured Homer, with a translation, and learned him all in twenty-one days. I learned grammar exclusively from observation of the relation of Homer's words to each other; indeed, I made my own grammar of the poetic dialect as I went along. I devoured all the other Greek poets within four months.[11]

Scaliger very likely exaggerated a little in this retrospective Gasconade. Gibbon believed him: 'Scaliger ran through the *Iliad*

in one and twenty days, and I was not dissatisfied with my own
diligence for performing the same labour in an equal number of
weeks.'[12] E. V. Blomfield, himself the product of the school of
Porson, put the negative case convincingly:

> After having made himself master of Homer, he proceeded to the next of
> the Greek poets in chronological order, and pursuing the same plan, read
> through all of them in the incredibly short space of four months. For this
> again we have only his own word; and whoever has turned over the leaves
> of Stephen's *Corpus Poetarum*, will be struck with a mixture of horror and
> incredulity at the very thought of such an undertaking.[13]

The literal truth of the account is less important than Scaliger's
real accomplishment. For it is clear that within two or three
years he mastered Greek and read through the entire corpus of
Greek literature, while still pursuing the Latin studies to which
his father had initiated him.

Our first objective records of his progress are impressive. In
1560 he obtained a copy of Euripides, which he signed and
dated in Greek.[14] The many marginal annotations that he made
in the next few years — ranging from corrections of misprints to
original conjectures — show how closely he read what he later
called 'mes trois Tragiques'.[15] By 1561 he had become proficient
enough to spend much of his time on Greek verse composition.
In particular, he translated much classical Latin into Greek. He
was encouraged to do so by the works of Muret, from which, it
seems, he learned the value of the comparative study of Greek
and Latin. One of his earliest Greek poems was a rendering of
Catullus 66 — itself, of course, a Latin translation from a lost poem
by Callimachus. Muret had suggested in his Catullus commentary
that the loss of the Greek was a blow to Latin scholarship; had
it survived, one could have 'compared the Greek with the Latin,
not only with respect to individual words, but also with respect
to figures of speech, metre, and, finally, the whole structure of
the poem'.[16] Scaliger not only agreed that the loss of the Greek
was unfortunate; he set out to remedy it. He took Muret's
advice so seriously that he repeated the idiosyncracies of Muret's
Latin text in his Greek. Instead of 'Proximus Hydrochoi fulgeret
Oarion', the text of 66.94 given by older editions, he accepted
Muret's version, 'Proximus Arcturos fulgeat Erigonae', and
translated it word for word as: ἐγγύθεν ἀρκτοῦρος λαμπέτω
ἠριγόνας.[17] And for 66.48 he gave the appropriate fragment
from Callimachus in the emended form that Muret had suggested:
Ζεῦ πάτερ, ὡς Χαλύβων πᾶν ἀπόλοιτο γένος.[18] In September

1562 he dedicated the finished version, along with one of Catullus 65, to Muret, then visiting Paris for the last time.[19]

Some of Scaliger's other Greek poems were also inspired by an interest in the comparative method. A case in point is his undated version of Catullus 4, with its prominent Graecism in line 2: 'Ait fuisse navium celerrimus'.[20] Even more striking is his version of two elegies of Propertius, which he dedicated to Willem Canter as early as 1561.[21] Here he was translating a Latin poet who had clearly proclaimed his heavy debt to the Greeks.

As materials for comparative study his versions could not have much appeal. But the fact that he could produce them proved that he had mastered the Parisian circle's central critical principle — and also that he could write astonishingly fluent Greek. It is not surprising, then, that he was soon on good terms with the best scholars in Paris. No doubt Muret and Buchanan, both of whom had known his father in Bordeaux, helped him; but his own works were also an impressive visiting card. By 1563 we find him at the very centre of the Parisian scene, dedicating a Greek version of the *Moretum* to Ronsard.[22]

Scaliger found time for activities well beyond the realm of classical studies. He began to study Hebrew, in response to the suggestion of Guillaume Postel, who interested him in Oriental languages in 1562. The two men were then sharing a bed in the house of a Parisian printer.[23] They spent less than a week together, for Postel was arrested on suspicion of heresy and confined in a monastery, and Scaliger had to teach himself the language.[24] He evidently used the Bible as he had used Homer for Greek, comparing the Hebrew text with the Vulgate; for a few years later he spoke biblical Hebrew to the Jews that he met in Italy and the South of France.[25]

Scaliger also changed religions. As a boy he had been instilled with strict Catholic orthodoxy by Julius Caesar and his tutors. By 1562 he had decided to convert to Calvinism, and he took instruction from two ministers in Paris.[26]

Most of the fragmentary evidence we possess, however, shows that Scaliger's main interests were those he shared with the other Parisian classicists. He became close to Dorat. His translation of the *Orphica*, which he achieved in five days in 1562, very likely reflects Dorat's teaching. For Dorat regarded the poems as the works of the original Orpheus, and believed that they contained portentous secrets of ancient natural magic; and Scaliger, in his original subscription to the work, described Orpheus as 'vates vetustissimus'.[27] Certainly he heard Dorat discuss problems in Theocritus; whether he attended Dorat's formal lectures we cannot say.[28] In any event, he made a strong impression. In 1563, Dorat found him a job as the literary companion to a young Poitevin nobleman, Louis Chasteigner de la Rochepozay; and by 1564, Dorat trusted him enough to ask him to pass on a request for funds to Louis's older brother François — who promptly obliged — as well as respectfully to ask his opinion about the interpretation of a phrase in Pindar.[29]

Turnèbe was as impressed by Scaliger's abilities in Latin as Dorat had been by his facility in Greek. In 1563 to 1564 they discussed passages in Varro *De lingua latina*. Turnèbe also heard with benign approval Scaliger's emendation of Catullus 74.3. Here the vulgate read 'patrui perdespuit ipsam uxorem'. Scaliger brilliantly guessed that *perdespuit*, though not impossible, was a *lectio facilior* — a trivialization introduced by a scribe who mistook a less familiar word for it. The original reading, he argued, must have been *perdepsuit* ('he kneaded over' — i.e. 'he made love to'). Though unattested, the word was historically plausible, for Cicero had indicated that its root verb *depso* could have an obscene connotation. Scaliger's emendation gave the entire epigram a much clearer point: 'Gellius had heard that his uncle used to utter rebukes if anyone spoke of or played at love. Lest this happen to him, he made love to his uncle's own wife, and made his uncle into the God of silence himself.'[30] Accordingly, Turnèbe included Scaliger's conjecture in the vast mass of *Adversaria* that he was preparing for the press: 'Scaliger, a learned young man, has a plausible suggestion which, I recall, he once mentioned to me: the reading should be *patrui perdepsuit ipsam uxorem*, not *perdespuit*.'[31]

Lambin respected Scaliger as an authority on both languages. In 1564, while he was working on his second edition of Horace, he and Scaliger discussed the word *Genitalis*, which Horace had used in *Carmen Saeculare* 16 as an epithet for the goddess of birth, Ilithyia. Lambin knew that Genitalis was the Latin equivalent of γενέθλιος — 'connected with birth'. What he did not know was that Plato had used γενέθλιος in the *Laws*, for the vulgate text of the passage in question was corrupt, and it was a conjectural emendation of Scaliger's that restored the word to it. As Lambin told the story:

Joseph Scaliger showed me not long ago that Plato used the word in Book V of the *Laws*. He had then come to Paris to see to the printing of his

Coniectanea on Varro *De lingua latina*. Now these are Plato's words: ξυγγένειαν δὲ καὶ ὁμογνίων θεῶν κοινωνίαν ἅπασαν ταὐτοῦ φύσιν αἵματος ἔχουσαν τιμῶν τις καὶ σεβόμενος εὔνους ἂν γενεθλίους θεοὺς ἐς παίδων αὐτοῦ σπορὰν ἴσχοι κατὰ λόγον. There the vulgate reading is: εὔνους ἂν καὶ γενέσθαι οὓς θεούς.³²

And he proved the superiority of Scaliger's emendation to the vulgate by the simple expedient of translating it into Latin; one who properly reveres all the gods that protect his race 'deos genitaleis propitios erga liberorum suorum sationem merito et probabiliter habuerit' — 'will, as is reasonable, find the gods of childbirth favourably disposed towards the generation of his children'.

With younger Paris scholars Scaliger was on even closer terms. Indeed, he set up what amounted to a working partnership with Dorat's pupil Willem Canter. When Muret came back from Italy, he brought with him a copy of a fragment of the *Deipnosophistae* of Athenaeus, from a manuscript in the collection of the Farnese family.³³ This section had been omitted from the printed editions of the full text. Muret passed it on to Canter for publication, and Canter turned to Scaliger for help with the many recondite and problematic words in it. The text appeared in Canter's *Novae lectiones* of 1564, with Scaliger's conjectures in the margins.³⁴ Scaliger lent Canter his annotated Euripides — a course of action that he later regretted, for Canter copied out and published some of his conjectures without clearly identifying Scaliger as their author. All Scaliger could do was to decorate the offending passages in his copy of Canter's work with indignant comments: 'The man is ashamed to mention me'; 'He took this from my Euripides, which I made available to him.'³⁵ But even this unfortunate incident did not break the friendship; as late as 1572, Scaliger proudly declared his affection for Canter in print.³⁶

These scattered references confirm Scaliger's precocity as a master linguist and his remarkable ability at divining textual corruptions and emending them by conjecture. Even in the 1560s, few humanists in their early twenties could argue convincingly for the creation of an unattested Latin form or the rewriting of a piece of Plato's Greek; fewer still could command wide assent for their ideas from the most eminent professional philologists. Yet such anecdotes are frustrating as well. Inevitably, they have something of the effect of music played on a piano in a far-away room; the individual notes are fleetingly attractive, but the tune escapes identification. Scaliger's abilities are clear; but his central interests and motivations are not.

In 1564 Scaliger completed and gave to the printer a full-scale scholarly work, his *Coniectanea* on Varro *De lingua latina*. This was a selective text-critical and exegetical commentary, studded with digressions into the correction and explication of the most diverse Greek and Latin writings. It occupied Scaliger for years. He began it around 1560; as his friend François Vertunien later wrote: 'He composed Coniectanea on Varro at the age of 20. "In those days", he said [to me], "I was as mad as a young hare."'[37] The numerous discussions of Near Eastern words that appear throughout show that he continued to work on it after meeting Postel. He clearly regarded the book as a sort of representative specimen of his best work in progress, for in his preface he stated that he had equally good sets of observations on other texts ready for publication, but had singled out those on Varro as a testimony of his gratitude to Louis Chasteigner, to whom he dedicated the whole.[38]

Scaliger clearly set out to bring off a demonstration of virtuosity. He lost no chance to prove his mastery of Greek, even where he had to fetch the occasion for doing so from rather far. One example will illustrate his method. In V.113 Varro says that '*Lana* [wool] is a Greek word, as Polybius and Callimachus write.'[39] Here is part of Scaliger's comment:

Varro is quite right to use the testimony of Callimachus. For Aeschylus also, when he used this word, explained it, as being a little out of the ordinary. These are his words, from the *Eumenides*:

Λήνει μεγίστῳ σωφρόνως ἐστεμμένον,
Ἀργῆτι μαλλῷ · τῇδε γὰρ τρανῶς ἐρῶ.

('Reverently crowned with a great wool fillet — with a white fleece, that is, for as to this I can speak plainly.')
For it is his custom, when he uses rare or hard words, to add an explanation. For example, in the *Seven Against Thebes*:

Ἅλω δὲ πολλὴν (ἀσπίδος κύκλον λέγω)
Ἔφριξα διῃῄσαντος · οὐκ ἄλλως ἐρῶ.

('I shuddered as he whirled around his great orb (I mean the circle of his shield). I cannot deny it.')[40]

Neither the second quotation nor the discussion of Aeschylus' practice of epexegesis was strictly relevant to the text of Varro. But as a comment on Aeschylus' style, the discussion was both original and illuminating — so much so that it was repeated by the best sixteenth-century Aeschylus scholar, Isaac Casaubon, in his unfinished commentary on the *Agamemnon*.[41] Page after page coruscated with similar gems of linguistic and stylistic analysis, which established Scaliger beyond question as a masterly critic of Greek poetry.

Even more decisively, the *Coniectanea* proved Scaliger's mastery as a Latin textual critic. Using Antonio Agustín's edition as his base, Scaliger devised and argued for a great number of elegant and plausible conjectures. At VII.107, for example, Varro discussed miscellaneous 'words in the poets, whose origins [can] be set forth'. Among them, in Agustín's text, was the decidedly curious *caudatus*, which Varro interpreted as meaning 'sweet'.[42] In the commentary that he was working on when he died in 1565 — itself in part the result of discussions with Scaliger — Turnèbe explained the word with all the misplaced zeal of a late antique schoolmaster: 'CAVDACVS] A very old word. It seems to be derived from *gaudium*. For the ancients often used *c* for *g*. For we rejoice (*gaudemus*) in sweet things.'[43] Using a parallel discussion in another Roman grammarian, Scaliger brilliantly emended: 'CAVDATVS.] In the older printed texts, *Cauadatus*. Clearly the reading must be *Clucidatus*, from Festus, who explains it as meaning sweet and pleasant. Elsewhere in Festus it is spelled *Glucidatus*, with the same meaning, from γλυκύς (sweet).'[44] Similar emendations did a great deal to smooth down the rocky passages throughout Agustín's text, which was based on a bad manuscript and presented many difficulties. At every turn he emended passages from other Latin texts as well. He took the opportunity to print his conjecture *perdepsuit* in Catullus 74.3.[45] More typical, however, is his note on V.94. Here he supported his correction of *verbum* to *cervum* — itself highly plausible — by citing the following parallel instance:

This error springs, as is not uncommon, from ignorance of the old style of writing. Incompetent scribes were not aware of this. For they misread the genuine reading *Cerbum* as *verbum*. The same error is remarkably common in the manuscripts of Nonius. For instance, in an example [quoted] from Sisenna, *Ferabite* is found instead of *fera vite*: 'Et partim fera vite, partim lauro et arbusto ac multa pinu ac murtetis abundat.' ('And it abounds partly in wild vines, partly in laurels and orchards, and in pine and in myrtle groves.') Some have even said in their magnificent dictionaries, compiled with so much effort, that ancient authors used *Ferabite* for *agrestis* (rustic).[46]

Canter liked the subsidiary emendation of Nonius so much that he published that as well, attributing it to an unspecified friend, and provoking Scaliger to another baleful marginal note.

Scaliger's conjectures reveal more than his cleverness. They show that he had learned from Turnèbe, in both method and substance, much more than he admitted in his preface or in his discursive remarks. He gave Turnèbe credit for having given him manuscript readings and discussed conjectures with him.[47] The picture of detailed co-operation is confirmed by Turnèbe's own approving citation of one of Scaliger's emendations.[48] But the many tacit correspondences between Scaliger's work and Turnèbe's expose debts that Scaliger wished to conceal.

At V.88, for example, Varro wrote that according to Hypsicrates, the Greek word for *cohors* (farmyard) was *chortos*. Here Scaliger wrote: 'Dicit esse Graece cohorton apud poetas dictum.] Without question, read *Chorton*, removing one letter. In the poets χόρτος means ὁ περίβολος (the enclosure).'[49] He cited supporting passages from Euripides and Homer. On the same passage Turnèbe wrote:

But the Greek grammarians interpret χόρτον (for I read this, not *cohorton*, nor κόνθον) in Homer, αὐλῆς ἐνὶ χόρτῳ, the circumference and wall of the farmyard. From this derived Euripides' phrase σύγχορτα ναίω πεδία, for next-door and nearby fields.[50]

Again, Scaliger rightly argued that in Agustín's text, two large sections of Book V (32-41 and 23-32) had been transposed. He boasted loudly of the originality of his correction:

I am less sorry for the sufferings of this passage, though it has been terribly mistreated, than I am surprised that those who have undertaken the correction of this author have paid no attention to it; so it is clear enough that there is a remarkable corruption here.[51]

Turnèbe proposed the same correction, and thanked Buchanan for it.[52] There are other identical results as well in the two commentaries.[53]

Two inferences cannot be escaped. The first is that Turnèbe had far more to do with Scaliger's training than has generally been realized. Scaliger's marvellous gifts for conjectural re-creation did not develop with the spontaneity that his own account suggests. He learned from an older master how to identify and attack corruptions. The second is less pleasing. It is that Scaliger was a young man in a great hurry — and, more important, that he was in a hurry to prove the validity of his father's contention that the abilities of a della Scala were limitless and his originality complete. He understood the notion of intellectual property perfectly well when it suited him — he became quite angry, as we saw, when Canter pillaged his work without giving him due credit. But it did not suit him to admit that the critical approach that he applied to Varro — to say nothing of many specific results — was not his own. In short, Scaliger's aim in this first work was not simply to produce a piece of solid, professional textual scholarship, but to prove that he was the aristocratic virtuoso that his father had wanted him to become, even at the expense of scholarly candour.

Scaliger's work on exegetical problems is still more revealing. He paid special attention to Varro's many quotations from Latin drama.[54] As we saw, Poliziano had suggested one way to deal with these. If the Greek original of a Latin fragment could be located in an extant play, the Latin work would be identified — a Latin passage by Ennius that corresponded to lines in Euripides' *Medea*, for example, could be assigned to the *Medea* that Ennius was known to have written.[55]

Since Scaliger's teachers shared this interest, it is likely that he learned the basics of Poliziano's method of identification from them. In VI.81, for instance, Varro attributed these lines to Medea:

> Ter sub armis malim vitam cernere
> Quam semel modo parere
> ('I would rather risk my life three times in battle than give birth once.')[56]

Here is Scaliger's note:

QVOD AIT MEDEA] Varro in the γεροντοδιδάσκαλος:
'Don't you see that Ennius writes:
Ter malim sub armis vitam cernere,
quam semel modo parere?' The words of Euripides that Ennius is translating are the following:
— ὡς τρὶς ἂν παρ' ἀσπίδα
Στῆναι θέλοιμι μᾶλλον ἢ τεκεῖν ἅπαξ
('I would rather stand three times by my shield than give birth once.')[57]

And here is Turnèbe on the same fragment: 'TER sub armis malim] Ennius here translates Euripides with remarkable elegance: ὡς τρὶς . . .'.[58] The parallel came from a well-known text, but the coincidence is at least suggestive. And there is other evidence to suggest that Scaliger acquired this interest too from his elders. In trying to assign plays to authors, and in trying to determine whether Ennius had written one play or two about Medea, Scaliger was also attacking problems that had attracted Turnèbe before him.[59] As we have seen, the Estienne were completing their systematic assault on archaic Latin at much the same time that Scaliger was embarking on his.[60] Scaliger's work was independent of the Estienne's *Fragmenta*, which he — along with his contemporary Fruterius — regarded as uncritical and incomplete.[61] But the very fact that the subject had interested so many of his elders suggests that here too Scaliger owed them more than he admitted.

At the same time, however, Scaliger made comparative exegesis serve new ends; and it is these new ends that draw together several of the scattered threads of his earlier activities. He compared Latin fragments with Greek originals far more comprehensively than had his elders, and in a different context. For he saw these comparisons not only as a method for identifying fragments, but also as a literary tool of genuine though vaguely defined interest. His note on the *Medea* fragment in VI.81, for example, continues thus:

I shall set out some other passages which you will compare with the words of Euripides. For I think that this sort of exercise is by no means a waste of time. In Probus, Ennius says:

Iuppiter, tuque adeo summe sol
Qui res omnes inspicis,
Quique tuo lumine
Mare, terram ac caelum
Contueris: hoc facinus dispice.
Priusquam fit, prohibe scelus.[62] Euripides:

Ἰὼ γᾶ τε, καὶ παμφαὴς ἀκτὶς
Ἀελίου, κατείδετε, εἴδετε τὰν
Οὐλομέναν, πρὶν φοινίαν
Τέκνοις προσβαλεῖν χέρα
Αὐτοκτόνον. Then
Ἀλλά νιν, ὦ φάος διογενές, κάτειργε,
Κατάπαυσον, ἔξελ' οἴκων φοινίαν.

('O earth, and all-illuminating splendour of the sun, look down, see this wretched woman before she destroys herself by murdering her children . . . But restrain her, divine light, stop her, expel the wretch . . .' [*Medea* 1251-60]).
In Cicero, *pro Rabirio Postumo*,
Si te secundo lumine hic offendero,
from the *Medea* of Ennius, is from this:
Εἴ σ' ἡ 'πιοῦσα λαμπὰς ὄψεται θεοῦ [352].
This, in the same work: *Animum advorte, et dicto pare,* he made from Ἀλλ' ἔξιθ' ὡς τάχιστα. In the same work *Praeter rogitatum ne querare* is clearly from μὴ λόγους λέγε. Others have noted the rest of the fragments cited by grammarians; therefore I shall omit them.[63]

There are many similar notes, in which all the parallels were Scaliger's own discoveries — the result of knowing the tragedies almost by heart. Both his contemptuous assumption that any

competent scholar would see the literary interest of these comparisons and the sheer amount of material he assembled went
far beyond what his teachers had tried to do. Scaliger even
suggested that it was precisely here — in the ability to identify
the Greek sources of early Latin — that the best test of philological excellence lay: 'Let these suffice', he concluded after
setting down another awesome list of parallels:

> to give practice to capable intellects in studies of this kind. For no one
> is competent in them unless he has trained his mind perfectly in both
> languages. And I have little interest in what the ruck of little schoolmasters
> think about them.[64]

Scaliger also tried to piece together these scattered remains of
Roman drama. Once he had assembled three or four quotations
from a given play, he would 'glue them up', as he put it, into a
coherent speech, even when the grammarians who had preserved
them offered no evidence at all about their immediate context.[65]
He repeatedly pointed out that he had made several such
attempts at reconstruction and tried to convey the aesthetic
pleasure so gained: 'I take the greatest delight in these remains,
which resemble the debris from a sunken ship.'[66] Though he
knew that there was little or no evidence to support these reconstructions, he defended them as the only way of making the
fragments usable for literary purposes:

> There was no reason not to collect these widely scattered fragments. For,
> even if we grant that Pacuvius did not assemble them in this way, let us
> none the less use them for the moment as a sort of cento. Scattered as we
> find them in the grammarians, they are like maimed and dead limbs. But
> connected as they are here, if nothing else, they will at least take on some
> beauty and value.[67]

More striking than either of these novel practices was a third,
which to some extent combined the other two. Once Scaliger
had established the texts of his Latin fragments and, in some
cases, assembled them into coherent sections of verse, he decided
that they were inaccurate as translations. He acidly criticized
the Romans for their errors, omissions, and departures from the
wording of the originals. Occasionally he even supplied alternative Latin renderings which he claimed to be more faithful:

> And although Ennius translated word for word, his procedures were rather
> careless. Take the following:
>> *Haec tu etsi pervorse dices, facile Achivos flexeris.*
>> *Nanque opulenti cum loquuntur pariter atque ignobiles,*
>> *Eadem dicta, eademque oratio aequa non aeque valet.*

('Even if you say these things poorly, you will easily sway the Greeks. For when the wealthy and the ignoble speak similarly, the same words and the very same speech do not have the same effect.')
I think that this would be rather more elegant:

> *Haec tu etsi inepte dixeris, flexis facul:*
> *Ignobilium etenim atque opinatum virum*
> *Oratio indidem aequa non aeque valet.*

Euripides:

> Τὸ δ' ἀξίωμα κἂν κακῶς λέγῃ τὸ σόν,
> Πείσει · λόγος γὰρ ἔκτ' ἀδοξούντων ἰών,
> Κἀκ τῶν δοκούντων, αὐτὸς οὐ ταυτὸν σθένει.[68]

It is not surprising that Scaliger found this too loose. Gellius had made the same criticism in *Noctes Atticae* XI.iv.4: 'neque omnes ignobiles ἀδοξοῦσι, neque omnes opulenti εὐδοξοῦσιν.'

What is puzzling is the apparent contradiction between Scaliger's great affection for the fragments of early Latin and his heated criticism of their errors. Why go to all the trouble of assembling them into possible speeches and casting about through hundreds of lines of Greek for their sources, only to point out that they were inaccurate and replaceable? What possible purpose could lie behind this strange juxtaposition of contrasting methods and feelings?

Scaliger himself solves these riddles for us. In a note on VII. 19, he argued on the basis of several parallels that Ennius had translated Aeschylus' *Eumenides*. He then wrote:

Now we have translated that whole play by Aeschylus in the ancient style of Pacuvius. In this respect great blame must be attached to those translators who make the ancient poets so unlike themselves, so that I am ashamed to read Homer speaking the language of Silius Italicus and Sophocles [speaking] that of Seneca. But I shall discuss these matters elsewhere.[69]

This passage reveals that Scaliger's interests were less historical than literary. He regarded the Latin poetry of the second century BC as the proper medium for translating the classics of Greek poetry. He may well also have reasoned that the second-century translations had naturalized Greek literature in Rome; they had been the common currency of the writers of the Roman Golden Age. But they had been imperfect and were in any case now lost. Accordingly, he set out to enrich the Latin culture of his own time by replacing and improving upon the lost originals. In mastering Varro he hoped to improve his own ability to write archaic Latin verse; in reconstructing the lost plays of Pacuvius, Scaliger hoped to recover his style. Seen in this light, these centos of fragments take on a clear meaning. Even if they were not historically justifiable, they could at least give some idea of extended passages in the archaic poets. They could stand as a model for imitation. The stringent comparison of Latin fragments with Greek originals could serve as a preventative against too much freedom in translation. One central end of the *Coniectanea*, then, was not the purification of ancient texts but the reconstruction of an ancient poetic genre.

This project had the merit of combining several of Scaliger's aptitudes: his splendid memory for verbal detail, his intimate knowledge of Greek poetry, and his fluency at adapting works written in one language into a second. This was the tune that his years of five-finger exercises in Paris had enabled him to compose and play.

This interpretation is strengthened by other episodes. Around 1564 he collaborated with Canter on an edition of Lycophron's *Alexandra*, perhaps the most learned and certainly the most obscure Hellenistic Greek poem. Canter prepared the Greek text, a commentary, and a literal Latin translation.[70] Scaliger devised emendations and interpreted difficult words. But his main share in the venture was a rendering of Lycophron's deliberately recherché Greek into equally recherché Latin. He used so many archaic or rare terms that he had to provide glosses in the margin to explain them to the ordinary educated reader. To be sure, he was not able fully to reproduce the qualities of his original. Where Lycophron had used more than 1,350 rare words, including 326 not found elsewhere, Scaliger was able to find only 140 Latin equivalents so arcane as to need explanation. Even of these, 'between a quarter and a third are conveniently taken' from one source, Festus *De verborum significatu*.[71] The work nevertheless conveyed at least something of the ghoulish obscurity of the original. More important, it read — at least in the 1560s — like a genuine piece of archaic Latin, the sort of thing that might have been written by a Roman poet in Lycophron's own time. 'This is my opinion', wrote Canter: 'had you written this in Latin when the poet wrote it in Greek, it would be very hard to tell which was the other's translator.'[72]

Further confirmation comes from Scaliger's translation of Sophocles' *Ajax*. This was also apparently completed in the period around 1565, though it was not printed until 1573.[73] Here too Scaliger's aim was clearly to write archaic Latin. He used as many arcane or distinctively pre-classical words as possible: *obgannuit, ninguida, salisubsuli*.[74] He dressed ordinary words in primitive spellings: *ast, maxumus, advorsum, par-volum.*[75] And, like the archaic poets, he freely coined new compound words — while avoiding those compounds that had also been used by classical and post-classical poets. Thus, to translate λιθόλευστον Ἄρη ('death by stoning') in 254 he used *Saxipetas . . . populi . . . manus* ('the stone-throwing hands of the people'). *Saxipetas* was unattested: but Scaliger deliberately formed it to avoid using the equally appropriate *saxiferas*, which had been used by the over-rhetorical Valerius Flaccus.[76] Sometimes he even introduced archaic compounds when the Greek offered no direct pretext for doing so. At 1142 Menelaus says:

ἤδη ποτ' εἶδον ἄνδρ' ἐγὼ γλώσσῃ θρασύν

('I saw a man over-bold in speech').
This perfectly plain Greek Scaliger translated as

Vidi tolutiloquente lingua praeditum.[77]

Tolutiloquens is an unattested form that Scaliger coined from the attested noun *tolutiloquentia*, 'volubility', which is found only in a fragment quoted by Nonius from the comic writer Novius.[78] Sometimes the effects of this method are merely curious, as when the choral lines

ἀλλ' ὀξυτόνους μὲν ᾠδὰς
θρηνήσει

('but she will sing sharp dirges')
become the horrible

Ast luctificum integrabit
lessum

('Verily she will begin again the mournful moan').[79]
Sometimes they are unintentionally comic, as when the tragic exclamation οἴμοι τάλαινα in 800 and elsewhere is replaced by *perii* ('I am lost'), which would infallibly call to the mind of a sixteenth-century reader not tragedy but the misadventures of parasites in Plautus and Terence.[80] The style of the *Ajax*, of course, has none of Lycophron's wilful obscurity. Scaliger himself, echoing ancient critical opinion, prized Sophocles especially because he was so *sanus* and *sobrius*.[81] That he still saw archaic Latin as the appropriate medium for his version is all the more revealing.

The most elaborate evidence for what Scaliger had in mind comes from a late but reliable source: the *De tragoediae constitutione liber* of his Leiden pupil Daniel Heinsius, which came out in 1611. Heinsius stated explicitly the stylistic views that Scaliger had only hinted at:

But learned antiquity has an honour all its own, and this sort of thing can be unbelievably charming . . . Thus the incomparable Joseph Scaliger and Florent Chrestien made elegant translations of some plays of the ancient Greeks in the style of Accius and Pacuvius. These are to be read with care, so that the difference between them and the rest may be clear, and so that the grace and charming squalor of pristine antiquity may allure the soul; finally, so that if possible some passages may be adapted, as Virgil did from the works of Ennius. We too once translated some things in this way. And while composing that passage we found among our papers the first part of Sophocles' *Electra*, translated in an archaic idiom. We thought that we should give it here for the use of students. . .[82]

It seems clear that by the 1560s Scaliger had already worked out what he passed on to the favourite student of his old age: an elaborate programme for improving Latin literature by cross-fertilization from Greek, one that both fitted into and derived from the preoccupations of the Parisian circle that he hoped to join.

Yet another side of Scaliger's *Coniectanea* did not fit the Parisian mould so neatly. Varro's principal subject in Books V–VII was etymology. Something of a linguistic nativist, he had tried as often as he could to find Latin roots for Latin words. Scaliger disliked these views and criticized them at length. He insisted that Varro had taken too narrow a view of the origins of Latin. Many Latin words were derived from Greek and even from Near Eastern roots. At V.124, for example, Varro derived *simpulum* (ladle) from *sumo* (take). Scaliger disagreed: '*Simpulum* is Syriac. For as *Abub, Ambub*, 'flute', gave rise to *Ambubaiarum collegia* (guilds of flute-girls); *copher* to *camphor*; . . . so *sephel* gave rise to *sempel*, and from that they made *simpulum*.'[83] In fact, he disagreed with Varro on so many counts that he appended to the *Coniectanea* several pages of etymologies that Varro had omitted or of which he had given incorrect accounts.[84] And he defended himself fiercely against unnamed detractors: 'I know that in saying this I will be hated by those who not only are ignorant of Hebrew and Syriac learning but hate it as well. But I find it as easy to despise these men as they do to hate that sort of learning.'[85]

Scaliger's attempts at etymology were original only because he tried so hard to find Near Eastern roots. He built his arguments and etymologies on the same weary set of unproven assumptions that grammarians had used since antiquity: that certain consonants, for example, were more easily exchangeable than others.[86] Without knowledge of Sanskrit he could not in most cases be correct; and if his notion that *Ambubaia* was cognate to Aramaic *'abûb* is still considered valid, his derivation of *simpulum* from Hebrew *sēpel* was far-fetched even when he proposed it.[87] Moreover, in using Varro *De lingua latina* as a pretext for etymological investigations, he was doing nothing new. Turnèbe had done the same.[88] M. Vertranius Maurus, a jurist from Aix-en-Provence, had published a commentary on the *De lingua latina* in 1563; he too had taken the opportunity to attack Varro's linguistic chauvinism.[89] Etymology, and the history of languages in general, was one of the most fashionable sub-disciplines of sixteenth-century scholarship. It attracted speculations from theologians and historians as well as from philologists.[90] A commentator on the most influential Roman etymologist could hardly avoid the question.

None the less, Scaliger's work had its novel points. The combination of Near Eastern philology with Greek and Latin studies was not common among the Paris philologists. Indeed, there is evidence that Scaliger's master Turnèbe opposed this part of his enterprise, unregenerately continuing in his *Adversaria* to derive *ambubaia* from *ambu* and *Baiae*.[91] In 1572, when Turnèbe was safely dead, Scaliger protested bitterly about his refusal to accept the possibility of a Near Eastern etymology:

Let us not believe the learned man who thinks the word is derived from Baiae. I do not want to be believed by him, ignorant as he is of the Syrian language, but by those who are expert in it. The fact that I could not persuade him of this point, when I had explained it in my commentaries on Varro, irks me less than his total surprise at my seeking that root in farthest Syria. For what he, in his ignorance of the Syrian language, tried so hard to mock, is not surprising at all to those who know the language.[92]

Even in his mid-twenties, avid for reputation by displaying brilliance in a more or less conventional mode of argument, Scaliger could not resist the temptation to try to add something out of the ordinary. Already his range of knowledge and interests was too broad to be accommodated within the pattern that his teachers had set. For the next twenty years, his life consisted of a search for a philological method that would enable him to pursue all the studies that he considered valid. Reluctantly, and after long hesitation, he was forced to abandon the methods of his first masters.

To sum up what Scaliger had achieved by 1565: he had shown that he was an inventive conjectural critic of Latin and Greek, devised an ambitious literary programme, and begun to make an effort at combining classical and Near Eastern philology. Reactions to his work were varied. We have already seen that his Near Eastern etymologies were unacceptable to his elders. His contemporaries, on the other hand, seem to have regarded them with more sympathy; Bonaventura Vulcanius, later to be Scaliger's colleague in Leiden, set out to provide analogous corrections for Isidore's *Etymologiae.*[93] His conjectural emendations were clearly most impressive — novel enough for Canter, a competent critic, to take the trouble to pilfer them.[94] Though the appearance of the fragments of Turnèbe's commentary in 1566 may have shown some readers the extent of Scaliger's debt, the edition seems to have been a tiny one, and I have not found any overt reaction to it.

Reactions to his exegetical and literary arguments were naturally mixed. His programme could be judged only in terms of the quality of the poetry he produced. Despite their lexical richness, Scaliger's translations were too crude to win full approval from the best contemporary judge. 'Muret', he recalled as an old man, 'had a good deal of fun mocking my *Ajax*. He was a great man; he must have seen something there that I did not.'[95]

Such reservations did not affect French views of Scaliger's emendations and explications of specific passages in Varro. Scaliger continued to work along the scholarly as well as the literary lines laid down in the *Coniectanea.* In particular, he made collations towards a new edition of the lexicon of Nonius Marcellus — only to abandon the project when Plantin brought out an edition that failed to meet Scaliger's criteria of excellence but was protected from competition by an imperial privilege.[96] Whatever the crudities of his aesthetics, Scaliger had established himself as the chief authority on both archaic Latin and the Roman grammatical tradition. When Pierre Daniel discovered the eighth-century bilingual glossary of Philoxenus, he showed it to Scaliger as well as to Turnèbe, and apparently gave Scaliger permission to make a partial transcript for publication. When Lambin was preparing his edition of Plautus in the early 1570s, he literally begged Scaliger for help in the shape of conjectural emendations.[97] The reputation won by the *Coniectanea* was, perhaps, slightly odd; but it was a reputation.

From 1565 onwards the peaceful tenor of Scaliger's life changed, largely if not entirely for the worse. His patron went on a journey to Rome. Like many other diplomats of the sixteenth century — who bore, as Bernays remarks, no very clear resemblance to their modern counterparts — he liked to while away his journeys by bringing a humanist along to read classical texts with him.[98] So for the next two years Scaliger's time was spent in travel. As he and Chasteigner slowly crossed and re-crossed the Alps, they read Greek and Latin texts together.[99] In Italy, where he travelled in both 1565 and 1566, he reached as far south as Naples; but most of his time was inevitably spent in Rome and in the cities of the North.[100] Despite his Italian descent, he came as a foreigner, and depended on Muret to guide him and introduce him to leading scholars.[101] He met Onofrio Panvinio, a leading antiquary, in dramatic circumstances:

In 1565, in the month of October, Muret arranged an appointment with Onofrio, who wished to meet Joseph, . . . When he had brought Joseph — who knew nothing of what was to happen — Onofrio came up to him. After he greeted Joseph, they had scarcely exchanged a few words when Joseph immediately guessed who he was. . . . Then he embraced Joseph and said: 'This is a happy day for me, to see the remnant of the della Scala family.'[102]

But he seems for the most part to have made his friends among the Italians who were best known for their pro-French sympathies — notably Paolo Manuzio and his son Aldo. Characteristically, Paolo tried to draw Scaliger into his feud with the allies of Vettori. He had learned that Orsini was preparing a collection of Greek lyric poetry. He and Scaliger agreed to co-operate on a 'project' as soon as the book appeared.[103] Presumably this would have taken the form of a reprint heavily emended by conjecture, designed to reveal that Orsini was too conservative in his editorial technique. Nothing concrete came of these discussions, however, except a lasting friendship between Scaliger and the Manuzio.[104]

More interesting to Scaliger than Italian scholars were the material remains of the ancient world that he encountered everywhere in Italy. He marvelled at the size of Roman walls.[105] He admired collections of ancient sculpture — though all he ever said about them was that the genitalia of the herms were very large.[106] He copied down the texts of a great number of inscriptions from the collections of the Farnese and others, concentrating on those in Greek.[107] In fact, he became so adept at deciphering the letters of worn inscriptions and emending and supplementing difficult texts that the results hidden in odd corners of his work sometimes surpassed those of eighteenth- and nineteenth-century scholars.[108]

But his main reaction to the Italian scene was one of disappointment and anger.[109] No doubt his paranoid fears of Venetian assassins, out to kill the last of the della Scala, contributed to his dislike of the country.[110] But there was more to it than that. Like the good young Huguenot that he was, he found the Italians slick, irreligious, and dishonourable. Late in life he recalled that the word *Mysterium* had been written on the papal tiara, and took this observation as the proof that the Pope was the Whore of Babylon.[111] So he spent as much time as he could manage in the wealthy and extraordinarily cultured Jewish communities of North Italy, especially in Mantua and Ferrara, where he marvelled at the freedom in which the Jews were allowed to live. It would be amusing to know how the Jews reacted to this strange young man, for we have only Scaliger's account:

I disputed at Rome and elsewhere with the Jews. They liked me very much and were very surprised that I spoke Hebrew well, and they said to me that I spoke the Hebrew of the Bible, and that very few of them could speak in that fashion, but that they spoke the language of the older Rabbis, *Rabbotenu Zicronam.*[112]

From Italy, Scaliger and Chasteigner went North. In Scotland, Scaliger noticed with interest the use of fossil coal and listened with pleasure to the lullabies sung by children's nurses.[113] Here too court life proved too wicked for his taste:

Mary Stuart, Queen of Scotland, had a handsome husband, yet she took pleasure in disgusting adulteries. . . . While I was there she and her husband had fallen out over the death of the famous David. Buchanan's History is entirely true; she did not speak to her husband. . . . She was a pretty thing.[114]

England was even less rewarding. He found the English barbarous and fanatical; their libraries held no interesting manuscripts, the fellows of their colleges lived a life of idleness, and they all had a pathological hatred for the French.[115] Only Elizabeth impressed him, not by her beauty but by her fluency in several languages.[116]

By 1567 he was back in France. He made a beginning on a new project: an edition of and commentary on the *Appendix Vergiliana*, along with an assortment of Latin epigrams, some dealing with or attributed to Virgil and others anonymous but appealing for literary reasons.[117] In preparation for this he collated or copied manuscripts from Pierre Pithou's library, including a fourteenth-century manuscript of the *Culex* and the only manuscript of a fifth-century grammarian's versified life of Virgil.[118] For unknown reasons, he had to leave Paris for the Limousin, but he sent the completed manuscript of his edition to Pithou, who was to oversee its publication.[119]

At this point the civil war interfered decisively with Scaliger's work. Pithou was unable to find a publisher and had to return Scaliger's manuscript.[120] Scaliger was swept up in the horrors of the worst of the Religious Wars, the second and third of 1567 and 1568. What property his father had left him in Agen was stolen, and he was forced to become a soldier. There was no longer time for scholarship, and even his edition of the *Appendix* was lost.[121]

In 1570, when peace came, Scaliger found himself at Valence, in the Dauphiné. Here the second formative period of his life was spent. Cujas took him in, supported him and taught him Roman law, an experience which brought Scaliger into contact with the mature historical scholarship of the best French jurists.

For the two years that Scaliger spent in Valence, Cujas was engaged on what he saw as his most important work: his historical reconstruction of the works and the thought of the jurist Africanus.[122] He collected the passages from Africanus that occurred in the *Digest*, he identified the lost works from which they had been excerpted, and explained the passages themselves in terms both of their original context and of their new context in the *Digest*. The project had both a scholarly and a practical end. On the one hand, by reconstituting the lost works of Africanus and other jurists, Cujas was contributing to the reconstruction of Roman legal history. He showed in an exemplary manner how arbitrarily preserved fragments could be made to yield a great deal of information about the lost original from which they came; at best, such studies could lead to the recovery of a world that had seemed lost, the world of the Roman jurists. At the same time, the reconstructed historical context of each fragment also helped the practising jurist in his normal tasks. For by understanding each fragment as clearly as possible, he would also arrive at the most thorough possible historical understanding of the *Digest* passages in which the fragments were quoted. Cujas, wrote a friend:

told me that he advised those who are already advanced in the study of law to work through Africanus again carefully. For anyone who has made himself completely familiar with him can deal with the other jurisconsults at his pleasure, since Africanus dealt only with the most difficult and obscure legal problems.[123]

For Scaliger, who had long been fascinated by the problems of reconstructing lost literary works, Cujas's instruction was immediately accessible and attractive. 'I came from Agen to Valence', he wrote:

that is, from the stormiest waves to the most tranquil harbour of all virtues and human letters, Jacques Cujas. Seasick as I was from the ship of state, he refreshed me with the taste of honourable studies; exhausted as I was, he revived me; given up for lost, and despairing as I was with regard to myself and my affairs, he called me back to the light.[124]

In Cujas, Scaliger found someone who shared his taste for and competence in the most exacting technical studies, who matched his virtuosity as a textual critic, and who could introduce him to a vast new field of historical and antiquarian research with which he had — so far as our evidence goes — previously had little acquaintance.[125]

Not surprisingly, they paid special attention in their discussions to the fragments of the oldest Roman laws, the *leges regiae* and the Twelve Tables. Here Scaliger's knowledge made him Cujas's equal. 'There is no one', he later remarked: 'who can teach me anything about the laws of the Twelve Tables, not even Cujas, who will not deny that he learned many things about them from me.'[126] Cujas agreed. As early as 1570, in the first year of their *contubernium*, he published one of Scaliger's conjectural emendations of a law from the Twelve Tables. He attributed it to 'the most learned Joseph Scaliger, with whom one disagrees at one's peril'.[127]

Their discussions embraced more than early law. Cujas, whose generosity with his books was proverbial, threw open his library to Scaliger. In this great collection there were no fewer than two hundred manuscripts of texts of every kind.[128] Scaliger, so Cujas pretended to complain, 'deflowered them'. He used manuscripts of Martial, Priscian, Dositheus, and Victorinus.[129] He copied Cujas's manuscript of the *Satiricon* of Petronius, which is now lost, but was more complete and accurate than those that have survived.[130] In 1572, when Élie Vinet asked Scaliger and Cujas to speed up the printing of his edition of Ausonius, Scaliger took the opportunity to collate Cujas's great Ausonius manuscript, a ninth-century codex in Visigothic script.[131]

Moreover, by living with Cujas, Scaliger placed himself at the centre of a rich and fine-spun web of allies and correspondents.

He could be sure that when any one of them discovered a new text or a new manuscript of an old one, Cujas would hear of it and be allowed to use it. Thus, when Pithou discovered in 1570 a manuscript of a strange late antique legal work, the *Collatio legum Mosaicarum et Romanarum*, he very soon sent a transcript to Cujas, and later lent him the original for collation. Scaliger thus came in contact with another codex of great age and striking script, which shows some of the same features (open *a* resembling *u*, for example), as Cujas's Ausonius. The contact was close; for Scaliger made a copy of it for his own use.[132]

The personal contacts that Scaliger made in this period brought emotional as well as scholarly rewards. In particular, he became acquainted with the young Jacques-Auguste de Thou. Something of the quality of their friendship, at once dignified, warm, and erudite, emerges from de Thou's description of his studies:

This friendship, begun in the daily intercourse of Valence, has been continued since, either by personal communication or by correspondence, for the space of thirty-eight years uninterrupted. This friendship is the pride and pleasure of my life. All the calumny and misrepresentation which it has occasioned me, are, in my opinion, balanced by the satisfaction of an intercourse so honourable and so delightful to me. I know that I have been reproached with it by mischievous men; but I both glory in it publicly, and cherish it in my own breast. As for Scaliger's sentiments on religion, I solemnly affirm that I never heard this great man dispute on the controverted points of faith; and I am well assured that he never did discuss them but upon provocation, and then reluctantly. Independently of his religious opinions, were there not in Scaliger the most transcendent attainments of human erudition? And did not the singular endowments bestowed upon him by Heaven claim the veneration of all worthy men?[133]

From this time Scaliger's warmest relationships came to be his friendships with the intellectuals of the *noblesse de robe longue*. In de Thou he found a life long friend and benefactor; in Claude Dupuy, *conseiller* in the Parlement of Paris, he found an adviser on points of scholarship, provider of rare books, and intermediary with Italian scholars. With Pithou, the most literary of the *robins*, his relations also continued to be close; he supplied emendations, for example, for Pithou's edition of the *Pervigilium Veneris* in 1577.[134]

In 1572 the idyll ended. Jean Monluc, the irenic Bishop of Valence, was sent by Catherine de' Medici to try to win the throne of Poland for her son, the Duke of Anjou. Monluc was known to like Protestants;[135] Cujas persuaded Scaliger that it

would be worth his while to go.[136] Cujas and Scaliger travelled
to Lyons, where Scaliger hastily finished reworking his edition
of the *Appendix Vergiliana*, the manuscript of which he had
recovered and enlarged. On 22 August 1572 Scaliger finished his
revisions, scribbled two dedicatory prefaces, and gave the work
to his printer.[137] Then he left for Strasbourg, where he was to
meet Monluc. On the early morning of 24 August, the Massacre
of St Bartholomew took place at Paris. By then Scaliger was at
Lausanne. He continued on his journey; but at Strasbourg the
news of the massacre reached him, and he fled at once to
Geneva.[138] On 8 September 1572 he was made a citizen of
Geneva; and on 31 October he became professor of philosophy
in the Academy.[139]

The Geneva period was critical for the development of
Scaliger's mind. His time with Cujas had exposed him to a great
variety of studies, manuscripts, and men. But he had not had
time at Valence to digest the new information and the new
methods he encountered. Hence the one substantial piece of
work that he produced there, his edition of the *Appendix Vergiliana*, ended as a fascinating but confused hodge-podge of
clever but unconnected insights and remarkably elementary
mistakes.

As we have seen, Cujas was the one French scholar who clearly
understood the Italian method of evaluating and publishing
manuscript evidence. Yet it is clear that Scaliger — at least
during his time with Cujas — did not fully grasp either the
Italians' method or Cujas's own critical response to it. The texts
in his *Appendix* were, wherever possible, a simple reprint of the
existing vulgate: in most cases, the edition of the *Appendix* that
Theodore Poelman had published at Antwerp in 1566.[140]
Scaliger made no attempt to emend this text even where he was
convinced that his manuscripts afforded better readings. Even
when he was sure that lines in the vulgate text had been transposed, he did not transpose them in his edition, but simply
recorded his belief in the commentary.[141] As to the texts that
he published for the first time, here too his procedures were
careless. He rarely gave any indication of the manuscript sources
on which he had drawn, nor did he make any attempt to distinguish between manuscript readings and his own conjectures.
Consider one small example. Scaliger's working transcript of the
Vita Vergilii a Foca Grammatico versibus edita survives, in
Leiden University Library MS Scal. 61.[142] In the margins of the

transcript he entered six conjectures.[143] Of these he retained four in the margins of his printed text, but the other two he simply adopted, omitting the manuscript reading.[144] The reader had no way of knowing that the text did not reproduce that of the un-identified manuscript from which it came.

This careless and slapdash method of working, designed to produce a readable text rather than a historically justifiable one, recalls the methods of Scaliger's Parisian teachers rather than the professionalism of Cujas. So do the contents of his commentary. Scaliger ventures dozens of conjectures, sometimes three or four for the same word.[145] He heaps up Greek parallels.[146] He takes pains to point out that the critic must be above all an expert on style, and that such knowledge can only be acquired by those aristocrats among critics who can write Latin and Greek as natives. Only absolute control of poetic style could enable the critic to determine the authorship of the various poems that make up the *Appendix*. His discussion of the *Moretum* is typical:

The authorship of this elegant poem is uncertain. That it is not by Virgil is sufficiently clear to those who have made themselves familiar with Virgil rather than with our grammarians. The opinion of the grammarians is refuted completely by the style, which is so different from Virgil's. What shall I say of the scholar, my close friend, whom I could never induce to stop attributing this work to Virgil? Clearly, this is the way of things: unless you have trained your mind rigorously in this sort of exercise, your judge-ment on these matters must often be wrong.[147]

Scaliger also refers with clear approval both to Lambin's com-mentary on Horace and to Dorat's theory about the origins of Hesiod's *Scutum*.[148] In short, the *Appendix* resembles in most respects the *Coniectanea*: it is another exercise in the Parisian mode.

Like the *Coniectanea*, the *Appendix* also shows deviations from Parisian norms. Scaliger heatedly defends his earlier attempts to derive Latin words from Near Eastern roots.[149] And at one point, a mention of the osprey in the *Ciris* leads him into a long digression on the history of falconry.[150] He argues that whereas the Greeks had not known the art, it had been cultivated in Gaul in the fifth century AD.[151] He even reflects on the idea of progress in the arts:

This sort of hunting was in my view unfamiliar to the ancients, but today, among our nobility, it has reached the highest grade of perfection. For, like other things, this too has moved from quite insignificant beginnings to that high degree of sophistication which it now possesses.[152]

This digression clearly shows the impact on Scaliger of Cujas and his students, who took much interest in the material culture of the ancients. Scaliger's room-mate at Valence, Montjosieu, was

a splendid student of mechanics, if anyone ever was. He was the first to work out all the marks and numbers on ancient coins, and the unknown writing of inscriptions. He is such a diligent painter that he could make a more accurate portrait of someone he had seen only once, without being in his presence, than any other painter could of someone who was in his presence. But what is extraordinary in him is his consummate mastery of ancient music, which he knows better than anyone, and about which he will soon publish a book of the proper size.[153]

Montjosieu later won fame as an expert on the techniques of ancient painters and architects. Clearly his company affected Scaliger. But the very isolation of the pages on falconry also shows how little Scaliger had yet digested of the rich diet offered by Cujas.

In Geneva he had time to reflect; and, very gradually, contact with the jurists began to change the main direction of his work. The change was not immediate, for Geneva, crowded with the most dedicated Calvinist intellectuals in Europe, offered many distractions. Scaliger taught, both by giving public lectures in the Academy and by taking private pupils. He disliked lecturing and did poorly at it. Just after he left Geneva, his friend Goulart wrote to Josias Simler that 'Scaliger will not return to us. For he suffered from a perpetual illness here; and if he lectured now and then, the audience was scanty.'[154] His private pupils found him more rewarding. A young *robin*, Claude Groulart, who entered Geneva at the same time as Scaliger and studied with him for fifteen months, said to de Thou that he 'made more progress with Scaliger in a month than with others in a year. For no difficulty held him up and he never wasted time.'[155]

Scaliger also made friends among the leaders of the city. He came to know Theodore Beza, once a brilliant Neo-Latin love-poet and now the head of the Geneva Company of Pastors. While he found Beza deficient in knowledge of Hebrew and inclined to unfair attacks on Erasmus, he admired his piety and eloquence.[156] With the Scots divine Andrew Melville he found a common ground in Latin poetry; Melville supplied him with a splendid conjectural emendation in Manilius and liminary poems for an edition of Julius Caesar Scaliger's poetry.[157]

Moreover, with Henri Estienne he formed what amounted to

a working partnership. Like everyone else, he found Estienne personally exasperating, particularly because of his deplorable habit of altering the books he accepted for publication without telling their authors that he had done so.[158] Nevertheless he supplied Estienne with advice and brief critical appendices for his collection of the fragments of the pre-Socratics and for an anthology of Greek works bearing on the life of Homer.[159] And he provided translations of a number of epigrams from the Greek Anthology to accompany Estienne's panegyric on the Frankfurt book-fair, the *Francofordiense Emporium* of 1574.[160]

Despite these preoccupations, however, he continued to concentrate on the criticism and explication of Latin texts. One project of this period developed from his earlier literary interests. Beginning to study Manilius, he discovered that the text suffered from numerous corruptions and, in particular, from transpositions of lines and passages. He set out to correct these in an edition of and commentary on the text. 'I have already corrected it and restored all the transposed passages to their proper places', he wrote to Pithou, 'and I am so bold that I am not at all ashamed to take on so great a project.'[161]

Scaliger's other Latin undertakings, however, increasingly reveal the impact of Cujas. First, he published an edition of the works of Varro with Estienne.[162] This was a reprint of Agustín's *De lingua latina* and Vettori's *De re rustica* as far as the texts were concerned. His *Coniectanea* on the *De lingua latina* he simply reprinted, adding an appendix in which he explained several passages in enormous detail, paying far more attention to details of Roman topography and history than he had in the original work.[163] It is his notes on the *De re rustica* that are especially revealing. Vettori had based his edition on one particularly valuable manuscript, the readings of which he had recorded in detail in his *Castigationum explicationes*.[164] Scaliger reprinted Vettori's notes in full; and in his own notes he repeatedly accepted Vettori's views or based his own emendations on Vettori's collations. 'For this correction', he wrote at one point, 'as for innumerable others [drawn] from that excellent manuscript, we are indebted to that excellent scholar Vettori.'[165] In the earlier *Coniectanea* he had often discussed manuscripts and the habits of scribes, but always in general terms. He had never confronted, reading by reading, a major edition from Vettori's school. In now doing so he clearly showed that he had learned from Cujas to use the detailed findings of the Italians as the basis for a bold and sophisticated conjectural criticism. Geneva gave him the time to digest and apply the lesson.

By August 1573 the Varro was completed, and Scaliger turned to an even more Cujacian project.[166] He wrote to Pithou, asking for the loan of manuscripts of Roman grammatical works from late Antiquity, which he hoped to use as the basis for an anthology:

> Your brother mentioned to me that he had left with you a Censorinus, and a Probus on Juvenal. He assured me that if I asked you for them, you would not refuse me, indeed, that you would willingly make them available to me. Well, since I have decided to publish Gellius, Macrobius, and Censorinus together, and have much to say on those authors, it would be most helpful to me if you were willing to let me use both the aforementioned manuscripts and your learned conjectures and notes . . . [167]

Later he renewed the request, and at the same time mentioned a new and related project for an edition of Juvenal, Persius, and the old scholia on them.[168] Neither plan was carried out; but this heightened interest in late antique technical works is itself revealing.

In the summer of 1573 Scaliger also completed an edition of and commentary on Ausonius.[169] This work, more than any of the others from this period, represented a clear attempt to apply Cujas's method to the criticism of a classical text. Ausonius had long interested philologists. This quirky late Roman aristocrat, who wrote Latin and Greek with equal facility, rewarded those diligent enough to plough through his works with vast amounts of historical, geographical, mythological, and even scientific information.[170] Construing him had much of the fascination of completing a difficult crossword puzzle; sometimes, indeed, he deliberately wrote in riddles. Humanists from Poliziano onwards had tried their hand at parts of his work.[171] In 1556 or 1557, moreover, a new manuscript of Ausonius had been discovered by Étienne Charpin; and in 1558 an edition of some of the new material from it appeared at Lyons. It was poorly edited; much of the new material, in particular, was incomprehensible or nearly so.[172] Accordingly, every major French philologist tried, either by gaining access to the new manuscript or by devising conjectures, to improve passages. Pithou, Turnèbe, and Canter each took a hand in the game.[173] Finally, Élie Vinet of the Collège de Guyenne managed to borrow the manuscript from Cujas, into whose collection it had come. By 1567 he had completed a new edition, which he sent to Gryphius in Lyons for publication.[174]

At this point Scaliger intervened. Through a mutual friend, one Jacques Salomon, he learned of some of Vinet's original conjectures, and he let Vinet know that he approved of them.[175] Gryphius — for reasons unknown — procrastinated for five years. Vinet, not unnaturally, wrote to Scaliger, who had declared himself an ally, and asked him to try to speed matters up.[176] As we have seen, Scaliger was in Lyons in the summer of 1572. Instead of merely fulfilling Vinet's request, he evidently decided to rework the edition completely. He made an independent collation of Cujas's manuscript, which he entered in the margins of a copy of Poelman's 1568 Plantin edition.[177] And in the summer of 1573, while at Basel, he completed his revised version and dedicated it — with considerable effrontery — to Vinet, who then abandoned all hope of printing his edition in Lyons and set out to prepare an even more polished version, which he eventually published at Bordeaux.[178]

Both text and commentary of the Ausonius suffered from serious defects. Though now middle-aged, Scaliger was still in a hurry. He appropriated Vinet's conjectures and printed them, raucously praising his own originality. In his note on *Mosella* 438, for example, Scaliger wrote:

I shall not allow an egregious blemish, which is at present found at the end of the work, to remain in this excellent poem:
Haec ego vivifica ducens ab origine gentem.
For it should read *Vivisca.* For Bordeaux (*Burdigala*) was the capital of the *Bituriges Vivisci.*[179]

In the preface to his own edition, Vinet pointed out that Scaliger had praised this particular conjecture as one of Vinet's best.[180] It was shown long ago that this was only one among many silent borrowings.[181]

Scaliger's collation of his manuscript, though accurate as far as it went, was hurried and incomplete. Sometimes he corrected the titles of poems against the manuscript, sometimes not.[182] For *Epistula* XIV, which is over one hundred lines long, he gave only 27 variants; of these, five belonged to a line that Poelman had omitted. Elsewhere, where he gave both the scribe's original version of a phrase and the scribe's marginal correction of it, he repeated a word that was the same in both cases.[183] Subtracting these, we find an average of one variant for each five lines of text; hardly enough to make a new recension possible. Indeed, only half of these did he introduce — or use as the basis of conjectures that he introduced — into his text of the *Epistula*: one new reading in every ten lines of text.[184] The inadequacies of his collation, in short, limited the textual improvements that he could make.

Even in this unlikely context Scaliger spent much time rehearsing his well-known views about archaic Latin. Ausonius, like other Romans of the late Empire, occasionally tried to imitate the Latin of the second century BC. It was just these deliberate archaisms that Scaliger found attractive. Accordingly, he made his *Ausonianae lectiones* the occasion for another series of polemics on the virtues of a style that lacked the 'scholasticus tumor' of most late antique formal writings.[185] Here too he made it clear that an appreciation of these points was what set the true critic off from the grammarian:

> Not all may bear judgement on these matters. 'I hate the profane crowd, and shun it.' It is no wonder that these mysteries are unknown to those who have never entered their inmost sanctuaries. Therefore let them be silent, if they are wise. I have no higher opinion of their judgement of poets than I do of their own poems. . . . I will add one thing. I can stand anything, but I cannot abide the judgement of a schoolmaster.[186]

Clearly Scaliger still saw himself as a literary specialist in the Parisian mould.

What is interesting is precisely that this description does not fit the facts. In two respects at least, the Ausonius was no longer a piece of main-line Parisian literary scholarship. For one thing, Scaliger showed far more interest than his teachers in palaeographical detail. Though he did not describe his manuscript comprehensively or give its location, he made it clear that he had based his text on a particular manuscript in 'Lombardic script.'[187] He took the trouble to discuss some of the manuscript's more interesting points. For example, he gave full details about a scribal correction that he had noted at *Epistula* XIV.70:

> I will not conceal the fact that in that old manuscript the first reading was *Anticipesque vinum*. The quantity of the syllable shows that this is wrong. But the learned scribe noticed the slip that his excess haste had caused, and he corrected it to *Anticipesque tuum*.[188]

Again, in his collation of the manuscript he noted that he could not tell whether the first word in line 101 of the poem was *Tostam* or *Tortam*, making the entry '*Tŏstam.v.*'[189] In his commentary he made this point the pretext for a brief discussion of the script: 'It is unclear whether *Tostam* or *Tortam* was the reading of that manuscript. For in Lombardic script there is no difference between R and S.'[190]

Secondly, and more important, Scaliger investigated the context of the text in a manner less narrowly literary than his own comments might suggest. He knew that Ausonius' poems were the product of a specific culture: that of late Roman Gaul. He also realized that they were in themselves a rich source for the history of that culture. Seeing that the best way to illuminate their historical background was to draw upon the widest possible range of other late antique texts, he drew in his commentary on every source to which Cujas had led him in order to bring Ausonius' world back to life. To correct and identify the vast number of place-names in Ausonius' *Mosella* he used inscriptions, many of which he had copied in the course of his own journey from Southern France to Geneva.[191] He supplemented them with the findings of other antiquaries who had studied the topography of late antique Gaul — notably those of Erasmus' brilliant biographer Beatus Rhenanus — as well as with the major ancient literary source, the *Notitia Imperii Romani*.[192] To illuminate the condemnation of the heretic Priscillian and his followers he used not only Sulpicius Severus but also an unpublished account of Priscillian's conduct at the Synod of Bordeaux.[193] To explain why Arles was called 'the Rome of Gaul' in the *Ordo urbium nobilium*, he printed the first edition of a constitution by the Emperor Constantine III, whose capital it had been.[194] To shed light on Ausonius' poems on the professors of Bordeaux he made brilliant use of the *Hermeneumata Pseudo-Dositheana*, a set of bilingual dialogues written for the use of Greek-speaking students, which is still the source that most graphically reveals what it was like to be a schoolboy in late Roman society.[195] Casaubon rightly described Scaliger's work as a study in the reconstruction of late antique history and topography: 'In these *Ausonianae lectiones* Scaliger deals with many problems about our Gaul and the fortunes of her administration just before the time of the Empire's decline. He also gives many learned and clever treatments of many problems about place-names.'[196] Clearly Scaliger had mastered the non-literary sources which had long been a chief province of the humanistic jurists.

Yet even the Ausonius did not exhaust Scaliger's energies or satisfy his ambitions. This particular combination of literary and juristic method was novel only in technical sophistication. As we saw, by the 1560s it was quite common for young *robins* to combine a classical and a legal training. The products of this regime had already applied a historical approach to late antique literary works. Scaliger's friend Daniel, for example, had published in 1564 the *editio princeps* of the *Querolus*, a late antique adaptation of a play by Plautus. He had reasoned from the style of the play that it had probably been written in the time of Theodosius.[197] And he had explicitly argued that the way to illuminate such a work was to amass contemporary parallels — notably from the Theodosian Code:

Das honoratam quietem.] We may state at the outset that, whenever possible, we will refer expressions and single words to the style of the time of Theodosius as diligently as we can, so that we may prove that this work was written in his time. Accordingly, no one should imagine that we have merely filled space arbitrarily. Here, for example, *dare honoratam quietem* is related to *donari quiete honoratissima*, in Law LV *de decurionibus*, in *Theodosian Code*, Book XII.[198]

Scaliger's work surpassed Daniel's only in its learning. And as we have seen, Scaliger was never satisfied with exercises in a conventional mode, however elegantly executed.

Moreover, Ausonius was not the ideal subject for an ambitious scholar. Though historically interesting, his poems did not offer as much purchase as legal or technical texts for the application of Cujas's methods. Moreover, even as literature they were peripheral as well as interesting. Scaliger fiercely attacked the literati of his time for their failure to appreciate them:

We must not be worried about those who do not like this poet. For they are the same ones who say that the Garonne is a little stream, Bordeaux a hamlet, Aquitaine itself no more than an ordinary diocese; they speak of the very Senate of Bordeaux as no more than a division of a town council. Can you stop yourself from laughing when you hear them say these things? . . . And yet one hears them not from the ordinary crowd but from those who hold high office, who enjoy great prominence, who wish to have literary reputations . . . We are neither sharp-witted nor completely obtuse; and if those important men are willing to abandon a bit of their pride, we can teach them both what Aquitaine is and what it is to be a critic in literature.[199]

The very heatedness of this outburst shows that Scaliger knew his views to be unpopular.

What he needed was a text central to the classical culture of his time and appropriate for his new historical approach. He found it in one of the most difficult, corrupt, and controverted works in Latin prose: the *De verborum significatu* of Festus.

Here, for the first time, he confronted powerful and fully established traditions of criticism and exegesis; and it is to these traditions that we must turn before we can grasp the meaning of Scaliger's first mature work.

V Scaliger's Festus: Classical Philology and Legal Humanism

— jene staunenerregende Leistung seines Genie's . . .
— J. Bernays

The complex story of the transmission of the text of Festus has often been told, but by no one has it ever been told in livelier terms than by Antonio Agustín when he published his edition in 1559. Agustín's preface is not only a remarkable literary text, but also a clear and accurate introduction to most of the problems that any editor of Festus must face:

In these twenty books, which he entitled *de verborum significatione*, or *priscorum verborum cum exemplis*, Sextus Pompeius Festus abridged the books of Verrius Flaccus on the same subject. For he omitted the words which were, in Verrius' own words, 'too old, and dead and buried and were of no use and authority'. He dealt with the same words [that Verrius had discussed] more clearly and more briefly, setting out the original words in a smaller space. He also provided a critical treatment of examples found in other sources. He often corrected Verrius' errors, and he always explained most learnedly why he did so.

Now this book had the misfortune to suffer harm of several kinds very long ago. For we could not find out either who this Festus was, or when he wrote this work. Only one or two references to it are to be found here and there in Charisius and Macrobius.

While the whole book was still extant in the time of Charlemagne, one Paulus thought it would be useful if he made a sort of epitome of the parts he liked best. Ignorant men liked his book so much that it took Festus' place in every library.

One codex survived the slaughter. But that was like a soldier whose comrades have been defeated and massacred, and who creeps along at random with his legs broken, his nose mutilated, one eye gouged out, and one arm broken. This book supposedly came from Illyria. According to Pio and Poliziano, Pomponio Leto had some pages of it; Manilius Rallus [had] the greater part. Angelo Poliziano received the book from them, went over it, and copied it, and he tried to use it in his *Miscellanea* to emend a verse of Catullus. Using this same copy by Poliziano, Pier Vettori has begun, with his customary learning, to emend the vulgate text of Festus at various points in his *Variae lectiones*.

The remains of the codex passed to Aldo Manuzio, who tried to combine them with the epitome of Paulus, thus making one body from two sets of parts. But so much was omitted [or] changed in publication that it was still necessary for other critics to intervene. Achille Maffei, the brother of Cardinal Bernardino, has another copy, similarly conflated from both texts; it is fuller than the Aldine. Thus there have been three recensions of the same text, all imperfect. There is the old MS of half of Festus; of this, nothing remains before the letter *M*, and from that letter to the end barely half of what there used to be. The second text is Paulus's epitome. As we show in this edition, even the most ignorant can see from a comparison of the texts how carelessly that was put together. The third text is that conflated from the other two, like those of Aldo and Maffei, and our own.[1]   App. V

The story Agustín told and the conclusions he drew are still for the most part acceptable. So far as the earliest history of the text is concerned, he was very accurate indeed, and only one or two details need be added. Verrius Flaccus was the best-known antiquarian and grammarian in Augustan Rome.[2] He served as tutor to Augustus' grandsons and wrote treatises on a variety of recondite topics, including a grammatical work *De obscuris Catonis* and a brief treatment of Etruscan antiquities. But his fame rested above all on his *De verborum significatu,* an enormous lexicon of unusual, difficult, or archaic words, shot through with rich veins of information on early Roman customs, institutions, and beliefs. Left unfinished at Verrius' death, the work was so large, and in part so disorderly, that it must have been very difficult to consult and virtually impossible to copy. It was nevertheless used by Gellius. Unfortunately, the unwieldiness of Verrius' work set the second-century grammarian Sextus Pompeius Festus to preparing an epitome in twenty books. Festus often disagreed with Verrius on points of organization and interpretation, and he omitted much that we should like to have.[3]

In the fifth and sixth centuries, as classical culture and classical education for the most part collapsed, teachers needed short and convenient works of reference. Festus' work — which was not, so far as the evidence indicates, much used in late Antiquity — served their needs far better than its enormous source. Consequently, the epitome was copied, and survived, while the original was lost.

As teachers concentrated more and more on the needs of elementary pupils, for whom Latin was a second language, even Festus' work was too large and too scholarly to be widely useful.

Elementary glossaries were needed. To provide them, teachers made various skimpy epitomes of Festus. The most successful was the one to which Agustín referred: that composed in the ninth century by Paulus Diaconus, monk of Monte Cassino and historian of the Lombards. As he put it in his prefatory letter to Charlemagne, Paulus 'omitted what was superfluous and unnecessary, and explained certain difficult matters entirely in [his] own words, leaving some things as they had been'.[4] He removed most of Festus' quotations and added little new matter.

Agustín did not realize that Paulus' epitome was by no means the only one. As we shall see, a whole series of glossaries were derived from Festus between the sixth and tenth centuries, many of them retaining Festan material that Paulus omitted.[5]

Agustín's history of the reappearance of Festus is only slightly less accurate. Presumably he did not think it worth the trouble to mention the various editions of Paulus that appeared from 1471 on.[6] As he said, only one codex of Festus' work survived the Middle Ages. This is now in Naples, where it bears the shelf-mark IV.A.3.[7] It was written in the second half of the eleventh century, probably at Rome.[8] Originally it contained sixteen gatherings, the first seven of which had been lost before it came to light in the fifteenth century. The nine that remained had also been damaged by fire, so that some leaves were missing, and on many leaves most or all of the outer column of the text was also lost.[9] Manilius Rallus, a Greek from Sparta who became a successful Roman Catholic churchman and Neo-Latin poet, brought it to Italy at some time before 1477. He is said to have found it in Dalmatia.[10]

Rallus lent this codex to Pomponio Leto, who found it most helpful for his pioneering research into Roman antiquities. He drew on the new codex for his university lectures on Varro and other authors.[11] Unfortunately, he treated the codex with his usual lack of scruple — he kept the eighth, tenth, and sixteenth gatherings, which have subsequently disappeared, and must be reconstructed from a number of surviving transcripts.[12]

Beroaldo mentioned the new text and published a passage from it in the *Annotationes centum*.[13] Poliziano had seen it in 1484; in *Miscellanea* I.73 he described it with his characteristic precision and used an entry to support an emendation in Catullus.[14] From the appearance of these works in 1488 and 1489, the existence of the fuller text of Festus was widely known.

Agustín thought that the first publication of the codex was that in Aldo Manuzio's 1513 edition of Perotti's *Cornucopiae*. In fact, the first edition was supervised not by Aldo but by G. B. Pio, and it appeared in Milan in 1500.[15] The circumstances are obscure, for Pio himself, as he explained in his *Posteriores annotationes*, had to leave Milan while it was in the press:

While teaching at Milan, we assembled much material to illustrate this writer. Some came from the manuscript that Pomponio Leto . . . had received from Illyria, which was very old and therefore most trustworthy. To that I would have added more, had Prince Giovanni Bentivoglio not compelled me unexpectedly to return to my home, Bologna, while this work was in the press.[16]

The Milanese printer Gabriel Conagus was left to explain the editorial principles that had been used:

Reader — All the fragments which have been found of Sextus Pompeius Festus, beginning from the letter M up to the end, have been printed together with, not separately from the rest [i.e. from the epitome of Paulus]. This was done deliberately, so that readers would not be troubled with boredom, owing to repetition, and because we added some things that were not in Pio's codex, but in another of the same kind.[17]

As this note suggests, the text that Pio and Conagus had produced fully deserved Agustín's sharp criticism. They had simply conflated the epitome of Paulus with the fuller text of Festus that began with the letter M. A reader could not tell which entries came from which source; where both works had entries for a single lemma, the two articles were printed next to one another with no indication of authorship. Moreover, Conagus tampered unsystematically with the order of the entries, and he simply omitted the many entries in the codex of Festus that were too fragmentary to be entirely comprehensible.[18] The resulting text was both confusing to use and devoid of historical justification. For want of anything better it became the vulgate and •was reprinted in Milan in 1510 and in Paris in 1511 and 1519, as well as in several editions of Perotti's *Cornucopiae*. By the middle of the sixteenth century, the prevailing text of Festus was thus an interpolated one.

At this point, however, Festus' afterlife became more complex and lively than Agustín's account suggests. After Pio's edition appeared, antiquarians in both France and Italy began to study Festus with zeal. By the time Agustín wrote, they had done much to emend and explicate what is still a difficult text.

Sixteenth-century antiquarians were passionately interested

in the early history of Roman law. The more sober among them, notably Cujas, saw these studies as useful chiefly because they could aid in the explication of Justinian's *Corpus iuris*. Others, such as Louis le Caron, saw the Twelve Tables as something more than one of the sources on which Roman jurists had drawn. For them, the Tables were a perfect legal code, the statutory counterpart to the perfectly balanced constitution of the early Roman state. The fragments of the Tables glittered before their eyes like the pieces of an ancient, shattered, crystal vessel. Its restoration was for them a task of almost sacred importance, on which they placed extravagant hopes for the reform of society in their own time. Both groups laboured to identify the sources of Festus' quotations from early law, to separate the words of the laws themselves from his commentary, and to correct and interpret the legal texts they isolated.

Perhaps the best-known, though not the first, of these reconstructors was François Baudouin. In 1550, he published a systematic collection of the extant fragments of the Twelve Tables. With more prudence than many later scholars, he refused to try to establish the original order of the fragments.[19] He merely printed the texts of the sixty-three that he regarded as unquestionably genuine, commenting at length on each. Naturally, he drew some of his material from Festus, though not sure that most of the legal material Festus preserved was relevant to his purposes. A jurist rather than a pure antiquarian, Baudouin was interested in the content of early laws, not in their language or other incidental points. Indeed, he regarded archaic Latin not as charming, but as rustic and crude.[20]

Festus normally cited the Twelve Tables in order to illustrate points of legal idiom. Often he did not quote an intelligible section of a law, but merely the two or three words that he wished to gloss. Baudouin argued that such brief quotations, and indeed any quotations that were not clearly intelligible, were useless to the jurist and should be ignored:

Festus mentions many words from the Twelve Tables which we would never have understood without his explanations: PEDEM STRVIT, for *fugit*; SARPVNTVR VINEAE, for *putantur*; RVPITIAS, for *damnum dederis*; PORTVM, for *domus*. Clearly, if we had those chapters in their entirety, no linguistic difficulty would prevent us from understanding their meaning thoroughly. But it did not seem of any use to include among the laws of the Twelve Tables mutilated fragments, which could yield no sense. Had I set out to do this, I would have produced not a mass of laws but one of empty words ... But we are interested in laws, not words.[21]

Others were less willing to forgo even the smallest trace of the marrow concealed within Festus' bones. Le Caron was both less cautious than Baudouin and more interested in the details of archaic legal language. He kept at Festus, trying to find or interpret passages that Baudouin had missed, and he published his results in 1555, in his edition of J. U. Zasius's Catalogue of early Roman laws.[22] Baudouin had pointed out that according to Festus, in the Twelve Tables 'pedem struere' meant 'flee'. Le Caron also noticed this passage. He knew that in the Roman army those who fled from battle were executed, and so concluded that Festus must have been referring to an article of the Twelve Tables that read: *Qui in bello pedem struit, capite punitor.* ('He who flees in battle shall be executed.')[23]

Within a year, another French jurist, of far higher technical proficiency, disputed le Caron's attempted reconstruction. In his *Selectarum ex iure civili antiquitatum libri duo*, Barnabé Brisson printed and explained a number of new fragments from the Tables, some derived from Festus. One of them contained the expression *pedem struere*: 'Si calvitur pedemve struit, manum endo iacito.' ('If the defendant delays or flees, the plaintiff shall lay hand on him.')[24] He took care to point out that this came not from the vulgate text but from an old manuscript or manuscripts: 'This [section] was previously very corrupt. That diligent antiquary M. Aimar de Ranconnet restored it to its pristine form with the help of old MSS.'[25] And he argued briefly but cogently that Festus' other reference to the phrase *pedem struere* must refer to this law. Le Caron's law about deserters could be dismissed as a mere fabrication: 'We must also reject this text that he [le Caron] cites: *Qui in bello pedem struit capite punitor.* For we showed above that the words *pedem struit*, which led him to invent all this, belonged to a different section.'[26] Brisson's reconstruction was in turn accepted by Cujas, himself a great player of the game of reconstruction.[27]

This episode was not isolated. Section after section in Festus was spiritedly debated among the jurists, and many still plausible emendations and interpretations resulted.[28]

Literary scholars also worked on the text of Festus. As Agustín pointed out, Pier Vettori corrected a number of passages. He had found Poliziano's transcript of both the main body of the Festus manuscript and the sections Pomponio Leto had kept. As he explained, this codex was neither complete nor fully legible, since Poliziano had made it for his own use rather than for publication: 'He wrote so quickly, and with so minute a hand, and often with only letters to indicate entire words — for that was his habit when he took notes like these for his own use only — that these remains were scarcely legible.'[29] But even this imperfect copy was better than the printed texts, riddled as they were with errors and omissions:

I think that some ignorant fellow, who had had little experience with manuscripts, must have made a copy, and that some printers used his manuscript, corrupt and incomplete as it was, for their base text. For when he didn't find a complete and full explanation of [a given word] . . . he left out even what sections of it remained.[30]

Accordingly, Vettori printed several passages from Poliziano's manuscript, carefully calling attention to all the gaps in the original codex, whose presence Poliziano had recorded.[31] The new material that Vettori obtained enabled him to shed light on some of the central problems of sixteenth-century scholarship — for example, the curious trace of euthanasia — or early voting practices — preserved in the phrase 'sexagenarios de ponte'.[32] This Vettori was unable to interpret in a fully satisfactory way, but at least he was able to show that the phrase had puzzled the Romans themselves by the time of Festus.[33]

It was only natural that scholars should seek to provide a more reliable edition of so rich a text, and a full commentary on it. In the late 1550s, both Carlo Sigonio and Antonio Agustín undertook editions. After a few months of competition, Sigonio agreed to give up his project in favour of seeing Agustín's through the press. Agustín's text, published in 1559, became the dominant one for the next two centuries and more.[34]

To a considerable extent, this pre-eminence was justified. Agustín's edition was undoubtedly a dramatic improvement. He traced the history of the text, as we have seen, and used it as the basis of his editorial practice. Since Verrius Flaccus was the ultimate source of most of Festus' material, Agustín began his work with a comprehensive collection of testimonia and quotations.[35] He then printed Paulus' epitome and Festus side by side, carefully indicating the authorship of each entry: 'In addition, we have done something that others have failed to do: that is, we inform the reader what is from Festus, and what from Paulus.'[36] He reproduced the text of the sole codex of Festus in a most craftsmanlike manner. He carefully explained how it had entered the library of Ranuccio Farnese, where he had used it.[37] Though he did not describe its appearance comprehensively, he recorded a substantial number of details about it. For example, he twice quoted the titles that indicated the beginnings or ends of books in the Farnesianus, and he remarked several times that the scribe had entered the letter *R* (for 'require') in the margin to indicate passages in need of correction.[38] Most important, he reproduced the text of the Farnesianus in its entirety, even where it was incomprehensible because of physical damage, scribal error, or idiosyncratic abbreviations. He represented the hundreds of gaps caused by fire and wear by rows of dots. A system of typographical symbols enabled him to enter conjectures, variants, and supplementary material from the earlier editions, as well as to single out interpolations for deletion:

[Words] placed in the margin with a cross or other sign indicate a variant reading from some codex.
If a semicircle is added at the end, it means that the passage can be corrected as shown in accord with some scholar's conjecture.
Wherever three dots [∴] are added before or after F., they mean that the words are in fact Festus', but not drawn from the old codex.
Words enclosed between two semicircles in the text are to be deleted, even though they were found in all codices.[39]

Agustín did not confine himself to reproducing his manuscript. He also proposed a large number of conjectural emendations that are still acceptable, and he elicited suggestions from the other leading scholars in Rome as well. He went over the whole text with Faerno, who suggested a number of corrections in the fragments of verse that Festus quoted.[40] Fulvio Orsini made several suggestions regarding material in Greek.[41] Sigonio, not surprisingly, provided a comprehensive re-working of the entire article on *spolia opima*.[42]

Finally, Agustín's practice of keeping the entries from Festus and Paulus separate made it possible to compare the two texts in detail. This enabled him to supplement the text of Festus at many points and to establish the general purport of entries too mangled to be reconstructed. It allowed him to show that the codex of Festus which Paulus had employed must have been fuller than the Farnesianus.[43] Most important, it enabled him to learn a number of interesting facts about Festan entries that were entirely lost. For example, by comparing the surviving entries in Festus with the corresponding entries in Paulus, he established that Festus, being a good pagan, had used the present tense when describing Roman religious ceremonial. Paulus, being an equally good Christian, replaced it with the imperfect: 'Paulus frequently uses such words as "he used to", "they used to be burned", "he replaced", in order not to seem to be of the same religion as Festus.'[44] This made it possible to reconstruct one significant detail about the articles on religion between A and M: where Paulus used the past tense, Festus had almost certainly used the present.[45] Similarly, comparative study enabled Agustín to recognize what Paulus himself had added to the entries as he compiled them. It was relatively elementary to point out that Paulus, not Festus, must have been the one who had included a quotation from Saint Paul's Epistle to the Romans, and who had used the late word *camisia*.[46] But it took closer observation to remark that Festus himself never cites Martial, so that Paulus's one citation of Martial I.30 might well be his own addition.[47] And sometimes such comparisons had far-reaching results. Paulus defined *Municipalia sacra* as 'those rites which were performed before the founding of the city'.[48] Festus had in fact written that 'Those *sacra* are called *municipalia* which they [the *municipia*, provincial cities that had accepted Roman citizenship] had from the beginning, before they had accepted Roman citizenship.'[49] It was clear what had gone wrong. As Agustín put it: 'Paulus did not understand what "ante civitatem Ro. acceptam" meant, and he took it to mean "ante urbem conditam". The municipal rites belong not to the city of Rome but to the *municipia*.'[50] The point was worth making, for it showed that Paulus was capable of falling into elementary errors in understanding historical and legal material. Other puzzling or incorrect statements in his epitome might, accordingly, reflect not what Festus had written, but simply Paulus's ignorance and confusion. Thus, Agustín wanted to delete the statement in Paulus — still the subject of controversy — that the thirty-five tribes 'were also called *curiae*', considering it an interpolated gloss rather than a summary of what Festus had written.[51]

In one respect at least Agustín's editorial work was not impeccable. The entries in Festus, as preserved by the Farnesianus, follow a peculiar order, the reasons for which have long been debated. Under each letter there are two series of entries. In the first, the words discussed are arranged in accordance with the alphabetical order of the first two, and sometimes the first three letters. In the second, words are simply grouped by the first letter. Sometimes there is an entry for a particular word in each series, with the result that Festus appears to repeat or contradict himself. Verrius himself left the entries in this order. Presumably, he intended to integrate the material in the later series into the more elaborate order of the earlier; why he did not do so we do not know.[52] Festus followed the same order — or lack of it. Agustín was well aware that the apparent disorder of Festus' entries probably stemmed from the arrangement employed by Verrius; but he none the less refused to leave it unreformed.[53] After all, as de Zulueta pointed out, Agustín was a canonist and a most successful Counter-Reformation prelate — in short, a practical man. Apparently, he could not bear to leave the material in Festus in an inconvenient form merely for the sake of fidelity to a manuscript.[54] So he rearranged all entries in both Festus and Paulus into a strictly alphabetical order.[55] As a result, his edition could not be an exact transcript of the Farnesianus. Moreover, the rearrangement made it impossible for him even to reproduce the entries exactly, since the changes in their order naturally affected the lengths of the spaces between words in the many gaps. As a result, it became all too easy for both Agustín and those who used his edition to devise conjectural supplements that were either too long or too short for the actual lacunae in the codex.[56] To this extent, Agustín defeated his own purpose of re-establishing the text of Festus by returning to the text of the archetype. But his edition still provided much new or partly new material, arranged in a most useable form.

To his critical text Agustín added a short commentary. His notes are pithy and business-like. Many are simply cross-references to other passages in the text; many more are lists of references to relevant passages in other classical works.[57] But a good many deal *in extenso* with problems of criticism or interpretation. While some handled problems that had become traditional in Festan studies — e.g. the language and content of the Twelve Tables — others ranged widely through Roman literature and antiquities. In effect, Agustín used his text as the springboard from which to launch investigations into two subjects above all: the nature of early Roman institutions and rites and the historical development of the Latin language.

On the one hand, Agustín explained, at varying degrees of length, many of Festus' technical legal and religious terms. No clear principle seems to have guided his choice of topics, for he wrote at considerable length both about such well-known institutions as that of the *rex sacrorum* and about more obscure ones, like *diffarreatio* (the form of divorce employed by those who had contracted marriage by the solemn ceremony of *con-farreatio*, which Agustín analysed in detail).[58] All the notes revealed wide reading, above all in the Greek and Latin historians of Rome, but also in literary texts. Taken together, they made one point clearly: the text of Festus was very well adapted to serve as the basis for a detailed — if necessarily selective — survey of Roman antiquities.

On the other hand, Agustín discussed at even greater length many passages that bore upon the history of Latin. He pointed out that certain words were used in more senses than Festus mentioned.[59] He tried to clarify and reduce to clearly stated rules the linguistic changes which Festus had merely recorded without clear comments, or without giving a sufficient expla-nation.[60] And he modifed and amplified Festus' remarks on the spelling of both common and proper nouns, drawing on his wide knowledge of inscriptions.[61] Here, even more than in his antiquarian excursuses, he was touching on a subject that lay at the heart of contemporary scholars' interests; these notes above all attracted the attention of most of Agustín's early readers.

Naturally Agustín's Festus was too technical to be a bomb-shell; but it was at least a good-sized firecracker. In France it caused a remarkable acceleration of Festan studies. Turnèbe found Agustín's commentary most stimulating. He admired Agustín's knowledge of legal Latin: 'Antonio Agustín rightly and cleverly appreciates that in the law of the Twelve Tables, *si adorat furto quod nec manifestum erit, adorare* means "lay accusation."'[62] More important, he found in Agustín's discussions of word derivation a stimulus to further reflection on the history of Greek as well as Latin dialects. In his note on the word *picati*, for example, Agustín argued — after consulting Orsini — that Latin *pica* was a regular transliteration of Greek φίξ ('sphinx'): 'It is clear that *Picas* is used for *phicas*, as *Poenos*, and *Alpes*, and *Pilippum*, and *triumpum*.'[63] This comment stimulated Turnèbe to reflect upon a nearby passage, in which Festus derived the verbs *pilare* and *compilare* from a Greek word, which the manuscript omitted. 'There is no doubt', wrote Turnèbe,

that *pilare* and *compilare* are derived from the Aeolic Greek word πιλητής, that is, 'thief', which Hesiod calls φιλητής. But it is the practice of the Aeolians to change aspirates into thin sounds, as in the previous word, where Doric φίξ and Aeolic πίξ equal σφίγξ, and they give rise to Latin *pica* and *picatus*.[64]

Curiously enough, Willem Canter published a cruder but quite similar argument in the same year, 1564:

That Festus derives the word *pilare* from φιλητής should not disturb any-one, even though the first letters in the two words do not agree. For that change of an aspirate into a thin sound often happens in such cases.[65]

These passages make clear how interesting Agustín's material was, especially for philologists who had previously had to use the vulgate text without commentary of any form. Others joined in. Pierre Pithou suggested an interpretation in his *Adversaria* of 1565.[66] French-trained Flemings and Germans such as Lucas Fruterius, Hadrianus Junius, and Hubertus Giphanius also tried their hands.[67] In 1567, Festus received an unmistakable token of wide esteem. Le Caron claimed to have found a manuscript of Festus 'much more complete than the one Agustín published.'[68] This supported some of the conjectures that he had made long before, and that Brisson had demolished. Le Caron promised to bring out an edition based upon it. It seems likely that the claim was unfounded. If the codex existed at all, it was very likely an apograph of the Farnesianus, possibly made by or for Pomponio Leto.[69] But one point is clear: Festus had become an author to be reckoned with in the North.

When Scaliger came to work on Festus, he could draw on several traditions of interpretation. He was himself intimately acquainted both with the text and with recent Latin scholarship. Festus he had used for more than a decade, above all as a source for archaic or rare terms to be used in verse composition. In Geneva, moreover, as we saw, he had hatched two plans for major critical editions of other late antique scholarly works. Though neither project was carried out, the preparatory studies meant that Scaliger was as deeply versed as anyone could have been in the material that an editor of Festus must master. His competence in this study was acknowledged by Henri Estienne in 1573. Not only did Estienne publish Scaliger's edition of Varro, but he also published in a work of his own Scaliger's correction of a passage in Donatus' Life of Virgil.[70] And Scaliger's general interest in archaic Latin, as we have seen, remained un-abated during his time in Switzerland.

Scaliger's Festus was a product of his last, broken months in Geneva and its environs. In July 1574 he wrote to Pithou from Basel that 'in the last few days, I have done a little something on Festus, which is already being printed.'[71] He finished the

commentary in September and left it in Geneva with his friend
Goulart, who was to pass it on to the printer. The dedication,
dated October 1574, he wrote in France, at the home of the
Chasteigners in Abain.[72] And, as the speed with which he worked
might lead one to expect, the result was not in fact a new edition
of the text. Rather, he followed the same form that he had used
for the works of Varro. He reprinted Agustín's text, wrote a
critical and exegetical commentary, and had the two issued together, though they were printed months apart. His conjectures
were not introduced into the body of the text.[73]

In his preface, Scaliger frankly admitted that he had no
material to work with save that assembled by Agustín:

> We have, then, exposed [Paul's] egregious errors and stolid ignorance, in
> which area we have done our work by conjecture alone. For that was the
> only aid we used up to the eleventh book. From there began the fragments
> which have been published thanks to the benevolence of Antonio Agustín.
> Their nature is such that one recognizes in them scraps and ruins of the
> original structures, but in such a state, that it is easier to divine what was
> built upon those foundations than to reconstruct the building itself from
> them.[74]

In short, he promised to do for Festus just what Cujas had done
with the Torelli's edition of the Pandects and Estienne with
Vettori's Aeschylus — to rearrange by conjecture the manuscript
material published by Italians. The benefits at which he aimed
were as typical of French scholarship as the means he employed.
For he argued that his commentary would help above all to
enrich the study of early Roman law:

> We have dug out from obscurity much that even we ourselves did not know.
> Nor will you find in any of the ancients so many venerable monuments of
> antiquity, especially from the most ancient law of the Romans, both civil
> and priestly; also from the laws of the kings, from the XII Tables, from the
> ancient treaties, and others which it would be tedious to enumerate. If
> anyone calls all this useless, I should like him to tell us what he considers
> useful in letters. For if knowledge of antiquity is of no value, then I do not
> see what value letters have for us.[75]

Scaliger's interest in early law seems here to derive from his
antiquarian tastes rather than from an interest either in reforming
his own society or in explicating the *Corpus iuris*. But the
general direction of his interests clearly reveals the influence of
his compatriots.

So far as the commentary proper is concerned, one's initial
impression of Scaliger's work is one of prodigal ingenuity and

staggeringly broad erudition — a phenomenon that would seem to call for psychological rather than historical explanation.

Again and again Scaliger cut knots that had baffled Agustín. Agustín had suspected the letters *D.T.* in the Farnesianus of being corrupt; Scaliger, thanks to what was now quite extensive experience in palaeography, simply resolved them into 'dun-taxat'.[76] Agustín had thought that the verses in which Ennius referred to the Wain were lost; Scaliger supplied them from Varro, who had quoted them twice in the *De lingua latina*.[77]

Scaliger's view of Festus' scholarly attainments was more sceptical and more accurate than Agustín's. In only one passage does Festus describe his own intentions:

Cuius [scil. Verrii] opinionem, neque in hoc, neque in aliis compluribus refutare minime necesse est, cum propositum habeam ex tanto librorum eius numero intermortua iam et sepulta verba atque ipso saepe confitente nullius usus aut auctoritatis praeterire, et reliqua quam brevissime redigere in libros admodum paucos. Ea autem, de quibus dissentio, et aperte et breviter, ut sciero, scripta in [h]is libris meis invenientur, (qui) inscribuntur, 'priscorum verborum cum exemplis' [242.28-244.1 L.].[78]

Agustín took this as a description of the aims and character of the *De verborum significatione*: 'This passage is the argument of the whole book.'[79] He realized that this interpretation entailed difficulties. For example, both the Farnesianus and Gellius had given the work the title *de verborum significatione* rather than *priscorum verborum cum exemplis*.[80] He persisted in his view, basing upon it an interpretation of the *De verborum significatione* as a scholarly and independent piece of work containing much that did not come from Verrius. Festus, he said, was quite right to disagree with Verrius and to omit useless information — after all, 'he always gave the reason why he did so most learnedly'.[81]

Scaliger argued that Agustín had misread the passage. In the last sentence, he pointed out, Festus must be referring not to the *De verborum significatione* but to a different work:

For Festus would not have called these extant books his own, since they are by Verrius. Nor did he set out to refute Verrius in them except in a very few passages, and then only in passing. . . . Anyone can see that the books *Priscorum verborum cum exemplis* are not the same as those that we have . . .[82]

Unlike Agustín, he showed no sympathy at all for Festus' attacks on Verrius, or even for the fate he had suffered at the hands of Paulus:

Festus . . . should not have resented being dealt with by Paulus as he had done by Verrius. Except in one respect: if Festus had to perish in this fashion, he should have chosen a worthier tree to be hanged from, as the proverb [Pliny *N.H. praef.*] has it.[83]

Scaliger, then, treated Festus as a grammarian rather than a scholar, and saw his criticisms of Verrius as empty attempts at self-aggrandizement. These views dominated virtually all historical assessments of the *De verborum significatu* until very recent times; for only after Scaliger wrote was it clear that Festus had drawn exclusively upon Verrius in making his lexicon.

More important, Scaliger was simply more ingenious than Agustín. The text was extremely corrupt, and no help could be expected from manuscripts; desperate remedies were needed. Scaliger was both willing and able to burn and cut, and if his desperate scalpel sometimes sank too deep, much of his surgery was curative as well as brilliant. Often he was able to cure by conjecture passages whose wounds Agustín had left untouched. Festus, for example, cited at one point Hippocrates' opinion on the etymology of Latin *aurum*.[84] Hippocrates was not, perhaps, best known as a Latin grammarian, but Agustín had not discussed the point. Here Scaliger's knowledge of the grammatical tradition provided him with an ingenious suggestion: 'The citation of Hippocrates is wrong. Read Hypsicrates, who is cited by Varro and Gellius [in book 16], and who wrote on the Roman words that are derived from the ancient Greek language.'[85] Again and again, using nothing but Paulus and mother wit, Scaliger rebuilt whole passages that Agustín had left in fragments. One article in Scaliger's reprint of Agustín's text read:

Meta . . . stices dicitur aput p . . . . .
. . . quod propter necessitatem metri . .
. . . t. quod idem barbaris. . . . . .
. . . ta oration . . scrib . . . .[86]

Here Agustín simply vapoured: '*Meta . . . stices*] It seems that the text gave Metaphrastices, but wrongly, for Metaphrastice, or Metaphrasis, or for Metastasis, or Metabasis.'[87] Scaliger reconstructed the entry with contemptuous ease:

Meta . . . . . stices] Write: Metaplasticos dicitur apud poetas usurpari id quod propter necessitatem metri mutant. quod idem barbarismus dicitur in soluta oratione conscribenda. ('In the poets, words which they change because of the metre are said to be used *metaplasticos*. This is called *barbarismus* in the writing of prose.')[88]

Fluency in conjecture and attention to detail could hardly be raised to a higher level.

Contemporaries offered a litany of praise to Scaliger's brilliance and originality. Goulart told Simler that Scaliger had 'healed Festus miraculously in many passages, filling a great many gaps that had long cried out for Scaliger's help, and his alone, with his happy dexterity of wit'. Casaubon, marvelling at Scaliger's restoration of the proverb 'Sabini quod volunt somniant', wrote 'Foelix divinatio et plane divina' in the margin of his copy. Later, G. J. Vossius would accuse Scaliger of presenting as conjectures what must really have been new variants surreptitiously drawn from manuscripts. Here slander rose to be a curious form of flattery. Vossius could not believe that Scaliger had invented so much that was convincing.[89] At last, Scaliger had found a text that enabled him to make his gifts for composing quasi-antique Latin serve text-critical rather than literary ends.

As usual, second thoughts modify first. Scaliger's Festus included not only his own commentary but Agustín's, just as his Varro had. Presumably he meant to show the extent of the improvement he had wrought. Certainly, the fact that Scaliger consistently refers to Agustín as 'viri docti', and then almost always in order to criticize him, suggests that he meant to reveal the flaws in Agustín's work. In fact, comparative study reveals a complex and troubling picture. Scaliger was deeply indebted to Agustín for the method he employed in both textual criticism and exegesis. Much of what he added to Agustín's method was not his own invention but that of the French jurists of the '60s. Most important, we shall see that Scaliger's chief innovations were either extremely technical or of dubious utility. All these facts had their part in shaping Scaliger's philological aims and allegiance. Considered in this light, Scaliger's Festus becomes of interest to the historian as well as to the student of the psychology of creativity.

To begin with the text itself, it is clear that Scaliger's critical work depended heavily upon Agustín's. He simply took over, without giving credit to, many of Agustin's emendations — and by no means always the best of them. For example, Paulus defines *Ambarvales hostiae* as 'those offerings which were sacrificed by two brothers [*a duobus fratribus*] before the altars'.[90] Since the word *ambarvalis* was evidently connected with brothers of some sort, Agustín decided that it might be derived from the title of the twelve *fratres Arvales*, and that *ambarvales hostiae* might be the victims that they sacrificed in their well-known ceremonies. Accordingly, he suggested (not without reservations) that *duobus* be emended to *duodecim*.[91] Scaliger accepted this argument with all too few reservations, merely adding a facile palaeographical explanation for the 'error': '*Ambarvales*] A duobus fratribus. Possibly for XII. He [Paulus? the scribe?] had read II and he missed the sign for the number 10.'[92] All he left out was a reference to Agustín.

Scaliger also took over from Agustín the principle that Festus and Paulus must constantly be compared. He used the material in Paulus above all as the raw material for filling gaps in Festus, and at the same time he tried to identify and delete material that Paulus himself had interpolated. Both methods, as we have seen, were Agustín's, and they could in any case be employed only because Agustín had performed the heavy work of separating Paulus and Festus. Furthermore, Scaliger took over a number of Agustín's specific arguments, again without giving credit. 'It is remarkable', he wrote at one point:

how much Paulus liked the name Curia. He attached it to everything. He wants the *Centuriae* to be curiae, and the tribes too; for example, in the entry *Centumviralia*, and the entry *Curia*. Therefore, in the entry *Centumviralia* above, Paulus added a piece of excess matter to Festus with these words: QVAE CVRIAE DICTAE SVNT. Likewise here, ITEM CVRIATA. And in the entry *Curia*, QVIBVS POSTEA SVNT ADDITAE QVINQVE. We can delete all of these with as much confidence as he added them.[93]

All three of these interpolations had already been exposed – if in milder language – by Agustín.[94] Considering that he reprinted the very notes in which Agustín had anticipated him, it is hard to see what Scaliger can have intended to achieve. Here too ambition or egotism blinded him to debts that are obvious to any careful reader.

What Scaliger added to Agustín's text-critical method was, above all, a greatly enlarged mass of parallel passages from other grammatical works. He made great play with the glossaries – especially the Greco-Latin glossary of 'Philoxenus', which Daniel had discovered at St Germain. These works had aroused wide interest among the French. Turnèbe had used them in his *Adversaria* to illustrate material from Festus, and Estienne had published two glossaries and excerpts from others in 1573.[95] Scaliger used them in a much more sophisticated way. Paulus defined *ador* as *farris genus*, a kind of grain. He then explained that the word *adoriam* meant 'praise' or 'glory', 'because they

thought that he who had a large supply of grain was glorious'.[96]
Scaliger found a divergent explanation in the Philoxenus glossary.
And this one also, once emended, apparently derived from
Festus:

Adoream] The old glossary, thanks to which we have excavated so much
that was buried in the dust of antiquity: Adoriosus, ἔνδοξος, Ασπομωϊος
αδορνικηας πεμπιος. Read: Adoriosus, ἔνδοξος, ὡς Πομπήϊος ['Glorious,
according to Pompeius.'] Ador, νίκη, ὡς Πομπήϊος ['Victory, according to
Pompeius']. There can be no doubt that he means our Pompeius Festus.[97]

Here and elsewhere he showed that the authors of some glossaries had drawn directly upon Festus and upon other ancient
sources, now lost or unidentified but clearly genuine.[98] Accordingly, their quotations from Festus could be used as a control
upon, and often as a supplement to, the epitome of Paulus. 'From
this', he wrote: 'we can easily see how much that Lombard
arbitrarily changed, mutilated, or distorted. For that glossator's
notes were obviously taken from this passage in its complete
form.'[99] And he used further material from Philoxenus throughout his commentary.[100] This insight was crucial for the establishment of a usable text of Festus, and the way Scaliger pointed
has been followed by every subsequent editor, from Fulvio
Orsini in 1581 to 1582 to W. M. Lindsay in 1930.[101] Scaliger,
keenly aware of his originality, later complained bitterly that
Orsini had stolen from him the idea of comparing Festus and
the glossaries.[102]

Scaliger was also the first to mine another crucial lode of source
material. In addition to the glossaries, Daniel had discovered a
manuscript of a recension of Servius' commentary on Virgil con-
siderably fuller than the vulgate. This recension, known ever
since as Daniel's Servius, contained much material on Roman
religion and institutions which the vulgate lacked.[103] In 1574
Daniel sent off a first lot of selections from the commentary to
Scaliger, who thanked him effusively and asked for more:

Sir: A few days ago I received your letter, . . . along with some fragments
of your Servius, which came at just the right time to help with my Festus,
which is now at press along with my notes. . . . I'm most grateful to you
for your Servius. And I wish that you had added [the sections dealing with]
Rites and *Ceremonies*, which would have been most helpful for my Festus. It
still would not be too late if you wanted to send them to me right away. . .[104]

Less than a month later Scaliger wrote again to thank Daniel for
'les fragments des aucteurs cites par vostre Servius'. 'I have made

very good use of your fragments in my Festus', he said, 'and
have profited greatly from them.'[105] The excerpts that Daniel
sent must have been a selection like that now in the Ambrosiana,
the text of which is very similar, though not identical, to the
text of the passages cited by Scaliger.[106] At all events, Scaliger
indeed profited greatly from them.

Like the glossaries, Daniel's Servius provided a substantial
amount of stones which could be mortared together in the gaps
that Festus showed. Under *resignare*, for example, Agustín's
text — here faithful to the manuscript — read as follows:

Resignare antiqui pro rescribere ponebant, ut
adhuc subsignare dicimus pro subscribere. Cato
de Spoliis, ne figerentur, nisi quae de
ho . . . . .
re . . .[107]

It was clear that Festus had quoted Cato, but no amount of
conjecture could have restored the passage. Scaliger, however,
found that Daniel's Servius had quoted the same passage in its
entirety. He was therefore able to fill in part of the missing
section with a supplement that is still accepted: 'quae de hoste
capta essent: Sed tum ubi indivisi sunt, revertantur resignatis
vectigalibus.'[108] At the same time, Daniel's Servius provided a
stock of illustrations and explanations that illuminated obscurities throughout the text. In some respects, the new stockpile of
quotations from Roman grammarians that the Servius contained
was even more exciting than the glossaries. For if it was not quite
so relevant to establishing the text, the new material helped
even more towards its explication and towards the reconstruction
of the lost sources that Verrius himself had drawn upon.

Scaliger had done more than bring new material into play. He
placed all his sources, from Cato through Festus to Paulus and
the glossaries, in a new and coherent historical perspective. He
realized that Festus must be studied not merely in the light of
the other classical writers on grammar and antiquities, but in that
of the whole thousand-year tradition of Roman grammatical
writing. Only by doing so could one reassemble the extant
scraps of the writers upon whom Festus had drawn, as well as
the large body of late glossators who had drawn upon Festus,
and whose quotations could be used to reconstruct his text. In
sum, he had performed a masterly piece of historical reconstruction: he had re-created a tradition which had previously been
studied only unsystematically and arbitrarily.[109]

Scaliger's exegetical notes at first appear more remarkable than those devoted to textual criticism. One example will give an idea of them. The following text, though complete, was one of the more puzzling passages in the Farnesianus: 'Marspedis, sive sine R. littera Maspedis imprecaticie sesita vallium, quid significet ne Messalla quidem augur in explanatione auguriorum reperire se potuisse ait.'[110] The general purport is clear: 'Even the augur Messalla, in his explication of the auguries, says that he could not find out what *Marspedis . . .* means.' But the words *imprecaticie sesita vallium* are incomprehensible. Agustín suggested that *sesita* be emended to *solita*, but did not attempt to explain how the sentence could then be construed.[111] He also tried to interpret the term *Marspedis*: 'I would think that it meant *filium Martis*, if the authority of Messalla did not deter me.'[112] Scaliger set about the passage with a will. First he supplied a splendid emendation of Turnèbe's for the problematic words: 'Following Adrien Turnèbe, one of the most learned scholars of our time, read *in precatione Solitaurilium* ['in the prayer at the *suovetaurilia*.'] .' He then explained just what *Marspedis* meant and when it was employed:

Despite Messalla's doubts, it is perfectly clear that in the formula of the suovetaurilia, for purifying land by the ambarval sacrifice, only Mars is mentioned: MARSPITER TE PRECOR, etc., as is clear from Cato, [*De re rustica*] section 141. I suspect that the ancients said MARSPEDIS instead of [MARSPITER].

As to the opinion of learned men that *Marspedis* means 'son of Mars', that is, Martis παῖδα, this is plainly an instance of what Horace describes: 'a human head on a horse's neck' [*Ars poetica* 1]. Therefore it deserves to be rejected. But one should note that in the *Suovetaurilia*, or other prayers of rustics, Mars is Silvanus. Therefore he is sometimes called by both names at once, Mars Silvanus. Cato: 'Perform the vow for the health of cattle as follows: To Mars Silvanus in the forest during the daytime etc.' [*De re rust.*, § 83]. On Mars Silvanus the books on the boundaries of fields give the following: 'Every estate has three Silvani. One is called domestic, and consecrated to the estate. The second is called *agrestis*, and consecrated to the shepherds. The third is called *orientalis*; he has a sacred grove at the *terminus*, where the boundaries between two or more begin. Therefore the grove is between two or more' [*Grom. vet.* 302]. Cato must be referring to the third one. The first is also called the Silvanus of the *lares*, as in an inscription at Rome:

SILVANO
SANCTO
LARVM
PHILEMON
P. SCANTI

ELEVTERI
D.D.[113]

The second — that is, the Silvanus agrestis — is mentioned in another inscription which we have copied out here, relying on our most learned friend Aldo Manuzio:

SILVANO
AG. SACRVM
IN MEMORIAM
C. RVFI. ANTHI
IlIllI VIRI
TALLVS. LIB.
D.D.[114]

Ovid also refers to the same one: 'Do not let me suffer for having sheltered my flock in a rustic shrine while hail was falling' [*Fasti* IV. 755-6]. Therefore *Mars pedis* and *Mars pater* in Cato must be understood as the *Mars Silvanus orientalis* of farmers, at the boundary of two or more fields. All this comes from the law of the Athenians. For in the oath which the ephebes swore, there was added ἵστορες θεοὶ ἄγραυλοι ['The rustic Gods be witnesses']. Then it names them: ἐννάλιος, ἄρης, ζεύς [Iulius Pollux, *Onomasticon* VIII. 106]. There Zeus is also the one referred to by Cato as

App. V *dapalis.*[115]

This note is in most respects typical. The disdainful opening reference to Agustín, the wealth of literary, grammatical, antiquarian, and epigraphical material that is brought to bear on a single point; above all, the extraordinary capacity for leaping from a mass of scattered fragments of evidence to a coherent and even elegant conclusion — all these features reappear again and again. By modern standards Scaliger treats his evidence rather too brusquely, especially in regard to the Greek origin of the Roman rite. But the argument is at worst both clever and coherent — and the notion that Silvanus was an alternate title for Mars is very acute.[116]

The cumulative effect of several dozens of notes like the one just quoted is fairly daunting. Scaliger, certainly, did not produce in the end a comprehensive reconstruction of Roman life like that provided in Sigonio's *De antiquo iure civium Romanorum*. He had no interest in bringing a dead world back to life in its entirety. Indeed, there is little evidence to suggest that Scaliger thought of the early Romans as three-dimensional, historical individuals, or of their culture as a single, coherent organism that ought to be resurrected as a whole. The evidence — if treated critically and in detail — could not support such an approach. Rather, Scaliger performed a series of elegant microscopic reconstructions, each time fitting back together only a few stones of the vast but ruinous mosaic that seems to have been his vision of Rome. The piecemeal nature of his work is most important. It meant that his commentary could not be decisively superior to Agustín's except in detail and in the scope of individual excursuses. By the nature of the material, he could not arrive at a single, coherent set of results that would drive the earlier work off the market.

Moreover, the material in Festus limited the subject-matter on which Scaliger's notes could touch. Many of them dealt with the two subjects that had become traditional in Festan studies: the development of the Latin language and the early history of Roman law. The first of these subjects, as we have seen, had engaged both Agustín and his French readers. And many of Scaliger's observations in this field closely resemble those of his predecessors on both sides of the Alps. On the one hand, he imitated Agustín in his close attention to orthography and its development during Roman history, in his interest in the early Latin dialects, and in his attempts to formulate rules for changes in spelling and pronunciation.[117] His use of inscriptions and coins also had parallels in Agustín's commentary.[118] On the other hand, he imitated Turnèbe in paying more attention than Agustín to the dialects of Greek.[119] True, Scaliger added new material of his own. He referred to phenomena in the vernacular languages of the sixteenth century that offered parallels to developments in Latin.[120] As in the *Coniectanea* on Varro, so here, he introduced material on the Near Eastern languages as well. For example, he provided the obvious Hebrew parallel to old Latin *vira* (woman), formed from *vir*.[121] He even devoted a digression to the nature and origin of the language of the Phoenicians.[122] But all this material was merely a matter of additional detail and wider scope; Scaliger was not able to build upon it a coherent history of the Latin language, or even a coherent set of principles by which such a history could be constructed.[123]

For early law as for the history of language Scaliger's work derived from the existing scholarly tradition — in this case, from the work of earlier French jurists. For example, under *nancitor* Festus wrote: 'Nancitor in duodecim nactus erit, praedatus erit. Item in foedere Latino pecuniam quis nancitor, habeto et siquid pignoris nanciscitur sibi habeto.'[124] Agustín did not discuss the passage. But Scaliger did so at some length:

Nancitor] PEQVNIAM . QVIS . NANCITOR . HABETO . ET . SI . QUID. PIGNERIS . NANCITOR . SIBEI . HABETO. *Nancitor*, for *nancitur*. And *nancitur* for *nanciscitur*; like *apiscitur*. QVIS for QVI, an archaism. It was a chapter in the Latin treaty, that the creditor should be satisfied within ten days after a suit was tried. Here, however, it calls for him to have the pledge, if after that time he has not been satisfied. Or rather it means that whatever agreement a Latin had made with a Roman before the war, whether it was a loan or a pledge, should stand.[125]

Scaliger's interpretation was broadly correct. The passages cited by Festus derive from the commercial provisions of the Latin treaty.[126] Their fragmentary nature may go some way to explain why he wavered so uncharacteristically about their precise meaning. Even more important, however, was what Scaliger did not say. As early as 1555 le Caron had suggested that these fragments belonged either to the Twelve Tables or to the Latin treaty, pointing out that 'Festus bears witness that the ancients said *quis* instead of *qui*'.[127] In 1556 Brisson had argued sharply and cogently that the fragments were from the treaty.[128] In 1560 Sigonio had cited them as part of the treaty in his *De antiquo iure Italiae*.[129] Scaliger, then, simply combined le Caron's observation about the archaic language of the fragments with Brisson's thesis about their provenance. All he added was a slightly more refined analysis of the archaic forms involved. Here and in many other passages, Scaliger continued normal French tradition in the study of archaic law.

In one respect, however, Scaliger's approach to the legal material in Festus was an innovation. He tried several times to reconstruct not only the content but even the language of laws to which Festus had merely referred. For example, under the word *pollucere* Festus listed a variety of foodstuffs that could lawfully be sacrificed to a god whose name the codex does not preserve. These included *pisces, quibus est squama, praeter scarum* ('scaly fish, except the *scarus*').[130] Scaliger knew from a fragment of Cassius Hemina preserved by Pliny that Numa had made a law against the sacrifice of fish that were *not* scaly.[131] And he decided, not unreasonably, that both passages must refer to a single enactment, which he reconstructed as follows: 'I think that the law must have been drawn up in these words: PISCEIS . QVEI . SQVAMOSEI . NON . SVNT . NEI . POLLV-CETO . SQVAMOSOS . OMNEIS . PRAETER . SCARVM POLLVCETO.'[132] In his Festus commentary — where he repeatedly attempted such reconstructions — Scaliger was having his last fling with the composition of archaic Latin. Not surprisingly, his versions of the laws were more successful with the public than his attempts at the original composition of archaic verse. Philologists and antiquarians alike wished to know as much as possible about every detail of Roman life. They were passionately interested to know the exact words that the Romans had used on official occasions. And, until Brisson published his great *De formulis et solemnibus Populi Romani verbis libri VIII* in 1583, there was no standard work on the subject. Brisson far surpassed Scaliger in the richness of his collection; he treated not only sacred and legal formulas but the commonplaces of everyday speech, ending with instructions on how to say goodbye (which he promptly applied in his own farewell to the reader).[133] In the meantime Scaliger's back-formations filled a need and even helped to create something of a fashion. For in 1576 Justus Lipsius, who was most impressed by the ingenuity of Scaliger's work, included the re-created laws in a little collection of *Leges regiae et leges x. virales* that he published for teaching purposes.[134] Thus removed from their original context, Scaliger's back-formations came to attract imitators even among scholars who were not otherwise his admirers. For when Fulvio Orsini brought out Agustín's treatise *De legibus et senatusconsultis* in 1583, he added an appendix of reconstructed *leges regiae* and fragments of the Twelve Tables. It is clear that Scaliger was his ultimate but indirect model. For among the laws that Orsini attributed to Numa appears — with no word about Scaliger — the very fish story that Scaliger had invented nine years before, tricked out in even more antique spelling:

PISCEIS . QVEI . SQVAMOSEI . NON . SIENT . NEI . POLVCETO . SQVAMOSOS . OMNEIS . PRAETER . SCAROM . POLVCETO .[135]

(This law lived on into the eighteenth century in the standard compendia). Geronimo Blancas, another friend of Antonio Agustín's, was even inspired to publish in 1588 an archaic Latin version of the medieval False Fueros of Sobrarbe, in which the following remarkable bit of composition occurs:

E . MAVRIS . VINDICABVNDA . DIVIDVNTOR . INTER . RICOSHOMINES . NONMODO . SED . ETIAM . INTER . MILITES . AC . INFANTIONES . PEREGRINVS. AVTEM. HOMO. NIHIL . INDE . CAPITO .[136]

Scaliger could indeed congratulate himself on bringing off a *tour de force* splendidly apposite to the tastes of his contemporaries, with their increasing interest in Tacitus on the one hand and in inscriptions and archaic Latin on the other. No wonder that he spoke in his prefatory letter of excavating venerable monuments from the dust.

And yet, it seems that Scaliger's commentary did not satisfy all his wishes. This is not surprising. As we have seen, he drew most of the material he attacked and most of the tools he employed from Agustín's work, and at some level he must have been aware of his debt. Moreover, much of what he added to Agustín both in point of method and of material was not his own discovery but that of other French scholars. If he knew that he had used the glossaries and Daniel's Servius in a more sophisticated way than anyone else could have done, he must also have known that few of his readers would appreciate his highly technical innovations in method. In fact, even his reconstruction of early Roman laws was not entirely original; le Caron had done the same, though he set to work with vastly inferior historical and linguistic knowledge. Moreover, Scaliger must also have realized that many of his reconstructions, whether of institutions, of the text of Festus, or of early law, were too speculative to command universal assent, or even that of many whose opinion he valued. His sense of uncertainty expresses itself in many of his notes. Along with the customary brays of triumph statements occur that are diffident and almost humble. 'I was wrong', he wrote at one point, referring to an earlier work: 'and I ask my courteous readers to pardon me for this, and anything else like it that I may have said. For these things are common to all who both know that they are men and feel that nothing human is foreign to them.'[137] One particularly eloquent passage shows precisely what Scaliger saw as the limitations of an approach that rested so heavily upon conjecture. Under *Punici*, Festus had a long passage of which very little survives — in each of some fifteen lines, the codex retains only two or three words.[138] Scaliger proposed a reconstruction of the passage, which he printed with Festus' words in Roman type and his proposed supplements in italics. He then set out to justify and explain what he had done:

We have set off what is Festus' from what is ours, so that we may convince the reader that we neither believe nor wish to persuade others that what does not belong to Festus belongs to him. I have imitated the men who love and study old images and statues. They sometimes have an elegantly carved marble statue which, perhaps because of its age, is mutilated and lacks a section, as often happens. They seek out skilled craftsmen to fill the missing space with their own work. All who see the statue know both what portion of the old craftsmanship has been lost and what has been added by the new. Yet the addition is often so important that without it the remaining proportion and symmetry of the whole statue would be impossible to detect. This is what we have done in this passage of Festus. For without the limbs we have added, it would be very difficult to tell what the trunk was. Now so far as we can tell, we have done something most useful for scholars. For by our diligence we have restored this building, that was almost levelled to the ground, from its foundations, and set it in good repair.[139]

The passage ends on a characteristically arrogant note. But the arrogance is not unqualified. Scaliger's excessive care to justify his actions, his insistence on his innocence of any intention to trick or cheat the reader, above all his realization, made plain by the analogy he chose, that he could not hope to restore what Festus had actually written, but only to give some idea of what he probably had said — these reveal his awareness of the limits of the method he had had to employ. In the second half of the commentary, Scaliger expresses his reservations with more and more frequency, and he takes more and more care to explain that he can only reveal the sense of partially lost passages, not their exact wording. Evidently, he came to realize as he went on that not all sherds can be fitted back together into pots.

Moreover, one passage suggests that Scaliger was even coming to have more general doubts about the validity of the French tradition in scholarship, and to feel increasing respect for the mass of manuscript evidence that lay behind the work of the Italians. In *Miscellanea* I.2, Poliziano had defended and explained the manuscript reading of Catullus 98.3-4:

Ista cum lingua, si usus veniat tibi, possis
    Culos, et crepidas lingere carpatinas.[140]

Characteristically, Muret had attacked him. 'Poliziano's reading, *crepidas carbatinas*', he wrote, 'is unacceptable for several reasons. First because it goes against the old manuscripts'.[141] He had insisted that 98.4 should read:

    Culos, et trepidas lingere cercolipas.

Equally characteristically, Statius had defended the manuscript reading, saying, 'It is with great pleasure that I agree with Poliziano.'[142]

What is important for our purposes is Scaliger's reaction to this controversy. In his note on the word *Cercolopis*, he wrote:

Cercolopis] Read *cercolips*, without any question — that is, an ape that doesn't have a tail. . . . Catullus also mentions these apes in an epigram:
- *et trepidas lingere cercolipas*. Anyone can see how clear the sense is here. For what could be fouler than the buttocks of an ape, especially a *cercolips*? But Poliziano preferred *carbatinas*. He did not invent this, but

had seen it so [written] in MSS. For the Catullus manuscript . . . of Cujas reads that way. But there have been some who accused Poliziano of dishonesty.[143]

Here we see Scaliger struggling to decide between Poliziano and Muret. Evidently he prefers Muret's reading of the line in question. But he has already come to see by experience that Poliziano was far more reliable than Muret as a collator of manuscripts.

I would not wish to push any one of these texts too far. Taken together, however, they produce an impression of doubt, of hesitation, almost of bafflement. Certainly Scaliger was no longer satisfied with the methods or the standards in which he had been trained. Even the Festus, a triumph when judged by French standards, gave him qualms. As we shall see, in 1575 a notorious and humiliating contretemps transformed those qualms into convictions of a new kind.

VI Scaliger's Catullus: the Synthesis that Failed

It was Scaliger's old benefactor Muret who made him turn against the methods in which he had been trained. Probably in 1565 or 1566, Muret had passed on to Scaliger two poems in archaic Latin, which he had attributed to Trabea and Accius. Scaliger accepted them as authentic and printed them in his notes on Varro *De re rustica* of 1573, praising them as gems of old Latin. 'Who is so hostile to the Muses', he wrote, 'and so devoid of humanity as to be displeased by the publication of these verses?'[1] In 1575, however, Muret included them in a collection of his own orations and poems. In a dry preface he explained that they were not archaic Latin at all, but compositions of his own, adapted from a Greek comic fragment:

I had tried, for my own amusement, to express the noble sentiment of the ancient Greek comic poet Philemon, which I had found in Plutarch and Stobaeus, in a style and metre as close as possible to that of the ancient Latin tragic poets. I then decided to see if I could set out the same sentiment in the manner of a comic poet. I thought that both attempts went off quite well. For a joke, therefore, I assigned the name of Accius to the former set of verses, that of Trabea to the latter, in order to test the judgements of others and see if there was any savour of antiquity in them. I found no one who did not take them for ancient. Indeed, I found one man, endowed with extraordinary learning and very acute judgement, who took them from me and published them as ancient poems. Lest anyone continue to be deceived, I thought that I should expose the whole affair and give the poems themselves here.[2]

Scaliger's humiliation must have been intense. He had made his name by becoming the chief expert on early Latin verse and the sole master of formal composition in it. Yet he had unhesitatingly declared Muret's verses genuine. Muret had shown him up as a scholar, by fooling him, and as a poet, by surpassing him. If Scaliger had written poems that his contemporaries found consistently archaic in tone, he had not written anything that they simply accepted as old Latin.

Some public response was called for. Scaliger, after all, was an aristocrat. During the later 1570s, he was also trying very hard to behave like one. He dressed in a short cloak, wore a ruff, and refused to let himself be seen reading or working.[3] But during the sixteenth century, an aristocrat, at least in France, had to preserve an untarnished public face. If he allowed himself to be defeated without fighting back, his honour was damaged. Physical blows could be avenged by a challenge to a duel.[4] But how could one reply to literary treachery?

Scaliger had already begun to worry about the reliability of standard French methods and to take an interest in Vettori's work. Muret's actions made him see that his suspicions had been more than justified. A method like Muret's, which stressed literary analysis and eloquence at the expense of absolute rigour and honesty in assessing and reporting the evidence, could lead too easily to deliberate deceit. Vettori's method seemed immune from this defect. Scaliger therefore decided to change allegiance; to publish an edition in the style of Vettori. Muret had edited Catullus, Tibullus, and Propertius. Accordingly, Scaliger chose them as his subject. One of his motives in doing so is neatly revealed by a letter that he wrote to Claude Dupuy, after hearing a false report that Muret had died:

M. Cujas just wrote me that M. Muret was dead, and that someone had written to him about it from Italy. I would like very much to know if it is true, and I ask you humbly to tell me. For I would be very sorry if he passed away before I could pay him back for his verses by Attius and Trabea. I shall set about copying my little annotations on Catullus, Tibullus, and Propertius, and will send them to you at once, so that you may be my Aristarchus.[5]

Desire for revenge was not Scaliger's only concern. His distrust of Parisian method continued to grow during 1576. More and more he came to see even his own Festus as flawed by excessive boldness in venturing conjectures. 'M. d'Abain', he wrote to Dupuy in June: 'has given copies of my Festus to Sigonio and to good old Pier Vettori. . . . God grant that they like it. For they don't think much of French wits. And to tell you the truth, they're partly right, partly wrong.'[6] The simple fact that he had access to important manuscripts may also have played a part in his decision. He knew that Cujas owned a fifteenth-century manuscript of all three elegists, which he was able to borrow.

Cujas also owned a much older fragment of Tibullus, which Scaliger had studied before he left Valence in 1572.[7] Certainly he could not have hoped to defeat Muret decisively without having a cache of new material to draw upon.

There were at least two other good reasons for choosing the elegists. First, their texts were central to the normal humanist curriculum and essential for anyone who hoped to write successful Neo-Latin verse. By choosing them instead of, for example, another rather peripheral author such as Ausonius, Scaliger ensured that his views would receive the required attention. Second, there was no competent work in the style of Vettori on their texts. Achilles Statius had published editions of Catullus and Tibullus based on collations of several manuscripts each. But his editions, though rich in apparatus, lacked method and direction. After Scaliger borrowed a copy of Statius's work from Dupuy, he realized that his own edition could only gain by the comparison. 'You would not believe how boastful I have become', he wrote to Dupuy, 'now that I have read the commentaries of M. Achilles. He has given me hope that I can do something good. I wouldn't have dared to say that before.'[8] In short, the new edition would not only complete Scaliger's revenge but also fill a gap in the existing philological literature.

The edition that finally appeared early in 1577 does not at first seem serious work. Scaliger claims in his preface that he has eliminated interpolations from Catullus and brought true readings, which medieval scribes had corrupted, 'into the light, from the bowels of antiquity'.[9] He also claims to have done the same for Tibullus and Propertius, spending less than a month on all three.[10] As to the commentary proper, he says that its preparation took him less than three weeks, as was reasonable for a work that dealt only with problems of verbal criticism.[11] In short, Scaliger presents the book as a spare-time rather than a long-term project.

Nothing could be farther from the truth, as Scaliger's private letters to his friends, written in French, clearly show. His work on the commentary began as early as November 1575.[12] He was still at it in early February 1576; on 11 May he hoped to be able to put it into final form in the near future; on 29 June he was busy doing so; and he did not send the completed work to Dupuy for publication until 8 August.[13] The work, then, took more than half a year to write. Moreover, it became highly controversial within months after its appearance. In July 1577

Scaliger wrote to Dupuy that 'there are many men, and others who look like men, and others who are not men at all, who are complaining about my Catullus'.[14] It has continued to attract attention ever since. Jacob Bernays saw it as Scaliger's most methodical edition, the one that marked his complete triumph over the vanity and incompetence of Italian correctors. And more recently, Sebastiano Timpanaro has shown that Scaliger's Catullus was one of the most remarkable anticipations of Lachmann's method before the eighteenth century.[15] In short, consideration of the edition's content bears out the evidence of Scaliger's correspondence: the edition was intended to be taken seriously.

The three elegists posed problems of method that were to some extent analogous, and Scaliger's solutions, as we shall see, also resembled one another. But he himself regarded the section of the edition that dealt with Catullus as particularly original and provocative. Accordingly, it will be best to begin by considering the Catullus and to turn more briefly at the end to the others.

In some respects, the Catullus did not represent a drastic departure from Scaliger's earlier work. He did not abandon the comparative method; indeed, he larded his pages with ample strips of Greek poetry and prose. He used them for two purposes: to show how Catullus drew on Greek poetic models and to explain mythological, historical, and geographical references. His learning is as overpowering as usual. Aratus 359 (θεῶν ὑπὸ ποσσὶ φορεῖται, 'is borne under the feet of the gods') provided a neat Hellenistic parallel to 66.69 (*me nocte premunt vestigia divum*, 'at night the footsteps of the gods oppress me').[16] Euripides was brought in to support a changed word-division in 36.9.[17] A fragment of Sappho preserved in Daniel's unpublished Servius enabled Scaliger to provide the Greek literary background to Catullus 61:

COLLIS *o Heliconei*] A. Ticida wrote a Hymenaeum in this metre. Sappho wrote an epithalamium, not a Hymenaeum. The unpublished form of Servius says: 'Sappho, in the book entitled *Epithalamia*:
- - χαῖρε δὲ νύμφα
χαῖρε τίμιε γαμβρέ [Serv. Dan. *ad* Georg. I.31].'
('Hail, bride, hail, honoured bridegroom.')
This is also in the same metre.[18]

Extensive quotations from Strabo served to illuminate the mysterious Persian fire-worship that Catullus had referred to in 90. 5-6.[19]

Both Muret and Statius had used Greek material in much the same way. Muret, for instance, had published in his commentary the poem by Sappho of which Catullus 51 is a translation.[20] Where Muret's commentary was rather brief and fragmentary, that of Statius was long and full. For Statius ransacked all Greek poetry for it; his reading was almost as wide as Scaliger's.[21]

Following Muret and Statius, Scaliger was able to omit the more obvious Greek sources and parallels and concentrate on matter more likely to be new to his readers.[22] His use of Greek was exceptional only in so far as much of the material he quoted was recondite.

Though he continued to use the methods of his Parisian masters, Scaliger nevertheless departed from their normal editorial habits. His notes record an extensive collation of one manuscript. In fact, he based his text on this collation. He said that he trusted his manuscript because it had been written just before the invention of printing, and so it was free from the interpolations that correctors had introduced into later ones. Furthermore, the manuscript retained traces of archaic spellings.[23]

Scaliger's collation was not completely accurate, and his evaluation of his manuscript was not completely sound. The manuscript survives as British Library MS Egerton 3027, which includes Tibullus, Propertius, and the *Priapea* as well as Catullus. Scaliger entered his collation of it in the margins of a copy of the 1569 Plantin edition of Catullus, Tibullus, and Propertius, which is now in Leiden University Library (shelf-mark 755 H 23). By comparing the manuscript and the original collation with Scaliger's published notes, it is possible to reconstruct his working methods and evaluate his accuracy.[24]

Scaliger had seen the manuscript at Valence, but Vertunien's vivid testimony suggests that he borrowed it in 1576 to prepare the new edition. It also shows how quickly Scaliger worked: 'No one is readier and more skilful at collating old books than Joseph Scaliger, as I observed in the case of the manuscript of Catullus, Tibullus, Propertius that Cujas sent him. He collated this with his own [books] in two or three days at most.'[25] He worked carefully nevertheless. He entered in the margins of his Plantin text a large number of variant readings from the manuscript, writing *v* — *i.e. vetus lectio* or *codex* — beside them in order to identify their source unambiguously. He also underlined many readings in the Plantin text which agreed with his manuscript; again he wrote *v* beside them. He took care to record unusual spellings and abbreviations: for example, at 61. 176 he correctly copied the manuscript reading *aderãnt*, and at 66. 91 he correctly copied the abbreviation *u̅r̅s̅*. Furthermore, he entered in the Plantin text numerous details of no direct text-critical use but important, for example, in identifying his manuscript or in reconstructing the textual tradition. Thus, he copied out the epigram with which Benvenuto Campesano, a fourteenth-century Vicenzan notary, had celebrated the rediscovery of Catullus.[26] He also copied out the colophon from the Propertius section of his manuscript, which included the scribe's name and the manuscript's date.[27] There were errors and omissions. He copied the date in the Propertius colophon as 1469 instead of 1467; at 61.151 he wrote *serviet* for *servit*; and at 62.9 he failed to record the manuscript reading *canent* — an omission which had disastrous consequences when he tried to emend the line.[28] For the most part, however, the collation that he entered in his Plantin text was comprehensive, detailed, and accurate.

When Scaliger came to write his commentary on Catullus, he introduced a number of errors into his report of the manuscript readings. He often misread his own notes. At 61.195 he had correctly entered the manuscript reading *venus* in his Plantin Catullus; but in the published commentary he gave the reading of the *manuscriptus liber* as *venis* (which was the reading given in the text of the Plantin edition). At 98.4 he ignored the manuscript reading *carpacias*, which he had also copied correctly. At least eighty of his reports disagreed with the manuscript reading. At least half the time Scaliger was silently correcting or altering the scribe's spelling habits; he would not have regarded these discrepancies as mistakes. But there remain at least twenty cases in which — usually because he misread his notes — he seriously misrepresented the manuscript.[29]

Moreover, Scaliger did not carry over into his published notes the precision and meticulousness of his original collation. Presumably he felt that minor details, which might help an editor to prepare a text, would be of no further use even to professional critics. At any rate, he paid little attention to details of spelling and punctuation. At 61.99, for example, he said that the *vetus lectio* was *proca turpia*; in fact, the manuscript gave *procatur pia*, as he could have found by checking his own notes.[30] At 66.91, he had copied in his notes the manuscript reading *u̅r̅s̅*. In the published commentary, he noted only that the manuscript reading could be either *veris* or *vestris*. In other words, he thought that the abbreviation $\overline{uns}$ was ambiguous, but did not think it necessary to record the problematic abbreviation in his published commentary.[31] Also, the terms with which he identified readings in his published notes — unlike the v of his original collation — were sometimes ambiguous. Usually he used the phrase *vetus scriptura* to introduce readings from the manuscript. But he used other phrases as well, and sometimes he did not make clear whether he was reporting a manuscript reading or a conjecture based on a reading.[32] Despite these lapses, Scaliger gave a better collation of his one manuscript than Statius gave of any of his seven.[33] But he certainly fell short of the standards set by Poliziano, Vettori, and Faerno.

Scaliger's judgement about the value of his manuscript was no sounder. Admittedly, the manuscript gave him an idea of the correct reading in places where the printed texts, or at least some of them, had conjectural emendations. But he could have learned more by using Statius's notes carefully. For Statius, as B. L. Ullman showed long ago, had access to the fourteenth-century manuscript now called R by editors. And this was a far more independent and faithful witness to the textual tradition than Scaliger's manuscript.[34] According to R. A. B. Mynors, Scaliger's manuscript is of critical value only because it preserves certain intelligent conjectures of unknown origin.[35] Its 'archaic' spellings were probably introduced by the fifteenth-century humanist who wrote the manuscript, the erotic poet Pacificus Maximus Asculanus.[36] Scaliger, then, was wrong to assert that his manuscript was better than those which other editors had employed and to base his text on it.

Though Scaliger was wrong about his manuscript, the way he used it and the reasons he gave for doing so are historically important. None of Scaliger's teachers, as we saw, attempted to base their editions on selected manuscripts that represented the earliest form of the text. Nor did they publish systematic collations of manuscripts — at least, not in anything like the detail that characterized Scaliger's Catullus commentary. Scaliger learned his method of using manuscripts not from the French but from the Italians. His edition of Catullus, based on a single manuscript which he believed to be especially authoritative, containing an extensive collation of that manuscript, was Scaliger's attempt at an edition that was in large part in the style of Vettori.

Scaliger never said that he was imitating Vettori. But a great deal of evidence indicates that that is just what he was doing.

In the first place, the inclusion of a detailed collation of a manuscript by itself implied adherence to Vettori's principles. Secondly, Scaliger employed other methods of Vettori's. For example, he tried to demonstrate that his manuscript was especially valuable because of its retention of word forms that had been archaic in Catullus' own time, and that Catullus had deliberately employed. Some of these archaisms the scribe of Scaliger's manuscript had copied correctly: for example, *quot* instead of *quod* (16. 12); *uno* instead of *uni* (45.14); *prosternit* instead of *prostravit* (64. 110).[37] To prove that these were legitimate archaic forms and not mere corruptions, Scaliger cited parallels from manuscripts known to be very old. This was precisely the procedure that Vettori had used to validate archaic forms in his own manuscripts.[38] At one point, Scaliger even quoted Vettori as an authority on such matters. In his note on 55. 13, he wrote:

... Our codex, excellently:
   Sed te iam ferre Herculei labos est.
There *Herculei* is in the ancient genitive. That most honest and learned old gentleman Pier Vettori found it written thus in the old manuscripts of Cicero's letters, *Themistoclei, Theophanei,* ... [39]

In his note on Cicero, *Familiares*, V. 12, Vettori had written:

Themistoclis fuga) The old exemplars [give] *Themistocli*, according to the old declension, in which they used the dative in place of the genitive in nouns of this kind. Thus *Ulyssi* for *Ulyssis*, *Achilli* for *Achillis*; thus also in our better codex of the *Epistolae ad Atticum*, in Book XIII, *Non vides ipsum illum Aristoteli discipulum*, for *Aristotelis* ... [40]

Other archaisms, however, the scribe had misread and miscopied. These had to be reconstructed from his erroneous readings, a task which could only be undertaken by a critic who had mastered epigraphy as well as palaeography. For inscriptions, even more than manuscripts, were an excellent source of unquestionably genuine archaic word-forms. In 2. 8, for example, Scaliger's manuscript read 'Credo ut quom . . .'. He thought that the line should begin 'Credunt'. He realized that, had *credunt* been spelt, archaically, 'credont', the scribe could easily have changed what he read into 'Credo ut'. To prove that verbs in the third person often terminated in *-ont* rather than *-unt*, he adduced epigraphical evidence: '. . . They wrote thus not infrequently, as in a stone in Narbonne:

VIVONT
A.   SEMPRONIO
GALLAECI.   L. LAETO
PVRPVRARIO
ET. SEMPRONIAE. MODESTAE
VXORI

In other inscriptions as well in that city one reads VIVONT for *vivunt*. . . . .'[41] This was exactly the method which Vettori had used for reconstructing archaic forms from scribal corruptions.

Scaliger said repeatedly that he intended to expunge the interpolations from the text of Catullus and return to the original tradition of the manuscripts. He frequently pointed out that small errors in copying could make whole passages incomprehensible. He insisted that it was possible to reconstruct Catullus' idiosyncratic spelling habits. All these statements had close counterparts in Vettori's notes on the *Familiares* — the very work that Scaliger cited.[42] This coincidence of method and substance makes it clear that Scaliger modelled his use of manuscripts on that of the Italians.

This interpretation is confirmed by the case of Catullus 66.94. In modern editions the line reads 'Proximus Hydrochoi fulgeret Oarion' — 'Let Orion shine next to Aquarius.' In the fifteenth century it seemed to present two problems. The first was metrical: if Orion's name appeared in its normal Latin spelling, the line did not amount to a full dactylic pentameter. The second was astronomical: Orion, a southern constellation, is near Taurus; Coma Berenices, a northern constellation, is near Virgo; neither is anywhere near Aquarius. The first Catullan commentator, Parthenius, solved the first problem by a bold invention: 'One should read Aorion [sword-bearer]. . . for ἄορ means sword; hence *aorion*, as it were, ensifer.' He ignored the second, harder one and went on his way rejoicing:

[The line means:] If I [the *coma*] became the queen's *coma* again, then the stars Aquarius and Orion would be separated by no interval and would become very close. For the *coma*, as was explained in part above, is located at the tail of Leo, in Virgo, so that it is not very far from Aquarius, which Orion is near.[43]

Poliziano rightly saw that Parthenius had been too bold. The line could be scanned with ease if Orion's name appeared in the Greek form 'Oarion', and Poliziano defended this reading elaborately against 'those who violate good books'. But he did not explain how the line's astronomy could be saved. Palladius and Guarino flailed away at it to no better effect. Marullus, meanwhile, had transformed it, replacing 'Oarion' with 'Erigonae' and 'Hydrochoi' with 'Arcturos' (which gave the astronomically plausible sense 'Let Arcturus shine near Virgo'). Muret accepted this wholesale rewriting, since it served his larger end of discrediting Poliziano. He quoted Marullus's verses on the passage and added a grave warning about Poliziano's efforts to replace the manuscript reading with what was really his own conjecture:

From this it can be seen how dangerous it is when famous men, who have great literary reputations, make mistakes. Because of Poliziano's authority, there is no printed edition, so far as I know, which does not reject the true reading and give that spurious and interpolated verse:
  Proximus Hydrochoo fulgeat Oarion.[44]

Only Muret could have turned Poliziano's own philological language against its creator with such deftness.

The line can be explained, but only by a scholar willing to abandon the tunnel vision of a word-by-word commentator, to examine the economy of the poem and the place in it of the *coma's* final plea. Achilles Statius did this difficult job of rethinking. He saw that the apparent astronomical error was crucial to the line's intended effect. The *coma* was saying that she would not mind seeing the heavens in chaos, if only she could return to earth: 'the point is . . . that she does not care what position which stars take, even if those that are located very far apart become near neighbours, so long as she may be on top of the queen.'[45] Modern commentators disagree on the syntax of the line, but all accept this paraphrase of it. Scaliger thought too little of Statius to learn from him and did not accept his interpretation. He tried to defend the *coma's* call for a conjunction of Orion and Aquarius on the feebler general ground that a poet had licence to be inaccurate about astronomy. The argument did not satisfy him. He found it hard to believe that Callimachus could have made so gross an error: 'We cannot conceal our surprise at the fact that . . . Orion seemed to Callimachus to be so close to Aquarius.'[46] But if Scaliger could not interpret 66.94 with much clarity, he defended Poliziano's version of it with force, making it the occasion for a hearty defence of Poliziano and a brutal attack on Marullus:

Therefore, the meaning of this passage, which the correctors polluted, not without being guilty of great temerity, is perfectly simple. The most ridiculous of all is Marullus. Though he has little or no understanding of this kind of literature, he ridicules Poliziano, a man not only greater than he, but also one to whom no one in our time is comparable. Poliziano did not fabricate this. Rather, he tried to defend the old reading, which he saw being polluted by the little masters, in their audacity. And clearly all the oldest editions, as I said, and all the extant manuscripts read no differently. But that Greekling thought he had the same liberty with regard to good authors that he wanted with regard to his own verses. He also dared to attack the learned Poliziano's note with a completely inept epigram. Those who think so much of that man, and make so much of him, would have to give up some of their obstinacy, if they examined his edition of Lucretius carefully. For no ancient author has been treated so badly by any corrector as Lucretius has by that rash Greekling. We will not imitate him. If any traces of his and similar correctors' audacity and temerity remain in good books, it is our plan to destroy them utterly and to expunge them completely from the midst of good authors. I have not yet been able to find out who was the author of this silly change, unless it was Marullus himself. For that passage was changed shortly before Poliziano wrote. That gave [this] most learned man the occasion for defending the old reading, which he saw being attacked before his very eyes by impudent little men. Indeed, Marullus had a rapid and fluent wit, but seemingly one suited more for spewing out extemporaneous verses, some good and some bad, than for emending good authors.[47]

Here too Scaliger repeated all the Vettorian *topoi*: the manuscript reading must remain unless there is compelling reason to change it; arbitrary conjectures are the lowest form of pseudo-scholarship; Poliziano is the best of critics, the model whom all must imitate if they hope to accomplish anything solid.

Scaliger's diatribe was more than a restatement of familiar themes. It was also an imitation of a somewhat less heated attack which Vettori had made on Marullus — once again, in his notes on the *Familiares*. In his discussion of the phrase *Te perterrefacto* (XI. 20), Vettori pointed out that the old manuscripts gave *pertimefacto*. In Cicero and elsewhere, he continued, this word had been altered by correctors who failed to realize that it was good Latin. For example, in Lucretius II. 44 *timefactae* had been replaced by *tumefacto*. 'We think', he wrote,

that Marullus of Byzantium bears the guilt for this crime. For we saw his copy, which, though it had first had TIMEFACTAE, had that word changed into TVMEFACTO. Now Marullus was a man of remarkable wit, and a most elegant poet, so ardent a student and admirer of Lucretius that he almost never put down [his work]. Furthermore, he laboured hard to cleanse [the text of] Lucretius, [which] was swarming with gross corruptions; and he restored many things successfully. Sometimes, since he indulged his own wit too much, he corrupted things which he meant to correct. For he paid little attention to manuscripts, since he found such corrupt ones everywhere. And [since he] considered correct whatever he had approved with his own judgement, he was deceived in many passages.[48]

The attacks are not closely parallel. But Scaliger obviously derived from Vettori the knowledge that Marullus had resorted to conjecture in his corrections of Lucretius — and that by doing so he had corrupted the text; and he also took from Vettori the thesis that Marullus was a good poet but no critic. By drawing on Vettori to defend Poliziano and attack Marullus, Scaliger was implicitly taking sides with Vettori and against Muret. He knew that his point would be taken by the better-informed among his readers. The Flemish scholar Gerard Falkenburg wrote in his copy of Muret's commentary: 'See Scaliger on this passage of Catullus, where he very rightly criticizes the follies of this silly little Greek.'[49]

Another case shows Scaliger going even farther in the same direction. None of Poliziano's restorations had won assent from more critics or a place in more editions than had 'Chalybon' in 66.48. This Scaliger rejected, supporting his action with an argument so obtuse as to sound like a parody: 'Certainly Catullus did not write *Chalybon*. Why? Because it is too great a departure from the traces of the original reading.'[50] He searched energetically for an alternative that came closer to the transmitted text; but though he did propose a revised version of the line in his commentary, he lacked the confidence to insert it in his text, which therefore became a monument to his new excess of conservative feeling: 'Iuppiter, ut * . . . omne genus pereat.'[51] One would not expect the sovereign restorer of Festus to prefer such counsels of despair to a perfectly plausible conjecture. In this case, Scaliger was not reviving Poliziano's editorial principles so much as reducing them to absurdity.

Extremism of this degree was unusual. For the most part, Scaliger tried to fuse French methods with Italian ones. On the one hand, he wished to adopt and naturalize in France the Italians' method of manuscript recension, clearly hoping that it would enable him to show that Muret's philology was unsound and that Muret himself was not accurate or honest enough to be a competent textual critic. On the other hand, he did not wish to reject the heart of the Parisian method along with the polemical excrescences that Muret had affixed to it. Literary texts had to be interpreted in a literary fashion; textual criticism was not enough. In a way, his Catullus amounted to a re-uniting of the sundered halves of Poliziano's original programme.

Scaliger did more than put existing methods together. He also invented a completely new one. He argued that all the

manuscripts of Catullus were descended from one lost archetype.
As he wrote,

Now that manuscript which we employed, and which we have already
mentioned, seems to me to be far superior to the other manuscripts of this
poet. All of them, however, were copied from one exemplar. That exemplar,
found in France by someone from Verona, engendered all those manuscripts
of the poet which exist in Italy.

He further argued that it was possible to reconstruct several
characteristics of the lost archetype. It had been written in a
difficult minuscule, so that the scribes of the extant manuscripts
made many errors: 'But I surmise that the French exemplar was
written in Lombardic script. For the errors, which were spread
about in the later manuscripts by ignorant scribes, seem definitely
to have sprung from that wretched script.' It was even possible
to reconstruct the spelling habits of the scribe of the archetype.
For the archaic forms which he had used also deceived later
copyists:

Moreover, not only the script, but also the archaic word-forms resulted in
mistakes. For the scribe had consistently written QVOR [for *cur*], QVOM
[for *cum*], LVDEI [for *ludi*], LVCEI [for *luci*], ADEPTA'S [for *adepta
es*], M'ALIUS [for *me alius*], . . .[52]

Scaliger's contention that all surviving manuscripts of Catullus
were descended from one archetype written in Lombardic script
and preserving archaic and unusual forms, was pursued in detail
in his commentary. He argued that later scribes must have confused *a* with *u*, tall *i* with *l*, and *c* with both *g* and *t* in copying
the archetype.[53] Therefore, the forms of the confused letters
must have been similar in the script of the archetype. Scaliger
used this palaeographical theory to explain the origin of many
corruptions. At 6.12, for example, he emended the reading of
his manuscript, 'Nam mi ista praevalet', to 'Nam, ni stupra,
valet'. A scribe, he explained, had misread the *u* in *stupra* as an
a: 'in this book *u* was often written instead of *a*. And Lombardic
script does not distinguish between these two letters.'[54]

These details were not pure invention. So far as the forms of
individual letters are concerned, he based his hypothetical lost
archetype on a manuscript which he had actually used — the
ninth-century Visigothic manuscript V of Ausonius. It was
while studying this manuscript that Scaliger had first become
interested in letter forms.[55] Moreover, the script of this manuscript has all the characteristics which Scaliger attributed to the

lost Catullus manuscript: *a* and *u*, tall *i* and *l*, *c* and *t*, *c* and *g* can all be easily mistaken for one another.[56] The Leiden Ausonius is a concrete embodiment of the Catullus archetype imagined by Scaliger.

He identified the archaic forms that he thought the archetype had contained in much the same way that he reconstructed its script — except that direct analogy with V played no great role. He emended the reading of his manuscript to what he thought was a genuine archaic form that could easily have deceived a scribe. At 55.16, for example, his manuscript read 'committe, crede lucet', which is obviously a corruption. An earlier scribe, he argued, must have misread the reading of the archetype, which was 'committe, crede lucei'. He had not realized that the unfamiliar *lucei* was merely an archaic form of *luci*: 'In the French exemplar, I think it was *Lucei*, in the old way of writing.'[57] As emended, the line made perfect sense, for, as Scaliger pointed out, *committere luci* was an idiom meaning 'to reveal'.[58]

Similar arguments about the script and spelling of the archetype filled Scaliger's notes. In the end, the picture he drew of the hypothetical lost archetype was clearer in many respects than his account of the manuscript he had actually collated. He was certainly more interested in the palaeographical details of the lost archetype than in those of his own manuscript.

Scaliger's arguments were not all valid. Timpanaro has shown that he committed a logical error in claiming that characteristics of the archetype could be reconstructed from errors common to all the extant manuscripts. All scribes would not have made exactly the same errors. If all the manuscripts contain them, then they must have been present in the archetype as well. The identical letter-forms and archaic spellings that gave rise to the errors must have been not in the archetype but in the exemplar from which the archetype was copied.[59] In the second place, his corrections were often incorrect. Sometimes he labelled as corrupt readings that have turned out to be perfectly valid. More often the corruptions that he saw were real, but his suggested emendations were either impossible or at least less likely than others.[60] Thirdly, his excessive love for archaic forms often led him to find archaisms where none need have been. In 55.22 his manuscript read *nostri* instead of the correct *vestri*. 'One must be devoid of common sense', he wrote, 'not to see that this must read "*Dum vostri sim particeps amoris.*"'[61] Catullus and the scribe of the archetype, he thought, had used the archaic form *vostri* instead of the classical *vestri*. Later scribes, not recognizing the archaism, had misread *vostri* as *nostri*: 'For those who changed *vostri* to *nostri* did not keep in mind that this author's diction is archaic.'[62] In fact, it is unnecessary to assume that the archetype read *vostri*. In most scripts, the abbreviation for *noster* and *vester* are nearly identical. *Vester* is usually abbreviated as *ūr*, *noster* as *n̄r*. *Vestri* is *ūri*, *nostri* is *n̄ri*. Scribes often mistook them for one another. Consequently, one need not assume that Catullus or an ancient scribe wrote *voster* in order to explain why a later scribe wrote *noster* where the context demanded *vester*.[63]

Here too what Scaliger tried to do was more important than whether he succeeded or failed. His attempt to reconstruct the characteristics of a lost archetype was highly original. The Italians had shown how to identify an extant *archetypus* by putting manuscripts in genealogical order, but none of them had tried in print to project the idea of the archetype into the past, or to draw analogies from extant manuscripts in order to reconstruct a lost one.[64]

This innovation can be seen to be Scaliger's most original attempt to synthesize the methods of the jurists with those of the philologists. In the tradition of philology there was no precedent for so detailed an effort at reconstruction of a lost witness. As we saw, Scaliger's own early attempts at philological reconstruction were not intended to serve even historical ends. But in the legal humanism of Scaliger's time there were many precedents for them. Baudouin had called for the reconstruction of lost historical sources on which the extant sources had drawn. In practice, moreover, he had tried to learn as much as possible about the banquet-songs in which were preserved Roman traditions about the early history of the city, and which the classical Roman historians might have used (in the end, he decided that they had not done so).[65]

Furthermore, the reconstruction of what was lost had been the speciality of Cujas, Scaliger's guide to mastery of legal science. Instead of a group of medieval manuscripts, Cujas worked on the *Digest* of Justinian. Just like Scaliger, he set out to decompose by analysis the evidence that lay before him and to reconstruct from it the original works which Justinian and Tribonian had cut apart. Scaliger put together scattered instances of confused letter-forms in order to reconstruct the script of a lost archetype. Cujas put together scattered fragments of opinions in order to reconstruct the lost works of a Roman jurisconsult.[66] Each was setting out to reverse the process by which a product of Roman culture had been corrupted. Each did so by considering the process of corruption as a historical problem. By working out how the corruption occurred, they could arrive at the incorrupt original.

True, Scaliger never said either that his work on the archetype of Catullus was historical, or that it was prompted by legal historians of the preceding generation. But there is other evidence to suggest that he was as eager as Le Roy or Cujas to apply historical method to a wide variety of phenomena. In his *Coniectanea* on Varro, he had tried to study the way in which Latin words developed from Greek.[67] In his *De emendatione temporum* of 1583, he would reconstruct each ancient calendar from the references to it, often fragmentary, in ancient historians, poets, and scholiasts — just as he reconstructed a lost archetype on the basis of errors preserved in extant manuscripts.[68] In the 1590s he would try to reconstruct the original 'linguae matrices' from which the European languages of his own time had developed. In the *Thesaurus temporum* of 1606, he would argue that all ancient alphabets arose out of the Phoenician.[69] All these reconstructions rested on the same 'demand for a genetic causal link'.[70] All rested on the same principle: that all things, poetic texts as well as alphabets, change in the course of time, giving rise to apparently different progeny, and that it is the scholar's duty to uncover the identical origin of these progeny by identifying their real similarities.[71]

Scaliger transformed the art of criticism. He showed that a critical edition could not rest on a genealogical examination of the extant manuscripts alone. Rather, it had to rest on a reconstructed history of the textual tradition; and where the oldest manuscripts were no longer extant, errors in the surviving ones and even literary evidence had to.be called into play. He had thus arrived at the fundamental insight of nineteenth-century German critics like Jacob Bernays and Karl Lachmann, who made Scaliger's method the accepted one.[72] When Lachmann, in 1850, reconstructed the lost archetype of Lucretius, 'telling his astounded contemporaries how many pages it had, and how many lines to the page',[73] he was doing in more detail what Scaliger had done almost three centuries before.

Scaliger did for Tibullus and Propertius more or less what he had done for Catullus. The nature of their poems imposed differences of emphasis: as Propertius was the more erudite and allusive, Scaliger paid more attention to his use of Greek sources.[74] The nature of Scaliger's working materials also imposed differences. For Propertius he had only the one fifteenth-century manuscript. For Tibullus, on the other hand, he had Cujas's fragment, which apparently began at III.iv.65, and also a manuscript of excerpts. Accordingly, he made much play with the great age of his sources. 'Therefore', he wrote, after describing the *fragmentum Cuiacianum*: 'we have outdone the Italians in one regard: we have obtained older remains of this poet than they did.'[75] But for the most part, he was merely cutting the same cloth to fit slightly different shapes.

He continued to make the same mistakes, in particular, to cite his manuscripts inaccurately and imprecisely. In the first edition he wrote, at Tibullus III.iv.65: 'SAEVVS *amor docuit*) This elegy is to be found along with the whole [third] book, and the fourth as well, in the library of Cujas', even though he had rightly described the fragment in the introduction to his commentary as extending 'from the fourth elegy of the third book down to the end'.[76] In later editions he changed the note on III.iv.65 to read 'This elegy, along with *the rest of* the third book (my italics)'.[77] But he never ironed out all the inconsistencies. And the reader often could not know for certain whether a given Tibullan reading came from the *fragmentum*, the newer Cujas manuscript, or the *florilegium* that Scaliger had also consulted. At IV.vi.19, for instance, he noted in his collation that the word *veniet* was found in *v* — *v* being the siglum by which he referred to Cujas's newer manuscript. In his published notes he said that *veniet* was 'in libris nostris' — 'in our manuscripts'. The reader therefore had no way of knowing that *veniet* was only the reading of the newer manuscript; and decades later Nicholas Heinsius, one of the most acute of Scaliger's readers, was fooled by this ambiguity.[78] Similarly, at IV.xi.5 he noted in his collation that the reading of the *fragmentum* was *At*, while that of the newer codex was *Ah*. But his published note said only that 'Our manuscripts read *Ah mihi* . . . '.[79] Here too design outran execution.

The most important continuity between Scaliger's work on these texts and that on Catullus was in the realm of critical theory. For both Tibullus and Propertius he tried to reconstruct textual histories. In both, he argued, both individual couplets and larger sections of poems had been transposed. In Propertius, he argued explicitly, these transpositions had been the work of the scribe who wrote the archetype:

Propertius was discovered within the memory of our grandfathers in a wine cellar. From this manuscript all the extant Italian codices were copied. That is why no old copy of the poet is to be found. The man who first copied it, whoever he was, was terribly foolhardy or careless. For in addition to the horrible corruptions with which he besprinkled this outstanding poet's entire book, he committed a great crime when in the second and third books he removed whole pages and a great many verses from their proper places, plunging many, many passages into obscurity.[80]

Scaliger set about discovering and correcting these transpositions with great energy. His new confidence in his ability to reconstruct texts historically led him to take a step that he had not taken when he discovered transpositions in the *Appendix Vergiliana*: he rearranged the texts of the poems themselves in accordance with his theory about their transmission.[81] It was no exaggeration when he called his work a *nova editio* of Catullus, Tibullus, and Propertius. That is just what it was: not a polished-up vulgate but a completely altered edition of the text.

Scaliger has often been criticized by nineteenth- and twentieth-century scholars for these high-handed tactics. The incoherences that he detected, they argue, were not really present. Propertius and Tibullus had written in a style which seemed disjointed and abrupt by sixteenth-century standards. Scaliger read them in his terms rather than their own; his corrections of their texts were really attempts to improve the poets. And he offered no explanation of how or why a scribe could have made such gross errors. Hence, his editions of Tibullus and Propertius are often cited as examples of his rashness and of the crudity of his critical methods.[82]

These criticisms miss one historically interesting point. Scaliger did have one piece of evidence for his theory. In *Tristia* II, Ovid adapted a long section from Tibullus (I.vi.5–32). He then wrote, describing Tibullus' teachings on love:

> Scit cui latretur, quum solus obambulat ipse,
>   Cur totiens clausas excreet ante fores.

('He knows at whom the dog barks, when he walks out alone, and why he coughs so often before the closed door.')

(459–460)

Scaliger took this couplet as a summary of Tibullus I.v.71–6, a not dissimilar passage.[83] He inferred that in Ovid's time, I.v.71–6 had followed directly after I.vi.5–32.[84] In short, he had historical grounds for thinking that the texts of the elegists might have suffered from transpositions, even if he did not have a plausible explanation for them.[85]

Furthermore, by forming his text of the poets in accordance with his theory of their transmission, Scaliger was not rash but consistent. He was showing, as he had in the Catullus, that the editor must begin in every case by reconstructing the history of his text, and that that history must be the basis of his editorial practice. The more detailed aspects of his reconstruction of the Catullus archetype were not generally applicable; but such an attempt at reconstruction was a necessary preliminary in all cases.

In the edition of the *tresviri amoris* Scaliger created a new synthesis of French and Italian methods, adding to them a touch of the jurists' historical methods. This synthesis was applicable to editing any text, whether literary or technical, with equal relevance. It did not depend entirely on the availability of new manuscript evidence. An editor could use other sorts of evidence, if all the manuscripts at his disposal were corrupt, to arrive at a lost anterior stage in the transmission of his text: the stage that most closely approximated that in which the author had left it. Scaliger had also finally created a work that took no unfair advantage of the ideas of others. He had learned much from Vettori, but he had taken over Vettori's insistence on open admission of debts along with his method of recording collations, and he freely owned himself Vettori's disciple. Here was Poliziano's method, recast in a more generally applicable form and in an acceptable literary genre, the systematic set of *castigationes* on a text.

Unfortunately, Scaliger immediately ceased to employ his synthesis of historical and philological method. For in 1577 to 1578 he suffered yet another humiliation, that sent him into a new set of allegiances. At the same time, an encounter with new disciplines stimulated him to attempt a different and, perhaps, even more original work of historical reconstruction.

VII Scaliger's Manilius:
From Philology to Cultural History

Early in 1577 Scaliger's interests began to shift again. He was largely confined to the company of his friend Vertunien, to whom he gave lessons in Greek. Since Vertunien was a doctor, it was only natural that the works they read included a medical text as well as a book of the Greek Anthology. Vertunien recalled their lessons years later:

During the first Estates of Blois, in the first war of the *Ligue*, we both withdrew to Touffou, an estate four leagues from this city [of Poitiers], which belonged to the late M. de la Rochepozay. Lying down in his room, he [Scaliger] told me that to make me expert in Greek, there was no better way than to make translations from one language into the other. Accordingly, he had me translate Hippocrates' book *On Wounds to the Head*. . . . And every evening, as he went to bed, he translated one or two of the epigrams from Book VII of the Anthology for me word for word. I was to return them to him the next day in Latin verse. As for him, when he first woke up he made his translations in his head; that was the only way he ever wrote his poems. But as for me — I am a very bad poet — I worked very hard, making two and three drafts by candle-light so that I could give him [a version] in the morning. Once I had finished it and he had corrected it for me, he had me take down his version. Thus in the nine or ten months that we were in exile there, we finished the whole book.[1]

Book VII of the Anthology was nothing new to Scaliger. But reading Hippocrates reawakened in him a long-standing interest in natural science, one that had expressed itself in several letters to Vertunien and to the Plinian scholar Jacques Daléchamps.[2] He decided that he had found a new and crucial key to the interpretation of the Hippocratic text. It was riddled with interpolated words and phrases, which previous editors had failed to notice. Scaliger worked through it twice, the second time more carefully. He made a number of emendations and excised both words and phrases, dictating to Vertunien a few notes on specially problematic or interesting points.[3] Vertunien prepared a Latin translation of and commentary on the corrected text, which were well advanced by 30 June and complete by the end of the year. Mamert Patisson printed them, along with Scaliger's comments and the Greek text, during 1578.[4]

Characteristically, Scaliger did not confine his notes to philological questions. He identified the inconsistencies, irrelevancies, and Ionic forms that 'tortores isti', the scribes, had introduced. He also crowed about his prowess in divination.[5] He ridiculed the medical men who had dealt with the text before him and had failed to notice the interpolations:

How did the infinite number of excrescences that so terribly distort this little book escape the notice of those learned men? Many men have studied it with close attention, and some have published commentaries on it in Latin or French . . . All, to put it in a nutshell, have wasted their time. For they failed to notice all the spurious material which complete incompetents have stuffed in here.

Indeed, he went so far as to claim that mere doctors could not hope to understand or correct texts. 'From this', he wrote: 'the careful reader may gather how vain it is for those ignorant of this study of criticism to attempt literary works.'[6]

Long before, Scaliger had tried to convince Vertunien of the antiquity and authority of criticism in a personal letter:

There is no reason for you followers of Asclepius to boast of the antiquity of your Medicine . . . The branch of learning that the ignorant call Grammar — and that they do not understand — it too, I say, has its ancient champions, Linus, Palamedes, Cadmus, and others . . . [The highest branch of criticism] winds its way into the hidden shrines of wisdom, when, that is, it separates the spurious verses of the poets from their true and genuine ones, corrects what is corrupt, claims what is misattributed for its true authors; works on and polishes all sorts of Poets, Orators, Philosophers.[7]

These claims Scaliger now developed in public and polemical statements. The critic, he claimed, could do much to heal the wounds of a text even if he had not been trained in the technical skills it treated: *Nam sola Critice sine Anatomia rem transegerit.* Anyone who denied Scaliger's contentions must be 'thick as a post'; even a *mediocris grammaticus* would see the validity of his diagnosis.[8]

These claims were not tactful, and their context made them even more wounding. Vertunien repeated Scaliger's abuse of the doctors in the preface to his commentary:

I shall try to restore Hippocrates' true meaning, using Scaliger's emendations. [I shall] show everyone how far all the doctors and surgeons who have dealt with this work — men admirable in other respects — were from under-standing Hippocrates, because of their ignorance of the art of Criticism.[9]

In his preface to the whole work, Vertunien also promised to translate the rest of Hippocrates' *Opera* as emended by Scaliger. He claimed once again to have exposed the errors 'that earlier translators introduced because of their ignorance of the art of criticism' — though he admitted their contribution to medicine.[10]

Vertunien's and Scaliger's work amounted to more than a new edition of Hippocrates on wounds to the head; it was itself a blow to the head of the medical profession. It was a manifesto that proclaimed that the doctors did not know how to interpret the authoritative classical texts on which their claims to pro-fessional authority rested.

What made matters worse was that here, as elsewhere, Scaliger claimed more than he deserved. He was right to say that the treatise contained interpolations. But he was hardly the first to notice them. In fact, Galen himself had pointed out that non-Hippocratean material on the influence of airs, waters, and places had crept into the last part of the treatise.[11] The Renaissance editors of Hippocrates knew this Galen passage. In both the 1526 Aldine edition of Hippocrates' *Opera* and the 1538 Basel edition — the text that Scaliger used — this material was set off from the body of the work by a space and a legend in Greek: 'Galen says that this was added to the book.'[12] At the very end of the work, a second, shorter section (the last section of the currently accepted text) was also set off by a space and labelled as spurious in both editions.[13] The Florentine physician Guido Guidi, who published a translation of the work in 1550, had ex-posed another interpolation that occurred at the beginning of the work, at least in the Latin translation by Fabio Calvo.[14] An anonymous edition of the Greek text of the work that appeared at Paris in 1556 simply omitted the material on airs, waters, and places.[15] Janus Cornarius also left it out of his 1558 translation of Hippocrates' works.[16] And Gabriele Falloppia, who published a very detailed *In Hippocratis librum de vulneribus capitis ex-positio* in 1566, also discussed textual interpolations at some length, consulting manuscripts of the Greek original to prove his points.[17]

Vertunien and Scaliger could not deny these facts. As to Galen, Vertunien offered a limp excuse: he had only happened on the relevant passage after Scaliger independently discovered the interpolations: 'Our Aristarchus, Scaliger, smelled these [additions] out [and] explained them, as you see. By chance I then happened on this passage by Galen. Scaliger was greatly pleased that he had divined even as he skimmed along something that Galen himself had noticed.'[18] As to Guidi and Falloppia, Vertunien ungraciously admitted only what could not be denied: they had preceded him in calling attention to the interpolations at the beginning of the work.[19]

What apparently did not occur to either Scaliger or Vertunien was that their claims sounded somewhat arrogant, given that they had merely elaborated upon a discovery made by the very doctors they despised. Presumably both knew that their work was bound to provoke controversy of a sort. But they seem to have been unprepared for the sharpness of the doctors' response. Louis Duret, a professor in the Collège Royal, had cured Scaliger by blood-letting in 1575.[20] He was enraged by Scaliger's sneers at his colleagues — especially, perhaps, by the ingratitude they showed. He tried to have the edition suppressed; he claimed that Scaliger had plagiarized from him; and he induced a younger doctor, Jean Martin, to denounce the book in public lectures.[21]

Scaliger had his revenge. In a wicked pseudonymous pamphlet he tore Duret apart for everything from slipping from Latin into French while lecturing to relying supinely on grammars and dictionaries.[22] Martin fared even worse. He had had the poor judgement to attack Scaliger's interpretation of a passage from Herodotus (I.74) and the even poorer judgement to interpret the ὅρκια (oaths) mentioned there as Bacchic orgies. 'This most learned master of the Parisian school', wrote Scaliger:

this second Duret, this pillar of the art of medicine, translates ὅρκια as 'orgies of Bacchus'. O poor Scaliger, who removed so much spurious matter from Hippocrates but did not notice this priestly rite, invented by Martin the Bacchant. What oblivion can poor Joseph now seek for himself and his art of criticism, which he vainly asks the Parisians to consider? Now Martin will be the master of the orgy. Why does he want to be a doctor when he has made so much progress in the orgies of Bacchus? O wretched lexica, where were you when Martin translated ὅρκια as orgies? Curse you for not helping him in his time of need.[23]

Having crushed Martin, Scaliger sprayed a final burst of venom over Duret's translation of the Aphorisms of Hippocrates, the Latin style of which, he remarked, 'has a certain divine quality to it'.[24]

The polemic was undeniably amusing. For our purposes it is

also important, because of the attitude that it reveals: namely, that Scaliger was more competent than professional scientists to explicate and correct classical scientific texts. For it was while he was engaged in the polemic over Hippocrates that Scaliger came across the copy of Manilius' *Astronomica* that he had worked on while in Geneva.[25] He decided that this text too had been either neglected or mistreated by modern practitioners of its subject. Hence, it too called for the ministrations that only a critic with Scaliger's gifts could provide. 'I know', he wrote to Dupuy: 'that there are great astrologers and mathematicians in France today. But I bet that they will be long in divining Manilius' meaning in these difficult passages.'[26] In short, even at its outset the new work had a polemical edge to it.

Events honed this edge. The doctors found allies among the philologists in their campaign against Scaliger. Jean Passerat, *lecteur royal* and friend of Ronsard, ridiculed Scaliger's Catullus all over Paris.[27] Scaliger, confined as he was to Touffou, could only foam impotently at the mouth. He was livid at the thought that a mere teacher, 'who had read only eight books', should dare to defame *un homme bien nourri*. 'So long as I live', he promised Dupuy, 'I shall make war on pedants.'[28] But even this threat did not prevent the notorious Cicero scholar Simeon Bosius (Dubois) from joining the chorus of Scaliger's critics with yet another series of sarcastic remarks about the Catullus.[29]

Still more wounding were the comments that now began to filter back from Italy. When he praised Vettori in the Catullus, Scaliger did not know for certain — though he clearly had his worries — what Vettori thought of his earlier works. No doubt he hoped that the boldness of his conjectures had not blinded Vettori to his learning and assiduity. In the event, Vettori saw Scaliger's works as another confirmation of his worst fears about French philology. One Ioannes Bisonnerius, who visited Florence during the spring of 1575, wrote as follows to Muret:

But to come to Pier Vettori, whom I saw at Florence, you should be aware that he seemed to me to have some sort of personal quarrel with you. For although I mentioned you several times, he would not respond at all. But he severely criticized those with whom conjectures weigh more heavily than authority [scil. manuscript] in correcting the writings of good authors. And on that ground he seriously reproves Joseph Scaliger, because he makes assertions in his *Coniectanea* on Varro so boldly that it seems as if he had spoken with Varro himself. Vettori argued that one should rarely or never depart from authority. Conjectures, like false witnesses . . . should be completely abhorred.[30]

Just in the period from 1576 on, Scaliger's patron Louis de Chasteigner was in an excellent position to inform Scaliger about Vettori's views, for he was serving as French ambassador in Rome.[31] There he spent a good deal of time with Muret, who read several classical texts with him.[32] He knew Orsini well enough to try (unsuccessfully) to have one of his works printed by Mamert Patisson.[33] He exchanged stately, empty letters with Vettori himself.[34] Naturally, Vettori spoke no evil — at least in the extant letters — of his exalted correspondent's protégé. But it was in the clear interest of Muret — whom Scaliger had, after all, attacked on behalf of Vettori — to see to it that Chasteigner learned of Vettori's views. For if he passed them on to Scaliger, a second conversion might well result. Very likely something along these lines happened. True, there is no solid evidence as to the channel of transmission. But we know that Scaliger heard something, for he quickly repented of the homage that he had offered Vettori. He bitterly complained to the Florentine exile Jacopo Corbinelli that Vettori had denigrated his works and called Turnèbe a barbarian.[35]

I do not know what Vettori thought of the Catullus edition. But it may well have seemed to him less an act of homage to his work than a parody of it. At least one Italian steeped in Vettori's principles disapproved of the work: namely, Guido Lolgi, who had collated manuscripts of Livy and Terence with Faerno, and who claimed that the Catullus had cost Scaliger 'mezza la riputatione'.[36] Other allies of Vettori's may also have criticized the work. Dupuy's Paduan friend Giovanni Vincenzo Pinelli — not Vettori's man, but one *au courant* and in sympathy with his work — described the edition as too rash, and expressed a pious hope that Scaliger would proceed more temperately in the Hippocrates.[37] And in any case, given Scaliger's sense of what his honour required of him, even a report of Vettori's criticism of his early work could have been enough to break him of his recently-acquired allegiance.

Accordingly, Scaliger set out to make his Manilius a declaration of yet another change of editorial principles. In a caustic preface he said just what he now thought of the Italians.[38] But he wanted to dedicate the edition to Henri III. Sensible men did not present attacks on Florentine scholars to the son of Catherine de' Medici. So he suppressed the preface, which survives only in a summary of it by Corbinelli.[39] The work itself nevertheless clearly reveals his intentions. It is both an assertion of the critic's supremacy in the study of ancient texts and a rejection of Vettori's critical method.

This interpretation does not quite agree with the standard judgement of Bernays and, following him, Pattison. They argued that Scaliger was not especially interested in emending the text. Rather, he wished to use it as a 'Leitfaden für Darstellung der alten Astronomie' — 'a peg on which to hang a representation of the astronomical system of the first century AD'.[40] We shall see that these views, though partly true, are greatly exaggerated. For, as Housman remarked, anyone who reads Scaliger's Manilius can see that emending the text was one of his central concerns.[41] Moreover, it is clear from Scaliger's letters in French, which were not available to Bernays, that Scaliger began by working on textual problems. As we saw, he found the printed text in which he had entered some emendations in 1573. 'I thought', he wrote to Dupuy on 30 June 1577:

that there were some quite apposite things [in the annotations]. I shall try to see to it as best I can, and to cleanse an author so corrupt as he is. Then you will be the judge, if you will, and M. Houllier, who is not unaware of how hard it is to correct an author who speaks of nothing but numbers and equations of planetary hours with equinoctial hours.[42]

This passage is revealing in two ways. It confirms the thesis that Scaliger began by trying to correct the text. It also shows that at this point Scaliger still regarded astrology from the standpoint of an outsider, seeing it as something rich but strange, and made all the stranger by its forbidding technical terminology.

Scaliger's letters enable us to watch the development of his interest in and knowledge of ancient astronomy. As late as 31 July 1577, he had not seen the Greek text of Ptolemy's *Tetrabiblos* or the Greek scholia on it — works which, as we shall see, were to be crucial to his thinking about the history of astronomy and astrology. He had to ask Dupuy to lend him copies.[43] These he received by 26 August.[44] Between then and 10 March 1578, when he sent his work to Paris for publication, he produced his extensive commentary on the corrected text and worked out his elaborate thesis about the nature and sources of Manilius' doctrines.

In order to approach the Manilius historically, I shall begin, like Scaliger, with the text proper, the foundation on which any interpretation had to rest. From there I shall proceed, as he did, to the general exegetical problems that it posed. Only then will we be in a position to evaluate the nature, scope, and originality of his views on the history of astronomy. These, in turn, will help us to understand more fully the motives that drove him to produce so complex, subtle, and difficult a piece of work.

The correction of Manilius required, not the literary taste that Scaliger lacked, but the training in formal rhetoric and poetics that his father had given him and the solid knowledge of technical disciplines that he had acquired on his own. His Manilian emendations show him very nearly at his best — inventive, resourceful, and, for the most part, patiently attentive to the details of the text before him.

Not all of Scaliger's emendations demand unstinted praise, however. It did not take a Scaliger to see that the scribes had frequently replaced *census*, a word Manilius liked, with the more common *sensus*. Nevertheless, this insight enabled him to restore I.12 and II.69 to their proper readings:

et cupit aetherios per carmina pandere census

('And it [the world] wishes to lay open the wealth of the heavens through poetry.')

ac tantum mundi regeret prudentia censum

('And [unless] prudence governed the great riches of the world . . .').[45]

As Housman rightly pointed out, 'such corrections are less of an honour to Scaliger than a shame to his predecessors.'[46]

It is more impressive to follow Scaliger through one of the clusters of apt conjectures that burst like fireworks from some pages of his commentary, shedding a brilliant light on passages where all had once been darkness. Consider the following set of notes that occur early in Book III, where Manilius described the twelve *sortes* or *athla*, the divisions of a circle that the astrologer superimposed on the original horoscope in accordance with a complex set of rules, and which determined 'the various activities, experiences, and circumstances'[47] of the life of his client:

Nonus locus occupat omnem Fatorum sortem [III.131-2]) Write, *Natorum sortem* ['the whole lot of children']. For he says that it [the ninth *sors*] contains the raising and education of children.
Omniaque intrantum [III.133]) Read *infantum*. . . .
Nunc oppressa movent [III.141]) The punctuation is wrong. Read:
  Quaque valetudo constat nunc libera morbis,
  Nunc oppressa, movent ut mundum sidera cunque.
('It [the eleventh *sors*] controls one's health, keeping one free of disease or infected, however the stars move the world.')
Non alias sedes [III.142])

This is also incorrect. It should be cleansed as follows:

Non alia est sedes, tempusve genusve gerendi
Quae sibi deposcat;

('There is no other station [than this one] that claims control over the time and manner of taking action.')[48]

What intervention on this scale meant for the text can easily be seen if we compare two versions of the passage to which these notes of Scaliger's refer: namely, Pruckner's text of 1551, which served as Scaliger's base, and Scaliger's own, with his emendations incorporated.

Pruckner:	*Scaliger:*
III.131–44 nonus locus	Nonus locus occupat omnem
occupat omnem	
Fatorum sortem dubiam,	Natorum sortem dubiam, patri-
patriosque timores,	osque timores,
Omniaque intrantum mixta	Omniaque infantum mista nu-
nutritia turba.	tricia turba.
Huic vicinus erit vitae qui	Huic vicinus erit, vitae qui
continet actum,	continet actum,
In quo servorum mores, et	In quo servorum mores, et
qualibet omnis	qualibet omnis
Formetur domus exemplis,	Formetur domus exemplis,
quoque ordine certo	quoque ordine certo
Ad sua compositi discedant	Ad sua compositi discedant
munera servi.	munera servi.
Praecipua undecima pars est in	Praecipua undecima pars est in
sorte locata,	sorte locata,
Quae summam nostri semper,	Quae summam nostri semper,
viresque gubernat.	viresque gubernat.
Quaque valetudo constat nunc	Quaque valetudo constat nunc
libera morbis,	libera morbis,
Nunc oppressa movent, et	Nunc oppressa, movent ut
mundum sidera, cumque	Mundum sidera cunque.
Non alias sedes tempusve	Non alia est sedes, tempusve
genusve medendi,	genusve medendi
Quae sibi deposcat, vel cuius	Quae sibi deposcat, vel cuius
tempore praestet	tempore praestet
Auxilium, et vitae succos	Auxilium, et vitae succos
miscere salubreis.	miscere salubreis.

It would be hard for two versions of the same passage to differ more. Pruckner's text, one soon discovers, reads as if no one had ever tried to edit it. Impossible readings and unintelligent punctuation combine to make the passage nearly impossible to understand. What are the things 'intrantum mixta nutricia turba' — 'mixed up with the nursing tribe of those who enter'? What does *oppressa* in line 141 modify — *valetudo*, as the parallel adjective *libera* would suggest, or *sidera*, as the punctuation indicates? And how can one possibly construe the relative pronoun *Quae* in 143, if the clause in which it occurs begins with *cumque*? To read a text in this condition is approximately as pleasant and rewarding as walking barefoot through a field of nettles.

Scaliger's version is far from perfect, but it is dramatically better than Pruckner's. The mysterious crowd of nursing entrants has become, thanks to a happy conjecture, the crowd of things involved in the raising of children (*infantum* for *intrantum*). The repunctuation of 140-1 makes the reference of *libera* and *oppressa* immediately clear. Scaliger has made the passage yield a continuous sense — a fundamental service that his predecessors had certainly not provided. He has done more. He has restored characteristic Manilian turns of thought and language. Thus, by restoring the phrase *movent ut mundum sidera cunque* in 141, he has provided a neat determinist parallel to line 126, *sidera ut inclinant vires et templa gubernant* ('as the planets modify and the temples govern the powers of this *athlum*') — and a neat linguistic echo for 119, *utcunque regunt dominantia sidera* ('as the ruling stars dictate'). Similarly, *Non alia est sedes* not only makes line 142 construable, as *Non alias sedes* had not; it also restores a characteristic Manilian device, a positive statement formulated in a negative way — a neat and necessary method for filling out many lines. Scaliger's text, in short, was the first that readers of Manilius had ever seen to offer a continuous sense, a coherent doctrine, and a consistent poetic diction. If there are long passages where his first edition did not need to make major changes in Pruckner's text, there is no book that does not contain many passages as richly altered for the better as the one we have examined.[49] Often, too, the bursts of small lights break off to admit a single spectacular flare. Consider the note on IV.688:

Thebas divisit rege vel uno] We have corrected this to: — *Thebae divis, et rege vel uno Thessalia, Epirusque potens* ('Thebes great in its gods, and Thessalia great even in one of its kings, and powerful Epirus'). For the city of Thebes was the nursery of the gods Bacchus, Melicerta, and Hercules . . . *Thebae divis et rege vel uno*: Sophocles, as quoted in Dicaearchus' *Description of Greece*: 'You speak to me of the seven-mouthed gates of Thebes, the only place where mortal women have given birth to gods.'[50]

This splendid correction has since been confirmed by manuscript evidence that Scaliger did not know when he proposed it. Readers of Housman's *editio maior* will be aware that it is by no means unique in the work.

Scaliger knew that he was reshaping Manilius. Without hesitation he entered both emendations and directions for the rearrangement of transposed lines and passages into the copy of Pruckner's 1551 edition that he prepared as a *texte belge* for his printers.[51] On the title-page he boldly declared that he was solely responsible for this genuinely new recension of the text: *Iosephus Scaliger Iul. Caes. F. recensuit ac pristino ordini suo restituit.* Though he sometimes characterized his conjectures as suggestions, any attentive reader could see that such disclaimers were the commonplaces of false modesty. 'Mirum hoc, bis mirum', Isaac Casaubon commented in the margin of his copy at one such passage: 'While the great man admits that he makes this correction with hesitation, he nevertheless dared to thrust forward his own conjectures — which he himself describes as doubtful — as the true reading, as though they were some sort of oracle.'[52] Qualified contemporaries soon took something of the measure of his achievement. The esoterist and Orientalist Guy le Fèvre de la Boderie was working on a French translation of Manilius I when he received a copy of the new edition from Scaliger. He wrote at once to offer thanks and praise: 'So far as I could tell at first sight — for I have not had the time to read him through — Manilius has certainly had a complete change of dress.'[53] Four more centuries of critical work have served to pile up impressive confirmations of these first impressions. Housman found more than two hundred of Scaliger's emendations worthy of acceptance into his text or approval in his apparatus.[54] Few would quarrel with his summary evaluation: 'Perhaps no critic has ever effected so great and permanent a change in any author's text as Scaliger in Manilius'.[55]

Scaliger's work seems even more remarkable when one considers that he claimed to have completed it under a stringent self-denying ordinance. He deliberately refused to consult any manuscript evidence. As early as 1574, Giphanius had offered to procure for him a collation of the tenth- or eleventh-century Gembloux manuscript (G) of Manilius, then in the hands of the diligent but painfully slow-working Jacobus Susius.[56] This offer Scaliger did not take up. His refusal led Bernays and Pattison to see him as relatively uninterested in textual problems.[57] But their judgement was the result of insufficient attention to the work's immediate context. In fact, Scaliger's refusal stemmed from what he saw as his mistreatment at the hands of the Italians. He relied on conjectural emendation rather than manuscript evidence because he wanted to defy those who had criticized his rashness. Though he cancelled his preface, he nevertheless used one clever literary device to indicate his change of heart. Vettori's notes almost always followed the same pattern. Beginning with careful reports of the manuscript readings, he then either defended them elaborately or emended them hesitantly. Even when he suggested emendations, he tried to follow the *ductus literarum*, preferring to change only one letter. As we saw, he called these notes *castigationum explicationes* — explanations of his corrections. It is clear by now that Scaliger's notes on Manilius could not have been more different. He gave the reading, not of his own text, but of Pruckner's, as the lemma. Then he wrote 'Read' or 'Correct this to . . . ', followed by the suggested emendation. His celebrated note on I.422 is typical: '*Tumidi quoque magnos*] Mendosissime. Lege — *tum Di quoque.*'[58] Sometimes, but by no means always, he gave the reason for his emendation in a sentence or two. The manuscripts he did not mention; attention to the *ductus literarum* of the vulgate text occasionally helped him to the truth but did not prevent some remarkable flights of fancy. But he chose Vettori's favourite title for this wholly un-Vettorian effort. Among the other things that the title-page of the Manilius promises are *castigationum explicationes.*[59] Scaliger can only have chosen this title in order to emphasize the differences between his work and Vettori's.

Here too, then, an affront to Scaliger's dignity stimulated him to change his entire mode of self-presentation as a scholar — and, in consequence, his scholarly method. In 1575 to 1576 he had sought to prove his diligence and accuracy, especially in the use of manuscript material. In 1577 to 1578 he abandoned these ideals for his earlier ones of ingenuity and disdainful, aristocratic boldness.

Unfortunately, with Scaliger's early ideals there came a return to his early vice. His need to show his brilliance in conjectural emendation again led him to be less than candid about the extent to which he had drawn on the work of others and, though indirectly, on manuscript evidence. In 1576 the Flemish scholar Louis Carrion had published a set of *Antiquae lectiones.*[60] These included many readings from G, some of which Carrion passed off as his own conjectures. The evidence strongly suggests that even though Scaliger disdained to consult a full collation of G, he had no objection to helping himself from the hors-d'œuvre assembled from it by Carrion. More than forty of the alterations that Scaliger made in Pruckner's text had already been suggested by Carrion; most of them were readings of G.[61] In at least one case, moreover, the agreements are too striking to be the result of coincidence. At V.372 Pruckner's text reads:

At nitidos clamare suis ratione sedentem.

In the margin of his working copy Scaliger wrote, without hesitation: *nidis damnare suis, ramove*. He also changed *At* to *aut*. And he printed the emended form of the line in his text. What he did not say was that Carrion had already published V.372 in the same form, drawing *ramove* from the text of G and *nidis damnare* from interlinear notes in the same hand.[62] And in two other cases he took over elaborate conjectures from Turnèbe, without acknowledging — indeed, while indignantly denying — that they were not original with him.[63]

These plagiarisms — if that is the right term — detract relatively little from the originality of Scaliger's work. His own ingenuity supplied the vast majority of the emendations that have continued to win acceptance or attract serious interest. Furthermore, textual criticism — though important enough in his eyes, apparently, to warrant sharp practice — dominated neither his attention nor his exposition of the text. More than in any of his earlier editions, Scaliger concentrated on exegesis. That was the field in which he could prove his superiority to his other major set of opponents — the doctors who bulked so large among the astrological practitioners of his time. The exegetical method that he devised turned out to be one of his most original creations.

More than any of the other texts that Scaliger had edited, save perhaps the *Aetna*, the *Astronomica* called for systematic exposition. Manilius had dressed a deeply technical subject-matter in a rococo cloak of metaphors. When not squeezing long series of calculations into amusingly varied but absurdly inappropriate hexameters, he had managed to touch on a wide range of mythological, historical, and scientific matters, seldom with total clarity. Even in the later sixteenth century, when more and more scholars were trying to combine mathematical and scientific skills with the literary learning of the humanists, few could grapple seriously with the detailed problems of such a text and end up victorious; not many more could read even the simplest sections with complete ease. To explain every point in Festus would have been impossible; to do so for the elegists unnecessary. But Manilius, difficult as he was, had received only one previous commentary. That curious document of late fifteenth-century Italian polymathy, the enormous word-by-word exposition by Pico's friend Lorenzo Bonincontri, had become so rare by the 1570s that Scaliger could not buy or borrow a copy, and did not see it until after his edition was published.[64] A work so firmly out of print could hardly serve as cicerone to many. If Scaliger wished to find readers he had to provide the sort of point-by-point guidance that he had previously dismissed as elementary and uninteresting. There was no exegetical tradition to provide a context within which he could confine himself to specialized notes on select topics. Remarkably enough, he did very well at a task as unfamiliar to him as it had always seemed uncongenial.

Throughout his commentary Scaliger was a capable, indulgent, and perceptive guide. At the beginning of each book, and at other key points, he followed the traditional practice of summarizing the material to come (Bonincontri had done the same).[65] Then he took the reader by the hand and led him through the text, pausing to pull brambles out of the path and bending occasionally to pick or point out an especially pretty flower. He emphasized literary parallels in Greek and Latin.[66] He identified the recurrent patterns in Manilius' thought and diction. After repunctuating II.522-3, for example, he analysed clearly, if abruptly, Manilius' habit of closing discrete sections of his work with one-line summaries — a habit that earlier editors had disregarded, to their cost:

Linea sic veri] Place a full stop after *linea*. *Sic veri per totum* [*consonat ordo*]) This is a characteristic Manilian peroration. Compare the earlier one:
  Sic iniungunt commercia Mundi.
Sic, inquam, alternis paret natura figuris. Similarly, *Sic erit ex signis odium tibi, paxque notanda.* And so on, almost everywhere.[67]

Throughout the poem, usually by supplying brief paraphrases, he solved the mysteries that allusive and difficult phrases posed to the careful reader. One small example of this process occurs at V.65, where Manilius described the gregarious man 'who takes one word everywhere he goes'. Scaliger commented only — and rightly — 'Hoc est, Have'.[68] Again, at IV.267-8 Manilius listed among the crafts of those born under Aquarius that of 'changing the face of the universe and the seats of the stars, and turning heaven in a new rotation'.[69] Scaliger's penetrating note was only three words long: *Sphaeram Archimedeam intelligit*, 'He means Archimedes' sphere [i.e. his spherical model of the universe]' — though Scaliger unfortunately changed his mind in the second edition of his commentary, leaving the correct interpretation to be rediscovered independently by Paul Tannery in the 1890s.[70]

In one respect, Scaliger's exegetical method fell within a well-established French tradition. He followed the example of Lambin's commentary on Lucretius and Turnèbe's on Cicero's *De legibus*, and put much effort into establishing the precise sources of Manilius' philosophical doctrines. Where Manilius wrote *Cum spiritus unus / per cunctas habitat partes* ('Since one spirit inhabits all parts of the world' (II.64–65)), Scaliger rightly commented: 'This is Stoic doctrine word for word'.[71] More wisely than many nineteenth-century Germans, however, he did not exaggerate the extent to which Manilius had gone to school to Posidonius and his shadowy brethren. Some of his notes amounted to little histories of the Greeks' solutions to particularly perplexing problems — for example, that of why the universe is spherical.[72] In such cases Manilius' views found their proper place within an historical tradition that Scaliger correctly saw as too complex to be amenable to summary treatment.

Despite his tendencies to generalization and abstraction, Manilius dealt for the most part not with general concepts but with celestial bodies and their movements. Accordingly, most of Scaliger's notes treated astronomical or astrological points. What is unusual about them is not their content *per se* but the level at which they were pitched. Scaliger condescended for the first time to give his reader clear elementary treatments of technical problems — and even clear definitions of technical terms. He listed and discussed the symbols for the signs of the zodiac and the planets; for the names of the latter he even supplied a handy mnemonic verse from an unpublished Greek description of the heavens, the so-called *Sphaera Empedoclis*.[73] He displayed in a neat diagram the aspects of the signs (i.e. their geometrical configurations), and he handily tabulated the possible equilateral triangles, squares, and hexagons into which they could be grouped.[74] He even cast his own horoscope as an example for the student.[75]

Moreover, he frequently launched forth from the text into

detailed accounts of important terms, concepts, or methods. Book I, which is for the most part an elementary introduction to geocentric astronomy, led him to define basic terms at length. A full and rather repetitious page was devoted to explaining what the meridian and horizon are in astronomy, and why Manilius had treated them together.[76] Similar passages worked out Manilius' arithmetic. If anything, Scaliger showed even more patience in the exposition of astrological procedures. In Book III, for example, Manilius explained how to apply the circle of the twelve *sortes* or *athla* to that of the zodiac. To do this one need only know where to place the first *sors*, the *sors Fortunae*. The rest, being equal in length and fixed in relation, automatically find their correct places.[77] Here is Scaliger's exposition of the rule for finding the position of the *sors Fortunae* for a daytime nativity:

Count [the number of degrees] from the Sun to the Moon in the order of the signs. Count off that number of degrees from the horoscope. Where the number leaves you is the *sors Fortunae*. The ascendant is at Taurus 17;4°. The place of the Moon is in Cancer 13;6°; that of the Sun in Capricorn 4;9°. The distance of the Sun from the Moon in the order of the signs is 188;57°. If I count this off from the place of the horoscope, the number will end in Scorpio 26;1°. There is the *sors Fortunae*.[78]

With Scaliger's help, even the rare reader who had never worked through the *Sphere* of Sacrobosco or a *Theorica planetarum* could fight his way through Manilius' thorniest descriptions and directions.

Like a good guide, too, Scaliger did not hesitate to supply background information. He drew heavily on other astrological works: the *Mathesis* of Firmicus Maternus, the *Tetrabiblos* of Ptolemy, the Greek commentaries on Ptolemy and the Latin version of Abu Ma'shar that Hieronymus Wolf had published in 1559.[79] His illustrative quotations sometimes amounted to little more than interesting parallels that served to drive home an explanation. His characteristic notes on the *sors Fortunae*, for example, went on as follows:

Hermes, in the *Enchiridion*: 'When we want to find the progress of the *sors Fortunae* in the whole year of variation, we take [the distance] from the Sun to the Moon, and the same amount from the horoscope.'
Petosiris and Necepso: 'When you take the *sors Fortunae*, count the days from the Sun to the Moon, and count off the same amount from the horoscope, in the order of the signs.' This was the method of the ancients.[80]

But others clearly helped to establish a broader context for

Scaliger's text, calling attention to a good many features of ancient astrological practice, and sometimes calling the world of the ancient astrologers back to a flickering, momentary life. In I.55 Manilius remarked straightforwardly enough that astrologers had to know their clients' birth-dates. Here opportune quotation from a non-astrological source made plain a curious implication of that theoretical requirement:

Nascendi quae cuique dies] Here is Sextus Empiricus' account of the methods by which they found this out: 'For by night, they say, the Chaldean sat on a high peak watching the stars, while another man sat beside the woman in labour till she should be delivered, and when she had been delivered he signified the fact immediately to the man on the peak by means of a gong; and he, when he heard it, noted the rising Sign as that of the horoscope. But during the day he studied the horologes (or sun-dials) and the motions of the sun.'[81]

Scaliger's exegesis suffered from a number of defects, often those of its own qualities. He could explain the elementary astronomy that the reader needed, but he sometimes missed astronomical points of a rather technical kind. He could solve many of the riddles that Manilius had worked into his text, but sometimes he read into the text riddles that the author had not intended. He could often supply just the parallel that many lines required; but all too often a spurious resemblance led him to discover subtleties that Manilius had never devised, doctrines that he had never held, and mistakes that he had never made. Each point requires explication.

Scaliger's knowledge of astronomy was neither so orderly nor so deep as it was broad. A gifted and well-read amateur, he sometimes missed what would have been obvious to the professionals whom he spurned. At II.201–2, for example:

Ne mirere moras, quum Sol adversa per astra

Aestivum tardis attolit mensibus annum.

('Don't be surprised at the tarrying, when the Sun bears the summer part of the year with its slow months through signs that rise hindparts foremost.')

Scaliger commented: 'Here is a pretty invention: he uses the orientation of the signs to explain the Sun's tarrying during the long days. These things are all causeless if you consider the matter itself rather than the myths about the constellations.'[82] In the 1650s a professional astronomer, Ismael Bouillau, contributed to the third edition of Scaliger's Manilius a brief treatment of a number of textual and exegetical points. It is instructive to watch him handling these same lines:

He proposes to those untrained in geometry and unskilled in astronomy an absurd reason for the greater length of the spring and summer: namely, that Taurus, Gemini, Cancer rise facing backwards. In fact the position of the apogee of the Sun — or, as we now say, the aphelion of the Earth — which was near Gemini 10° in the time of Manilius, brought this about. By no means is the astrologer-poet devising a cause for the tarrying of the long days, as Scaliger holds; nor is he concerned with the increase in the days. He relates the [orientation of the signs] to the length of time in which the Sun passed through the northern signs, 186½ days, which were assigned to a period of six months, while the other six-month period of the southern signs was around 178½ days long. That is why the three spring months had to be called 'late'; for they, like the three summer ones, consisted of 93¼ days more or less, and passed over a longer period than the autumn and winter months, each three of which were made up of roughly 89¼ days.[83]

Bentley — like Scaliger an amateur in astronomy, but a much more expert one, whose study of the *Principia* Newton himself took seriously — neatly summed up the point that Scaliger had missed: 'The author here gives a poetic, rather than astronomical, reason why the summer portion of the year consists of 186½ days, the winter portion of around 178½, as Bouillau rightly explains.'[84] We shall see that this was by no means the only time that Scaliger's technical equipment proved inadequate to bring him *per aspera ad astra*.

If Scaliger's cleverness enabled him to penetrate a good many genuine mysteries, it also led him more than once into doing what he would have called 'seeking *nodum in scirpo* [a knot on a bulrush]' — finding subtleties where a less clever man might well have seen that all was clear. Late in Book I, Manilius gave a series of explanations, philosophical in character, for the origin of the Milky Way. Then he suggested a mythological one: Phaethon's ride in the chariot of the Sun. He then wrote:

Nec mihi celanda est vulgata fama vetusta
Mollior, e niveo lactis fluxisse liquorem
Pectore reginae divum caelumque colore
Infecisse suo; quapropter lacteus orbis
Dicitur, et nomen causa descendit ab ipsa

('Nor must I conceal an old legend softer than the well-known one: that a stream of milk flowed from the white breast of the queen of the gods and dyed the sky with its colour. Therefore it is called the Milky Way; the name derives from its real cause.' [I.750-754]).

Scaliger commented:

> By *mollior fama* he means the common legend. Rhetors persuade, philosophers demonstrate. Rhetors use epicheiremes, philosophers proofs. But rhetors also sometimes use proofs, and philosophers epicheiremes. For epicheiremes can be very effective after proofs. Thus Manilius after his proofs about the Milky Way produces epicheiremes drawn from common knowledge, such as the tales of Phaethon and of Juno's milk. Aristotle sometimes does this, and is not embarrassed to come out with common myths, not because they are true, but because they are generally derived from the truth.[85]

This interpretation reveals Scaliger at his worst. He departs much too far from the text; if both the Phaethon story and that of Juno's milk are *molliores famae*, then line 750 should precede the Phaethon story. As the text stands — and Scaliger did not change it — 750 sets a distinction between the two stories: the second is *mollior* than the first, not both than the philosophical ones. Moreover, Scaliger reads too much into one word. It is most unlikely that Manilius, that great coacervator of synonyms and repetitions, would have used one general word like *mollior* to make the elaborate and technical point about levels of argumentation that Scaliger had in mind. As Casaubon perceptively remarked in his margin, 'The great man is certainly being too clever by half here. This never occurred to Manilius. And there can be no doubt why the poet calls the next legend *mollior.*'[86] Such were the dangers of unbridled ingenuity applied to the verses of an empty-headed astrologer.

Consummate learning sometimes proved as dangerous as excess cleverness. As Housman remarked, scraps of what Scaliger had read hung before his eyes, blotting out the text that lay before him.[87] Often they led him like mocking wills-o'-the-wisp into a morass of error and confusion, where a commentator less heavily armed with learning could have kept to the high road. Take, again, his discussion of the placement of the *sortes Fortunae*. After describing how to perform this operation for daytime nativities, Manilius directs the reader concerned with a night-time nativity to do as follows:

> Verte vias, sicut naturae vertitur ordo.
> Consule tum Phoeben imitantem lumina fratris
> Semper et in proprio regnantem tempore noctis;
> Quotque ab ea Phoebus partes et signa recedit
> Tot numerare iubet fulgens horoscopus a se.   (III. 196–200)

The question was simple. What did Manilius mean by *Verte vias*?

The scholiast on Ptolemy's *Tetrabiblos* had discussed the problem of how to find the *sors* for a nocturnal birth. According to him, the ancient astrologers Nechepso and Petosiris had held that in a nocturnal geniture one must proceed ἀνάπαλιν ('in the reverse order'). He then explained what they had meant by this direction. Scaliger, who quoted the scholium in part, took it as explaining what Manilius had had in mind:

Now Manilius' phrase *Verte vias* is clearly identical in meaning to that of the Egyptians: νυκτὸς δὲ τὸ ἀνάπαλιν. The Greek masters explain that as follows: 'What does "in the reverse order" mean? That you must count from the Moon to the Sun, and you must measure off the degrees not in the order of the signs but against it.'[88]

The scholiast, however, goes on to point out that this method yields results identical to those of the method for daytime nativities — a point that Scaliger repeats — and that astrologers had therefore abandoned it for another, according to which one should count the degrees from the Moon to the Sun in the order of the signs, and then measure that distance off from the horoscope, again in the order of the signs, to find the *sors Fortunae*.[89] The important point here is simply that Manilius' method can be taken as agreeing with this later one. He says that one should change the method of counting 'as the order of nature changes' — that is, one should take the Moon, rather than the Sun, as the starting-point for computation, just as in nature the Moon, not the Sun, is dominant at night. But he does not say that one must count degrees against the order of the signs; and there is no reason to infer that that was what he meant.[90] This interpretation has two decisive advantages over Scaliger's. It does not make Manilius present as different two methods that actually yield identical results, and it does not involve reading into Manilius' text something that he does not say. In this case Scaliger's erudition has come between him and the text. A scrap of a scholium, not considered in context, has led him into an unnecessary misinterpretation.

Yet we must journey a good deal farther to arrive at the heart of the matter. As we shall see, there were specific as well as general reasons why Scaliger wished to make Manilius' doctrines agree with those of the Egyptians Petosiris and Nechepso. What he wanted was to recapture the mind of Manilius and to explain it in terms of its historical context. He came to see the *Astronomica* as a vital historical document, the clearest record of a lost

Near Eastern system of astronomy and astrology, one that later Greek astronomers had rightly rejected, and that the astronomers of his own time — even the phoenix of the human race, Pico della Mirandola — had ludicrously misunderstood. By recapturing the historical identity of the *Astronomica*, Scaliger could knock the professional astrologers off their pedestal of authority, formed as it was by ancient texts which they imagined themselves able to interpret.

Scaliger began his commentary with a brief critical discussion of the evidence on Manilius' life. Taking up the discussion where Pietro Crinito and Lilio Gregorio Giraldi had left it in their lives of the Latin poets, he refined their analysis of the internal evidence of the *Astronomica*.[91] He rightly argued against Giraldi that Manilius could not have been the Manilius Antiochus who had come to Rome in the times of Sulla with the grammarian Staberius Eros.[92] He refuted with equal justice any attempt to infer other biographical facts from the *Astronomica*, save the obvious point that Manilius must have written shortly after the defeat of Varus.[93]

This sceptical argument, however, was only the modest foundation for a structure as lofty, complex, and — in part — as fanciful as the folly of an eighteenth-century country house. In addition to fixing the details of Manilius' life, Crinito at least had tried to assess his astrological learning and to identify its sources:

M. Mallius is thought to have been born of a well-known family. He flourished in Rome at the same time that Augustus ruled the city of Rome with supreme success. And there can be no doubt that he was well received by that great prince because of his outstanding learning and intellect . . . His special interest and occupation lay in mathematics, and in them he did so well as to win the warmest praise for his ingenuity. He wrote five books on astronomy, in hexameters. In them he is said chiefly to have followed Hipparchus, Eudoxus, and Aratus.[94]

Through these spider-webs woven by Crinito's fancy Scaliger tore his way with impatient vigour. Manilius had been no expert astrologer and friend to Augustus, but a drivelling incompetent: 'Anyone who reads our *Castigationes* and Manilius' own poem may rightly doubt whether he ought to call him a mathematician. For he will have to confess that he wrote things about which he knew nothing at all.'[95] As to Crinito's account of Manilius' sources, its warp was invention and its weft error:

He also asserts with equal parts of error and rashness that Manilius followed Eudoxus and Hipparchus in his *Astronomica*. The dilettante had read that Hipparchus and Eudoxus wrote *Astronomica*. But he did not know that Hipparchus refuted virtually the whole contents of Eudoxus' *Astronomica*. Is it then possible that [Manilius] chose as his model two writers who are opposed to one another?[96]

Throughout his commentary Scaliger returned to Manilius' errors and to the sources he had drawn on. He saw the two themes as intimately related, for he held that many errors could be traced with mathematical precision to the peculiar nature of the sources on which Manilius had depended. Just as the errors in the manuscripts of Catullus had stimulated Scaliger to reconstruct the lost archetype from which they sprang, so Manilius' mistakes provoked him to create a bold and elegant historical hypothesis.

Many of the passages that Scaliger singled out for abuse had little wider significance. He denounced Manilius for errors of every kind, many of them so elementary that they revealed nothing more than stupidity on the one hand, ignorance of arithmetic, geometry, and astrology on the other. In the course of his account of the celestial sphere, Manilius described the Tropic of Capricorn; when the Sun is there, he wrote, at the winter solstice, *longa stant tempora luce / vixque dies transit candentem extenta per aestum* (I.586-7) — the days are so long that each has barely ended before the next begins. Scaliger thrashed this description for both implicit and explicit errors:

Vixque dies transit] It is unworthy of a mathematician both to believe that the day is so long under the Tropic of Capricorn that there is almost no night, and to think that the days are longer under it than in our region. Take, for example, the parallel through Syene, where the longest day at the point of the solstice is no more than 13½ hours.[97]

He slated Ausonius and Lucan for equally elementary errors.[98] Elsewhere he berated Manilius for such varied ineptitudes as giving a wrong account of the form of the sign Taurus; allotting the decans, or 10°-long sections, of Pisces to the domination of the wrong signs; contradicting himself; and presenting material in the wrong order.[99]

A surprising number of his more elaborate comments end with a variant of this formula: 'From this it is absolutely clear that what we have said so often is true: Manilius was totally ignorant of the subject that he was treating.'[100]

Scaliger's criticisms were not uniformly well founded. Sometimes he attributed to Manilius gross blunders that could more easily have been explained as the results of scribal error.[101] (In fact, Scaliger never explicitly took up the problem of how to formulate criteria for distinguishing between an author's errors and a scribe's, though he always acted as if he had firm and exact ones.) He continually displayed the same sort of critical, carping attitude that he had shown towards Festus — and that, as he rightly but inconsistently complained, Hipparchus had shown towards the poet Aratus.[102]

Yet many of Scaliger's points were better than trivial. A simple case will give a hint of what he intended. In his description of the sphere, Manilius says that the celestial equator is four *gradus* of 6° each from the Tropic of Cancer (I.581). Scaliger remarks: 'Now more recent authors compute the sum as ½° less. For they set the maximum declination of the Sun at 23;30°.'[103] What is important here is not the correction but the manner of its delivery. Instead of reproving Manilius for his imprecision, Scaliger explained it by reference to the poet's historical context. Manilius gave a round number because he was following outdated and imprecise treatments of astronomy.

A more complex case will enable us to broaden the hint into an interpretation. In Book III Manilius gave a rule for determining the rising times of the signs at a given latitude.
Let

D stand for the longest day at that latitude; N for the shortest night; r for rising time; dr for change in rising time.

Then

$$\frac{D}{6} = rLeo; \quad \frac{N}{6} = rTaurus$$

and

$$\frac{rLeo - rTaurus}{3} = dr.$$

Then rTaurus − dr = rAries = rPisces; rTaurus + dr = rGemini = rCapricorn etc.[104]

Scaliger misunderstood the rule in his first edition (though not in the second).[105] He saw immediately that it was a simple arithmetical device that worked by adding a constant amount to or subtracting it from the rising-time of a given sign in order to determine those of the signs adjacent to it. He knew that Ptolemy condemned such rules: 'the common practice, which rests on equal increases in the rising-times, is nowhere near the truth.'[106] Why had Manilius followed this incorrect practice? The answer was clear: 'Our [poet] makes the [decreases in rising-time] equal because he follows the ancient Egyptians.'[107] Manilius' astronomy was imprecise and crude because it was based upon Egyptian sources rather than the sophisticated mathematical planetary theory of Hipparchus. Much of Scaliger's commentary was devoted to proving and refining this hypothesis.

It is a striking coincidence that this guess of Scaliger's about Manilius' sources came near the truth. The rising-time formula of the *Astronomica* came from the Near East — from Babylon, through an intermediary as yet undiscovered.[108] Scaliger had no way of knowing the cuneiform sources in which the Babylonian procedures appear. His argument amounted to divination — a splendid inductive leap.

Before he leapt Scaliger built himself the strongest spring-board that he could from the evidence he had. He tried to show that Manilius had drawn most of his astronomical knowledge from Eudoxus; that Eudoxus, in turn, had learnt astronomy on his trip to Egypt (though he had added innovations of his own); and that a vast array of other evidence existed to show that the astrological doctrines that Manilius purveyed came from the Near East for the most part.

To prove the Eudoxan origin of Manilius' astronomy Scaliger adduced two pieces of technical evidence. The first was Manilius' treatment of the Arctic Circle, which he had described as a fixed circle of the celestial sphere, its circumference uniformly distant by *sex gradus* of 6° from the North Pole (I.567). Scaliger knew from Strabo that in early Greek astronomy, the Arctic Circle had not been fixed, but rather had varied with the observer's latitude.[109] Its centre was at the North Pole; its circumference was at a tangent to the observer's horizon. It contained all the circumpolar stars — those permanently visible at the observer's latitude. And the angular distance from the North Pole to its circumference was by necessity equal to the observer's geographical latitude:

Sexque fugit solidas) Let ninety circles be drawn parallel to the celestial equator. The circle at a tangent to the horizon at the point where the meridian and horizon intersect will be the Arctic Circle of the place in question. But because the horizons are movable, so too are the Arctic Circles. Thus in Cnidus, where the pole is elevated to 36°, Eudoxus wrote that the Arctic Circle is distant by that number of degrees from the North Pole. At another *clima* there will be another Arctic, in accordance with the changed elevation of the Pole. And it is necessary that the distance from the Pole of the point that defines the Arctic be equal to the *altitudo* of the place.[110]

Why had Manilius treated the Arctic Circle as a fixed component of a generally valid celestial sphere? Where had he stumbled on the figure of 36°? The answers to both questions are contained *in nuce* in the previous quotation. From Hipparchus' commentary on Aratus, Scaliger knew that Eudoxus had written a systematic description of the *Phaenomena*. From Diogenes Laertius and other sources he knew that Eudoxus came from Cnidus — where latitude and, accordingly, the polar elevation were 36°.[111] What had happened was obvious. Manilius, like other late authors, had foolishly mistaken Eudoxus' Cnidian Arctic for a universally valid one:

Hence we can see the incompetence of the Greeks and the old Romans who followed them: Manilius, Hyginus, Martianus Capella. They set out the Arctic Circle of their sphere in accordance not with the inclination of their own locality but with that of Cnidus. For that was how it was first passed on by Eudoxus, who was the first to provide the Greeks with a treatment of the sphere. And they were quite wrong to think that that Arctic was suitable to any inclination. For, as Strabo writes, 'The Arctics are neither visible to all, nor are they the same for all places.'[112]

However elementary this mistake, it showed that Eudoxus was Manilius' proximate source.

A more complex but more decisive piece of evidence was provided by III. 247–74. Here Manilius stated that at the latitude of the Nile Delta, the longest day consisted of 14½ hours. This statement Scaliger rebutted on simple astronomical grounds:

Atque haec est illas demum mensura per horas] Write, *per oras*. He says that in the parallel through Alexandria the longest day is 14½ hours long. This is completely wrong. Indeed, I am astonished that it was said by one who both was a mathematician and promised, as we shall see below, [to explain] the art of establishing the length of hours. Ptolemy sets the longest day at Alexandria, under Cancer, at 14 hours. The difference comprises 30 minutes, which correspond to at least 6° [of latitude]. Thus, this sum of hours corresponds to at least 6° of latitude beyond Alexandria. Moreover, if we make a more precise reckoning, we see that the longest day under Cancer in the parallel of Alexandria is not 14 full hours long. The greatest arc of daylight at Alexandria in Cancer is 205;4°.

$$\frac{205;4°}{15} = 13.41 \text{ hours.}$$

And that is clearly true. It is thus even farther from amounting to a full 14½ hours, as Manilius holds.[113]

The correction of Manilius' error mattered less to Scaliger than the discovery of its origin. Manilius had again gone wrong by failing to realize that he was dealing with one of the calculations

Eudoxus had made at Cnidus — the latitude of which, 36°, determined a longest day of precisely the period, 14½ hours, that Manilius had attributed to the longest day at Alexandria.

Well then, let us grant that the [longest day] is of 14 hours, and that it cannot occur within a latitude of 36°, as in fact it cannot. We must at least admit that that ratio of hours occurs at a latitude of 36°. Nor can that be doubted. For in the *clima* of Cnidus and Rhodes the longest day is of 14½ hours, as Ptolemy also says. And clearly the diurnal arc of the longest day in those regions is very close to that number. The diurnal arc of the longest day at the latitude of Cnidus is therefore 216;50°. This sum, when divided by the ratio of hours to degrees, yields 14.36 hours, which very nearly equals the example we set out. We therefore see that this sum of hours was noted down at the *clima* of Cnidus. This is true. For all the spheres of the Greeks were constructed according to the calculations of Eudoxus. But he was a Cnidian, as everyone knows. And he was the first of all the Greeks to pluck astronomy out of the inner mysteries of Egyptian philosophy and bring it home to his fellow-countrymen.[114]

Scaliger knew that this argument raised problems as well as solving them. His knowledge of Eudoxus' work came for the most part, as ours still does, from the quotations, summaries, and criticisms of it found in Hipparchus' commentary on Aratus. Scaliger had not only read this work with great care, entering conjectural emendations, some of them excellent, in the margins of his copy;[115] he had also excerpted from it the direct quotations from Eudoxus, arranging those that came from the *Phaenomena* and those that came from the *Enoptron* (*Mirror*) in distinct series (Leiden, MS Scal. 22, fols. 19^r-20^r). From this preparatory study — itself astonishingly precise and painstaking, even for him — he learned that Eudoxus had given not one but two ratios of the longest day to the shortest night: 5:3 and 12:7. Hipparchus had criticized Eudoxus acidly on this count, pointing out that where the ratio was 5:3, the longest day would last some 15 hours, and the latitude would be about 41°, that of the Hellespont — and nowhere near the 36° of latitude of Cnidus.[116] How could Scaliger be sure that Eudoxus was responsible for Manilius' figure of 14½ hours?

Scaliger's answer, though over glib, was not wholly implausible. According to Diogenes Laertius, Eudoxus spent a good deal of time in the area of the Hellespont, where he was greatly admired.[117] The ratio of 5:3 fitted the latitude of the Hellespont, as we saw. So Scaliger simply concluded that Eudoxus had used different values for the longest day because he wrote his works in different places: 'But Eudoxus wrote what he wrote about the longest day when he was in [the area of] the Hellespont; what he wrote about the Arctic, he wrote while he was in his fatherland. Therefore they are different, just as the places where he wrote them are also different.'[118] Hipparchus' criticisms thus arose from ignorance of Eudoxus' peripatetic life-style, and were unjustified. This answer unfortunately did not explain the origin of the second Eudoxan ratio mentioned by Hipparchus, 12:7, which is not very close to the 29:19 generated by the latitude of Cnidus. But a further epicycle would easily have saved Scaliger's theory: perhaps Eudoxus wrote major works in three places, using three different sets of values.

A second problem remained. Given that Manilius had followed Eudoxus, why had he thought that the value of 14½ hours fitted the longest day at Alexandria? This discrepancy Scaliger transformed into a new buttress for the fragile structure of his thesis:

Eudoxus, then, spent much time, along with Plato, among the Egyptian priests, who preserved the secrets of astronomy. Finally he published for his fellow-countrymen what he had learned from them. Because he owed this material to Egypt, it was hard to establish the custom that it be attributed to Eudoxus rather than to the Egyptians from whom he had derived it. Laertius: 'Some [say] that the Egyptians wrote [the dialogues that Eratosthenes attributed to Eudoxus] in their own language, and that he translated them and published them for the Greeks.' Thus, what they cited from Eudoxus, they attributed to the Egyptians. Thus Manilius here thinks that what Eudoxus wrote about the *clima* of his fatherland, Cnidus, refers to Egypt. For he thought, as did others, that Eudoxus' teaching was that of the Egyptians.[119]

The technical astronomical evidence, even in its discrepancies, confirmed Scaliger's arguments.

Scaliger fleshed out these bare quantitative bones with much non-technical information about the lives and works of ancient astronomers. That astronomy had begun in the Near East was a commonplace, known from any number of reliable sources:

Now Aristotle also bears witness that the Babylonians and Egyptians discovered astrology: 'The Egyptians and Babylonians, from whom we have many proofs about each of the stars'. Ptolemy, himself an Egyptian, explains why the Egyptians were adept at those studies: 'Because they are more closely familiar to Gemini and Mercury; on this account they are thoughtful and intelligent and especially capable at mathematics.' And about the Babylonians: 'Because they are familiar to Virgo and Mercury, and so the study of mathematics and the observation of the planets are their special traits.'[120]

True, astrology's ultimate origins were made obscure by a cloud of contradictory witnesses. It seemed that one Thot or Tat had taught the Egyptians, and received divine honours for doing so; but it also seemed that Joseph had taught them, presumably on the basis of a Hebrew astronomical tradition, that the world was created *in posterioribus partibus Librae.*[121] Whatever the origins of Near Eastern astrology, however, the channels by which it had passed to the West were easily traced in standard texts:

Eudoxus was the first to bring astronomy from the Egyptians to his Greek fellow-countrymen. Berosus brought horoscopic astrology from his fellow-countrymen, the Chaldeans, to the Greeks. Vitruvius: 'Their discoveries, of which they left written records, show how ingenious, how brilliant, and how great were those who sprang directly from the nation of the Chaldeans. And Berosus first settled in the island and state of Cos and opened a school there.' Pliny writes that the Athenians dedicated to him at public expense a statue with a gilded tongue, on account of his divine predictions.[122]

Scaliger also felt able to identify some of the doctrines that the Greeks received. One was that the planets move in the direction opposite to that of the daily rotation of the fixed stars:

The path of the five planets, as well as the Sun and Moon, is from West to East. The Greeks were late in finding this out. Seneca says in Book VII of the *Quaestiones naturales* that the path of the planets was not yet understood at the time of Democritus, and that Eudoxus was the first to transmit it to Greece. This is true. For those three who made a joint expedition to Egypt, Plato, Eudoxus, Euripides, learnt it from the Egyptians and were the first of all the Greeks to teach it to their fellow-countrymen — Plato in his *Timaeus*, Eudoxus in the *Mirror*, Euripides in the *Thyestes*:
    'For, having shown the opposite path of the planets . . . ' (fr. 861 Nauck).[123]

Again, apropos of I.867 Scaliger mentioned that Democritus and Anaxagoras had held comets to be the results of excessively close conjunctions of the planets. Here a slight confusion entered Scaliger's argument, for he took this as evidence of a pre-Eudoxan transfer of non-technical ideas: 'This', he remarked, 'they apparently learned from the Egyptians.'[124] But the general thesis remained clear.

Scaliger did not hold that the Greeks had ignored the night sky until the Egyptians and Babylonians taught them how to read it systematically. Even among the heroes of the archaic age there had been astronomers of a sort:

Palamedes was the first to lay out the watches of the night, during the Trojan War. And Euripides bears witness, in the *Iphigenia in Aulis*, that in that period they were already accustomed to mark off the sections of the night by astronomical signs:

'What star is this that passes over?
Sirius, near the seven-pathed Pleiades,
still streaking through the midst of the heavens.'
And our Manilius clearly alluded to this passage.[125]

These exceptions did not disprove Scaliger's rule, any more than the case of Democritus and Anaxagoras. What rudimentary knowledge the Greeks had amassed on their own or gained through hearsay was not significant by the side of the enormous amount that they had learned from the older peoples to the East — at least until the Greeks began to manipulate their benefactors' data in new ways.

Finally, the evidence of Manilius' superstitions served to confirm that of his scientific doctrines. The system of μελοθεσίαι — that is, the system by which different parts of the body are assigned to the governance of particular signs — Manilius treated at II.453 ff.[126] Scaliger showed that the system itself was an Egyptian creation: 'The μελοθεσίαι are considered in two ways, either with regard to whole signs, as here, or with regard to single degrees. That ancient Egyptian patriarch Necepso treated this in a special work devoted to the subject. See Firmicus, Book VIII.'[127] In IV.294–386 Manilius explained the division of the signs into sections of 10°, each under the dominion of a sign. Most other astrological writers also referred to such divisions, which were under the control of powers called decans.[128] In particular, the scholiast on the *Tetrabiblos* remarked that 'Teucer the Babylonian sets out the effects of the decans, and their *paranatellonta*, and the πρόσωπα.'[129] From this text Scaliger inferred that here too Manilius preserved Near Eastern doctrine that Ptolemy had omitted.[130]

Above all, in Book V Manilius described in great detail the *paranatellonta* — the stars that 'rise alongside' given degrees of the signs — and their effects.[131] Firmicus Maternus also treated the *paranatellonta* in Book VIII of his *Mathesis*, relying very heavily on Manilius. But he said that they formed only one part of a larger system, which he called *Sphaera barbarica*, or *Chaldaici operis disciplina*. This system also included, in Firmicus, a treatment of the effects of all 360 degrees of the zodiac, and of certain *clarae stellae* of the zodiac, when they appeared in a horoscope. He indicated more than once that the same ground had been covered, albeit imperfectly, by two venerable Egyptian

wise men, Petosiris and Nechepso.[132] Across this slender tight-
rope of evidence Scaliger confidently ran, arriving at a bold
conclusion that strikingly confirmed his other results. Manilius
V was half of a treatment of the *Sphaera barbarica*. Its other
half, had it been completed, would have covered the effects of
each degree and of the *clarae stellae* of the zodiac. Both parts
together would have been closely parallel to Firmicus' Book VIII
in its entirety.[133] Firmicus attributed his material in some
measure to the Egyptians. Hence Manilius, his predecessor and
source, must also have drawn his doctrines from them, though
he did not say so: 'The inventor of these subtle and clever bits
of nonsense was that ancient Egyptian Aesculapius. The sphere
is called "barbaric" — that is, Egyptian.'[134]

Astronomical evidence supported this astrological case. In
Book V Manilius made more astronomical errors than usual; in
some cases he placed stars as far as 90° from their true locations.[135] Scaliger argued that these errors too had come about
because Manilius had failed to bear in mind the origins of his
information. In Daniel's unpublished Servius he found a quotation from the lost *Sphaera barbarica* of Cicero's friend Nigidius
Figulus. This described a constellation as 'the ploughman, whom
the Egyptians call Orus'. 'You see', explained Scaliger, 'that in
that sphere Nigidius dealt with matters belonging to the phenomena [as observed] in Egypt.'[136] The *Sphaera barbarica*, in
short, treated the heavens as seen in Egypt, not in Greece. Thus
the last section of Manilius' work was barbaric or Egyptian in
two senses; not only had its astrological system been devised by
Aesculapius the Egyptian, but its astronomical data had also
been compiled in Egypt. This, in turn, could help to explain
some of Manilius' apparent mistakes:

And clearly the risings of the fixed stars that are treated in those accounts
of effects are suitable only to an Egyptian sky. For Cepheus never sets
completely in Greece. For it shaves and, in the words of Aratus, 'skims
over' (650) the point of the Greek horizon. But in the barbaric sphere
effects are observed from its rising and setting. The same can be said of
Cassiopeia and of others contained within the circle of stars perpetually
visible in Greece. For in Egypt, and in the area to the south of it, they rise
and set.[137]

Further evidence for the Near Eastern origins of Manilius'
astrology came from an unexpected set of sources. Just as Scaliger
had shown that late antique compilations preserved essential
evidence about the earliest Latin grammatical works, so now he

pointed out that medieval Arabic astrologers preserved traces of ancient doctrines that Ptolemy had omitted, and that resembled those of Manilius. The doctrine of decans, for example, was '*Abrogata . . . a Ptolemaeo, et ab Arabibus relata*'.[138] So too were the various systems of dodecatemories — a complicated set of procedures for dividing the signs into twelve smaller sub-units, each of which was allotted to the governance of a sign. 'Ptolemy', wrote Scaliger:

criticizes the whole theory of dodecatemories as empty and fallacious. And in general he says that all the Egyptians' inventions concerning individual degrees are 'unreasonable, and many talk a great deal of nonsense about them, and no reasonable account of them can be given'. For the Egyptians, with their useless learning, were much given to playing at and revelling in inventions of that sort . . . But the Arabs — who omit nothing that the ancients meddled with in their spare time — have kept this doctrine.[139]

Again medieval sources had enriched and bolstered Scaliger's reading of a classical text.

Scaliger knew very well what he was about. He took care to single out as his own this innovation in method and to rebuke his contemporaries for their sad lack of historical understanding: 'Whatever the Arabs set out that does not agree with Ptolemy, our astrologers take to be the Arabs' invention. In fact, I have found that much of what is commonly attributed to the Arabs really comes from the most ancient Greeks, from whom the Arabs took it over.'[140] Here Scaliger's insight led him to see the long series of astrological treatises much as scholars have come to see it again in the last hundred years: as an elaborately connected set of lenses and prisms, each of which bends, breaks up, or distorts the original band of light that all of them transmit, and none of which can simply be pulled out of its context for isolated study without destroying the device that gives each of its parts meaning. In his Festus, Scaliger sketched the lines of historical inquiry that have since been filled in by the editors of the *Corpus Glossariorum Latinorum*, the *Glossaria Latina*, and — sad conjunction — the Harvard Servius. In the Manilius he spied out the vast unsettled areas that would later be claimed, inhabited, and cultivated by Bouché-Leclercq, Boll, Cumont, Housman, Warburg, and Saxl.

A final set of arguments completed Scaliger's thesis. More than once he tried to show that astronomy had become much more sophisticated after the Greeks set to work upon it. If their data and their elementary concepts had come from the Near East, the mathematical methods and geometrical models of Ptolemaic astronomy were their own. Sometimes he had to manufacture the opportunity to make this point, but that did not stop him. At I.471 Manilius remarked that when the Moon is full, the stars are concealed by its light, and *fugiunt sine nomine signa* — 'the constellations flee without a name'. Here Scaliger remarked: 'Ptolemy, Hipparchus, and Chrysippus before them computed the number and order of the stars' — as, he implied, Manilius' cruder sources had not.[141] Again, at III.275 ff., Manilius tabulated the rising-times of the signs for the latitude of Rhodes in terms of stades (half-degrees of the celestial equator). Scaliger commented:

Octonis stadiis) A stade is half a degree, as we said. Therefore if Taurus and the rest grow by eight stades, they will grow by four degrees. But uniform increases are very inaccurate, and were later corrected by more recent [astronomers], Ptolemy and others. It is the Egyptians' invention. From them that notable master Eudoxus passed it on, as he had received it, to his successors — that is, according to constant increases. Hear Ptolemy's opinion on this subject: 'The common practice, which rests on equal increases in the rising-times, is nowhere near the truth.' More recent [astronomers] were therefore right to correct it.[142]

Though he offered few comments of this kind, Scaliger clearly saw them as important. First, they eliminated any possibility that Manilius had after all drawn on the work of Hipparchus or other independent Greek astronomers. Second, they established the originality of his argument. For to say that the Greek or Roman astronomers had learned from the Near East was hardly novel; nor was the anecdotal segment of Scaliger's evidence very fresh. By insisting that much of what the Near Easterners had taught was wrong — and that only this fact could explain Manilius' doctrines — Scaliger placed even his old evidence in a new context. The ancient anecdotes had all rested on the assumption, as widespread in Antiquity itself as in the Renaissance, that priority in time implied superiority in doctrine.[143] For Scaliger, priority meant crudity. Astronomy had advanced rather than declined as time passed. That was why Manilius' relics of an older astronomy were so historically interesting.

Though ingenious, Scaliger's set of arguments skipped lightly over a good many minor — and some major — problems. He took as factual many biographical anecdotes about Greek and Eastern sages that are more plausibly seen as back-formations. He ignored astronomical errors and inconsistencies which his theories could not account for. He over-simplified the problem of the *Sphaera barbarica*, which — as his own quotation from Nigidius Figulus could have told him — actually included non-Greek constellations, not merely the *paranatellonta* and *clarae stellae* of the Greek sphere as seen in Egypt.[144]

But in its general outlines Scaliger's historical argument was a momentous achievement. Here at last he arrived at the synthesis that he had been seeking since his youthful work on Varro: to bring together fruitfully in one work his two lines of study, classical and Near Eastern. He showed that both Arabic and Western astrologers could be treated as the joint inheritors of a common classical tradition. More important, he placed Egypt and Babylon on the one hand, Greece and Rome on the other in a single, coherent historical series, in which each culture was credited only with those achievements that could be shown to be its work. In an intellectual world where it was normal to exalt the *prisca theologia* of Hermes and other Near Eastern magi, Scaliger set out to redress the balance: to show that the Greeks had not merely learned but created. For him, complex intellectual disciplines were not given out by a beneficent God to the virtuous Jews and Egyptians and Druids of the world's beginning, and then corrupted over time. Rather, they were the product of history itself. They came into being only as the result of centuries of trial and error. In astronomy and astrology, it had been the Greeks, not the Babylonians and Egyptians, who performed most of the observations and, above all, tabulated and systematized the results. The ancient Near East had been not a world of gold, populated by calm sages, but a world of iron, haunted by superstitious fears and only fitfully illuminated by the work of certain science-minded priests — themselves prone to spin out unfounded speculations. In Scaliger's Manilius, then, one of the great clichés of Renaissance culture met its refutation.[145]

Two pieces of evidence show how central this line of argument was in Scaliger's work. In 1582, François de Lisle, a *parlementaire* and a Neo-Latin poet of sorts, attacked his Manilius in a verse pamphlet, the metre of which was evidently meant to express horror (it certainly inspires it).[146] Scaliger's attacks on the crudity of the astronomy taught by Roman poets — Lucan in particular — had aroused de Lisle's anger. And it was precisely by reference to his belief in the progress of astrology through time that Scaliger defended himself in a pamphlet of his own.

In the Manilius commentary, Scaliger had abused Lucan for

saying that there was a perpetual noon at Syene.[147] He had precedent for doing so: Macrobius had made the same point in his commentary on the *Somnium Scipionis* (II.vii.16). De Lisle none the less denounced Scaliger. He had given an incorrect reading of the text and, worse still, had dared 'to pretend that the poet was so ignorant of the heavens and of holy Mathematics'.[148] Scaliger's rebuttal took the form of a venomously sarcastic summary of his historical thesis:

First he objects that I falsely criticized Lucan for setting a perpetual noontide under the tropic. O man with too much time on his hands! Not only did Lucan believe this, but it was the opinion of all the ancients, before Eratosthenes and Hipparchus after him opened up the holier shrines of astronomy. So carelessly did he read our commentaries, in which we said that the ancients placed not only noon, but also perpetual day under the tropics. Does not Manilius put the longest day under Capricorn?

> *sed finibus illis,*
> *Quos super incubuit, longa stant tempora nocte.*

Ausonius, speaking of the Ethiopians and of our Tropic, explained this more clearly in accordance with the opinion of the ancients: *Semper ubi aeterna vertigine clara nitet lux.* What do you dare to mutter in opposition to these facts? Do you deny that at the very origins of astronomy, this was the opinion of the ancient Greeks Eudoxus, Meton, Cleostratus, and Euctemon? Clearly I hold Lucan blameless, because his opinion is that of those ancients. But I do not see how I can defend one who followed Eudoxus and Meton rather than Hipparchus. That our Manilius did this is clear. How seriously do even learned men err from lack of historical knowledge, when they attribute to the ancients the discoveries of later men.[149]

Again and again de Lisle defended Lucan by arguing that he had understood the essentials of Hipparchan astronomy — including the precession of the equinoxes and the epicyclic explanation for the second anomaly in the motion of the planets in longitude (their stations and retrogradations).[150] Moreover, he explicitly connected his argument with a more general one. Since the ancients had had a complete and perfect philosophy, they must have had sound astronomical doctrines; and if they failed to mention them, that was because they wished to preserve astronomy and *sacra Mathesis* from being made accessible to the unworthy:

> Then was the custom to profess the thing
> Alone; nor name nor figure did they bring
> To bear. A later age, perhaps less wise,
> Perhaps less worthy, did new names devise,
> New figures. The word was all their novelty.

The knowledge came from deep antiquity.
Do you believe the ancients never knew
These things that are so obvious to you?[151]

It had been the custom of ancient philosophers to hide their pearls from swine, as de Lisle gravely explained in a most revealing marginal comment: 'Archimedes [and] Plato advised this practice by their teaching, and so did the Jewish Cabalists and Talmudists by their example.'[152] In this familiar Renaissance mingling of Neo-Platonic and Cabalistic motifs we see the very structure of beliefs that Scaliger's Manilius was designed to attack. De Lisle read the work as its editor had intended. Scaliger's replies to every point were uncompromising restatements of his views. 'Hinc illae lacrymae', he wrote, while showing that Lucan had not known of the precession: 'this is what deceived you and other incompetents, who have sought out in Manilius and Lucan things that were completely unknown to them.'[153] Whether Scaliger was correct in all his criticisms — he was not[154] — is not at issue here. What is relevant is that both he and his critic saw his historical thesis about astronomy as crucial — as the aspect of his work by which it would stand or fall.

The other piece of evidence, though late, is powerful. In 1599 to 1600 Scaliger published a second, much revised edition of the Manilius. To it he added *Prolegomena de astrologia veterum Graecorum*, which began with an extension of his thesis to cover all of ancient culture:

Although the Greeks taught many things in all areas of learning, everyone considers Greece to have been the teacher rather than the parent of the liberal arts, because she developed discoveries that were not her own but those of the Chaldeans. Those who express this view seem to me either to forget the antiquity of the Greeks or to ignore their splendid literary achievements. For if we examine the matter from its ultimate origins, we will see that the arts were not only discovered and perfected by the Greeks in antiquity, but also passed from them to those [Near Eastern] nations on whom, so those gentlemen hold, the Greeks drew. For since the growth of great things is slow, and one age does not suffice for their complete exploration, they have a rather rudimentary character at first, and are not passed on to us in a state of perfection. Therefore those who come after fashion something to add to their ancestors' inventions, and the ancients always leave for posterity something that needs correction or explanation. Since the Greeks did this in every study, as their special effort was to illustrate, correct, or develop the discoveries of their ancestors, who will deny that the arts, which the Greeks made better day by day, ought to be attributed to no nation other than those very Greeks, who dug them up little by little and, so to speak, from the depths? For [as to] the Chaldeans and

Egyptians, from whom, they claim, the Greeks learnt everything — what, pray tell, do they have today that they did not learn from the Greeks?[155]   App. VII

This thesis he supported with the example of astronomy:

That the Greeks used a Chaldean or Egyptian master in Astrology must be taken in the following sense: that they were late in beginning work on it, being led to do so partly by Eudoxus, whom the Egyptians taught that the planets always resist the motion of the universe; partly by the eclipse observations of the Chaldeans, which were only moderately old, as they began from the beginning of Nabonassar, which is later than the first Olympiad. But [to believe] that they learned Geometry from the Egyptians, because they received figures from them, or Astrology, because the Chaldeans showed the Greeks the eclipse observations set down in their annals, is as if someone believed that he had learnt eloquence from him [from whom he learned] the elements of Grammar, or Philosophy, from his tutor in the principles of Logic. Therefore the barbarians taught the Greeks the history of eclipses. The Greeks investigated the causes of eclipses, and finally found them at a late date. Conon of Samos, who compiled the solar eclipses observed by the Egyptians, and Hipparchus — a man, as Pliny says, in the intimate councils of nature — were the first to take this course. The latter was the first to adapt the Chaldeans' observations of eclipses of both stars to the months of all Greek nations. From this divine work Ptolemy drew the whole history of lunar eclipses. . . . And certainly, as we admit that the Greeks were latecomers to Astronomy, so we affirm with constancy that the Chaldeans had only an approximate, not an accurate knowledge of it.[156]   App. VII

The thesis was stated more cogently and prominently than it had been in the first edition. But these differences of form were the only significant ones. We have seen that a careful, if hostile, reader had found the same argument in the first edition.

One problem remains. Why did Scaliger pick the incongruous medium of a commentary on Manilius to advance so sweeping an argument? Or, to put it another way, what made him use astronomy and astrology as a pretext for advancing a thesis about the history of ancient culture? Two sets of texts that Scaliger knew may help us to find some partial answers.

In the first place, Scaliger's was more than a generalized refutation of a fashionable error. Down to many of its minute details, it was an attack on one of the main traditions in Renaissance mathematical thought: namely, that of Petrus Ramus, which dominated mathematical and astronomical teaching in the Collège Royal that Scaliger knew. Ramus, as is well known, had called for an astronomy without hypotheses — an astronomy that merely recorded and predicted events in the heavens without relying on the geometrical models of Greek planetary theory, based as they were on inherently unverifiable assumptions. It is less well known that he believed that such an astronomy had actually existed in Babylonia and Egypt. The new astronomy to whose inventor he promised to resign his chair would, in his view, be the revival of a lost Near Eastern science.

Ramus took this vision of the history of astronomy seriously. Indeed, he cited it as one of the strongest pieces of evidence·in favour of his programme of reform. Late in the 1580s, Tycho Brahe recalled how Ramus had buttonholed him and tried unsuccessfully to make him a disciple:

As to the opinion of Petrus Ramus, the most famous philosopher of our time, that astronomy can be established without hypotheses by logical reasoning, it is unfounded. Sixteen years ago [in 1570], when we were together at Augsburg, he laid this notion before me. At the same time he urged me, after I had reduced the course of the stars to exact order by means of hypotheses, to strive to attempt the same [enterprise] without them. This was his argument why it could be done: he had read that the Egyptians once had a very easy [way to gain] knowledge of astronomy. And since the method of hypotheses seems difficult and involved, they must have learned the paths of the planets by another way, shorter and simpler, and therefore without any hypotheses.[157]

In both his now-famous letter to Rheticus of 1563 and his *Scholae mathematicae* of 1569, Ramus worked this argument out in detail. The history of astronomy became a neat morality play, set, cast, and directed to provide support for his rejection of all hypotheses. While Plato played an equivocal role, Eudoxus was the villain of the piece:

Please recall the hypotheses . . . from the four schools of astronomers defined by Pliny: the Chaldeans, Egyptians, Greeks, and Latins — if any are attributed to the Chaldeans and the ancient Egyptians and the Greeks in Plato. Plato certainly applied no hypotheses to astrology, as Proclus notes in his commentary on the *Timaeus*. But when he denied that there is any anomaly or confusion in the motion of the stars, he offered mathematicians a pretext (according to the commentators on Aristotle *De caelo*) to seek out hypotheses by which they might save the planetary phenomena. Therefore Eudoxus of Cnidus was the first to devise the hypotheses of the planets' motion in the direction opposed [to the daily rotation], which Aristotle, along with Callippus, corrected and emended. . . . Consider, whether astrology was ever devoid of hypotheses, and by how easy a calculation, once the motions of the stars had been marked and observed, any future conjunction and aspect of the stars could be predicted for the next hundred or thousand years. For . . . it seems not only completely illogical, but highly profane, for inventions — especially those that are obviously false and absurd — to form part of this holy and celestial body of knowledge. But . . . the hypotheses concerning epicycles and eccentrics are inventions, false and absurd . . . [158]

So ran the letter to Rheticus, which first appeared in print in 1576, and thus was not stale news when Scaliger was at work on Manilius. Ramus's thesis was the negative mould that shaped Scaliger's historical construction. Each of Scaliger's main points contradicted one of Ramus's. Where Ramus exalted the ancient Near East, Scaliger denigrated it. Where Ramus criticized the over-sophisticated mathematics of the Greeks, Scaliger ridiculed the crude mathematics and astronomy of the Babylonians and Egyptians. Where Ramus made Eudoxus the perverter of astronomy, Scaliger made him its true founder — and collected the fragments of his lost works in order to reconstruct the details of his achievement. It is not surprising that Scaliger did not attack Ramus by name. He respected Ramus's learning, and, even more, the devotion to Protestantism that had led him to a martyr's death in 1572.[159] What he was attacking was not so much Ramus himself as the *cénacle* of Ramist mathematicians, some of them also doctors, that had established itself in Paris in the 1550s and '60s: Peña, Forcadel, Nancel, Risner, de Monantheuil.[160] These men he condemned on the same grounds as the earlier editors of Hippocrates: they did not understand the very ancient texts on which they lectured, and from which they derived their claim to professional authority. To some extent, it is now clear why Scaliger saw himself as attacking a professional establishment. In the context of the Parisian scene, the denizens of which were his favourite audience, that is just what he was doing in the historical sections of his commentary.

Even when Scaliger's unnamed adversaries are identified, analysis is not complete. For here, as so often before, Scaliger was less original than some of his whoops of self-congratulation suggest; and the source that he drew upon sheds still more light on his intentions. In the hectic last year of his life, Pico della Mirandola had devoted himself to writing the first part of a huge attack on the seven enemies of the Church: his *Disputationes adversus astrologiam divinatricem*, which he left unpolished at his early death in 1494. In Books XI and XII of this work he suggestively analysed the history of astrology. On the one hand, he denounced the Egyptian and Babylonian inventors of the art for their failure to develop a sound scientific method. Good astronomers and mathematicians, they had suffered from the error that afflicts 'all those who are totally absorbed in a single discipline: to be very eager to see everything in its terms'. '*Omnia illis erant stellae*, that is, they liked to explain everything by the stars.'[161] Unhampered by natural philosophy, which their obsession with mathematics had prevented them from developing, urged on by the lust for gain, and stimulated by evil demons, they had divided the sky into constellations, zodiac, and signs, and assigned properties both to stars and to points on the zodiac. They had gone about their work not by the proper method of trial and error, but by the arbitrary application of mathematical procedures and the random creation of explanatory analogies (if a star is red, it must share the properties of the red planet Mars).[162] They had persistently refused to heed the crucial distinction between universal and particular causes. The system they built, Pico wrote, was like a spider's web: 'If you look at it from afar, you are deceived by the apparent size of the threads, its attractive structure and fascinating novelty. If you look at it more closely, you despise it. If you touch it with your hand, you tear it apart and destroy it.'[163]

On the other hand, he also qualified his praise of their mathematical skills and achievements. The Babylonians had claimed to have thousands of years' worth of observations of the heavens. But the best available evidence, that of Ptolemy's *Almagest*, refuted these claims:

When Hipparchus and Ptolemy, the founders of astronomy, produce the observations of the ancients in order to lay the foundation of their doctrine, they produce none older than those [made] in Babylon and Egypt under King Nabuchodnosor [Nabonassar]. Hipparchus flourished around the six-hundredth year after his reign; from him to our time no more than about sixteen hundred years have passed. Their claim to have observations from so many centuries is therefore false and mendacious.[164]

Moreover, their observations were necessarily inaccurate, for they had not mastered the motion of the Sun and Moon, against which all the other motions had to be measured:

If they erred so grossly as to the motion of the Moon, which is so easy and so familiar to us, what must we think of the less evident and slower motions of the other planets? But there is no need of conjecture. Read Ptolemy's book entitled *The Great Composition*, and it will be clear beyond a shadow of doubt that all the ancients were completely wrong — by the whole width of the sky, as the saying goes — about the motions of the heavenly bodies. As to the motion which we mentioned, that of the planet nearest to us, you will recognize that the ancients not only did not grasp the truth, but did not even [come] near it. Hipparchus was the first to observe the Moon's motion more correctly, while on the island of Rhodes at around the year 200 BC. But even he [did not arrive] at complete certainty. Therefore he was corrected by Ptolemy, who, surpassing

Hipparchus, approached the truth but did not quite reach it. The Spanish astronomers finally corrected it.[165]

Here we confront themes that we have already met in Scaliger. The Greeks in general and Ptolemy in particular are seen as the founders of real astronomy — i.e. mathematical planetary theory. And this discipline in turn is seen as having been perfected by generations, even centuries of human effort, not as something that God revealed in its fullness to the ancient theologians.

These general similarities do not prove the case. But even more striking parallels occur in the details of the *Disputationes*. Like Scaliger, Pico pointed out that the Egyptians and Babylonians had used an inaccurate method for computing the rising-times of the signs.[166] Like Scaliger, he treated Ptolemy as more rational and coherent, even in his astrological doctrines, than other writers on the subject.[167] Like Scaliger, he pointed out that Ptolemy had ignored and omitted the theory of the division of the signs into decans.[168] True, Scaliger only cited Pico's work in order to criticize it, while praising Pico himself with unexampled fulsomeness.[169] But we have seen that it was ever Scaliger's habit to sink his teeth into the hands that fed him most generously.

One of these parallels is especially suggestive about the nature of Scaliger's debt. In VI.3 Pico quoted and discussed Manilius' account of the *athla*. Wrongly taking this as merely an alternative system for the houses in a horoscope, he rightly pointed out that Manilius' astrology differed sharply from that found in other sources, even though it was apparently at least as old as the normal variety:

If we examine Manilius, who says that he sometimes imitated the teaching of the ancients — and than whom the Latins have no older author on astronomical matters (or, to be more accurate, fables) — we find a treatment of the twelve *loci* so different from any opinion now current that the entire method of prediction is completely changed ... What of those other twelve heavenly *loci* treated by Manilius? Aren't they completely different from any sort of astrology now practised?[170]

He anticipated Scaliger in rebuking the interpreters of Manilius for failing to recognize how idiosyncratic his doctrines were.[171] Scaliger referred to this passage, but only in order to express surprise at Pico's confusion of *athla* with houses.[172] It is highly likely, however, that Pico's discussion first called his attention to the idiosyncratic nature of Manilius' astronomy, and thus provided him with the central thesis of his commentary. At all events, Pico provided Scaliger with much of the ammunition that he fired off against Ramus. As with Festus, his innovation here consisted less in the devising of completely new methods than in refining and extending the ideas of others.

Scaliger's use of Pico may be revealing in another sense. After suppressing his original preface, he replaced it with an ornamental but uninformative poem in which the Muse Urania thanks Henri III for supporting Scaliger's work.[173] Neither there nor elsewhere did he state the purpose of his work explicitly. Pico, however, made the purpose of his work as clear as clear could be. He wished to expose the divinatory astrology of the ancient world and of his own time as a bundle of lies, errors, and contradictions. In his view, the philosophical errors and unreconciled disagreements of the astrologers were powerful evidence against the validity of their art.[174] Similar points occur here and there in Scaliger's commentary. Certainly he used the ancient astrologers' ignorance of the sky of the Southern Hemisphere as grounds for criticism.[175] And at I.312 he criticized Ptolemy sharply for the un-Aristotelian suggestion that the Moon caused dampness because it was affected by vapours rising from the earth. He also took the time to refute Cardano's attempt to save Ptolemy's account, thereby showing that his objection held for the astrology of his own time as well as for that of Antiquity.[176]

One parallel is arresting. Pico admitted in III.4 that the sky influenced events on earth. But he argued that this influence took the form only of a general infusion of life-giving force, not a shaping of every person and event:

It is thus clear that nothing happens in the corporeal world without the influence of the heavens. But the fact that a given event takes place comes not from the heavens but from secondary causes, with all of which the heavens do what those causes themselves are born to do, whether they pertain to the species or to the individual.[177]

In Book IV Manilius explained first the influence of each sign on those born under it and then the general influence of the heavens on different lands. Scaliger reproached him for moving in this fashion from the particular to the general, instead of following the proper order, as Ptolemy did. 'For', he explained, 'no one doubts that universal effects are better founded than individual ones.'[178]

These coincidences suggest that Scaliger may well have seen himself as carrying on one part of Pico's campaign for a reformed astrology, one that would abandon the arbitrary inventions of the ancients and concentrate on the general effects of the heavens, using the most sophisticated mathematical techniques in order to measure them precisely. If so, the Manilius really was a blow not only at Vettori and at Ramist mathematicians, but at most contemporary astronomers, as well as those doctors (almost all of them) who practised astrology.

This interpretation is supported by Scaliger's *Prolegomena* of 1599. For there, after restating his historical thesis, Scaliger explicitly cited Pico's *Disputationes* and connected his own work with them:

We are not the ones to believe that the stars and the brilliant celestial bodies are idle. But we utterly deny that their effects are limited by these ridiculous devices and arbitrary divisions. Later practitioners have made so many changes in this art, that when compared with the methods of earlier ones it cannot seem to be the same art. Indeed, in many respects it is contrary. And yet those earlier men seemed to make true predictions; and the later ones, who follow an opposite method, are also said to be truthful. But to refute all this would take much time and many books. Since Count Pico della Mirandola and others have done this, it will suffice that they have pressed a strong attack home on the citadel, and that the practitioners, who would have been wiser to remain silent, have defended it feebly.[179]   App. VII

Perhaps, then, Scaliger saw himself as supplying the historical details needed to prove Pico's arguments — the highlights and shadows that Pico's brilliant but rapid historical sketch had omitted.

From Scaliger's point of view the Manilius was undoubtedly a splendid piece of work. His friend Vertunien, the man in the best position to know Scaliger's thoughts and feelings, said in a liminary epigram that this was the first work into which Scaliger had really put his back:

What marvels noble Scaliger in play
    Can bring forth — these an ingrate world denies,
Though Virgil, Festus, Varro and the sweet
    Catullus and his friends refute such lies.
Manilius alone, e'en envy will admit,
    Shows to what heights his earnest work can rise.[180]

Scaliger himself was so pleased with the Manilius that he arranged, after much hesitation, to present it in person to the king. He even provided and had printed a French verse translation of the preface, which he inserted in the presentation copy to make it more attractive to a patron who, though clever, was no scholar.[181] The king professed much pleasure in the gift, though Scaliger's sole reward was the promise of a pension, which in the event was never paid.[182] Twenty years later, Scaliger still took delight in boasting about the brilliance with which he had set the *Astronomica* in its historical context. 'There is no Jesuit', he told his favourite pupil, 'and there is no other living scholar, who could have done for Manilius what [I] did, and especially in the *Sphaera barbarica* (Book V).'[183]

Unfortunately, from the standpoint of most readers the work was supremely ill adapted to win favour. Scaliger developed his arguments as he wrote; hence he never stated them explicitly and in full, but scattered partial statements throughout his commentary. Reading the Manilius commentary is a little like wandering through a maze, perpetually catching glimpses of a splendid statue at the centre, but never seeing more than part of the head or a hand, and never arriving at the clearing where the statue can be seen as a whole. It is revealing that the older and wiser Scaliger of 1599 put a short, coherent summary of his main points before his readers at the outset and only then led them through the text itself.

The content of the work was even less happy than its form. Astrologers could not be pleased to see their art assailed and its founding myth refuted; nor could they view with any pleasure the prospect of a revival of Pico's ideas. Moreover, Scaliger's attacks on the mathematical and astronomical competence of Greek and Roman authors were too sharply phrased to be widely acceptable — especially to those Ramists who saw the ancient scientific poems as ideal vehicles for teaching natural philosophy. And the boldness of Scaliger's conjectures could only widen the gap between him and the Italian textual critics.

Scaliger clearly felt that he was now trapped in a methodological cul-de-sac. At the end of July 1579, furious and desperate, he brilliantly defined his situation in an open letter to the Belgian Ioannes Stadius, himself both astronomer and humanist, and at that time a claimant to the chair of mathematics that Ramus had founded in his will. The Italians, Scaliger complained, had begun to persecute him as early as 1573, when his notes on Varro *De re rustica* appeared:

From that time on a man of the greatest reputation and culture, who has treated this area of letters with great success and acclaim, has never ceased to defame me to men of our nation. I alone was born to destroy letters; letters would perish if I survived; I trust too much in my wits.[184]

This was to Vettori's address. Next came Sigonio, who had labelled Scaliger's work on Festus as mere divination and guess-work. That was merely the customary incivility of the Italians, who 'generally call all races located outside Italy barbarians'.[185]

The edition of Catullus, Tibullus, and Propertius had only made matters worse, for it had enraged the French as well as the Italians:

It seemed that I had brought Hesiod's Goddess of Strife into the world. Not to speak of the Italians, I so inflamed the Senate of the Parisian masters, that they frequently assembled to deliberate about important public matters. Weighty opinions were delivered. It almost came to the extreme decree: 'Let the Magistrates see that no harm befall the Republic.' For Hannibal was at the gates.[186]

The Hippocrates had spread still more Greek fire on the troubled waters. Here Scaliger had made discoveries 'which the good doctors had not seen or even suspected, not even in their dreams'.[187] But here too benefactions had won neither honour nor gratitude. The doctors had first defamed Scaliger as a plagiarist and then, seeing that tactic fail, reviled him as incompetent to treat medical texts:

In this the whole *faex* of pedagogues collaborated. For there was no one who thought himself a doctor — always excepting the learned ones, lest anyone think that I include all of them here — who could hide his pain and anger at the thought that I, who was no doctor, should undertake to correct Hippocrates and Celsus.[188]

Scaliger saw no reason to hope that his Manilius would find a better reception. The professionals had a vested interest in responding with calumny and abuse:

There will be those who have read only Ptolemy and the more recent writers, and they will see that I follow a different method of calculation and a different astronomy from the common ones. Thereupon they will cry that I am entirely ignorant of astronomy. This, I think, will be the action of those who believe that they are astronomers just because they go about laden with Ephemerides to earn their livings. And they will not consider that Manilius' astronomy is very different from Ptolemy's, nor, what is most important, that Ptolemy himself established a new astronomy, or rather restored the true one, no differently than Aristotle, who did not establish his own Physics before he overturned the foundations of Democritus, Pythagoras, and the rest.[189]

Scaliger appealed to Stadius for fair judgement of the Manilius.[190] Nothing Stadius could have done would have been enough. Scaliger had begun and carried through his great spasm of commentary-writing in order to win the glory that his name deserved. He had failed. He was moving ever farther from the sorts of interests that could appropriately be pursued in commentaries on texts. To write the history of aspects of ancient culture he would have to abandon the commentary for the treatise.

It soon became clear that Scaliger's resentment against the reading public was largely unjustified. Each of his early works had won far more respectful attention than he realized. In 1581, when Justus Lipsius published his *Menippean Satire* against the critics of his age, he made it clear that in his eyes Scaliger was the master practitioner of their art. The work depicts a meeting of the Senate of Roman writers, as seen in a dream by Lipsius and described in vivid detail, down to careful reproductions of the forms of the Senate's procedures and *senatusconsulta*.[191] Cicero, Sallust, and Ovid in turn are seen denouncing the critics who have wounded them. Only then does Varro rise to defend his modern colleagues, and to argue forcefully that every Roman writer has benefited from their work. 'I myself', he cries: 'have I not given the civic crown to Joseph Scaliger for [saving] me? I gave it, gladly and rightly. *Magna enim haec res P.C. mihi credite, magna, et non unius e plebe doctorum.*'[192] Not only was Scaliger the only modern critic to be praised — Lambin was savagely lampooned[193] — but Lipsius also dedicated the satire to him.[194] The civic crown was no mean award for his *Jugendwerk* on Varro.

The Festus also received praise from abroad, though of a more equivocal kind. In 1581 to 1582 Fulvio Orsini published an edition of the Farnese manuscript of Festus. He took great trouble, even changing publishers in mid-stream, to reproduce every detail of the *archetypum exemplar*.[195] 'We saw to it as best we could', he wrote: 'that the pages were set out in the order in which Festus wrote them, with the number of lines in each column, and of letters in each single line, neither increased nor decreased, as they are in the exemplar.'[196] In other words, Orsini produced the sixteenth-century equivalent of a modern photographic facsimile edition. As to the many gaps in the manuscript, Orsini indicated them carefully and filled many of them with conjectural supplements set in a different type face. Orsini admitted that for this supplementary material he had drawn on the earlier work of Agustín and Scaliger.[197] But in many cases he took Scaliger's conjectures over; he merely rearranged them to fit the actual gaps in his manuscript more exactly.[198] Hence, when Scaliger saw the book he remarked that it was 'tousjours le mien'.[199] To be sure, Orsini added insult to injury — at Vettori's direct request — by referring to Scaliger only as *vir doctus*.[200] Scaliger had done exactly the same to Agustín. No one was better qualified than he to see that plagiarism was only another form of flattery. Though irritated, he took the episode as something of a perverse compliment: 'I am glad that what little I do is so good that even our enemies use it.'[201] Even in the stronghold of conservative criticism, his conjectures had won attention and acceptance.

The Catullus edition found understanding readers as well as sceptics. In his 1584 edition of Callimachus, Bonaventura Vulcanius indicated whole-hearted agreement with Scaliger's arguments. He included in his work Scaliger's text of and commentary on Catullus 66.[202] To do so was to take Scaliger's side against Muret; for the last edition of Callimachus, Henri Estienne's, had included Muret's text and a slightly abridged version of his notes.[203] Moreover, Vulcanius defended Poliziano's rendering of the *Lavacra Palladis* as systematically as Scaliger had defended his honesty in collation. At line 91 Teiresias' mother reproaches Venus for blinding her son: 'You have exacted too much for a small matter.' Vulcanius commented:

ἦ μεγάλ' ἀντ' ὀλίγων ἐπράξαο] Poliziano translated this as *Magna nimis parvis mutas*. This I like far more than the version Henri Estienne says that he prefers: *Magna rei parvae merces*. I shall try to explain why by comparing the two versions. When Poliziano translates ἦ μεγάλ' by *magna nimis*, he conveys the force of Callimachus' ἦ, which emphatically expresses the disparity of the things exchanged. Then surely anyone would prefer to render ἀντ' ὀλίγων by *paucis*, so that the two agree in number, rather than by *parvae rei*. Further, *mutas* corresponds better to ἐπράξαο, since it is a verb for a verb, and figuratively expresses the exchange of compensations, than does *merces* [payment, reward, bribe], which it would be absurd for a goddess to take from a man.[204]

As to Scaliger himself, Vulcanius made clear that he was an exemplary critic in both Latin and Greek: 'He not only cared for Catullus' wounds . . . but also shed much light on Callimachus. But I wish that that great man would also apply his surgical skill to the poor tattered fragments of Callimachus that I have collected.'[205]

Among the less learned Scaliger's name stood immensely high. He enjoyed great respect in the pleasant Poitevin salon of

Madame and Mademoiselle des Roches.[206] And the ordinary bourgeois of Poitou saw him as an awesome figure, 'celuy qui n'ignore rien'.[207]

Most of this recognition was still in the future when Scaliger wrote to Stadius. No amount of uninformed praise could have satisfied his monstrous, wounded pride. In the circumstances it was almost fortunate for him that his dear friend and patron François de Chasteigner fell ill in the summer of 1579 and died on 9 September. Scaliger's efforts on behalf of his friend exhausted him; Chasteigner's death filled him with a *grande melancholie*.[208] For a time, he ceased to work. When he began again, he pursued a new set of interests which derived but differed widely from his earlier ones. At last he was to win his glory, but as a chronologer rather than a critic. And that is another story.

VIII Scaliger at Thirty-nine

The Scaliger we have now come to know does not much resemble the bearded, venerable figure of Meursius's *Athenae Batavae* — or the single-minded seeker after truth unforgettably described by Bernays and Pattison. He wanted fame and honour more than truth. He was a good listener and reader rather than a sovereign inventor of new methods. He chose and abandoned subjects and approaches for trifling and personal reasons.

Through the first part of his career, Scaliger could not escape from the dilemma to which his character and situation confined him. He loved to find masters, in the classroom and in books. He found it easy to learn how to use the new tools they offered. Sometimes he acknowledged that he had employed equipment forged by others. But he could not admit the full extent of his dependence. A nobleman could not owe so much of his eminence to others. He could not bear to be corrected or disowned by those whom he had chosen to follow — and from whom he had decided to borrow. Hence the curious, jagged trajectory of Scaliger's intellectual life, as he appropriated method after method, used them in novel combinations, and then found himself driven to reject the great men who betrayed him, claimed their property when they saw it in his work, or criticized his applications of it as illegitimate. Scaliger, the best of students, was the worst of disciples. He thrust his former masters away as forcefully as he had once clasped them to him.

Naturally Scaliger's work became more sophisticated and independent as he grew older. He learned as he aged. From early efforts to apply the textual criticism of Turnèbe and the poetic skills of Dorat, he moved to the rich historical scholarship of Cujas. His work with Cujas enabled him to treat the text of Festus with all the resourcefulness and flexibility that Cujas had previously applied to that of the *Digest*. But Scaliger remained the servant of his emotions, not their master; and public humiliation at Muret's hands made him shift his ground again. In the

Catullus he tried to avenge himself, correcting the French methods he had been trained in by the Italian ones that he knew from books. The edition was original in conception if not impeccable in execution. Here too Scaliger's putative masters, the Italians to whom he was trying to declare allegiance, rejected him; and here too public rejection reshaped Scaliger's private world of thought and feeling. Claiming to abandon all that he had known — but making rich use of it in practice — he produced his Manilius, the richest and most fascinating of all his early works. This lay outside all normal traditions of sixteenth-century philology; yet it too rested in part on unacknowledged borrowings of facts from Carrion and ideas from Pico. To that extent even the Manilius fits the consistent pattern of Scaliger's early life and work.

Clearly Scaliger was all too human. This should not surprise anyone. Few scholars could survive with credit our effort to spy on them through keyholes, to watch their books taking shape *in vitro* as raw materials were catalysed by raw emotions. And after all, even an all too human Scaliger is better than the splendid, stylized icon that his previous biographers painted and gilded.

The course of Scaliger's early life inspires general questions as well as biographical conclusions. How far are his career and situation symptoms of wider problems?

The careers of Poliziano, Vettori, and Dorat showed, at the outset of this study, that Renaissance philology always remained a field populated by rhetoricians — men trained to polemize and constrained to do so by their situation. Philological treatises were cast as much in personal as in substantive terms, designed as much to win support from inexpert patrons as assent from expert readers, and aimed as much to contribute to broadly literary enterprises as to recover a lost past. Many books were nothing more than single broadsides in hot and protracted battles. Few scholars felt any need to enumerate all the evidence that supported or opposed their position, to give fair hearings to their critics, or to refrain from sniping at irrelevant minor breaches in the armour of the other side.

Much of what Scaliger did can be explained by the impact of these conditions on him. Intellectually, he knew that he needed to master the widest possible array of existing methods. But it was socially awkward and tactically inadvisable to say that he was borrowing so much. It was emotionally impossible to admit that a Scaliger could be less independent and original than Julius

Caesar Scaliger had demanded — or to accept harsh, public criticism. It was perfectly possible — and even normal — to conceal his debts and even to deny them. No one has ever said that a good rhetorician should produce evidence that weakens his own case.

In the conditions that obtained, it was inevitable that Scaliger would find himself in conflict. When he did, it was only natural for him to follow the same rhetorical standards of argument that his rivals and enemies applied. He was as willing as they to argue *ad hominem*. More important — and more unexpectedly — he was as willing as they to exaggerate the originality or tenability of his positions, or to shift his ground entirely in order to evade attack or reply more effectively. These tactics were all acceptable within the rules of rhetoric — and those rules governed the game of philology. The strange graph of Scaliger's early work moved against a professional as well as an emotional axis. And Scaliger's fate in turn reveals something about the character of philology itself: that it formed part of a traditional curriculum and embodied a traditional set of mental and linguistic categories. To that extent, to judge Renaissance scholarship by its success or failure in anticipating the professional philology of the nineteenth century is to obscure matters rather than to clarify them.

The historian sets out 'to dig up the dead cat, to excavate the maggot from the cheese, to locate the canker in the rose'. In tracking Scaliger through manuscripts and margins, in reading his mail and verifying his references, I have found plenty of cankers and maggots. But I have also tried to see him as a figure in a coherent cultural landscape. Some of his least excusable actions have revealed themselves to be not the excesses of a bizarre personality but the normal components of a period style in scholarship.

Notes

Introduction

1. H.-J. Martin, *Livre, pouvoirs et société à Paris au XVIIe siècle (1598-1701)*, i (Geneva, 1969), pp. 190 ff.

2. E. H. Gombrich, *In Search of Cultural History* (Oxford, 1969), p. 37.

3. A. D. Momigliano, 'Jacob Bernays', *Quinto contributo alla storia degli studi classici e del mondo antico* (Rome, 1975), i, pp. 127-58; H. I. Bach, *Jacob Bernays* (Tübingen, 1974), pp. 127-31.

4. M. Haupt, 'Ueber Joseph Scaliger und die von Haase vorgeschlagene Umstellung tibullischer Versreihen', *Opuscula*, iii (Leipzig, 1876), pp. 30-41.

5. G. V. Pinelli to C. Dupuy, 22.ii.1578; Paris, Bibliothèque Nationale, MS Dupuy 704, fol. 53ᵛ.

6. Pinelli to Dupuy, 22.viii.1578; Paris, Bibliothèque Nationale, MS Dupuy 704, fol. 59ʳ; Pinelli to Dupuy, 22.x.1578; ibid., fol. 67ʳ; Pinelli to Dupuy, 17.iv. 1579; ibid., fol. 69ʳ.

7. H. I. Marrou, *A History of Education in Antiquity*, tr. G. Lamb (New York, 1956), pp. 228-34, 375-8.

8. A. D. Momigliano, 'Pagan and Christian Historiography in the Fourth Century A.D.', in *Essays in Ancient and Modern Historiography* (Middletown, 1977), pp. 107-26.

9. For the importance of the concept of intellectual property in the formation of disciplines see R. K. Merton, 'Priorities in Scientific Discovery. A Chapter in the Sociology of Science', *American Sociological Review*, xxii (1957), pp. 635-59.

10. See e.g. D. R. Kelley, 'Guillaume Budé and the first Historical School of Law', *American Historical Review*, lxxii (1967), p. 814.

11. On the conventions of the preface see in general K. Schottenloher, *Die Widmungsvorrede im Buch des 16. Jahrhunderts* (Münster Westfalen, 1953); E. R. Curtius, *European Literature and the Latin Middle Ages*, tr. W. R. Trask (New York, 1953), pp. 79, 83-9; cf. E. J. Kenney, 'The Character of Humanist Philology', in *Classical Influences on European Culture, A.D. 500-1500*, ed. R. R. Bolgar (Cambridge, 1971), p. 128.

12. For Scaliger's attempt to define the duties of a critic see his letter to F. Vertunien, most readily accessible in G. W. Robinson, 'Joseph Scaliger's Estimates of Greek and Latin Authors', *Harvard Studies in Classical Philology*, xxix (1918), pp. 145-7; he follows Sextus Empiricus, *Adversus Mathematicos*, I. 91-3. For Sextus and his widespread influence in 16th-century France, see R. H. Popkin, *The History of Scepticism from Erasmus to Descartes* (rev. edn., Berkeley, 1979).

13. For attempts to write the history of philology solely on the basis of general treatises about the nature of the study see A. Bernardini and G. Righi, *Il*

concetto di filologia e di cultura classica (Bari, 1953); J. Jehasse, *La Renaissance de la critique* (St Etienne, 1976). On the first manuals of textual criticism (not a distinguished lot) see E. J. Kenney, *The Classical Text. Aspects of Editing in the Age of the Printed Book* (Berkeley, 1974), Ch. II.

14. Here and elsewhere, my argument is much indebted to G. Lloyd, *Magic, Reason and Experience* (Cambridge, 1979), Ch. II.

15. R. Darnton, *Mesmerism and the End of the Enlightenment in France* (repr., New York, 1970), p. viii.

Chapter I

1. See D. R. Kelley, *Foundations of Modern Historical Scholarship. Language, Law and History in the French Renaissance* (New York and London, 1970), Ch. II, for a particularly eloquent statement of these views.

2. *Opus Epistolarum Des. Erasmi Roterodami*, ed. P. S. Allen *et al.* (Oxford, 1906-58), ii, p. 350; v, pp. 243-7; and esp. xi, p. 177.

3. Ibid., ii, p. 460 on Budé; ii, p. 26 on Zasius; ii, p. 237 on B. Amerbach.

4. For a reference to the *Miscellanea* as a purely secular work see ibid., ii, p. 171; on Erasmus's seal see E. Wind, 'Aenigma Termini. The Emblem of Erasmus', *JWCI* i (1937-8), pp. 66-9; and J. K. McConica, 'The Riddle of "Terminus"', *Erasmus in English*, ii (1971), pp. 2-7.

5. M. W. Croll, *Style, Rhetoric, and Rhythm* (Princeton, 1966), pp. 24-5.

6. *Scaligerana II*, p. 510, s. v. POLITIAN: 'Mon Pere disoit de lui, que c'est le premier de son tems, qui a osé lever le nez au Ciel pour les lettres: il s'est servy d'un Ausone que Petrarque avoit escrit.'

7. Cf. e.g. Kelley, *Foundations*, pp. 47-9.

8. G. Billanovich, 'Petrarch and the textual tradition of Livy', *JWCI* xiv (1951), pp. 178-9; cf. 137-42.

9. S. Rizzo, *Il lessico filologico degli umanisti* (Rome, 1973), pp. 230-3.

10. Lorenzo Valla, *Collatio Novi Testamenti. Redazione inedita*, ed. A. Perosa (Florence, 1970), pp. xxvii-xxxiv.

11. For what follows see e.g. R. Sabbadini, *Il metodo degli umanisti* (Florence, 1922).

12. For Valla's method in the *Elegantiae* see e.g. M. Baxandall, *Giotto and the Orators* (Oxford, 1971), pp. 8-11; H. J. Stevens, Jr., 'Lorenzo Valla and Isidore of Seville', in *Traditio*, xxxi (1975), pp. 343-8. For Tortelli's *De orthographia* see R. P. Oliver, 'Giovanni Tortelli', in *Studies Presented to David Moore Robinson*, ii (St. Louis, 1953), pp. 1257-71. And on the intellectual relations between Valla and Tortelli, which at times amounted to collaboration, see O. Besomi, 'Dai "Gesta Ferdinandi Regis Aragonum" del Valla al "De Ortho-graphia" del Tortelli', in *IMU* ix (1966), pp. 75-121.

13. For what follows see J. Monfasani, *George of Trebizond. A Biography and a Study of his Rhetoric and Logic* (Leiden, 1976), pp. 262-5, 289-94, where it is also shown that George of Trebizond was, unlike his predecessors, indepen-dent of older traditions of commentary on Cicero.

14. See L. Frati, 'Le polemiche umanistiche di Benedetto Morandi', in *Giornale Storico della letteratura italiana*, lxxv (1920), pp. 32 ff. Cf. Livy IX. xvii-xix.

15. On the roles of philology and rhetoric in Valla's thought see H. H. Gray, 'Renaissance Humanism: the pursuit of eloquence', in *Journal of the History of Ideas*, xxiv (1963), pp. 511-12; Gray, 'Valla's *Encomium of St. Thomas Aquinas* and the humanist conception of Christian Antiquity', in *Essays in History and Literature presented to Stanley Pargellis*, ed. H. Bluhm (Chicago, 1965), pp. 49-50.

16. For a contrary view of the nature of conjectural criticism see E. J. Kenney, *The Classical Text* (Berkeley, 1974), Ch. VI, building on the earlier arguments of G. Pasquali and others.

17. It is significant that modern textual critics refer to a MS that has been corrected against another as one that has suffered 'contamination'.

18. G. Billanovich and M. Ferraris, 'Le "Emendationes in T. Livium" del Valla e il Codex Regius di Livio', in *IMU* i (1958), pp. 245-64.

19. G. Billanovich in *JWCI* xiv, pp. 178-9.

20. See e.g. L. D. Reynolds and N. G. Wilson, *Scribes and Scholars. A Guide to the Transmission of Greek and Latin Literature*, 2nd edn. (Oxford, 1974), pp. 132, 134.

21. Cf. Kenney, *The Classical Text*, Ch. I.

22. This generational change in the character of Italian humanism has often been remarked on: see e.g. C. Marchesi, *Bartolomeo della Fonte (Bartholomaeus Fontius). Contributo alla storia degli studi classici in Firenze nella seconda metà del Quattrocento* (Catania, 1900), p. 2; F. Gilbert, 'Biondo, Sabellico, and the Beginnings of Venetian Official Historiography', *Florilegium historiale. Essays Presented to Wallace K. Ferguson*, ed. J. H. Rowe and W. H. Stockdale (Toronto, 1971), pp. 275-93.

23. On Leto see V. Zabughin, *Vergilio nel Rinascimento italiano da Dante a Torquato Tasso*, i (Bologna, 1921), pp. 188, 192. On de' Tirimbocchi see *Scholia in P. Ovidi Nasonis Ibin*, ed. A. La Penna (Florence, 1959), pp. xxxix-xl.

24. See H. Caplan, *Of Eloquence. Studies in Ancient and Mediaeval Rhetoric*, ed. A. King and H. North, (Ithaca, N. Y., 1970), p. 268. These humanists were imitating their ancient models here too, for the commentators and scholiasts of late Antiquity had also cannibalized the works of their predecessors. This is hardly surprising, considering that in both cases the commentators were practising arts teachers who had to cover a vast amount of material in their lectures and could hardly have done original research to support all or even most of what they said (nor is the situation very different in modern arts teaching: normal 20th-century school commentaries are mostly derivative in content). On ancient commentators' use of their sources see J. E. G. Zetzel, 'On the history of Latin scholia', in *Harvard Studies in Classical Philology*, lxxix (1975), pp. 335-54.

25. On the classical scholarship of the late-medieval friars see B. Smalley, *English Friars and Antiquity in the early Fourteenth Century* (Oxford, 1960).

26. A good account of Servius' method is given by R. R. Bolgar, *The Classical Heritage and its Beneficiaries . . .* (Cambridge, 1954; repr. New York, 1964), pp. 41-2 and p. 396 n. ad loc. Despite its untrustworthiness on many points of detail (cf. the remarks of C. Dionisotti in *IMU* i (1958), pp. 427-31, and J. Hutton in *Gnomon*, xxviii (1956), pp. 63-6), this work contains many interesting remarks on the history of the commentary, which should not be ignored.

27. M. Filetico, dedicatory letter to Cardinal Giovanni Colonna in Filetico's edition of selected letters by Cicero with Filetico's notes, quoted by G. Mercati, 'Tre dettati universitari dell' umanista Martino Filetico sopra Persio, Giovenale ed Orazio', in *Classical and Mediaeval Studies in Honor of Edward Kennard Rand*, ed. L. W. Jones (New York, 1938), p. 228 no. 46, and by C. Dionisotti, '"Lavinia venit litora". Polemica virgiliana di M. Filetico', in *IMU* i (1958), p. 307: 'et quoniam tunc quidam sane doctissimi viri assuefecerant iuventutem ut nil audire cuperent ni super unaquaque propemodum dictione sensum et expositionem adiungerent, . . . eorum ego instituta sequerer necesse fuit.'

28. See esp. Poliziano, *Commento inedito alle Selve di Stazio*, ed. L. Cesarini Martinelli (Florence, 1978), p. 20.

29. Here too, the humanists were doing what their classical predecessors had done; many of the shorter glosses in Servius are merely synonyms or periphrases of a word in the text. The inherent defects of the humanists' style of commentary have often been discussed; see e.g. *Scholia in Ovidi Ibin*, ed. La Penna, p. xlvii and n. 6; E. Barbaro, *Castigationes Plinianae et in Pomponium Melam*, ed. G. Pozzi, i (Padua, 1973), *Introduzione*, pp. cxlix-cl.

30. On the 'modus modernus', which was first used for civil and canon law texts, see K. Haebler, *The Study of Incunabula*, tr. L. E. Osborne (New York, 1933), p. 91.

31. D. Calderini, 'Epilogus et προσφώνησις de observationibus', 1475, quoted by C. Dionisotti, 'Calderini, Poliziano e altri', in *IMU* xi (1968), p. 167: 'De commentariis nulla mihi posthac erit cura magnopere. . . . Interea acriore studio et maiore ocio duo perficimus et expolimus opera: quorum alterum est e Graeco in latinum conversum, . . . alterum est latinis litteris elucubratum quod observationes inscripsimus, tribus voluminibus, quorum primum continet tercentum locorum ex Plinio explicationem, secundum quicquid observavimus parum ab aliis traditum apud poetas omnes, tertium quae collegimus et observavimus apud Ciceronem, Fabium, Livium et scriptores omnes reliquos.' This and the following paragraph are based on Professor Dionisotti's article; cf. also Barbaro, *Castigationes Plinianae*, ed. Pozzi, i, *Introduzione*, Ch. v, 'Il Barbaro e gli umanisti', pp. cxii-clxviii, esp. pp. cxlix-cl, clxiv. For a 15th-century assessment of Calderini that stresses his ability to solve technical problems of interpretation — as well as his lack of scruple — see Paolo Cortesi, *De hominibus doctis dialogus*, ed. and tr. Maria Teresa Graziosi (Rome, 1973), p. 54.

32. On Plinian studies in the later 15th century see Pozzi, loc. cit. (n. 31); C. G. Nauert, in *CTC* iv, pp. 297-422.

33. D. Calderini, 'Ex tertio libro observationum', in *Lampas, sive fax artium liberalium, hoc est, thesaurus criticus*, ed. J. Gruter, i (Frankfurt, 1602), p. 316: '*Harpastrum* quid sit longa commentatione Graecis auctoribus explicamus in Epistolam quarti libri sylvarum, multaque de eo docuimus, quae adhuc (ut opinor) incognita fuerunt, ea siquis volet legere, illic requiret'; ibid., p. 314: 'Repetamus praeterea particulam commentariorum nostrorum in Iuvenalem, ubi carmen exit illud in mulierem curantem cutem et expolientem faciem in gratiam adulteri:
> *Interea foeda aspectu ridendaque multo*
> *Pane tumet facies, et pinguia popeana spirat.* (Juv. *Sat.* VI, 461-3)
. . . Haec scripsi, siqui fortasse Iuvenalis carmen parum intellige[ntes] de *Popeano* ambigant, quod ego, ut arbitror, primus fortasse elucubravi, ut sexcenta alia, quae in commentationibus nostris requires.'

34. F. Beroaldo the Elder, *Annotationes centum*, GKW 4113 (Bologna, 1488), fol. a ii[v]: 'Sane has annotationes nullo servato rerum ordine confecimus, utpote tumultuario sermone dictantes, et perinde ut cuiuslibet loci veniebat in mentem, ut quilibet liber sumebatur in manus, ita indistincte atque promiscue excerpentes annotantesque. Fetus hic plane precox fuit, utpote intra menstruum tempus et conceptus et editus.' This statement may merely be a commonplace, an imitation of Gellius' similar confession of haste and disorderliness (*Noctes Atticae, praefatio*, x). None the less Beroaldo seems genuinely less bold than Poliziano in asserting the merits of the new genre; and this difference in tone probably reflects some difference in opinion.

35. F. Beroaldo, *Annotationes in commentarios Servii Virgiliani commentatoris*, GKW 4115 (Bologna, 12.xi.1482), sigs. [a vi[v]- a vii[r]], against Servius on *Aen.* I.373; [a vii[r-v]] against Servius on *Aen.* I.410; b iii[v]-b iiii[r], against Servius on *Aen.* II.707; e ii[r-v], against Servius on *Geor.* III.124. I give one example of Beroaldo's method, [a vii[r-v]] against Servius on *Aen.* I.410:

SERVIUS. Incusare proprie est superiorem arguere; accusare vero vel parem vel inferiorem.
PHILIPPVS. Quis non videt falsam ac penitus inanem esse differentiam, quam Servius nobis persuadere contendit? Nemo fere eruditorum in latina lingua ita loquitur. Nemo hanc differentiam observat; quinimo saepissime secus legitur. Caesar in primo Commentario, omnium ordinum adhibitis ad id consilium centurionibus, vehementer eos incusavit. Certe Caesar militibus suis maior est non minor, et tamen contra Servii disciplinam dicit se illos incusasse, et profecto latinissime locutus est. Incusare enim significat reprehendere vel culpare sine aliquo discrimine. . . . Accusare vero ab auctoribus idoneis usurpatur, nusquam observata fetutina illa et rancida Servii observatione; qua de re exempla ideo ponere supersedeo, quia talibus scatent scriptorum cuncta volumina.
This observation was well worth making, considering that the standard contemporary work on Latin usage – Junianus Maius, *De priscorum proprietate verborum*, Naples, 1475 – reproduced Servius' words without comment (admittedly, this was the author's normal practice); see sigs. [a vi^{ra}; s vii^{rb}].

36. Beroaldo, *Annotationes contra Servium*, fols. aiii^v-aiiii^r, bii^{r-v}, biiii^v, [bvi^{r-v}], cii^v-ciii^r, [civ^{r-v}], etc.

37. Ibid., fol. [bvii^{r-v}]: 'In illo quoque versu Maroniano, Explebo numerum reddarque tenebris [*Aen.* VI. 545], admiror Servium, cum more diligentis commentatoris varias interpretationes attulerit, omisisse id, quod a Macrobio relatum est, quod eruditionem maximam prae se fert, et Virgilianae sententiae optime quadrat. . . . [There follows a summary of Macrobius *In somn. Scip.* I. xiii.11-12]. Haec Macrobii interpretatio, tam subtilis, tam elegans, tam erudita, praetermitti non debuit a curioso commentatore, qui ex fontibus philosophorum, unde hauserat Macrobius, haurire potuisset; praesertim cum multa undique exquisiverit. Sed ut mihi videtur, nihil est cum praedicta Macrobii expositione comparandum.' For an amusing rebuttal see Francesco Florido Sabino, *Lectiones Subcisivae* II. 9-18, in *Lampas*, ed. Gruter, i, pp. 1121-43.

38. See E. Daxhelet, 'Notes sur l'humaniste italien Cornelio Vitelli', *BIHBR* xv (1935), pp. 83-97; Pozzi, loc. cit., cxxvi-vii.

39. W. G. Rutherford, *Scholia Aristophanica*, iii (London, 1905), p. 387.

40. Ibid., pp. 67-72; cf. N. G. Wilson, 'A Chapter in the History of Scholia', *Classical Quarterly*, xvii (1967), pp. 244-56; Zetzel, art. cit. (n. 24 above), pp. 337-9; Grafton, 'On the Scholarship of Politian and its Context', *JWCI* xl (1977), pp. 160-1 n. 30, 187-8.

41. R. P. Oliver, '"New Fragments" of Latin authors in Perotti's *Cornucopiae*', *Transactions of the American Philological Association*, lxxviii (1947), pp. 390-3, 405-6, 411, 412-24, and *passim*. This article is very useful as an analysis of Perotti's sources and methods.

42. J. Dunston, 'Studies in Domizio Calderini', *IMU* xi (1968), pp. 144-9; S. Timpanaro, 'Noterelle su Domizio Calderini e Pietro Giordani', *Tra Latino e Volgare: Per Carlo Dionisotti*, ed. Gabriella Bernardoni Trezzini *et al.* (Padua, 1974), ii, pp. 709-12.

43. On Leto and Ennius see Dunston, in *Antichthon*, i, pp. 91-2.
On Calderini's falsification of his note on Martial xiv. 41 see Dunston in *IMU* xi, pp. 134-7, correcting and amplifying R. Sabbadini, *Classici e umanisti da codici Ambrosiani* (Florence, 1933), pp. 59-62. On Marius Rusticus see Dunston, loc. cit., pp. 138-42, and G. Brugnoli, 'La "praefatio in Suetonium" del Poliziano', in *Giornale italiano di filologia*, x (1957), pp. 211-20, esp. pp. 216, 219-20; but see above all the new information and the suggestion for a new interpretation of the incident in A. Perosa, 'Due lettere di Domizio Calderini', *Rinascimento*, 2nd ser., xiii (1973), pp. 6, 13-15.

44. G. Merula, 'In Epistolam Sapphus contra Domitium annotationes', in *P. Ovidii Nasonis Heroides cum interpretibus Hubertino Crescent. et Iano Parrhasio* (Brescia, 1551), cols. 467-70, at 470: 'Hic ego aliquid subiungam ex occultis Graecorum commentariis sumptum, conduplicationem istam non tam ad emphasim esse factam ab Ovidio, quam ut geminando [ed.: germinando] eadem verba characterem Sapphus demonstraret, quae, ut Demetrius Phalaereus author est, gratiam suis carminibus ἐκ τῆς ἀναδιπλώσεως quesivit. Nam ubi περὶ χάριτος λόγου praecepta tradit, de charactere Sapphus, Haec, scribit, sermonis gratiae, quae per figuras fiunt manifestae, et plurimae sunt apud Sap.; quemadmodum anadiplosis, ubi nympha ad Partheniam ait:
    παρθενία παρθενία ποῖ με λιποῦσα οἴχῃ;
    Quae respondet ad eam per eandem figuram:
    οὐκέτι ἥξω πρὸς σέ, οὐκέτι ἥξω.
    Maior enim gratia apparet, quam si semel esset dictum et sine figura . . . '. Merula's argument has continued to be controversial: it was summarized and ridiculed by S. G. de Vries, *Epistula Sapphus ad Phaonem* (Berlin, 1888), p. 53 ad loc.; defended by J. Hubaux, 'Ovidiana, I. Ovide et Sappho', *Le Musée Belge*, xxx (1926), pp. 197-218, at 215-16; and has been seriously discussed in the recent work of H. Jacobson, *Ovid's Heroides* (Princeton, 1974), p. 285.

45. See L. Ruberto, 'Studi sul Poliziano filologo', in *Rivista di filologia e d'istruzione classica*, xii (1884), pp. 235-7.

46. Poliziano, *Miscellanea*, 'Praefatio ad Laurentium Medicem', *Opera* (Basel, 1553), p. 216 : 'Enimvero ne putent homines male feriati, nos ista quaequae sunt, de fece hausisse, neque grammaticorum transiluisse lineas, Pliniano statim exemplo nomina praetexuimus auctorum, sed honestorum, veterumque duntaxat, unde ius ista sumunt, et a quibus versuram fecimus, nec autem, quos alii tantum citaverint, ipsorum opera temporibus interciderint, sed quorum nosmet ipsi thesauros tractavimus, quorum sumus per literas peregrinati, quanquam et vetustas codicum, et nomismatum fides, et in aes, aut in marmore incisae antiquitates, quae tu nobis Laurenti suppeditasti, plurimum etiam praeter librorum varietatem nostris commentationibus suffragantur.' Cf. Pliny, *N.H.*, *praef.*, xxi: '. . . auctorum nomina praetexui.'

47. Calderini wrote: 'Opus Ovidii est plenum irae et obscuritatis. Ego vero quae aut a Graecis Apollodoro, Lycophrone, Pausania, Strabone, Apollonio et illius interprete, aliisque scriptoribus, aut a nostris tradita sunt, quae quidem ad huius explicationem pertinere videbantur, in hoc opusculum congessi.' *Commentarioli in Ibyn Ovidii*, Hain 4242 (Rome, 7 Sept. 1474), preface, fol. 2ᵛ. Poliziano wrote: 'Enarravit Domitius libellum Nasonis in Ibin, praefatus ex Apollodoro se, Lycophrone, Pausania, Strabone, Apollonio, aliisque Graecis, etiamque Latinis accepta scribere. Multa in eo commentario vana, ridiculaque confingit, et comminiscitur ex tempore, commodoque suo, quibus fidem facit, aut se frontem penitus amisisse, aut tam magnum sibi fuisse intervallum inter frontem et linguam (sicut ait quidam) ut frons comprimere linguam non potuerit.' *Miscellanea*, I. 75; *Opera*, p. 285.

48. Calderini, *Commentarioli in Ibyn Ovidii*, fol. 25ʳ *ad* 569: 'Agenor lapsu equi inserta ori manu extinctus est.'

49. The passages in question are *Odyssey* IV.285 ff. and Tryphiodorus, Ἰλίου Ἅλωσις 476 ff.; see *Publi Ovidi Nasonis Ibis*, ed. A. La Penna (Florence, 1957), pp. 153-4 ad loc.: cf. *Scholia in Ovidi Ibin*, ed. La Penna, p. xlviii.

50. Calderini, 'Ex tertio libro observationum', in *Lampas*, ed. Gruter, i, pp. 316-17: 'Incidi nuper in quasdam Laurentii commentatiunculas, quas in Fabium composuit, in quibus cum alia desideravi tum testium, quos citat aliquando, fidem atque adeo, ut unum subiiciamus, ubi Fabius de verbis peregrinis ita scribit: *Nam*

Mastrugam, quod Sardum est illudens Cicero ex industria dixit [*Inst. or.* I.v.8], Laurentius, locum indicans ubi id Cicero dixerit, haec addit: *Cicero pro Scauro, quem purpura regalis non commovit, eum Sardorum Mastruga mutavit* [*Quintiliani institutiones cum commento Laurentii Vallensis, Pomponii, ac Sulpitii*, Proctor 4865, Venice 18.viii.1494,sig. c iiii^r, quoting Isidore, *Origines* XIX.xxiii.5]. Equidem *Scauri caussam* actam fuisse apud Ciceronem, legi apud Valerium Max. et Pedianum: *Orationem* vero a Cicerone pro illo habitam, unde se haec accipere Laurentius profitetur, legi nusquam, neque exstare arbitror, vereorque ne Grammaticum aliquem ignobilem secutus haec verba recitaverit potius, quam legerit usquam apud Ciceronem.' Cf. *JWCI* xl, p. 159 n. 27.

51.　Ibid., p. 317: 'Mendosa est dictio [*medico*, for *melico*] apud Plinium, ut ego quidem arbitror, et heri observavi, cum de Simonide nonnulla apud Graecum scriptorem legi . . . '. The 'Greek writer' is merely the *Suda*, s.v. Σιμωνίδης.

52.　Poliziano, *Opera*, p. 304: 'Neque autem istos Eupolidis poetae versus ex ipsius statim fontibus hausimus, ut cuius opera aetate interciderint, sed eorum partem ex interprete quopiam Aristidae rhetoris accuratissimo, partem ex epistola Plinii Iunioris accepimus.'

53.　Poliziano, *Miscellanea*, I.45, *Opera*, p. 263: '*Patroclo iuniorem Achillem, contra quam aut Aeschylus prodiderit, aut vulgo existimetur.*'

54.　Petrarch said that he followed those 'whose verisimilitude or greater authority demands that they be given greater credence' — 'Ego . . . eorum imitator sum, quibus vel similitudo vel autoritas maior ut eis potissimum stetur impetrat.' The translation is that of B. G. Kohl, 'Petrarch's Prefaces to *De viris illustribus*', in *History and Theory*, xiv (1974), p. 139; the original is from Petrarch, *Prose*, ed. G. Martellotti *et al.* (Milan and Naples, 1955), p. 220. Petrarch uses much the same formula in his *Epistula posteritati*, where he says that in his study of history he occasionally has encountered conflicting accounts and that in such cases he has followed 'quo me vel veri similitudo rerum vel scribentium traxit autoritas' (*Prose*, ed. Martellotti, p. 6). For examples of Petrarch's use of historical sources see H. J. Erasmus, *The Origins of Rome in Historiography from Petrarch to Perizonius* (Assen, 1962), pp. 8–11; S. Prete, *Observations on the history of textual criticism in the medieval and Renaissance periods* (Collegeville, Minn., n. d.), pp. 19–20.

　　On Salutati see A. Von Martin, *Coluccio Salutati's Traktat 'Vom Tyrannen'. Eine kulturgeschichtliche Untersuchung nebst Textedition* (Berlin and Leipzig, 1913): 'Exkurs: Salutati als philologisch-historischer Kritiker', pp. 77–98; B. L. Ullman, *The Humanism of Coluccio Salutati* (Padua, 1963), pp. 95–9. On Bruni see A. D. Momigliano, 'Polybius' Reappearance in Western Europe', in *Polybe* (Vandoeuvres, 1974), pp. 356–7. For a brief but helpful discussion of Biondo see Dorothy M. Robathan, 'Flavio Biondo's *Roma Instaurata*', in *Medievalia et Humanistica*, n. s. i (1970), p. 204.

55.　In general, the humanists hesitated to attribute error to ancient writers. Thus, Salutati argues in the *De tyranno* that a statement in Valerius Maximus must be wrong, since there is incontrovertible evidence to the contrary in Livy. He explicitly states that in such cases it is proper to assume that the error is a textual corruption: 'et potius credant textum Valerii fuisse corruptum, quam eum in tam supinum errorem, qui in tante scientie virum cadere non debuit, incidisse'. He concludes by saying that Valerius Maximus should be emended to agree with Livy (Salutati, *Il trattato 'De Tyranno' e lettere scelte*, ed. F. Ercole (Bologna, 1942), p. 15). There were exceptions. Valla set out to expose a genealogical error in Livy; see Erasmus, *The Origins of Rome*, pp. 28–9; and Poliziano argued in *Miscellanea*, I.53; *Opera*, pp. 268–9, that Cicero had wrongly attributed a speech of Odysseus to Agamemnon. For the most part, however, the humanists failed to make a sufficiently clear distinction between textual criticism — the restoration of corrupt passages — and historical criticism

- the reconstruction of events. As a result, they often did the latter while thinking that they were doing the former. I thank H. J. de Jonge for pointing this out.

56. Poliziano, *Opera*, p. 259: 'Literas igitur Cadmi Phoenicis munus, et papyrum Niloticam, et atramentum scriptorium, et calamum librarium literatoris eius germanum instrumentum videtur mihi Ausonius sub haec involucra complicasse. Cadmus enim literas primus in Graeciam attulit e Phoenice.' For Greek traditions on the origin of the alphabet see R. Pfeiffer, *History of Classical Scholarship* ... (Oxford, 1968), pp. 19-22.

57. Ibid.: 'Omitto quod et Suidas, aut Zopyrion potius φοινίκεια vocatas literas ait. Omitto Plinium, caeterosque permultos, qui dicant eas a Cadmo in Graeciam allatas. Nam cum diversi quae legerant apud Herodotum passim meminerint, satis ipsi fecisse videmur, quod ista suae reddimus autoritati. Nec enim tam numeranda, sicuti putamus, veterum testimonia sunt, quam ponderanda.' Poliziano here alludes to Pliny, *Epistolae*, II.xii.5: 'Numerantur enim sententiae, non ponderantur ... '.

58. Beroaldo, *Annotationes centum*, sig. hi[v]: 'Litteras Cadmi filias vocat, quoniam Cadmus litterarum inventor fuisse perhibetur, qui e Phoenice in Graeciam sexdecim numero attulisse fertur a Plinio in vii Na. hi. Vnde antiqui Greci litteras Phoenicias cognominaverunt, ut autor est Herodotus in Terpsicore. Ait idem scriptor se vidisse in templo Apollinis litteras Cadmeas in tripodibus quibusdam incisas, magna ex parte Ionicis litteris consimiles. Quin etiam Cornelius Tacitus Cadmum autorem litterarum fuisse autumat, rudibus adhuc Graecorum populis. Non me preterit alia ab aliis scriptoribus de origine litterarum commemorari, quibus in presentia supersedebimus cum ad rem nostram non pertineant.'

59. In maintaining that Poliziano revolutionized philological method, I do not wish to imply that his emendations and interpretations were always superior to those of his predecessors. See below, text to nn. 138 ff.

60. Kenney, *The Classical Text*, pp. 5-6; cf. G. Funaioli, 'Lineamenti d'una storia della filologia attraverso i secoli', in *Studi di letteratura antica*, i (Bologna, 1946), p. 284.

61. Poliziano, *Miscellanea*, I.57; *Opera*, p. 271, quoted by Silvia Rizzo, *Il lessico filologico degli umanisti*, p. 162: 'Nam cum ipsa quoque mendosissima plerisque sint locis, vestigia tamen adhuc servant haud obscura verae indagandae lectionis, quae de novis codicibus ab improbis librariis prorsus obliterantur.'

62. Poliziano, *Miscellanea*, I.71; *Opera*, p. 282: 'Pudet referre quam manifestum, sed nondum tamen a quoquam (quod sciam) nisi nobis indicibus animadversum, mendum Vergilianis codicibus inoleverit libro Aeneid. octavo: Quod fieri ferro, liquidove potestur electro. Caeterum in volumine illo, quod est in intima Vaticana bibliotheca mire vetustum, et grandibus characteribus perscriptum, non potestur offendas, sed potest usitatius verbum.'

63. Poliziano, *Miscellanea*, I.97; *Opera*, p. 307: 'Locus apud Suetonium in Claudio ita perperam legitur in plerisque voluminibus: Si aut ornatum, aut pegma, vel quid tale aliud parum cessisset: cum veri integrique sic habeant codices: Si automaton, vel pegma. Inspice vel Bononiae librum ex divi Dominici, vel item alterum Florentiae ex divi Marci bibliotheca, quam gens Medica publicavit, veterem utrunque. Sed et utroque vetustiorem, quem nunc ipsi domesticum possidemus, ... ubique hanc nimirum posteriorem scripturam invenies.'

64. Pp. 147-64. On the quality of Poliziano's work as a collator, see R. Ribuoli, *La collazione polizianea del Codice Bembino di Terenzio* (Rome, 1981).

65. See Rizzo, pp. 233-4, 257, 271. Others came much closer than Beroaldo to Poliziano's standards. For the case of B. Fonzio see V. Fera, 'Il primo testo critico di Valerio Flacco', *Giornale italiano di filologia*, n.s. 10 [31] (1979), pp. 230-54.

66. Beroaldo, *Annotationes centum*, sig. [b vi^r] : 'Conditam pixidem vocat medicamentis refertam; quae dictio a condio, non a condo, deducitur. Ideoque pronuntiandum est media syllaba producta et ita versus legendus: Turgida nec prodest condita pixide Lide; ubi condita septimus est casus, et cum pixide copulatur. Ego nuperrime versum istum ita scriptum legi in vetusto codice, et olim Angelus Pollicianus, Latine Graeceque doctissimus, mihi retulit se ita locum istum in sincerae fidei libro scriptum animadvertisse.'

67. Poliziano, *Miscellanea*, I.46, *Opera*, p. 263: '. . . cacoethes legendum suspicamur, ut sit quod apud Graecos τὸ κακόηθες. Eo namque verbo frequentissimo usitatissimoque mala consuetudo significatur. Quod item in vetusto codice Langobardis exarato literis reperimus, cuius mihi potestatem legendi fecit Franciscus Gaddius Florentinus summi magistratus a secretis, prudens humanusque vir, nec literis incultus. Sed et ille versus ita in eodem: Turgida nec prodest condita pyxide Lyde.' The MS mentioned is now Vat. lat. 3286; it is in Beneventan script and was written in the 11th century. See Rizzo, *Lessico filologico*, pp. 124–5.

68. S. Timpanaro, *La genesi del metodo del Lachmann*, 2nd edn. (Padua, 1981), pp. 4–6; cf. G. Kirner, 'Contributo alla critica del testo delle *Epistolae ad Familiares* di Cicerone (1. IX–XVI)', in *Studi italiani di filologia classica*, ix (1901), pp. 400–6.

69. Poliziano, *Opera*, pp. 246–7: 'Nactus sum Ciceronis epistolarum familiarium volumen antiquissimum, de quo etiam supra dixi, tum ex eo ipso, alterum descriptum, sicuti quidam putant, Francisci Petrarchae manu. Descriptum autem ex ipso liquet multis argumentis, quae nunc omiserim: sed hic posterior, quem dixi, codex, ita est ab indiligente bibliopola conglutinatus, uti una transposita paginarum decuria, contra quam notata [text cit. *nota*; *notata* is the reading of the Venice 1498 edn. of Poliziano's works, and it is obviously correct] sit numeris deprehendatur. Est autem liber in publica gentis Medicae bibliotheca. De hoc itaque uno quantum coniiciam, cuncti plane quotquot extant [ed. 1498; extent 1553] adhuc epistolarum earundem codices, ceu de fonte capiteque manarunt, inque omnibus praeposterus et perversus lectionis ordo, qui mihi nunc loco restituendus, quasique instaurandus.'

70. Poliziano, *Opera*, p. 260: 'quibusdam etiam, saltem in praefatione, velut ab autore plane, et a cogitante, atque generante potius, quam a librario, et exceptore inductis, expunctis ac superscriptis, . . .'.

71. Ibid., p. 261: 'Igitur in Pandectis his, non iam Pisanis, ut quondam, sed Florentinis, in quibus pura sunt verba: nec ut in caeteris plena maculis et scabie, diffisum [ed. 1498; diffissum 1553] reperio, non diffusum'. Cf. ibid., p. 260: 'Diffisionis vocabulum, et item quod dici solitum in iudiciis diffindi diem, pene iam sublatum e medio, atque inscitia quadam improba importunaque bonis artibus exitiosa iam obliteratum restituere ipsi pro virili conabimur, et renovare diligentia nostra.' The point was hardly important except from a philological viewpoint, as the passage had been understood even in the corrupt form; see *Accursii glossa in Digestum vetus* (Turin, 1969), p. 60 note ad loc.: 'Diffusum id est differendum'.

72. See H. E. Troje, *Graeca leguntur: Die Aneignung des byzantinischen Rechts und die Entstehung eines humanistischen Corpus iuris civilis in der Jurisprudenz des 16. Jahrhunderts* (Cologne and Vienna, 1971), pp. 21–2, though Troje's interpretation of the episode differs from that proposed here.

73. Poliziano, *Opera*, p. 287: 'Caeterum in Pandectis istis Florentinis, quas etiam archetypas opinamur, negatio prorsus est nulla. Quo fit, ut interpres legum Florentinus Accursius, mendosum et ipse nactus codicem, pene dixerim miserabiliter se torqueat.'

74. On Valla's attacks on medieval jurisprudence see M. P. Gilmore, 'The Renaissance

conception of the lessons of history', in *Facets of the Renaissance*, ed. W. H. Werkmeister, 2nd edn. (New York, Evanston, and London, 1963), pp. 92–5; Kelley, *Foundations of Modern Historical Scholarship*, pp. 39–43. For Beroaldo see *Annotationes centum*, sig. [h iii^r] : 'Sexcenta sunt id genus apud iurisconsultos ab Acursio perperam enarrata.'

75. Aulus Gellius, *Noctes Atticae* I.vii.1 (tr. J. C. Rolfe): 'In oratione Ciceronis quinta in Verrem, libro spectatae fidei, Tironiana cura atque disciplina facto . . . '. To be sure, many of the MSS that Gellius and his fellow antiquaries prized seem to have been forgeries, but Poliziano had no way of knowing that. Cf. J. E. G. Zetzel, '*Emendavi ad Tironem*. Some Notes on Scholarship in the Second Century A.D.', *Harvard Studies in Classical Philology*, lxxvii (1973), pp. 225–43.

76. Aulus Gellius, *Noctes Atticae* IX.xiv.1–4.

77. R. Sabbadini, *Storia e critica di testi latini*, 2nd edn. (Padua, 1971), pp. 77–108.

78. See *Two Renaissance Book Hunters. The Letters of Poggius Bracciolini to Nicolaus de Niccolis*, tr. Phyllis W. G. Gordan (New York and London, 1974), pp. 74–8.

79. G. Pasquali, *Storia della tradizione e critica del testo*, 2nd edn. (Florence, 1952), pp. 61–3.

80. Giovanni Lamola to Guarino of Verona, 31 May 1428, quoted in Sabbadini, *Storia e critica*, p. 106: 'Ego tamen, quantum diligentiae ac ingenii peritiaeque in me fuit . . . adhibui, ut omnia secundum priorem textum restituerem. . .'.

81. Ibid.: '. . . ex eo accurato exemplari exemplum, quod vulgatum ubique est, traduxerunt . . . '.

82. Ibid.: 'Curavi etiam ut usque ad punctum minimum omnia ad veteris speciem exprimerem, etiam ubi essent nonnullae vetustatis delirationes, nam velim potius cum veteri illo delirare, quam cum istis diligentibus sapere . . . '. This letter is quoted in part and its sources and significance are discussed in Rizzo, *Lessico filologico*, pp. 175–7.

83. Giorgio Merula, preface to his edition of Plautus, Venice 1472, quoted by Rizzo, *Lessico filologico*, p. 314: 'his omnibus accedit unum tantum fuisse librum a quo, velut archetypo, omnia deducta sunt quae habentur exempla.'

84. Sabbadini, *Storia e critica*, p. 241.

85. Ibid., pp. 241–57; C. Questa, *Per la storia del testo di Plauto nell'umanesimo*, I: *La 'recensio' di Poggio Bracciolini* (Rome, 1968), pp. 7–21.

86. Rizzo, *Lessico filologico*, pp. 314–15.

87. Reynolds and Wilson, *Scribes and Scholars*, p. 128.

88. R. Weiss, *The Renaissance Discovery of Classical Antiquity* (Oxford, 1969), p. 71.

89. Poliziano, *Miscellanea*, I.77; *Opera*, pp. 286–7.

90. Poliziano used the first recension of Fra Giocondo's sylloge (1478–c. 1489), which was dedicated to Lorenzo; in it there were separate sections for inscriptions that Giocondo had seen and those that he had found in other sylloges, or that had been reported to him by others. After citing 2 inscriptions in which the form 'Vergilius' appears, and carefully specifying their locations, Poliziano writes (*Opera*, p. 286): 'Idque nos utrinque non sine aliquot arbitris etiam de proximo inspeximus. Neque enim antiquarum duntaxat inspectionum auriti testes, sed et oculati esse concupivimus.' On his use of Giocondo's sylloge he says (ibid., p. 287): 'In collectaneis autem, quae nuperrime ad Laurentium Medicem Iucundus misit, vir unus, opinor, titulorum monimentorumque veterum supra mortales caeteros non diligentissimus solum, sed etiam sine controversia peritissimus, relata quoque invenio elogia duo, quae Romae (sicut ille

indicat) in marmoribus inveniuntur: . . . '. On Giocondo, see Weiss, *Renaissance Discovery*, pp. 150-1.

91. Poliziano, *Opera*, pp. 248-9; cf. *The Tragedies of Ennius. The Fragments*, ed. H. D. Jocelyn (Cambridge, 1967), Frag. CV a, pp. 118-19; cf. p. 347.

92. Poliziano, *Miscellanea*, I.2; *Opera*, p. 228; I.69; *Opera*, p. 282 trans. in part in *JWCI* xl, p. 173.

93. Poliziano, *Miscellanea*, I.68; *Opera*, p. 282.

94. Marchesi, *Bartolomeo della Fonte*. Further examples in *JWCI* xl, p. 174.

95. Poliziano, *Opera*, pp. 247-8: 'Vertit hos nimirum quam potuit ad unguem poeta ingeniosissimus, et sunt tamen in graeco nonnulla, quae noster parum enarrate. Quin si veris concedendum, transmarinam illam nescio quam Venerem, ne attigit quidem noster.'

96. Ibid., 'Quod vitium, linguae potius minus lascivientis, quam parum copiosae'. Cf. Quintilian IV.i.77: 'Ovidius lascivire in Metamorphosesin solet'; cf. also X.i.88, 93.

97. Poliziano, *Miscellanea*, I.4; *Opera*, pp. 229-30: '. . . ea . . . quae de iusto atque iniusto, deque sui cuique notitia Socrates inibi cum Alcibiade agit, delibasse ex eo . . . Persius intelligatur.' Cf. *Auli Persii Flacci Satirarum liber*, ed. O. Jahn (Leipzig, 1843), pp. 166-7; R. Cardini, *La critica del Landino* (Florence, 1973), p. 173n.

98. Ibid.: 'Consimiliter quod ait ibidem, Tecum habita: nonne dialogi eiusdem pervidisse videtur voluntatem? Siquidem (quod Proclus enarrator affirmat) nihil hic aliud Plato, quam literam Delphicam respexit, monentem, se quisque ut norit.' Cf. Proclus Diadochus, *Commentary on the First Alcibiades of Plato*, ed. L. G. Westerink (Amsterdam, 1954), sect. 6, 11; sect. 19, 11-15.

99. Ibid.: 'Sic item, *Dinomaches ego sum*, ductum ex eo quod apud Platonem sic est, ὦ φίλε παῖ κλεινίου καὶ δεινομάχης [Persius IV.20; *Alcibiades* I.105D] .'

100. B. Bischoff, 'Living with the Satirists', in *Classical Influences on European Culture, A.D. 500-1500*, ed. R. R. Bolgar (Cambridge, 1971), pp. 83-94.

101. F. Jacoby, 'Zur Entstehung der römischen Elegie', *RhM*, N. F. lx (1905), p. 38 and n. 1.

102. Aulus Gellius, *Noctes Atticae* IX.ix.1-3 (tr. J. C. Rolfe): 'Quando ex poematis Graecis vertendae imitandaeque sunt insignes sententiae, non semper, aiunt, enitendum ut omnia omnino verba in eum in quem dicta sunt modum vertamus. Perdunt enim gratiam pleraque, si quasi invita et recusantia violentius transferantur. Scite ergo et considerate Vergilius, cum aut Homeri aut Hesiodi aut Apollonii aut Parthenii aut Callimachi aut Theocriti aut quorundam aliorum locos effingeret, partim reliquit, alia expressit.' (Rolfe's translation slightly altered.)

103. See esp. Macrobius, *Saturnalia* V.2-22. Cf. in general P. Courcelle, *Late Latin Writers and their Greek Sources*, tr. H. E. Wedeck (Cambridge, Mass., 1969), pp. 13-26.

104. De Bury probably knew only the preface and Books I-VII of Gellius; see Sabbadini, *Le scoperte dei codici latini e greci ne' secoli XIV e XV. Nuove ricerche* (Florence, 1914), p. 9 and n. 40.

105. R. de Bury, *Philobiblon*, ed. and tr. E. C. Thomas and M. Maclagan (Oxford, 1960), p. 111.

106. For an example see R. Sabbadini, *La scuola e gli studi di Guarino Guarini Veronese* (Catania, 1896), p. 219; others are listed in *JWCI* xl, p. 178, n. 99.

107. Domizio Calderini, *Elucubratio in quaedam Propertii loca quae difficiliora videantur*, first published at Rome on 13.viii.1475 (Hain 14983); my references are to the edition of the same collection of Calderini's works published at Brescia on 8.vi.1476 (Hain-Reichling 4244; Proctor 6949).

108. Calderini, *Elucubratio*, sig. [c viʳ], *ad* I.20: 'Theocritum in primis hoc loco imitatur et transfert, de fabula Hylae.'

109. Ibid., *ad* III.xxi.24: 'Theseae brachia longa viae. Muros longos intelligit: qui Graece [*space left for Greek*] dicebantur. Ii ex urbe in Pyreum usque excurrebant. Historia est apud Thucydidem diligentissime perscripta.'

110. Calderini, *Elucubratio*, sig. [c.vʳ], *ad* I.xiii.21: 'Hemonio: id est Thessalo. Sed dissentit a Strabone Propertius: nam Enipeum amatum a puella scribit Strabo esse in Pisana regione, cum tamen alter sit in Thessalia.' Cf. Strabo VIII.iii.32; IX.v.6. Strabo places a river Enipeus or Eniseus in Thessaly, but the river Enipeus with which Tyro fell in love he situates in Elis.

111. See in general D. O. Ross, Jr., *Backgrounds to Augustan Poetry. Gallus, Elegy and Rome* (Cambridge, 1975). IV.i.64 is normally interpreted as a statement of Propertius' intention to write aetiological poems about Rome, modelled in scope and method on the *Aetia* of Callimachus; see e.g. *The Elegies of Propertius*, ed. H. E. Butler and E. A. Barber (Oxford, 1933), pp. lxvi, 322.

112. Calderini, *Elucubratio*, sigs. [d5ᵛ-d6ʳ], *ad* IV.i.64: 'Romani Callimachi. Se Romanum Callimachum appellat. Nam Callimachum, poetam Graecum, versibus Latinis explicat.'

113. Ibid., sig. c2ᵛ, *ad* I.ii.1: 'Vita. Ex Callimacho, quom praecipue imitatur, verbum deductum est. Nam et ille blandiens Graeca voce amicam [ʒωήν] appellat.'

114. Beroaldo's note on IV.i.64 reads as follows (Tibullus, Catullus, Propertius [Venice, 9.xii.1491], Hain-Copinger *4763; Proctor 5029, sig. [s viᵛ]): 'Vmbria Romani. Appellat se Romanum Callimachum: quoniam qualis est apud Graecos Callimachus scriptor elegiarum, talis est apud Romanos Propertius: qui in primis Callimachum aemulatus est, et illum in scribendo habet archetypon. Ita Virgilius dictus est Mantuanus Homerus: cuius emulatus est non modo magnitudinem, sed simplicitatem orationis, tacitamque maiestatem.' The same point is made in his introductory remarks, ibid., sig. 1ʳ. On *vita* see sig. 1 iiʳ, *ad* I.ii.1: 'Vita. Vox est amatoria, Graece a Iuvenale dictum est [*space left for Greek words*] idest, vita et anima. Id genus multa reperies apud Plautum. Imitatio est Callimachi, a quo [*space left for Greek word*] id est, vita, amica appellatur.'

115. Poliziano, *Miscellanea*, I.80, *Opera*, p. 289: 'Iam illud quoque miror, cur et Domitius, et alii quidam post illum, quocunque momento, quacunque occasione scribere audeant, hoc aut illud imitatione Callimachi dictum fuisse a Propertio, cum praeter hymnos pauculos nihil prorsus extet ad nos poetae istius, nec autem plane quicquam quod amoris argumenta contineat.'

116. Calderini's own commentary on Juvenal — which A. C. Dionisotti kindly consulted for me — does not discuss the word in question.

117. Propertius IV.ix.57–8:
    Magnam Tiresias aspexit Pallada vates,
        Fortia dum posita Gorgone membra lavat.

118. Poliziano, *Opera*, pp. 288–95.

119. For the later history of the debate on the origins of Latin love-elegy, see *JWCI* xl, p. 181 n. 112. In addition to the material gathered there see A. Cartault, *À propos du Corpus Tibullianum. Un siècle de philologie latine classique* (Paris, 1906), p. 518.

120. For a modern comparative discussion of the Euripides and Ennius passages that Poliziano treated in *Miscellanea* 1.27 see O. Skutsch, *Studia Enniana* (London, 1968), pp. 166–9.

121. Poliziano, *Miscellanea*, I.24; *Opera*, p. 246: 'Quin ubi Callimachus in Apollinis ait hymno,

ὁ φθόνος ἀπόλλωνος ἐπ' οὔατα λάθριος [ed. 1498; λάτριος 1553] εἶπεν
οὐκ ἄγαμαι τὸν ἀοιδὸν, ὃς οὐδ' ὅσα πόντος ἀείδει [ed. 1498; ὀνείδει 1553]
                                                          [*Hymni* II.105–6],
in eum locum sic interpres propemodum: Per haec, inquit, illos accusat, qui sic
in eum cavillarentur, quasi magnum facere poema non posset. Vnde coactus
est Hecalen facere. Verba interpretis ita sunt: . . . '.

122. Before revealing the Platonic source of Persius' 4th Satire, Poliziano makes the
general claim that a good critic must also have complete mastery of all other
disciplines: 'Qui poetarum interpretationem suscipit, eum non solum (quod
dicitur) ad Aristophanis lucernam, sed etiam ad Cleanthis oportet lucubrasse.
Nec prospiciendae autem philosophorum modo familiae, sed et iureconsul-
torum, et medicorum item, et dialecticorum, et quicunque doctrinae illum
orbem faciunt, quae vocamus Encyclia, sed et philologorum [ed. 1498; philosophorum 1553] quoque omnium. Nec prospiciendae tantum, verum intro-
spiciendae magis, neque (quod dicitur), ab limine ac vestibulo salutandae, sed
arcessendae potius in penetralia, et in intimam familiaritatem, si rem iuvare
Latinam studemus, et inscitiam quotidie invalescentem profligare; alioqui
semidocta sedulitas cum magna sui persuasione detrimento sit [om. ed. 1498],
non usui.' (*Miscellanea*, I.4; *Opera*, p. 229). His reference to Cleanthes and
Aristophanes is also an allusion to Varro's similarly phrased claim that a good
grammarian must have mastered all existing approaches to the study of etymology: 'Quod non solum ad Aristophanis lucernam, sed etiam ad Cleanthis
lucubravi' (*De lingua latina* V.9) – a much discussed passage. Poliziano also
advances a polemical claim for the status of criticism by implication in his discussion of the relative ages of Patroclus and Achilles (*Misc.* I.45); for this was
one of the very topics that Seneca had ridiculed grammarians for discussing in
Epistulae morales 88.6. To take the question seriously was also to deny
Seneca's assessment of its worth.

123. On Argyropoulos see J. E. Seigel, 'The Teaching of Argyropulos and the
Rhetoric of the First Humanists', in *Action and Conviction in Early Modern
Europe. Essays in Memory of E. H. Harbison*, ed. T. K. Rabb and J. E. Seigel
(Princeton, 1969), pp. 237–60; on this controversy see the excellent study by
E. Garin, ''Ενδελέχεια e 'Εντελέχεια nelle discussioni umanistiche', *Atene e
Roma*, ser. III, v (1937), pp. 177–87.

124. Poliziano, *Miscellanea* I.1; *Opera*, p. 227: 'Quid autem prohibet, quo minus
Cicero ipse videre matricem quoque librorum Aristotelis, qui fuerint ipsius
aetate publicati; si non incorruptam, certe (sicuti diximus) conscribellatam
potuerit?'

125. I cannot enter here into the important controversies about the philosophical
aspirations and achievements of the humanists; see in general C. B. Schmitt,
*A Critical Survey and Bibliography of Studies on Renaissance Aristotelianism
1958-1969* (Padua, 1971), for an orientation in some of the major issues. I am
inclined to take the humanists' claims somewhat more seriously than does the
leading American authority, Professor Kristeller, and a little less seriously than
does the leading Italian authority, Professor Garin.

126. See in general E. Bigi, *La cultura del Poliziano e altri studi umanistici* (Pisa,
1967).

127. Poliziano, ep. ded. in L. B. Alberti, *De re aedificatoria*, GKW 579 (Florence,
29 Dec. 1485), sig. aᵛ.

128. On what Renaissance readers expected from Neo-Latin poetry – and on its
general social and cultural functions – see the excellent treatment by C. Ree-
dijk, *The Poems of Desiderius Erasmus*, Diss. Leiden (Leiden, 1956), Ch. II:
'Not From Mere Foolishness . . .', pp. 35–41.

129. See J. Hutton, *The Greek Anthology in Italy to the Year 1800* (Ithaca, N.Y.,
1935).

130. Poliziano, *Opera*, p. 241: 'In tragoedia Senecae, quae Hercules furens inscribitur, hic senariolus legitur: Sublimis altas luna concipiat feras. Alias enim codex habet vetustus ex publica Medicae familiae bibliotheca, non altas, ut in vulgariis exemplaribus. Cuius intellectum loci non [non ed. 1498; om. 1553] temere aliunde quam ex Achille desumpseris, quem autorem Iulius quoque Firmicus in Matheseon libris et citat et laudat. Is igitur in commentariis Arateis, cum de luna verba facit, ita scribit ad verbum:

  εἶναι δὲ ἐπ' αὐτῆς οἴκησιν ἄλλην ποταμούς τε καὶ ὅσα ἐπὶ
  γῆς, καὶ τὸν λέοντα τὸν νεμιαῖον ἐκεῖθεν πεσεῖν μυθολογοῦσιν.

  Id est: In ea etiam habitari, fluviosque esse et caetera, sicut in terra. Quin Nemeaeum quoque illinc cecidisse leonem fabulantur. Ex quo nos in Nutrice:
  Nemeaeaque tesqua
  Lunigenam mentita feram.'

131. See e.g. Erasmus, *De conscribendis epistolis, Opera omnia*, new edn., I.2 (Amsterdam, 1971), p. 266: 'Caeterum cui palma debeatur in hoc genere, non est huius instituti pluribus verbis persequi. Si quis omissis Graecis, patiatur quenquam ullo in genere anteponi, M. Tullio, et Plinio, et Politiano primas detulerim. Sed hac sane in re fruatur suo quisque iudicio'; cf. also the *index nominum*, s.v. Poliziano, Agnolo Ambrogini, and *JWCI* xl, p. 185 and n. 130.

132. F. Simone, 'La Notion d'Encyclopédie: Elément caractéristique de la Renaissance française', in *French Renaissance Studies 1540-70*, ed. P. Sharratt (Edinburgh, 1976), pp. 245, 259-60 nn. 78-82.

133. See Ch. VII, below.

134. Poliziano, *Miscellanea*, I.41; *Opera*, p. 261: 'Cuius tamen voluminis [i.e., the Florentine Pandects] legendi ac versandi per otium mihi est uni facta copia, Laurentii Medicis opera causaque, qui vir, suae reipublicae princeps, dum studiosis obsequatur, etiam ad haec usque officia se demittit.' Cf. also n. 90, above.

135. I follow, with reservations, H. Baron, *The Crisis of the Early Italian Renaissance*, 2nd edn. (Princeton, 1966); for an important critique see Q. Skinner, *The Foundations of Modern Political Thought* (Cambridge, 1978), i: *The Renaissance*, Parts 1 and 2.

136. For the poetic uses to which Poliziano put his scholarship see e.g. A. Perosa, 'Febris. A Poetic Myth Created by Poliziano', *JWCI* ix (1946), pp. 74-95; Bigi, *La cultura del Poliziano*, pp. 89-90 and n. 50; M. Martelli, 'La semantica di Poliziano e la *"Centuria secunda"* dei *"Miscellanea"'*, *Rinascimento*, ser. II, xiii (1973), pp. 21-84; L. Cesarini Martinelli, 'In margine al commento di Angelo Poliziano alle *Selve* di Stazio', *Interpres*, i (1978), pp. 96-145. My view is indebted especially to D. Quint's introduction to his translation of *The Stanze of Angelo Poliziano* (Amherst, 1979); for a very different view see Cardini, *La critica del Landino*, pp. 48 ff.

137. See above, text to nn. 31 ff.

138. See Dunston in *IMU* xi, pp. 143-4.

139. S. Timpanaro, *'Atlas cum compare gibbo'*, *Contributi di filologia e di storia della lingua latina* (Rome, 1978), pp. 333-43.

140. Poliziano, *Commento inedito alle Selve di Stazio*, pp. 5-7; *Miscellanea*, II.48, *Miscellaneorum centuria secunda*, ed. V. Branca and M. Pastore Stocchi, *ed. minor* (Florence, 1978), pp. 86-9.

141. Poliziano, *Epistolario*, III.18: 'Iuvit enim, quantum potuit, rem literariam . . .'.

142. Poliziano, *Epistolario*, III.19: 'Ego vero sic Domitium studiosis, quasi foveam viatoribus ostendo.'

143. Ibid.: 'Adde, quod illustribus factum id quoque exemplis, nisi cui tamen levis est auctor Horatius, Ennium, Plautum, Lucilium, Dossennium, totamque illam

cohortem poetarum veterum semel jugulans, et quidem reclamante populo. Quid? non in Senecam quoque Aulus Gellius magna libertate verborum incurrit? . . . Non omnes denique philosophorum scholae maxime cum prioribus digladiantur?'

144. *Miscellanea*, II.1; *ed. minor*, p. 3.

145. See e.g. Poliziano, *Epistolario*, III.18, and the others listed by Branca and Pastore Stocchi in their *introduzione* to *Miscellanea II, ed. minor*, separately paginated, p. 3 n. 3.

146. See *Michaelis Marulli Carmina*, ed. A. Perosa (Zürich, 1951), pp. 59, 66, 67, 73, 76, 78-9, 88-9, 185; cf. 218.

147. See L. Perotto Sali, 'L'opuscolo inedito di Giorgio Merula contro i *Miscellanea* di Angelo Poliziano', *Interpres*, i (1978), pp. 146-83.

148. See Dionisotti in *IMU* xi, pp. 183-5 (on Matteo Bosso, who wrote: 'Solet enim Policianus codices, quasi vina, magis vetustate quam ratione probare, ut cum eo ridens ingessi quandoque ioco mordaci'). Cf. E. Bolisani, 'Vergilius o Virgilius? L'opinione di un dotto umanista', *AIV* cxvii (1958-9), pp. 131-41, for a similar case.

149. C. Dionisotti, *Gli umanisti e il volgare fra Quattro- e Cinquecento* (Florence, 1968), pp. 1-14, 38-52.

150. See P. Crinito, *De honesta disciplina*, ed. C. Angeleri (Rome, 1955), *Introduzione*, pp. 37-40.

Chapter II

1. See C. Dionisotti, introduction to *Prose e rime di Pietro Bembo* (Turin, 1960), pp. 9-10; R. Ribuoli, *La collazione polizianea del Codice Bembino di Terenzio* (Rome, 1981).

2. P. Bembo, *De Virgilii Culice et Terentii fabulis liber*, in Bembo, *Opere*, IV (Venice, 1729), pp. 303-19. For the authorship of the *argumenta* to Terence see pp. 314b-315a; for the *scholia Bembina*, p. 318a. On archaisms in spelling, see e.g. pp. 315a-b, 316b.

3. For Bembo's account of his MS of the *Appendix* see *Le Culex. Poème pseudo-Virgilien*, ed. Ch. Plésent (Paris, 1910), pp. 39-45, listing Bembo's errors on pp. 43-4 n. 3. For Bembo's errors and mis-statements on the *Bembinus* of Terence see K. Dziatzko, 'Zur Geschichte der Bembo-Handschrift des Terenz', *RhM*, N. F. xlvi (1891), pp. 47-8, correcting and supplementing E. Hauler, 'Paläographisches, Historisches und Kritisches zum Bembinus des Terenz', *Wiener Studien*, xi (1889), pp. 275-8; S. Prete, *Il codice di Terenzio Vaticano latino 3226. Saggio critico e riproduzione del manoscritto* (Vatican City, 1970), pp. 14-15. A more general account of the work is to be found in V. Zabughin, *Vergilio nel Rinascimento italiano da Dante a Torquato Tasso*, ii (Bologna, 1923), pp. 75-7.

4. R. Sabbadini, *Le scoperte dei codici latini e greci ne' secoli XIV e XV* (Florence, 1905), pp. 159-60, 170; G. Mercati, *Prolegomena de fatis Bibliothecae Monasterii S. Columbani Bobiensis . . .*, in *M. Tulli Ciceronis De re publica libri e codice rescripto Vaticano latino 5757 phototypice expressi* (Vatican, 1934), esp. pp. 112-13; M. Ferrari, 'Le scoperte a Bobbio nel 1493: vicende di codici e fortuna di testi', *IMU* xiii (1970), pp. 139-80.

5. Aulo Giano Parrasio, 'Epistula de Lutatio', in F. Lo Parco, *Aulo Giano Parrasio. Studio biografico-critico* (Vasto, 1899), p. 165: 'quom plus apud omnes sanae mentis homines valere debeat antiquorum codicum fides, quorum magna mihi copia Neapoli, Romaeque contigit, quam particula vulgatis inserta codicibus ab iis qui testimonium inscriptionis ab se perversae sibi ipsi confinxerunt'. Cf. his

'Epistula ad Pium', ibid., p. 162: '. . . is me perducere non potuit, ut ei, magis quam vetustiorum codicum fidei, crederem.'

6. Parrasio, 'Epistula de A. Marcellino', ibid., p. 163: 'Ammiani Marcellini Rerum gestarum libri penes me sunt omnes quot extant, ex antiquissimo codice Romae excripti; . . .'.

7. Parrasio, 'Epistula de Livii indice', ibid., p. 159: '. . . ut deprendimus in antiquissimo codice, qui manavit ab exemplari Francisci Petrarcae, viri, sua tempestate, doctissimi'.

8. See Lo Parco, *passim.*

9. Mercati, *Prolegomena*, p. 114 n. 1.

10. *Flavii Sosipatri Charisii Artis grammaticae libri V*, ed. K. Barwick (repr. with corrections; Leipzig, 1964), pp. viii–xi.

11. For the Roman scene in this period see e.g. F. Ubaldini, *Vita di Mons. Angelo Colocci*, ed. V. Fanelli (Vatican City, 1969), pp. 38–75, with monumental commentary by Fanelli; G. Tiraboschi, *Storia della letteratura italiana*, vii.1 (Florence, 1809), pp. 141–4; both Ubaldini and Tiraboschi quote and discuss Sadoleto's letter.

12. F. Philippi, 'Zu Tacitus' Annalen', *Philologus*, xlv (1886), 376–80. E. J. Kenney, who followed not Philippi's article but a glancing reference to it in an essay by E. A. Lowe, misconstrued Leo's attitude towards classical MSS; see his *The Classical Text* (Berkeley, 1974), p. 85; but cf. the additional note by A. C. Griffiths, ibid., p. 157.

13. Those with the necessary patience can glean much information on the bibliophilic activity of Colocci and his friends from the *Atti del Convegno di studi su Angelo Colocci, Jesi, 13–14 settembre 1969* (Jesi, 1972). The truly dedicated will find references to further secondary literature in V. Fanelli, 'La fortuna di Angelo Colocci', ibid., pp. 19–34.

14. F. Beroaldo, prefatory letter to Leo X, in *P. Cornelii Taciti libri quinque noviter inventi atque cum reliquis eius operibus editi* (Rome, 1515), fols. 2ᵛ–3ʳ.

15. Beroaldo, prefatory note *ad lectorem*, ibid., fol. 3ᵛ: 'At quae loca in se maiorem in corrigendo difficultatem habere videbantur, sicut erant reliqui, appositis interiori margini stellulis, quae vitiosum codicem testarentur.'

16. Ibid., fol. [74ʳ] : 'Neque vero quemque mirari volumus, si quasdam dictiones inveniet ab usu cotidiano paulum remotiores, sed tamen antiquitatem redolentes, quas invertere, et secus quam erant in vetusto codice publicare, non modo temerarii sed plane indocti viri fuisset. Vt Sulla pro Sylla, Donusa pro Donysa, Sibulla pro Sibylla, Inclutos pro inclytos . . .'.

17. Ibid., fol. [74ᵛ] : 'Hoc quoque monitum lectorem volo, contulisse me hos quinque libros, iam formis excusos, cum vetere codice, et si quid ab eo variatum per impressorem fuerat, hic inferius annotasse. Ex qua diligentia sperare lector poterit reliqua omnia bona fide publicata.' (A page of corrections follows.) Here is Beroaldo's parting shot: 'Nomine Leonis X Pont. Max. proposita sunt premia non mediocria his qui ad eum libros veteres neque hactenus editos attulerint.' (fol. [QQviiiᵛ])

18. Beroaldo *ad lectorem*, ibid., fol. 3ᵛ: 'Namque errores qui poterant nulla temeritatis nota emendari, consultis primo nonnullis eruditis, et acris iudicii viris, correxi.'

19. See *Dizionario biografico degli Italiani*, s.v. Beroaldo, Filippo, iunior, by E. Paratore.

20. The best study of Valeriano's life and works is K. Giehlow, 'Die Hieroglyphenkunde des Humanismus . . .', *Jahrbuch der Kunsthistorischen Sammlungen des allerhöchsten Kaiserhauses*, xxxii (1915). On his critical work on the text of

Virgil see Zabughin, *Vergilio nel Rinascimento italiano*, ii, pp. 72-5, 96-100 nn. 6-30.

21. G. P. Valeriano, letter to Parrasio in Valeriano, *Castigationes et varietates Virgilianae lectionis* (Rome, 1521), p.[213]: 'Castigationes et varietates Maronianae lectionis, quas per litteras toties, ut ederentur, efflagitasti, publicavi demum, Iane . . .'.

22. Valeriano, *Castigationes in Bucolica*, ibid. (with separate pagination), p. i. For the text see Appendix to Ch. II, below.

23. Ibid.

24. Ibid., pp. lxix–lxxi, *ad Georg.* IV.563. See e.g. p. lxx: 'Et, ne tedium afferat singulorum nomenclatura, sexcenta huiusmodi praeteribimus; ut minus me moveat, quod in Pandectis quoque illis, quae nunc Florentiae publice asservantur, libro ipso Iustiniani Principis, ut creditur, archetypo, non aliter quam per E nomen id notetur.' It is clear that the terms in which Valeriano describes the Florentine Pandects come directly from Poliziano. For other cases where Valeriano gives precise information about the owners and the handwriting of MSS see A. Malaman, 'Le "Castigationes Virgilianae lectionis" di Pierio Valeriano e il Codice Romano Vaticano di Virgilio', *AIV* c (1940-1), pp. 81-91. Valeriano does not say that he is imitating Poliziano, and he attacks his views on the spelling of 'Vergilius'; but the coincidences listed here seem to me to prove his indebtedness on points of method beyond any doubt.

25. Valeriano, *Castigationes*, notes on the *Aeneid*, p. 197: 'TEVCRVM Arma Quiescant ET RVTVLVM. Nostro Dirimatur Sanguine Bellum. In Romano codice, in Oblongo Vaticano, in Porcio, in plerisque aliis antiquis legere est Teucrum Arma Quiescant ET RVTVLI. Oratione non invenuste variata. In Mediceo ultima syllaba est aliena manu corrupta, quum omnino RVTVLI. prius fuisse appareat. Quod vero in exemplaribus vulgatis. DIRIMATVR. tertia persona passivi legitur. in omnibus his antiquis. DIRIMAMVS. prima plurali, activa voce, scriptum observavi.'

26. Valeriano explicitly attributes the following readings to R; *Castigationes* (*ad Bucolica*), pp. xvii–xviii: Ac, tibi (18); Ac, simul, parentum (26); tellurem, infindere, sulco (33); suboles (49); laetantur (52); Orphi (57); Pan, etiam, Arcadia (*licet . . . una habundet littera*, remarks Valeriano; R reads Arcadiae) (59); tulerunt (61); Cui (attributed not to R but to *antiquissima . . . omnia exemplaria*) (62); cubilest (63).

27. Ibid., p. xvii *ad Buc.* IV.1: '. . . loco lemmatis scriptum est in Romano codice. SAECVLI NOVI INTERPRETATIO.'

28. At IV.63 Valeriano gives *cubilest*; R reads *cubilist*.

29. Ibid., *ad Buc.* IV.17: 'Quamvis vetustissimi cod. aliquot. PATRIS. legunt, magis tamen acceptum. PATRIIS. intelligo.' Ibid., p. xviii, *ad* IV.51: 'Sunt antiqui cod. in quibus. TERRAM. unitatis numero legas. Sed multo magnificentius est plurali dicere.'

30. The following readings, attributed by Valeriano to 'several old MSS.', are not in R:

Line	Reading	Valeriano's identification of the sources
1	Sicilides	*antiquos plerosque codices*
3	sunt	*in codicibus plerisque antiquioribus*
4	Cymaei	*veteres plerique codices*
51	Terram	*antiqui cod.*

31. Valeriano omits these readings from R:
ll. 3: canibus; 14: formine; 18: nulla; 28: flavescit; 31: vestia, frusdis; 36: adque; 48: magnus; 55: vincet.

32. *Miscellanea* I.83, e.g., deals with the Egyptian god Harpocrates. On Poliziano's

interest in symbols, see in general E. Wind, *Pagan Mysteries in the Renaissance*, 2nd edn. (London, 1968), pp. 74-5 n. 74, 164, 235. As Crinito and others in Florence shared Poliziano's interest, I cannot agree with Erwin Panofsky's view that Valeriano's work on hieroglyphs stems from a tradition of scholarship cultivated by 'North Italians, or at least non-Tuscans and non-Romans' (*The Iconography of Correggio's Camera di San Paolo* (London, 1961), pp. 30-6).

33. Valeriano, *Hieroglyphica, sive de sacris Aegyptiorum literis commentarii* (Basel, 1556), dedicatory letter to Book XXXIII, to Urbano Bolzani, fol. 233^r: 'Comperimus vero te in honestissimo studiosorum coetu Pindari oracula interpretantem, forteque locum illum explicabas, Nemeis, Diniae, μαστεύει δὲ καὶ τέρψις ἐν ὄμμασι θέσθαι πίστιν [VIII.43-4]. Hic tu horum adventu plurimum exhilaratus, opportune de laetitia, quae statuerit in oculis fidem, disseruisti. Gestit enim, interpretabaris, voluptas ex oculis fidem facere: laetitiam scilicet oculi patentioris figura hieroglyphice apud Aegyptios significari, in iisque iucunditatis praecipuam esse sedem, quia gaudium se primum ab oculis prodat.' The digression continues for some time, merging into a discussion of the *tabula Bembina*.

34. Ibid., dedicatory letter to Book XXVII, to Giovanni Grimano, fol. 194^{r-v}.

35. Giles personally encouraged Valeriano in his work; see the exchange of letters between them with which Book XVII begins (ibid., fol. 123^{r-v}). This Christian humanist inspiration helps to explain why Valeriano deals with so many biblical passages; cf. his *Locorum quorundam sacrae scripturae, qui hic passim exponuntur, index*, ibid., fol. [*6^{r-v}].

36. Valeriano cites this MS of a Latin Dioscorides on fol. 420^v; cf. *Castigationes*, p. 207, *ad Aen.* XII.411. For his MS of Horapollo (Vat. gr. 871) see Giehlow, art. cit. (n. 20, above), p. 114 n. 3. Valeriano also discusses statues, gems, and inscriptions in great detail; see ibid., p. 114 n. 4, and Book XLII, fol. 318^{r-v}, where he reproduces an inscription with all abbreviations and then provides a transcript in normal Latin.

37. For the Florentine Pandects see the dedicatory letter to Book XLV of the *Hieroglyphica*, to Tommaso Campegio, fol. 334^r, using the MS to emend *anchora* to *cura* in *Digest*, XIV.i.2.

38. For the effects of the sack see e.g. Ubaldini, *Vita di Colocci*, pp. 75-7.

39. 'Oratione di Piero Vettori, fatta alla militare ordinanza fiorentina l'anno M.D. XXIX . . .', in R. von Albertini, *Das florentinische Staatsbewusstsein im Übergang von der Republik zum Prinzipat* (Bern, 1955), p. 405. For Vettori's early career and its political context see ibid., pp. 132-3, 136, 144, 146.

40. Ibid., pp. 89-90; D. Cantimori, 'Rhetoric and Politics in Italian Humanism', *JWCI*, i (1937-8), pp. 83-102, is still essential for the culture of these young aristocrats.

41. Poliziano's MS subscription in his copy of *Scriptores rei rusticae* (Venice, 1472), fol. 85, quoted in Alessandro Perosa, *Mostra del Poliziano nella Biblioteca Medicea Laurenziana: manoscritti, libri rari, autografi e documenti. Catalogo* (Florence, 1955), p. 26: 'Contuli ego Ang. Politianus Catonis hos ac Varronis rerum rusticarum libellos cum vetustissimo codice ex Divi Marci Florentina bibliotheca, sic ut ne ea quidem non ascriberem siqua depravatiora viderentur. Hoc enim nobis emendandi novos codices institutum placuit, ne quid ex nostro temere adiceremus, neu quid omitteremus quod in antiquioribus exemplaribus invenissemus. Quod si hoc priores librarii institutum probassent, non tantum profecto negoci laborisque posteris reliquissent. Sicubi ergo nostrum adhibuimus iudicium, relictis tamen antiquae lectionis vestigiis aliquibus, suum cuique liberum reliquimus. Vale, lector, et nostrum hunc laborem boni consule. Florentiae in divi Pauli, ipso bacchanaliorum die MCCCCLXXXII, . . . '. Poliziano's other subscriptions are published and discussed ibid., pp. 13-92. In general, the more recent edition of these texts in Ida Maïer, *Les manuscrits*

d'Ange Politien (Geneva, 1965), pp. 331–62, is less accurate and less intelligently annotated than Perosa's edition.

42. Pier Vettori, MS subscription in his copy of Varro *De lingua latina*, quoted in *M. Terenti Varronis De lingua latina quae supersunt*, ed. G. Goetz and F. Schoell (Leipzig, 1910), p. xiv: 'Petrus Victorius ac Iacobus Diacetius contulimus cum vetusto codice ex Divi Marci Bibliotheca literis longobardis exarato, tanta diligentia sive potius morosa observatione ut vel quae in eo corrupte legebantur in hunc transtulerimus. Die XIIIJ. Aprilis. MDXXI.' Already in March Vettori had left a subscription with details about the sources of a collation in a copy of Lucretius. But this was merely a collation of two printed books with marginalia, and it therefore did not follow the form used by Poliziano as closely as the Varro subscription did. It reads as follows: 'contuli cum duobus codicibus, altero Ioviani Pontani, altero vero Marulli poetae Bizantii, impressis quidem, sed ab ipsis non incuriose, ut patet, emendatis, quos commodum accepi ab Andrea Cambano patritio Florentino M.D.XX. Idibus Martiis. Petrus Victorius', quoted in *T. Lucreti Cari De rerum natura libri sex*, ed. H. A. J. Munro, 4th edn. (London, 1900), i, p. 11.

43. On Modesti see Perosa, *Catalogo*, pp. 37–8, 55, 107–10, 174–5; Maïer, *Les Manuscrits d'Ange Politien*, p. 383 n. 1.

44. Pier Vettori, *Explicationes suarum in Catonem, Varronem, Columellam castigationum* (Lyons, 1541–2), pp. 142–3, quoted by Perosa, *Catalogo*, pp. 27–8.

45. Poliziano, *Opera*, p. 141: 'Quapropter operae precium me facturum credidi, si commentarios aliquos evigilarem, quibus in integrum corrupta diu lectio restitueretur, et linguae Latinae vis, quae tota pene in legibus est, explicaretur.'

46. The most elaborate record of one of Poliziano's lecture courses is his *Commento inedito alle Selve di Stazio*, ed. L. Cesarini Martinelli (Florence, 1978). For his work on Suetonius cf. G. Gardenal, *Il Poliziano e Svetonio* (Florence, 1975), the review of Gardenal by S. Rizzo in *ASNP*, ser. III, v (1975), pp. 1686–8, and L. Cesarini Martinelli, 'Il Poliziano e Svetonio: osservazioni su un recente contributo alla storia della filologia umanistica', *Rinascimento*, ser. II, xvi (1976), pp. 111–31.

47. P. Vettori, *Explicationes suarum in Ciceronem castigationum* (ed. Paris, 1538), p. 41 *ad Fam.* XVI.18: '. . . cum nostrum totum studium fuerit ad priscam et genuinam scripturam hos libros reducere. Nec enim castigare, aut emendare receptos Ciceronis codices voluimus: sed ope priscorum exemplariorum importunas, et ineptas quorundam audaciorum castigationes eicere, et delere: . . .'.

48. Ibid., p. 27: 'Tum enim cum rem habebas quaestiunculis te faciebam attentiorem) Pervetus ille codex Mediceus solus rectam lectionem servat: nam qui ab eo descriptus videtur, quem aiunt Francisci Petrarcae manu exaratum, ut fit, ab illa integritate degenerat. Sic omnia fatis in peius ruere, ut inquit prudentissimus poeta [Vergil, *Georgics* I. 200] QVAESTIVNCVLIS enim legit, e quo vulgatam lectionem perfluxisse arbitramur. Ille incorruptior QVAESTICVLIS adhuc retinet, quae vox huic sententiae mire quadrat: . . .'.

49. Ibid., p. 41: 'Nos tam novam, et nostris auribus inauditam structuram verborum recipere, et probare ausi non sumus: nec tamen culpam mereri nobis videmur, quod hanc rem, quantulacunque est admonere non piguit.'

50. Ibid.: 'Iidem [prisci] codices Vmmium habent, ubi vulgati Mummium: quod nomen nostri librarii corruperunt, quare corrigatur. Ne autem hoc nomen quia rarum est, amplius ut novum repudietur, adscribemus epitaphium quod Pisis in antiquo lapide vidimus: in quo valde simile huic et quasi ab eo derivatum nomen legitur.' Vettori then prints *CIL* XI, 1504, which contains the name 'Ummidiae'.

51. Wilhelm Rüdiger, *Petrus Victorius aus Florenz: Studien zu einem Lebensbilde*

(Halle a.S., 1896), p. 16 n. 3. Cf. J. A. Ernesti, 'Historia critica Operum Ciceronis typographorum formulis editorum', *Opuscula Philologica Critica* (Leiden, 1764), pp. 142-3.

52. Vettori, *Expl.*, p. 19: ' . . . ut videant omnes non posse quemlibet vetera exemplaria tractare'.

53. For inscriptions see n. 50, above; for comparative study of old MSS, ibid., p. 41: 'aliis autem locis semper ubi M. habebant vulgati codices, ∞ in cunctis priscis exemplaribus a nobis inventam notam reposuimus: neque solum in his vidimus epistolarum antiquis libris hoc semper servatum esse, sed etiam in Livianis quibusdam vetustissimis exemplaribus quae in Divi Marci bibliotheca servantur: quod idem et M. Varronis in eadem bibliotheca mirae antiquitatis codex retinet, et Columellae non negligenter scriptus a Nicolao Nicolo liber, quem olim Politianus viderat et laudat. Sed quid opus est haec tam accurate vel ambitiose potius testimonia colligere? nullos unquam vidi antiquiores codices, qui non semper loco millenarii numeri hanc notam retinerent.'

54. Ibid., p. 12: ' . . . V pro B scriptum est, quod ex multis antiquorum monimentis colligitur saepe priscos usurpasse'; p. 19: 'Hoc loco vetustissimus ille Mediceus codex, et alter etiam non malus, non aeque tamen antiquus, pro tempore habent TAM, fractam omnino, et parum commodam hoc loco vocem: ipsi unius literae mendum ibi esse existimamus, deceptumque librarium TAM, pro TEM scripsisse. Non semel autem in priscis exemplaribus, sic concisam hanc vocem reperies: ut prima ad Atticum epistola in vetere illo nostro codice . . .'; p. 40: 'nec mirum videri debet in Latinis libris antiquitus exaratis Graecas voces aliquantum perversas esse, et inquinatas: cum enim sermonem illum ignorarent, vix poterant ab erroribus cavere: videmus enim illos quasi descripsisse, pinxisseque Graecos characteres non negligenter, si consideres eos, eorum quae scribebant sententiam non percepisse.'

55. Ibid., p. 26: ' . . . nec mirum est in voce parum frequenti antiquiores etiam librarios deceptos esse'; p. 32: 'nec semper oportet cunctas rariores et infrequentiores voces condemnare et explodere: nimis enim anguste latos Latinae linguae terminos contraheremus, quos maiores nostri eruditiores, et meliore iudicio praediti, semper summo studio proferebant'; p. 33: 'Vetera omnia exemplaria PERTIMEFACTO: quae vox, quia rara est, cum eam fortasse pro Latina non haberent, non hinc tantum indignissime deiecta est, sed aliis etiam suis sedibus deturbata.'

56. Ibid., p. 14: 'si auctoribus sermo qui eorum aetate vigebat, conservandus est, et non ad posteriorum normam et consuetudinem conformandus.'

57. Ibid., p. 38: 'Hoc loco veteres codices manci sunt ad unum omnes, ut suspicer hunc locum, ut multos alios restitutum esse, suppletumque ab aliquo arbitrio suo potius, et coniectura, quam veterum, et integrorum codicum auxilio.'

58. Ibid., p. 27: 'Vetustiores codices ARTIS loco AREIS habent, sed tamen EX praepositionem retinent. . . . Ego institutum meum ab antiqua scriptura modice declinandi tenens, ET ARTIS legi: . . . '; p. 10: 'Nos raro admodum tantum nobis tribuimus ut aliquid quod non in vetustis codicibus invenerimus, receperimus: siquando tamen id accidet, ut aliquantulum, non longe tamen a vetustis vestigiis discesserimus, semper ingenue fatebimur: . . . '.

59. Ibid., p. 23: 'Non recte autem facere mihi videntur, qui ea quae non assequuntur suo ingenio, statim delent: existimare enim debent . . . multa . . . quae abdita adhuc sunt, cum novi cotidie Graeci maxime auctores e tenebris eruantur, in lucem propediem esse proditura.'

60. Ibid., pp. 22-3: ' . . . apud Graecos maxime Romanarum historiarum auctores, qui cum externis gentibus scriberent, quae Romanos ritus ignorabant, diligentius, minutiusque haec pertractarunt quae Latini scriptores ut passim, vulgoque nota praeteribant'.

61. Pier Vettori, *Posteriores Petri Victorii castigationes in Epistolas, quas vocant Familiares* (Lyons, 1541), p. 3: 'Cum enim in primis laborassem, ut quae a me immutata fuerant, constituerem: non pauci voluissent etiam obscuriores aliquos locos illustrari, quamvis scripturae immutatio nulla facta esset. Statui igitur horum studio quantum possem, ac cum primum possem, satisfacere: maxime cum ex assidua Ciceronis lectione cognossem, non sine causa id a me postulari.'

62. For Greek materials see ibid., p. 126, *ad Fam.* XVI.10: '*Nostra ad diem dictam fient.* Modus loquendi sumptus a Graecis: illi enim ἐς ῥητὴν ἡμέραν. Vtuntur eo saepe Romanarum rerum Graeci scriptores, Plutarchus, Dion, Appianus . . .'. Cf. pp. 43–4, *ad Fam.* VII.1. For Vettori's use of MSS see ibid., p. 43: 'tantae autem hi apud me autoritatis sunt, et, nisi fallor, apud alios propter fidelitatem erunt, ut testimonio duorum illorum magis credam, quam reliquorum omnium.' Vettori cites and discusses the Medicei on, e.g., pp. 8, 11, 12, 15, 43, 128; he uses inscriptions and other MSS of great age to justify the orthography of the Medicei on pp. 29–30, 45–7, 129–30.

63. Giannotti to Vettori, 3.'ix.1541; Giannotti, *Lettere italiane (1526–1571)*, ed. F. Diaz (Milan, 1974), p. 89.

64. See M. Dopchie, 'Un collaborateur de Pier Vettori', *BIHBR* xxxvii (1966), pp. 111–12.

65. Dopchie, 'L'humanisme italien et l'Agamemnon d'Aeschyle', ibid., pp. 99–108; E. Fraenkel, introduction to his edition of Aeschylus, *Agamemnon* (Oxford, 1950), i, pp. 34–5. Dopchie's remarks must be used with great caution; for instance, on pp. 104–5 n. 3, she suggests that Vettori drew information about Mei and Barbadori's work on Aeschylus not simply from having supervised them but from Josias Simler's *Epitome* of Gesner's *Bibliotheca*. This intrinsically absurd theory is refuted by the fact that the passage by Vettori in question comes from Book XXV of the *Variae lectiones*; this appeared not in 1568, as Dopchie says, but in 1553, while Simler's work came out in 1555. Simler is dependent on Vettori.

66. See C. V. Palisca's introduction to his edition of G. Mei, *Letters on Ancient and Modern Music to Vincenzo Galilei and Giovanni Bardi* (n.p., 1960). Palisca must also be used with caution; he promotes G. Faerno to the rank of cardinal, and his translations are not reliable.

67. 'Lucrezia the courtesan'; subscription to Parisinus graecus 1750, quoted by Dopchie, art. cit. (n. 64, above), p. 113; previously quoted and discussed by e.g. O. Crusius, in *Philologus*, Supplementband vi (1891–3), p. 219.

68. B. Schneider, *Die mittelalterlichen griechisch-lateinischen Übersetzungen der Aristotelischen Rhetorik* (Berlin, 1971), pp. 73–6.

69. Vettori makes interesting attempts to unravel Cratander's editorial procedures and assess his sources. I give one case, from *Castigationum explicationes*, p. 40, *ad Fam.* XV.19: "Ἡδονὴν vero et Διαξίαν) Sic omnes habebant vulgati codices, prorsus mendose. Germani videntur exemplar habuisse, quod minus incorruptum hunc locum conservarit: credimus enim illos, ut testati sunt, ex vetusto codice collegisse, quas in marginibus collocarunt, lectionum varietates: ἀταξίαν enim legunt.' The whole note should be read; it provides impressive evidence of Vettori's mastery of the history of Greek philosophy.

70. Vettori, *Castigationes*, pp. 128–33, on the *Tusculan Disputations*; see also pp. 133–4, on the Greek originals of the Latin philosophical terms used by Cicero in the *De natura deorum*. In general, however, one must agree with Ernesti's judgement, *Opuscula*, p. 143: 'Atque etiam plus curae posuit in Epistolis, quam libris Philosophicis, et Rhetoricis, et Orationibus. Nam in illos non multum, in has nihil notarum dedit . . .'.

71. Vettori, 'Lectori hor. libror.', *Variarum lectionum libri XXV* (Florence, 1553),

p. 407: 'Cum diligenter olim legissem principes quosque Latinae linguae auctores, et in legendo plura notassem, quae aut expressa de Graecis scriptoribus videbantur, aut eorum doctrina poterant adiuvari, et non mediocriter (nisi fallor) illustrari . . . '. Cf. ibid.: 'Studui autem ea potissimum e reconditis Graecorum literis, tanquam e fonte omnium scientiarum, haurire, quae sententiam aliquam Látini scriptoris ornarent.'

72. Vettori himself points up the lack of order in the work, ibid.: '. . . si ordo hic vocari potest, cum quicquid animadversione dignum offendis apud diversos auctores, variaque etiam in materia, seligis, et in commentariis confuse scribis.' It should be noted that Vettori also provides a table of contents made up of chapter titles, and detailed indices.

73. See e.g. VIII.24 on Torelli and Agustín; X.1 on Faerno; VII.15 ('Franciscus Medices acerrimi iudicii vir fuit, et reconditae atque elegantis doctrinae . . .').

74. See e.g. VI.2, VI.17, X.1, XIV.16, XV.20.

75. Ibid., XX.13, p. 309: 'Accurate videndum est quid valeant in epistola Ciceronis ad Trebatium verba haec, sumpta (ut opinor) e Medea Ennii: Quibus illa manibus gypsatissimis persuasit, ne sibi vitio illae verterent, quod abesset a patria; neque enim quicquam apud Euripidem invenitur, unde fabula expressa est, quod Medeae manus, partemve ullam corporis, hoc aut illo colore tinctam fuisse, aut alio modo affectam ostendat.'

76. Ibid., pp. 309–10: 'Ipse sane arbitror significare verbis illis Ennium voluisse pulchritudinem corporis, candoremque; atque illum quidem fucatum, industriaque adiutum. Nam gypsi candor eximius est, quod docet etiam Plato in Phaedone . . . Nam hac etiam materia usos veteres in se armisque suis dealbandis, cum aggredi noctu hostes volebant, ut suos ab adversariis dignoscerent, testatur Herodotus in Urania . . . '. Cf. *The Tragedies of Ennius. The Fragments*, ed. H. D. Jocelyn (Cambridge, 1967), pp. 359–60.

77. Ibid.: 'Addidisse autem id Ennium mirari non debemus; haec enim erat consuetudo veterum poetarum in vertendis fabulis Graecorum, ut quaedam adiungerent, alia autem relinquerent . . . '.

78. M.-A. Muret, *Variarum lectionum libri XVIIII*, ed. F. A. Wolf (Halle a. S., 1791), VIII.17, pp. 232–5 (first publ. 1580 in the Plantin edition of Muret's *Variae lectiones*).

79. Vettori, *Variarum lectionum libri XXV*, III.3, pp. 32–3, at p. 32; cf. II.15, pp 24–5.

80. Ibid., X.22, p. 153; see Appendix to Ch. II for text.

81. Horace, *Opera*, ed. D. Lambin, 2nd edn. (Paris, 1567), II, p. 382 *ad A. P.* 467: 'IDEM FACIT OCCIDENTI] Graecum loquendi genus, τ'αὐτὸ ποιεῖ τῷ κτείνοντι. sic Lucret. lib. 2. de primis corporibus. *Qui poterunt igitur rerum primordia dici, Et Lethi vitare vias, animalia cum sint, Atqu' animalibu' sint mortalibus una, eademque? Id est, ταυτὰ τοῖς ζώοις. Idem lib. 3. quorum unus Homerus Sceptra potitus eadem aliis sopitu' quiete est. Idem lib. 4. Nempe eadem facit, et scimus facere omnia turpi.*'

82. See below, nn. 88, 91.

83. Cf. E. Cochrane, *Florence in the Forgotten Centuries, 1527–1800* (Chicago and London, 1973), pp. 78–80.

84. B. Weinberg, *A History of Literary Criticism in the Italian Renaissance* (Chicago, 1961), i.

85. B. Cavalcanti, *Lettere edite e inedite*, ed. C. Roaf (Bologna, 1967), Introduzione, pp. xxxix–xlvi and the relevant letters, which are listed on p. xxxix.

86. For the tradition of trying to identify Aristotle's imitative arts, see the splendid collection of material in P. O. Kristeller, 'The Modern System of the Arts',

Renaissance Thought II. Papers on Humanism and the Arts (New York, Evanston, and London, 1965), pp. 179–80 n. 92. For comments on Iphigenia's behaviour see P. Vettori, *Commentarii in primum librum Aristotelis de Arte Poetarum* (Florence, 1560; repr. Munich, 1967), pp. 145–7, to be compared with F. Robortello, *In librum Aristotelis de Arte Poetica explicationes* (Florence, 1548; repr. Munich, 1968), pp. 173–4, and V. Maggi and B. Lombardi, *In Aristotelis librum de Poetica communes explanationes; Madii vero in eundem librum propriae annotationes* (Venice, 1550; repr. Munich, 1969), pp. 170–2, esp. p. 171. Vettori's solution was later paraphrased by Jean Racine, who owned and annotated heavily a copy of his commentary; see Racine, *Principes de la tragédie*, ed. E. Vinaver (Manchester and Paris, 1951), p. 29, ll. 261–3 and p. 66 n. ad loc. For a similar case, cf. Vettori's note on what Aristotle considers to be the ἄλογον that takes place 'outside the tragedy' in the *Oedipus*: *Commentarii*, pp. 150–1 ad 1454 a 37–1454 b 8; here Vettori follows Maggi, pp. 172–4, rather than Robortello, pp. 179–81. It should also be noted that the general format of Vettori's edition, in which tiny snippets of Greek text and Latin translation are separated by huge sections of Latin commentary dealing with both simple matters of explication and more complex ones of textual criticism, is also derived from the tradition established by Robortello and Maggi.

87. See J. E. Sandys, *Harvard Lectures on the Revival of Learning* (Cambridge, 1905), pp. 170–1.

88. Vettori, *Variarum lectionum libri XXV*, XV.13, pp. 227–8: 'Turpe (ut videtur) erratum, et quod facile fallere posset, occupavit versum Horatii ex epistola de arte poetica ad Pisones. Id autem huiuscemodi est, ut moribus potius poetae notam inurat, quam studio lectoris moram afferat. Quod enim in excusis pluribus libris est, At nostri proavi Plautinos, et numeros, et Laudavere sales, non convenit tenuitati hominis, ac patre libertino nato. Quod si ita locutus fuisset, explosus undique risu esset, et ab omnibus merito exagitatus. Id tamen magnopere ab ingenio ipsius abhorrebat, qui semper prae se tulit, ac confessus est, humilitatem suam. Legi igitur debet cum scriptis exemplaribus, At vestri proavi. Scribebat enim ad eos, qui antiqua nobilique familia orti essent.'

89. Anonymous marginal note in a 16th- or early 17th-century hand, in the author's copy of the *Variae lectiones*, p. 227: 'Quid si nostros proavos vocavit, non de suis intelligens poeta, id est, ex quibus ipse originem duxisset, sed communiter de omnibus, qui multis aetatibus, ac seculis antecesserunt, se ipsum ceteris Romanis admiscens; et per proavos intellexerit omnes illos veteres, quos saepe ita et poetae, atque alii scriptores elegantes appellavere? Quem morem hodie vulgo observamus. Quare nihil prohibet quo minus vetus lectio retineatur.'

90. See C. O. Brink, *Horace on Poetry*, ii: *The 'Ars Poetica'* (Cambridge, 1971), p. 307.

91. See esp. Bentley's copy of *Q. Horatius Flaccus cum commentariis et enarrationibus commentatoris veteris et Iacobi Cruquii Messenii* (Leiden, 1597), British Library, shelf-mark 680.d.26; in his note ad loc., p. 644a (misnumbered 446), Cruquius writes: '*at vestri proavi*. sic habent scripta quae legi omnia, non etiam *nostri*, ut est in vulgatis olim.' Bentley underlined most of the comment and wrote, on one of the blank leaves preceding the title-page: 'At *nostri* proavi. Recte Codd. Antiquis. [*Antiquis* is lined through] omnes sui *vestri*. Nimirum erat Horatius *Libertino patre* natus, et non Romano.'

92. Antonio Agustín, *Emendationum et opinionum libri IV*, in *Thesaurus juris Romani*, ed. Everardus Otto, 4 (Leiden, 1729), col. 1431: 'Ex his apparet, errorem Pisani librarii omnes librarios secutos. et negare audeo, extare aliquem Digestorum librum, quo non idem error sit. Quibus consequens est, ex Florentinis ceteros omnes descriptos. quod si verum est, ut esse ostendi, ad eorum

librorum scripturam omnes libri emendandi . . . sunt, . . . '. On the methods used by Agustín see Juan Miquel, 'Mechanische Fehler in der Überlieferung der Digesten', *Zeitschrift der Savigny-Stiftung für Rechtsgeschichte, Romanistische Abteilung* lxxx (1963), 272-4; F. de Zulueta, *Don Antonio Agustín* (Glasgow, 1939), pp. 37-44.

93. Ibid., col. 1495: 'Qui errores cum in omnibus libris sint, eandem esse omnium originem ostendunt. Quae cum ita se habeant, ad horum librorum scripturam caeteros emendandos esse fateamur.'

94. Ibid., col. 1457: 'Cum omnes libros e Florentinis ortos esse antea scripserimus: illi vero ita scripti sint, ut non orationibus solum, sed ne verbis quidem ipsis distincti sint: quod, ut in antiquis monumentis apparet, Romani homines his punctorum, et spaciorum intervallis non uterentur: mirandum non est, si in separandis orationibus est erratum. Admonuit me hujus rei Laelius Taurellus meus, . . . '.

95. Ibid., col. 1432: 'Item illud cognoscimus e Graecia eos libros in Italiam allatos. . . . Magis probo eos libros, cum jus civile Byzantii traderetur, scriptos post aliquot annos, quam Justinianus e vita migravit. Fuisseque studiosi alicujus viri in Graecia, non publicos, mihi sit verisimile. Maximum ejus rei signum est, quod numerorum et verborum notis usi multis locis librarii sint, quas notas Justinianus tribus constitutionibus fieri prohibuit, . . . '.

96. Agustín, *Emendationes et opiniones*, col. 1439: 'Fuit autem id a me necessario factum, ut in uno genere librorum versarer: et accidit percommode, ut tanta diligentia Norici essent ab Haloandro scripti. Nam si omnibus juris studiosis prodesse voluissem, ut cupio et spero: omnes omnium librorum errores me, quod infinitum erat, significare oportebat. Nunc his libris comparatis, qui jam multis exemplis exscripti in omnibus bibliothecis ad manum habentur, nostrae emendationes omnibus facile, ut desidero, erunt utilitati.'

97. In a long letter of 1567 to Latino Latini, Agustín argued that Roman orthography could only be reconstructed from inscriptions and coins; the letter is printed in *Anecdota litteraria ex MSS. codicibus eruta*, II, ed. G. C. Amaduzzi (Rome, n. d.), pp. 317-24. As to manuscripts, Agustín argued on p. 323: 'Quod si quis objiciat nullum exstare exemplum veterum librorum Ciceronis, Caesaris, Sallustii, in quo haec scribendi ratio conservata sit, ac ne illa quidem, quae omnes laudant, exempla Terentii, et Vergilii Bembi, et si qua alia exstant, et in pretio a doctissimis viris habentur; huic argumento facile respondemus, nulla exstare optimis temporibus scripta volumina, sed aut Iustiniani, aut Theodosii, aut, ut omnia illis concedamus, Constantini Maximi temporibus, quibus linguam latinam concidisse fatentur. Et quamvis in his veteribus libris multa melius scripta sint, quam in iis, qui vulgo circumferuntur; tamen ab optima ratione scribendi longe absunt.' Towards the end of his life Agustín arrived at a related conclusion about historical sources, namely, that medals and inscriptions were more reliable than any written history; see A. D. Momigliano, *Studies in Historiography* (London, 1966), p. 16; C. Mitchell, 'Archaeology and Romance in Renaissance Italy', in *Italian Renaissance Studies*, ed. E. F. Jacob (London, 1960), p. 457.

98. *Digestorum seu Pandectarum libri quinquaginta ex Florentinis Pandectis repraesentati* (Florence, 1553), 'Lectoribus' (unpaginated): 'Primum igitur omnium sciendum, in nullo nos quod quicquam momenti haberet, ne latum quidem unguem ab eius fide discessisse: ut quoad fieri posset, eiusdem vera species repraesentaretur.'

99. 'Illustrissimo optimoque principi Cosmo Medici Florentinorum duci, domino suo Franciscus Taurellius salutem', ibid.: 'Graece vero tradita, quae frequentia sunt, ut quam emendatissima prodirent, vir, ut scis, omni doctrina praeditus, gloriaeque tuae in primis studiosus Petrus Victorius operam dedit.' For a case

in which one of Vettori's corrections anticipated Mommsen see H. E. Troje, *Graeca leguntur* . . . (Cologne and Vienna, 1971), p. 45.

100. 'Lectoribus', ibid.: 'Praeter haec si quas unas vel plures maiusculas minoribus litteris admixtas extra consuetum scribendi morem invenietis, vel si quas ipsis maiusculis insertas minores, scietis non temere sed dedita opera positas: quo significaretur vel unam litteram poni pro duabus, ut celeRimo, CorneII, adIcere, pro adiicere, Cornelii, celerrimo: vel alteram pro altera . . . vel unam syllabam pro pluribus, ut sENTia pro sententia . . . Quae cum infinitis similibus ne vos fallant, diligenter potius animadvertetis, quam nobis quicquam detrahatis.'

101. Ibid.: 'Quae varie in eo volumine scripta sunt, si quidem sine vitio, pariter varie reddidimus; unde Compraehendere et Comprehendere, Extare et Exstare, Plebiscitum et Plebisscitum invenietis.' On the changes introduced by the Torelli see Troje, *Graeca leguntur*, pp. 45–6.

102. V. Fanelli, 'Le lettere di mons. Angelo Colocci nel Museo Britannico di Londra', *Rinascimento*, x (1959), pp. 107–35.

103. S. Morison, 'Marcello Cervini, Pope Marcellus II. Bibliography's Patron Saint', *IMU* v (1962), pp. 301–19.

104. P. Petitmengin, 'Le *codex Veronensis* de Saint Cyprien', *Revue des études latines*, xlvi (1968), pp. 330–78; P. Paschini, *Tre ricerche sulla storia della chiesa nel Cinquecento* (Rome, 1945), pp. 155–281. The first major product of Roman scholarship after recovery from the sack was the edition by Niccolò Majorano and Matteo Devaris of Eustathius (1542–50); see Paschini, 'Un ellenista del Cinquecento: Niccolò Majorano', in his *Cinquecento romano e riforma cattolica* (Rome, 1958), pp. 224–6.

105. I am not certain when Vettori and Faerno first came in contact with one another. In a letter of 21.XI.1570 to Fulvio Orsini, Vettori mentions the fact that he and Faerno had disagreed about a point in the text of Caesar 'XX anni fa'; *Lettere di Piero Vettori*, ed. G. Ghinassi (Bologna, 1870), p. 61. As Vettori discusses the point in question in *Variae lectiones* XXII.10 – and as the letter shows that he and Faerno had discussed the point *before* Vettori's work was written – their acquaintance certainly began well before 1553.

106. The best general work on Faerno is still P. Paschini, 'Gabriele Faerno cremonese favolista e critico del '500', *Atti dell'Accademia degli Arcadi*, xiii (1929), pp 63–93. More recent secondary literature is referred to below.

107. L. Latini, *Epistolae, coniecturae, et observationes sacra, profanaque eruditione ornatae*, ed. D. Magri, II (Viterbo, 1667), p. 43: 'In Livio nolim tibi persuadeas, eum vel ita audacem, vel ita sibi placentem esse, ut praeter vetustorum Codicum fidem (nisi sicubi corruptissimi planissime appareant) quicquam mutet, aut addat . . . '.

108. Marc-Antoine Muret, *Scholia in Terentium*, quoted in Luigia Ceretti, 'Critica testuale a Terenzio in una lettera del Faerno a Paolo Manuzio', *Aevum* xxviii (1954), pp. 537–8: 'Sed mirabilis hac in re Faernus fuit; ut equisones solent, inspectis equorum dentibus de eorum aetate pronunciare, ita ipse, inspectis veterum librorum chartis, de illorum antiquitate iudicabat, ut non dubitaret dicere hunc illo esse decem, aut viginti, aut triginta annis vetustiorem, neque id ita sibi videri dicebat, sed ita adfirmate et adseveranter loquebatur, quasi ipse cum illi omnes scriberentur, interfuisset.'

109. *Epistola Gabrielis Faerni viri doctissimi, qua continetur censura emendationum Livianarum Caroli Sigonii* (Milan, 1557), fol. B ii^r: ' . . . non . . . per difetto d'ingegno, che lo ha assai bello, ma parte per essersi abbatuto in mali libri, parte per non saper quanto nell'emendare gli autori si habbia a promettere della congettura'. Cf. ibid.: '. . . nelle congetture si vuol andar un poco piu riservatamente, di quello, che ha fatto lui'.

110. Ibid., fol. Biii^r: 'Se le mutationi saranno circa altre parole, la vulgata sia sempre di maggior autorità, eccetto alcuni luoghi acconci egregiamente, liquali facilmente compareranno à chi haverà ingegno, et massime quelli, dove la congettura non muta piu d'una lettera, come è quel luogo nel. XXIIII. libro Ne libera efferatur Resp. dove il Sigonio con aggiunger un p, alla vulgata, ha illuminata tutta quella sententia . . . '. On the circumstances in which this letter was published – to Faerno's surprise and against his will – see L. Ceretti, 'Gabriele Faerno filologo in otto lettere inedite al Panvinio', *Aevum*, xxvii (1953), pp. 319-21. For Sigonio's reply see his *Patavinarum disputationum . . . liber secundus* (Padua, 1562), fols. 68-72.

111. Faerno did not live long enough to write a preface for the edition, which was brought out posthumously by Vettori. Hence we do not know whether he believed that some or all of the extant Terence MSS could be arranged genealogically.

112. On the tradition of Terentian commentary in the Renaissance see M. T. Herrick, *Comic Theory in the Sixteenth Century* (repr., Urbana, 1964); H. W. Lawton, *Térence en France au XVIe siècle. Éditions et traductions* (Paris, 1926), pp. 291-329. The novelty of Faerno's approach is clearly revealed by comparing the extracts from commentaries on *Andria*, IV.1 given ibid., pp. 323-9.

113. The MSS used by Faerno are identified by Ceretti, art. cit. (n. 110, above), p. 309: Bembinus (Vat. lat. 3226), 5th century; Vat. lat. 3868, 9th century; Vat. Basilicanus H 19, 10th century. For a discussion of a correction in Bembinus see Faerno, *Emendationes in sex fabulas Terentii* (Florence, 1565), p. 69 *ad Eun.* 943: '*Pro fidem diem*. Solus liber Bembinus habet hanc collocationem verborum: quamvis deinde eadem fere manu, eorum inversio sit notata ab indicante legendum, pro deum fidem, ut habent omnes alii libri et Donatus.' For another example see Prete, *Il codice di Terenzio Vaticano latino 3226*, p. 16 and n. 36. On the scholia, *Emendationes*, p. 76, *ad Heaut. prol.* 4: '*Ex integra Graeca*. In libro Bembino, ut per omnes alias comoedias, antiquissima manu glossemata ex Donato in margine ascripta sunt, ad locorum quae incidunt expositionem, ita in hanc ipsam Heauton timorumenon multa visuntur, quae Donati similiter putamus esse, cuius in hanc fabulam commentarii interciderunt. Sed sive Donati sint, sive cuiuspiam alius, optima certe et eruditissima sunt. Quorum aliqua ponere non gravabimur . . .'. Cf. Prete, *Il codice*, p. 49 and nn. 2-3, who, however, is wrong to say flatly that 'il Faerno pensa che gli scoli derivino da Donato . . . '.

114. See n. 119, below.

115. I compared Faerno's notes on the *Adelphoe* in *Emendationes*, pp. 117-49 with the reproduction of Bembinus given in Prete, *Il codice*.

116. Faerno, *Emendationes*, p. 127, *ad Ad.* 351; p. 138, *ad Ad.* 667.

117. Faerno to Vettori, 7.i.1558; London, British Library, MS Add. 10266, fols. 109^r-110^r.

118. Faerno to Vettori, 24.xii.1553, ibid., fol. 105^r; Faerno to Vettori, 30.xi.1556, ibid., fol. 107^r-v.

119. Faerno to Vettori, 29.iv.1558, ibid., fols. 119^r-120^r: 'Quanto al sciscitor [which Vettori had spelt *siscitor* in his new edition of the *Familiares*, justifying the spelling by Poliziano's testimony that it was also found in the Bembinus at *Eun.* 548], io ho havuto più di sei mesi nelle mani quel Terentio antico del Bembo, ne mi pare haver mai notato questa tal scrittura [*siscitor*]: ne ho anchora una copia cavata da un riscontro che ne fecero insieme Mons. Antonio Augustino, et M. Metello dottor Borgognone, che annotorono ogni minima minutia; dove questa parola non è alterata niente di quello ch'ella sta nello stampato. . . . Quanto a quello che ha annotato il Politiano, mi fate vacillare se

cosi è, et vo dubitando che piu tosto noi tre si siamo ingannati che lui solo.' Faerno was right to be worried, for Poliziano's collation was correct; at *Eun.* 548 Bembinus reads: . . . LVBET PRIVS QVID SIT SISCITARI (fol. 17ʳ; Prete, *Il codice*, plate 31).

120. P. Vettori, *Epistolarum libri X. Orationes XIIII. Et liber de laudibus Ioannae Austriacae* (Florence, 1586), p. 69: 'Nec tamen non ego plurimos calamo exaratos, sedulo collegi, et e publicis bibliothecis, privatisque domibus, deprompsi. Cuius rei mihi testes esse possunt multi honesti et eruditi viri, qui ad me salutandi causa hoc tempore venerunt: viderunt enim circumfusum undique multis harum epistolarum voluminibus; eaque passim explicata iacere, ut statim omnia, quae usus ferret, invenirentur. Utinam diligentia hac, conquisitioneque acri talium librorum aliquid proficeretur.'

121. Ibid., p. 70.

122. Ibid.: '. . . primae meo iudicio Laelio Taurellio deferendae sunt, qui utilissimum opus . . . summo studio ac diligentia purgavit, cuncta exquisite minuteque conferens cum antiquissimo celeberrimoque Pandectarum exemplari: hic enim tanta cum fide se gessit, adeoque caute negotium illud administravit, ut nihil unquam iudicio suo, quo plurimum valet, tribuere voluerit: ac non nulla etiam, quae sane vitiosa suspicaretur, ut in exemplari invenit, reliquerit: . . . Hunc igitur et doctissimum, et omni in re prudentissimum virum, in hac re mihi imitandum proposui . . . '.

123. Ibid.: 'Cum etiam, ut veterem scribendi rationem sequerer: ac ne digitum quidem ab ea, quam in exemplari hoc optimo invenissem, discederem, mihi auctor idem fuerit, quod ipse sane curiose fecerat, in illo praeclaro legum opere edendo. Quanquam Gabrielem etiam Faernum, qui et Terentii fabulas et Ciceronis Philippicas, a se cum antiquissimis libris collatas, divulgare cogitat, eiusdem animi esse inveni.'

124. Faerno to Vettori, 29.i.1558; London, British Library, MS Add. 10266, fol. 111ᵛ; Faerno to Vettori, 12.ii.1558, ibid., fol. 113ʳ; the latter is quoted at length in *JWCI* xxxviii (1975), pp. 162-3 n. 27.

125. Cf. n. 123, above for the text. Vettori's wording may reflect his realization that Faerno and he were for once not seeing eye to eye; but few if any readers would have noticed that he described Faerno's editions as 'collated with old manuscripts' rather than 'based upon them'.

126. Faerno to Vettori, 26.ii.1558, London, British Library. MS Add. 10266, fol. 115ʳ⁻ᵛ: 'Quanto a quello, per provinciam imperii tui, non e dubio che la stampata lettione sta bene, et quella antica male. Et quante volte si vedde che anco li libri perfettissimi danno ne le scartate. Onde non bisogna sempre fidarsene. Anzi qualche volte uno modernissimo, pur che sia scritto, contiene la vera, dove gli antichi errano.'

127. Faerno to Vettori, 29.iv.1558, ibid., fol. 119ᵛ: 'Quanto a quello che mi scrivete, che sono alcuni che vorebbono che le filippice si stampassero come stanno su questo libro antico novamente per me trovato, vi dico che non metterebbe conto, perche questo libro non sta sempre bene, come quello che fu scritto da uno che non intendeva niente, ma dipingeva. Et vi si veggono dentro de notabili errori, dico anco in quelli lochi, dove gli altri libri, et la vulgata sta bene.' Faerno's negative assessment of the scribe's abilities was quite just; cf. A. C. Clark, 'The Textual Criticism of Cicero's *Philippics*', *Classical Review*, xiv (1900), p. 39: 'I have myself spent some time over it [scil. collating the MS], though with little result, except to realise more clearly the remarkable ignorance of the writer. No glimmer of intelligence appears amid his errors, and, but for such a passage as xiii.6, where for *seiungamus tamen* he reads *seiungamus amen*, he shows no knowledge even of ecclesiastical Latin.'

128. Faerno, loc. cit.: 'Ma dove questo varia dalli altri libri in megliorare, non sempre ha la lettion netta e iusta, ma spesso solo i vestigii, dalli quali poi si cava la bona con un poco di giudicio.'

129. Ibid.: ' . . . basta che nelle annotationi darò conto in quelli lochi dove il libro varia in bene dalla vulgata con qualche errore, daro conto, dico, in che modo stii la scrittura antica, et come la interpreti io, et le raggioni perche, se vi sarà qualche difficulta, o obscurita.'

130. Faerno, dedicatory letter to Vettori, in *Marci Tullii Ciceronis Philippicae et orationes pro Fonteio pro Flacco in Pisonem, omnes ex antiquissimo exemplari a Gabriele Faerno emendatae* (Rome, 1563), fol. [Avi^{r-v}] : 'Sed et tu nonnulla in his orationibus coniecisti; non pauca et ego; quorum nos hic antiquus liber veros coniectores probavit. Ex quo re ipsa admonemur, in emendandis auctoribus, non esse perpetuo libris scriptis inhaerendum: sed aliquid etiam hominum ingenio iudicioque tribuendum. Quod propterea libentius commemoramus, quia superioribus litteris tuis mihi significasti, esse istic nonnullos, ad quos huius antiqui exemplaris nuper inventi fama pervenerit, qui has orationes postulent edi, ad eum prorsus modum ut in eo scriptae inveniuntur, neque quicquam omnino variari. Qui si ipsi in hunc librum incidissent, sententiam, mihi crede, mutarent: non enim bene habet semper hic liber . . . '. Faerno says that in his *emendationes* he has given explicit reasons 'ubicumque a Manutiana editione defleximus' (fol. [Avii^{r}]); this approach resembles that of Vettori's first edition of the *Familiares*. As to Vettori's conjectures that anticipated readings of the Basilicanus, Faerno was again quite right. In *Variarum lectionum libri XXV*, XV.12, p. 227, Vettori suggested that the vulgate reading of *Phil.* X.v.11, 'certissimo modo erat etiam illius exercitus', should be emended to 'Certus (si modo erat) etiam illius exercitus'. Here the Basilicanus reads 'certus, si modo erat ullus, exercitus'. I owe this point to Claude Dupuy, who wrote as follows in the margin of his copy of Vettori's work (Paris, Bibliothèque Nationale, rés. Z 86): 'In cod. vat. legitur, Certus si modo erat ullus, exercitus. ad quam scripturam Vict. coniectura proxime accedit.'

131. Faerno's attitude towards Vettori strikingly resembles that of O. Jahn towards his master Lachmann; for Jahn also chose the medium of a dedicatory letter — in his *editio maior* of Persius (1843) — to declare both that he was personally loyal and that he found his master's methods too rigid. See S. Timpanaro, *La genesi del metodo del Lachmann*, 2nd edn. (Padua, 1981), pp. 88-9. Thus the school of Vettori, if the phrase is not exaggerated, encountered the same intellectual problems as the school of Lachmann 3 centuries later. This is strong evidence in favour of the thesis that the 16th century saw the growth of a professional philology.

Chapter III

1. E. Barbaro, *Castigationes Plinianae et in Pomponium Melam*, ed. G. Pozzi *et al.* (Padua, 1973-9). For a brief discussion of Barbaro's method see V. Branca, 'Ermolao Barbaro and Late Quattrocento Venetian Humanism', in *Renaissance Venice*, ed. J. R. Hale (London, 1973), pp. 222-5.

2. A. Manuzio, 'Adnotationes in Horatium', in *Aldo Manuzio Editore*, ed. G. Orlandi with an important introduction by C. Dionisotti (Milan, 1975), i, pp. 172-80. The notes appeared in Aldo's 1509 edition of the *Odes* of Horace.

3. See esp. K. Krautter, *Philologische Methode und humanistische Existenz. Filippo Beroaldo und sein Kommentar zum Goldenen Esel des Apuleius* (Munich, 1971).

4. C. Dionisotti, 'Calderini, Poliziano e altri', *IMU* xi (1968), pp. 173-8.

5. Erasmus, Adage 670; *Adagiorum Chiliades* (ed. Basel, 1536), pp. 256-8. Cf. *Opus Epistolarum Des. Erasmi Roterodami*, ed. P. S. Allen *et al.* (Oxford, 1906-58), i, pp. 293-4.

6. See the texts collected and discussed by F. Simone, 'La notion d'Encyclopédie: Elément caractéristique de la Renaissance française', in *French Renaissance Studies, 1540-1570*, ed. P. Sharratt (Edinburgh, 1976), pp. 244, 257 nn. 58-60.

7. G. Kisch, *Erasmus und die Jurisprudenz seiner Zeit. Studien zum humanistischen Rechtsdenken* (Basel, 1960), pp. 177-226, 495-503.

8. For interesting details on the use made by later scholars of the *Commentarii* see T. H. L. Parker, *Calvin's New Testament Commentaries* (London, 1971), pp. 147-50; D. Donnet, 'La "Syntaxis" de Jean Varennius et les "Commentarii" de Guillaume Budé', *Humanistica Lovaniensia*, xxii (1973), pp. 103-35.

9. G. Budé, *Commentarii linguae Graecae* (Paris, 1529), p. 873: 'Nos autem in hisce Commentariis libenter id fecimus, ut copiam linguae Latinae, quanta est illa cunque, ex Graecorum divitiis cantatissimis partem optimam manasse ostenderemus.'

10. Ibid., p. 50: 'Cicero enim omnium maxime transferre scriptorum Graecorum elegantiam, Graecorumque verborum vim in Romanum sermonem voluit . . .'.

11. Ibid., p. 874: 'Ita enim Graecis permultis dictionibus usus est, quasi aut plane Latinis, aut certe communibus: etiam (quod fortasse mireris) in orationibus, in librisque oratoriis.'

12. Ibid., p. 50: 'Arist. in tertio Ethic. . . . [*Nicomachean Ethics* III.15, 1119 b 1-2], quod Cicero imitatus est pro Mil. . . . [ix.23].'

13. Ibid., pp. 766, 50.

14. Ibid., p. 882: 'Neque vero cum eam copiam ex Graecia in Italiam importavit, commercium inde abstulit, ut idem aut simile quod ipse ausus esset, posteris non liceret, qui quidem eodem animum studiumque intendissent.'

15. H. Omont, 'Le premier professeur de langue Grecque au Collège de France. Jacques Toussaint (1529)', *Revue des études grecques*, xvi (1903), pp. 417-19. On the foundation of the royal lectureships see esp. A. Lefranc, 'Les commencements du Collège de France (1529-1544)', in *Mélanges d'histoire offerts à Henri Pirenne* (Brussels, 1926), ii, pp. 291-306; Lefranc, *Histoire du Collège de France* (Paris, 1893), pp. 101-6.

16. Cf. M. Augé-Chicquet, *La Vie, les idées, et l'œuvre de Jean-Antoine de Baïf* (Paris, 1909), pp. 20-30; J. Hutton, *The Greek Anthology in France and in the Latin Writers of the Netherlands to the Year 1800* (Ithaca, N.Y., 1946; repr. with corrections, New York, 1967), pp. 5, 16-17.

17. Cf. *Procli Sphaera, Thoma Linacro Britanno interprete, cum annotatiunculis ex publicis praelectionibus Iacobi Tusani Regii Graecarum literarum professoris exceptis* (Paris, 1553), sig. Biiii^v (on the Zodiac) with J. Stoeffler, *In Procli Diadochi, authoris gravissimi, Sphaeram mundi, omnibus numeris longe absolutissimus commentarius* (Tübingen, 1534), fol. 59^r; Toussain, sigs. Biiii^v-Bv^r (on the Milky Way) with Stoeffler, fol. 69^{r-v}; Toussain, sig. Bv^r (on the 5 geographical zones) with Stoeffler, fols 73^v-74^r. Naturally, Toussain has some material unknown to Stoeffler, e.g. a Greek epigram on an image of Berenice (sigs. Bv^v-[Bvi^r]): but one's general impression is one of dependence on the earlier commentator; and Toussain certainly falls far short of Stoeffler in mastery of the text's astronomical content.

18. The record of Toussain's lectures takes the form of: *Hermogenis Rhetoricae artis de Statibus translatio e fidelissimis Iacobi Tusani Regii Graecarum litterarum professoris praelectionibus diligenter excepta* (Paris, 1545), which appears to be a faithful and literal translation of the τέχνη ῥητορικὴ τελειοτάτη of Hermogenes (ed. Paris, 1544), a copy of which is bound with Toussain's

translation in a British Library *Sammelband* (shelf-mark 11340.f.5). It seems likely that Toussain edited the Greek text as well, for the use of those who attended his lectures; both works were printed by Bogardus in the same format, and the translation is introduced by a Latin version of the life of Hermogenes from the *Suda*, the Greek text of which occupies the corresponding position in the edition of the Greek text of Hermogenes. It should be noted that Toussain's lectures on the pseudo-Aristotelian *De mundo* had a certain philological content, at least to judge from the report in P. Vettori, *Variarum lectionum libri XXV* (Florence, 1553), XXV.13, p. 398: 'Arnoldus autem Arlenius, quem probum et eruditum virum cognovi, narravit mihi, dum hic potissimum locus excuderetur, Iacobum quoque Tusanum Lutetiae Parisiorum hunc librum accurate interpretantem, dixisse ipsum verum Aristotelis partum non esse, et quod hic esset elegans copiosumque prooemium, et quod in extremo auctor eius Platonem γενναῖον appellet, cum minime soleat ille tam praeclarum testimonium doctori suo impartiri.'

19. Toussain explains the origin of the work in a letter headed 'Iacobus Tusanus candido lectori Salutem', in Toussain, *Annotata in G. Budaei epistolas tam priores quam posteriores* (Paris, 1526), verso of title-page.

20. Ibid., fol. VI^v: 'Mirum quantum me totum. Mirum quantum pro maxime positum est. Livius lib. I. Mirum quantum illi viro haec nuncianti fides fuerit, et a Graecis tractum, qui θαυμαστὸν ὅσον dicunt, et θαυμάσιον ἡλίκον. Demosth. ταῦτα δὲ θαυμάσια ἡλίκα καὶ συμφέροντ' ἐδόκει τῇ πόλει.'

21. Ibid., fol. XIII^r–v: 'Nisi etiam Iliadis molestiarum. Ex proverbio Graeco ductum est: ἰλιὰς κακῶν. Demosth. καὶ κακῶν ἰλιὰς περιειστήκει θηβαίους: malorumque Iliade Thebani circunventi erant. Quod proverbium a magnitudine poematis tractum est [Cf. Erasmus, *Adagiorum Chiliades*, adage 226; ed. Basel, 1536, p. 108: *Ilias malorum*; Erasmus cites several other Greek uses of the proverb, but not that given by Toussain]. Quod sequitur, οὐδ' οὕτω κακῶς, ne sic quidem male, et subintelligendum, cessit. Huius proverbii meminit Plato in Symposio . . .'.

22. P. de Nolhac, *Ronsard et l'humanisme* (Paris, 1921), pp. 36–43, 341–2; Frances A. Yates, *The French Academies of the Sixteenth Century* (London, 1947), Ch. II.

23. See esp. L. de Baïf, *De re navali commentarius* (Basel, 1537).

24. *Ex Platonis Timaeo particula, Ciceronis de Vniversitate libro respondens*, ed. J. Perion (Paris, 1540) (Perion reproduces only those sections of Plato's Greek that have corresponding ones in the Latin); *Ciceronis in Arati Phaenomena interpretatio*, ed. J. Perion (Paris, 1540).

25. Ibid., pp. 105 (misnumbered 106)–106 (misnumbered 104): 'Haec habui de versibus coniungendis graecis Arati, cum latinis Ciceronis et Vergilii, quae dicerem. Nam praeterea multos Vergilii, quos ab Hesiodo, Homero, et Theocrito transtulit, commemorare possum, sed haec satis multa sunt hoc tempore, . . . Quod si visum esset ea, quae ab Arato Angelus Politianus transtulit, adhibere, plura Latinorum carmina Arateis graecis respondissent. Duae enim aut tres potius paginae Rustici eius extremae refertae sunt prognosticis Arateis, quorum pleraque Cicero et Vergilius transtulerunt. Nunc mihi hi duo Latini sermonis principes satis multi visi sunt ad rem declarandam, . . .'.

26. Ibid., p. 90: 'Ἐκ Διὸς ἀρχόμεσθα,] A Vergilio sic conversus est in Damoeta, Ab Iove principium, Musae [*Ecl.* III.60]. Tres autem versus qui sequuntur ab eodem in miram brevitatem redacti, contractique sunt eam, qua versum superiorem absolvit, Iovis omnia plena. Aratus singulas res enumeravit, quae plenae sunt Iovis, ut rura, ut coetus hominum, ut maria, ut portus: in quo usus est copia et ubertate dicendi. Virgilius uno vocabulo universa complexus est. Itaque plura significavit quam Aratus. . . . ' Cf. p. 95 for a similar comparison.

27. A full treatment of Perion's programme is contained in a forthcoming article by C. B. Schmitt.

28. Perion also irritated Parisian philologists; Nicholas de Grouchy spent many years publishing corrected versions of Perion's translations of Aristotle. And Lambin claimed that he had refuted Perion's views so effectively in an open argument that the latter was unable to offer a real rebuttal: D. Lambin, *De utilitate linguae Graecae, et recta Graecorum latine interpretandorum ratione, oratio* (Paris, 1572), pp. 18-22.

29. Lambin to Prévost, 11.iii.1553, quoted in H. Potez, 'Deux années de la Renaissance (d'après une correspondance inédite)', *Revue d'histoire littéraire de la France*, xiii (1906), p. 495 n. 1: 'Delectavit me in primis epistolae tuae locus de comoediis et tragoediis Gallicis. Libenter enim audio linguam nostram, quam ceterae nationes barbaram et inopem esse dicant, antiquorum poetarum veneres et ornamenta capere, interpretari, et exprimere posse. Qua in re gloriebantur Itali se nobis esse superiores. Sed propediem, ut video, intelligent sibi rem esse cum adversariis pugnacibus et lacertosis.'

30. Lambin to Nicole le Clerc, late 1554, ibid., pp. 665-6 n. 4: 'Hoc ego iuratus tibi confirmo, Perionium . . . in hoc utilissimo et elegantissimo Aristotelis opusculo ita turpiter et toties lapsum esse ut me Galliae nostrae apud exteras nationes pudeat. Saepe enim in Italia interfui querelis doctissimorum virorum, qui dicerent in Perionii scriptis nihil esse, praeter inanem quamdam orationis speciem.'

31. On Dorat see in general Nolhac, *Ronsard et l'humanisme*, pp. 52-84; M. Pattison, *Essays*, ed. H. Nettleship (Oxford, 1889), i, pp. 206-10. Further studies are listed in S. Guenée, *Bibliographie de l'histoire des universités françaises des origines à la révolution*, i (Paris, 1981), pp. 474-5.

32. C. Binet, *La Vie de P. de Ronsard*, ed. P. Laumonier (Paris, 1910), p. 12.

33. Ibid., p. 13: 'Ce fut ce qui l'incita à tourner en François le Plutus d'Aristophane, et le faire représenter en public au collège de Cocqueret, qui fut la première Comédie Françoise joüée en France.'

34. Much MS material remains to be studied before Dorat's method can be described with confidence. Meantime, the best case study is G. Demerson, 'Dorat, commentateur d'Homère', *Études seiziémistes offertes à V.-L. Saulnier* (Geneva, 1980), pp. 223-34.

35. Ibid., p. 234.

36. P. Sharratt, 'Ronsard et Pindare: un écho de la voix de Dorat', *BHR* xxxix (1977), p. 104.

37. See *Scaligerana I*, s. v. Auctores, p. 20.

38. For the authors in whom Dorat was most interested see e.g. Nolhac, *Ronsard et l'humanisme*, pp. 78-9.

39. Hesiod, *Scutum Herculis* 1-2.

40. W. Canter, *Novarum lectionum libri quatuor* (Basel, 1564), IV.3, pp. 179-81: 'Dubitari a multis intelligo, quid sibi velit Hesiodi ἀσπίδος initium, . . . etc. cum hoc et abruptum videatur, et absurde idcirco a multis expositum sit. Quem nodum ut commodius dissolvamus, paulo altius est res repetenda. Hesiodus inter caetera, quae Pausanias in Boeoticis [*Graeciae descriptio*, IX. xxxi.5] enumerat, scripsit etiam μεγάλας ἠοίας, ut vocat idem Pausanias, et praeterea Athenaeus [*Deipnosophistae*, x.32, 428b], et Apollonii, Pindari, Sophoclis interpres: in quibus praeclarissimas quasque mulieres et heroinas perpetuo carmine celebravit, ut vel singulas pro exemplo nobis proponeret, vel unam aliquam praeclarissimam cum reliquis compararet. Hinc enim dictae sunt ἠοίαι, quod singulae similitudines ab his vocibus, ἢ οἵη, inciperent: sicut et in Homeri Boeotia factum cernimus, et apud Hebraeos in Pentateucho. . . . earum

fragmentum est id, quod hodie extat, Scutum Herculis, quo una comparatio earum, quibus opus totum constabat quamplurimis, continetur. itaque et ab ἢ οἴη, sicut etiam reliquae, incipit. Exemplum unum et alterum ab interprete Pindari citatum adducam: . . . [Canter goes on to cite examples from the scholia to Pindar, *Pyth.*, IV.36, IX.6 (*Scholia vetera in Pindari carmina*, ed. A. B. Drachmann, vol. ii: *Scholia in Pythionicas* (Leipzig, 1910), *Pyth.* IV.36.c; IX.6.a).] His omnino simile est nostrum illud, ἢ οἴη προλιποῦσα, etc. . . . Haec si cui minus erunt verisimilia, is me sciat auctorem habere huius opinionis doctissimum virum, Ioannem Auratum.'

41. Dorat, *Poematia* (Paris, 1586), Pt. II, p. 157, quoted by Nolhac, *Ronsard et l'humanisme*, p. 21 n. 2:

> Orphaeus, Musaeus, fur et Homerus erant:
> Fur erat Hesiodus, clypeum furatus Achillis:
> Herculis est, olim tegmen Achillis erat.
> Ipsas quinetiam furatur uterque Sibyllas,
> Seque Sibyllinis ornat uterque modis,
> Neve putes, mendax quia semper Graecia, Graecos
> Furaces Latiis vatibus esse magis.
> Ennius ipse pater magnum furatur Homerum,
> Maeonides alter visus et inde sibi est.

On Dorat's Latin poetry see G. Demerson's edition of *Les Odes latines* (Clermont-Ferrand, 1979).

42. See B. Weinberg's introduction to his collection of *Critical Prefaces of the French Renaissance* (Evanston, Ill., 1950), pp. 16-17. Du Bellay had other sources besides the teaching of Dorat. In particular, he drew heavily on the writings of earlier Italian literary theorists, notably Sperone Speroni; see P. Villey, *Les sources italiennes de la 'Deffense et illustration . . .'* (Paris, 1908). But it seems clear that his general beliefs about imitation – and his ability to put them into practice – were owed at least in part to Dorat, whom he praised fluently and with whom he seems to have studied. Cf. Nolhac, *Ronsard et l'humanisme*, index, s.v. Bellay (Joachim du).

43. Muret's commentary appeared for the first time in the 2nd edition of the *Amours* (1553). It is readily accessible in several modern editions, e.g. *Les Amours . . . d'après le texte de 1578*, ed. H. Vaganay with an important introduction by J. Vianey (Paris, 1910); *Œuvres de Ronsard. Texte de 1587*, ed. I. Silver, vol. i (Paris, 1966). See also Nolhac, *Ronsard et l'humanisme*, pp. 92–101. For the place of poetry in 16th-century court life and the reasons why French poets needed a language of elaborate conceits and recondite allusions, see L. Forster, *The Icy Fire. Five Studies in European Petrarchism* (Cambridge, 1969), Chs. I-II.

44. M.-A. Muret, preface to his *Juvenilia* (1552), Muret, *Opera Omnia*, ed. D. Ruhnken (Leiden, 1789), i, p. 660, quoted by Nolhac, *Ronsard et l'humanisme*, p. 17: 'Qui se vernaculo nostro sermone poetas perhiberi volebant, perdiu ea scripsere, quae delectare modo otiosas mulierculas, non etiam eruditorum hominum studia tenere possent. Primus, ut arbitror, Petrus Ronsardus, cum se eruditissimo viro Ioanni Aurato in disciplinam dedisset, eoque duce veterum utriusque linguae poetarum scripta, multa et diligenti lectione trivisset, transmarinis illis opibus sua scripta exornare aggressus est; cuius postea exemplum insecuti I. Antonius Baifius, I. Bellaius aliique permulti, brevi tempore tantos fecere progressus, ut res vel ad summum pervenisse iam, vel certe haud ita multo post perventura esse videatur.'

45. While in Italy, Estienne seems to have discussed his Anacreon with, among others, Vettori and Francesco Robortello; see *Anacreon, with Thomas Stanley's Translation*, ed. A. H. Bullen (London, 1893), p. xvi; *Anacreontis Teïi quae*

vocantur συμποσιακὰ ἡμιαμβεῖα, ed. V. Rose (Leipzig, 1890), p. viii, xix n. 34. Cf. also W. Rüdiger, *Petrus Victorius aus Florenz. Studien zu einem Lebensbilde* (Halle a. S., 1896), p. 47.

46. H. Estienne, 'Observationes in Anacreontis carmina', in *Anacreontis Teii Odae* (Paris, 1554), pp. 78-9. For the text see Appendix to Ch. III, below.

47. Ibid., p. 69: 'Haec observatione sunt digna, ut et ipsi discamus caute imitari veteres, et si quid apud illos occurrat, quod in rem nostram sit, ita in usum nostrum illud vertere, ut non aliunde tamen petitum, sed domi natum videatur.'

48. Nolhac, *Ronsard et l'humanisme*, pp. 107-8.

49. Hutton, *Greek Anthology in France*, pp. 98-101.

50. J. Brodeau, *Miscellaneorum libri sex* (Basel, 1555). The prefatory letter by one Baptista Sapinus explicitly compares Brodeau to Poliziano and declares that Brodeau is justified in criticizing his predecessors. Sapinus is careful to say that Brodeau is *not yet* to be compared with masters like Poliziano; but the tone of the piece clearly indicates that these apparent concessions should not be taken at face value. In VI.11, pp. 226-7, Brodeau criticizes one point in Poliziano's translation of Herodian. In I.5, pp. 11-12 and II.2, pp. 46-7, Brodeau defends Cicero against Vettori, who had accused him — following Poliziano's precedent — of making mistakes in his use of Greek terms and reading of Greek sources. A comment in I.8, p. 14, seems to suggest a certain anti-Italian bias: 'Venio nunc ad Alciatum, qui lib. Parerg. 2. colorem rubrum cum rufo confundit ... Decepit, ut opinor, Alciatum vernaculum idioma: siquidem Itali tam rubrum, quam rufum, rossum promiscue vocant.' Brodeau also engages in systematic comparison of Latin and Greek; in I.21, pp. 26-7, e.g., he shows that Horace *Carm* I. xxxvii.1-2 is derived from Alcaeus (frag. 20; Loebl-Page 332; preserved by Athenaeus).

51. On the French Greek scholarship of the 1550s and 1560s see R. Pfeiffer, *History of Classical Scholarship from 1300 to 1850* (Oxford, 1976), Ch. IX; Pfeiffer, 'Dichter und Philologen im französischen Humanismus', *Antike und Abendland*, vii (1958), pp. 73-83; J. Hutton, 'The Classics in Sixteenth-Century France', *Classical Weekly*, xliii, no. 9 (30.i.1950), pp. 131-9. On Turnèbe, L. Clément, *De Adriani Turnebi regii professoris praefationibus et poematis* (diss. Paris, 1899) is still the most informative, with a useful bibliography of Turnèbe's publications. J. Hutton's *Greek Anthology in France* and Nolhac's *Ronsard et l'humanisme* are also mines of information, as the many footnote references to them in this chapter show. The many articles by L. C. Stevens (e.g. 'A Re-Evaluation of Hellenism in the French Renaissance', *Studies in Philology*, lviii (1961), pp. 115-29, repr. in *French Humanism 1470-1600*, ed. W. Gundersheimer (New York and Evanston, 1969), pp. 181-96) are ill digested and unanalytical, and can safely be ignored. U. von Wilamowitz-Moellendorf, on the other hand, compresses a remarkable number of striking observations on French philology into pp. 221-7 of his *Einleitung in die griechische Tragödie* (Berlin, 1907), which should be consulted by all students of the French Renaissance. For Turnèbe's work on Cicero's Greek sources see Ch. VII, below, n. 71.

52. For Lambin's family background and early life see H. Potez, 'La jeunesse de Denys Lambin (1519-1548)', *Revue d'histoire littéraire de la France*, ix (1902), pp. 385-413. For his later financial problems and struggles to find adequate jobs, see Potez, 'Deux années de la Renaissance, d'après une correspondance inédite de Denys Lambin', ibid., xxvii (1920), pp. 214-51.

53. C. Dupuy to O. Giphanius, 12.viii.1570, Paris, Bibliothèque Nationale, MS Dupuy 16, fol. 16ʳ⁻ᵛ. Dupuy says of Lambin: 'qui etsi me offenderit, et notam nomini meo non levem inusserit; tamen hanc ille culpam a me deprecatus est, et ego hominis potius inconsiderantiae, ut ita dicam, παιδαγωγικῇ, quam malitiae tribuo.'

54. For Lambin's observation see his edition of Horace (Paris, 1567), i, 91, *ad Carm.* I.xxxvii.1: 'NVNC EST BIBENDVM] videtur haec ab Alcaeo esse mutuatus, cuius hi versus reperiuntur apud Athen. lib. x. Νῦν χρὴ μεθύσκειν, καὶ τινὰ πρὸς βίαν Πίνειν.' For Brodeau see n. 50, above.

55. Ibid., p. 83 *ad Carm*, I.xxxiv.2: 'INSAN. DVM. SAP.] ... Venuste autem *insanientem sapientiam* dixit Graecorum exemplo, apud quos crebrum est hoc genus loquendi. Eurip. in Hecuba, νύμφην ἄνυμφον, παρθένον τ'ἀπάρθενον [612]. ...'. There follow Greek parallels from Sophocles, Oppian, Aristophanes, and Homer, and Latin parallels from Horace himself, Cicero, Catullus, and Ennius. Cf. Vettori, *Variarum lectionum libri XXV*, X.12, pp. 147-8: 'Arbitror autem Latinum poetam, quod apud Graecum erat, unde vertebat, γάμον ἄγαμον, innuptias nuptias dixisse. Saepe nanque poetae Graeci hac forma sermonis utuntur, ut Euripides, quum induxit Helenam ita exclamantem in fabula, cui ipsa nomen dedit. ἰὼ τροία τάλαινα δι' ἔργ' ἄνεργ' ὄλλυσαι [363]. ...'. There follow a number of further parallels, some of which Lambin has borrowed.

56. I follow the analysis of E. Fraenkel, *Horace* (Oxford, 1957), pp. 184-8.

57. Horace, ed. Lambin, i, p. 61 *ad Carm.* I.xxii.1.: 'SCELERISQUE PVRVS.] sceleris purum accipio eum, qui castas, et puras a sanguine manus habet: qualeis Hippolyti dicit esse Phaedrae nutrix apud Eurip. Ἁγνὰς μὲν ὦ παῖ χεῖρας αἵματος φέρεις [*Hipp*.316]. Contra Adrastus ille apud Herodot. Clione. Is, qui fratre suo interfecto sese ad Croesum contulerat, non habebat puras manus ...'.

58. Ibid., p. 61 *ad Carm.* I.xxii.2: 'Maura autem iacula dixit quia Mauri optimi erant iaculatores.'

59. Ibid., pp. 62-3 *ad Carm.* I.xxii.17, at p. 63: 'Atqui hanc esse temperatam, et habitabilem, qui nostra et avorum nostrorum aetate navigarunt, compererunt.'

60. Scaliger, *Epistolae*, p. 87 (Scaliger to Lipsius, 12.ii.1577): 'Plautum Lambini si vidisti, non admiraris, certo scio. Est enim germanus plane illius Horatii Lambiniani, qui commentariorum mole laborat.' For a discussion of this passage see e.g. E. J. Kenney, *The Classical Text* (Berkeley, 1974), p. 64 n. 2.

61. Horace, ed. Lambin, i, p. 63 *ad Carm.* I.xxii.23: 'DVLCE RIDENTEM.] sic Catullus ad Lesb. ... Quod quidem Sappho Graece dixerat (nam ab ea transtulit in usum suum Catullus) ... Idem Catull. ... Hom. ... et Pindar. in Pyth. carm. 9. ... et Apollon. 3. Argon. ... similia sunt haec Horatiana ... Quanquam illud *canet indoctum, sed dulce bibenti*, potest dici esse dissimile, propterea, quod verbum canere cum quarto casu coniungi solet, et vocis agentis est.'

62. *Scaligerana II*, p. 416, s. v. Lambinus: 'LAMBINUS in Horatium. Plessaeus de Missa. Tableaux de Sainte Aldegonde. Mercerus in Job. Testamentum Bezae. Calvini opera, praestantissima. Lambinus avoit fort peu de livres.'

63. Horace, ed. Lambin, ii, p. 359 *ad A. P.* 141: 'DIC MIHI MVSA VIRVM] principium Odyss. ... etc. Libet mihi hoc loco occasionem et ansam nacto ex P. Ronssardi, viri clariss., poetae Regii, Franciade, poemate Gallico, plane cum Iliade Homerica et Aeneide Virgiliana comparando, versus aliquot Gallicos decerpere, eosque ab Io. Aurato, viro singulari doctrina ornato, poeta Regio, Latinos factos, commentariorum meorum lectoribus legendos exponere, ut intelligant exterae nationes quae et qualia ingenia efferat nostra Gallia, et quantopere apud nos floreant bonae litterae, liberalesque doctrinae.' It is clearly significant that one of the two selections Lambin made was the opening invocation of the Muse. In suggesting that the samples would move readers to demand that Ronsard's work be published, Lambin is presumably setting up a parallel with Virgil. The selections follow on pp. 359-61.

64. Frances A. Yates, *Astraea. The Imperial Theme in the Sixteenth Century* (London, 1975), Part III.

65. S. Proxenus a Sudetis, *Commentarii de itinere Francogallico*, ed. D. Martínková

(Budapest, 1979), p. 82: 'Ludovicus Cospaeanus venit in nostrum diversorium. Ei tradi..i epithalamion domino Iohanni Aurato exhibendum, ut de eo censuram ferat. A prandio emeram poemata Michaelis Hospitalis et Ioachimi Baillei, emturus adhuc plura poetarum Gallicorum, si potero. Cospaeanus retulerat, quod alias saepius N. Maignan, Iohanne Aurato non esse alium doctiorem in tota Europa in explicandis et intelligendis poetis Graecis. Ronsardum ómnia sua accepta ferre Aurato. Reliquos professores ex aequo omnes, in Graeca lingua si quod est dubium, ad eum confugere.'

66. B. Vulcanius to Th. Canter, 17.xi.1585, in *Epistolarum ab illustribus et claris viris scriptarum centuriae tres*, ed. S. A. Gabbema (Haarlem, 1663), pp. 712-13: 'It ad te tandem Ronsardus quem petiisti. Morae causa fuit, quod per quem commode mitterem non habebam. Neque nautis pluvioso hoc coelo committere volui, ut nec debui. Interea ego succisivas aliquot hebdomadarum horas ei perlegendo impendi. Idque majore nescio an voluptate, an fructu. Ita mihi accurata in eo felicissimaque poetarum tam Graecorum, quam Latinorum imitatio placuit. Atque ita quidem placuit, ut nisi aetas mea et erumpentes paulatim cani id suo quodam jure prohiberent, darem operam, ut tale aliquod exemplum nostratibus etiam hominibus proponerem. Neque enim lingua nostra ita est aut sterilis aut barbara, quin parem in compositione vocabulorum dexteritatem, et easdem Veneres, si quis in eo non invita plane, quod ajunt, Minerva allaboret, admittat. Atque utinam Hautenus noster, qui Plauti Comoedias aliquot nostro idiomate eleganter admodum, vel Lipsio judice, transtulit, publici aliquando juris faciat.'

67. M.-A. Muret, *Variarum lectionum libri XVIII* (Halle a. S., 1791-1828), VII.7; vol. i, pp. 180-1: 'Eodem prope modo memini correctum olim esse ab Io. Aurato, homine doctissimo, mihique amicissimo, versum quendam Callimachi ex hymno in Apollinem; qui cum vulgo ita legatur:

Οὐδ' ὁ χορὸς τὸν Φοῖβον ἐφ' ἓν μόνον ἦμαρ ἀείσει.
Ἔστι γὰρ εὔυμνός τις · ἂν οὔρεα Φοῖβον ἀείδει,

legendus est, ut is, quem modo dixi, vir eruditissimus admonuit, hoc modo:
Ἔστι γὰρ εὔυμνος, τίς ἂν οὐ ῥέα Φοῖβον ἀείδοι;

Hoc enim dicit poeta, neminem esse usque eo rudem et indisertum, cui non facillimum sit laudare Apollinem. Nam ita multa in eo laudanda esse, ut nemini, ne infantissimo quidem, qui eum celebrare instituerit, deesse possit oratio.'

68. H. Estienne, *Annotationes in suam hanc editionem alterius voluminis poetarum*, in *Poetae Graeci principes heroici carminis, et alii nonnulli* (Geneva, 1566), separately paginated, pp. xxxviii–xxxix; see Appendix to Ch. III for text.

69. Aeschylus, *Agamemnon*, ed. E. Fraenkel (Oxford, 1950), i, p. 35.

70. See e.g. L. D. Reynolds and N. G. Wilson, *Scribes and Scholars*, 2nd edn. (Oxford, 1974), pp. 157-8; see also Nolhac, *Ronsard et l'humanisme*, pp. 75-7, 132-7. *Editiones principes* include H. Estienne's *Anacreontea*, J. du Tillet's Ulpian, P. Daniel's *Querolus*, P. Pithou's *Collatio legum Mosaicarum et Romanarum* and *Pervigilium Veneris*. New MSS brought into play for the first time include what is now Leiden MS. Voss. Lat. fol. 111 of Ausonius (see Ch. IV, below); the lost Codex Turnebi of Plautus, on which see W. M. Lindsay, *The Codex Turnebi of Plautus* (Oxford, 1898); the St. Germain manuscript of the Philoxenus glossary; and a good many miscellaneous codices.

71. *Aeschylus*, ed. A. Turnèbe (Paris, 1552), ep. ded. to Michel de l'Hopital:
τρεῖς μέντοι τῶν τραγῳδιῶν οὐκ ἂν ὀκνοίημεν διϊσχυρίσασθαι οὐκ ὡς ἔτυχεν
ἡμῖν διωρθῶσθαι. ἀντίγραφον γὰρ εὖ μάλα παλαιὸν παρὰ τοῦ λαμπροτάτου
προέδρου Αλμάρου Ραγκωνήτου κομισάμενοι, ἀφορμῆς ἐτύχομεν εἰς τὴν ἀκρίβωσιν
τῆς ἐκδόσεως τῶν τριῶν καλλίστης.

72. Ibid., p. 210: Τὰ ἄλλως εὑρεθέντα ἔν τισιν ἀντιγράφοις.

73. Ibid., ep. ded.: οὐκ ὀλίγα μέντοι ἄττα . . . εἰς τὸ ὑγιὲς ἀποκατεστήσαμεν.

74. See e.g. Vettori, *Explicationes suàrum in Ciceronem castigationum* (Paris, 1538), p. 5 *ad Fam.* I.9; p. 38 *ad Fam.* XV.ii.17: 'Hoc loco veteres codices manci sunt ad unum omnes, ut suspicer hunc locum, ut multos alios, restitutum esse, suppletumque ab aliquo arbitrio suo potius, et coniectura, quam veterum et integrorum codicum auxilio.' Cf. also n. 82, below.

75. Sophocles, ed. A. Turnèbe (Paris, 1553), quoted by R. Aubreton, *Démétrius Triclinius et les recensions médiévales de Sophocle* (Paris, 1949), p. 28: βιβλίον γὰρ παρὰ σοῦ εὐτυχήσαντες Δημητρίου τοῦ Τρικλινίου σημειώσεσι, στιχογραφίαις, ἐξηγήσεσι, διορθώσεσιν εἰς εὔρυθμον καὶ ἐμμελὲς εὖ μάλα διηκριβωμένον.

76. Ibid., pp. 240-5; Turnèbe's MS was Parisinus graecus 2711 (T); he reproduced its readings inexactly and apparently used another MS as well (ibid., pp. 27-45).

77. No competent study of Lambin's life and work is available. The articles by H. Potez cited above remain the most valuable sources for his biography.

78. See Lambin's letter, headed 'Idem lectori S. D.' in his edition of Horace, i, sig. † iiij^v: 'A Gabriele Faerno, homine candidissimis moribus, unum item commodato accepi.'

79. Ibid.: 'In bibliotheca Pontificis Rom. Vaticana, quae mihi beneficio Gulielmi Sirleti, et Hieronymi eius fratris, et Federici Brutii, quoties mihi commodum erat, patebat, quinque libros antiquissimos, manuque scriptos reperi. Donatus Iannoctius Florentinus unum, qui fuerat amplissimi, atque ornatissimi viri Rhodolphi Cardinalis, eoque mortuo cum aliquot aliis Graecis, ac Latinis ad ipsum testamento pervenerat, mihi commodavit. A Gabriele Faerno, homine candidissimis moribus, unum item commodato accepi. Accesserunt duo, quorum alter erat Rainutii Farnesii clarissimi Card.; typis ille quidem excusus, sed cum antiquissimis, atque optimis codicibus comparatus, atque ex eorum fide, ac testimonio quam plurimis locis emendatus; alter Ludovico Vrsino, Farnesiorum consobrino, adolescenti pudenti ac probo, ab Annibale Caro donatus fuerat; in quo desiderabantur sermonum libri. Horum utriusque mihi facta a dominis copia est, opera Fulvii Vrsini, hominis eruditissimi. Postremo mihi ex Italia reverso, commentariis meis iam absolutis, liber item calamo scriptus, vetustissimus, a Io. Tornesio, typographo Lugdunensi, nuper insperanti Lugduni oblatus est. . . .'.

80. See e.g. ibid., p. 26 *ad Carm.* I.vii.15: 'DETERGET] detergit quidem reperi scriptum in duobus libris calamo scriptis Don. et Faer. sed *deterget* tamen reposui, secutus lib. 2. Vaticanos, et Vrsini, et Tornes.'; ibid., p. 43 *ad Carm.* I.xiii.6; ibid., p. 126 *ad Carm.* II.xv.9-10. It does not take much acquaintance with Lambin's commentary to see that he was far more interested in and able at exegesis than textual criticism; cf. Kenney, *The Classical Text*, pp. 63-6 and Grafton, 'From Politian to Pasquali', *Journal of Roman Studies* lxvii (1977), pp. 172-3.

81. After discussing and emending some epigrams attributed to Plato, Vettori published one of the *Anacreontea* found by Estienne in *Variarum lectionum libri XXV*, XX.17, p. 313. His introductory comments are revealing in more ways than one, and supply an approximate date for their meeting: 'His autem suavissimis politi philosophi versibus addere libet suave itidem, lepidumque Anacreontis carmen, quod, cum paucis ab hinc mensibus hac transiret Henricus Stephanus Roberti filius, probus adolescens, ac liberali doctrina supra aetatem instructus, ipse mihi dedit; inventum a se forte (ut aiebat) in antiqui libri tegmine . . .'.

82. P. Vettori, ep. headed 'Petrus Victorius lectori S.', in *Aeschyli Tragoediae VII* (Geneva, 1557), sig. a ii^r; repr. in Vettori, *Epistolarum libri X. Orationes XIII. Et liber de laudibus Ioannae Austriacae* (Florence, 1586), *Epistolae* (separately paginated), pp. 66-7. Vettori had Sirleto collate the other manuscript, which

was in the library of Alessandro Farnese. 'Nos autem', he writes, 'postea varietatibus illis diligenter ponderatis, in eam opinionem venimus ut nostrum librum non deteriorem illo putaremus; ac magnam partem eorum quae variata in eo offenduntur, immutatam ab aliquo crederemus, qui in suos quosdam versus restituere chori cantus voluerit. Saepe enim addita aut dempta illic quaedam cognovimus, quae consilium ipsius adiuvarent.'

83. *Aeschyli Tragoediae VII*, p. 354: '... simulatque hae tragoediae excusae fuerunt, illas omnes varias lectiones [scil. those collected by Vettori in an exemplar ... cum antiquis libris ac praesertim cum pulcherrimo ac vetustissimo quodam suo (oculatus ipse sum testis) ... collatum] in unum colligere coepi: aliis etiam quibusdam, quas ex non omnino malo codice habebam, additis. Collectas autem eas quum iamiam daturus essem ad calcem operis excudendas, commodum vir quidam mihi amicissimus supervenit: qui quum eas percurrisset, Quae ergo a te ratio, inquit, in tanta lectionum varietate, dum librum ipsum excuderes, inita est? Unumne tibi exemplar ubique sequendum proposuisti, an potius delectum aliquem habuisti? Cui quum respondissem, me plus fidei illi Victorii libro quam ulli alii habuisse, nec id tamen ita ubique sequutum esse, ut in eius lectiones quasi iurasse videri possem: Tunc ille, Tui ergo fuerit officii, dixit, varias has lectiones non ita nudas edere, sed una rationem consilii tui omnibus exponere, et aliquibus (si omnibus minus possis) eam probare ...'.

84. Ibid., pp. 354-5: 'Exemplar autem quod potissimum sequutum me dico, sequutus omnino et ubique fuissem, illud videlicet quod caeteris omnibus vel antiquitatis nomine praeferendum esse merito censebatur: nisi, me illi prorsus addicendo, reliquis exemplaribus temere et sine ratione nonnullis in locis fidem esse derogandam praevidissem.'

85. Ibid., p. 355: 'Cuiusmodi cum alii, tum vero insignes paginis 61 et 279 et 312 habentur: in quibus si illud exemplar quod dico sequi voluissem, ego certe prudens et sciens pulcherrimas sententias, corruptas, ut erant in quibusdam editionibus, reliquissem. Cui malo ut occurrerem: siquando alio in libro lectionem diversam loco poetae congruam inveni, etsi deerat libri huius Victoriani consensus (quippe quum eam ex illo adnotatam non haberem) non dubitavi in contextum eam recipere, et alteram, quam nemo non mendosam esse iudicasset, in calce libri adnotandam servare, id nimirum faciens, quod ipse Victorius, si adfuisset, mihi facturus videbatur.'

86. In the 3 notes to which Estienne refers as cases where he was obliged to alter Vettori's text (p. 366 *ad Prom.* 1014; p. 382 *ad Eum.* 224; p. 384 *ad Suppl.* 124), sense is always the major consideration, though on p. 382 he says that he has found the correct reading *in alio non pessimo codice*, and on p. 384 that he has found his better reading *in exemplari non omnino malo*, and that the scholiast seems to have had a text with the better reading. In the 2nd note he suggests that Vettori may have missed the correct reading in his collation — and incidentally gives some interesting information about Vettori's habits of work: 'Quod autem attinet ad illam lectionem, Δίκας δὲ Παλλάς, fieri potest ut habeatur in illo veteri libro, ex quo tamen eam adnotatam non habuerim: quod dum conferretur editio libri impressi cum eo, pronuntiatio fefellerit: id est, ex mala pronuntiatione eius qui legebat, δὲ Παλλάς a δ'ἐπ'ἄλλας distingui non potuerit.'

87. It would be interesting to know precisely how far the printed edition differed from the text that Vettori had given to Estienne — and, indeed, whether that text was merely a printed text with collations, as Estienne describes it. It would also be interesting to know Vettori's feelings when he saw the printed text. His only remark about the edition known to me is in a letter to Sirleto, in *Prose fiorentine raccolte dallo Smarrito*, new edn., 18 vols. in 5 (Florence, 1751-4), iv. 4, p. 7: 'Mi pare di conoscere, che [Enrico Stephano] ha indugiato tanto a darlo fuora, perchè vi ha voluto fare da dietro certe annotazioni, e così usare un po' di saccenteria.'

88. It is worth pointing out that much of the editorial effort of French scholars went into texts to be used in teaching, for which care in editing was less relevant than speed in printing. Thus, Dorat's 1548 edition of Aeschylus' *Prometheus*, a copy of which has recently been discovered, was intended expressly for the auditors at his lectures; and Dorat described his editorial method as follows in his letter to the reader: 'Notavi igitur quaedam sed obiter, quae et ratio pedum, et sensus ipse, et poetica phrasis subindicabant, reliqua accuratius persecuturus inter interpretandum: ita ut inoffense de reliquo perlegi possit.' See M. Mund-Dopchie, 'Le premier travail français sur Eschyle: le Prométhée enchaîné de Jean Dorat', *Les Lettres Romanes*, xxx (1976), pp. 261–74, at p. 269. Lambin apparently edited a text of Pindar for similar purposes (information kindly supplied by A. C. Dionisotti). Élie Vinet, the great Bordeaux humanist, also published many such works for use in the Collège de Guyenne and elsewhere; see L. Desgraves, *Élie Vinet* (Geneva, 1977), for a list of Vinet's editions and the texts (sometimes slightly mangled) of his prefaces. For a good case study in the skills of the French at conjectural emendation see J. Masson, 'A Lost Edition of Sophocles' *Philoctetes*', *Journal of Philology*, xvi (1888), pp. 114–23.

It is not surprising that these rather cavalier editorial habits attracted some sharp criticism in the formative years of 19th-century philology. For a spirited defence of Estienne's work in particular see D. Wyttenbach's preface to his edition of Plutarch's *Moralia*; cf. also K. Sintenis, 'Zur Ehrenerklärung für H. Stephanus', *Philologus*, i (1846), pp. 134–42; E. B. England, 'H. Stephens's *Vetustissima Exemplaria*', *Classical Review*, viii (1894), pp. 196–7, with the note by A. Tilley, 'Henri Estienne', ibid., p. 251, and a reply by R. Y. Tyrrell, 'The Bacchae of Euripides', ibid., pp. 294–6.

89. See in general C. Phillipson, 'Jacques Cujas', in *Great Jurists of the World*, ed. J. MacDonell and E. Manson (Boston, 1914), pp. 83–108.

90. See J.-A. de Thou, *Mémoires*, ed. C. Bernard (Paris, 1823), pp. 248–9.

91. J. Cujas, *Observationum et emendationum libri xvii* (Cologne, 1578), III.38, pp. 149–50; I.9, pp. 7–8.

92. Ibid., I.1, p. 2: 'Abest quidem negatio a Florentino libro, cuius quanta sit apud omnes auctoritas non ignoro, sed plus ipse rationi iuris tribuo, quam ulli scripturae, qua quidem nulla res est quae facilius depravari possit: nec tamen etiam scriptorum librorum auctoritate careo . . .'. Cf. Bentley on Horace *Carm.* III.xxvii.15: 'Nobis et ratio et res ipsa centum codicibus potiores sunt, praesertim accedente Vaticani veteris suffragio.'

93. Ibid., II.1, p. 43: '. . . atque ea re sum omnibus studiosis auctor, ut etsi editis Pandectis Florentinis, nihil ad Pandectarum restitutionem praeterea quicquam desiderandum esse plerique vociferentur, quotquot poterunt alias tamen quascumque manu scriptas Pandectas conquirant, certoque iudicio earum scripturam expendant, et examinent. Nec enim fidem habendam esse censeo his, qui caeteras omnes ex Florentinis dimanasse profitentur.' For a detailed study of the implications of Cujas's method see J. Miquel, 'Mechanische Fehler in der Ueberlieferung der Digesten', *Zeitschrift der Savigny-Stiftung für Rechtsgeschichte, Romanistische Abteilung*, lxxx (1963), pp. 272–4; and cf. H. E. Troje, *Graeca leguntur* (Vienna and Cologne, 1971), the most detailed and penetrating study yet published of the scholarship of Cujas and his contemporaries.

94. Cf. B. Ricci, *De imitatione libri tres*, 2nd edn. (Venice 1545), fol. 18ᵛ: 'Si mihi igitur interpres sit aliquando agendus, nihil mihi aut Donati prudentia, aut Servii Honorati diligentia (ut reliquos minorum gentium interpretes omittam) quicquam obstiterit, quo minus Asconium Pedianum mihi deligam, cuius ad rationem interpretandi totum me conferam, atque adiungam. Quod a meo Manutio in epistolis ad Atticum exponendis video fieri sane quam praeclare.'

On Manuzio see in general P. Costil, 'Paul Manuce et l'humanisme à Padoue à l'époque du Concile de Trente', *Revue des questions historiques*, ser. III, 21 [117] (1932), pp. 321-62.

95. B. Cavalcanti to P. Vettori, 24.viii.1540, in Cavalcanti, *Lettere edite e inedite*, ed. C. Roaf (Bologna, 1967), pp. 102-3.

96. P. Manuzio, 'Scholia', in Manuzio, *Commentarius in M. Tullii Ciceronis Epistolas ad Diversos*, ed. C. G. Richter (Leipzig, 1779-80), ii, p. 955: 'Sed nullus est tam antiquus codex, qui non multis locis corruptus tamen sit. Itaque uno, aut etiam altero manuscripto libro qui se putant veteres scriptores posse restituere, meo iudicio falluntur. Vetustis exemplaribus ad eam rem plurimis opus est. Quae licet inquinata sint, tamen ex singulis boni aliquid excerpentes, usu saepe venire videmus, ut ex multis libris, qui mali sint, bonus tamen liber efficiatur unus.'

97. Ibid., p. 925, *ad Fam.* I.ix.13: '*Bonorum omnium consensio*] Antea, *consensus. Nos, consensio*, restituimus ex veterum librorum fide. Alii, vetustos omnes libros, *consensus*, habere scripserunt. Quod aliter esse deprehendimus.' Ibid., *ad* I.ix.15: 'itaque Ubaldinus Bandinellus . . . iampridem arbitratus est legendum, *illa furia* . . .'. Cf. Vettori, *Castigationum explicationes*, p. 5 ad loc.: 'Nos furia legimus, non tamen in hac parte ab antiquis codicibus adiuti sumus.' See also Manuzio, 'Scholia', p. 929 *ad* III.x.6. Cf. also Cavalcanti, *Lettere*, ed. Roaf, pp. xxxvi-xxxvii and the letters there listed.

98. Cavalcanti to Vettori, 24.viii.1540;*Lettere*, ed. Roaf, pp. 102-3. D. Giannotti, *Lettere italiane (1526-1571)*, ed. F. Diaz (Milan, 1974), pp. 54-68, 73-4.

99. See above all M. W. Croll, *Style, Rhetoric and Rhythm* (Princeton, 1966), Ch. III.

100. *Catullus et in eum commentarius M. Antonii Mureti* (Venice, 1554), fols. 104^v-105^r, *ad* 66.94.

101. See esp. the series of letters from Manuzio to Muret in *Epistolarum Pauli Manutii libri XII* (Leipzig, 1603).

102. Vettori, *Variarum lectionum libri XXV*, XIII.18, p. 198.

103. See F. Duaren, *Disputationes anniversariae* II.xli (1554), in Duaren, *Opera*, ii (Lyons, 1584), p. 1434.

104. Vettori, *Variarum lectionum libri XXV*, I.22, p. 14.

105. Muret, *Variarum lectionum libri XVIII*, IV.14, vol. i, pp. 111-4; for the text see Appendix to Ch. III, below.

106. See the letter from G. Faerno to P. Manuzio (undated, but probably early 1557), published with extensive commentary in L. Ceretti, 'Critica testuale a Terenzio in una lettera del Faerno a Paolo Manuzio', *Aevum*, xxviii (1954), pp. 522-51, esp. p. 540.

107. Faerno to Vettori, 30.xi.1556; British Library, MS Add. 10266, fol. 107^{r-v}: 'E stato un Muretto che ha ruinato tutto Terentio con volerlo emendare. Et il nostro Paolo Manutio l'ha stampato, del quale mi maraviglio piu che di esso Muretto, perche doveva pur saper iudicar tanta cosa. Questo e un francese di assai bon ingegno, ma senza iudicio, perche el si inganna prima nell arte metrica . . . poi non sa che cosa siano libri antichi, ma pur che siano scritti gli basta, et dio volesse chel havesse anco seguitati questi cosi fatti, et non havesse di sua testa fracassato tutto quel poeta . . .'.

108. *Aevum*, xxviii, pp. 550-1: 'Il Goveano et Muretto valeranno creddo in qualche altra sua professione, ma, quanto all'emendar delli autori, sono in tutto giù della bona via.'

109. Ibid.: 'Aggiungesi al peccato anchora il detrimento all'honor della vostra stampa il qual da certo tempo in qua (ve lo dirò pur io liberamente da amico) si come

doveva crescer, è scemato non poco presso alli homini intelligenti, per haver voi, non solo in questo autore, ma anco in altri di grande importantia, a persuasione d'alcuni che si fundano o nel suo cervello, o in un libro solo, o anco in più, ma poco boni, mutato a gran torto la vulgata in infiniti luoghi . . .'.

110. Faerno to Vettori, 25.xi.1559, British Library MS Add. 10266, fol. 128^{r-v}.

111. This, at any rate, was Manuzio's interpretation; Manuzio to Muret, 20.ix.1561, in *Miscellaneorum ex MSS. libris Bibliothecae Collegii Romani Societatis Jesu tomus* . . . (Rome, 1754-7), ii, p. 399: 'Le dedica al Vittorio, quasi per ristorarlo dell'honore toltogli dalle vostre varie lettioni.'

112. D. Giannotti to P. Vettori, 9.v.1560, in Giannotti, *Lettere italiane*, ed. Diaz, p. 164: 'Egli ragiona di voi molto honoratamente, et sono certo che se havesse a mandare fuori quelle sue varie lettioni, in qualche luogo sarebbe nello scriver di voi piu temperato . . .'.

113. Cf. Muret's preface, where — perhaps satirically — he dates the MS by the similarity of its script to that of the Florentine Pandects and its orthography to that of the Vercelli MS of the *Familiares*, 'cuius exemplum abhinc triennium divulgavit P. Victorius'; Muret, *Scripta selecta*, ed. J. Frey (Leipzig, 1887-8), i, pp. 221-4. Muret takes care to point out that he has *not* reproduced such orthographical curiosities as '*emptus sumptus* et similia per litteram p: in quo ita immoderata fuit aetas illa, ut *sollempnia* et *sompnum* et *temptare* plerique omnes tum scriberent'. For Manuzio's reaction to Faerno's death see his letter to Muret of 12.i.1562, *Miscellaneorum* . . . *tomus II* (n. 111, above), p. 400: 'Già molti dì vi scrissi, che il Faerno era morto ὡς ἀπόλοιτο καὶ ἄλλος . . .'.

114. G. B. Titi to P. Manuzio, 19.xi.1565, in *Inedita Manutiana, 1502-1597*, ed. E. Pastorello (Florence, 1960), p. 250: 'Collegi igitur ea quae Victorius sine caussa repudiasse videtur, cum praesertim professus sit, se ubique eius libri fidem, atque auctoritatem sequi . . .'.

115. Titi to Manuzio, 3.vi.1566, ibid., p. 280: 'Ho dubitato più volte che il Mediceo et altri libri simili non siano stati copiati da libri longobardi, da persone, che non pur sapevano poco Latino ma che male intendevano quella lettera, masime per le molte abreviationi. et oltra molt'altre cose, me ne da segno ancora il vedere in questi nostri libri, come il Mediceo il Cesare Vatic. et altri, quel r longobardo, come aperte certe partim, virtus et simili. altramenti non saprei a che mi dar la colpa di tanti errori che in questi nostri libri si leggano, percioche ne in quelli di lettere maiuscule scritti inanzi à Longobardi, ne nei longobardi stessi non sono tanti errori.'

116. Titi to Manuzio, 15.iv.1566, ibid., p. 273.

117. Ibid., p. 251: '. . . queretur, clamabit Deos, hominesque testabitur: me quoque se deseruisse, et ad te descivisse . . .'. Cf. ibid., p. 273: '. . . percioche caso si risapesse che havessi scoperto questa cosa io, mi bisogneria partire di questo paese . . .'.

118. *Fragmenta poetarum veterum Latinorum*, ed. R. and H. Estienne (Geneva, 1564).

119. H. Estienne, ibid., p. 432: 'Scio quosdam existimasse, a grammaticis, quum Medeam exulem citant, non intelligi Medeam quae hodieque extat: sed quum ex locis qui ex illa proferuntur, et qui in ea inveniuntur, alii Medeae exuli, alii simpliciter Medeae adscribantur, dubitare cogor.' Cf. ibid., p. 118: 'Ex locis qui sequuntur, quidam ex Medea, sine adiectione, nonnulli ex Medea exule citantur: quum tamen utrique in una eademque tragoedia reperiantur.' For Vettori's view see *Variarum lectionum libri XXV*, XIV.16, p. 213: 'Duo hi senarii Ennii sunt e Medea Euripidis, translata ab ipso: non tamen Medea hac, quae in manibus nunc est: quaeque ut distingueretur ab altera, exul a Latinis grammaticis quondam vocata est.'

120. L. Fruterius to W. Canter, s.d., in *Lampas, sive fax artium liberalium*, ed.

J. Gruter, V (Frankfurt, 1605), p. 385: 'Legi nuper, quod et te fecisse non dubito, Henr. Stephani, vel potius Patris eius fragmenta, in quibus et Auratus laborat scio, et Turnebus laboravit, ut non ignoro, in libris alteris Adversariorum, quae adhuc excuduntur brevi omnino (ut dicunt) proditura. Et ego aliquid, nisi me fallo, praestiti, et multum fortasse. Tu videbis, ex infinitis locis duos tresve adscribam . . .'. Fruterius filled the margins of his copy of the *Fragmenta* with corrections, which Erycius Puteanus copied in the margins of *his* copy of the work, now in the Bayerische Staatsbibliothek, Munich (Libri impressi cum notis manuscriptis, 31). Puteanus's recension of the notes was published with valuable commentary by W. Meyer, 'Des Lucas Fruterius Verbesserungen zu den Fragmenta poetarum veterum Latinorum a. 1564', *RhM*, xxxiii (1878), pp. 238–49.

121. A. Manuzio Jr., *In Q. Horatii Flacci Venusini Librum . . . commentarius* (Venice, 1576), pp. 61-3, at p. 63: 'Haec autem hoc loco ideo collegi, ut ostenderem, olim me de Poetarum fragmentis edendis cogitasse. Quod cum alii anteverterint, ne tamen vigiliae meae pereant, quaecumque eae sint (cum tamen locupletiores multo, quam alias, esse dignoscam), edentur aliquando.'

122. A. Turnèbe, *Adversaria*, 2 vols. (Paris, 1564-5), II.3, vol. i, fols. 23^V-24^r; I. 1, ibid., fols. 1^r-2^r; I.2, ibid., fol. 2^{r-v}; I.19, ibid., fols. 9^r-10^r; I.22, ibid., fols. 12^r-13^r; II.1, fol. 22^{r-v}; etc.

123. Ibid., I.5, fol. 4^{r-v} at 4^r: 'Etsi plenum est periculi et aleae coniecturae confidere suae in tractandis auctoribus, multis tamen in rebus sola coniectura nitimur, quam et in re capitali nostra medicus aucupatur.'

124. Ibid., II.9, fols. 28^r-29^r, at 28^V; cf. however V.26, ibid., fol. 100^r: 'Vt moribus antiquis stabat res Romana, sic Romana lingua stat antiquis exemplaribus, a quibus cum recedunt editiones, merito doctis suspectae sunt, et prope falsi condemnantur.'

125. See esp. I.3, I.4, I.5, I.6, I.10, I.12, I.25; in IV.11, fol. 70^r Turnèbe praises Muret's edition of the *Philippics* effusively.

126. See e.g. Vettori, *Castigationum explicationes*, p. 12, *ad Fam.* V.2: '. . . quam scripturam volui hic notare, etsi proculdubio depravatam, ut possint ex his vestigiis studiosi veram lectionem indagare, et suo loco inventam reponere. Vnusquisque igitur nunc in veritate pervestiganda se exerceat.'

127. P. Vettori, *Variarum lectionum libri XXXVIII* (Florence, 1582), XXXVI.11, p. 425: 'Quod vero excogitavit Adrianus Turnebus . . . magis remotum perspicitur a vestigiis veteris lectionis, et ut arbitror, falsum et explodendum est. Utinam autem hic vir, sane doctus ac multae lectionis, non tam cupidus undique fuisset omnia emendandi: melius nobis, melius existimationi suae consuluisset . . .'.

128. D. Lambin, *Emendationum rationes*, in *M. Tullii Ciceronis Opera omnia, quae exstant* (Paris, 1565-6), iii, p. 457 *ad Fam.* VII.20: 'P. Victorius suum, nos nostros, hoc est Memmianos, codices secuti sumus . . .'.

129. Ibid., p. 455 *ad Fam.* III.11: 'Ad te nihil. alterum enim etc.] sic reposui libris omnibus reclamantibus . . .'; p. 454 ad II.16: 'nonne omnia potius cur in sent.] sic legendum, *cur in sent. perm.*, non, *ut in sent.* quamvis omnes libri reclament. sic enim loquimur: omnia acciderunt, cur hoc, vel illud facerem'; p. 455 *ad* IV.4.

130. Ibid., ii, p. 715: 'studium populus Ro. tribuerit absenti, ut desid. etc.] diu dubitavi quo pacto hunc locum edendum curarem, quia Faernum, et Muretum, quibus testibus antiquae scripturae utimur, hic pugnantia loqui video . . . utri credam, cum alterum necesse sit falsum dicere? utrique non possum, cum duo contraria non possint simul esse vera. Neutri igitur potius.' And indeed, he

goes on to steer a compromise course, retaining *Tribuerit* (rather than *-et*) because it is found *in libris vulgatis*, even though Faerno also claimed to have found it in the Basilicanus.

131. J. Ruysschaert, 'Le séjour de Juste Lipse à Rome (1568-1570)', *BIHBR* xxiv, (1947-8), pp. 139-92.

132. See Ch. II, above, n. 108, and Ceretti in *Aevum*, xxviii, pp. 531-2.

133. Nolhac, 'La bibliothèque d'un humaniste au XVIe siècle', in *Mélanges d'archéologie et d'histoire*, iii (1883) p. 233.

134. See Ch. V, below, n. 122.

135. B. L. Ullman, *The Identification of the Manuscripts of Catullus cited in Statius' edition of 1566* (Diss. Chicago, 1908), pp. 10-17, 64.

136. There is no full study of Orsini's scholarly work, but see in general Nolhac, *La Bibliothèque de Fulvio Orsini. Contributions à l'histoire des collections d'Italie et à l'étude de la Renaissance* (Paris, 1887).

137. C. Pichena, *Ad Cornelii Taciti Opera notae, iuxta veterrimorum exemplarium collationem* (n.p., 1600), *ep. ad lectorem*, pp. 5-6. Deceived by the subscription in the Apuleius that forms part of Laur. LXVIII. 2, Pichena took it to have been written in the 4th century AD. Vettori was dead, indeed. For a general assessment of Pichena's work see J. Ruysschaert, *Juste Lipse et les Annales de Tacite* (Turnhout, 1949), pp. 33-4.

138. Cf. Ch. II, above, n. 87. Lipsius was, of course, Muret's most famous and influential convert.

139. On Muret's continuously close relations with his Parisian friends and younger French scholars see in general Nolhac, *Ronsard et l'humanisme*, pp. 146-52, as well as the evidence cited below.

140. Of the several recent studies on the culture of the *noblesse de robe*, D. R. Kelley, *Foundations of Modern Historical Scholarship. Language, Law and History in the French Renaissance* (New York and London, 1970) is the most informative and acute. Much the best way to gain an impression of that culture, however, is to read the *Mémoires inédits de Henri de Mesmes*, ed. E. Fremy (Paris, n.d.), a very striking autobiography of a well-known scholar and patron of scholars.

141. On Cujas's students see G. Berriat-Saint-Prix, *Histoire du droit romain suivie de l'histoire de Cujas* (Paris, 1821).

142. For Fruterius's notes on the *Fragmenta*, significantly preserved in a copy, see n. 120, above. Another copy, with notes in the hand of Claude Dupuy, is in the Bibliothèque Nationale, Paris. It contains many conjectures and some ascriptions for verses that the Estiennes had found no home for. At the bottom of the title-page is written 'Ex Emendatione Jos. Scalig.'; and where the title describes the fragments as 'undique a Rob. Stephano summa diligentia olim congesta' a characteristically malevolent note reads: 'Imo summa negligentia ut pudeat'. Presumably Dupuy's notes were copied from the annotated copy listed in the Catalogue of Scaliger's library: *The Auction Catalogue of the Library of J. J. Scaliger*, ed. H. J. de Jonge, Catalogi Redivivi, 1 (Utrecht, 1977), p. 34 of the original text. I do not know the present location of Scaliger's copy. As to the general interests of Scaliger's generation, see e.g. P. Pithou, *Adversariorum subsecivorum libri II* (Paris, 1565), a work which reveals extraordinary knowledge of the world and literature of late Antiquity.

143. The *Sammelband* that belonged to Fruterius bears shelf-mark 758.E.34 in Leiden University Library; it contains *Catullus et in eum commentarius M. Antonii Mureti; ab eodem correcti, et scholiis illustrati, Tibullus et Propertius* (Venice, 1558); see C. L. Heesakkers, *Praecidanea Dousana* (Amsterdam, 1976),

p. 117 n. 27. References hereafter will treat the 3 texts as individual books, as each has its own title-page and foliation.

144. Ibid., *Catullus*, fols. 5^r, 8^v, 18^r, and *passim*.

145. Ibid., *Catullus*, fol. 18^v *ad* 10.1–2: 'Visere ad aliquem est veterum locutio etiam Gellio familiaris'; fol. 38^v ad 25.2: 'f.inula, ut est in vetustissimis q. impressis. vox est formata ab ina, quae tenuissimam chartae pelliculam significat. Vide Festum in voce Ilia.'

146. Ibid., *Catullus*, fols. 113^r, 114^v.

147. Ibid., *Catullus*, fol. 114^v.

148. Ibid., *Catullus*, fol. 146^r.

149. Ibid., *Tibullus*, fol. 19^r ('O black night, who rearest the golden stars').

150. Ibid., *Propertius*, fol. 22^v: 'politian. ἀρκεῖ δ᾽ἐν μεγάλοις καὶ τὸ θέλημα μόνον' ('In great matters the will is enough by itself.')

151. Ibid., Catullus, fol. 116^r: ἦν γὰρ ὁ πολιτιανὸς παιδεραστής. Cf. ibid., fol. 129^r on Muret's note on 74.6 (on *fellatio*): φοῦ τῆς ἐσχάτης ἀτοπίας.

152. e.g. ibid., *Catullus*, fol. 6^v, on Muret's note attacking Poliziano's view that the *passer* of poems 2 and 3 is to be taken in an obscene sense: 'Politian. a Sannazario derisus'.

153. Fruterius to Lambin, in *Lampas*, ed. Gruter, V, p. 399: 'Interim vide, mi Lambine, ne nimis matures, quae res et tibi et Lucretio ipsi damnosa esset. Cupio vehementer ut liceat mihi unam rem a te petere, et etiam auferre, nimirum ut quae vetusti codicis sit lectio semper admoneas in Commentariis tuis, sive ea sit sana, sive insana (ut Plauti verbo utar), sive etiam obscura et incognita. Sic fiet, ut de fide tua nulli non sis gratus futurus: tum occasionem dabis studiosis, ut ex corrupta illa lectione tua integram et synceram conentur educere, quod vir omnino Maximus Victorius sua fide facit, idque rectissime.' Cf. also on Vettori Fruterius, *Verisimilia*, I.10, in *Lampas*, ed. Gruter, II (Frankfurt, 1604), p. 821; III.3–4 bis, in *Lampas*, V, pp. 342–60; III.17, p. 379; III.18, p. 380; and, for a defence of conjectural emendation, III.8, p. 366.

154. O. Amaduzzi to C. Dupuy, Rome, 24.iii.1571; Paris, Bibliothèque Nationale, MS Dupuy 699, fol. 29^r: 'Fulvius Vrsinus (cuius nomine plurimam tibi dico salutem) adeo·honorificas de te a Petro Victorio habuit literas, ut nil quicquam amplius desiderari possit . . .'.

155. For Muret see e.g. his letter to Cujas, 14.iv.1571, in Cujas, *Opera* (Paris, 1658), IV.1, p. 1131. Dupuy became especially close to Paolo Manuzio's son, Aldo the Younger. He recorded some of Aldo's emendations in his philological journal of his time in Italy: Paris, Bibliothèque Nationale, MS Dupuy 808, fols. 3^r–8^r, at fols. 3^r, 3^v.

156. MS Dupuy 808, fol. 3^r: 'Apud Columellam de re rusti. lib. 12 cap. 34 Latinus Latinius vir doctissimus vidit illa, qui scylliticum acetum facere volunt, esse imperite avulsa a librario ex fine superioris capitis; pro illis autem, decem bambatae, reponit, de embammate, quae esse debet inscriptio capitis xxxiiii. Turnebus enim in adversar. lib. xvii. cap. xiii. frustra se torquet in explicanda voce nihili, bambatae. In vetustis autem codicib. vulgata inscriptio capitis xxxiiii. non exstat, et in iisdem caput ipsum xxxiiii.^{um} cum xxxiii.^{o} cohaeret.'

157. Ibid., fol. 4^r: 'In Sulpicia gente duo cognomina usurpare fuisse primum Bernardinus Rutilius admonuit in vita iurisconsultorum, nec tamen probat: quamquam observationem eius certissimam esse, iis quae sequuntur Fulvius Vrsinus mihi confirmavit. Cornelius Nepos in vita Pomponii Attici, namque Amicia Pomponii consobrina nupserat M. Servio fratri Sulpicii. ita habet v. c. Vrsini, ita priores editiones, a quibus Paullus Manutius primum, alii dehinc temere discederunt. Praeterea idem duos nummos perantiquos ita inscriptos habet,

L. SERVIVS RVFVS . . .'. Orsini also passed on conjectures to Dupuy: ibid., fols. 4ᵛ, 7ʳ.

158. Ibid., fol. 6ʳ: 'Cicero ad Atticum libro xii. ep. iiii. de Catone; Quin etiam (inquit) si a sententiis eius dictis, si ab omni voluntate, consiliisque quae de Rep. habuit, recedam, ψευδῶςque velim gravitatem constantiamque eius laudare: etc. pro ψευδῶς P. Victorius emendat ψιλῶς a v. c. qui scriptus est Fr. Petrarchae manu adiutus, qui scriptum habet ψειλως: qua in re saepius erratum esse in illo cod. idem mihi aliquot exemplis comprobavit. Opponit autem Cicero τὸ ψιλὸν ornato.'

159. Ibid., fol. 5ᵛ: 'In eadem orat. [*scil. in Pisonem*] 39. a. b. [editionis Faerni] notandus locus hic, atque id quod nondum potestate poterat, obtinuit auctoritate; propter similem in 11. oratione in Rullum, qui a Mureto perperam in variis lectionibus immutatus est.' Dupuy describes the manuscript as 'v. c. S. P. Vaticani ex quo Faernus orationem illam infinitis locis meliorem fecit . . .'. Cf. also Ch. II, above, n. 130.

160. O. Amaduzzi to C. Dupuy, Rome 24.iii.1571; MS Dupuy 699, fol. 29ʳ⁻ᵛ: '. . . eidem (Vrsino) dixi te non poenitenda quaedam habuisse a Mureto in Cornelium Tacitum, prout ego te talia ab eo accipientem ultimo, quo hinc discessurus eras, die apud ipsum vidi; quae omnia illi daturum te promisisse ipse respondit: seque multa sua in Ciceronem (ut par pari referret) tibi missurum . . . Latinus non minorem tibi quam Fulvius impartitur salutem . . .'. The notes in question may well have been those recorded in MS Dupuy 808, fol. 5ᵛ.

161. Paris, Bibliothèque Nationale, Rés. Z. 86. At Vettori, *V. L.* I.22 Dupuy summarizes Muret, *V. L.* IV.14; at Vettori, VI.8 Dupuy cites supporting evidence from Muret II.9; at Vettori, VI.9 Dupuy summarizes Muret's attack in VIII.6; at VI.12 Dupuy cites Muret's commentary on Catullus; at VI.16 Dupuy cites Muret, VII.20; at XXIII.5 Dupuy summarizes Muret's attack in IV.5; at XXV.13 Dupuy summarizes Muret's attack in II.8 (these are only a few instances; Dupuy has notes on other passages in Muret and from Brodeau, Turnèbe, and others as well).

162. C. Dupuy to P. Delbene, 27.v.1570; MS Dupuy 16, fol. 14ʳ⁻ᵛ: 'Neque vero magnam tibi quandam de doctoribus Italis exspectationem commovebo, ut eorum te congressu et recitationibus sitim tuam restincturum possis. Etenim Italia, cui litterarum παλιγγενεσίαν reliquae nationes acceptam referunt, nullum omnino hodie iurisconsultum habet, iuris, inquam, Romani illius puri puti, quod suos apud nos nactum est assertores; glossarum, commentariorum, consiliorum, nugarumque id genus, quas miserae et credulae iuventuti magno fastu et inutili ostentatione decantant, peritos plures fortasse quam par sit. In aliis vero disciplinis, si quinque aut sex exceperis, qui praeterea excellat reperias neminem.' Dupuy advised Delbene to try instead to study 'vera germanaque prudentia iuris' with Cujas.

163. Delbene to Dupuy, 29.i.1571, MS Dupuy 808, fols. 85ʳ⁻86ᵛ; Delbene to Dupuy, 27.i.[1571], ibid., fols. 87ʳ⁻89ᵛ.

164. Ibid., fol. 89ʳ: 'Is vero cum de singulis fere Galliae nostrae eruditissimis hominibus me interrogasset, unum Auratum prae caeteris admirabatur, et in astra tollebat. Huiusque suae opinionis autores laudabat summos viros, M. Antonium Muretum, et Josephum Scaligerum. . . . De stilo, scribendique genere singulorum fere clarorum nostrae et superioris aetatis virorum, quid sentiret, libere aperuerat; maximaque audientem me delectatione affecerat . . .'.

165. See J.-A. de Thou, *Mémoires* (Paris, 1823), pp. 248–9.

Chapter IV

1. For Scaliger's relations with his tutors – Girard Roques, Simon Beaupé, and

Laurens de Lamarque – see the letters from them to his father published in whole and part in J. de Bourrousse de Laffore, 'Jules-César de Lescale (Scaliger)', *Rec. Soc. Agen*, Ser. II, 1 (1860; but published 1861), pp. 24–69, at pp. 53–64. On 8.viii.1555 Laurens de Lamarque wrote that 'Vos enfantz proffitent, desquelz Joseph est la fleur . . .' (p. 60); on 22.viii.1555 he wrote that 'Joseph sera homme scavant sur toutz les aultres. Il n'oyt rien de moy quil ne le comprenne incontinent . . .' (ibid.). Interesting details on the themes and letters that Joseph and his brothers wrote come from the earlier letters of their first tutor, Roques; see e.g. that of 12.xii.1553: '. . . car il est tres vray que Joseph ha compose un theme tout a ung coup en prenant le francoys quil navoit accoustume, car il le prenoit et puis sur icelluy il faisoit le latin, qui me faict esperer quelque grand advancement avec le temps de luy' (p. 58).

2. Scaliger, *Autobiography*, p. 29.

3. See in general V. Hall, Jr., 'Life of Julius Caesar Scaliger (1484–1558)', *Transactions of the American Philosophical Society*, New Ser., xl (1950), pp. 85–170; C. B. Schmitt, 'Theophrastus', in *CTC* ii, p. 271.

4. Scaliger, *Autobiography*, p. 30.

5. Ibid.

6. See the definitive treatment by M. Billanovich, 'Benedetto Bordon e Giulio Cesare Scaligero', *IMU* xi (1968), pp. 187–256.

7. Scaliger, *Epistola de vetustate gentis Scaligerae, Epistolae*, p. 45.

8. See *M. Manilii Astronomicon liber I*, ed. A. E. Housman, 2nd edn. (Cambridge, 1937), p. xiii: '. . . it is arrant gasconading when he says in the Scaligerana "se et patrem nihil unquam scripsisse, quod scivissent ab aliis dictum aut scriptum".'

9. See Vertunien's report, *Scaligerana I*, s. v. Scaliger, p. 149: 'Hoc amplius ab eo didici, ei a puero ad patris usque mortem, quae contigit illo 18 aut 19 annum agente, fluxam lubricamque alvum fuisse, ab eo vero tempore, cum per 18 dies nihil ipsa reddidisset ob ingentem moerorem, semper adstrictam fuisse, ab eodemque tempore non nisi aquas et flumina in somnis habuisse.' I am grateful to Dr L. Erlich for discussing with me the clinical significance of Scaliger's experience. For a more extended treatment of Vertunien's report see Bernays, *Scaliger*, pp. 117–19.

10. Scaliger, *Autobiography*, pp. 30–1 (wording altered). Cf. Gargantua's letter to Pantagruel, in Rabelais, II.8.

11. Scaliger, *Autobiography*, p. 31.

12. E. Gibbon, *Memoirs of My Life*, ed. G. A. Bonnard (New York, 1966), p. 118.

13. 'Biographical Memoir of Josephus Justus Scaliger', *Museum Criticum; or, Cambridge Classical Researches*, i (1826), p. 345. As Blomfield points out: '. . . the singular vanity and egotism of this eminent man leads us to receive with caution the commendations which he bestows upon himself . . .' – an analysis which will be repeatedly confirmed in the course of the present study.

14. Scaliger's first copy of Euripides was Hervagius's 2nd edition (Basel, 1544), now in the Bodleian Library (shelf-mark Auct. S. 4. 11). For a list of the more important conjectures contained in it see C. Collard, 'J. J. Scaliger's Euripidean *Marginalia*', *Classical Quarterly*, xxiv (1974), pp. 242–9. Scaliger's inscription (on the recto of the blank leaf before the title page) reads: ἔτει ἀπὸ χριστοῦ γεννήσεως ᾱ φ ξ χιλιοστῷ πεντακοσιοστῷ ἐξηκοστῷ τῇ θ μεταγειτνιῶνος μηνός. λοδοϊκὸς ὁ λιλίος. ἰωσὴφ ὁ σκαλανὸς ὁ ἰουλίου καίσαρος ἰωσὴφ ὁ καίσαρος σκαλανοῦ αἰσυμνᾷ ἄρχει. Εὐριπίδης μηδείᾳ. *Yôsēp sulāq* ἰωσηππος ὁ σκαλανὸς Josephus Scaliger.' Scaliger's glossing of αἰσυμνάω (Eur. *Med.* 19) suggests an early stage in his studies; (*yôsēp sulāq* in Hebrew characters).

15. *Scaligerana II*, s. v. SOPHOCLE, pp. 576–7: 'Lors que j'avois 18 ou 20 ans, j'avois fort bien leu mes trois Tragiques . . .'.

16. *Catullus et in eum commentarius M. Antonii Mureti* (Venice, 1554), fol. 101^r: 'Iuvaret Graeca cum Latinis componere . . . non in singulis modo vocibus, sed in figuris etiam luminibusque orationis, in ipsa ratione numerorum, ac denique in tota structura poematis . . .'.

17. Leiden University Library, MS Scal. 62, fol. 27^r. When Scaliger later turned against Muret (see Ch. VI, below), he changed the Greek text of 66.94 to make it match Poliziano's Latin: ἐγγύθεν ὑδροχόου λαμπέτω ὡαρίων (= *Proximus Hydrochoï fulgeret Oarion*). It was in this changed form that Scaliger's Greek version was published: *Poemata omnia*, ed. P. de Lagarde (Berlin, 1864), p. 217. In the MS ἀρκτοῦρος and ἠριγόνας are lined through, and ὑδροχόου and ὡαρίων are written in below.

18. Leiden University Library, MS Scal. 62, fol. 26^r.

19. Ibid., fol. 25^r: 'Ex Catullo Ad M. Ant. Muretum suum.' Fuller text in *Poemata*, p. 217: 'Oblata haec Catulliana M. Antonio Mureto Lutetiae anno 1562 mense Septembri.'

20. Ibid., fol. 45^r.

21. Ibid., fol 27^r: 'Ex Propertio Cantero.' Fuller text in *Poemata*, p. 226: 'Oblata haec Propertiana Guil. Cantero Lutetiae anno 1561 mense Septembri.'

22. Scaliger, *Poemata*, pp. 228–31, at 231: 'Conversum anno 1561, oblatum vero Petro Ronsardo Lutetiae anno 1563.' Cf. Nolhac, *Ronsard et l'humanisme* (Paris, 1921), pp. 202–5.

23. See in general C. M. Bruehl, 'Josef Justus Scaliger. Ein Beitrag zur geistesgeschichtlichen Bedeutung der Altertumswissenschaft', *Zeitschrift für Religions-und Geistesgeschichte*, xii (1960), pp. 201–18; xiii (1961), pp. 45–65, at xii, pp. 209–12.

24. Cf. Scaliger to S. Ubertus, 12.iii.1598, *Epistolae*, p. 706, and *Scaligerana I*, s.v. Lingua, pp. 113–14 (Vertunien's report). Scaliger denigrates Postel's knowledge and says that they spent less than a week together. Vertunien reports that they stayed together for 3 days 'apud Bibliopolam quendam' and that Postel's encouragement was what induced Scaliger to take up Oriental languages as well as Greek, in order to gain access to 'miranda . . . mysteria' and the 'excellent authors, and most worthy to be read, among the Jews, who had not yet been translated . . .'.

25. Cf. Scaliger, *Autobiography*, p. 31: 'I had devoted two entire years to Greek literature, when an internal impulse hurried me away to the study of Hebrew. Although I did not even know a single letter of the Hebrew alphabet, I availed myself of no teacher other than myself in the study of the language.' Cf. also n. 112, below.

26. *Scaligerana II*, s. v. Scaliger; Bernays, *Scaliger*, pp. 125–9. On the religious element in Scaliger's upbringing, his tutor Roques's letter of 3.viii.1553 is also revealing: 'Je ne suis moingz curieulx a les accoustumer a toute bonne, saincte et catholique costume et institution laquelle est de nostre foy nourrice, nous faisant par choses visibles croire les invisibles' (*Rec. Soc. Agen*, Ser. II, 1, p. 57).

27. The translation is preserved in Leiden University Library, MS Scal. 62, fols. 1^r–24^v; Scaliger's subscription is on fol. 24^v: 'Initiorum Orphei vatis vetustissimi finis Anno Domini 1562. Ego I. S. vertebam intra quinque dierum spatium.' The sentence beginning *Ego* is scored through. As to Dorat's views, I have ventured to deduce them from those of Willem Canter, his pupil and a man much given to repeating the ideas of others. Canter treats the Orphica as genuine in *Novarum lectionum libri quatuor* (Basel, 1564), i.3, pp. 22–5, where he presents Dorat's solution to a riddle in the *Oracula Sibyllina* (I.141–6). See p. 22: ' . . . cum antiquissima quaeque scripta fere soleant esse rudiora, et ornamentis, quae recentiores addiderunt, paucioribus expolita: sicut ex Orpheo, Musaeo, et aliis

cognoscitur: debet idem et Sibyllinae poeseos autoritatem non tam diminuere, quam augere.' Even more revealing is *Novarum lectionum libri septem* (Canter's 3rd edition) (Antwerp, 1571), II.3, pp. 91-2: 'Orphei qui circumferuntur hymni, tametsi a paucis recipiuntur, nobis tamen propter antiquitatem et elegantiam suam valde placuerunt semper, ut et aliis nonnullis, qui in his etiam non parva naturalis Magiae mysteria putant latere.'

28. Scaliger, 'Emendationes ad Theocriti, Moschi, et Bionis Idyllia', in *Theocriti, Moschi, Bionis, Simmii quae extant*, ed. D. Heinsius (n. p., 1604), p. 228: 'τὸ δὲ λύχνιον ἐν πρυτανείῳ] Ioannes Auratus, vir doctissimus, et nunquam sine laude nominandus, putabat hic intelligi de Prytaneo Athenarum. Quod non videtur convenire piscatoribus Siculis . . .'. The line in question is *Idyll. Incert.*, III, 36.

29. Jean Dorat to François Chasteigner de la Rochepozay, 1.iv [1564?], in André Duchesne, *Preuves de l'histoire de la maison des Chasteigners* (Paris, 1633), p. 124; for the text see Appendix to Ch. IV, below.

30. Catullus 74.1-4:
    Gellius audierat patruum obiurgare solere,
      Si quis delicias diceret aut faceret.
    Hoc ne ipsi acciderit, patrui perdepsuit ipsam
      Vxorem et patruum reddidit Harpocratem.
    For *depso* see Cicero *Fam.* IX.xxii.4, and cf. n. 45, below.

31. Turnèbe, *Adversaria*, XXI.17, previously quoted by H. de la Ville de Mirmont, *Le Manuscrit de l'Île Barbe* (*Codex Leidensis Vossianus Latinus 111*) *et les travaux de la critique sur le texte d'Ausone. L'œuvre de Vinet et l'œuvre de Scaliger*, 3 vols. (Paris and Bordeaux, 1917-19), i, p. 169 n. 5: 'Scaliger autem, adolescens eruditus, non male putat, quod aliquando me ex eo audisse recordor, legendum esse *patrui perdepsuit ipsam uxorem*, non *perdespuit.*'

32. Horace, *Opera*, ed. D. Lambin (Paris, 1567), i, p. 328 *ad Carm. Saec.* 16: 'SEV GENITALIS] γενεθλία θεά. dea nascenteis faetus adiuvaris: seu partus maturans, seu ad gignendum valens, seu faetus utero inclusos in lucem proferens. Taleis autem deos, γενεθλίους Graeci vocant. Qua voce usum esse Platonem lib. 5. de rep. [rectè Leg. v.729c] non ita pridem mihi indicavit Iosephus Scaliger, cum Lutetiam, ut coniectanea sua in Varronem de lingua Latina excudenda curaret, venisset. Platonis autem verba sunt haec, . . . ubi vulgo legitur, . . .'. The passage is 729c. Modern editors accept Scaliger's emendation but attribute it to David Ruhnken, who drew the correct reading from Stobaeus. Lambin also respected Scaliger's expertise in his own special field of comparative exegesis. See his note on *Carm.* I.xii.45: 'CRESCIT OCCVLTO VELVT, etc.] Haec videntur esse ex Pindaro sumta, et imitata, ut indicavit mihi Scaliger, Nem. εἶδ.η. Αὔξεται δ'ἀρετά, χλωραῖς ἐέρσαις ὡς ὅτε δένδρον ἀίσσει, etc. id est, Crescit autem virtus, ut cum arbor, recentibus et virideis herbas elicientibus roribus, surgit, etc.' (ibid., p. 41).

33. The section in question is *Deipnosophistae*, XV.674a-96a.

34. Canter, *Novarum lectionum libri quatuor*, III.2, pp. 128-73; see esp. pp. 127-8: 'Istud autem fragmentum a M. Antonio Mureto, cum nuper ex Italia in Galliam rediisset, primum ad nos devenit, sicut erat ab eo ex Vaticana bibliotheca descriptum. Deinde cum Iosepho Scaligero, iuvene doctissimo, idem communicavimus: et ab eo multorum locorum emendationes, quibus ad marginem positis literam S affiximus, vicissim accepimus: ipsi in reliquis, quoad eius a nobis fieri potuit, corruptiora quaedam restituere conati, quemadmodum margines indicabunt.'

35. Scaliger's presentation copy of the 2nd edition of Canter's work (*Novarum lectionum libri septem*, Basel, 1566) is in Leiden University Library (shelf-mark 766. D. 1.). A very legible copy of the marginalia, with additions, has been

entered in another copy of the same work (ibid., shelf-mark 766. D. 2); and
P. Burman transcribed them in his copy of the 3rd edition of Canter's work
(ibid., shelf-mark 766. D. 4). At the beginning of II.7 ('In Euripide nonnulla
declarata'), p. 92, Scaliger has written: 'Accepit ex Euripide nostro cuius copiam
ei fecimus.' In III.3, p. 132, Canter emends *Ferabite* (which he rightly describes
as a *monstrum* rather than a *vocabulum*) to *Fera vite* in Nonius Marcellus 113
M. He attributes the correction to *amicus quidam*. Scaliger underlined those
words and wrote in the margin: 'Pudet hominem meminisse nostri'. The second
emendation surely belonged to Scaliger (see n. 46, below). But at least one of
Canter's points – namely, that in *Rhesus* 397 τούπίσ' should be read as τὸ ἐπί
σε – was not taken from Scaliger, as there is no corresponding note in his
Euripides (Bodleian Library Auct. S. 4. 11, Basel 1544, fol. kk2ʳ).

36. Scaliger, *Commentarii et castigationes*, in *Publii Virgilii Maronis Appendix*
(Lyons, 1572), p. 307 *ad Cirin* 21: 'Quare et Aristoteles librum suum, quem
de Heroum tumulis confecerat, Peplum vocavit. Eum nuper edidit doctus
iuvenis Gul. Canterus, summa necessitudine mihi coniunctus.' Canter's edition
of the *Peplus* appeared at Basel in 1566.

37. *Scaligerana I*, p. 21: 'Confecit Conjectanea in Varronem anno aetatis vigesimo.
Et lors, dit-il, *étois-je fou comme un jeune lièvre*. Notas in lib. de Re Rustica
anno 25. et in Catalecta Virgilii anno 27.'

38. Scaliger, *Coniectanea*, ep. ded., in *M. Terentii Varronis Opera quae supersunt*
(Geneva, 1573), p. 7: 'Cum igitur, Ludovice Castanaee, iuvenis nobilissime et
eruditissime, in animo habuissem, haec Coniectanea saltem sola non edere,
quod multa eiusmodi in alios bonos autores habeam, et poterant una cum illis
publicari: tamen placuit haec in gratiam tuam edere . . .'.

39. 'Lana Graecum, ut Polybius et Callimachus scribunt.'

40. Scaliger, *Coniectanea*, in *Varronis Opera*, separately paginated, p. 52 *ad* V.113:
'LANA Graecum.] Posset putare quispiam hic intelligi λάχνη, et extrita media,
factum lana, ut ab ἀράχνης, araneus. Sed non ita est. λῆνος enim prius dice-
batur, et Doribus λᾶνος. Apollonius lib. IIII,
βεβρίθει λήνεσσιν ἐπηρεφές – Et λανισταί, οἱ κτενισταί
apud veteres dicebantur, qui carebant (hoc est carminabant) lanam. Nec sine
caussa ad hoc testimonio Callimachi utitur Varro, cum et Aeschylus ipse, cum
hanc vocem usurparet, eam, ut a vulgi opinione paulo remotiorem interpretatus
sit. Cuius haec verba ex Diris . . . [*Eumenides* 44-5].
Solet enim interdum ille poeta, cum quaedam insolentia verba aut durius-
cula ponit, eorum interpretamentum subiicere: ut in ἑπτὰ ἐπὶ Θήβαις . . .
[489-490] . . .
Porro ante haec quaedam deesse sensus ipse satis docet.'

41. Aeschylus, *Agamemnon*, ed. E. Fraenkel (Oxford, 1950), i, pp. 36-8.

42. 'Multa apud poetas reliqua esse verba quorum origines possunt dici, non dubito,
ut apud Naevium . . .' (Scaliger's text, p. 90).

43. A. Turnèbe, *Commentarius*, in *Varronis Opera*, separately paginated, p. 122 *ad*
VII.107: 'CAVDACVS.] Verbum perquam antiquum, a gaudio ductum videtur.
Nam c pro g, saepe antiqui dicebant: suavibus enim gaudemus.'

44. Scaliger, *Coniectanea*, p. 171 ad VII.107: 'CAVDATVS.] In illis qui olim
excusi sunt, *Cavadatus*. Manifesto legendum *Clucidatus*, ex Festo, qui id interpretatur dulce et iucundum. Et alibi apud eundem *Glucidatus* scribitur, eodem
sensu, παρὰ τὸ γλυκώ.' Cf. Paul. *ex* Fest. 48.13 L.; 87. 24-5 L.

45. Scaliger, *Coniectanea*, pp. 63-4 *ad* V.138, at p.64: 'Porro Varro apud Nonium
videtur in obscoenum significatum accepisse, *Hic alius*, inquit, *tibi molit ac
depsit*. Depsere enim etiam obscoenum verbum: ut etiam Cicero ad Paetum
ostendit. Apud Catullum vero mendum est: *– patrui perdespuit ipsam Vxorem
– legendum enim perdepsuit.*'

46. Scaliger, *Coniectanea*, pp. 40-1 ad V.94: 'QVOD sequitur verbum adventum, et in ventum.] Diverse castigatur, vel potius cruciatur, hic locus ab aliis. At haec erat vera lectio: *Quod sequitur cervum ad ventum.* Error natus, ut solet, ex ignoratione veteris scripturae, quam non animadverterant imperiti librarii. *Cerbum* enim scriptum erat, pro quo *verbum* legerunt. Idem error mirum quam frequens sit in Nonianis codicibus: ut in exemplo Sisennae, *Ferabite*, pro *fera vite. Et partim fera vite, partim lauro et arbusto ac multa pinu ac murtetis abundat.* Nec defuerunt qui in suis magnificis Thesauris tanto labore consarcinatis *Ferabitem* pro agresti sumi apud veteres autores admonuerint.' Cf. n. 35, above.

47. Scaliger, *Coniectanea*, p. 11 *ad* V.8: 'QVARTVS, ubi est aditus, et initia, Regis.] Non videtur eruditissimo Adr. Turnebo aliquid mutandum: neque ego mehercule censeo . . .'; p. 12 *ad* V.15: 'AB EO praeco dicitur locare, quoad usque id emit quoad in aliquo consistit precium.] Legendum proculdubio, Quod usque idem it, quoad in aliquo consistit precium. Et, nisi valde fallor, memini olim quoque ita sensisse doctiss. Adr. Turnebum, cum haec cum illo communicarem . . .'; p. 68 *ad* V.158: 'QVOD ab iis viris dicuntur aedificata.] *Viocuris* se vidisse scriptum in vetusto exemplari admonuit me doctissimus Adrianus Turnebus: ex cuius fide haec reponimus. Viocuris vero, id est, Aedilibus.' All three of these points are to be found in Turnèbe's notes.

48. Above, no. 31.

49. Scaliger, *Coniectanea*, p. 40 *ad* V.88: 'DICIT esse Graece cohorton apud poetas dictum.] Certissimum est, una litera dempta *Chorton* legendum. χόρτος, ὁ περίβολος apud poetas. Ἰλιάδ. λ,
Πίονα μηρί' ἔκηε βοὸς Διὶ τερπικεραύνῳ
Αὐλῆς ἐν χόρτῳ——
Item Ἰλιάδος ω,
Αὐλῆς ἐν χόρτοισι κυλινδόμενος κατὰ κόπρον.
Inde Euripidi σύγχορτα πεδία. In editione Romana emendarunt κούρθον. Miror cur non novas aures quaererent, quibus talia persuaderent, qui nova vocabula commenti sunt. Est enim haec vox plane apud omnes autores inaudita.'

50. Turnèbe, *Commentarius*, p. 47 *ad* V.88: 'χόρτον autem (sic enim lego, non cohorton, nec κόνθον) explicant grammatici Graeci in Homero, αὐλῆς ἐνὶ χόρτῳ, cohortis ambitum ac septum. A qua etiam significatione illud Euripidis manavit σύγχορτα ναίω πεδία, pro finitimis et vicinis agris.'

51. Scaliger, *Coniectanea*, p. 15 *ad* V.23: 'FVNESTA manet, et dicitur humilior.] Non tantum doleo vicem huius loci, quanquam pessime est acceptus, quantum admiror non esse animadversum ab iis qui hunc autorem purgandum susceperunt; ut satis constet insigniter esse depravatum.'

52. Turnèbe, *Commentarius*, p. 15 *ad* V.23: 'Quae post aliquot paginas sequebantur, huc traduxi, sententia ita postulante, atque connexui hunc in modum, Et dicitur humilior, demissior, infimus, humillimus. Cuius me rei admonuit Georg. Buccananus, vir doctiss.'

53. Cf., e.g., Scaliger, *Coniectanea*, p. 104 *ad* VII.6 with Turnèbe, *Commentarius*, p. 102 ad loc.

54. See in general *The Tragedies of Ennius. The Fragments*, ed. H. D. Jocelyn (Cambridge, 1967), pp. 47-63.

55. See Ch. I, above, n. 91.

56. 'Ab eodem est quod ait Medea . . . quod, ut decernunt de vita eo tempore, multorum videtur vitae finis.'

57. Scaliger, *Coniectanea*, p. 98 *ad* VI.81: 'QVOD AIT MEDEA.] Varro γεροντοδιδασκάλῳ, *Nonne vides apud Ennium esse scriptum, Ter malim sub armis vitam cernere, quam semel modo parere* – Verba Euripidis, quae vertit Ennius, sunt haec . . .'.

58. Turnèbe, *Commentarius*, p. 98 *ad* VI.81: 'TER sub armis malim.] Ennius ex Euripide vertit sanequam eleganter, – ὡς τρὶς ...'.

59. See *The Tragedies of Ennius*, ed. Jocelyn, p. 359, n. 2.

60. See Ch. III, above, nn. 118–20.

61. Ibid., n. 142.

62. This passage is quoted by Probus, *ad* Verg. *Ecl.* VI.31–3; see *The Tragedies of Ennius*, ed. Jocelyn, pp. 121–2. The three lines that follow are quoted by Cicero *Pro Rab. Post.* xxviii–xxix; on Scaliger's arguments and those of later critics see Jocelyn, p. 349.

63. Scaliger, *Coniectanea*, pp. 98–9 *ad* VI.81: 'Ponam et alia quae comparabis cum verbis Euripidis. Non enim in eiusmodi exercitationibus male horas collocari puto. Ait itaque Ennius apud Probum, ... Euripides, ... Deinde, ... Apud Ciceronem pro Rabirio Postumo, ... ex Medea Ennii: ex illo, ... Item quae ibidem, ... fecit ex illo, ... Ibidem, ... Plane ex illo, ... Reliqua quae citantur a grammaticis, ab aliis animadversa sunt: quare ea non ponam.'

64. Scaliger, *Coniectanea*, pp. 106–7 *ad* VII.9, at p. 107: 'Haec satis sint ut exerceantur magna ingenia in eiusmodi investigandis. Nam in illis nemo sapit, nisi qui animum in utraque lingua subegit. Neque magnopere laboro quid de illis iudicent magistelli de trivio.'

65. As a sample of Scaliger's method we may take his note on pp. 169–70 *ad* VII. 107: 'VITVLANTES.] Naevius Lycurgo,

> *Vos, qui regalis corporis custodias*
> *Agitis, ite actutum in frondiferos lucos, ubi*
> *Ingenio arbusta innata sunt, non obsita.*
> *Ducite eo argutis linguis mutas quadrupedes:*
> 5 *Vt in venatu vitulantes ex aviis*
> *Locis, nos mittant Poenis decoratos feris.*
> *Alii sublime alios saltus illicite, ubi*
> *Bipedes volucres lino linquant lumina.*

Quod toties in his Coniectaneis fecimus, hic praestitimus: quatuor exempla ex Lycurgo Naevii a Nonio diversis locis citata hic in unum conglutinavimus, et verba mendosa emaculavimus.'
    In this reconstruction Scaliger has assembled the following:

lines 1–3	= Non. 323.1	= Naev. *Lyc.* fr. V Ribbeck
line 4	= Non. 9.24	= Naev. *Lyc.* fr. VI Ribbeck
lines 5–6	= Non. 14.9	= Naev. *Lyc.* fr. VIII Ribbeck
lines 7–8	= Non. 6.17	= Naev. *Lyc.* fr. VII Ribbeck.

66. Scaliger, *Coniectanea*, p. 168 *ad* VII.104: 'Hi luculentissimi versiculi a nobis non solum emendati sunt, sed et, quod quatuor locis dispersi sunt apud Nonium, in unum corpus collecti et digesti. Valde enim delectant me hae reliquiae veterum autorum, tanquam quaedam ex naufragio tabellae.' Cf. ibid., pp. 99–100 *ad* VI.86, at p. 100: 'Quis enim antiquitatis studiosus his reliquiis non delectatur? Quanquam haec sunt, veluti ex magno naufragio parvae tabellae.'

67. Ibid., p. 113 *ad* VII.12: 'Haec sane tot locis sparsa congregasse nihil impediverit. Nam ponamus ita Pacuvium olim non digessisse: tamen interim pro quodam quasi centone nobis sunto. Quia, ut leguntur sparsa apud grammaticos, sunt illa quasi membra quaedam manca et mortua: hic vero ita coniuncta, si nihil aliud, aliquam tamen speciem et dignitatem obtinebunt.' Cf. ibid., pp. 76–7 *ad* VI.4: 'Hic plane ῥαψῳδοί fuimus. Nam testimonia tria, quae divulsa adducit Nonius, in unum coniunximus ...'.

68. Ibid., pp. 174–5 *ad* X.70, at p. 175: 'Et cum ad verbum transferret, satis negligenter ea [ed. 1: illa] tractabat: ut illa, ... Concinnius puto, ... Euripides ... Sed de his satis.' Scaliger's source is Gellius (cf. the text) for both the Latin and the Greek original (*Hec.*, 273–5).

69. Ibid., pp. 118-19 *ad* VII.19, at p. 119: 'Illam vero Aeschyli fabulam totam nos vertimus veteri stylo Pacuviano. In quo maxime sunt reprehendendi isti, qui in veteribus poetis vertendis, eos tam dissimiles sui reddunt, ut pudeat me legere Homerum Sillii Italici, Sophoclem Senecae verbis loquentem. Sed de his alias.' On Scaliger's translation of the *Eumenides*, which he entitled *Dirae*, and which is now lost, see V. R. Lachmann and F. E. Cranz, 'Aeschylus', *CTC* ii, pp. 12-13.

70. For Canter's description of his part in the work see *Lycophronis Chalcidensis Alexandrae, sive Cassandrae versiones duae* (Basel, 1566), *Prolegomena*, sig. β^V-sig. β2^V. That Scaliger's part of the work was completed well before publication is clear from Canter's letter to him, ibid., p. 102: 'Redit ad te tandem Cassandra tua, vir doctissime, quanquam serius forte, quam velles, aut potius, quam uterque vellemus.' (According to the colophon, the book appeared in May.)

71. *Selections from the Brief Mention of Basil Lanneau Gildersleeve*, ed. C. W. E. Miller (Baltimore, 1930), p. 70. As a sample of the version I give the beginning of Cassandra's monologue:

    Heu heu cremata lacrymosa patria,
    Primum quidem feralibus Trinoctii
    *Stlatis gigantis, ore quem quondam suo   *navibus, Fest.
    Consi voravit campo*manduces canis,   *Fest.
    Qui vivus ustus excavator viscerum
    Intra lebetis ignis expertes focos
    *Formo capronas verticis fudit solo,   *calido, Fest.
    Prolis peremtor, patriae pestis meae: . . .

72. Canter to Scaliger, s.d., in *Lycophronis Versiones duae*, p. 102: 'Quid enim de eo sint iudicaturi doctiores, brevi, credo, cognosces. Equidem sic sentio: si haec eodem tempore a te Latine, quo a Poeta Graece, fuisset conscripta, dubitari a permultis, uter alterius esset interpres, potuisse. Vtinam porro Hymnos Orphei, Eumenides Aeschyli, et si quid aliud pari diligentia vertisti, cum studiosis communicare digneris.'

73. *Sophoclis Aiax Lorarius, carmine translatus per Iosephum Scaligerum Iulii filium* (Paris, 1573) gives a Greek text and Scaliger's version on facing pages. The exact dating of the version is unclear. One of the poems in honour of Scaliger by J. Gardesius with which the work concludes is headed 'Eiusdem in eundem, qui Lycophronis Cassandram, Aeschyli Eumenidas, ac postremo Sophoclis Aiacem Latinis versibus transtulit' (p. 102); this shows that 1564 must be the *terminus post quem*. But in *Scaligerana II*, s.v. Muret, pp. 464-5, Scaliger writes: 'O que Muret a mesdit de mon Ajax Lorarius! Il s'en est tant mocqué; c'estoit un grand homme, il faut bien qu'il y ait veu quelque chose que je n'y ay pas veu . . .'. This suggests that the two men discussed the version; and that could only have happened during Scaliger's Italian tours of 1565 and 1566. Given the work's close similarity to Scaliger's other enterprises of the mid-1560s, I have tentatively assigned it to the same period.

74. True, the word *Salisubsilus* appears in Catullus 17.6; but it could legitimately be considered archaic, because it was also found in a quotation attributed to Pacuvius by the Catullus commentator A. Guarinus; see A. F. Naeke, *Opuscula philologica*, ed. Fr. Th. Welcker, i (Bonn, 1842), pp. 107-9.

75. In fact he was by no means consistent; if he used *praevorteres* in line 2 rather than the more classical-sounding *praeverteres*, he also used *Vestro*, which he considered a later form of *Vostro*, in line 43.

76. Cf. Val. Flac. V.608.

77. Cf. also 1169, where 'et gnatus huius atque particeps tori' misrepresents παῖς τε καὶ γυνή. Scaliger occasionally brings off a real coup in his choice of words;

in 332 the archaic compound *expectorarier* is a fine match for διαπεφοιβάσθαι, also a rare compound.

78. Cf. Non. 4 M.

79. *Ajax*, 630-2.

80. Erasmus and Buchanan, more wisely, had not attempted to reproduce choruses and exclamations as precisely as Scaliger did.

81. Scaliger, *Coniectanea*, pp. 155-6 *ad* VII.82: 'QVOD ἀνδρὶ μάχεται.] Crebri sunt in hac licentia ac nimis invenusti Graeci Poetae: sed maxime Euripides: ut de Polynice, quod sit νεικέων ἐπώνυμος: de Pentheo, μὴ πένθος εἰσοίση δόμοις. Aeschylus de Prometheo, quod eum oporteat προμηθέως ex malis evolvi: de Artapherne nimis putide, quod φρένας ἔχοι ἀρτίας. Nam quis sanus Persico nomini etymon Graecum attribuat? Sic Euripides de Thyeste, − ἐπώνυμα δεῖπνα θυέστου, ut citant grammatici. et de Apolline,

'Ω χρυσοφεγγὲς ἥλι' ὥς μ' ἀπώλεσας.

'Όθεν σ' 'Απόλλων' ἐμφανῶς κλῄζει βροτός.

Citat Macrobius. Sophocles etiam aliquando, ut de Aiace. Sed parcius, ut decet sanum et sobrium poetam, et qui sane principem locum in theatro Graeco obtinet. In Graecis hoc tolerandum erat. At quis ferat in Ennio? . . .'.

82. D. Heinsius, *De tragoediae constitutione liber* (Leiden, 1611), bound with *Aristotelis de poetica liber*, ed. D. *Heinsius* (Leiden, 1611); both repr., Hildesheim and New York, 1976, *cap.* xvii, pp. 222-3: 'Sed nec eruditae vetustati deest suus honos, et est incredibilis venustas in hoc genere; modo reliqua conveniant, neque fiat, *Vt cum multa iura confundit cocus* [Plaut. *Mostel.* 277]. Ita eleganter quasdam veterum Graecorum fabulas Acciano et Pacuviano charactere vir incomparabilis Iosephus Scaliger et Florens Christianus convertêre. Quae vel ut discrimen inter hos et reliquos appareat, cum cura sunt legendae. Tum ut lepor, et venustas pristinae antiquitatis squalor, animum demulceat. Postremo, ut si res ferat, quaedam transferantur, quemadmodum ex Ennianis Maro. Sed et nos nonnulla olim sic vertimus. Et cum ista scriberemus, inter chartas nostras primam Sophocleae Electrae partem, antiquissimo sermone expressam invenimus. Quam in iuventutis gratiam hic apponendam duximus . . .'. For a similar interpretation see *Sophoclis Aiax cum scholiis tam antiquis quam novis*, ed. Io. Gottfrid. Hoerius (Leipzig, 1766), sig. [b6ʳ-b7ᵛ] ; for further corroboratory evidence see Scaliger's Prologue to the translation of Aeschylus' *Prometheus* by Chrestien, much of which is quoted and discussed by V. R. Lachmann and F. E. Cranz in *CTC* ii, p. 18.

83. Scaliger, *Coniectanea*, p. 57 *ad* V.124: 'SIMPVLVM A sumendo.] Id est bibendo. *Vnde sumi pote, puteus.* Id est, unde bibi potest. Cicero, *si sumpserit meracius*, id est biberit. Apud eundem, Fluctus in simpulo excitare, τὸ πομφολυγεῖν proverbium. Est autem Syriacum. Nam ut Abub, Ambub, αὐλός: ambubaiarum collegia: a copher, camphora: a sadon, sindon: a sabeca, quod est apud Danielem, sambuca: sic a sephel, sempel, et inde simpulum fecerunt.'

84. *Verborum etymologiae perperam a Varrone traditae, hic veris suis originibus redduntur, aut praetermissae explicantur; M. Terentii Varronis opera*, pp. 177-90.

85. Scaliger, *Coniectanea*, p. 57 *ad* V.124: 'Scio ego me dicere hoc cum magno odio eorum qui non solum literas Hebraicas et Syriacas ignorant, verum etiam oderunt. At tam mihi facile est eos contemnere quam ipsis proclive est eas odisse.' Cf. also ibid., pp. 62-3 *ad* V.137: 'HAS phancillas chermonesice dicunt.] . . . Fortasse legendum, *Has falcillas chermes Poenice dicunt*. Scio enim Chermes falces vocatas olim a Syris et Phoenicibus, quorum colonia sunt Poeni in Africa. Et fieri potest ut hoc dixerit Varro ex Magonis libris, qui Poenice scripti erant de re Rustica. Haec vero asseverare ut vera nolumus. Scimus tamen ex eiuscemodi coniecturis saepenumero veritatem erutam fuisse.'

Scaliger presumably has in mind ḥerəmēs (Deut. 16:9, 23:26). Mago's works were translated into both Latin and Greek, and Varro probably used the latter; see Pauly-Wissowa, s.v. Mago (5): M. Aus Karthago.

86. See e.g. H. Aarsleff, 'The Study and Use of Etymology in Leibniz', *Akten des Internationalen Leibniz-Kongresses. Hannover, 14.–19. November 1966*, iii (Wiesbaden, 1969), pp. 173–89, esp. 183–6.

87. Scaliger later worked out much more sophisticated criteria for establishing relations between languages; see *Epistolae*, pp. 489–90, and *Opuscula* (Paris, 1610), pp. 119–22.

88. See e.g. *Adversaria*, XIX.28 (ed. Paris, 1573–80), II, pp. 162–3.

89. M. Vertranius Maurus, *Libellus de vita M. Varronis deque notis ad eius libros de lingua Latina*, in *M. Terentii Varronis pars librorum quattuor et viginti de lingua Latina* (Lyons, 1563), p. 237 *ad* V. 65: '*Nam tum est conceptum, exinde cum exit, quod oritur*] Q. Ennium, nescio an ex libro Annalium sexto, ibi, Tum cum corde suo divum pater atque hominum rex Effatur – qui Iovem antonomasticῶs, ut ait Fabius, hoc in libro intelligit, autorem habet Varro, et eius appellationis caussam studiose quaerens, non animadvertit ad illud Homericum, πατὴρ ἀνδρῶντε, θεῶντε: sed nimio Latinae linguae studio raptus Iovem dici patrem putavit, quod omnia patefeceret . . .'. In other respects Scaliger and Vertranius Maurus do not have much in common; the latter is more interested than Scaliger in Roman history and antiquities, far less so in archaic Latin, comparative study of Greek and Latin poetry, and the relations between Latin and Near Eastern languages. Scaliger had read him before he completed the *Coniectanea*; cf. p. 170 *ad* VII.107: '. . . Persuaserunt Itali Vertranio, legendum *Persicus.*' A copy of Vertranius's edition, heavily emended by Scaliger and bearing the legend 'EX IOS. SCALIGERI IVLII CAESARIS F. RECOGNITIONE' on its title-page, is now in the Burgerbibliothek, Bern (shelfmark G 233). The book also bears the inscription 'Petri Danielis Aurelii 1565 / Iseppo de lascala / Iseppo de la Scala'. H. Hagen took this to mean that Daniel owned the book before Scaliger (*Catalogus codicum Bernensium* (*Bibliotheca Bongarsiana*), Bern, 1875, p. 550). Though it is plausible at first sight, I suspect that this suggestion is wrong. In an undated letter to Daniel, Scaliger refers to 'my Varro' (Hagen, *Zur Geschichte der Philologie und zur römischen Literatur. Vier Abhandlungen*, Berlin, 1875, pp. 30–2). I believe that the letter should be dated 1565 (see Appendix to Ch. IV, below). If that is correct, then Scaliger's copy of Vertranius was probably meant to serve as a *texte Belge* for a printed edition of the *De lingua latina*, which in the event was not published; and Daniel simply kept the book. When Scaliger's edition of the text of the *De lingua latina* finally appeared in 1573, it followed Agustín's text, not Vertranius's.

90. See e.g. J. B. Trapp, 'The Conformity of Greek and the Vernacular', *Classical Influences on European Literature, A. D. 500–1500*, ed. R. R. Bolgar (Cambridge, 1971), pp. 239–44.

91. Turnèbe, *Adversaria*, XI.23. Cf. the next note.

92. Scaliger, *Commentarii et Castigationes*, in *Virgilii Appendix*, pp. 521–2 *ad Copam* 4: '*Ad cubitum raucos*] . . . Porro Copa nostra, quum Syra sit, id quod nomen Syriscae satis convincit, non male *Ambubaia* dici potest. Nam Syriace *ambubaia*, ἡ αὐλητρίς. Ne interea doctissimo viro credamus, qui putat a Baiis dictum. At ego nolo illi credi, linguae Syriacae ignaro: sed illis, qui eius peritissimi sunt. Nam quod illi persuadere non potui, quum id in Commentarios meos in Varronem retulissem, non tam me movet quam quod adeo illi mirum videretur, nos ex ultima usque Syria id nomen petere. Non enim illis, qui Syriace sciunt, mirum videri debet: quod ille eius linguae nescius, adeo eludere voluit.' Cf. also ibid., p. 523 *ad Copam* 7. I owe these points to Isaac Casaubon. In his copy of Scaliger's edition of the *Appendix* (British Library, shelf-mark 1000.

e. 16), Casaubon wrote 'ambubaia. Turnebo. 1.xi c. 23' in the margin of p. 521. He also wrote 'Hoc verissimum est' at p. 523, where Scaliger returned to the charge. And in the index, sig. Nn 3^V, he added the following entry: 'Σηᾳι Scaligeri digressiunculam in Turnebum. p. 521.'

93. *Correspondance de Bonaventura Vulcanius pendant son séjour à Cologne, Genève et Bâle (1573–1577)*, ed. H. de Vries de Heekelingen (The Hague, 1923), pp. 41–2: 'In etymis frequenter ignoratione linguae Graecae lapsus [scil. Isidorus], ideoque necesse erit annotationes meas adiicere, quibus eius errores castigentur, quod ipsum in Varrone quem nuper Henricus Stephanus edidit Josephus Scaliger praestitit.'

94. See n. 35, above.

95. *Scaligerana II*, s.v. Muret, pp. 464–5: 'O que Muret a mesdit de mon Ajax Lorarius! il s'en est tant mocqué; c'estoit un grand homme, il faut bien qu'il y ait veu quelque chose que je n'y ay pas veu . . .'.

96. *Scaligerana II*, s.v. Glossaires, p. 349: 'Les GLOSSAIRES ne valent rien pour le Grec, mais seulement pour le Latin. P. Daniel qui n'estoit pas des plus doctes, les avoit trouvez à S. Germain, les montra à Monsieur Turnebus et à moy.' The reference to Turnèbe provides a *terminus ante quem* of 1565 for the discovery and Daniel's communication of it to Scaliger; this is confirmed by Scaliger's statement that 'J'en avois fait un extrait, que je voulois montrer à Muret et Manuce en Italie . . .', which dates the discovery before Scaliger's Italian travels of 1565–6. See also Scaliger to Daniel, undated, in Hagen, *Zur Geschichte der Philologie*, 31: 'Nam de tuo optimo Lexico, quod mihi commodasti, hoc vere dicere possum, me hactenus nullum librum tractasse, ex quo plus fructus coeperim. Infinita quidem in eo errata sunt, sed illa sunt, ex quibus illum fructum coepi. Adeo feliciter mihi versatus esse videor in illis emendandis. Sed nisi reliquum ad me miseris, vix mihi satisfecero de illis quaternionibus, quos iam accepi, cum ipsi auxerint mihi desiderium eorum, qui inter manus tuas restant. Quare oro te, mittas ad me illos, ut, simulac eos exscripsero, tibi emendatos remittam.' Scaliger's work on Nonius is dated by a subscription found in a Venice 1513 and Basel 1526 edition of Perotti's *Cornucopiae*, Festus, and Nonius (Leiden University Library, 761.A.9; ibid., 761.A.10, the latter autograph but incomplete): 'Nonius Marcellus collatus ad vetus exemplar optimum cuius copia nobis facta est anno a Christo nato MDLXV. V calendas Novemb. Josephus Scaliger contuli. . . . In eo exemplari quaecunque offendimus, margini apposuimus. Nam in quibus litera N signata est, haec sunt Nostrae Coniecturae. Item ubi C est Cuiacii Iurisconsulti Codex' [the last sentence added later in 761.A.10]. H. Nettleship printed Scaliger's subscription and notes from a copy entered in a Bodleian Library exemplar of H. Junius's Nonius edition. See *Journal of Philology*, xxi (1893), pp. 211–32; xxii (1894), pp. 74–83. Scaliger evidently abandoned work when Junius's edition reached him (it came out in 1565); for it had an imperial privilege forbidding anyone else to edit Nonius for 6 years. See Scaliger, *Poemata Anecdota*, ed. H. J. de Jonge (Leiden, 1980), p. 16.

97. Lambin to Scaliger, 16.viii.[1571], in *Epistres françoises des Personnages illustres et doctes a Monsr. Ioseph Iuste de la Scala*, ed. Iaques de Reves (Harderwyck, 1624), pp. 284–5; Lambin to Scaliger, 21.iii.1572, ibid., pp. 133–5.

98. Bernays, *Scaliger*, pp. 130–1.

99. By 1564–5 Scaliger and his patron had read Statius and Propertius together. See Scaliger, *Castigationes in Propertium*, in *Catulli, Tibulli, Propertii nova editio* (Paris, 1577), p. 185 *ad* II.ii.12: 'VIRGINEM *Brimo*] Ita olim emendavit lumen literatorum Adr. Turnebus. Sed antequam ille Adversaria sua publicaret, nos ita emendaveramus ex ipso Etymologici loco, ex quo ipse quoque coniecturam suàm fecerat. Testis huius emendationis nostrae nobilissimus atque

eruditiss. Ludovicus Castanaeus eques Regius Torquatus, et Christianissimi Regis ad summum Pontificem Legatus. Quum enim illi Propertium explicarem, ita eius libri orae a me annotatum fuit. neque hoc solum, sed paulo ante, quum eidem quinque libros Silvarum Statii enarrarem, ostenderam illi eundem errorem esse in libro secundo . . .'. In a letter to Casaubon Scaliger also recalled that he and Chasteigner had discussed passages in Polybius 'Inter equitandum': *Epistolae*, p. 352; Bernays, *Scaliger*, p. 131.

100. See in general Bernays, *Scaliger*, pp. 38–9, 131–6.

101. *Scaligerana I*, s.v. Muretus, p. 126: 'Mihi dixit Dom. d'Abain tanti fuisse Jos. Scaligerum Mureto, cum Romae esset ante sex annos, vix ut unquam ab illo Muretus divelli potuerit, cujus doctrinam totus stupebat et admirabatur maxime'; *Scaligerana II*, s.v. Abain, p. 172: 'ABAIN. Madame d'Abain estant à Rome avec son Mary Ambassadeur, alla voir le cabinet du Pape; Muret les mena et moi aussi.' Muret regularly served as a guide for learned French visitors; see Nolhac, review of Ch. Dejob, *Marc-Antoine Muret*, in *Revue Critique*, n.s., xiii (1882), pp. 483–8, esp. p. 486.

102. Scaliger, *Confutatio fabulae Burdonum*, quoted by Bernays, *Scaliger*, p. 133.

103. Scaliger, *Lettres françaises*, pp. 13–14: 'Car desja moi estant à Rome je fus adverti de Paulus Manutius touchant ledict livre, et ce qu'il contient, dont nous en avons faict nostre project du despuis.'

104. Scaliger's emendations to the Hymn of Cleanthes, which had formed part of Orsini's collection, appeared in Henri Estienne's 1573 *Poesis philosophica*, which also included the Hymn; see C. G. F. Mohnike, *Kleanthes der Stoiker* (Greifswald, 1814), pp. 12–14. They may have been a remnant of his original 'project'.

105. Scaliger, *Castigationes in Propertium*, p. 229 *ad* IV.i.125: '. . . Oportet fuisse insigne opus illud moeniorum Ameriae . . . Sane hodie quaedam supersunt eorum murorum reliquiae, immanibus saxis quadratis, qualia sunt hodie in mole Adriani Romae, praestantiam eorum testantibus.'

106. Scaliger, *Castigationes, Virgilii Appendix*, p. 455: 'Et quantum ad Deos viales, ut vocat Plautus, nihil intererat, Mercurii, an Priapi essent. Quin et Mercuriis ipsis et Terminis vialibus veretra longa, et immania, ut Priapis, attribuebantur. Quod et ego Romae in aedibus Cardinalis de Caesiis vidi, et patet ex dicto Philosophi . . .'. See also *Scaligerana I*, s.v. Tibia, p. 161.

107. For Scaliger's work in epigraphy see E. Ziebarth, *Heinrich Lindenbruch und Joseph Justus Scaliger*, Festschrift Wilhelms-Gymnasium (Hamburg, 1905), p. 95; Bernays, *Scaliger*, p. 136.

108. Ibid., p. 137.

109. One should not, however, confuse this immediate reaction with Scaliger's life-long attitudes, which, as will be shown below, varied greatly from year to year.

110. *Scaligerana II*, s.v. Scaliger, pp. 551–2: 'Scaliger a esté à Verone, sed alio nomine, nam esset occisus'; p. 553: 'Si les Venitiens me tenoient, ils me coudroient dans un sac'; p. 558: 'Ego sum ultimus Scaliger. Veneti dicunt nullum superesse. Muretus dicebat mihi ne nomen meum Venetiis dicerem.'

111. See H. J. de Jonge, 'The Study of the New Testament', in *Leiden University in the Seventeenth Century. An Exchange of Learning*, ed. Th. H. Lunsingh Scheurleer (Leiden, 1975), pp. 79–80; cf. J. Bernays's comments, published by A. D. Momigliano, 'Jacob Bernays', *Mededelingen der Koninklijke Nederlandse Akademie van Wetenschappen, Afd. Letterkunde*, n.s., xxxii (1969), p. 175.

112. *Scaligerana II*, s.v. Judaei, p. 407: 'J'ay disputé à Rome et ailleurs avec les Juifs: ils m'aymoient et estoient fort estonnez que je parlois fort bien Hebreu, et me disoient que je parlois l'Hebreu de la Bible, et que paucissimi ex illis ita loquebantur, sed lingua majorum Rabbinorum loquebantur, Rabbotenu Zicronam.'

Scaliger's comments on the Jews occupy pp. 402–10; they have been reprinted in W. Den Boer, *Scaliger en Perizonius: hun betekenis voor de wetenschap* (The Hague, 1964), pp. 43–6.

113. Bernays, *Scaliger*, p. 138.

114. *Scaligerana II*, s.v. Marie Stuard, p. 442.

115. Bernays, *Scaliger*, p. 139.

116. *Scaligerana II*, s.v. Elizabeth, p. 303.

117. Cf. n. 37, above for Scaliger's statement that he wrote his notes on the *Catalecta* at the age of 27.

118. Pithou's MS of the *Appendix* is now in the Bibliothèque Nationale, Paris (MS lat. 8207); see Ch. Plésent, *Le Culex. Poème pseudo-Virgilien* (Paris, 1910), p. 11 n. 3, and Scaliger to Pithou, 23.viii.1573, *Lettres françaises*, p. 22. Scaliger's transcript of the *Vita Vergilii a Foca Grammatico urbis Romae versibus edita* is now Leiden University Library, MS Scal. 61, fols. 46^r–47^v; it comes (directly or indirectly) from Bibliothèque Nationale, Paris, MS lat. 8093.

119. Scaliger to Pithou, 14.iv.1568 (9?), *Epistolae*, pp. 136–8; Scaliger to Pithou, 6.v.1568 (9?), *Epistolae*, pp. 143–4. On the order in which these letters should be arranged see Bernays, *Scaliger*, p. 273. I am not able to date them to any year with absolute confidence.

120. Scaliger to Pithou, 24.vi.1572, *Epistolae*, p. 140: '. . . quum ergo me Deus amicis restituisset, offendi domi jam ante biennium allatum mihi fuisse illum librum Parisiis, ab amico meo Carolo Sevino.' That Pithou had had trouble in seeing to the publication of the edition seems clear from Scaliger, *Epistolae*, p. 141.

121. Scaliger, *Epistolae*, pp. 139–40: 'De Catalectis nostris idem possum dicere, vel potius deplorare, quod de me ipso. In meo enim exilio aut in militia quamdiu fui, putavi penitus intercidisse illa.'

122. On the context, aims, and limitations of Cujas's work see H. E. Troje, 'Humanistische Kommentierungen klassischer Juristenschriften', *Ius Commune*, iv (1972), pp. 51–72.

123. J. Regnauld to Dupuy, Lyons, 23.viii.1572; Paris, Bibliothèque Nationale, MS Dupuy 808, fol. 138^r: 'Monsr Cuias apporta pareillement le reste de son Africanus et trois livres d'Observations . . . Entre aultres propos que nous eusmes ensemble il me dict qu'il conseilloit a ceulx qui sont desia provects en la science du droict de bien remascher cest Africain, que qui se l'a rendu familier manie les aultres Jurisconsultes a son plaisir, n'ayant led. Africain traicté que les plus difficiles et scabreuses questions de droict qu'il avoit prinses et tirees des . . . Questions de Juliain: que pour son regard il n'a jamais tant profficté en aulcune estude qu'il ait faicte en celle la . . .'.

124. Scaliger, *Epistolae*, p. 139: Cf. the very similar passage in *Scaligerana I*, s.v. Cujacius, pp. 74–5.

125. *Scaligerana I*, s.v. Auctores, p. 23: 'Ego cum Cujacio nostro, nihil quicquam scire eum existimaverim, qui nihil novit quam quod vulgus et mediocriter docti'; ibid., p. 20: 'Non omnibus datum, etiam doctis, sed rarae cujusdam foelicitatis est, bonos auctores corrigere, et suae dignitati atque nitori restituere: nec quenquam hodie novi qui id praestare possit praeter Dom. Cujacium, et Dom. Auratum.'

126. *Scaligerana I*, s.v. Cujacius, p. 75: 'Nullus est qui de legibus XII. Tabul. quicquam docere me possit, ne Cujacius quidem; qui non inficiabitur me illi multa de iis indicasse, quae hactenus illum latuerant.'

127. Cujas, *Paratitla*, on *Digest* XLVII.3, quoted by Bernays, *Scaliger*, p. 144: 'In XII. tab. scriptum opinor: "Tignum iunctum aedibus vineaeque concaptum ne

solvito" vel potius ut doctissimus Iosephus Scaliger censet, a quo pudet dissentire, "concapes".' Cujas later changed his mind; ibid., pp. 144-5.

128. C. Philippson, 'Jacques Cujas', in *Great Jurists of the World* (Boston, 1914), p. 96. For a contemporary description of Cujas's library, which was equipped with a book wheel and a barber's chair, see R. Calderini de Marchi, *Jacopo Corbinelli et les érudits français* (Milan, 1914), p. 176.

129. *Scaligerana II*, s.v. Cujacius, p. 286: 'Monsieur Cujas disoit que j'avois depucellé les Manuscrits . . .'. Cf. Bernays, *Scaliger*, pp. 142-4.

130. *Scaligerana II*, s.v. Cujacius, p. 285: 'Il prestoit aussi des livres MSS. à tous ceux qui luy en demandoient, il avoit presté à P. P. son Petrone, et à moy aussi . . . C'est le premier Petrone que nous ayons eu. Je l'ay copié sur cet exemplaire; je l'ayme mieux qu'un imprimé.' Scaliger's transcript is now Leiden University Library, MS Scal. 61, fols. 4-44. It is not a simple transcript of Cujas's MS but a conflated text designed to be read. Many variants are given in the margins, attributed to *al. c., v. c.*, and the like. Cf. *Petronii Arbitri Satyricon*, ed. K. Müller (Munich, 1961), pp. xiv-xix, with the rev. edn. (Munich, 1965), pp. 392-4.

131. The MS is now Leiden University Library, MS Voss. Lat. fol. 111. Scaliger entered his collation in a copy of Th. Poelman's edition of Ausonius (Antwerp, 1568), now in the Bodleian Library (shelf-mark Auct. S. 5. 22, olim Linc. 8°.A. 141); see below, n. 177.

132. Scaliger's copy of the *Collatio* is in Leiden University Library, MS Scal. 61, fols. 108[r]-126[r]; see *Mosaicarum et Romanarum legum collatio*, ed. M. Hyamson (London, 1913), pp. xiii-xviii, xlix-li, for a handy discussion of the discovery and early attempts to date, analyse, and edit the work. Much further information is collected in E. Volterra, 'Collatio legum Mosaicarum et Romanarum', *Atti della R. Accademia Nazionale dei Lincei*, Memorie della Classe di Scienze morali, storiche e filologiche, ser. VI, iii (1930), pp. 8-23.

133. Quoted by Mark Pattison, 'Joseph Scaliger', *Essays*, ed. H. Nettleship (Oxford, 1889), i, p. 153.

134. D. R. Kelley, *Foundations of Modern Historical Scholarship* (New York and London, 1970), p. 259.

135. As Scaliger grew older, his views on the relationships among languages became much clearer and more explicit; see esp. his *Diatriba de Europaeorum linguis, Opuscula* (Paris, 1610), pp. 119-22.

136. Regnauld to Dupuy, 23.viii.1572, Paris, Bibliothèque Nationale, MS Dupuy 808, fol. 138[v]: 'Led. Sr Cuias ne se peut induire d'ambulare per Suevos, Scythicas pati pruinas, ne Roaldes semblablement. Scaliger integer aevi καὶ ὦ γόνυ χλωρόν [Theocritus XIV. 70] a la persuasion dud. Sr Cuias sy est acheminé . . .'.

137. In Scaliger's dedicatory letter to Cujas (22.viii.1572) he makes clear that he has had to break off his editorial work in order to join Monluc: 'Scis enim, ut hodie repentino nuncio in Germaniam proficiscendi mihi necessitas imposita sit' (sig. A3[r]). That the date of Scaliger's letter really was his last day in Lyons is clear from Regnauld to Dupuy, 23.viii.1572, MS Dupuy 808, fol. 138[v]: 'Scaliger partit hier de ceste ville pour aller a Strasbourg . . .'. Cf. also Scaliger's note on *Aetna* 645: ' . . . unus mensis, in quo haec omnia opuscula recensuimus . . .' (*Virgilii Appendix*, p. 420).

138. *Scaligerana II*, s.v. Scaliger, p. 552: 'J'estois à Lauzanne, lors que le massacre fut fait, et le sceus à Strasbourg, d'ou je vins incontinent à Geneve.'

139. Pattison, 'Joseph Scaliger (Fragment)', *Essays*, i, pp. 156-7; *Registres de la Compagnie des Pasteurs de Genève*, iii, ed. O. Fatio and O. Labarthe (Geneva, 1969), pp. 91, 93. Scaliger had already begun to lecture on 21 Oct. (ibid., p. 92). Cf. Ch. Seitz, *Joseph-Juste Scaliger et Genève* (Geneva, 1895).

140. Scaliger's first letter to Pithou suggests that he had copied out the text of Poelman's edition, adding the variants given in Poelman's margins later: 'Quantum ad textum Opusculorum, et reliqua Appendicis Virgilianae, nihil decrevi attentare. Tu tantum quae tibi videbuntur leviuscula mutabis, et non nisi quae tuto mutari possunt. Ego chartae meae quam legent operae, notas Codicis Antverpiensis apposui. Tamen sunt multa quae temere mutata sunt a nescio quo * * * , quae tu restitues. Caetera bene habent' (*Epistolae*, p. 138). Bernays rightly points out that the Codex Antverpiensis is not a MS but Poelman's edition, and that the 'nescio quis * * * ' must be Poelman himself (*Scaliger*, pp. 274-5). Scaliger's text of the *Aetna*, which I collated against Poelman's, was unchanged except in orthography and punctuation. Mr M. D. Reeve informs me that Scaliger's *Priapea* are also reprinted directly from Poelman's — at least one clear misprint included. Nicolaas Heinsius argued in a letter to Theod. Ryckius, 21.i.1674, that Scaliger did not consult the Aldine edition at least for the *Ciris* (Leiden University Library MS Br. Q.14, p. 341, kindly brought to my attention by Dr F. F. Blok).

141. *Vergilii Appendix*, p. 279, *ad Cul.* 148; after explaining that lines 157 and 160-4 should be moved so that they follow line 145, Scaliger writes: '*His suberat*] vetus scriptura: *His superat.* malim, *superet.* Non erat hic locus haec explicandi, cum in alium locum reiecerimus: sed vulgatam editionem sequimur, ut in sequentibus.' Scaliger's work is inconsistent in other ways as well. At *Aetna* 6 Scaliger's text follows Poelman's in reading *Amphinomus*; but his note ad loc., p. 419, reads: '*Amphion*] Lege, *Amphinomus.* Et quaedam editiones ita correxerunt.' In short, Scaliger did not even bother to make the lemmata in his commentary agree with his base text.

142. Above, n. 118; for a modern text see *Vitae Vergilianae*, ed. I. Brummer (Leipzig, 1912), pp. 49-53.

143. In MS Scal. 61, fols, 46ʳ-47ᵛ, Scaliger gives these conjectures: *Hic* for *Haec* (line 9), *clara* for *data* (line 12), *fronte* for *fronde* (line 23), *omne* for *omnem* (line 37), *oras* for *auras* (line 50), and *Scironem* for *Sironem* (line 63).

144. In the printed text (*Virgilii Appendix*, pp. 141-5), *fronte* is simply introduced into the text of line 23, and *omne* into that of line 37; the others are recorded in the margins. Moreover, Scaliger's printed version of the poem continues for 14 lines beyond the last line recorded in MS Scal. 61; at the end of the text he wrote: 'Caetera deerant in exemplari' (*Virgilii Appendix*, p. 145). Yet he gives no explanation for the apparent discrepancy between what were apparently two versions of the poem on which he drew. The case is not unique. On pp. 185-6 Scaliger prints 2 epigrams which he drew from what is now Leiden University Library MS Voss. Lat. fol. 111, fol. 37ᵛ (Riese, *Anthologia Latina*, i, 648-9). In his transcript of the first, Scaliger wrote *adtrito* in the text of line 11, and entered the conjecture *ac trito* in the margin; in line 9 of the 2nd he wrote *mendosae* in the text and [*mendos*]*e* in the margin (Leiden University Library, MS Scal. 61, fol. 127ʳ). Both conjectures are incorporated into the texts of the printed version; their origin is not revealed.

145. Scaliger himself ended a series of conjectures on *Moretum* 15 with the following wry comment: 'Sed ego nae abutor otio meo. Et versiculum, qui ita conceptus est in membrana, sic interpretor . . .' (*Virgilii Appendix*, p. 425).

146. See e.g. *Virgilii Appendix*, pp. 413-14 *ad Aetn.* 580: '*Et sacer ad bellum*] Alioque *Numerus* ad contemptum.
    Nos numerus sumus, et fruges consumere nati.
    Ex Graecorum proverbiis, ἀριθμός. Quod etiam de uno dici, non tantum de pluribus, annotavimus apud Euripidem Heraclidis.
    Εἰδὼς μὲν οὐκ ἀριθμόν, ἀλλ' ἐτητύμως
    ἄνδρ' ὄντα τὸν σὸν παῖδα — [997-8]'
    Cf. p. 416, *ad Aetn.* 590.

147. *Virgilii Appendix*, pp. 421–2: 'De auctore vero huius elegantissimi Catalecti, non constat. Neque enim Virgilii esse, satis norunt, qui Virgilium magis, quam Grammaticos nostros triverunt. Valde enim confutat eorum iudicium stilus tam diversus a Virgiliano. Quid dicam de homine erudito, summoque amico nostro, a quo extorquere nunquam potui, ne hoc opusculum Virgilio adscriberet? Profecto ita est: nisi valde ingenium in hac exercitatione subegeris, necesse est perperam de his rebus saepe iudicare.' For Scaliger's discussion of the style and authorship of the *Priapea* see F. R. Hausmann, 'Kaspar Schoppe, Joseph Justus Scaliger und die Carmina Priapea . . .', *Landesgeschichte und Geistesgeschichte. Festschrift für O. Herding* (Stuttgart, 1977), pp. 382–95; Hausmann in *CTC* iv, p. 443.

148. For Lambin, see ibid., p. 417, *ad Aetn.* 604: '*Quanquam sors*] Editiones veteres: *quam sors et*. Lego:
    Nec minus ille pius, quam forset nobilis ignis.
    forset. Vide doctissimos D. Lambini in Horatium commentarios' (Horace, ed. Lambin, Lyons, 1561, ii, pp. 95–6 *ad Sat.* I.vi.49). This passage caught Casaubon's eye. He commented as follows in his margin: 'Elogium Scaligeri de Lambini comm. in Horatium.' For Dorat see pp. 515–16, *ad Catal.* IX.61, esp. p. 516: '. . . et sane μεγάλας ἠοίας imitatur cum ait. *Non illa, Hesperidum* etc. *non edita Tyndaris* etc. *Non supero fulgens* etc. *Non defensa diu* etc. *Regia non Semele* etc. Hesiodus vero semper exempla sua incipiebat, ἠ ο'ίη, ut et noster Auratus docuit. Vnde ἠοῖαι vocatur illud poema.' Casaubon wrote in his margin: 'vide Canter. Nov. ἠοῖαι opus Hesiodi unde dictum.'

149. See above, n. 92.

150. *Virgilii Appendix*, pp. 344–6, *ad Cir.* 536.

151. Ibid., pp. 344–5: 'Non enim veteribus illis Graecis notum fuisse, satis patet ex verbis Aristotelis in historia animalium . . . Ex quibus cognoscimus tum apud veteres Graecos hoc genus aucupii ignotum fuisse, cum id in Barbaris admiretur Aristoteles: tum accipitrem potius illicis avis locum tenuisse, quam praedatricis. In illis tamen videmus quasi incunabula eius aucupii. Nam aetate Sidonii Apollinaris videtur maiore in cultu, ac cura fuisse: ut omnia solent ex parvis, et minimis augeri.'

152. Ibid., p. 344: 'At Falco et leporem, et Agrettam, seu Egrettam capit. Plerique ex nobilitate Gallica etiam Falcones ad leporis capturam instituunt. Quod sane genus aucupii mihi videtur veteribus satis leviter notum, hodie vero apud nostratem nobilitatem ad summum gradum perfectionis pervenisse. Vt enim alia, ita et hoc ex parvis admodum initiis ad hanc, quam hodie obtinet, summam artem progressum est.'

153. *Scaligerana I*, s.v. *Dominus de Saint* JOUSY, p. 105: '*Dominus de Saint* JOUSY excellentissimus mechanicus, si quis alius. Notas numerosque omnes antiquorum numismatum, ignotamque scripturam inscriptionum, omnium primus divinavit. Pictor adeo industrius, ut semel modo visum absens exprimere ac reddere melius possit, quam quivis alius pictor praesentem. Sed quod eximium in eo est, Musicae antiquorum summa peritia, quam callet omnium optime, de eaque librum justae magnitudinis propediem editurus est. Fuit convictor Jos. Scaligeri, Valentiae Delphinatum.' Chronological considerations – and the details of the description – have led me to assume that Scaliger was referring to Louis de Montjosieu rather than Pierre du Faur de Saint-Jorry, the other antiquary and student of Cujas's whose name could easily have been transformed into 'Saint Jousy'. For a discussion of Montjosieu's scholarship see A. Ellenius, *De arte pingendi* (Uppsala and Stockholm, 1960). Naturally, Scaliger was not the first or the only French philologist to take up such problems. Cf. e.g. J. Brodeau, *Miscellaneorum libri sex* (Basel, 1555), VI.3, pp. 217–18: 'Salis usum multis gentibus Troiano saeculo incognitum fuisse, testatur Odyss. λ. Homer. . . .' (Brodeau goes on to argue that Homer knew of cavalry as well as chariot warfare).

154. S. Goulart to J. Simler, 22.ix.1574; L. C. Jones, *Simon Goulart, 1543–1628* (Geneva and Paris, 1917), pp. 326–7: 'Perpetuo enim morbo hic laboravit: et si aliquoties praelegit, rarum fuit auditorium.' Cf. Scaliger's account in *Scaligerana I*, s.v. *Auctores*, p. 20: 'Dominus enim Scaliger non discurrit, ut dicebant Germani Genevae, sed bene interpretatur auctoris mentem' (Vertunien's report). Admittedly Scaliger did not pretend he had enjoyed teaching; see ibid.

155. *Thuana*, s.v. Groulart; quoted by Bernays, *Scaliger*, p. 154.

156. *Scaligerana I*, s.v. Beza, p. 28: 'Beza magnus vir procul dubio, olim Poeta, nunc concionator extemporaneus. Davidem propediem est editurus'; *Scaligerana II*, s.v. Beza, pp. 230–2, esp. p. 231: 'Il n'estoit pas docte en Hebreu. Beze reprend souvent et à tort Erasme, il s'amuse et s'abuse à le reprendre, il n'a pas bien entendu les langues . . .'. Cf. also *Registres de la Compagnie des Pasteurs*, III, pp. 107–8; the Company of Pastors upheld Scaliger against a complaint levelled by his colleague Corneille Bertram.

157. Scaliger, *Commentarius*, in *M. Manilii Astronomicωn libri quinque* (Paris, 1579), separately paginated, p. 235 *ad* IV.588: '*Nascentemque ipsumque diem*) Andreas Melvinus Scotus, iuvenis eruditus admonuit me hic legendum esse, *lapsumque diem*'; Julius Caesar Scaliger, *Poemata* (n.p., 1574), I, sig. [*3ᵛ].

158. *Scaligerana I*, s.v. Dalechampius, p. 76: ' . . . cujusmodi habemus Henricum Stephanum, qui omnes quotquot edidit, editve libros, etiam meos, suo arbitrio jam corrupit et deinceps corrumpet . . .'; cf. ibid., s.v. Erotianus, pp. 88–9.

159. *Homeri et Hesiodi Certamen* (Geneva, 1573); *Poesis Philosophica* (Geneva, 1573). Scaliger's working copies of both works – the latter including many additional philosophical fragments entered in Scaliger's hand – are in the Bodleian Library (shelf-mark 8°.C. 238 Auct).

160. See J. Hutton, *The Greek Anthology in France and in the Latin Writers of the Netherlands to the Year 1800* (Ithaca, N.Y., 1946), p. 153.

161. Scaliger to Pithou, 10.ix.1573, *Lettres françaises*, p. 26: 'Aussi j'adjoustai en mes lettres touchant le Manilius, lequel j'ai desja corrigé et mis en son lieu toutz les lieus transposés, qui sont en ce grand poète, et je suis si audacieux jusques là, que je n'ai poinct eu honte d'entreprendre un si grand labeur. Mais avec l'aide de Dieu· nous en sommes venus à bout'; cf. Scaliger to Pithou, 23.viii.1573, ibid., pp. 21–2.

162. A 1569 edition of Varro's works and Scaliger's commentaries is sometimes listed in bibliographies; see e.g. the *Index editionum M. Ter. Varronis* in *M. Ter. Varronis De lingua Latina libri qui supersunt cum fragmentis ejusdem* (Zweibrücken, 1788), p. xxxvi. I have not been able to find a copy of this work or an entry for it in a modern library catalogue; nor is there any clear reference to such an edition in Scaliger's works. So I have ventured to assume that listings of it result from the repetition of some early bibliographer's error. The same conclusion is reached by V. Brown, in *CTC* iv, p. 467.

163. Scaliger, *Appendix ad Coniectanea sua in libros M. Terentii Varronis de lingua Latina*, in *Varronis Opera*; the Bipontine edition of the *De lingua latina*, mentioned in the previous note, mixes this set of notes in with the *Coniectanea* without mentioning their disparate origin, and must therefore be used with great care.

164. Vettori's MS included the work of Cato as well as that of Varro, and was in the library of San Marco in 1482. It is now lost. For an exhaustive study of the use that Poliziano and Vettori made of it – and a critical assessment of Vettori's accuracy in collation – see *M. Porci Catonis De agri cultura*, ed. A. Mazzarino (Leipzig, 1962), *Prolegomena*, esp. pp. xxxi–lxv.

165. Scaliger, *Notae ad libros M. Terentii Varronis de re rustica*, in *M. Varronis Opera*, pp. 210–11 *ad* I.ii.5: 'SI NON diffinderem meo insititio somno:] Hanc

restitutionem, ut et alias innumeras in hoc auctore, ex illo peroptimo exemplari debemus eruditissimo Victorio.' Cf. p. 219, *ad* I.xxiii.2: 'QVAE cibi sunt maioris.] Rectissime, ut et alia, haec restituit P. Victorius.' Cf. also *JWCI* xxxviii (1975), p. 168, n. 49.

166. Scaliger to Pithou, 23.viii.1573, *Lettres françaises*, p. 22.

167. Ibid., pp. 20–1.

168. Scaliger to Pithou, 10.ix.1573, ibid., pp. 25–6.

169. Scaliger's preface is dated Basel, 29.viii.1573. On 23.viii.1573 he wrote to Pithou that 'Je suis aprés pour faire imprimer l'Ausonne tout renouvellé et aultre qu'il n'est aujourd'hui avec des grans castigations et explications sur le dict Poète' (*Lettres françaises*, p. 23). But though he thought the printing would be finished soon, Gryphius stopped work, causing him 'la plus grand peine du monde' (ibid., pp. 30, 31). Scaliger's commentary seems to have been published in 1574; the text, however, did not appear until 1575.

170. Cf. E. Vinet, *Praefatio*, in Ausonius, *Opera* (Bordeaux, 1580): 'Nullam Ausonius disciplinam ignoravit. Omnes Latinos Graecosque scriptores, quorum maior pars intercidit, ad unguem novit. Hinc in eius scriptis multa se ostendit, et varia eruditio, ut cuivis legenti non statim queant intelligi.'

171. On the earliest humanists' dealings with Ausonius see R. Weiss, 'Ausonius in the Fourteenth Century', *Classical Influences on European Culture, A.D. 500–1500*, ed. Bolgar, pp. 67–72. For the efforts of Poliziano and Beroaldo to solve one Ausonian riddle see Ch. I, above, nn. 56–8.

172. H. de la Ville de Mirmont, *Le Manuscrit de l'Île Barbe*, i, pp. 46–62.

173. Ibid., *passim*, esp. pp. 63–125.

174. Ibid., pp. 126–8.

175. Ibid., pp. 166 ff. Vinet had known Scaliger for many years; cf. his letter to P. Daniel of 15.ii.1566, in Hagen, *Zur Geschichte der Philologie*, p. 33: 'Monsieur Scaliger fait bien, de se pourmener, cependant qu'il est jeune et qu'il en a bon moien.'

176. E. Vinet, *Praefatio*, in Ausonius, *Opera*, ed. cit., sig. A3^r: '. . . nec multo post eas datas litteras, ex Aginnensi suo ad audiendum Cuiacium se contulit. Docebat ille tunc Valentiae: ad quem et ad Scaligerum scripsi de Ausonio ad Gryphium iam ante annos quinque misso. Rescripsit Scaliger Valentia et Lugduno mense Aprili et Augusto. Promisit omnem operam, quo posset Ausonius, cuius erat studiosissimus, in lucem castigatior exire, et meis commentariis illustratus.'

177. Ibid.: 'Ceterum quum veterem illum librum, quem eo tempore remiseram Cuiacio, nactus esset, conferendum cum meo exemplari censuit, siquid forte deprehenderet, quod me fugisset. Barbarica nanque scriptura erat. Quaedam litterae agnitu difficiles; multae fugientes; plerique multorum verborum versus in modum unicae dictionis descripti, et nonnulla interdum verba in duo plurave divisa.' See also above, n. 131.

178. Scaliger writes: 'Caeterum, mi Vinete, quia tu primus me ad haec scribenda impulisti, neque aliter, quam a te admonitus, videbar ea scripturus fuisse, hoc quicquid est lucubratiunculae meae, tibi do dedicoque . . .' (*Ausonianarum lectionum libri duo*, ed. 1588, p. 6).

179. Ibid., I.5, p. 24: 'Non patiar insignem labem in tam excellenti poemate residere, quae hodie in epilogo eiusdem operis legitur:
     Haec ego vivifica ducens ab origine gentem.
     Legendum enim *Vivisca*. Burdigala enim caput Biturigum Viviscorum.'

180. In Scaliger's copy of Poelman's *D. Magni Ausonii Burdigalensis Opera* (Bodleian Library, shelf-mark Auct. S. 5. 22), the printed text of *Mosella* 438 reads:
     Haec ego vivifica ducens ab origine gentem.

Scaliger underlined *vivifica* and wrote *vivisca* in the margin. This is not, unlike most of his notes, a reading from *V*, which lacks most of the *Mosella*. And Vinet claimed it for his own in the preface to his edition of 1575, where he summarized a lost letter from Scaliger to Salomon: 'Cui (= Salomon) quum rescripsisset Scaliger, ac mihi multa salute ascripta, locum illum de Vivisca, pro Vivifica, mire probasset . . .' (repr. in *CTC* iv, p. 207). Moreover, Scaliger also wrote *Magni* (for *magnum*) in the margin at *Mosella* 290, *magnes* (beside *Achates*) at 316, and *Afflatamque* (for *Afflictamque*) at 317. The first and third of these could have come to him from an early draft of Vinet's commentary, which presents the first as a conjecture ('*magni*, mallem') and the second as a variant reported by Poelman 'in libris duobus antiquis'; see *Ausonii Burdigalensis . . . Opera*, ed. Vinet (Bordeaux, 1580), sigs. Ee3ʳ, Ff2ʳ⁻ᵛ; the interpretation of *Achates* as *magnes* is also Vinet's, ibid. Only one of Scaliger's notes on the *Mosella* – 'transtris, et dum' for 'transire deum' at 206 – has no direct counterpart in Vinet. All in all, then, it seems likely that Scaliger was here too claiming the ideas of others as his own. It is interesting that he much later, accused Vinet of plagiarizing him in the 2nd edition of his commentary (1590); see *Epistolae*, p. 439.

181. H. de la Ville de Mirmont, *Le Manuscrit de l'Île Barbe*, II–III, *passim*. This splendid repertory of conjectures and collection of information about their authors is invaluable but needs to be treated with caution. The author's hatred of Scaliger leads him to draw a great many unconvincing inferences from his sources. It is relevant to point out that Scaliger stole from Poelman as well as Vinet. In his working copy of Poelman's edition, he acidly criticized the appended selection of Greek epigrams imitated by Ausonius, which contained poems written after Ausonius' lifetime: 'Atqui Palladas, et Agathias post Ausonium fuerunt' (p. 342). But he reprinted Poelman's collection – including the offending pieces by Agathias and Palladas – in his own edition, pp. 303–18, without indicating that he had drawn his material from Poelman. And he changed the order of the epigrams, very probably in order to cover his tracks.

182. On pp. 62–3, e.g., he noted that where Poelman's edition gave the title of an epigram as *Nerva Imp.*, the MS read *Tetrarcha*; but he did not note that where an earlier epigram was headed *T. Vespasianus* in the printed edition, the MS read merely *Vespasianus*, or that where yet another epigram was headed *Sergius Galba* in the printed edition, the MS read *Galba* only. The entire collation is shot through with similar inconsistencies.

183. Scaliger records the following readings for *Ep.* XIV: abest *e* (line 2); *leviora, nomismata* (line 17; MS *lebiora*); *oculis* (line 29); *villica, linq* (line 56; MS *vilicalini*); *Corroco* (line 60); *ligari* (line 61); *curbi* (line 62); *dependere* (line 68); *Scillito, corpurgeris* (line 69; MS *corpus geris*); *Anticipesque vivum v.* sed eadem manu correctum infra. *Anticipesque tuum* (line 70: MS of corr.: *Anticipetque*); *protinus* (line 80); *Et post, semipedem, duos Iambos* (line 87; om. Poelman); *Teo* (line 94); *Tostam, et agnam* (line 101); *taberna* (line 104). In line 57 Scaliger changes *Collaque* to *Colaque*; in line 60 he adds *-que* to *lethalis*; in line 85 he underlines Poelman's marginal variant reading *Phaleucii* (MS *Phaleucius*). Since he does not write his normal *v.* by these notes I have not counted them as part of his collation proper.

184. Scaliger's text follows the MS or incorporates changes based on it in the following instances: abest *e* (line 2); *villica lini* (line 56); *Carroco* (line 60); *Scillite, cor purgeris* (line 69); *Anticipesque tuum* (line 70); *protinus* (line 80); *Et post semipedem duos iambos* (line 87); *Tostam* (line 101); *taberna* (line 104). His text also gives *Colaque* in line 57 and *Phalaecus* in line 85.

185. Scaliger, *Ausonianae lectiones*, I.21; ed. 1588, p. 85: 'Epigramma de Penelope fragmentum est, et reliquiae iusti poematis, ut apparet, in quo castigat stili sui

ubertatem, et luxuriem Ausonius. Denique nihil fere in eius poematis reperias, quod eius saeculi scholasticum tumorem referat. Ita omnia ad imitationem veterum, tanquam ad examen quoddam exiguntur.' Cf. also I.20.

186. Scaliger, *Ausonianae lectiones*, I.20, p. 81: 'Sed non omnium est de his sententiam ferre. Odi profanum vulgus, et arceo. Quid mirum si mysteria haec non norunt, qui ad eorum penetralia nunquam accesserunt? Quare taceant, si sapiunt. Quorum ego iudicia de poetis non pluris facio, quam ipsorum poemata. Quanquam, ut ingenue fatear, pro illis ne manum quidem verterim. Eos igitur missos faciamus. Vnum addam. Omnia ferre possum. Paedagogicum iudicium ferre non possum.'

187. See esp. *Ausonianae lectiones*, I.28, p. 113: 'Certe ego tantum illi veteri exemplari tribuo, ut melius neque fidelius me nancisci posse sperem. Erat enim vetustissimis Longobardorum characteribus exaratum.'

188. Scaliger, *Ausonianae lectiones*, II.12, p. 171: 'Non dissimulabo in veteri libro primum scriptum fuisse, *Anticipesque vinum*. Mendose, ut apparet ex modulo syllabae. At doctus librarius agnovit commissum manus nimis properantis, et emendavit, *Anticipesque tuum*.' The reader will note that Scaliger misread what he had recorded in his collation – for there he gave the MS reading correctly as *vivum*.

189. See n. 183, above.

190. *Ausonianae lectiones*, II.13, p. 173: 'Sed dubium est, utrum in illo libro *Tostam*, an *Tortam* scriptum esset, quia characteres Longobardici nullam differentiam inter R, et S, faciunt.'

191. See e.g. *Ausonianae lectiones*, I.1, I.2, I.5, I.30.

192. For an interesting application of the *Notitia* see *Ausonianae lectiones*, I.30, p. 120. That Scaliger saw himself as contributing to a well-established field of late antique topographical studies is clear from II.6, pp. 142-3: 'A Rheni ostiis, et paludibus ad Garumnae usque ostia, vel ad Santonos usque, veteres vocarunt eum omnem tractum litus Saxonicum, quod omnem illam oram Saxones piratae myoparonibus infestam haberent. Id quod nemo paulo in historiis declinantis imperii exercitatior ignorat.'

193. Scaliger, *Ausonianae lectiones*, I.10, pp. 44-5:
   Minus malorum munere expertus Dei.
   Caussam addit:
   Errore quod non deviantis filiae,
   Poenaque laesus coniugis   [*Comm. Proff. Burd.*, V, 35, 37-8].
   Non enim cuivis nota est historia. Nam Euchrotia Delphidii uxor cum aliis in synodo Burdigalensi damnata est Treveris a Maximo tyranno, quod Priscilliani haeresi nomen dedissent. Sed quia nihil ἀνέγγυον, neque ἀμάρτυρον producere debemus, proferam verba ex vetustiss. scheda, ubi huius rei mentio sit . . .'.

194. Scaliger, *Ausonianae lectiones*, I.24, pp. 93-8, esp. p. 94: 'Constantini autem de Arelate constitutionem communicavit mihi Fr. Roaldus, Doctor meus, vir totius antiquitatis peritissimus, et fidissimus iuris interpres. Nolui igitur lectorem tam egregio antiquitatis monumento fraudare, ut praeter luculentos locos in illa, quibus Ausonius non parum illustratur, sit, quo plurimum illi viro se debere omnes studiosi fateantur.'

195. Scaliger, *Ausonianae lectiones*, I.15, pp. 60-1: 'Proscholus autem ab eodem Ausonio redditur subdoctor. Erat enim in schola ille, qui non docendis tam pueris, quam eorum moribus praefectus erat. Ut scilicet concinne ad magistrum accederent, ut togam componerent, ut omni gestu, incessu, vestitu compositi essent. Nam ante scholae auditorium erat locus Proscholii nomine, ab auditorio ipso velo tanquam aliquo intergerrivo pariete disseptus. Ibi pueri conveniebant eius loci praefectum, quem Proscholum vocabant, ut admonerentur officii sui

ante, quam ad magistrum reducto velo accederent. Quod sane institutum non possum non valde commendare. Id ego didici ex veteribus puerorum colloquiis utraque lingua scriptis. In quibus ita loquitur puer: ὡς δὴ ἦλθον, πρὸς τὴν κλίμακα ἀνέβην διὰ τῶν βαθμῶν ἀτρέμα,ὡς ἔδει. καὶ ἐν τῷ προσχολίῳ ἀπέθηκα βίῤῥιον καὶ κατέψηξα τρίχας. καὶ οὕτως ἡρμένῳ κέντρωνι εἰσῆλθον. καὶ πρῶτον ἠσπασάμην καθηγητάς, συμμαθητάς.’

196. Casaubon, note on verso of p. 255, in his copy of the 1588 edition of the *Ausonianae lectiones* (Eton College Library, shelf-mark Bc.8.21): ‘Multa in Ausonianis his L. tractat Scal. de nostra Gall. et fortuna administrationis eius sub tempora inclinantis imperii. Multa item de appellationibus multorum locorum docte et acute . . .’. On Scaliger’s interest in the legal history of the later Empire see esp. his *Epistolae*, pp. 414-24 (elaborate discussions of the *praetor* and *praefectus praetorio*, with special attention to Ausonius and to changes in the natures and powers of these offices).

197. *Querolus, antiqua comoedia*, ed. P. Daniel (Paris, 1564), sig. Fjʳ⁻ᵛ: ‘De tempore nihil adeo certi adferri potest. Quod si coniecturis est locus, Theodosii temporibus aut proximis scriptam, duabus de causis arbitror: primum quod stilum Theodosiani seculi maxime redolet, deinde quod ad Rutilium inscripta est, si modo is sit Rutilius, quem seculo Theodosii fuisse constat, ut de illo optime coniicere mihi videor. Sed ut hae sunt coniecturae duntaxat, quae temporis suffragio fortasse confirmari poterunt, sic in iis probandis minus laborandum esse duxi.’

198. Ibid., sig. Fiiʳ: *‘Das honoratam quietem.*] Hic initio liceat antestari, nos locutiones ipsas atque etiam vocabula, cum usus venerit, ad stilum Theodosiani temporis quam fieri poterit sedulo esse relaturos, ut illius saeculo scriptum fuisse hoc opus convincamus, ne quis forte putet a nobis quomodocunque paginam impletam: ut hic, *dare honoratam quietem*, pro quo, *donari quiete honoratissima*, in L. LV. de decurionib. lib. XII. Cod. Theodos.’

199. Scaliger, *Ausonianae lectiones*, pp. 5-6: ‘Quosdam esse, quib. hic poeta non placet, id vero animum nostrum exercere non debet. Sunt enim iidem, qui dicunt Garumnam fluviolum esse, Burdigalam oppidulum, Aquitaniam ipsam non maiorem esse, quam sunt illae praepositurae quae uno tantum Episcopatu, aut dioecesi continentur: ita ut Senatus ipse Burdigalensis eorum sermone sit tantum una decuria senatuli municipalis. Cum eos ita loquentes audis, risum potes abstinere? Et non ridebis, cum Ausonium bonum poetam negant? Et tamen non a plebe haec audias, sed ab illis, qui honoribus amplissimis funguntur, qui in luce hominum versantur, qui in literis aliqui videri volunt . . . Nos, qui neque acuti, neque adeo hebetes in iis rebus sumus, eos amplissimos viros, siquid de supercilio remittere velint, possumus docere et quid sit Aquitania, et quid sit in literis Criticum esse.’

Chapter V

1. A. Agustín, ‘De M. Verrii Flacci, et Sex. Pompei Festi libris’, in M. *Verrii Flacci quae extant, et Sex. Pompei Festi de verborum significatione lib. xx* (Venice, 1560), sigs. Iijʳ-Iiijʳ (For the text, see Appendix to ch. V).

2. M. Schanz and K. Hosius, *Geschichte der römischen Literatur*, ii, Handbuch der Altertumswissenschaft, VIII.2 (Munich, 1935), pp. 361-7; Pauly-Wissowa, s.v. Verrius, 2) M. Verrius Flaccus, by A. Dihle.

3. Ibid.; see also *Der kleine Pauly*, s.v. Festus. 6. F. Sex. Pompeius.

4. *Epistola Pauli pontificis ad Carolum regem*, in Aldo Manuzio’s edition of Perotti’s *Cornucopiae* (Venice, 1513), cols. [1123-4] (I use this text as it would have been that known to Renaissance critics): ‘. . . ex qua ego prolixitate

superflua quaeque, et minus necessaria praetergrediens, et quaedam abstrusa penitus stilo proprio enucleans, nonnulla ita, ut erant posita, relinquens . . .'.

5. For a brief but expert account of the glossaries see M. L. W. Laistner, *Thought and Letters in Western Europe, A.D. 500 to 900*, 2nd edn. (Ithaca, N.Y. and London, 1957), pp. 222-4.

6. M. Flodr, *Incunabula Classicorum* (Amsterdam, 1973), pp. 172, 218-19.

7. A facsimile of the MS was published in 1893 by A. Therewk de Ponor.

8. I follow E. A. Lowe, 'The Naples Manuscript of Festus; its Home and Date', *Berliner philologische Wochenschrift*, 1911, xxix, cols. 917-18 = *Palaeographical Papers, 1907-1965*, ed. L. Bieler (Oxford, 1972), i, 66-7. W. M. Lindsay later argued that the MS might have been written in Dalmatia; see his 'The Farfa Type', in *Palaeographia Latina*, iii (1924), pp. 49-51, at p. 50; his arguments do not seem to be decisive.

9. For a detailed description of the MS see *Sexti Pompei Festi de Verborum significatu quae supersunt cum Pauli Epitome*, ed. W. M. Lindsay (Leipzig, 1913), pp. iii-x (hereafter referred to as *Festus*, ed. Lindsay).

10. Ibid., p. xi.

11. V. Zabughin, *Giulio Pomponio Leto. Saggio critico* (Rome and Grottaferrata, 1909-12), i, p. 222; M. Accame Lanzillotta, 'L'opera di Festo nel "Dictatum" Varroniano di Pomponio Leto (Vat. lat. 3415)', *Giornale italiano di filologia*, n.s. 11 [32] (1980), pp. 265-99.

12. *Festus*, ed. Lindsay, pp. xi-xviii.

13. P. Beroaldo, *Annotationes centum*, GKW 4113 (Bologna, 1488), fol. [ciiii^v]: 'Legimus in codice Festi Pompei vetusto, ex quo epitoma, quod passim legitur, circumscriptum fuit, Manium consecrasse Dianae Aricinae lucum Aricinum: . . . a quo Manio multi et clari viri orti sunt et per multos annos fuerunt. Vnde proverbium invulgatum est: multi Manii Aritiae' (Festus 128.15-18 L.). Cf. also fol. [ciiii^r] for a summary of Festus, 446.16-23 L. Naturally, Beroaldo also makes very heavy use of Paulus's epitome.

14. Poliziano, *Opera* (Basel, 1553), p. 284; the relevant passage is also quoted in *Sexti Pompei Festi de verborum significatione quae supersunt cum Pauli Epitome*, ed. K. O. Mueller (Leipzig, 1839), p. ii n. 2 (hereafter referred to as *Festus*, ed. Mueller). Poliziano's transcript is *U* (Vat. lat. 3368); see *Festus*, ed. Lindsay, pp. xii-xiv.

15. *Festus*, ed. Mueller, pp. xxxv-xxxvi; that Conagus's edition first appeared in 1500 (not 1510, as Mueller had stated), was first established by R. Reitzenstein, *Verrianische Forschungen* (Breslau, 1887), p. 98-9.

16. G. B. Pio, *Annotamenta*, in *Annotationes linguae Latinae Graecaeque conditae per Ioannem Baptistam Pium Bononiensem* (Bologna, 1505), *cap.* xvi, sig. D^{r-v}: 'Pompeio Festo plurimum debent qui latinas literas assectantur. Hic enim facta quadam veluti centuria collegit antiquorum verba ardua, nodosa, complicata, quae tanta facilitate felicitateque enucleavit ut melius nil supra fieri possit et excogitari. Multa nos ad illustrandum hunc nobilissimum scriptorem contulimus cum Mediolani doceremus. His, quae nobis venerunt ex codice pervetusto, et ob hoc fidelissimo, qui ex Illyria Pomponio Laeto extra ingenii aleam posito fuerat oblatus, plura additurus eram et fortassis meliora, ni me Bononiam, patriam meam, princeps florentissimus Ioannes Bentivolus praeter spem redire coegisset, dum opus hoc esset sub incude.'

17. *Nonius Marcellus, Festus Pompeius, Varro*, ed. G. B. Pio (Milan, 1510), sig. [pviii^r]: 'Lector. Si fragmenta Sesti Pompei Festi quae omnia reperta hic apposita sunt, ab M littera incipiendo usque ad calcem, non sequestrata posita sunt, sed coniuncta aliis; id industria factum est, ne replicando legentes taedio afficiantur, et quia quaedam addita sunt quae non erant in exemplari Pii nostri,

sed in alio eiusmodi. Quae adeo dura sunt ut omnino recte constare non videantur; tamen ob temeritatem vitandam, et ne quid ipsorum fragmentorum omitteretur, iusta exemplar impressa sunt. Quae si Pius ipse, qui propter sui absentiam ea castigare nequivit, sed nec ipsius exemplar revidere, dum imprimeretur, affuisset, correctiora haberentur. Itaque ne ipsi Pio attribuas eas additiones, quae sunt incorreptiores, ab alieno exemplari sumptas, inferius annotatae sunt.' See also *Festus*, ed. Mueller, pp. xxxv-xxxvi, where the text is reproduced in its original punctuation.

18. Cf. *Festus*, ed. Lindsay, p. xxii, for Mommsen's description of the 1500 edition; his strictures certainly hold for the 1510 edition accessible to me.

19. Fr. Baudouin, *Libri duo in leges Romuli, et leges XII Tab., quibus fontes Iuris Civilis explicantur*, 2nd edn. (Paris, 1554), p. 36: 'Ne ignoraremus tamen omnia, reliquias collegi, quas potui: et sexaginta duo consarcinavi capita, non iisdem fortasse verbis, quibus edita primum fuerant (id enim praestare non possumus) sed eadem tamen, quae fuit Decemvirorum, sententia.'

20. Ibid., p. 35: 'Neque vero ignorare debemus, Romanam saepe linguam mutatam esse, vel potius, quae rudis et aspera prius erat, sensim excultam et perpolitam fuisse.'

21. Ibid., pp. 35-6: 'Commemorat Pompeius Festus multa 12. Tabularum verba, quae, nisi interpretaretur ipse, nunquam intelligeremus, veluti, PEDEM STRVIT, pro, fugit. SARPVNTVR VINEAE, pro, putantur. RVPITIAS, pro damnum dederis. PORTVM, pro domo. Ac sane si integra illa capita éxtarent, nulla nos verborum difficultas deterreret, quin sententiam pervestigaremus. Sed mutila fragmenta, ex quibus nullus sensus eligi posset, non visum est esse operae precium inter leges 12 Tab. referre. Quod quidem si facere instituissem, non tam legum, quam inanium verborum congeriem ostentassem . . . Multa huius generis ex veterum monumentis repetere possem de significatione verborum antiquorum, quibus usae sunt 12. Tabulae: sed legum, non verborum studiosi sumus.' After this policy was challenged by le Caron and others (on whom see below), Baudouin restated it in even stronger terms in the 3rd and heavily revised edition of his work: *Commentarii de legibus XII Tabularum* (Basel, 1557), *cap.* XLIX, esp. p. 250: 'Supersunt apud Festum nonnulla XII Tabularum fragmenta: sed ita lacera, itaque mendosa, ut cur ea nunc colligere debeam, nihil esse causae putem. Festus admonet, portum appellari domum in hac, quam recitat, lege XII Tab. CVI TESTIMONIVM DESIT, OB PORTVM OBVAGVLATVM ITO. Quid illud sibi velit, ingenue fateor me nescire. Sunt apud eum multa verba ex XII Tabulis repetita. Sed de rebus nunc magis, quam de verbis agimus.' The law in question is cited at 262.20-2 and 514.6-8 L.; le Caron had discussed it – and sneered at his predecessors for omitting it – in 1555 (op. cit., in n. 22, fol. 183^{r}): 'Hanc legem a Festo Pompeio duobus locis repetitam, caeteros neglexisse miror.'

22. L. le Caron, *Ad leges duodecim tabularum liber singularis*, in J. U. Zasius, *Catalogus legum antiquarum, una cum interpretatione* (n. p., 1555), fols. 154^{r}-187^{v}. On le Caron's interest in Roman law, see D. R. Kelley, 'Louis Le Caron philosophe', in *Philosophy and Humanism. Essays in Honor of Paul Oskar Kristeller*, ed. E. P. Mahoney (Leiden, 1976), pp. 35-6; Kelley shows that this branch of study was rather a peripheral one for le Caron.

23. Le Caron, *Liber singularis*, fol. 187^{r}: '*Qui in bello pedem struit, capite punitor.* Huius legis describendae (quam ex Romana historia collegi) monuit me Festus. Cum enim legissem veteres eum, qui ignavia exercitum deseruisset, capite punisse, atque in locum Festi incidissem, in quo scribit, Pedem struit, significare fugit: ut in 12. ait Servius Sulpitius [232.3-4 L.], hoc caput restituere conatus sum; an foeliciter, aliorum sit iudicium.'

24. B. Brisson, *Selectarum ex iure civili Antiquitatum libri duo* (Paris, 1556); i.3,

fol. 8^r, from Festus 408.37–410.1 L. Here as elsewhere my translations are greatly indebted to those of Warmington, in the Loeb *Remains of Old Latin*, III. Brisson deserves a detailed study; for the moment see the useful indications in D. J. Gordon, '*Hymenaei*. Ben Jonson's Masque of Union', *JWCI* viii (1945), pp. 128–32, 140–5 = *The Renaissance Imagination. Essays and Lectures by D. J. Gordon*, ed. S. Orgel (Berkeley, Los Angeles, and London, 1975), pp. 174–8, 282–9, where his work on ancient marriage customs is placed in its proper context within the Renaissance antiquarian tradition.

25. Brisson, *Antiquitatum libri*, fols. 8^v–9^r: 'Secundum caput ex Sex. Pomp. huc translatum est, quod mire antea depravatum, V. C. Aemarus Ranconnetus, antiquitatis diligentissimus investigator, librorum veterum beneficio integritati suae restituit. . . . Permittebat ergo . . . lex manus iniectionem in eum qui vocatus sequi detrectaret vel fugeret. Nam ita pedem struit in xii Tab. accipi Festus tradit.'

26. Ibid., I.5, fol. 16$^{r–v}$: 'Nec minus explodendum est quod idem refert, *Qui in bello pedem struit capite punitor*. Nam verba haec pedem struit, quibus ille ad haec fingenda ductus est, ad aliud caput pertinuisse supra docuimus.'

27. J. Cujas, *Observationum et emendationum libri xvii* (Cologne, 1578), VII.16, pp. 308–10, at p. 308: 'De manus iniectione loquuntur saepe XII tab. Vt alio capite, SI CALVITVR, PEDEMVE STRVIT MANVM ENDO IACITO. . . .'.

28. A good many of the relevant passages are assembled in the section headed *Annotationes et castigationes doctorum virorum in Sex. Pompeium Festum eiusque epitomam nunc primum in lucem editae* of the 1584 and 1593 editions of Scaliger's Festus (I use the latter, which was published by P. Santandreanus). Cf. *Festus*, ed. Mueller, p. xxxvii. Mueller's introduction and apparatus are also of great value as guides to earlier Festan literature.

29. P. Vettori, *Variarum lectionum libri xxxviii* (Florence, 1582), XVII.2, pp. 192–3, at p. 193 (misnumbered 195): 'Cum vero supra ipse affirmarim me librum habere Sex. Pompeii, exscriptum de antiquissimo exemplari, totam rem accuratius, ut fides eius auctoritasque augeatur, commemorabo. Angelus Politianus in lxxiii capite Miscellaneorum, narrat se Romae accepisse a Manilio Rallo fragmentum quoddam Sex. Pompeii, sane quam vetustum, nonnullasque itidem pagellas eiusdem exemplaris a Pomponio Laeto, quae omnia, ut ostendit illic, cum descripsisset, paucis ab hinc annis ego incidi in adversaria quaedam ipsius in taberna libraria, quibus continebantur etiam hae reliquiae Festi, atque emi, manu Politiani cognita. Tanta tamen ille celeritate in scribendo usus fuerat, litterisque adeo minutis, ac saepe etiam per notas totis vocibus indicatis, quod suum propriumque hominis erat, cum huiuscemodi aliquid, quod ipsius tantum usibus serviret, in commentariis adnotaret, ut vix intelligi possint.'

30. Ibid., XXII.21, pp. 269–70, at p. 270: 'Id autem factum puto, quia inde etiam olim descripserit imperitus aliquis homo, nec in veteribus libris versatus; cuius tamen postea scripto, corrupto videlicet et manco, usi fuerint aliqui typographi pro exemplari. Nam idem etiam, quod multis locis factum est, cum plenam integramque explicationem alicuius rei non invenerat, quamvis partes illius aliquae restarent, ipsas relinquebat.'

31. See, in addition to the chapters already cited, ibid., XVIII.7, XXV.9; cf. *Festus*, ed. Lindsay, p. xiii.

32. See Festus 450.22–452.22 L.; Paul. *ex* Fest. 66.5–6 L.

33. Vettori, *Variae lectiones*, XVIII.7, at p. 208: 'Nam antiquitus etiam de hoc quaeri solitum, variasque moris huius iam tunc rationes allatas Sex. Pompeius in xvii libro testatur.' The phrase remains puzzling; cf. R. M. Ogilvie, *Early Rome and the Etruscans* (n.p., 1976), pp. 137–8.

34. L. Ceretti, 'I precedenti e la formazione dell' "Editio" di S. Pompeo Festo di Antonio Agustín', *AIV* cxi (1952–3), 153–64.

35. Agustín, 'De Flacci et Festi libris', sig. Iiiij^r: 'Et quoniam Verrius Flaccus primus huius operis auctor fuit, quaecumque eius opera extant, quaeque de eo ab aliis referantur, initio collocavimus.' Agustín's collection was a characteristically professional piece of work; he distinguished between fragments that could and that could not be assigned to specific works by Verrius, and he gave careful references to the sources on which he drew (chiefly Gellius, Macrobius, Festus himself, and other grammatical writers, especially Charisius).

36. Agustín, 'De Flacci et Festi libris', sig. Iiiij^r: 'Sed nos hoc amplius fecimus, quod illi neglexerunt: ut lectores admoneremus, quae Festi, quaeque Pauli essent.'

37. Ibid.: 'Omnia quoque fragmenta Festi describi curavimus, ne quid desiderari posset; in quibus interpretandis quam operam posuerimus ex his, quae in commentariis adscripsimus, iudicare lector possit. Habuimus autem hoc monumentum antiquitatis ex locupletissima bibliotheca amplissimi viri Rainutii Farnesii Cardinalis, cui propter singularem bonarum literarum amorem, ingeniumque praeclarum, atque in utraque lingua maximos progressus, et non vulgarem eruditionem, a Michaele Silvio Cardinali ex testamento relictum est.'

38. Agustín, *Annotationes*, sig. [pvii^v] *ad* 356.5-7 L.: 'Rideo] Hoc loco in antiquo libro est Sexti Pompei Festi lib. xviij'; sig. [Qv^v] *ad* 444.12-23 L.: 'Scirpus] In veteri libro est hoc loco. Sex. Pompei Festi de verborum significat. lib. xviij. Incipit lib. xviiij"; sig. Q^r *ad* 322.11-13 l.: 'Ruspari] In ultimis verbis mendum esse notatum est R. littera adiecta in veteri libro'; sig. R^r *ad* 452.27-32 and Paul. *ex* Fest. 453.2; sig. Rij^r *ad* 382.2-5 L. and Paul. *ex* Fest. 383.1 L.

39. Agustín, 'Notarum explanatio', ibid., sig. [Vvi^v]: 'In margine posita cum cruce, vel alia nota, significant variam scripturam ex aliquo libro. Quod si in fine addatur semicirculus, significatur ex docti alicuius viri coniectura ita posse emendari. Vbicumque ante F vel postea adduntur tria puncta, significatur verba quidem esse Festi, sed non ex antiquo libro sumpta.
   Duobus semicirculis inclusa in contextu, reiicienda esse, licet in omnibus libris reperta fuerint.'

40. Agustín, *Annotationes*, sig. [Mvii^r] *ad* 124.2-12 L. and Paul. *ex* Fest. 125.8-13 L.; sig. [Nv^v] *ad* 190.32-192,1 L. and Paul. *ex* Fest. 191.10-13 L.; sig. [Ovi^r] *ad* 250.5-8 L.; sig. [Pvi^v] *ad* 344.11-15 L. and Paul. *ex* Fest. 345.3-5; sig. [Pvii^v] *ad* 320.24-322.10 L. and Paul. *ex* Fest. 321.7-8 L.; sig. Qiii^r, *ad* 439.10-18 L.; sig. Rii^v *ad* 380.25-32 L. and Paul. *ex* Fest. 381.2-5 L.; sig. [Rv^r] *ad* 394.33-37 L. and Paul. *ex* Fest. 395.6 L.; sig. Sii^r *ad* 482.7-27 L. and Paul. *ex* Fest. 483.5-6. At sig. [Ovi^r] Agustín calls Faerno '. . . optimo numerorum censori'.

41. Ibid., sig. Nii^v *ad* 162.17-24 L. and Paul. *ex* Fest. 163.9-10 L.: 'Nepotes] Maximam partem horum verborum Festi ex verbis Pauli interpretaberis praeter id, quod de Tuscis initio dicitur, quodque in fine πόδεσσιν scriptum est. De Tuscis nihil aliud habeo, quam me opinari Tuscos eo nomine usos. Graecum autem esse cognovi, cum mihi Fulvius Vrsinus eius linguae peritissimus, a quo multa in hoc libro emendata sunt, ostendit Apollonium lib. iiij et Theocr. Idyll. xvij in hac significatione hoc verbo uti. Eustathius quoque idem affirmat, in Δ Odyss. Fieri etiam potest, ut Apollonii carmen retulerit Festus cuius finis est: Tεοῖσι νεπόδεσσι ἑτοίμη. Quem vero significet illis syllabis (chus inter), an Aristarchum, vel Callimachum, aliumve, nobis incertum est.' Cf. sig. O^r *ad* 235.8-10 L.; sig. Oii^r *ad* 226.2-4 L.; sig. Riiii^v *ad* 414.23-31 L.; sig. S^v *ad* 504.1-3 L.

42. Ibid., sig. [Nvi^{r-v}] *ad* 202.14-204.23 L.: 'Opima] Carolus Sigonius, a quo multa in hoc libro emendata sunt, quod deest post illa verba, intra annos, ita posse sarciri existimat . . . [A long series of conjectures follows.] . . . Sed mihi hoc non satis probatur . . . Quod vero ad interpretationis rationem attinet, vehementer probo eius opinionem.'

43. Ibid., sig. [Ovii^r] *ad* 268.1–2 L. and Paul. *ex* Fest. 269.1–2 L.: 'Primanus) Emendatiore, ut opinor, libro usus est Paulus, nam nos in veteri neque Catonis verba neque significationem habemus, cum tamen nihil in hac parte lacerum existat . . .'; sig. Piii^r *ad* 310.28–35 L. and Paul. *ex* Fest. 311.6–8 L.: 'Quando) Verbis Festi pauca desunt. Sed omnia exempla videntur ad tempus pertinere. Ideo miror unde Paulus epitomen confecerit, nisi meliorem librum, quod ex aliis cognosco, habuerit.'

44. Ibid., sig. L^r *ad* Paul. *ex* Fest. 17.3–5 L.: 'Acerra) Paulus libenter utitur his verbis: solebat, incendebantur, reponebat, ne videatur cum Festo in religione consentire.'

45. For modern discussion of this point see *Festus*, ed. Mueller, p. xxxii; A. D. Momigliano, *Studies in Historiography* (London, 1966), p. 256 n. 25.

46. Agustín, *Annotationes*, sig. Liiii^V *ad* Paul. *ex* Fest. 32.14–17 L.: 'Barbari] . . . locum Apostoli ex epist. ad Rom. I nemo credat Festi fuisse, sed Pauli, qui epitomen confecit'; sig. [Rvii^r] *ad* Paul. *ex* Fest. 407.6–8 L.: 'Supparus] Camisiam dixisse Festum non arbitror, ut nec minare, licet utroque verbo Paulus utatur.'

47. Ibid., sig. Siiii^V *ad* Paul. *ex* Fest. 506.16–21 L.: 'Vespae] Suspectus locus, quo refertur Martialis, quem non alio loco nominaverat, et Festo fuit, ut arbitror, posterior'; cf. Reitzenstein, *Verrianische Forschungen*, pp. 21–2 n. 1, and Agustín, sig. Qiii^r *ad* 436.14–21 L. and Paul. *ex* Fest. 437.6–9 L.

48. Paul. *ex* Fest. 147.5–6 L.: 'Municipalia sacra vocabantur, quae ante Urbem conditam colebantur.'

49. Festus 146.9–12 L.: 'Municipalia sacra vocantur, quae ab initio habuerunt ante civitatem Romanam acceptam; quae observare eos voluerunt pontifices, et eo more facere, quo adsuessent antiquitus.'

50. Agustín, *Annotationes*, sig. [Mvii^V] *ad* 146.9–12 L. and Paul. *ex* Fest. 147. 5–6 L.: 'Municipalia] Paulus non intellexit, quid esset ante civitatem Ro. acceptam; et ante urbem conditam interpretatus est. Neque enim municipalia sacra sunt urbis Romae sacra, sed municipiorum.'

51. Ibid., sig. Liiii^V *ad* Paul. *ex* Fest. 47.13–18 L.: 'Centumviralia] illa verba; quae, et curiae dictae sunt; non esse Festi existimo. Vide Curia'; cf. sig. [Lvi^r] *ad* Paul. *ex* Fest. 42.16–24 L., the note to which Agustín's cross-reference alludes.

52. This order has been often and elaborately studied; see esp. Reitzenstein, *Verrianische Forschungen*. Cf. now the critique of all previous theories in A. Moscadi, 'Verrio, Festo e Paolo', *Giornale italiano di filologia*, n.s. 10 [31] (1979), pp. 17–36.

53. Agustín, 'De M. Verrii Flacci et Sex. Pompei Festi libris', sig. Iiii^{r-v}: 'In hac editione mutatus est verborum ordo Verrii, Festi, et Pauli: ut lector facilius, quid de quaque re scriptum sit, reperiat. Nam veteres nescio quo modo primam literam indicasse contenti, omnia verba ab eadem inchoata in unum locum conferebant. Nostri melius omnibus syllabis ordinem adhibuere literarum. Ita facile verba reperies; quae tamen si obiter dicta sint, praesto erit quaerenti index obiter dictorum.'

54. F. de Zulueta, *Don Antonio Agustín* (Glasgow, 1939), p. 28. It had in fact been customary since ancient times to treat the texts of technical works – scholia, handbooks, lexica – with far more freedom than those of literary works whose exact wording had to be preserved; see J. E. G. Zetzel, review of L. D. Reynolds and N. G. Wilson, *Scribes and Scholars*[2], *Classical Philology*, lxxii (1977), p. 182.

55. Cf. n. 53, above. Where Paulus and Festus both have entries for a single lemma, Agustín arbitrarily places one or the other first.

56. Agustín's transcriptions of individual articles were for the most part very accurate; see *Festus*, ed. Mueller, pp. xxxvi-xxxvii and p. xxxvi n. 3. But his reproduction of the spaces between words and entries was inevitably inexact. Cf. F. Orsini's comments in his letters to P. Vettori, in Nolhac, 'Piero Vettori et Carlo Sigonio: Correspondance avec Fulvio Orsini', *Studi e documenti di storia e diritto*, x (1889), pp. 91-152, esp. pp. 123-4.

57. See e.g. Agustín, *Annotationes*, sig. Miiiᵛ *ad* Paul. *ex* Fest. 94.9-11 L.: 'Italia] Licet a vitulis, vel ab Italo rege multi dicant Italiam esse appellatam. De Attalido nihil aliud accepi. Thucyd. lib. vi. Varro lib. ii. cap. v. de re rust. Columel. lib. vi. in prin. Verg. lib. I. Aen. Dionys. lib. I. Antiq. Gell. lib. xi. cap. I. Apollodorus in Bibliotheca. Steph. de Vrbibus.'

58. Agustín, *Annotationes*, sig. Qiiʳ *ad* 422.11-15 L. and Paul. *ex* Fest. 423.4-5 L.; sigs. [Lviᵛ-Lviiʳ] *ad* Paul. *ex* Fest. 65.17-19 L. See also sigs. Qiiᵛ-Qiiiʳ *ad* 440.13-28 L. and Paul. *ex* Fest. 441.4-5 L., on the *ludi saeculares*.

59. Agustín, *Annotationes*, sig. [Lviʳ⁻ᵛ] *ad* Paul. 64.6-7 l.: 'Delubrum] Duplex est huius nominis significatio, nam et pro Dei simulacro, et pro loco Deo consecrato ponitur. Varro apud Macrob. lib. III. Servius lib. II. et Iv. Aen. Asconius hanc Festi interpretationem reprehendens in Divinat.'

60. Agustín, *Annotationes*, sig. Lʳ *ad* Paul. 17.22-23 L.: 'AB oloes] Oli, pro olli, et olli pro illi: oloes autem illoes est, et pro illis accipitur Graeca terminatione . . .'; sig. Liiiiᵛ *ad* Paul. 22.5-8 L.: 'Aureliam] A sole Auselii, origo dura; forte ab aureo sole: nam aurum dicebant ausum Sabini, ut mox videbimus. sic a Corneo Cornelius, a Cereo Cerelius'; sig. [Pviʳ] *ad* 346.7-12 L. and Paul. 347.3-4 L.: 'Refutare] In Festi verbis erat Pacuvii exemplum. et quod A. in V. verteretur, ostendebatur, cum a claudo recludere sit compositum. Sed hic A tollitur, non mutatur, vel non sola mutatur, sed AV in V longum vertitur.'

61. Agustín, *Annotationes*, sig. [Lviʳ] *ad* Paul. 48.12 (a discussion of *Crustumina* and *Crustumeria*): ' . . . prima syllaba CLV. in monumentis aliquot videmus, in aliis CRV. pro tribu. Eligat ex his lector, quod sequatur. mihi Crustumina tribus placet, et Crustumeria urbs Latinorum'; sigs. Miiiᵛ-Miiiiʳ *ad* Paul. 108.5-6 L. (for a similar use of numismatic evidence); sigs [O viiiᵛ-P ʳ] *ad* 294.9 ff. L. and Paul. 295.4-6 L.

62. A. Turnèbe, *Adversaria*, X.15 (Paris, 1564-5), I, fol. 192ʳ: 'Antonius autem Augustinus rectissime et ingeniosissime vidit in ea lege 12. tab. *si adorat furto quod nec manifestum erit*, adorare esse agere . . .'; cf. Agustín, *Annotationes*, sig. Nᵛ *ad* 158.27-160.1 L. and Paul. 159.14-16 L.: 'Crederem scribi oportere nec esit; et verbum adorat significare agat; ut idem Festus scribit verbo Adorare.'

63. Agustín, *Annotationes*, sig. Oiiʳ *ad* 226.2-4 L.: 'Picati] Apud Hesichium φίκα, φίγα, et σφίγγα. Hesiodus in Theogonia φικ' ὀλοήν [326]. Lycophron in fine Alexandrae φίκειον τέρας [1465]. Picas vero pro phicas dici, ut Poenos, et Alpes, et Pilippum et triumphum manifestum est. Haec etiam Fulvius noster.'

64. Turnèbe, *Adversaria*, III.10; I, fol. 51ʳ⁻ᵛ: 'Picae apud Festum sunt Sphinges: unde et apud eum Picati: quanquam et pici, ex se picatos propagare possunt, qui Latinis sunt avidae illae volucres ferae griphes vocatae, aurum e cavernis penitus egerentes. Pilare et compilare dubium non est, quin a verbo Graeco deducantur Aeolico πιλητής, id est fur, qui φιλητής ab Hesiodo vocatur: sed Aeolum est aspirationes in tenues mutare, ut et in superiore vocabulo, pro σφίγξ, dorice φίξ, et Aeolice πίξ, unde Latinum verbum pica et picatus.'

65. Canter, *Novae lectiones*, I.3; *Annotationes et castigationes doctorum virorum in Sex. Pompeium Festum* (see n. 28 above), pp. 70-1: 'Ceterum quod ἀπὸ τοῦ φιλητοῦ deducit Festus, verbum, *Pilare*, neminem turbare debet, tametsi primae utriusque litterae sunt dissimiles: quandoquidem ista aspiratae in tenuem mutatio frequens in talibus contingit: quemadmodum et Festus ipse in verbo,

Picati, docet, cum quod Graeci φῖκα, id Latini picum dixerint. Alioqui nemo nescit Aeoles aspirata tenuiter efferre solere.'

66. P. Pithou, *Adversariorum subsecivorum libri II* (Paris, 1565), I.10, fols. 17ᵛ-18ʳ.

67. Fruterius was particularly interested in Festus. The Leiden University Library has a MS set of conjectures and interpretations headed *Iani Dousae P. et Lucae Fruterii emendationes ac notae ineditae in Festum* (MS BPL 168D, saec. xviii, manu ignota). The notes are often keyed to specific pages and lines in Scaliger's 1575 edition, and were very likely copied from a *Handexemplar* annotated by Dousa. Dousa, in turn, seems to have made use of a copy of Agustín's edition heavily annotated by Fruterius. These included both straight conjectures (e.g. fol. 62ʳ *ad* Paul. 104.4 L.: *'Mulier auguratrix*. F. argutatrix.') and attempts to fill some of the gaps in the Farnesianus (e.g. fol. 69ʳ *ad* 144.29-146.2 L.: *'Non comitia* etc. Haec sic impleri posse existimabat Fruter. noster **non comitia habebantur**, nec aliud **quicquam** in rep. fiebat, **nisi quod ultima necessitas**. et praesentanda etc. [bold characters in the original]'). Fruterius incorporated many of his best Festan conjectures into his *Verisimilia* (Leiden, 1584), I.1, I.7, I.8, I.11, I.16, I.18, II.3, II.5, II.9, II,12, II.15; thus the conjecture *argutatrix* for Paul. 104.4 L. also appears in *Verisimilia*, I.11, pp. 34-6. I.8, pp. 26-8, records a very interesting discussion between Fruterius and Dorat of 231.5-7 L. For the contributions of Junius and Giphanius see the *Annotationes et castigationes doctorum virorum*.

68. L. le Caron, *Catalogus legum antiquarum* . . . (ed. Paris, 1578), fol. 10ᵛ: ' . . . (habeo enim manuscriptum Festi librum multo integriorem illo qui ab Augustino editus est) . . .'; this is quoted in *Festus*, ed. Mueller, p. vii n. 5, from an edn., Paris, 1567.

69. As Mueller points out (*Festus*, pp. vii-viii), the 'new readings' from le Caron's MS reinforce his own old conjectures with suspicious elegance, especially where Brisson and others had attacked them. See e.g. fol. 25ᵛ: 'In meo libro haec verba tum in xii. Tab. tum in foedere Latino repetuntur: quod siquis xii Tab. esse neget, non contendo.' This is anent the law 'Pecuniam quis nancitor habeto, et si quid pignoris nancitor, sibi habeto', which le Caron had assigned to the Twelve Tables in his 1555 commentary on Zasius, fol. 184ᵛ, and which Brisson had re-attributed to the Latin treaty in his *Selectae antiquitates* of 1556, I.5, fol. 16ʳ⁻ᵛ. See nn. 127-8, below for the texts. On le Caron's congenital inability to report honestly or accurately on his work see also P. F. Girard, 'Le manuscrit des *Gromatici* de l'évêque Jean du Tillet', *Mélanges Fitting*, ii (Montpellier, 1908), p. 278.

70. 'Henr. Stephanus lectori', in *Homeri et Hesiodi certamen* (Geneva, 1573), p. 180: 'Quoniam locus qui ex Tiberio Donato in Virgilii vita fuit allatus pag. 129, longe aliter legitur in vulgatis editionibus, admonendum te putavi, non absque veteris exempl. autoritate mutatum fuisse . . . Sed animadversione digna praecipue sunt verba illa, Paro quidam, pro Graeco vocabulo παρῳδήσας. Huius autem adeo insignis et memorabilis depravationis te commonefaciendum censui, simulque emendationis, non solum ut tantam mutationem minime suspectam haberes, sed etiam ut huius loci exemplo cautior in aliis evaderes. Ne hoc quidem dissimulare volo, me in ea emendatione, veteris quidem exempl. fide stetisse, sed ex relatu Iosephi Scaligeri. Ideoque illi hanc emendationem, sicut in aliis Latinis scriptoribus quamplurimas, debes.'

71. Scaliger to Pithou, 24.vii.1574; *Lettres françaises*, p. 31: 'Au reste en ces jours passés j'ai faict quelque petite chose sur le Festus, laquelle est desja sur la presse.' Scaliger returned to Geneva from Basel; but in September he learned that his mother had died, and on 19.ix.1574 the Geneva Company of Pastors gave him leave to resign his post and return home. See *Registres de la Compagnie des Pasteurs de Genève*, ed. O. Fatio and O. Labarthe, iii (Geneva, 1969),

pp. 143-4. That Scaliger did not really send the commentary to the printer until he left Geneva is clear from Goulart to Simler, 22.ix.1574, in L. C. Jones, *Simon Goulart, 1543-1628* (Geneva and Paris, 1917), p. 327; Goulart to Simler, 12.xii.1574, ibid., p. 329.

72. Scaliger, ep. ded., in *M. Verrii Flacci quae extant. Sex. Pompei Festi De verborum significatione libri XX* (n.p., 1575), sig. *iiii^r: 'Vale. Abenni in agro Iuliodunensi: XI Kal. Novembr. CIƆ IƆ LXXIV' (hereafter '*Festus*, ed. Scaliger').

73. Comparison of several entries in Agustín's edition with the corresponding passages in Scaliger's editions of 1575 and 1576 revealed almost no changes of any kind — and the few that did appear were all either typographical errors on the part of Scaliger's printers or corrections of those made by Agustín's. I give a few examples:

Festus reference	Agustin	Scaliger (75)	Scaliger (76)
Paul. 13.23. L.	Adscripticii	. . . titii	. . . ticii
Paul. 26.17 L.	Adoptaticius	. . . titius	. . . titius
180.21 L.	Laevimus	Laevinus	Laevinus

That the text was printed before the commentary is clear from Scaliger to Sainte-Marthe, 2.iii.1575; Paris, Bibliothèque de l'Institut, MS 290, fol. 252^r: 'Ie n'ai aulcunes nouuelles de mon Festus, lequel y a six mois qu'il deuoit estre paracheuè le texte en estant desia imprimè.' The edition seems to have come out in February; see Jones, *Goulart*, p. 336.

74. *Festus*, ed. Scaliger, ep. ded., sig. *iii^{r-v}: 'Itaque hominis prodigiosos errores, atque crassam ignorantiam deteximus, quatenus sola coniectura negotium confecimus. Eo enim unico praesidio usi sumus usque ad undecimum librum: a quo fragmenta incipiunt, quae beneficio probissimi, atque eruditissimi viri Antonii Augustini, Episcopi Ilerdensis, edita sunt. Ea eiusmodi sunt, ut in illis fundamenta quidem ac rudereta priscorum aedificiorum agnoscas, ita tamen, ut quid in illis fundamentis olim inaedificatum fuerit, facilius divinare possis quam aedificium ipsum a fundamentis excitare.'

75. Ibid., sig. *iii^v: 'Tantum autem profecimus ex huius praestantissimi scriptoris emendatione, ut ea e tenebris eruerimus, quae antehac nec nobis ipsis cognita fuerunt; nec temere apud ullum veterum reperias, tot nempe vetustatis veneranda monimenta, praesertim ex antiquissimo Romanorum tum civili tum pontificio iure: item ex Regiis legibus, ex duodecim Tabulis, ex antiquis foederibus, et aliis, quae enumerare labor esset. Quae qui inutilia dixerit, velim is nos doceat, quid utile vocet in literis. Si enim antiquitatis cognitio nihil prodest, non video quid nobis literae prosunt.'

76. Agustín, *Annotationes*, sig. R^r *ad* 452.27-32 L.: 'Simpludiarea] Haec verba mendosa sunt (D.T. ludi, corbitoresque) quod notatum est in veteri libro R. littera'; Scaliger, *Castigationes*, p. clxxi *ad* 470.5-13 L.: '*Senacula*] Notae D.T. significant Duntaxat. Infra: Simpludearia funera sunt, quibus adhibentur D.T. ludi. hoc est Duntaxat'; cf. ibid., p. clxxvi.

77. Agustín, *Annotationes*, sigs. Qvi^v-Qvii^r *ad* 454.36-456.11 L.: 'Post Seplasia] De Septentrionibus haec intelligenda sunt . . . Haec Varro, et Gell. lib. ii. cap. xxi. Eadem Festus hoc loco scripserat. Tantum addit Ennii versus, qui non extant'; Scaliger, *Castigationes*, pp. clxxi-clxxii ad loc., at p. clxxi: 'Intelligit autem locum Ennii ex Iphigenia, quem olim in coniectaneis illustravimus.
     Quid nocti' videtur? . . .'

78. 'There is no need at all to refute Verrius' opinion either here or at several other points, since I intend to omit from the vast number of his books the words which are dead and buried and by his own admission of no use or authority, and to assemble the rest, with the greatest possible brevity, into a few books. The clearest and shortest treatment I could manage of the points on which I disagree will be found in my books entitled "*priscorum verborum cum exemplis*".'

79. Agustín, *Annotationes*, sig. [O viii^r] *ad* Paul. 257.3-4: 'Profanum] Hic locus totius libri argumentum est.' Cf. Moscadi, art. cit. (n. 52 above).

80. See n. 38, above for Agustín's report of the title found in the Farnesianus; Gellius, *Noctes Atticae*, V.xvii.1, V.xviii.2 (Agustín knew both passages and drew on them in his collection of the fragments of Verrius); Macrobius, *Saturnalia*, III.viii.9.

81. Agustín, 'De M. Verrii Flacci, et Sex. Pompei Festi libris', sig. I ii^r: 'Saepius autem Verrii errores notavit: et cur id faceret, non minus docte semper reddidit rationem.'

82. Scaliger, *Castigationes*, p. cxxxv *ad* Paul. 257.3-4L.: 'Nam quod docti viri putant Festum de his, quos in manu habemus, loqui: et peccant ipsi, et alios in errorem inducunt. Nam neque Festus hos libros, qui extant, vocasset suos, cum sint Verrii. neque in istis libris instituit reprehensionem Verrii, praeter quam in locis admodum paucis, idque obiter. neque paucos hos libros vocasset, cum supra XIX. scripserit. neque haec est horum librorum inscriptio, cum a Macrobio vetere auctore, de verborum significatione citentur. His, et pluribus rationibus, atque adeo tenore verborum Festi inductus quilibet potest advertere libros PRISCORVM VERBORVM CVM EXEMPLIS non esse eosdem cum his nostris DE VERBORVM SIGNIFICATIONE.'

83. *Festus*, ed. Scaliger, ep. ded., sig. *iii^r: 'Festum enim, qui Verrii Flacci libros breviasset, aequo animo debuisse ferre, si quomodo ipse Verrium tractaverat, similiter ipse ab isto Paulo acciperetur. Hoc unum excipio: si Festo hoc modo pereundum fuit, digniorem arborem, ut est in proverbio, suspendio deligendam fuisse.'

84. Paulus 8.10-12 L.

85. Scaliger, *Castigationes*, p. xxvi *ad* Paul. 8.9-14 L.: '*Aurum*] Male citatur Hippocrates. Legendum enim Hypsicrates, qui a Varrone, et Gellio lib. XVI. citatur, scripsitque de Romanis vocibus, quae a vetere lingua Graeca derivantur.'

86. Festus 138.2-6 L.

87. Agustín, *Annotationes*, sig. [Mvi^v] ad loc.: 'Meta . . . stices] Metaphrastices scriptum fuisse videtur; sed mendose: pro Metaphrastice, vel Metaphrasi; vel pro Metastasi, vel Metabasi; interpretari autem existimamus, cum poetae propter necessitatem metri aliud pro alio ponunt.'

88. Scaliger, *Castigationes*, p. lxxxvii ad loc.

89. Goulart to Simler, 22.ix.1574; Jones, *Goulart*, p. 327. Casaubon, marginal note in his copy of the 1575 edition of Scaliger's Festus (Eton College Library, shelf-mark Be.8.17), *Castigationes*, p. clxii: 'Prov. Sabini quod volunt somniant. Foelix divinatio et plane divina.' Cf. the note on p. li: 'No. Subtilissima haec: sed parum certa.' G. J. Vossius to F. Gomarus. Vossius, *Epistolae* (Cologne, 1691), I, p. 117: 'Equidem longe mitius de Scaligero censeo: Sed tamen tantam licentiam probare non possum, non magis, quam candorem, cum dissimulat quae in Antiquis Varronis Codd. invenisset. Et cui persuaserit, se in Festo corrigendo, non usum esse schedis Laeti, dum ita supplet quae desunt, prout in iis saepe schedis legebantur? Non haec candidi animi fuere.' This reference was kindly supplied by C. S. M. Rademaker; Vossius's accusation seems unfounded.

90. Paulus 5.1-2 L.: 'Ambarvales hostiae appellabantur, quae pro arvis a duobus fratribus sacrificabantur.'

91. Agustín, *Annotationes*, sig. Liii^r ad loc.: 'Ambarvales] A duodecim fratribus scriberem, non a duobus, ex Plin. lib. XVIII. cap. II. Gellio lib. VI. cap. VII. et Fulgentio de obscuris, ut intelligatur de duodecim fratribus arvalibus, sed quae sequuntur Macrobius refert lib. III uti a Pompeio Festo conscripta: et in his nulla mentio fratrum; ideo videndum est, an arvis, et frugibus emendare oporteat.'

92. Scaliger, *Castigationes*, p. xvi ad loc.: '*Ambarvales*] A duobus fratribus. fortasse pro XII. legerat II. et fugit eum nota denarii numeri.'

93. Scaliger, *Castigationes*, p. xl *ad* Paul. 47.3–4 L.: '*Centuriata*] Mirum quam placuerit huic Paulo nomen Curiae. hoc enim omnibus rebus attribuit. Vult Centurias, Curias fuisse. item Tribus ipsas: ut in voce Centumviralia, et in voce Curia. Quare superius in voce Centumviralia, impactum Festo pittacium a Paulo iis verbis, QVAE CVRIAE DICTAE SVNT. Item hic, ITEM CVRIATA. et in voce Curia, QVIBVS POSTEA SVNT ADDITAE QVINQVE. Quae omnia ea confidentia tollere possumus, qua posita fuerunt.'

94. See above, n. 51.

95. See in general G. Goetz, 'Joseph Scaliger's glossographische Studien und Pläne', *Berichte über die Verhandlungen der Sächsischen Gesellschaft der Wissenschaften zu Leipzig*, Phil.-hist. Klasse, 1888, pp. 219–34.

96. Paulus 3.19 L.: 3.22–23 L.: 'Adoriam laudem sive gloriam dicebant, quia gloriosum eum putabant esse, qui farris copia abundaret.'

97. Scaliger, *Castigationes*, p. vii ad loc.: '*Adoream*] Glossarium vetus, cuius ope multa vetustatis situ sepulta eruimus: Adoriosus, . . . Lege . . . Ador . . . Quin intelligat nostrum Pomp. Festum dubitandum non est.' Scaliger had already corrected this glossary entry in 2 of his working copies: Leiden, MS Scal. 61, fol. 72^r, col. 2 and MS BPG 3, fol. 7^r (the latter = col. 6 of Scaliger's working copy of H. Estienne's *Glossaria duo*, 1573; see K. A. de Meyier and E. Hulshoff Pol, *Codices Bibliothecae Publicae Graeci* (Leiden, 1965), p. 7; *Corpus Glossariorum Latinorum*, ii, p. xix, i, pp. 248 ff., esp. 255). The correction does not appear in Scaliger's 3rd working copy, MS Scal. 25. A comparison of readings from all 3 working copies with those cited in the *Castigationes in Festum* suggests that Scaliger used all 3 while working on Festus; it is not possible to establish any chronological order among his 3 sets of notes, save that the MSS certainly antedate Estienne's edition.

98. See e.g. *Castigationes*, p. xxvii *ad* Paul. 3.12–15 L.: '*Axamenta*] Glossarium: Axamenta, στίχοι ἐπὶ θυσιῶν ἡρακλέους. Vbi notandum est sacrificia, quae Salii faciebant, non Marti, sed Herculi fieri: cum tamen Salii sint Martis sacerdotes. Quare scriptor doctissimus illius Glossarii secutus est auctores eos, quos et Virgilius, dum attribuit Salios Herculi, non Marti.'

99. Ibid., p. vii *ad* Paul. 3.22–23: 'Hinc, quam multa ad arbitrium suum mutaverit, mutilaverit, perverterit Longobardus iste, facile adverti potest. Nam quae Glossarius ille annotat, ex hoc integro loco deprompta fuerunt sine ullo dubio.'

100. See e.g. ibid., p. lv *ad* Paul. 72.20–22 L.: p. lviii *ad* Paul. 78.4–5 L. (where Scaliger wrongly but understandably attributes the glossary to 'is Philoxenus, qui temporibus Iustiniani Consul fuit cum Probo'); p. lxx *ad* Paul. 92.16–17 L.; p. clvi *ad* Paul. 350.13–16 L.; p. cxciii *ad* Paul. 503.8–11 L.

101. See esp. Goetz, art. cit. (n. 95, above); Lindsay's edition of Festus in the *Glossaria Latina* is a direct extension of the editorial principles Scaliger devised.

102. *Scaligerana II*, s.v. Glossaires, p. 349: 'Les GLOSSAIRES ne valent rien pour le Grec, mais seulement pour le Latin. P. Daniel qui n'estoit pas des plus doctes, les avoit trouvez à S. Germain, les montra à Monsieur Turnebus et à moy. Je m'en suis bien servy en mon Festus; je l'ay cité le premier. Fulvius Ursinus mea Simia se les fit avoir, et depuis les a citez.'

103. The precise authorship of DS and its relation to the shorter recension are still much disputed; on the discovery and the excitement it aroused see esp. H. Hagen, *Zur Geschichte der Philologie und zur römischen Litteratur. Vier Abhandlungen* (Berlin, 1879), p. 22 and nn.

104. Scaliger to Daniel, 1.vii.1574, in F. Kortüm, *De Societatis Atticae origine atque institutis*, Progr. Heidelberg (Heidelberg, 1844), Epilogus, pp. 8–9: 'Monsieur

et frere! je receus ces jours passés vos lettres et bienqu'elles fussent datées de long temps, ensemble quelques fragmens de votre *Servius*, lesquels me sont bien venus à propos pour mon *Festus*, lequel est sur la presse avecques mes notes . . . Je vous remercie bien fort de vostre *Servius*. Et eusse voulu que vous y eussiés adjousté *ritus et ceremonias*, qui m'eussent fort aidé pour mon *Festus*. Encores ce ne seroit pas trop tard s'il vous plaisoit me les envoier de bonne heure.'

105. Scaliger to Daniel, 24.vii.1574; Bern, Burgerbibliothek, MS 141, item 37: 'Ie me suis fort bien servi de vos fragmens en mon Festus, et en ai bien faict mon proffit' (previously quoted in part by Hagen, *Zur Geschichte der Philologie*, p. 22 n. 58).

106. See C. E. Murgia, *Prolegomena to Servius 5 — The Manuscripts* (Berkeley, 1975), pp. 15–19.

107. Festus 352.4–8 L.

108. Scaliger, *Castigationes*, pp. clvi–clvii ad loc.: '*Resignare*] Cato de spoliis, ne figerentur, nisi quae de hoste capta essent: Sed tum ubi indivisi sunt, revertantur resignatis vectigalibus. Haec citabat Festus. quae nos reperimus in fragmentis Servii, qui est penes Danielem nostrum' See also pp. xxxv–xxxvi *ad* Paul. 38.8 L.; pp. xliii–xliiii *ad* Paul. 52.2–4; p. xlix *ad* Paul. 48.12 L.; p. l *ad* Paul. 56.3–6 L.; pp. lxvi–lxvii *ad* Paul. 101.5–6 L.; pp. lxxxvii–lxxxviii *ad* 146.12–17 L.; p. clxiiii *ad* 438.47–439.10 L.; and Murgia's fuller list of Scaliger's excerpts from DS, loc. cit., p. 16 n. 31.

109. As late as 1882, after the full triumph of the German historical method, H. Usener ranked Scaliger's Festus along with Hermann's Aeschylus, Ritschl's Plautus, and Lachmann's Lucretius as a 'meisterhafte divinatorisch-kritische Restitution eines Literaturwerkes'; 'Philologie und Geschichtswissenschaft', in *Wesen und Rang der Philologie. Zum Gedenken an Hermann Usener und Franz Bücheler* (Stuttgart, 1969), p. 27.

110. Festus 152.37–154. 3 L.

111. Agustín gives *solita* as a conjectural emendation of *sesita* in the margin of his text ad loc.

112. Agustín, *Annotationes, ad loc.*: 'Mars pedis] Filium Martis significare putarem: nisi me auctoritas Messallae moveret.'

113. This inscription found a home later in J. Gruter's *Inscriptiones antiquae totius orbis Romani*, ed. J. G. Graevius (Amsterdam, 1707), I, p. lxvi.

114. Orelli, *Inscriptionum Latinarum selectarum amplissima collectio*, 1598.

115. Scaliger, *Castigationes*, pp. lxxxi–lxxxiii; see Appendix to Ch. V, below, for the text.

116. Cf. W. Warde Fowler, *The Religious Experience of the Roman People from the earliest Times to the Age of Augustus* (London, 1922), pp. 89 n. 39, 131–4, 142 n. 53.

117. See e.g. Scaliger, *Castigationes*, p. iv *ad* Paul. 17.22–23 L.: '*Ab oloes*] In lege Regia: SEI. PARENTES. PVER. VERBERIT. AST. OLOE. PLORASSINT. PVER. DEIVEIS. PARENTVM. SACER. ESTO. In hac lege, oloe, est olli, vel illi. Nam E, post in O, ut Apello, et Apollo. Deinde non geminabant literas'; pp. xviii–xix *ad* Paul. 10.20–21 L.: 'Quae per u, antea per oe extulerunt, ut in poenire, punire'; p. xli *ad* Paul. 37.15–16 L.; p. xliii *ad* Paul. 44.15–18 L.; pp. cxxxvii–cxxxviii *ad* 242.9–11 L.; p. cli *ad* 334.19–25 L.; p. clxvii *ad* 428.32–33 L.

118. Ibid., p. xxxv *ad* Paul. 41.8 L.; p. iii *ad* Paul. 21.19 L.

119. Ibid., p. xxviii *ad* Paul. 31.17–19 L.; p. xxxiv *ad* Paul. 41.11–12 L.; p. lv *ad* Paul. 73.10–16 L.; p. lxxvii *ad* 126.11–15 L.

120. See e.g. ibid., p. xliii *ad* Paul. 44.15-18.

121. Ibid., pp. cxlvi–cxlvii *ad* 314.11-20: '*Querquetulanae*] Lege: sed feminas antiqui quas nunc dicimus, viras appellabant. quae, inquit, nunc feminae a nobis dicuntur, eae virae dicebantur. neque immerito, cum masculinum sit vir: Ita enim et utrunque formant sexum Hebraei. Iss, vir: Issa, vira. hoc est femina.'

122. Ibid., p. clxxxv *ad* 404.29-35 L.: '*Sufes*] Sufes dictus est Poenorum lingua summus magistratus, ut Oscorum Medix. Calidius in oratione in Caecilium: Nonne vobis etc. Porro qui Hebraice sciunt, et non ignorant Poenos Tyriorum colonos esse, concedent mihi, Sufes idem esse, quod Graecis ἔφορον, ἐπόπτην, ἐπίσκοπον, ṣwph.'

123. Here, as before, Scaliger confines himself to occasional remarks, usually arguing in a rather traditional way for the passage of individual words from one language or family of languages to another; see e.g. ibid., p. lxxvii *ad* 126.11-15 L.: '*Mamphula*] Ego scio in Hebraeorum commentariis Manphul esse mancipem pistrinorum, dictum a Graeco μονοπώλης. Neque dubito quin Mamphula in traduces Syriacae linguae ex matrice Graecia, propagata sit. Sic in Daniele vetustissimo scriptore Graecum est Psanterin pro psalterio: Sic in Paralipomenis, seu Chronicis Rapsod παρὰ τὸ ῥαψωδεῖν.'; p. clxxiiii *ad* Paul. 453.18: '*Sicilicum*] Frustra in peregrino verbo Latinam etymologiam rimatur. est enim Syrum.'

124. Festus 166.29-31 L.

125. Scaliger, *Castigationes*, p. xciiii ad loc.: '*Nancitor*] PEQVNIAM. QVIS. NANCITOR. HABETO. ET. SI. QVID. PIGNERIS. NANCITOR. SIBEI. HABETO. Nancitor, pro nancitur. et nancitur, pro nanciscitur. ut, apiscitur. QVIS pro QVI, ἀρχαϊκῶς. Erat caput in foedere Latino, ut intra decem dies post contestatam litem, creditori satisfieret. Hic vero vult ipsum pignus sibi habere, si post illud tempus ipsi satisfactum non sit. Vel potius intelligit, quod ante bellum contraxerit Latinus cum Romano, sive mutuum sit, sive pignus, uti id valeat.'

126. Ogilvie, *Early Rome and the Etruscans*, p. 100.

127. Le Caron, *Ad leges duodecim tabularum liber singularis*, fol. 184ᵛ: '*Item in foedere Latino pecuniam quis nancitor habeto, et si quid pignoris nanciscit, sibi habeto.* Desumpsimus hoc caput ex epitome Festi Pompeii. Nam is quid Nancitor in duodecim tabulis significet, explicans scribit: Nancitor . . . Particulam quis veteres, pro qui dixisse testatur Festus . . .'.

128. Brisson, *Selectarum ex iure civili Antiquitatum libri duo*, I.5, fol. 16ʳ: 'Reiiciendum quoque est quod alter quidam ex Sex. Pomp. transcripsit. *In foedere latino pecuniam quis nancitor habeto, et si quid pignoris nanciscit sibi habeto.* Nam haec non xii. tab. sed foederis cum Latinis percussi verba sunt. Eaque verba, in foedere latino, a reliquis separanda et pro titulo accipienda vel puer intelligat eo Pompeii loco lecto.'

129. C. Sigonio, *De antiquo iure Italiae libri tres* (ed. Paris, 1573), I.3, fol. 12ʳ: 'Meminit huius quoque foederis Livius libro secundo: meminit et in Corneliana Cicero. quin etiam profert ex foedere Latino Festus haec verba: Pequuniam . . .'.

130. Festus, 298.29 L.

131. Scaliger, *Castigationes*, pp. cxxvi–cxxvii ad loc.: '*Pollucere*] Regis Numae lex fuit de polluctu, quae videlicet liceret polluceri, quae non liceret. De piscibus, qui squamosi essent, omnes, praeter scarum: idque propter raritatem . . . Cuius rei auctor Cassius Hemina apud Plinium, his verbis . . .'. Scaliger goes on to cite the relevant passage from *N.H.* xxxii.20.

132. Ibid.: 'Puto legem his verbis conceptam fuisse; PISCEIS. QVEI. SQVAMOSEI. NON. SVNT. NEI. POLLVCETO. SQVAMOSOS. OMNEIS. PRAETER. SCARVM. POLLVCETO.'

133. B. Brisson, *De formulis et sollemnibus Populi Romani verbis libri VIII* (Paris, 1583); Brisson's conclusion (p. 854): 'Atque ut tandem aliquando finem scribendi faciam, novissimis hisce Comoediarum verbis, Formularum libros claudere me iuvat. Vos ergo, candidi lectores (odi namque malignum vulgus et arceo), Bene valete, vigiliasque et lucubrationes nostras aequi, bonique consulite: et si meruerimus, plausum date.'

134. For Lipsius's impression of the work see *Epistolicae Quaestiones* III.20, in Lipsius, *Opera omnia quae ad Criticam proprie spectant* (Leiden, 1596), pp. 330-2, at p. 330: 'Ten' quaerere quid sentiam de Scaligeri Festo? ego vero quod de scriptis eius omnibus, nil posse divinius ... Dii boni! quam multa ille nova, quam multa vetera, non lecta, non visa, non audita aliis depromit! Daemonium hominis.' The series of conjectures that follows shows how well Lipsius had grasped Scaliger's innovations. See esp. p. 331: 'Ait: *Iovistae, compositum a Iove et iustae*. Ineptissimae ineptiae ... Lego, *Iosipse, compositum ab ios et ipse*. Ita enim antiqui, pro Isipse. Vnum testem habeo, sed luculentum, Glossas veteres ab H. Stephano, Iosipse, αὐτός.' As to Lipsius's *Leges Regiae et leges x. virales* (Antwerp, 1576) see the interleaved copy in Paris, Bibliothèque Nationale, MS Dupuy 449, fols. 7ʳff., which was given by A. Schottus to J. Bongars, in which Lipsius's text of the law about fish occurs on fol. 12ʳ: 'PISCEIS QVEI SQVAMOSI NON SVNT NEI POLLVCETO: SQVAMOSOS OMNEIS PRAETER SCARVM POLLVCETO.' A note on one of the interleaved sheets (fol. 11ᵛ) refers the law to 'nō Scaligeri in Festum in Pollucere'; it seems to be in Bongars's hand.

135. F. Orsini, *Notae ad leges et Senatusconsulta*, in A. Agustín, *De legibus et Senatusconsultis liber* (Rome, 1583), separately paginated, p. 7. For a late appearance of the same law in a standard work see G. V. Gravina, *Origines juris civilis* (Leipzig, 1708), p. 275.

136. See R. E. Giesey, *If Not, Not. The Oath of the Aragonese and the Legendary Laws of Sobrarbe* (Princeton, 1968), frontispiece, pp. 61-2, 148 ff.

137. Scaliger, *Castigationes*, pp. cxxii–cxxiii *ad* 230.15-18 L. and Paul. 231.14.L.: '*Pisatiles*] Pisatiles, sunt οἱ πισᾶται. Memoria lapsus sum olim, qui destitutus codice Festi annotavi Picenos olim a Naevio Pisatiles dictos, unde etiam hodie fluvium Pisatellum dici. Ego plane hallucinatus sum, cum haec memoriter scribebam. Petoque a candidis Lectoribus, ut et hoc, et si quae similia dicta sunt, quae mihi cum omnibus communia sunt, qui meminerunt et se homines, et a se nihil humani alienum putant, omnium mihi veniam facere.'

138. Festus 278.5-20 L. The passage contains more than one entry.

139. Scaliger, *Castigationes*, pp. cxxxix–cxl *ad loc.*: 'Distinximus quae Festi sunt, ab iis, quae nostra, ut lectori fidem faciamus, neque nos credere, neque persuadere aliis velle, quae Festi non sunt, ea esse Festi. Sed imitatus sum homines veterum signorum ac statuarum studiosos atque admiratores, qui ubi signum marmoreum elegantissime scalptum habent, atque id forte propter vetustatem aliqua parte sui, ut saepe fit, mutilatum sit, conquirunt peritos artifices, qui a se partem mancam suppleant. Omnes, qui illud signum vident, norunt et quid de veteri artificio deperierit, et quid de novo additum sit. Tamen id, quod additum est, tanti momenti est saepenumero, ut absque illo foret, totius signi reliqua proportio ac commensus lateret, atque obscurus esset. Sic in hoc Festi loco fecimus. Nam sine illis membris quae addidimus, quid ille truncus esset, facile discerni non poterat. Non mediocriter autem studiosos iuvimus, quantum iudicamus, qui solo prope aequatum aedificium diligentia nostra a fundamentis usque redivivum excitavimus ac sartum tectum praestitimus.'

140. Poliziano, *Opera* (Basel, 1553), p. 228: '*Quae sint crepidae apud Catullum Carpatinae, quod probe scriptum vocabulum perperam mutatur.*'

141. *Catullus et in eum commentarius M. Antonii Mureti* (Venice, 1554), fol. 129ʳ ad loc.: 'Quod autem Politianus legit, crepidas carbatinas, multis de causis non placet. Primum quia est contra fidem veterum exemplarium.'

142. *Catullus cum commentario Achillis Statii Lusitani* (Venice, 1566), p. 394 ad loc.: 'Ego vero in Politiani sententiam lubens eo.'

143. Scaliger, *Castigationes*, p. xl *ad* Paul. 47.23-4: '*Cercolopis*] Legendum sine ulla controversia, cercolips. hoc est Simia, quae caudam non habet. . . . Catullus quoque harum simiarum mentionem facit in epigrammate:
   — et trepidas lingere Cercolipas. Quam enim apertus sensus, omnes vident. Quid enim foedius, quam nates Simiae, praesertim Cercolipis? Politianus tamen maluit Carbatinas. Quod ipse non excogitavit. Sed ita in manuscriptis viderat. Ita enim habet manuscriptus Catullus clariss. et eruditissimi Cuiacii, I. C. ac senatoris amplissimi. Sed non defuerunt, qui in Politiano candorem animi requirerent.'

Chapter VI

1. Scaliger, *Notae ad libros M. Terentii Varronis de re rustica*, in *M. Terentii Varronis opera quae supersunt* (Geneva, 1573), p. 270: 'Quis enim tam aversus a Musis tamque humanitatis expers, qui horum publicatione offendatur?'

2. M. A. Muret, *Orationes XXIII . . . eiusdem Interpretatio quincti libri Ethicorum Aristotelis ad Nicomachum. Eiusdem hymni sacri, et alia quaedam poematia* (Venice, 1575), p. 56: 'Cum veteris Comici Graeci Philemonis nobilem sententiam a Plutarcho et a Stobaeo acceptam animi caussa exprimere tentassem et dicendi genere et numero veterum Latinorum tragicorum simillimo: placuit etiam experiri, numquid eandem comice explicare possem. Visum est utrumque non infeliciter successisse. Per iocum igitur prioribus versibus Attii, posterioribus Trabeae nomen adscripsi, ut experirer aliorum iudicia, et viderem num quis in eis inesset vetustatis sapor. Nemo repertus est, qui non ea pro veteribus acceperit. Vnus etiam et eruditione minime vulgari et iudicio acerrimo praeditus repertus est, qui ea a me accepta pro veteribus publicaret. Ne quis igitur amplius fallatur, et rem totam detegendam, et carmina ipsa hic subiicienda duxi.' The poems follow, under the headings 'Afficta Attio' and 'Afficta Trabeae', on pp. 56-7. Cf. also Bernays, *Scaliger*, pp. 270-2.

3. See R. Calderini de Marchi, *Jacopo Corbinelli et les érudits français d'après la correspondance inédite Corbinelli-Pinelli (1566-87)* (Milan, 1914), esp. pp. 133-6. For Scaliger's ruff see the engraving by H. Goltzius after a portrait dated 1575: *Icones Leidenses. De portretverzameling van de Rijksuniversiteit te Leiden* (Leiden, 1973), nr. 27; the plate is reproduced in Rijksmuseum Amsterdam, *Leidse Universiteit 400. Stichting en eerste bloei 1575-ca. 1650* (Amsterdam, 1975), nr. A110, p. 68. On the social significance of the large ruff ca. 1575, see W. L. Wiley, *The Gentleman of Renaissance France* (Cambridge, Mass., 1954), p. 81.

4. Ibid., Ch. x.

5. Scaliger to Dupuy, 8.ii.1576, *Lettres françaises*, pp. 44-5: 'Monsieur Cujas m'escrivit dernièrement que Monsieur Muret estoit mort, et qu'on lui avoit escrit d'Italie. Je vouldrois fort en savoir la vérité, et vous supplie très humblement m'en éclaircir, car je serois bien marri, qu'il s'en fust allé plustost, que je lui eusse rendu conte de ses vers d'Attius et Trabea. Je me mettrai après à transcrire mes petites annotations sur Catulle, Tibulle, Properce, et vous les envoierai incontinent, affin que vous en soyez l'Aristarchus.'

6. Scaliger to Dupuy, 29.vi.1576, *Lettres françaises*, pp. 50-1: 'Monsieur d'Abain a donné de mes Festus à Sigonius, et au bon homme P. Victorius, lequel luy a faict bonne compagnie pendent qu'il a esté à Fleurence. Dieu veille qu'ils le

trouvent bon! Car ils n'estiment guères *Gallicana ingenia*. Et, pour vous dire la vérité, ilz ont partie raison, partie tort.'

7. Scaliger to Pithou, 13.ii.1572, *Lettres Françaises*, pp. 17-18: 'Et ainsi l'ai-je trouvé en un fragment de Tibulle, lequel j'estime si fidele et certain que je ne pense jamais livre avoir esté manié plus asseuré que cellui-là. Je ne vous saurois asses louer icellui exemplaire, comme, Dieu aidant, je ferai connoistre en quelques autres livres que je delibère mettre en lumière, moiennant que je les aie mis au net en attendant qui les transcrive pour moi, n'aiant le loisir à cause de mon estude du droict.'

8. Scaliger to Dupuy, 29.vi.1576, *Lettres françaises*, p. 50: 'Vous ne sauriés croire, que je suis devenu glorieux, despuis que j'ay leu les Commentaires de Messer Achille. Car ce brave Commentateur m'a donné espérance de faire quelque chose de bon, ce que je n'osois affirmer par ci devant. Mais vous en aurés la preuve bient tost, Dieu aidant.' See also ibid., pp. 43, 45-6, 48 ('... pour le moins, nous ne ferons tant le fat qu'a faict Messer Achille Statio, auquel Dieu doint bonne vie et longue, car s'il n'impètre cella par noz bonnes prières, à peine l'obtiendra il par son bon entendement').

9. Scaliger, ep. ded. to Dupuy, in *Catulli, Tibulli, Propertii nova editio* (Paris, 1577), sigs. a ii^v-a iii^r: 'Multa enim quae ignoratione priscae lectionis Grammatistae contaminaverant, restituimus: non pauca, quae aliquot ab hinc saeculis vitio potius aetatis suae, quam suo imperiti homines illi praetermiserant, e penetralibus vetustatis in lucem protulimus.'

10. Ibid., 'Quid multa? nolui simplicem insaniam insanire. idem enim et in Tibullo et Propertio tentavimus: quia eos, ut scis, vulgatae editiones coniungere solent. et, nisi fallor, feliciter successit nobis: quanvis, Deum testem laudo, ne integrum quidem mensem illis tribus poetis recensendis impendimus.'

11. Ibid., sig. a iii^r-v: 'Tamen, ne quid dissimulem, meliorem partem harum Criticarum commentationum vindicat sibi stilus, et scriptio. Quum enim quae in animo habebam, ea chartae commendarem, cui rei viginti tantum dies dedimus, sub acumen calami, ut solet, longe plura cadebant, quam inter legendum auctores ipsos commentati fueramus. Id quod testatum volumus, ne forte quispiam putet nihil aliud nos, quam haec Aristarchea nec velle nec posse tractare.' These prefatory *topoi* are sometimes taken all too literally; see e.g. Tamizey de Larroque, in *Lettres françaises*, p. 56 n. 1; J. Jehasse, *La Renaissance de la critique* (St. Étienne, 1976), p. 194: 'Ce n'est là que divertissement de génie.'

12. Scaliger to Vertunien, 11.xi.1575, in R. L. Hawkins, 'The Friendship of Joseph Scaliger and François Vertunien', *Romanic Review*, viii (1917), pp. 117-44, 307-27, at p. 128: 'Praeterea ni grave est quaere diligenter ut possis requirere Catullum, Tibullum, Propertium cum commentario. Eo libro non amplius octo dies utar, ac bona fide remittam.'

13. Scaliger, *Lettres françaises*, pp. 35, 36, 41, 43, 45-6, 48, 50, 53-4, 56, 58.

14. Scaliger to Dupuy, 31.vii.1577, *Lettres françaises*, p. 69: 'Il y a beaucoup de sorte d'hommes, et de ceux qui ressemblent à hommes, et d'aultres qui ne sont hommes du tout, qui murmurent fort de mon Catulle.'

15. Bernays, *Scaliger*, pp. 45-6, 162-4; S. Timpanaro, *La genesi del metodo del Lachmann*, 2nd edn. (Padua, 1981), pp. 10-11, 17, 21, 37, 77-8, 83, 111, 115; cf. E. J. Kenney, *The Classical Text* (Berkeley, 1974), pp. 55-7. On Catullan scholarship in the Renaissance see also V. J. Rosivach, 'Sources of Some Errors in Catullan Commentaries', *Transactions of the American Philological Association*, 108 (1978), pp. 203-16; H. D. Jocelyn, 'On Some Unnecessarily Indecent Interpretations of Catullus 2 and 3', *American Journal of Philology*, 101 (1980), pp. 421-41.

16. Scaliger, *Castigationes in Catullum, Tibullum, Propertium* (Paris, 1577), in *Catulli, Tibulli, Propertii nova editio*, separately paginated, p. 78 *ad Cat*. 66.69: 'SED *quanquam me nocte premunt vestigia divum*) Aratus: . . .'.

17. Scaliger, *Castigationes*, p. 32 *ad Cat*. 36.9-10 (where he emends *Iocose et* to *Ioco se*): 'Repetitur autem bis *sese*, more Graecorum, praesertim Atticorum, ut ego innumeris locis apud Demosthenem notavi. Euripides Phoenissis [497-8]

    ἐμοὶ μὲν εἰ καὶ μὴ καθ' ἐλλήνων χθόνα
    τετράμμεθ' ἀλλ' οὖν ξυνετά μοι δοκεῖ λέγειν.

    Hic enim τὸ ἐμοί repetitur eodem modo, quo hic *Se.*'

18. Scaliger, *Castigationes*, p. 46 *ad Cat*. 61.1: 'COLLIS *o Heliconei*] A. Ticida hoc genere carminis Hymenaeon scripsit. Sappho non Hymenaeon, sed epithalamion. Servius nondum excusus: *Sappho*, inquit, *in libro, qui inscribitur* ἐπιθαλάμοι . . . Quod et ipsum est eiusdem generis metrum.'

19. Scaliger, *Castigationes*, pp. 95-6; see the interesting discussion of Scaliger's note in J. Selden, *De diis Syris*, 3rd edn. (Leipzig, 1672), II.8, pp. 322-4.

20. *Catullus et in eum commentarius M. Antonii Mureti* (Venice, 1554), fols. 56ᵛ-58ʳ; cf. M. Morrison, 'Henri Estienne and Sappho', *BHR* xxiv (1962), pp. 388-91, where the various early publications of Sappho's poem are discussed and the relevant section of Muret's commentary is translated.

21. *Catullus cum commentario Achillis Statii Lusitani* (Venice, 1566), *passim*; cf. R. Ellis, *A Commentary on Catullus* (Oxford, 1876), Preface, p. vi: 'In the accumulation of really illustrative passages, drawn from the stores of a most extensive reading, he anticipates the learning of a later period . . .'.

22. Cf. Scaliger, *Castigationes*, p. 76 *ad Cat*. 66.54: 'Possemus et illos versus Callimachi adducere ex Athenaeo, nisi iam eos Turnebus libris suis Adversariorum inseruisset.'

23. Scaliger, *Castigationes*, p. 111 (*in Tibullum, ad init.*): 'Huius poetae ea omnia quotquot in Italia extant, exemplaria, recentiora sunt, quam ut inter vetustos libros censeri debeant. Quin correctorum audacia multa perabsurda illis admista sunt. Eiusmodi unum vidimus, cuius copiam nobis fecit Iuris consultissimus Iacobus Cuiacius. Sed et meliora quaedam in eo, quam alii in suis, invenimus. Neque puto meliorem librum eo hodie extare: Nam quaedam etiam vetustatis retinet vestigia, quum paulo ante ineuntem typographicam artem scriptus sit: et nondum correctorum audacia ita licenter in bonis auctoribus pervagaretur.' Cf. ibid., p. 3: (*in Catullum, ad init.*): 'Porro liber ille, quo usi sumus . . . longe alios huius poetae manuscriptos bonitate superare mihi videtur . . .'.

24. The MS was first identified by R. Ellis and A. Palmer in their article 'Scaliger's *Liber Cujacianus* of Propertius, Catullus, etc.', *Hermathena*, ii (1876), pp. 124-58; Ellis summarized his findings in *Catulli Veronensis liber*, 2nd edn. (Oxford, 1878), pp. liv-lix. In my original reworking of the comparison between Scaliger's commentary and the MS, I tried to give an exact number of the MS readings he meant to report. I now believe that my count included too many words that Scaliger included only to complete lemmata for notes and not to report on the MS; accordingly I shall not repeat my attempt to give a proportion of correct to incorrect readings. For a full list of all the readings Scaliger reported, together with the MS readings and those of his collation (see below), see A. Grafton, 'Joseph Scaliger (1540-1609) and the Humanism of the Later Renaissance', unpublished diss. Chicago 1975, Appendix, pp. 221-49. As to the 1569 Plantin edition that contains Scaliger's collations, it is chiefly known to critics because it also contains his collation of the lost *fragmentum Cuiacianum* of Tibullus; see below and, in general, *Tibulli aliorumque carminum libri tres*, ed. J. P. Postgate, 2nd edn. (Oxford, 1915), pp. vi-ix.

25. *Scaligerana I*, s.v. Lingua, p. 113: 'Nullus est in veterum librorum collatione

Josepho Scaligero expeditior ac promptior, ut in codice Catulli, Tibulli, Propertii manuscripto, illique a Domino Cujacio misso observavi, quem intra duos aut tres ad summum dies cum suis contulit. Hoc autem exemplar descriptum erat anno Domini 1469, Nemausique a Dom. Cujacio inventum est.' That Scaliger saw Egerton 3027 in Valence is clear from the passages collected in *Catulli Veronensis liber*, ed. Ellis, p. lv. But Vertunien's remark that Cujas 'sent' him the MS implies that he did his collating after leaving Valence; hence the reconstruction offered in the text. The order of entries in Scaliger's collation (see n. 26, below) suggests that he collated the *fragmentum Cuiacianum* of Tibullus after Egerton 3027 — and thus that Cujas sent him the *fragmentum* as well as the other, less precious MS. Cf. Ch. V above, n. 143.

26. Leiden University Library, liber annotatus 755 H 23, verso of title-page (the famous epigram beginning *Ad patriam redeo*). Scaliger also noted that where the printed text read 'C. VALERII CATVLLI VERONENSIS AD CORN. NEPOTEM LIBELLVS', the MS added POETAE after CATVLLI and gave LIBER INCIPIT FELICITER rather than LIBELLVS. On the other hand, at the beginning of the Propertius section of the printed text, Scaliger recorded the MS heading NAVTAE MONOBIBLOS AD CINTHIAM but omitted *Liber primus incipit feliciter.*

27. Scaliger's transcript of the colophon (index to the Propertius section of 755 H 23, *ad fin.*) reads: 'Sexti Aurelii Propertii Nautae monobiblos ad Cynthiam feliciter explicit per me Pacificum Maximum de Asculo in Sapientia veteri Perusiae. anno 1469 6. die Februarii.' Palmer and Ellis wondered why the date given by Vertunien in the *Scaligerana* was 1469 rather than 1467, and feared that their identification of Scaliger's MS might be weakened. As we can see, Vertunien was simply repeating what Scaliger had mistakenly copied out in his notes — and, no doubt, told Vertunien.

28. His final version of the line was *cavent quo iure parent se*, which is surely indefensible.

29. e.g. the following:

Line	Scaliger's Reading	Collation	Manuscript
2.8	error		ardor
39.17	ex Celtiberia		*om.* ex
53.5	salaputium	salapautium	salapantium
59.1	Bononiensem		Bononiensis
	Rufulum	Ruffum	ruffum
63.53	apud miser	misere	caput misere
69.3	No s'illa rarae	illam amare	Non illam amare

(The last case is 'Ita reconcinnatum ex prisca scriptura.')

30. Scaliger, *Castigationes*, p. 49 *ad Cat.* 61.99: 'Vetus enim lectio disertim habet, *Proca turpia.*' Scaliger's collation reads, rightly, '*procatur pia v*'. He later wrote *proca* under the MS reading, for which, indeed, he may have mistaken it later on.

31. Scaliger, *Castigationes*, p. 79 *ad Cat.* 66.91: 'NON *votis esse tuam me*] Vetus lectio, *veris*, aut *vestris* praefert. Si *veris*, deest prima syllaba, ut supra dixi. Sin, quod verius est, *vestris*: profecto inversum est pro *Siveris* . . .'.

32. Cf. n. 29, above. Often, too, it is not clear whether Scaliger is giving the testimony of his MS alone or those of others. At 113.1, for instance (*Castigationes*, p. 106), he introduces a reading from his MS with the words 'veteres membranae'. At 2.7-8 (ibid., p. 7) he uses 'Vetus scriptorum librorum lectio'.

33. Cf. most recently G. B. Pighi, 'Achillis Statii lectiones atque emendationes Catullianae', *Humanitas* (Coimbra), iii (1950-1), pp. 37-160.

34. B. L. Ullman, *The Identification of the Manuscripts of Catullus cited in Statius's Edition of 1566*, Diss. Chicago 1908, pp. 10-17, 64.

35. *C. Valerii Catulli carmina,* ed. R. A. B. Mynors (Oxford, 1958), p. xi. Cf. *Catullus, A Critical Edition,* ed. D. F. S. Thomson (Chapel Hill, 1978), p. 50–1.

36. As a Neo-Latin poet of some skill (his *Hecatelegium* is a minor classic of pornography) and the author of a treatise on metres, Pacificus Maximus was certainly capable of using mock-archaic spellings and devising conjectural emendations.

37. Scaliger, *Castigationes,* pp. 15, 38, 64.

38. See Ch. II, above, n. 53. Scaliger also used the testimony of the Florentine Pandects (*Castigationes,* p. 91 *ad Cat.* 76.11); he there argued, mistaking the Torelli's editorial practice for a literal reproduction of the MS, that in the original MS an extra-large consonant had been employed to indicate that the syllable it preceded should be repeated (METVIRI = *Metutum iri*). Isaac Casaubon pointed out Scaliger's error in the margin of his copy of the *Castigationes,* Leiden University Library, shelf-mark 758 F 1¹ : 'Sed legisse memini illas magnas literas non ex archetypi imitatione profectas esse, sed ab exscriptore Taurello.' (Cf. also Ch. II, above, n. 100). But if Scaliger's execution of Vettori's principles proved wanting, his intention is clear.

39. Scaliger, *Castigationes,* p. 43 'SED *te quaerere iam Herculis labos est*] Et haec quoque de correctorum officina. Noster codex optime: *Sed te iam ferre Herculei. labos est.* ubi *Herculei* genitivus antiquus. ut apud Ciceronem in epistolis probissimus, ac doctissimus senex P. Victorius notavit scriptum in veteribus libris, *Themistoclei, Theophanei . . .*'.

40. P. Vettori, *Explicationes suarum in Ciceronem castigationum* (ed. Paris, 1538), p. 13: 'Themistoclis fuga] Vetera exemplaria THEMISTOCLI, ratione veteris declinationis qua dandi casum in huiuscemodi nominibus pro generandi ponebant, ut Ulyssi pro Ulyssis, Achilli pro Achillis: sic etiam in nostro probatiore codice epist. ad Att. lib. XIII, *Non vides ipsum illum Aristoteli discipulum,* pro *Aristotelis.*'

41. Scaliger, *Castigationes,* p. 7: 'Vetus scriptorum librorum lectio:
    Et solatiolum sui doloris
    Credo ut quom gravis acquiescet error.
    Magnum mendum, sed parva labe contractum. Nam vetus codex Gallicanus sine dubio habuit *credont* pro *credunt.* Ita enim non raro scribebant, ut in lapide Narbonensi:
    . . . [See text] . . .
    Et in aliis eiusdem urbis inscriptionibus legitur VIVONT pro *vivunt.*' The inscription is *CIL* XII.4507; it is there stated that *VIVONT* did not appear on the original stone.

42. For Scaliger see the passages quoted in n. 41, above and n. 47, below; see Ch. II, above and, in particular, Vettori, *Explicationes,* p. 24 *ad Fam.* IX.2: '. . . atque hoc eo libentius admonere placuit, ut videant eruditi lectores tam parva perversio in antiquis codicibus quam magnos errores pariat.'

43. Catullus, *Carmina,* Goff C–324 (Brescia, '1485,' 1486), sig. h^r: 'Aorion: haec est vera huius loci lectio. Alii autem legunt Oyrion, divisa diphthongo imperite: penultima enim fieret brevior, quum apud omnes poetas producatur. Sed legendum est Aorion, nulla diphthongo divisa: non enim ab Orione deducitur, quamquam idem est signum, sed Aorion, ensiger, dicitur. Τὸ ἄορ enim significat ensem: inde Aorion, quasi ensifer.' 'Proximus Hydrochoi fulgeret Aorion. i. si fierem regia coma, tunc Aquarius et Orion sydera nullo interstitio separata fierent propinqua. Nam haec coma, ut partim superius dictum est, ad Leonis caudam apud Virginem ita sita est ut ab Aquario, cui vicinus est Orion, non multum distet.'

44. *Catullus . . . Mureti,* fols. 104^v–105^r *ad* 66.94: 'Hinc autem videri potest, illustres homines, quique magnum nomen habent in literis, quanto periculo peccent. Effecit enim Politiani auctoritas, ut nullus iam, quod sciam, extet liber

impressus, in quo non, reiecta vera lectione, nothus ille et suppositicius versus
legatur,
Proximus Hydrochoo fulgeat Oarion.'
For Poliziano's views see *Miscellanea* I.69, *Opera* (Basel, 1553), p.
282 ('*Oarion
synceriter esse apud Catullum, quod Aorion isti legunt, qui bonos violant
libros*'). For Marullus see his *Carmina*, ed. A. Perosa (Zürich, 1951) pp. 59,
185, and index nominum s.v. Oarion. For Palladius see his note ad loc. in *Al.
Tibulli Elegiarum libri quatuor* . . . (Venice, 1520), fol. lxxxᵛ; for Guarino see
*Alexandri Guarini Ferrariensis in C.V. Catullum Veronensem per Baptistam
Patrem emendatum Expositiones* (Venice, 1521), fol. xcᵛ.

45. I quote from the variorum edn. of Catullus, Tibullus, and Propertius *ex Musaeo
Joannis Georgii Graevii* (Utrecht, 1680), 2nd pagination, p. 263 (misnumbered
363): 'Ut sit haec, aut hac potior alia sententia, se non laborare quae quem
sortiantur locum sidera, ut remotissimis e locis ad se invicem propius accedant,
dum sibi modo in reginae vertice esse liceat . . .'. A very similar position was
taken by Th. Marcilius, *In C. Valerium Catullum Asterismi*, ibid., p. 653: 'Si
coma, inquit, regia fieri possem, ut fui, me volente vel Orion esset proximus
Aquario. Non laborarem quo quicque sidus loco esset. Mihi enim locus inventus
esset, omni loco caelesti optatior.'

46. I quote from the 1600 Commelin edn. of Scaliger's *Castigationes*, p. 92 ad loc.:
'Non tamen dissimulare possumus nobis mirum videri non solum Callimacho
Orionem Aquario tam vicinum videri, sed etiam Siriam Pleiadi. Non tamen
propterea mutandum esse dicamus, siquid absurde ab illis dictum.'

47. Scaliger, *Castigationes*, pp. 80–1 ad loc.: 'Simplicissimus ergo sensus huius loci,
quem non sine magnae temeritatis conscientia correctores contaminarunt. Sed
omnium maxime ridiculus Marullus, qui quum nullum aut admodum exiguum
sensum harum literarum haberet, ridet Politianum virum non solum se maiorem,
sed et cum nullo nostrae aetatis comparandum, qui non haec commentus est,
sed veterem lectionem, quam a magistellis depravari videbat, ab illorum audacia
vindicare conabatur. Et sane omnes vetustissimae editiones, ut dixi, et quantum
scriptorum exemplarium extat, non aliter habent. At Graeculus ille putavit sibi
licere in bonis auctoribus, quod ipse sibi in suis versibus voluit licere. Ausus est
praeterea annotationem doctissimi Politiani ineptissimo epigrammate exagitare.
Sane quibus ille vir tantus videtur, tantique fit, debebant aliquid de pertinacia
remittere, si eius editionem Lucretianam diligenter perpenderent. Nullus enim
veterum auctorum ita male ab ullo correctorum acceptus est, ut Lucretius ab illo
audace Graeculo. At nos illum non imitabimur, et si qua extant eius ac similium
correctorum in bonis libris temeritatis atque audaciae vestigia, ea prorsus abol-
ere, atque de medio bonorum scriptorum penitus obterere nobis consilium est.
Quis autem huius ineptae mutationis auctor fuerit, nondum comperire potui:
nisi fuerit Marullus ipse. Nam tum recenter, quum illa scribebat Politianus, locus
ille mutatus fuit. Quod ansam praebuit homini eruditissimo veterem lectionem
asserendi, quam videbat ob oculos suos ita ab audaculis labefactari. Rapidum
quidem ingenium Marulli fuit, et torrens, sed quod versibus nunc bonis nunc
malis ex tempore effutiendis potius, quam bonis auctoribus emendandis natum
videtur.'

48. Vettori, *Explicationes*, p. 33: 'cuius criminis culpam putamus nos Marullum
Byzantium sustinere: vidimus enim eius librum, qui cum TIMEFACTAE ante
scriptum habuisset, in TVMEFACTO eam dictionem conversam habebat. Fuit
autem Marullus admirabilis ingenii vir, et elegantissimus poeta, Lucretiique in
primis ita studiosus, et admirator, ut fere nunquam e manibus dimitteret:
magnam praeterea operam in eo, cum foedissimis mendis scateret, purgando
collocavit, multaque foeliciter restituit. Quandoque tamen cum nimis ingenio
suo indulgeret, nonnulla quae corrigere voluit, depravavit: parum enim manu

scriptos codices, cum tam corruptos passim inveniret, sequebatur: quaeque suo iudicio probasset, ea recta iudicans, multis locis deceptus est.'

49. Falkenburg's note (it seems, at least, to be his) is in his copy of the 1558 edition of Muret's work, which Fruterius had owned before him (see Ch. III, above, n. 143), in the top margin of fol. 116ᵛ: 'Vid. Scaligerum ad hunc locum Catulli, ubi ineptias levissimi Graeculi non sine gravi causa perstringit.' Scaliger also took Poliziano's side against Marullus and Muret on the question of the *crepidas . . . carbatinas* in Catullus 98.4 (cf. Ch. V, above, *ad fin.*); *Castigationes*, pp. 101-2 ad loc.: 'ET *crepidas lingere carbatinas*] Liquida scriptura omnium ·veterum tam scriptorum, quam formis excusorum. Quum Politianus haec videret contaminari, non passus est . . . Quod autem hac in re Marullus Politianum ridet, nihil praeter solitum facit. Modo enim occasionem hominem insectandi nanciscatur, iure an iniuria, recte an secus id faciat, susque deque habet.'

50. Scaliger, *Castigationes*, p. 74 ad loc.: 'Certe *Chalybon* non scripsit Catullus. Quare? Quia nimium quantum discedit a vestigiis priscae lectionis.'

51. Scaliger's MS originally read *celi tum*; this is changed to *teli tum* in a darker ink. In his collation Scaliger reported the reading as *teli tum*; in *Castigationes*, p. 74 ad loc., he writes: 'Certe in nostro liquide scriptum fuit, *telitum*.' From this he inferred that the true reading had been

   Iuppiter, ut šicelicum omne genus pereat,

   and argued that Catullus had interpreted ' . . . τὸ χαλύβων in Graeco poeta non pro natione, sed pro ipso ferro . . . Nam chalybs passim apud Graecos etiam τὸ στόμωμα, acies ferri.'

52. *Castigationes*, p. 3: 'Porro liber ille, quo usi sumus, cuiusque iam mentionem fecimus, longe alios huius poetae manuscriptos bonitate superare mihi videtur: quum tamen omnes ex uno exemplari descripti fuerint. Id exemplar ab homine Veronensi, quisquis ille fuit, in Galliis repertum, omnes illos codices eius poetae, qui in Italia extant, propagavit.

   Suspicor autem illud Gallicanum exemplar Langobardicis literis scriptum fuisse, quia errores, qui in postremis codicibus ab imperitis librariis disseminati sunt, non aliter videntur, quam a morosis illis characteribus nati. Id quod suo loco diligenter admonebimus. Praeterea non character solum menda propagavit, sed et antiquaria lectio. Nam librarius semper scripserat QVOR, QVOM, LVDEI, LVCEI, ADEPTA'S, M'ALIVS . . .'.

53. Scaliger found *a–u* confusions in 6.12, 29.4, 66.43, 66.63, 67.32; *i–l* in 64.322, 80.8, 113.2; *c–t* in 25.7, 29.20, 34.22-3, 61.46, 64.308, 68.52, 95.7; *c–g* in 61.68.

54. Scaliger, *Castigationes*, p. 9: ' . . . in primo versu quod *Stupra* eruimus, hoc factum, quia saepe in hoc libro *u* pro *a* scriptum fuit. Et Langobardus character non distinguit has duas literas.'

55. See Ch. IV above, *ad fin.*

56. See *JWCI* xxxviii (1975), plate 24 and pp. 171-2 n. 60. Much later Scaliger described the Latin script of his Latin-Arabic dictionary, which is also Visigothic, as 'Lombardic', though by 1608 he considered this name to be inaccurate; see P. S. van Koningsveld, *The Latin-Arabic Glossary of the Leiden University Library* (Diss. Leiden, 1976), pp. 6-7, 66 n. 12. Scaliger's notional Lombardic script may also have owed something to that of the Berlin codex of the *Collatio*, which has features in common with Visigothic; see Hyamson's edition (Ch. IV above, n. 132) for a facsimile. For a different view see H. W. Garrod, 'Lombardic,' *The Classical Quarterly*, xiii (1919), pp. 51-52 (reference kindly supplied by M. Ferrari).

57. Scaliger, *Castigationes*, p. 43: 'COMMITTE. *lucet*.] In Gallicano exemplari puto fuisse: *Lucei* antiquo more scribendi.'

58. Ibid.: 'Committere luci est in medium proferre . . .'.

59. Timpanaro, *Lachmann*, p. 113.

60. Ibid., n. 3.

61. Scaliger, *Castigationes*, pp. 43-4: 'SIS *nostri quoque particeps*] Vetus scriptura, *Dum nostri sis particeps amoris*. Sensus communis expertem esse oportet, cui non pareat legendum, *Dum vostri sim particeps amoris*.'

62. Ibid.: 'Nam *vostri* in *nostri* mutaverant, qui non meminerant ἀρχαϊκόν esse characterem huius auctoris.'

63. See A. E. Housman's review of Schulze's edition of Baehrens's Catullus, in *Selected Prose*, ed. J. Carter (Cambridge, 1961), p. 76; for a contrary view see K. P. Schulze, 'Bericht über die Literatur zu Catullus für die Jahre 1905-1920', *Bursians Jahresbericht*, clxxxiii (1920), pp. 50-72. And on Scaliger's excessive predilection for inserting archaisms into the texts of the elegists see in general M. Haupt, 'Ueber Joseph Scaliger und die von Haase vorgeschlagene Umstellung tibullischer Versreihen' (1857), *Opuscula* (Leipzig, 1875-6), iii, pp. 32-3.

64. Poliziano anticipated Scaliger's attempt to reconstruct a lost archetype systematically, but only in the unpublished second *Centuria* of the *Miscellanea*; see *JWCI* xl (1977), p. 169. So, as we saw, did Paolo Manuzio's friend G. B. Titi (Ch. III, above, n. 115). But neither work could have been known to Scaliger; and no published work known to me could have served as his model.

65. See e.g. D. R. Kelley, '*Historia Integra*: François Baudouin and his Conception of History', *Journal of the History of Ideas*, xxv (1964), pp. 35-57; A. D. Momigliano, *Secondo Contributo alla storia degli studi classici* (Rome, 1960), p. 71 and n. 11.

66. See in general H. E. Troje, 'Humanistische Kommentierungen klassischer Juristenschriften', *Ius Commune*, iv (1972), pp. 51-72. Troje argues emphatically that Cujas saw his reconstructions not as an end in themselves but as an aid to the elucidation of the *Digest* (much as Scaliger's reconstructed archetype was itself intended as an aid to the reconstruction of the lost original text of Catullus — though Scaliger himself does not always keep the distinction between archetype and original text in mind).

67. See Ch. IV, above.

68. Scaliger, *Opus novum de emendatione temporum* (Paris, 1583); this work will be studied in detail in the 2nd volume of the present study.

69. Scaliger, 'Diatriba de Europaeorum linguis', *Opuscula* (Paris, 1610), pp. 119-22; *Animadversiones in Chronologica Eusebii, Thesaurus Temporum* (Leiden, 1606), pp. 102-13.

70. F. Meinecke, *Historism. The Rise of a New Historical Outlook*, tr. J. E. Anderson (London, 1972), p. 25 (on Leibniz; the whole section on Leibniz is of interest for purposes of comparison with Scaliger); see also Timpanaro, *Lachmann*, Ch. VIII, comparing stemmatic recension of MSS and historical Indo-European linguistics in the 19th century.

71. Scaliger, *Animadversiones in Chronologica Eusebii*, p. 103: 'Iones enim a Phoenicibus literas acceperunt, quae, ut in omnibus rebus evenit, usus tractatione et progressu longi temporis a primigenia forma desciverunt: ita tamen, ut earum origo dissimulari non possit.'

72. Cf. above all Timpanaro, *Lachmann*, and Kenney, *The Classical Text*.

73. L. D. Reynolds and N. G. Wilson, *Scribes and Scholars*, 2nd edn. (Oxford, 1974), p. 189.

74. For a particularly interesting case see *Castigationes*, pp. 206-7, where Scaliger argued that by the phrase *Et non inflati somnia Callimachi* (II. xxxiv. 32) Propertius meant to criticize the *Aetia* of Callimachus as too obscure to be a good

example for imitation: 'Haec aliter accipit vulgus, ac voluit Propertius. Ipsi putant a Propertio hic Callimachum laudari, quod eum non inflatum vocaverit. Ego contra inflatum eum vocari aio, ac propterea non laudari. Ait enim: mollem ac delicatum versum Philetae potius imitare, quam somnia inflati Callimachi. Somnia Callimachi vocat τὰ αἴτια, opus morosum ac obscurum . . .'. Scaliger, realizing that he then had to account for Propertius' claim to be *imitating* Callimachus in IV.i.64, accordingly goes on to revive Calderini's theory that Propertius was imitating lost love-poems by Callimachus: 'Propertius tantum deterret eum ab Aetiis Callimachi, cui poemati simile aggrediebatur ille Propertii amicus: non autem ab amoribus, aut Elegiis Callimachi, quas ipse imitari se, ut dixi, profitetur.' Evidently his allegiance to Poliziano did not extend to all questions of exegesis.

75. Ibid., p. 111 (*in Tibullum, ad init*.): 'Item fragmentum peroptimum, et quam emendatissimum a quarta elegia libri tertii ad finem usque commodavit nobis idem praestantissimus vir, summaque humanitate praeditus Iacobus Cuiacius. Qui liber, et si imperfectus, tanti apud me momenti est, ut non meminerim me ullum vetus exemplar emendatius legisse. Itaque hoc praeter Italos amplius consecuti sumus, ut vetustiores, quam illi huius poetae reliquias nacti simus.'

76. Scaliger, *Castigationes*, p. 149 ad loc.: 'SAEVVS *amor docuit*] Haec elegia cum toto libro, item et quarto extat in Bibliotheca clariss. viri Iac. Cuiacii. Quod fragmentum emendatissimum est, et eius ope multa menda in hoc poeta sustulimus.' For the introduction to the commentary see n. 75, above.

77. 'Haec elegia cum reliqua parte libri huius . . .'; quoted by A. Cartault, *À propos du Corpus Tibullianum. Un siècle de philologie latine classique* (Paris, 1906), p. 4 n. 3; see in general pp. 1–12.

78. I follow the excellent treatment by E. Hiller, 'Ueber die Lesarten der Tibull-Handschriften Scaligers', *RhM*, N. F. xxix (1874), pp. 99–100.

79. Ibid., p. 100. On Scaliger's use of the *excerpta Parisina* — which was not based on a systematic evaluation of their origin and worth — see Cartault, *Corpus Tibullianum*, p. 7.

80. Scaliger, *Castigationes*, p. 168 (*in Propertium, ad init*.): 'Nam avorum nostrorum memoria in cella vinaria inventus fuit. ex quo exemplari omnia illa, quotquot hodie in Italia habentur, descripta sunt. quo fit, ut vetustum eius poetae nullum exemplar inveniatur. Qui autem illud descripsit primus, nae ille audax aut negligens homo fuit, quisquis ille fuit. nam praeter innumera menda, quibus totum librum praestantissimi poetae aspersit, magni sceleris se obligavit, quum in secundo et tertio libro integras paginas et magnum numerum versuum suo loco luxaverit, et infinitis locis magnas tenebras offuderit. adeo, ut neminem esse putem (libere enim quod sentio fatebor) qui hunc poetam in secundo libro nisi per caliginem, quod dicitur, intelligat. Nos primi eam perturbationem versuum odorati sumus. et bene nobis successit labor iste. Parem enim diligentiam in eo restituendo, ac in Tibullo, posuimus.' Cf. ibid., p. 111.

81. For Tibullus see the hostile but useful account of Cartault, *Corpus Tibullianum*, pp. 9–11.

82. See e.g. Haupt, *Opuscula*, iii, pp. 34–6; Kenney, *The Classical Text*, pp. 55–6.

83. Scaliger, *Castigationes*, p. 126 ad Tib. I.vi.32: 'INSTABAT *tota cui tua nocte canis*] Post hunc versum pentametrum sequi debent tria disticha, quae superiorem elegiam claudebant: NON FRVSTRA QVIDAM IAM NVNC IN LIMINE PERSTAT, auctore Ovidio, qui ita secundo Tristium post multos huius elegiae ad verbum recitatos versus tandem ita ordine claudit:

  Scit cui latretur, quum solus obambulat ipse,
    Cur toties clausas excreet ante fores.

Cur legendum, ut posui, non *Cui*, ut est in vulgatis. docet nos Ovidius, quo sensu haec accipienda sint. μιμητικῶς enim de se ipse Tibullus ait, tanquam moneat virum. quod artificiosissime factum a poeta, ut nescio an locus illustrior in toto Tibullo sit. Quasi diceret: saepe ego obambulans ante fores excreo, ut illa me audiat.'

84. Ibid.: 'Absque Ovidio horum versuum sedem propriam ignoraremus, quanquam eos ex fine superioris elegiae expunxeramus. praeterea et verum huius loci sensum sine eiusdem ope divinare difficile erat. Vides, candide lector, non iam novum esse, coniectura nostra tot versus in hoc poeta suo ordini restitutos, quum videas huius rei nos fideiussorem locupletem Ovidium habere.'

85. Scaliger later added a second historical argument. In his *vita* of Tibullus, L. G. Giraldi mentions that Lucas Ripa had complained about the great obscurity of many passages in Tibullus. Giraldi commented: 'sed enim ego non inficias ierim ita pleraque in Tibullo videri ut senex Ripa dicebat, iis qui in mendosa exemplaria impegerint, sed postquam pervetustum codicem nactus sum, amici opera, et emendatum satis, id ego totum pernego. nam quae tum difficilia videbantur et duriora, ea partim fragmenta sunt et fenestrae, partim tralaticia et supposititia adeo, ut aliquo etiam sint interiectae fere elegiae. codicem vobis alias ostendam.' Scaliger, taking this perhaps more literally than it deserves, assumed that Giraldi had had the archetype and that it had already suffered the transpositions that he claimed to have discovered; and he incorporated this argument into later editions of his *Castigationes*: 'Lege vitam huius poetae apud Lilium Gyraldum. ibi videbis exemplar, ex quo omnia Tibulliana quae hodie extant propagata sunt, aliquot pagellis transpositis turbatum fuisse.' His inference that Giraldi's codex was the parent of the rest was clearly a bit cavalier. See Haupt, *Opuscula*, iii, pp. 34–5, from whom I derive both quotations, for a more detailed discussion. Modern scholars emphasize that transpositions are normally the result not of scribal intervention but of physical damage (transposition of leaves), which cannot be the case when distichs and other short passages are in question. For an effort to explain the origin of such errors in Tibullus see the passages from C. G. Heyne quoted in A. Grafton 'Prolegomena to Friedrich August Wolf', *JWCI*, 44 (1981), p. 113 n. 74. These show that Heyne did not entirely disapprove of Scaliger's approach (though cf. Timpanaro, *Lachmann*, p. 11 n. 24).

Chapter VII

1. Vertunien to P. Dupuy, 2.vii.1602; R. L. Hawkins, 'The Friendship of Joseph Scaliger and François Vertunien', *Romanic Review*, viii (1917), p. 130: 'Or vous veulx je dire l'occasion de ladite version. Nous estions tous deux retirez à Touffou, maison de feu Monsieur de la Rochepozay, à quatre lieues de ceste ville, pour la premiere guerre de la Ligue, 1577, durant les premiers Estats de Blois: où couchant en sa chambre, pour m'exercer à la langue grecque, il me dist qu'il n'y avoit rien meilleur que de faire des versions de l'une langue en l'autre: et partant me fit il tourner le livre d'Hippocrate Περὶ τῶν ἐν κεφαλῇ τρωμάτων (cuius libelli editio apud Mam. Patissonum tot turbas excitavit Lutetiae) et tous les soirs s'allant coucher me tournoit verbo ad verbum un ou deux des Epigrammes du 7 de l'Anthologie, pour luy rendre le lendemain en vers latins. Quant à luy, à son premier reveil, il faisoit sa version in mente, ne faisant jamais autrement ses poemes: mais moy, qui suis fort mauvais poete, je travaillois prou de la faire et refaire deux et trois fois à la chandelle, pour la luy rendre au matin. Ce qu'aiant fit, et me l'aiant corrigée, il me faisoit escrire la sienne: tellement que durant neuf ou dix mois, que nous fusmes exilez audit lieu, nous achevasmes tout ledit livre . . .'. Cf. *Scaligerana II*, s.v. ANTHOLOGIA, p. 195: 'Ego cum Vertuniano et altero vertebam Anthologiam versibus, et fere totam verti. Alter tam bene vertebat quam Marotus, quo nullus in vertendo fuit foelicior.' Given the imprecision of Scaliger's memory and of the Vassani, the

compilers of the *Secunda Scaligerana*, I have followed Vertunien's account. Apparently both copies that Vertunien made of Scaliger's version were lost: *Romanic Review*, viii, pp. 130-1.

2. See, respectively, Scaliger, *Epistolae*, pp. 103-16, 120-5, and Bernays, *Scaliger*, pp. 309-10.

3. F. Vertunien, ep. ded., in *Hippocratis Coi de capitis vulneribus liber, Latinitate donatus a Francisco Vertuniano* . . . (Paris, 1578), sig. ā iii^r: 'Ille igitur [scil. Scaliger], animi gratia et aliud agens (id enim certo affirmare possum qui viderim) Libellum istum cursim legere primum coepit, in quo cum e vestigio tot glossematis a stylo Hippocratis omnino abhorrentibus ipsius lectionem interpolatam animadvertisset, notassetque in meo libro, hoc primo conatu audentior audentiorque factus Libellum denuo, sed attentius relegere operae precium duxit. In quo tantula seges tantam mendorum messem tulit, paucis ut horis, hoc est, tribus ad summum, quantum nunc extat explicarit, mihique dictaverit.' For an English translation of Vertunien's preface see Hawkins in *Romanic Review*, viii, pp. 132-4.

4. Scaliger to Dupuy, 30.vi.1577, *Lettres françaises*, pp. 64-6, refers to the work as more or less complete: 'Car ce livre estant nettoié par moi de mille faultes et glossemes qu'on avoit fourré dens le texte de ce grand personage, il l'a tourné en bon latin, illustré d'un fort beau commentaire et reprins beaucoup d'erreurs des modernes.' Vertunien's preface is dated 'Idib. Decembris' 1577, from Touffou. Scaliger had received copies of the printed work by 10 March 1578 (*Lettres françaises*, p. 73), but he none the less complained about Patisson's idleness and torpor.

5. Scaliger, 'Castigationum in Hippocratis libellum de vulneribus capitis explicatio', in *Hippocratis Coi de capitis vulneribus liber*, pp. 29-39, at pp. 29-30: 'Quare, ut dixi, diu est, cum haec addita sunt a studiosis. Mirum vero cum tot tantorumque virorum in re medicina aetas nostra feracissima fuerit, nemini hoc ne minimum quidem oboluisse.'

6. Ibid.: 'Mitto haec, quae ab eruditis apposita sunt, quaeque nihil de sententia Hippocratis detrahunt. Illa vero infinita, quae huc inculcata sunt, et hunc libellum tot modis deformarunt, quomodo illos doctos homines fugere potuerunt? Multi ita hunc libellum assidua lectione triverunt, ut pars in eum Commentarios, alii Latine, alii Gallice ediderint: pars etiam ex illo quae expiscati erant, in suos Commentarios ad verbum transfuderint. Sed omnes, ut uno verbo dicam, operam luserunt, cum tot aliena, quae huc temere ab imperitissimis hominibus infercta sunt, non animadverterunt. . . Quare hinc potest colligere studiosus Lector, quam frustra aliquid in literis tractandis promittunt illi, qui huius partis, quae Critice vocatur, expertes sunt. Haec enim una pars illis ad perfectionem defuit, cum in caeteris magni viri essent. Aliter enim de illis aut loqui, aut cogitare neque possumus, neque debemus.'

7. Scaliger to Vertunien, 25 December 1574; *Epistolae*, pp. 117-18.

8. Ibid., p. 31 ('Nam sola Critice . . .'); p. 30: 'Stipitem esse oportet qui haec Hippocratis esse credat'; p. 38: 'Nam et mediocris Grammaticus iudicaverit haec, quae adposui, delenda esse . . . Sane in recensendis auctoribus opus est ingenio non solum acuto ad menda indaganda, sed et aequanimo, et facili ad ea quae vera sunt admittenda. Nam ἐριστικῶν et contentiosorum infinitus numerus est. Quos omnes ad officinariorum et φαρμακοτριβῶν clysteria ablegamus. Imo toto Hippocrate arcemus, si has literas humaniores ignorant.'

9. Vertunien, 'Commentarius in Hippocratis libellum de vulneribus capitis', ibid., p. 44: 'Quod quia ab uno IOSEPHO SCALIGERO, divini plane ingenii heroe, hactenus praestitum scio, conabor, ex eius emendationibus, genuinum Hippocratis sensum eruere, palamque omnibus facere, quantum, Critices (quae in eo

excellentissima est) ignoratione, omnes quotquot hunc Librum tractarunt Medici ac Chirurgi, alioqui nobilissimi, ab eius mente assequenda abfuerunt.'

10. Vertunien, ep. ded., sigs. ā iii^v-[ā iiii^r]: 'Vnum addam, quod tibi ac Asclepiadis omnibus scio fore gratissimum, si a te tuique simillimis hunc primum suum conatum probatum iri animadverterit Scaliger, idem in reliquo Hippocrate tentaturum: . . . Ego vero abunde me fecisse putabo, si me modulo meo metiens, . . . totum Hippocratem ab eodem emendatum, Celsi lingua, hoc est, Latina loquentem . . . tandem aliquando edendum curavero . . . Vnum modo me id praestitisse confido, ut clare ab omnibus Senis nostri sensa intelligantur, quae alii interpretes, Critices ignorantia, admiserunt errata corrigantur, quae vere ab iis sive de morbi natura, sive de eiusdem curatione prodita sunt, probentur, nec tamen repetantur.'

11. Galen, *Opera Omnia*, ed. C. G. Kühn, xv (Leipzig, 1828), p. 733, quoted by Vertunien, 'Commentarius', p. 43.

12. Hippocrates, *Opera* (Venice, 1526), fol. 194^r; (Basel, 1538), p. 451: Ταῦτα προσγεγράφθαι τῶδε τω βιβλίω, Γαληνός φησι.

13. Ed. 1526, fol. 196^r; ed. 1538, p. 456: Καὶ τάδε τὰ τελευταῖα ὑπό τινος προσγεγράφθαι δῆλον ἐστίν.

14. *Hippocrates de vulneribus capitis, Vido Vidio Florentino interprete* (Paris, 1550). The interpolated matter is given on p. 22, under the heading: 'In interpretatione Calvi leguntur haec in principio.'

15. Ἱπποκράτης περὶ τῶν ἐν κεφαλῇ τρωμάτων (Paris, 1556), fol. 17^r; the interpolated matter at the beginning is also omitted (ibid., fol. 2^r).

16. Hippocrates, *Opera quae ad nos extant omnia, per Ianum Cornarium Medicum Physicum Latina lingua conscripta et recognita* (Basel, 1558), p. 689; Cornarius's text does contain the interpolation at the beginning of the work (p. 680), though the 1538 edition of Hippocrates in Greek that he had edited did not.

17. G. Falloppia, *In Hippocratis librum de vulneribus capitis G. F. medici clarissimi expositio* (Venice, 1566), esp. fol. 8^v: 'Nullum capitis vulnus] In codice Cornarii habemus appendicem appositam, apud Graecos etiam codices varia addita sunt, et varia deficientia dicta sunt, usque ad illam partem Hominum capita [the beginning of the genuine text] omnia superaddita sunt. Hoc possum probare ex codice Graeco Cardinalis Florentini, quem donavit Gallorum Regi maiusculis literis manuscripto. Hoc etiam patet, quia Hipp. inordinate loqueretur, si adessent haec verba, at Gal. testatur in hoc libro nihil desiderari, itaque expungite verba illa, et incipite veram lectionem.'

18. Vertunien, 'Commentarius', p. 43: 'Quae cum subodoratus esset Aristarchus noster Scaliger, iis iam, ut nunc vides, explicatis, forte accidit ut in hunc Galeni locum inciderim, quo sane mirum quam gavisus sit, se, quod ipsi Galeno sub oluerat, cursim percurrendo, divinasse.'

19. Ibid., p. 44: '*Humana capita*] Quae, in quibusdam exemplaribus hunc textum praecedunt non esse Hippocratis, cum Vido Vidio et Gabriele Fallopio sentio. Cuius certe aequanimitatem hac in parte maxime miror, quod Cornarii interpretatione contentus meliorem eligere, aut praestare ipse noluerit.'

20. Scaliger to Vertunien, 11.xi.1575, *Romanic Review*, viii, p. 127.

21. Scaliger to Dupuy, 10.iii.1578, *Lettres françaises*, p. 74: 'Car Patisson n'a pas bien faict d'avoir monstré le livre de Monsieur de La Vau a mestre Louis Duret, car ceste pouvre beste se vante en pleine chaise que je lui ai dérrobé ses corrections.' Bernays, *Scaliger*, pp. 239–40.

22. The pamphlet was entitled *Nicolai Vincentii Pictaviensis Chirurgi epistola ad Stephanum Naudinum Bersuriensem*; I use the excerpts given by Bernays, *Scaliger*, pp. 241-51.

23. Ibid., p. 247: 'Orgia Bacchi ὄρκια interpretatur doctissimus scholae Lutetianae magister, alter Duretus, columen artis medicinae. O misellum Scaligerum, qui tot adulterina ac spuria ex Hippocrate sustulit, unum ritum sacrorum, quae Martinus bacchans commentus est, animadvertere non potuit. Quam latebram inscitiae nunc quaeret infelix Iosephus ille cum sua Critica, cuius rationem habere Scholasticos Parisienses frustra postulat. Iam Martinus erit Orgiastes. Quare ille se medicum esse postulet, qui in Orgiis Bacchi adeo profecit? O infelicia Lexica, ubi eratis, cum Martinus τὰ ὄρκια vertit Orgia? Male vobis sit qui Martino in tempore non adfuistis.'

24. Ibid., pp. 249-50: 'Sed aliquid divini latet in Dureti Latinitate quod vulgo notum non est'; 'Sed favet Gallis nostris Duretus, quorum more ille Latine loquitur.'

25. Scaliger to Dupuy, 30.vi.1577, *Lettres françaises*, p. 63: '. . . dernièrement en brouillant mes livres j'ai trouvé mon Manilius corrigé par moi du temps que j'estois *in Helvetiis*. Il m'a semblé qu'il y avait de choses, qui sont assés à propos.'

26. Ibid., p. 64: 'Je sais qu'il i a aujourd'hui en France de grands genethliaques et mathématiciens. Mais . . . je leur baille bon terme à diviner le sens de Manilius en ces lieux difficiles.'

27. So Scaliger thought, though Jacopo Corbinelli reported that Passerat spoke of the Catullus with the greatest respect; R. Calderini de Marchi, *Jacopo Corbinelli et les érudits français* (Milan, 1914), pp. 139-40; but cf. the next n.

28. Scaliger to Dupuy, 10.iii.1578, *Lettres françaises*, p. 75: 'Aussi je le fai d'autant que Passerat, et quelques aultres *pedantes* comme lui, qui n'ont aulcune science, que de petitz fatras de corrections, pourroient aussi dire comme Duret. Mais tant que je vivrai je ferai la guerre aux *pedantes*, et puisqu'ilz ne veullent cognoistre la différence qu'il y a d'un homme bien nourri à celle d'un *magister*, et que je ne les puis avoir par honnesteté, je leur abaisserai leur caquet par aultre moien.'

29. Corbinelli to Pinelli, 21.xi.1579, quoted by Calderini de Marchi, *Corbinelli*, p. 140 n. 1: 'Quel Simon Bosius è galantissimo spirito et si burla di Scaligero et dice liberamente che ha preso di molti granchi et che non intende che cosa sia *matrimo* et *patrimo* et che *Patrona virgo* è la vera lettione.'

30. Io. Bissonerius to M. A. Muret, 24.iv.1575; *Miscellaneorum ex Mss. libris Bibliothecae Collegii Romani Societatis Jesu tomus . . .* (Rome, 1754-7), II, p. 499: 'Sed ut ad Petrum Victorium veniam, quem Florentiae reperi, scito, eum, quantum deprehendi, privatas adhuc aliquas tecum simultates gerere. Nam cum saepe de te mentio a me esset injecta, ne verbum quidem unquam est prolocutus. Invectus est autem acerbe in eos, quibus in castigandis probatorum auctorum scriptis, conjecturae momenta potiora essent, quam auctoritatis; eoque nomine Josephum Scaligerum reprehendit graviter, quod in conjectaneis illis suis in Varronem adeo confidenter quaedam asserat, ut cum Varrone ipso collocutus esse videatur: contendebatque Victorius, nunquam aut raro discedendum esse ab auctoritate; conjecturas autem, tamquam ψευδεῖς μάρτυρας, ut de Etymologia quodam loco Galenus loquitur, prorsus esse aversandas. Qua in re quam bene sentiat tuum esto judicium.' Vettori owned Scaliger's 1573 Varro and a 2nd copy of his commentaries; see the card catalogue of his books in 4°, 8°, 12°, 16° in the Bayerische Staatsbibliothek, Cod. Bav. Cat. 209C. Both books seem to have been lost.

31. See *Dictionnaire de biographie française*, s.v. Abain, by J. Balteau.

32. Scaliger to Dupuy, 21.vi.1582, *Lettres françaises*, p. 125.

33. N. Audebert to C. Dupuy, 13.i.1579; Paris, Bibliothèque Nationale, MS Dupuy 712, fol. 2, printed in part by Nolhac, *La Bibliothèque de Fulvio Orsini* (Paris, 1887), p. 68 n. 1.

34. A. Du Chesne, *Preuves de l'histoire de la Maison des Chasteigners* (Paris, 1633), pp. 129–32 (3 letters from Vettori to Chasteigner).

35. Corbinelli to Pinelli, 21.iii.1579; Calderini de Marchi, *Corbinelli*, p. 143: 'Mi s'è doluto di Pier Vettori che dice che gl'ha detto che le son bagatelle le cose sue et si mescola dell'antichità et non gli riesce. Cosa che io non credo punto che sia vera perchè Pier Vettori non è di questa natura nè le cose sue son bagatelle. Ha non so che d'amarognolo col Sigonio.' Admittedly this text is anything but clear; but as Scaliger elsewhere complains that the Italians had called Turnèbe a barbarian, my reading of it seems plausible.

36. Ibid., p. 139.

37. Pinelli to Dupuy, 22.ii.1578, MS Dupuy 704, fols. 53^v–54^r.

38. Calderini de Marchi, *Corbinelli*, pp. 142–5.

39. Ibid., p. 144: 'Non nomina nessuno designanter, ma s'intende benissimo che si sdegna un po' con Pier Vettori, lodandolo però sempre con una buona modestia, è un po' contro al Sigonio et mi par che gli dia un certo motto d'Arpinate Bolognese, non me ne ricordo. Mette in invidia Pier Vettori che habbi anco chiamato Barbaro il Turnebo. Non ci veggo cosa nè troppo maligna nè che possi anco punto agguagliare l'aspettatione che s'ha da chi non ha vedute queste sue cose . . .'. Dr Timpanaro found the first version of the interpretation proposed here 'poco credibile', though he accepted my general description of the change that Scaliger's method underwent. See his *La genesi del metodo del Lachmann*, 2nd edn. (Padua, 1981), p. 11 and n. 25. Great though his authority is, I continue to find the argument credible. Dr Timpanaro's alternative explanation of the change — that Scaliger suffered 'un diminuire della pazienza e della capacità di attenzione costante che sono necessarie per collazioni complete . . . ' — can hardly survive even a brief inspection of Scaliger's later works. His first major book on chronology, the *De emendatione temporum*, came out only four years after the Manilius, and rested on a vast body of computations that required — *experto crede* — as much 'pazienza' and 'attenzione' as any collation. The second, the *Thesaurus temporum* of 1606, rested on very wide explorations in Greek and Latin MSS and required a vast effort of patient copying, which Scaliger himself carried out. Others of his late works — notably the indices that he drew up for Gruter's corpus of inscriptions, on which see A. Grafton in *Lias*, ii (1975), pp. 109–13 — also reveal an unimpaired willingness to undertake the most exacting of clerical and scribal labour. The change in Scaliger's work was one of method, not of mental habits.

40. Bernays, *Scaliger*, p. 47; M. Pattison, *Essays* (Oxford, 1889), i, p. 162.

41. Housman to Asquith, 22.iv.1926; *The Letters of A. E. Housman*, ed. H. Maas (London, 1971), p. 236.

42. Scaliger to Dupuy, 30.vi.1577, *Lettres françaises*, pp. 63–4.

43. Scaliger to Dupuy, 31.vii.1577, *Lettres françaises*, pp. 68–9, esp. 69: 'Mais ce seroit un grand blasme à moi d'avoir leu le Ptolémée tourné barbarement d'Arabic, et n'avoir veu le grec, et ne sai qui vouldroit entreprendre de m'excuser d'une si grande nonchallance.'

44. Scaliger to Dupuy, 26.viii.1577, *Lettres françaises*, p. 71: 'J'ai receu vostre Ptolémée avecques les scholies et vous remercie tres humblement . . . '; Scaliger to Dupuy, 10.iii.1578, ibid., p. 73: 'Je vous envoie mon texte de Manilius, avec mes castigations et commentaires sur icellui.' Scaliger goes on to explain why he has 'tant différé' to send the work, a statement that implies that he had been finished for some time. The 'barbaric' version of Ptolemy that Scaliger had to work through was a copy of Plato of Tivoli's translation which was included in the collection of astrological texts published by Pruckner (Basel, 1551); Scaliger's copy is now in Leiden University Library (shelf-mark 761 B 2). Scaliger evidently worked through the Latin *Tetrabiblos* twice, the first time

trying to reconstruct the Arabic words and proper names that lay behind some of the more curious Latin words, and the second time entering the original Greek. Thus, against the phrase 'Arbalui, Caurosiae, Fathathiae, Nudhiae' in II.3 (p. 24 of the 2nd pagination), Scaliger has written: ἀριανοί, γεδρωσοί, πάρθοι, μῆδοι. And on the prooemium to IV (p. 60), where the Latin text reads 'Primum est in substantia et valetudine . . .' Scaliger has underlined the last word and written 'ἀξίωμα. male' in the margin.

45. Scaliger, *In Manilii quinque libros Astronomicon commentarius et Castigationes* (Paris, 1579), bound with *M. Manilii Astronomicωn libri quinque* (Paris, 1579), p. 6: *'Pandere sensus*] Scribendum est, *census*. Sic saepe, ut in Apotelesmatis *— inque ipsos Mundi descendere census*. et in secunda Institutione *— hominis per sidera censum'*; pp. 68-9: *'Ac tantum mundi regeret prudentia sensum*] Sine ullo dubio *censum*, non *sensum* scripsit Manilius. Vt in Sphaerae prooemio: *— et aethereos per carmina pandere census*. Apud Gellium quoque in Favorini declamatione legendum, *caelestium rerum censu, atque ductu*. Scio equidem vulgatam lectionem defendi posse. Sed veritas paedagogorum pervicaciae anteferenda.'

46. *M. Manilii Astronomicon liber I*, ed. A. E. Housman, 2nd edn. (Cambridge, 1937), pp. xiii-xiv. The 5 volumes of Housman's edition have been to me an invaluable guide to Manilius; they are referred to hereafter simply as 'Housman', followed by volume and page numbers. In numbering of lines and, where possible, in translation I follow the extremely useful Loeb edition by G. P. Goold (Cambridge, Mass. and London, 1977); Goold's introduction is much the most painless entrance to the technical matters dealt with by Manilius, and I wish that it had been available when I began my work.

47. Housman, iii, p. v.

48. Scaliger, *Commentarius*, p. 140: *'Nonus locus occupat omnem Fatorum sortem*] Scribe, *Natorum sortem*. Ait enim eo τὴν παιδοτροφίαν omnem καὶ ἀνατριβήν contineri.*Omniaque intrantum*] Lege *infantum. Nutritia*, τὰ τροφεῖα, τὰ θρεπτήρια. Alibi:

   Et precium caelo sua per nutritia ferre.

   Continet patrios timores, inquit, καὶ πᾶσαν τὴν τεκνοτροφίαν, mista turba tamen, hoc est non sine turba et timore. Soliciti enim sunt paterni animi in affectus suos. Dixit ergo τὴν ἀνατριβὴν seu τεκνοτροφίαν rem esse soliciti timoris plenam.

   Nunc oppressa movent) Vitiosa interpunctio. Lege:
   Quaque valetudo constat nunc libera morbis,
   Nunc oppressa, movent ut mundum sidera cunque.
   Non alias sedes) Ne haec quidem sincera sunt. Nam
   ita purganda:
   Non alia est sedes, tempusve genusve gerendi
   Quae sibi deposcat. —
   Ait τὸν ἐπιλογισμὸν τῶν πρακτέων in ea esse . . .'.

49. Cf. Housman, i, p. xvi.

50. Scaliger, *Commentarius*, p. 238: *'Thebas divisit rege vel uno*] Emendavimus: — *Thebae Divis, et rege vel uno Thessalia, Epirusque potens —* Thebarum urbs Deorum nutricula, Bacchi, et Melicertae, et Herculis: Thessalia magnorum Regum, Achillis, et regum Macedoniae. Quorum vel unus satis erat ad eam illustrandam Alexander Magnus. Epirus Pyrrhum et alios tulit. . . . *Thebae divis et rege vel uno*] Sophocles apud Dicaearchum ἐν ἑλλάδος ἀναγραφῇ:
   Θήβας λέγεις μοι τὰς πύλας θ'ἑπταστόμους,
   οὗ δὴ μόναι τίκτουσιν αἱ θνηταὶ θεούς.'

51. Scaliger's working copy of Manilius also forms part of his copy of Pruckner (op. cit., n. 44, above), pp. 144-224 of the 2nd pagination. In it he has incorporated into the text many of his emendations (e.g. at IV.688 he has altered

the printed text's *Thebas divisit* to *Thebae divis, et*). And before line V.710 he has indicated in the margin that V.30-1 should be inserted, followed by asterisks to indicate a lacuna. At this point he writes: 'Laisses espace de six ou sept vers' (p. 223). And indeed, in the corresponding passage in the 1579 text (p. 135) there is a gap of 6 lines. Mr M. D. Reeve — who called my attention to these points — accordingly suggested that this must be the base text Scaliger prepared for his printer ('Scaliger and Manilius', *Mnemosyne*, ser. IV, xxxiii (1980), pp. 177-9). Scaliger's Pruckner does not contain by any means all of the changes that appear in his final text of 1579 (e.g. *Natorum* for *Fatorum* in III.132); nor are there the normal chalk-marks giving signature numbers that one expects in a book used as a printer's copy. Accordingly, it seems likely that either Scaliger himself or, less likely, Patisson eventually decided to transcribe the new text before printing it, and that the further emendations were introduced into the new base text at that time, along with the directions and changes that had already been made by Scaliger in his copy of Pruckner.

52. Casaubon's copy of the Manilius is Leiden University Library, 758 F 1². This note falls on p. 227 of the *Commentarius*, 11. 25 ff.: 'Mirum hoc, bis mirum. Cum fateatur summus vir se dubitanter ita corrigere, ausum tamen suas coniecturas ipso teste dubias tanquam oracula quaedam pro vera lectione obtrudere.'

53. Guy le Fèvre de la Boderie to Scaliger, 25.i.1579; *Epistres françoises des Personnages illustres et doctes à Monsr. Ioseph Iuste de la Scala*, ed. Iaques de Reves (Harderwyck, 1624), I.17, p. 28: 'Lequel certes, à ce que j'ay peu recognoistre de premiere veüe, parce que je n'ay encor eu le loisir de le par lire, a bien changé de manteau, auquel la clairté de vos doctes commentaires donne beaucoup de lustre.'

54. Housman, v, p. xviii.

55. Housman, i, p. xiii.

56. Giphanius to Scaliger, 7.ii.1574 (misdated 1578 by Burman), *Sylloges epistolarum a viris illustribus scriptarum tomus I [-V]* (Leiden, 1727), II, p. 306: 'Superioribus diebus, quibus ad socerum migravi, dum libros et chartas scrutor, incido in litteras *Caroli Langii*, illius, qui olim officia Ciceronis emendavit: iis litteris (quas abhinc sesquianno ad me dedit) scribit *Jacobum Susium* . . . habere antiquissimum exemplar Manilii Astrologi, idque cum edito formis comparare. Sed se ita nosse *Susium*, ut vix putet nisi longo fortasse post intervallo eam rem perfectum iri. In eo autem Poeta, quia te illis litteris scripseras versari, et operam dare, ut emendatior brevi edatur: rem gratam me tibi facturum putavi, si illud ad te perscriberem: nam si ita voles, opera *Langii*, de quo tamen jam ex eo tempore nihil accepi, curare fortasse tibi potero, ut si non ipsum exemplar, saltem varietates scripturae habere possis. Qua de re quid me facere velis, facies me certiorem.'

57. See the passages cited in n. 40, above.

58. Scaliger, *Commentarius*, p. 32; Housman called this 'a feat of easy brilliancy' (i, p. xiii).

59. Only once before had Scaliger used a similar title. The title page of Vertunien's Hippocrates advertises *Hippocratis textus Graecus a Iosepho Scaligero . . . castigatus, cum ipsius Scaligeri Castigationum suarum explicatione*. There he uses the singular *explicatio* rather than the plural that Vettori normally used. Considering that Hippocrates was even farther from Vettori's normal line of country than from Scaliger's, it seems unlikely that the title was intended to make a polemical statement.

60. L. Carrion, *Antiquarum lectionum commentarii III* (Antwerp, 1576); cf. M. Bechert, *De M. Manilii emendandi ratione* (Leipzig, 1878), pp. 6-7.

61. I compared Scaliger's text of Manilius with the relevant chapters in the editon

of Carrion's work in Gruter's *Lampas,* III; given the high rate of corruption in this text, it is possible that Carrion anticipated even more of Scaliger's corrections. It should be pointed out that Carrion himself viewed Scaliger with the greatest respect after the Manilius had appeared. See Paris, Bibliothèque Nationale, MS Dupuy, 699, fol. 133ʳ.

62. Op. cit., n. 44 above, p. 217 of the text of Manilius; cf. for similar tactics on Scaliger's part Ch. IV, above, n. 180. Cf. too Carrion, *Antiquae lectiones* II.14, *Lampas,* III, p. 49 (of the second pagination); 'liber Gemblacensis:
   Et medios inter volucrem pensare meatus
   Aut nitidos clamare suis, ramove sedentem,
   Pascentemve super surgentia dicere vina.
   Correctum in eodem, ut in plerisque illius bibliothecae libris:
   Aut nitidis damnare suis, ramove sedentem,
   Pascentemve super surgentia deicere lina.
   Suspicor legendum . . .
   Et medios inter volucrem prensare meatus,
   Aut nidis damnare suis, ramove sedentem
   Pascentemve super surgentia dicere vina.'
   The scribe of G entered *nidis* above *nitidos* with a break in the middle of the word: *ni/dis.* Carrion could have read it hastily as *nitidis*; he could also have hoped to pass off the MS's variant reading as his own conjecture.

63. In *Adversaria,* XXII.32 (Paris, 1564–5), II, fol. 240ᵛ, Turnèbe suggests that IV. 168–9 be emended to read:
   Et gravia annonae speculantem incendia, ventis
   Credere opes: (cf. Carrion, I.10);
   Scaliger accepted this at *Commentarius,* p. 213, remarking: 'Turnebus etiam ita olim emendavit. Si quis putat me ab eo suffuratum, en sibi suas res habeat.' In XXIII, 26, II, fols. 261ᵛ–262ʳ, Turnèbe suggests that V. 63 read:
   Indelassato properantia corda vigore;
   so did Carrion, using G, in II.5 (reading *videre*). Scaliger, *Commentarius,* p. 253, writes: 'Scribe', followed by Turnèbe's version, which he had also entered in his copy of Pruckner (changing *Inde relaxato* to *Indelassato, corde* to *corda, videre* to *vigore*).

64. L. Bonincontri, *In C. Manilium Commentum,* Hain *10706 (Rome, 1484); see B. Soldati, *La poesia astrologica nel quattrocento. Ricerche e studi* (Florence, 1906), Ch. II, esp. pp. 144–53, for a good account of Bonincontri's life and a brief discussion of the Manilius edition. In the section DE MANILIO with which his commentary begins, Scaliger remarks: 'Aiunt Bonincontrium quendam in hunc poetam commentarios edidisse: quem librum diligenter in Gallia, Italia, Germania conquisitum reperire non potui. Quod ipse in hunc poetam boni edere potuerit, non video, qui tot mendis inquinatum eum nobis reliquerit. Quod si illum nancisci licuisset, fortasse multa menda, quae in hoc auctore extant, ab eius commentariis propagata esse videremus. Sed quia illum auctorem non legi, de eo nihil aliud dicendum censeo.' (*Commentarius,* p. 4.) In fact, Scaliger was wrong to assume that Bonincontri was solely responsible for the state of the vulgate; on the one hand, he made a number of good emendations, and, on the other hand and more important, Bonincontri was neither the first editor nor the only one whose hand lay heavy on the text. For detailed discussion see A. Cramer, *Über die ältesten Ausgaben von Manilius' Astronomica* (Ratibor, 1893); *Manili Astronomicon liber II,* ed. H. W. Garrod (Oxford, 1911), pp. lxxv–lxxx.

65. See e.g. *Commentarius,* p. 5: 'M. MANILII ASTRONOMICON LIBER PRIMVS) Iste liber est Sphaera mundi, aut de Vniversitate. Secundus prima Isagoge apotelesmatice. Tertius secunda Isagoge. Quartus Signorum apotelesmata. Quintus Sphaerae barbaricae prima apotelesmata. Ac aliorum quidem quatuor

rationes suis locis redduntur. Huius autem haec est. Astronomiae partes duae sunt. Altera circa Stellarum motus versatur . . . Altera est circa effectus ipsos . . . '. Bonincontri had followed the ancient tradition that any commentary should include a summary of the work ('Solent Poetarum expositores', he remarks, 'primo de poete nomine indagare et eius vita. Deinde libri titulum, carminis qualitatem, librorum numerum, et quae sit scribentis poete intentio, quae a me recte cogitata saepius animo volvissem';*In C. Manilium commentum*, fol. 2ᵛ); accordingly, he wrote: 'Scribentis poete intentio est Rudibus adhuc astrologie Romanis astrorum imagines et xii. zodiaci signa, mundi dispositionem et ortus syderum ostendere, cum ipsorum vi ac potestate, sphere etiam celestis circulos demonstrare. In primo enim libro operis sui preponit scientiam;secundo invocat Augustum ad quem opus suum dedicavit; tertio de inventoribus huius scientie perscruptatur, ostendens operis difficultatem . . . '.

66. See e.g. *Commentarius*, p. 6 *ad* I.1; p. 8 *ad* I.26; p. 12 *ad* I.81; pp. 30–1 *ad* I.405 ff.; p. 82 *ad* II.241; p. 242 *ad* IV.764.

67. Scaliger, *Commentarius*, p. 105; '*Linea sic veri*] Pone τελείαν στιγμήν post τὸ *linea*. eod. *Sic veri per totum*] Epilogus Manilianus, ut supra: . . . Item: . . . Et sic fere semper.' Casaubon wrote at p. 252 of his copy of the commentary (Leiden University Library, 758 F 1²): 'Epilogi freq. in Manil.'

68. Scaliger, *Commentarius*, p. 253; cf. Housman, v, p. 9 ad loc.

69. *Quippe etiam mundi faciem sedesque movebit*
    sidereas caelumque novum versabit in orbem.

70. Scaliger, *Commentarius*, p. 221; cf. P. Tannery, 'Sur deux vers de Manilius', *Revue de Philologie*, n. s. xvii (1893), pp. 213–14 and Housman, iv, p. 35 *ad* IV.267, 268 (Housman abuses Scaliger for his error in the 2nd edition but does not mention that he had given the correct interpretation in the first place).

71. Scaliger, *Commentarius*, p. 68: 'Stoicorum est ne una quidem vocula minus. Quid est ἡγεμονικόν; πνεῦμα ἔξ ὅλου κινούμενον καθ' ἑκάστην τύπωσιν. Et revera Stoicis magis addictus est noster.'

72. Scaliger, *Commentarius*, pp. 17–18.

73. Scaliger, *Commentarius*, p. 20 *ad* I.263 ff.; pp. 35–6 *ad* I.807–8. Scaliger's working copies of the poem are preserved (Leiden MS Scal. 32, fols. 20ᵛ–22ᵛ; a copy of this, incorporating marginal corrections from the former into its text, in Scal. 22, fols. 20ᵛ–22ᵛ). In the passages cited above he quotes from the second, separate part of the poem (= E. Maass, *Commentariorum in Aratum reliquiae* [Berlin, 1898], p. 170).

74. Scaliger, *Commentarius*, p. 85 *ad* II.286.

75. Scaliger, *Commentarius*, p. 143 *ad* III.170; cf. p. 144.

76. Scaliger, *Commentarius*, p. 52 *ad* I.633: '*Hos volucres fecere duos*] Meridiani et Orizontes pro locorum inclinatione alii atque alii; cum contra Paralleli immobiles sint . . . Ambos autem coniunctim ponit. recte. Quia alter sine altera esse non potest. Omnis orizon Meridianum suum recte secat. Poli omnis orizontis sunt puncta Orientis et Occidentis. Poli Mundi sunt poli omnium Meridianorum. Ita omnis orizon per puncta ortus et occasus transit, ut omnis Meridianus per polos Mundi. In situ immobili rectae sphaerae imaginemur CLXXX circulos magnos ad polos mundi se intersecare, totidem ad puncta ortivum et occiduum: Qui verticem nostrum tanget, is erit meridianus noster. Qui illum ad rectos angulos intersecat, is est orizon, et tangit punctum finitionis oculi. Rursus, qui definiet aciem oculi nostri, is est orizon noster. Qui illum ad angulos rectos secat, is stringit punctum verticis nostri, et est Meridianus noster. Mutua ratio est, et reciproca descriptio: quod alter sine altero esse non potest. Merito igitur coniunxit eos.'

77. See in general Goold's introduction, pp. lxii–lxviii.

78. Scaliger, *Commentarius*, p. 145 *ad* III.187: '*Tunc si forte dies*] In diurna genitura hoc modo progredere. A Sole ad Lunam per signa consequentia numera. Eas partes ab horoscopo deme. In quo relinquet te numerus, ibi est Sors Fortunae. Ascendat 17.4' Tauri. Locus Lunae sit in 13.6' Cancri, Solis 4.9' Capricorni. Distantia Solis a Luna per signa consequentia, Signa 6. grad. 8.57'. Quam si a loco Horoscopi numeravero, numerus residebit in 26.1' Scorpii. Ibi est Sors Fortunae.'

79. Scaliger's text of Firmicus Maternus was that contained in his 1551 Pruckner collection (Leiden University Library, 761 B 2). He worked through the text carefully, collating it against a MS from the collection of Cujas; see *Commentarius*, p. 204 *ad* III.601: '. . . scriptus Firmici codex, qui est penes iuris civilis Apollinem Iac. Cuiacium' and the margins of Scaliger's copy, where the codex is referred to simply as 'v'. Scaliger also compared Book VIII of the *Mathesis* with Manilius, identifying passages where Firmicus had or had not drawn on the *Astronomica* (e.g. Scaliger's marginal note on p. 218, *ad* VIII.8: 'plus dicit, quam Manil.'; p. 221, *ad* VIII.15: 'non est apud Manil.'). He entered the Greek equivalents for Firmicus' Latin astrological terms (e.g. Scaliger's note on p. 16, *ad* II.3, 'Stellarum altitudo, deiectioque': ὕψωμα ταπείνωμα; p. 32, *ad* II.22, 'piger locus': ἀργὸς τόπος). And he filled the margins with his usual *signes de renvoi*. Scaliger read the Greek commentaries on Ptolemy and Abū Maʾshar *De revolutionibus nativitatum* in H. Wolf's edition, the title of which begins: *In Claudii Ptolemaei Quadripartitum enarrator ignoti nominis* . . . (Basel, 1559), and which he borrowed from Dupuy (by the end of his life, he owned his own copy). And he read Hipparchus' and Achilles' works on Aratus in the edition by Pier Vettori (Florence, 1567). His copy of this last work ended up in Weimar. There J. B. G. D'Ansse de Villoison found it; he printed its extensive marginal notes in his *Epistolae Vinarienses* (Zürich, 1783), Ep. III, pp. 73-80.

80. Scaliger, *Commentarius*, p. 145: 'Hermes in Enchiridio: ὅτε βουλόμεθα ποιῆσαι τὸν περίπαθον τοῦ κλήρου τῆς τύχης ἐν ὅλῳ τῷ ἐνιαυτῷ τῆς ἐναλλαγῆς, λαμβάνομεν ἀπὸ τοῦ ἡλίου ἐπὶ σελήνην, καὶ τὰ ἴσα ἀπὸ τοῦ ὡροσκόπου. Petosiris et Necepso: ὅταν κλῆρον τύχης λαμβάνῃς, ἡμέρας μὲν ἀπὸ ἡλίου ἐπὶ σελήνην ἀρίθμει, καὶ τὰ ἴσα ἀπὸ ὡροσκόπου ἐπὶ τὰ ἐπόμενα τῶν ζωδίων ἀπόλυε. Haec fuit veterum illorum methodus.' The 2nd passage Scaliger took from Wolf's edition of the *Tetrabiblos* commentaries, p. 111. For further details on the astrological authors and doctrines discussed here see in general the exhaustive work by A. Bouché-Leclercq, *L'Astrologie grecque* (Paris, 1899; repr. Brussels, 1963), which, however, is far more trustworthy on the Greek background than on Manilius himself.

81. Scaliger, *Commentarius*, p. 11: '*Nascendi quae cuique dies*] Id quibus rationibus collegerint, apponam ex eodem Sex. Empirico: νύκτωρ μὲν ὁ χαλδαῖος, φασιν, ἐφ' ὑψηλῆς τινὸς ἀκρωρείας ἐκαθέζετο, ἀστεροσκοπῶν, ἕτερος δὲ παρήδρευε τῇ ὠδινούσῃ μέχρις ἀποτέξαιτο. ἀποτεκούσης δὲ εὐθὺς δίσκῳ διεσήμαινε τῷ ἐπὶ τῆς ἀκρωρείας. ὁ δὲ ἀκούσας καὶ αὐτὸς παρεσημειοῦτο τὸ ἀνίσχον ζώδιον ὡς ὡροσκοποῦν. μεθ' ἡμέραν δὲ τοῖς ὡροσκοπίοις προσεῖχε καὶ ταῖς τοῦ ἡλίου κινήσεσιν [*Adversus mathematicos* V.27-8, tr. Bury].' Cf. ibid., pp. 10-11 *ad* I.53, where Scaliger uses *Adv. Math.* V.24-6 to illustrate the use of water devices to time the risings of signs.

82. Scaliger, *Commentarius*, p. 80: '*Ne mirere*] Pulchrum vero commentum: propter σχέσιν κατηστερισμένων moras longarum dierum ponere. Quae omnia ἀναιτιολόγητα sunt, siquidem rem ipsam, non fabulas ἀστροθεσιῶν spectare vis' (the point here is that the signs in question, Taurus, Gemini, and Cancer, were traditionally depicted as rising with their hind-parts foremost; Scaliger apparently took this as Manilius' attempt to explain why summer days are longer than winter ones).

83. I. Bouillau, in Scaliger, *Castigationes et notae in M. Manilii astronomicon*, in

M. Manilii Astronomicon a Iosepho Scaligero ex vetusto codice Gemblacensi infinitis mendis repurgatum (Strasbourg, 1655), p. 4:
> '*Nec mirere moras, quum Sol adversa per astra*
> *Aestivum tardis attollat mensibus annum.*]

legendum proculdubio *aversa*, ut cum superioribus conveniant. Causam longioris veris, atque etiam aestatis rudibus in Geometria et Astronomiae imperitis ridiculam offert, propterea quod Taurus, Gemini, Cancer aversi oriantur, cum Solis Apogaei, vel ut hodie loquimur Terrae Aphelii Manilii saeculo circa decimam Geminorum partem situs apparens hoc effecerit. Nullatenus autem moras longarum dierum αἰτιολογεῖ poeta astrologus, ut vult Scaliger, aut respicit ad incrementum dierum; sed illa refert ad longitudinem temporis, quo Sol Borealia signa percurrebat diebus 186½, qui semestri tempori imputabantur, cum alterum semestre australium signorum fuerit dierum 178½ circiter. Vnde tardi dici debuerunt menses tres vernales, qui, ut et tres aestivi, diebus 93¼ praeter propter constabant: et diuturniori tempore labebantur quam autumnales et hiberni, qui singuli terni diebus 89¼ ὁλοσχερῶς accepti conficiebantur. Haec autem loquendi formula *aestivus annus* significat tempus aestivum.'

84. *M. Manilii Astronomicon ex recensione et cum notis R. Bentleii* (London, 1739), p. 84 *ad* II.201: 'CVM SOL ADVERSA PER ASTRA . . . Ceterum poeticam hic causam, non astronomicam, auctor assignat, cur *annus aestivus* constet diebus 186½, hibernus 178½ circiter; ut recte explicat idem Bullialdus.'

85. Scaliger, *Commentarius*, p. 58 *ad* I.750–751: '*Famae vulgata vetustas Mollior*]
   Ita interpungimus:
   > *Nec mihi celanda est famae vulgata vetustas*
   Mollior: e niveo, etc. Molliorem famam vocat fabulam vulgi. Rhetorum est πείθειν, Philosophi ἀποδεικνύειν. Ita eorum sunt ἔνδοξα ἐπιχειρήματα: huius ἀποδείξεις. Sed et Rhetor interdum ἀποδείξει utitur, et Philosophus ἐνδόξῳ ἐπιχειρήματι. Nam ἔνδοξα ἐπιχειρήματα multum possunt post ἀποδείξεις. Sic Manilius post ἀποδείξεις de Lacteo circulo ἔνδοξα ἐπιχειρήματα e medio vulgi petita, puta fabulam Phaethontis et de lacte Iunonis adfert. Quod solet aliquando facere Aristoteles. Neque pudet eum fabulas vulgi in medium producere. Non quod in illis verum sit, sed quia a vero ortae sunt ut plurimum. De lacte Iunonis quod hic dicitur, praeter Grammaticos et Mythologos, habes plene apud Philoponum in primum Meteoron.' The differences between Scaliger's text and the modern one quoted above are not relevant here except in one respect; they show that Scaliger's excess learning diverted him from considering the really crucial point posed by these lines. As Bentley put the question: 'Quid enim est *vetustas vulgata famae*? quid *mollior vetustas*? Haec monstra sunt, nec ulli poetae adscribenda.' (quoted by Housman, i, p. 66 ad loc.)

86. Casaubon, marginal note ad loc. (Leiden University Library 758 F 1[2]): 'πείθειν et ἀποδεικνύειν. Sed profecto vir summus hic nimis est argutus, nec hoc unquam cogitavit Man. Neque dubium esse potest cur fabulam seq. mollem poeta appellet.' Casaubon did not always see farther than his friend. At V.165 ff. Manilius describes those who can 'with a deft kick keep in the air a flying ball, exchanging hands for feet and employing in play the body's support' . . . i.e. jugglers. Scaliger, in an excess of scholarly black humour, took the lines to refer to those born without arms, who train their feet to perform the tasks of normal people's hands: 'Vidi paulo ante, quam haec scriberem, hominem Hispalensem ex Hispania, qui truncus brachiis natus erat. Is pede et scribit, et suit, et, quod mirum est, tormenta sclopettaria tendit ac laxat: item quacunque parte corporis vult, pedes traiicit, et circumplectitur, quod Manilius dicit, ludere saltu, et per totum corpus vagas plantas disponere. Vidi mulierem ex Belgio, quae idem faciebat, truncam et ipsam lacteris . . .' *Commentarius*, p. 261. Here is Casaubon's comment on this bit of philologist's Grand Guignol: 'Ego similem vidi Genevae, anno 1587, qui et scriberet pedib. et alia multa

mirabiliter praestaret.' Since Casaubon mentions both Manilius V.165 ff., with Scaliger's commentary, and his own parallel experience in his *Commentarius et castigationes ad lib. Strabonis Geograph. XVII* (1587), p. 206, his reading of Scaliger's commentary can probably be assigned to 1587.

87. Housman, i, p. xiv.

88. Scaliger, *Commentarius*, p. 148: 'Quod igitur Manilius dixit, *Verte vias*, plane est, quod Aegyptii dicunt, νυκτὸς δὲ τὸ ἀνάπαλιν. Graeci magistri illud ita exponunt: τὸ ἀνάπαλιν δὲ τί ἐστιν; ἵνα ἀπὸ σελήνης ἐπὶ ἥλιον ποιήσῃς, καὶ μηκέτι εἰς τὰ ἑπόμενα, ἀλλὰ εἰς τὰ ἡγούμενα ἀπολύσῃς.' Scaliger's source is p. 111 of the Greek scholia on the *Tetrabiblos*.

89. Scaliger, *Commentarius*, p. 148: 'Nimirum contrario ordine μεθοδεύειν docet: hoc est a Luna ad Solem secundum signa consequentia. Et idem erit. Nam eodem recidit numerus.' The scholium in question reads: 'For one finds again the same *Sors Fortunae* as before, the one found by counting from the sun to the moon'; see Housman, iii, pp. viii–x and Addenda, p. 69.

90. There is a clear explanation in Goold's edition, pp. lxvi–lxviii. See also Housman loc. cit.

91. It is still not clear from the internal evidence whether Manilius wrote under Augustus or Tiberius; but see in general Goold's edition, pp. xi–xv, and D. Pingree's article on Manilius in the *DSB*.

92. L. G. Giraldi, *De historia poetarum tam Graecorum quam Latinorum dialogi decem*, dial. IV, *Opera omnia* (Leiden, 1696), II, col. 220: 'Sunt, qui Antiochenum ex Plinii verbis faciant, ut minus illis credendum sit, qui Romae illum ex illustri familia natum arbitrantur. Ego potius in Manliam familiam adoptatum crediderim, quam natum, si conjecturae standum. Plinius quidem lib. xxxv. Manlium astrologiae, ut ait, conditorem celebrat, et eum quidem Romam vectum eadem navi cum Plotio et Taberio Erote grammatico.' Scaliger, *Commentarius*, sec. DE MANILIO, p. 4: 'Castigandus tamen est, cum videtur concedere nostrum Manilium eundem esse cum Manilio Antiocho: quem una navi Romam cum Staberio Erote grammatico vectum Plinius auctor est. Is est Staberius Eros, euius Suetonius meminit libro de claris Grammaticis ita: *Staberius hero suo emptus de catasta*, ubi legendum *Staberius Eros emptus de catasta*. Atqui Romae Staberius Eros temporibus Sullanis ludum aperuit. Eius aequalis Antiochus quomodo ad excessum usque Augusti, ad quem a Sullanis temporibus minimum centum anni numerantur, pervenire potuerit, viderit ipse. Est enim manifestus ἀναχρονισμός.'

93. See esp. the opening of the section DE MANILIO, ibid., p. 3; that Manilius wrote soon after the defeat of Varus Scaliger inferred from I.898–9.

94. P. Crinito, *De honesta disciplina libri xxv. Poetis Latinis lib. v. Et Poematon lib. II* (Lyons, 1543), p. 456 (*De poetis Latinis*, III.xli): 'Mar. Mallius ex illustri familia natus creditur. Iisdem temporibus in Vrbe claruit, quibus divus Augustus Imperium Romanae urbis felicissime gubernavit. Neque dubitandum est fuisse illum tanto principi gratissimum propter egregiam disciplinarum cognitionem et ingenii excellentiam. Fabius Quintilianus nullam mentionem de poeta Mallio fecit: quocirca mirantur quidam, cur illum praetermiserit, praecipue cum de T. Lucretio et Aemilio Macro iudicium fecerit. Studium suum atque industriam collocavit in Mathematicis artibus, tantumque in his profecit, ut maximas ingenii sui laudes tulerit. Scripsit libros quinque de Astronomicis, carmine hexametro: in quibus magna ex parte Hipparchum, Eudoxum, atque Aratum sequutus traditur.'

95. Scaliger, *Commentarius*, sec. DE MANILIO, p. 4: 'Deinde qui nostras Castigationes et poema ipsius Manilii legerit, an eum mathematicum vocare debeat, merito dubitare possit. Nam eum illa, quae ignorabat, scripsisse, fateri cogetur.'

96. Ibid., p. 3: 'Petrus Crinitus, qui singulorum poetarum vitas, facta, ac opera singulis capitibus librorum suorum dicare instituerat, cum videret se de hoc poeta nihil certi afferre posse, quo iustum caput conficeret, confugit ad nugas suas, tanquam claudus ad equum: Augusto gratissimum fuisse propter ingenii excellentiam; studium suum in Mathematicis collocasse; maximas ingenii sui dotes tulisse; quae verba tanquam carmen legitimum tunc solet interponere, cum iusto capiti absolvendo materia deest. Sed et illud tam falso, quam confidenter extulit: Manilium Eudoxum et Hipparchum in suis Astronomicis sequutum fuisse. Homo nugator legerat Eudoxum et Hipparchum Astronomica scripsisse: sed nesciebat, nihil paene in Astronomicis ab Eudoxo dictum, quod Hipparchus non everterit. Fierine igitur potest, ut duos contrarios scriptores imitandos sibi proposuerit? Non magis profecto, quam si quis Thessalum et Galenum se in medicinis sequi profiteretur.'

97. Scaliger, *Commentarius*, p. 47 *ad* I.587: '*Vixque dies transit*] Mathematico indignum, sub Tropico Capricorni non solum putare diem adeo longam esse, ut minimum discrimen noctis intersit: sed et longiores sub illo dies esse, quam sub nostro: puta in parallelo διὰ συήνης, ubi longissima dies in puncto solstitiali non maior horarum 13.30'.'

98. Ibid., pp. 47-8.

99. Scaliger, *Commentarius*, p. 80 *ad* II.198-9: '*Aspice Taurum Clunibus*] Quod clunes Tauro tribuat, frustra est. Est enim omnino, ut dixi, ἡμίτομος . . . '; p. 225 *ad* IV.359 (on the order of the signs governing the decans of Pisces; cf. Housman, iv, p. 43 ad loc.); pp. 104-5 *ad* II.509 (Claiming that Manilius did not know the signs under which Augustus was conceived and born) etc. See esp. p. 192 *ad* III.482: 'Voluit autem Manilius otio uti, ne dicam abuti, more Platonis in suis numeris putandis. Nam quod uno verbo poterat, plurib. ambagibus maluit, ad fertilitatem ingenii ostentandam. Hoc Platonem factitare non ignorant, qui eum diligentius legerunt.'

100. Scaliger, *Commentarius*, p. 225 *ad* IV.359: ' . . . Dignus scutica error. Ut omnino fatendum sit, quod toties diximus, Manilium ea, quae nesciebat, scripsisse.' Similar phrases are found on p. 103 *ad* II.488; p. 104 *ad* IL.503; p. 193 *ad* III.485.

101. e.g., Pruckner's text of II.503, referring to Scorpio, reads: 'Ille videt Pisces, auditque per omnia Libram' — that is, Scorpio 'sees' Pisces and 'hears' Libra — that is, in turn, a line parallel to the diameter of the zodiac connecting Aries and Libra will connect Scorpio and Pisces, while a line parallel to the diameter of the zodiac connecting Cancer and Capricorn will connect Scorpio and Libra. The problem here, as Scaliger pointed out, is that Scorpio and Libra are next to one another in the zodiac, and hence cannot possibly 'hear' one another: 'Et hic quoque Manilium fugit ratio, qui ait Pisces [read: Scorpium] Libram audire. Nam si antiscia sunt ea, quae aequaliter ab aliquo quatuor punctorum cardinalium absunt, quomodo haerentia καὶ συναφῆ signa hic ullum locum habere possunt?' (*Commentarius*, p. 104) His conclusion was mordant: 'Nescivit, inquam, Manilius, quid scriberet.' Bouillau, attacking the same line, agreed with Scaliger's criticism of the vulgate but found it absurd to ascribe so elementary an error to Manilius rather than a scribe: 'Recte monet Scaliger falsum esse, Scorpium audire Libram: neque tamen Manilium tale σφάλμα διανοητικόν admisisse crediderim, sed potius hunc versum sic condidisse:
   Ille videt Pisces, audit quae proxima Librae.
Subaudi *eam*, nempe Virginem Librae connexam et coniunctam.' The line, so emended, means: 'Scorpio sees Pisces and hears her who is next to Libra (i.e., Virgo)'; and this solution, which is accepted by Housman and Goold, is certainly far more judicious than Scaliger's. For a discussion and diagrams of the relationships among the signs that include 'seeing' and 'hearing' see Goold, pp. xlvi-li.

102. Scaliger, *Commentarius*, p. 156 *ad* III.271: 'Itaque praecipiti quodam calore Eudoxum carpendi Hipparchus saepe erravit in iis, quae in Aratum animadvertit.' Scaliger also criticized Hipparchus' φιλελεγχία (excessive desire to find faults) in his marginal notes in his copy of Vettori's edition of the commentary on Aratus; see D'Ansse de Villoison, *Epistolae Vinarienses*, pp. 74 and esp. 76.

103. Scaliger, *Commentarius*, p.47 *ad* I.581: '*Quatuor et gradibus*] Quatuor gradus, inquit, Aequinoctialis distat a Tropico nostro: qui sexies multiplicati producunt XXIIII. Sed uno semisse minus numerant recentiores. Nam maximam Solis declinationem 23.30' ponunt.'

104. See Goold, pp. lxxiv–lxxv; Housman, iii, pp. xvii–xviii.

105. Scaliger, *Commentarius*, pp. 180–4; cf. Scaliger, *Castigationes et notae*, in *M. Manilii Astronomicon a Iosepho Scaligero ex vetusto codice Gemblacensi infinitis mendis repurgatum* (Leiden, 1599-1600), separately paginated, pp. 239 ff., for the correct explanation of the rule; cf. Bouché-Leclercq, *L'Astrologie grecque*, p. 266. n. 1.

106. Ptolemy, *Tetrabiblos*, I.20, quoted by Scaliger, *Commentarius*, p. 160 *ad* III. 282: 'Sed ὁμαλαὶ παραυξήσεις ἐπισφαλέσταται sunt, ac sero a recentioribus, Ptolemaeo et aliis, castigatae. Est autem Aegyptiorum commentum. Ab illis ita, uti acceperat, posteris tradidit egregius ille magister Eudoxus: hoc est κατὰ τὰς ὁμαλὰς παραυξήσεις. Audi de hac re sententiam Ptolemaei: ἡ κοινὴ πραγματεία ἡ πρὸς ὁμαλὰς ὑπεροχὰς τῶν ἀναφορῶν συνισταμένη μηδὲ κατὰ μικρὸν ἐγγύς ἐστι τῆς ἀληθείας. Merito igitur a recentioribus castigata fuit.' In the context of this chapter of the *Tetrabiblos* it is clear that the 'common method' Ptolemy censures is that of the Egyptians.

107. Scaliger, *Commentarius*, p. 184 *ad* III.413: '. . . Ex quibus, ne pluribus agam, decrementorum inaequalitas deprehenditur, quae noster aequalia facit, illos veteres Aegyptios secutus.'

108. O. Neugebauer, *A History of Ancient Mathematical Astronomy*, (New York, 1975), pp. 718, 722, where it is shown that Manilius mixes data from Babylonian Systems A and B; his general rule is from System A (this work is hereafter referred to as *HAMA*). .

109. See in general *The Geographical Fragments of Hipparchus*, ed. D. R. Dicks (London, 1960), frag. 40 and Commentary ad loc., pp. 165-6.

110. Scaliger, *Commentarius*, p. 43 ad I.567: '*Sexque fugit solidas*) Describantur Circuli Aequinoctiali paralleli xc. Is, qui punctum orizontis ad communem intersectionem Meridiani et Orizontis tanget, erit Arcticus illius loci. Quia autem orizontes mobiles sunt, sic et Arctici mobiles. Ita in Cnido, ubi polus ad xxxvi grad. attolitur, Eudoxus scripsit Arcticum circulum totidem partibus a polo mundi distare. In alio climate alius erit, nempe pro ratione elevationis polaris. Et quanta erit altitudo loci, in tantum a polo distare punctum illud necesse est, quod Arcticum describit.'

111. *Hipparchi in Arati et Eudoxi phaenomena commentariorum libri tres*, ed. K. Manitius (Leipzig, 1894), p. 8 ll. 15-20; Diogenes Laertius, *Vitae philosophorum* VIII.viii.86.

112. Scaliger, *Commentarius*, p. 46: 'Hinc Graecorum et Latinorum veterum, qui eos secuti sunt, Manilii, Hygini, Martiani Capellae, oscitantiam videmus, qui Sphaerae suae Arcticum non ad inclinationem loci sui, sed ad Cnidium clima descripserunt: quia primum ita ab Eudoxo traditus fuit, qui Graecis primus sphaeram publicavit. Et frustra eum Arcticum cuivis inclinationi convenire putarunt. Nam, ut scribit Strabo, οἱ ἀρκτικοὶ μήτε παρὰ πᾶσιν εἰσί, μήτε οἱ αὐτοὶ πανταχοῦ [II.ii.2, loosely quoted].'

113. Scaliger, *Commentarius*, p. 155 *ad* III.271: '*Atque haec est illas demum mensura per horas*] Scribe, *per oras*. Ait in parallelo δι' ἀλεξανδρείας longissimam

diem esse hor. 14.30′. Quod falsissimum est: ut mirer et a Mathematico dictum, et ab eo, qui horarum artem promittit, ut infra videbimus. Alexandriae maximam diem sub Cancro Ptolemaeus ponit xiiii hor. Differentia xxx scrup. horarii; quae minimum vi graduum est. Ita epilogismus ille horarum minimum est vi graduum citra Alexandriam. Quin si rationem propius putemus, diem maximam sub Cancro in Alexandrino parallelo non integrarum xiiii horarum esse deprendemus. Alexandriae arcus diurnus maximus in Cancro est ccv part. scrup. iiii, quae in xv divisa reddunt horas 13.41′. Et profecto verum est. Tantum abest, ut sit integrarum 14.30′, ut vult Manilius.’ In fact, a value of 14½ hours for the longest day is always assigned to Rhodes; Manilius’ assignment of it to Alexandria may well have been the result of a simple slip. See Goold, pp. lxix–lxx and *HAMA*, p. 718.

114. Scaliger, *Commentarius*, p. 155: ‘Sed age xiiii esse concedamus, et intra xxxvi gr. latitudinem non posse consistere, ut re vera non potest: fatendum est saltem sub elevatione xxxvi gra. illam horarum rationem esse. Quod neque ipsum dubitandum est. Nam in climate Cnidi est Rhodi maxima dies est horarum 14.30′, ut etiam testatur Ptolemaeus [*Almagest* II.6]. Et sane arcus diurnus maximae diei in illis tractibus minimum ab illo numero abest. Est ergo arcus diurnus maximae diei sub Cnidi inclinatione part. 216.50′. Quae ad horariam rationem redactae refundunt horas 14.36′, quae parum a proposito exemplo absunt. Deprehendimus igitur hunc ὡριαῖον ἐπιλογισμόν collectum fuisse sub Cnidio climate. Quod verum est. Nam omnes Graecorum sphaerae ad rationes Eudoxi conditae sunt. Fuit autem Cnidius, ut et vulgo notum est, ac primus omnium Graecorum Astronomiam e penetralibus Aegyptiae philosophiae erutam ad populares suos eduxit. In sphaera eum omnes Graeci secuti sunt: cum interea non viderent, quae ille de climate Cnidio collegerat, ea non posse ad omnia climata referri.’

115. For Scaliger’s working copy of Hipparchus, cf. above, n. 79. On the quality of Scaliger’s work, see Manitius’s preface to his edition of Hipparchus, p. v: ‘Ac primus quidem Iosephus Scaliger de Hipparcho optime meritus est.’ See e.g. p. 124, 11. 9–10 of the text and *Epistolae Vinarienses*, p. 76, where by changing τοῦτο γὰρ ἐγίνετο ἐν ἴσῳ χρόνῳ εἰ ἕκαστον τῶν ζῳδίων ἀνέτελλεν to εἰ ἐν ἴσῳ χρόνῳ, Scaliger has made nonsense into sense (the revised text means: ‘this would be true if each of the signs rose in the same amount of time’). As to the precision of Scaliger’s collection of fragments see e.g. MS Scal. 22, fol. 20ʳ, where all 3 of Hipparchus’ direct quotations from the *Enoptron* are transcribed under the heading Ἐκ τοῦ Ἐνόπτρου Εὐδόξου.

116. Hipparchus, *Comm. on Aratus*, ed. Manitius, p. 26 l.3–p. 28 l.18.

117. Scaliger, *Commentarius*, p. 156: ‘Diu enim in Hellesponti ora moratus est, et multa opera in ea conscripsit. Quo nomine animos earum nationum demeruit, ac multis honoribus ab illis affectus est. Auctor Laertius.’ This is apparently a rather loose recollection of *Vitae philosophorum*, VIII.viii.87.

118. Ibid.: ‘Itaque inepte omnes veteres in sphaera sua alium ponunt Arcticum, aliam elevationem poli: cum elevatio polica sit semper aequalis Arctico, ac utriusque unum punctum commune sit in orizonte septentrionali. Sed quod scripserat Eudoxus de maxima die, id scripserat cum in Hellesponto degeret: quod de Arctico, cum in patria sua esset. Diversa igitur sunt: quemadmodum et loca, in quibus illa annotavit, diversa. Itaque praecipiti quodam calore Eudoxum carpendi Hipparchus saepe erravit in iis, quae in Aratum animadvertit. Nam cum τὰ φαινόμενα ἐνόπτρου Eudoxi non semper convenire Graecanico themati videret, et potius ad Hellesponti inclinationem pertinere, non advertit Eudoxum ea Cyzici scripsisse, quae conveniunt Cyziceno parallelo, non autem Athenis, ubi non diu moratus est. Ac profecto mirum est haec defendendo Arato et Eudoxo apud veterem scriptorem Hipparchum non valuisse.’

119. Ibid., pp. 156-7: 'Eudoxus igitur cum Platone diu inter Aegyptios sacerdotes versatus, penes quos asservabantur arcana astronomiae, tandem ea, quae ab illis didicerat, popularibus suis publicavit. Quae quia Aegypto accepta ferebat, aegre mos obtinuit, ut ea Eudoxo attribuerentur potius, quam Aegyptiis ipsis, a quibus hauserat. Laertius: οἱ δὲ γεγραφέναι μὲν αἰγυπτίους τῇ αὐτῶν φωνῇ. τοῦτον δὲ μεθερμηνεύσαντα ἐκδοῦναι τοῖς ἕλλησιν [VIII.viii.89] Ita quae ex Eudoxo citabant, Aegyptiorum nomine citabant. Vt Manilius hic quae Eudoxus de Cnidi patriae suae climate scripsit, ea putat de Aegyptio dici. Quia doctrinam Eudoxi Aegyptiorum esse cum aliis credebat.'

120. Scaliger, *Commentarius*, pp. 9-10 *ad* I.44: 'Babyloniorum autem, et Aegyptiorum inventum esse Astrologiam adtestatur et Aristoteles: αἰγύπτιοι καὶ βαβυλώνιοι, παρ' ὧν πολλὰς πίστεις ἔχομεν περὶ ἑκάστου τῶν ἄστρων. Quare autem Aegyptii plurimum illis disciplinis valuerunt, Ptolemaeus, et ipse homo Aegyptius, caussam adfert, ὅτι μᾶλλον συνοικειοῦνται τοῖς Διδύμοις, καὶ τῷ τοῦ Ἑρμοῦ. διόπερ, inquit, διανοητικοί τε, καὶ συνετοί, καὶ ὅλως ἱκανοὶ περὶ τὰ μαθήματα. Et de Babyloniis: ὅτι τῇ παρθένῳ, καὶ τῷ τοῦ ἑρμοῦ συνοικειοῦνται. διὸ καὶ παρ' αὐτοῖς τὸ μαθηματικόν, καὶ παρατηρητικὸν τῶν ἀστέρων συνέπεται [*Tetrabiblos* II.3].'

121. Scaliger, *Commentarius*, p. 8 *ad* I.25 ff.: '*Quem primum*] . . . Neque enim homines soli per se id adepti fuissent, nisi ipsis Diis monstrantibus. Aegyptios astronomiam didicisse docente Mercurio omnes libri loquuntur. Cui propterea Aegyptii divinos honores habuerunt, et primum mensem Thot cognominem Mercurio fecerunt. Nam Thot, seu Tat, est Mercurius. Adiuvat et sententiam Manilii et castigationem nostram Firmicus his verbis: *Mundi itaque genituram hanc esse voluerunt, secuti Aesculapium et Anubim, quibus potentissimum Mercurii numen istius scientiae secreta commisit* [*Mathesis* III.i.1]'; p. 13 *ad* I.125: 'Aesculapius Aegyptius vetustissimus scriptor in sua Myriogenesi scripserat in posterioribus partibus Librae hanc πῆξιν ["coagulation"; in this context the creation of the world] factam: eumque esse natalem mundi. Firmicus de Libra: *Caeterae enim ad xxx numeros collocantur. In istis enim posterioribus partibus terra dicitur esse composita, ut barbarica ratio confirmat* [VIII.iv. 7]. Haec ille. Apparet Aegyptios hoc a Iosepho Patriarcha edoctos. Nam Hebraei ante legem Mosae principium anni a Libra auspicabantur. Quo nomine σκηνοπήγια solenne institutum. Postea ab aequinoctio verno. Quia eo tempore et ex Aegypto egressi sunt, et Opt. Max. Dei beneficio servitutis iugum a cervicibus suis depulerunt. Apud Firmicum *barbarica ratio* valet Aegyptiaca ratio. Hoc etiam alibi repetimus.' (*Barbarica ratio* does not occur in modern texts at this point.)

122. Scaliger, *Commentarius*, p. 10 *ad* I.44: 'Primus quidem Eudoxus ab Aegyptiis astronomiam in populares suos Graecos deduxit. Berosus autem a popularibus suis Chaldaeis Genethlialogiam in Graecos. Vitruvius: *Eorum autem inventiones, quas scriptis reliquerunt, qua solertia, quibusque acuminibus, et quam magni fuerint, qui ab ipsa Chaldaeorum natione profluxerunt, ostendunt. Primusque Berosus in insula, et civitate Coo consedit, ibique aperuit disciplinam* [IX.vi.2]. Plinius scribit, ob divinas praedictiones illi statuam inaurata lingua ab Atheniensibus publice dedicatam.'

123. Scaliger, *Commentarius*, p. 6 *ad* I.15 '*Et adversos stellarum*] Stellarum quinque, item Solis et Lunae ab occasu in ortum cursus est. Eum sero didicerunt Graeci. Seneca Naturalium libro septimo ait Democriti tempore nondum comprehensum fuisse Planetarum cursum, et ab Eudoxo primum in Graeciam delatum. Quod verum est. Nam tres isti profectionis in Aegyptum socii, Plato, Eudoxus, Euripides, ab Aegyptiis didicerunt et primi omnium Graecorum populares suos id docuerunt, Plato in Timaeo suo, Eudoxus ἐν ἐνόπτρῳ, Euripides in Thyeste:

δείξας γὰρ ἄστρων τὴν ἐναντίαν ὁδόν.
Et poetae Graeci ἀντιθέοντας ἀλήτας, obluctantes errones.'

124. Scaliger, *Commentarius*, pp. 62-3 *ad* I.867: '*Ob cuncta creavit*] Legendum: *ob iuncta*. Sive, inquit, id fiat κατ' ἔξαψιν καὶ συναυγασμόν. Est opinio Democriti et Anaxagorae: qui dicebant τὸν κομήτην nihil aliud, quam σύναψιν τῶν πλανητῶν ἀστέρων, ὅταν διὰ τὸ πλησίον ἐλθεῖν δόξωσι θιγγάνειν ἀλλήλων. Quod videntur ab Aegyptiis didicisse, qui credebant τῶν πλανητῶν καὶ πρὸς αὑτοὺς καὶ πρὸς ἀπλανεῖς συνόδους γίνεσθαι. Vnde decernebant, Cometen esse σύνοδον ἀστέρων δυοῖν, ἢ καὶ πλειόνων κατὰ συναυγασμόν. Qui hic intelligitur per *iuncta sidera*.' For Democritus and Anaxagoras see Aristotle, *Meteorology* I.vi.1, 342 b; cf. frags. 46 A 81, 55 A 92 Diels.

125. Scaliger, *Commentarius*, pp. 38-9 *ad* I.506: 'Noctis vigilias bello Troiano primus dependit Palamedes. Ac iam illis temporibus momina noctis signis notare solitos fuisse testis Euripides Iphigenia in Aulide:

τίς ποτ' ἄρ' ἀστὴρ ὅδε πορθμεύει;
σείριος ἐγγὺς τῆς ἑπταπόρου
πλειάδος ἀίσσων ἔτι μεσσήρης [6-8].

Et manifesto ad hunc locum allusit noster Manilius.' The Euripides passage was a favourite of Scaliger's; he had cited it also in the *Coniectanea* to VII.73 and in the Festus commentary (Ch. V, above, n. 77).

126. See in general Bouché-Leclercq, *L'Astrologie grecque*, pp. 318-20 (320-5 on the influence of the planets on the parts of the body).

127. Scaliger, *Commentarius*, p. 98 *ad* II.453: 'Porro αἱ μελοθεσίαι dupliciter considerantur, aut ἐν ὅλοις σημείοις ut hic, aut ἐν μονομοιρίαις. Quam pater priscus ille Aegyptius Necepso peculiari ad hanc rem dicato sermone tractavit. Vide Firmicum libro octavo.'

128. See in general Bouché-Leclercq, *L'Astrologie grecque*, pp. 215-40; W. Gundel, *Dekane und Dekansternbilder* (Glückstadt and Hamburg, 1936; 2nd edn., Darmstadt, 1969).

129. *In Quadripartitum enarrator*, ed. Wolf, p. 200: ἔγκειται δὲ καὶ τῶν δεκανῶν, καὶ τῶν παρανατελλόντων αὐτοῖς καὶ τῶν προσώπων τὰ ἀποτελέσματα, παρὰ Τεύκρου τοῦ Βαβυλωνίου. On Teucer's list of the *paranatellonta* see esp. F. Boll, *Sphaera* (Leipzig, 1903); the work was written in the 1st century AD.

130. Scaliger, *Commentarius*, p. 223 *ad* IV.294: 'Res admodum prisca est. Nam et vetustissimus auctor Teucer Babylonius de illis scripsit. Abrogata vero a Ptolemaeo, et ab Arabibus relata . . . '.

131. See esp. Goold, introduction, pp. xciii-xcvii.

132. Firmicus Maternus, *Mathesis*, VIII, esp. i.10, v. 1, xvii.11, xviii. For discussion see above all Housman, v, pp. xl-xlvi, where Scaliger's view is rightly refuted.

133. Scaliger, *Commentarius*, p. 249 (pref. to V): 'Hic liber continet alteram partem Apotelesmatum, quae a stellis claris cum aliquo Zodiaci signo surgentibus ducuntur: et vocantur prima apotelesmata sphaerae barbaricae. Nam duae sunt partes sphaerae barbaricae. Prima haec ipsa, quae versatur circa clara sidera, quae cum aliquo signo aut oriuntur, aut occidunt. Ea est, quam nunc tractat noster . . . Alterius partis duae rursus partes sunt. Quarum altera singulas partes et minutias signorum scrutatur, quas Aegyptii earum nugarum auctores μονομοιρίας vocarunt. Altera eas stellas, quae clarae sunt in corporibus eorum signorum. Vtraque pars Myriogenesis vocatur.'

134. Ibid.: 'Inventor harum subtilium atque argutarum ineptiarum Aesculapius ille priscus Aegyptius. Sphaera Barbarica vocatur, hoc est Aegyptia. Nam apud Firmicum barbarica ratio non semel pro Aegyptiaca positum est.'

135. Details in Housman, v, praef., and in Goold, Tables 5 and 6.

136 Scaliger, *Commentarius*, pp. 249–50: 'Nigidius φαινόμενα ad inclinationem utriusque caeli, Aegyptii scilicet et Graeci, scripsit. Alterum librum vocavit sphaeram barbaricam, alterum, Graecanicam. Apud vetustissimum Virgilianum interpretem Danielis nostri ita memini me legere: *Nigidius sphaerae barbaricae: Sub Virginis signo Arator, quem Oron Aegyptii vocant: quod Oron Osiridis filium ab hoc educatum dicunt* [*ad Georg.* I.19]. Vides Nigidium in ea sphaera tractasse, quae ad φαινόμενα Aegypti pertinent.'

137. Scaliger, *Commentarius*, p. 250: 'Et sane ortus stellarum fixarum, qui in illis apotelesmatis tractantur, caelo Aegyptio tantum conveniunt. Nam Cepheus in Graecia nunquam totus occidit. Radit enim, et, ut Aratus loquitur, ἐπιξύει punctum orizontis Graecanici. At in sphaera barbarica ex eius ortu et occasu apotelesmata observantur. Idem dicas de Cassiopea, item aliis, quae intra circulum ἀειφανερόν Graeciae continentur. Illa enim oriuntur et occidunt in Aegypto, καὶ ἐν τῇ κάτω χώρᾳ. Quia ad Austrum pergentibus polus deprimitur. Nam omnia signa, quae sunt intra xxxvi gradum a polo, in Graecia nunquam occidunt.'

138. See n. 130, above.

139. Scaliger, *Commentarius*, p. 115 *ad* II.693: 'Porro omnem Dodecatemoriorum doctrinam Ptolemaeus, ut vanam ac fallacem exagitat. Et in genere omnia de Monomoeriis ab Aegyptiis conficta, ἀναιτιολόγητα, καὶ περιττῶς ὑπὸ τῶν πολλῶν φλυαρούμενα, καὶ μὴ πιθανὸν ἔχοντα λόγον dicit. [I.22?] Multum enim eiuscemodi commentis lusit ac luxuriata est veterum Aegyptiorum περιεργία. Adeo ut Paulus Alexandrinus τρισκαιδεκατημόριον excogitaverit, et omnem de duodecimis doctrinam falsam et inconstantem esse convicerit. Arabes autem, qui nihil eorum, quae veteres in otio ἐπολυπραγμόνησαν, relinquunt, hanc doctrinam retinuerunt. Vocant autem Dorogen.'

140. Scaliger, *Commentarius*, p. 93 *ad* II.376: 'Et quaecunque Arabes praeter sententiam Ptolemaei decernunt, id Arabum commentum putant Astrologi nostri. Cum tamen plurima, quae Arabibus vulgo attribuuntur, vetustissimorum Graecorum esse compererim, a quibus Arabes desumpserunt.'

141. Scaliger, *Commentarius*, p. 37: 'Ptolemaeus, Hipparchus, et ante eos Chrysippus numerum stellarum et rationem putarunt.'

142. Scaliger, *Commentarius*, p. 160 *ad* III.282: '*Octonis stadiis*] Stadium est dimidium gradus, ut diximus. Ergo si octona stadia accrescunt Tauro et caeteris, quaterni gradus accrescent.' (For the remainder of the passage see n. 106 above.) On the stade, a device more or less peculiar to Manilius, see *HAMA*, p. 719.

143. Cf. W. von Leyden, 'Antiquity and Authority. A Paradox in Renaissance Theory of History', *Journal of the History of Ideas*, xix (1958), pp. 473–92. Views like Scaliger's were, of course, becoming more and more common in his times. See e.g. H. Weisinger, 'Ideas of History during the Renaissance', ibid., vi (1945); H. Baron, 'The *Querelle* of the Ancients and Moderns as a Problem for Renaissance Scholarship', ibid., xx (1959) (both essays are reprinted in *Renaissance Essays from the Journal of the History of Ideas*, ed. P. O. Kristeller and P. P. Wiener [New York and Evanston, 1968]); J. B. Bury, *The Idea of Progress. An Inquiry into its Growth and Origin* (repr. New York, 1955); P. Rossi, *Philosophy, Technology and the Arts in the Early Modern Era*, tr. S. Attanasio, ed. B. Nelson (New York, Evanston, and London, 1970), Ch. II.

144. See Housman, v, pp. xl–xlvi; the constellation called Horus and mentioned by Nigidius Figulus (above, n. 136) is clearly an Egyptian constellation, not a Greek one viewed from Egypt.

145. Cf. Grafton, 'Rhetoric, Philology and Egyptomania in the 1570s: J.J. Scaliger's Invective against M. Guilandinus's *Papyrus*', *JWCI* xlii (1979), pp. 167–94.

146. F. de Lisle, *Mathematica pro Lucano Apologia adversus Iosephum Scaligerum*

(Paris, 1582); I read this and several other works by de Lisle in a *Sammelband* in the Folger Shakespeare Library. For de Lisle's position as a *parlementaire* see his *Poemata* (Paris, 1576) ep. ded., fol. 2^r ('. . . porro ocium illud mihi vacatio et dimissio senatus Parisiensis confirmaret . . .'); fol. 2^v ('Et si enim nobis importuna clientum caterva et forensis strepitus haec otia perraro permittit . . .').

147. Scaliger, *Commentarius*, pp. 50-2 *ad* I.631, and esp. p. 48 *ad* I.587: 'Lucani autem duplex [scil. error], non solum diem longissimam ibi ponentis, sed etiam perpetuum meridiem. Hoc enim tinniunt illa:
    —umbras nunquam flectente Syene . . . '

148. De Lisle, *Mathematica Apologia*, pp. 9-10:
    Omnibus et prelis id constat, id ingerit ultro
    Et ratio, quae non patitur te fingere vatem,
    Vsque adeo expertem Coeli, sacraeque Mathesis,
    Qua nulli veterum cessit, nullique Nepotum,
    Vt Solem aeterna vertigine mobile corpus,
    Vel Tropicis, alio coeli vel carcere figat.
    Hoc voluit vates, Solem cum proximus Arcto,
    Maxime abest, a parte dies quae noctibus aequat,
    Semidiemque notat, rectum appendere Sieni,
    Tumque Sienenses umbras sibi flectere nusquam.

149. Scaliger, open letter to Mamert Patisson, first published as *Epistola adversus barbarum, ineptum et indoctum poema Insulani patroniclientis Lucani* (Paris, 1582) (see Bernays, *Scaliger*, p. 281); repr. in Scaliger, *Epistolae*, pp. 69-86, at pp. 73-4: 'Audiamus nunc Patroniclientem et absolvamus eum. Nam egomet me moror. Primum obiicit me falso in Lucano notasse perpetuam μεσημβρίαν sub tropico ab eo assignari. O hominem otio abundantem. Tantum abest, ut Lucanus hoc non crediderit, ut haec omnium veterum fuerit opinio, antequam Eratosthenes et post eum Hipparchus Astronomiae sanctiora adyta reserassent. Tam oscitanter legit commentarios nostros, in quibus non solum meridiem semper sub Tropicis, sed etiam aeternum diem collocari a veteribus diximus. An non sub Capricorno longissimam diem ponit Manilius? *sed finibus illis, Quos super incubuit, longa stant tempora nocte.* Quod Ausonius de Aethiopibus loquens et de nostro Tropico clarius explicavit ex veterum opinione: *Semper ubi aeterna vertigine clara nitet lux.* Quid contra haec audes hiscere? In ipsis incunabilis Astronomiae negas hanc veterum Graecorum opinionem fuisse, Eudoxi, Metonis, Cleostrati, et Euctemonis? Sane Lucanum culpa libero, quod cum illis veteribus ita sentiat; sed tamen quo modo eum defendam non video, qui Eudoxum et Metonem potius, quam Hipparchum sequutus sit. Quod Manilium nostrum fecisse manifestum est. Quam graviter homines etiam docti τῇ ἀνιστορησίᾳ peccant, ut cum ea maioribus attribuunt, quae posterorum inventa sunt.'

150. De Lisle explains the precession on pp. 14 (misnumbered 10)-15 (misnumbered 12), and the motion of the planets on p. 17:
    Nempe Planetarum duplex est denique motus:
    Alter ab occasu Mundo contrarius ortum
    Poscit . . .
    Alterius paulo est doctrina abstrusior, ut quem,
    Ipsa vix acie, solo sed acumine mentis
    Percipias: Is motus habet, quo vertitur orbem
    Privatum, antiquis Epicycli nomine dictum.
    Circulus is nempe est, privatim quo quasi ludit
    Quodque Astrum, interea dum primum mobile secum
    Impete communi, Epicyclos, astraque versat.
    Motus et is triplex . . . [i.e. sometimes forwards, sometimes retrograde,
    sometimes apparently non existent (when the planet is stationary)].'

151. Ibid., p. 19:
> Quod si Epicyclorum longo post tempore nomen
> Excussum, et nostro forte est vox posthuma Vati,
> Quid tum praeterea? Res non ita nomine demum
> Clauditur, ignoto ut nomine, protinus et rem
> Ignotam facias: Imo consulta vetustas,
> Ne tandem Coeli studium, ne sacra Mathesis,
> Vulgari temerata manu vilesceret usu,
> Suppressis voluit Naturae arcana latere
> Nominibus: tum mos res nudas nomine nullo,
> Nullis Schematibus profiteri: Serior aetas,
> Vel consulta minus, vel tantae indaginis impar,
> Ipsa novas rerum voces, nova schemata finxit.
> Posteritatis opus, vox est, res mystica priscae
> Est maiestatis. Tu ne ergo antiquitus omnes
> Ignorasse putes, tibi vel tritissima quae sint?
> Nam quid ego nostris plus iusto abblandiar annis?
> Si maiestatem veterum, et fastigia pendis,
> Ipsa superficies, rerumque umbratile nomen,
> Vix etiam ad miseros sunt derivata Nepotes.

152. Ibid.: 'Quod Archimedes, quod Plato consilio, atque etiam Iudei Cabalistae, et Thalmudistae exemplo docuere.'

153. Scaliger, *Epistolae*, p.81: 'Hinc illae lacrymae: hoc est quod vos et alios sciolos decepit, qui ea in Manilio et Lucano rimamini, quae illis penitus ignota fuerunt.'

154. De Lisle replied to Scaliger's criticisms of his work and abuse of his person in a work entitled *Francisci Insulani ad Iosephi Scaligeri epistolam responsio* (Paris, 1583); a further reply to de Lisle, not in Scaliger's hand, is preserved in MS Dupuy 810, fols. 88^r-90^v, under the title 'C. Thaletis Valerii Epistola ad Jos. Scaligerum admonens ut insano versificatori Francisco Insulano ne respondeat'; it is dated July 1583. This seems to be another of Scaliger's pseudonymous pamphlets, or at least one written in imitation of his style. See e.g. fol. 88^r: 'En hic Insulanus Thersites homo infimi subsellii ut audet Agamemnonem probro lacessere et lingua tolutiloquente abuti' — for the phrase *lingua tolutiloquente* cf. Ch. IV, above, text to n. 77. For a judicious treatment of Lucan's astronomical knowledge see J. Palmerius, 'κριτικὸν ἐπιχείρημα, sive Pro Lucano Apologia', in *M. Annaei Lucani Cordubensis Pharsalia*, ed. F. Oudendorpius (Leiden, 1728), pp. 911-66.

155. Scaliger, *Prolegomena de Astrologia veterum Graecorum*, in *M. Manilii Astronomicon*, ed. 1599-1600, sig. ∝ 2^{r-v}; see Appendix to Ch. VII, below for the text.

156. Ibid., sig. ∝ 3^{r-v}; see Appendix to Ch. VII, below.

157. Tycho Brahe to Chr. Rothmann, 20.i.1587; *Tychonis Brahe Dani Opera Omnia*, ed. J. L. E. Dreyer, vi (Copenhagen, 1919), pp. 88-9: 'Quod autem celeberrimus ille nostri Aevi Philosophus PETRVS RAMVS existimarit, sine Hypothesibus per Logicas rationes Astronomiam constitui posse, caret fundamento. Proposuit quidem ille mihi ante annos elapsos 16. cum Augustae Vindelicorum una essemus, hanc opinionem, et hortator simul erat, ut postquam per Hypotheses Siderum cursum in exactum ordinem redegissem, idem sine his tentare affectarem. Id enim fieri posse, hanc rationem addidit, quod legisset Aegyptios facilimam olim habuisse Astronomiae cognitionem; Cumque hypothesium ratio difficilis et intricata videatur, oportere eos alia compendiosiore et planiore via siderum cursus cognovisse, ideoque citra omnes hypotheses. At ego illi resistebam, ostendens sine hypothesibus Phaenomena caelestia non posse in scientiam certam redigi, neque ut intelligantur, excusari. Facilitatem

vero illam Aegyptiacam saltem in Aequatoriis Planetarum, quibus se a sup-
putatione taediosa liberarunt, cum Ephemeridum expedita ratio nondum in
usu foret, extitisse. Verum cum is, vir alias perspicaci ingenio praeditus, et
veritatis, si quis alius, amans, penetralia artis huius non penitus perspexisse
mihi videretur, varietatemque in motu siderum statis anni temporibus nequa-
quam recurrentem non animadvertisse, quicquam hac in parte obtinere ab ipso
nec potui, nec volui. Habet is plerosque adhuc asseclas, qui idem fieri posse
sperant, sed qui rem ipsam neque intelligant, neque unquam in effectum sint
deducturi. Cum enim omnia constent numeris, ponderibus, et mensura, sine
his etiam, quicquam in mundo visibili explicari nequit . . . '.

158. Ramus to Rheticus, 25.viii.1563; Ramus, *Professio regia* (Basel, 1576), fols.
1^v-2^r (transcript kindly supplied by M. S. Mahoney): 'At hypotheses . . . e
quatuor astrologorum sectis, quae a Plinio statuuntur, Chaldaeorum, Aegyptiorum, Graecorum, Latinorum, recordare quaeso, si quae Chaldaeorum, veterumque, tum Aegyptiorum, tum apud Platonem Graecorum memorentur. Plato
certe (quod Proclus in Timaeo animadvertit) hypotheses nullas in Astrologiam
adhibuit. Attamen, cum in stellarum motibus, ullam anomaliam vel confusionem
esse pernegaret, occasionem (aiunt Aristotelis interpretes in libris eius de coelo)
Mathematicis praebuit, hypotheses inquirendi, quibus planetarum φαινόμενα
defenderent. Itaque Eudoxus Cnidius primus hypotheses ἀνελιττουσῶν reperit:
quas cum Callippo Aristoteles correxit et emendavit. . . . et iudicato, utrum
Astrologia aliquando sine hypothesibus fuerit, et quam commoda ratione,
notatis et observatis stellarum motibus, possit in annum centesimum aut
millesimum praedici coniunctio et effectio syderum quaelibet futura? Enimvero, ut (quod summum hic arbitror) adiungam, videtur non solum Logicae
legibus valde contrarium, sed omnino profanum, in sacra et coelesti doctrina,
commenta, praesertim manifeste falsa et absurda, permisceri. At hypotheses
Epicyclorum et eccentricorum commenta, falsa et absurda esse: epistola tua,
nisi fallor, Copernico praeposita, manifeste ex epicyclo Veneris ostendit.'
For the sources Ramus drew on in this account, see T. L. Heath, *Aristarchus
of Samos. The Ancient Copernicus* (Oxford, 1913; repr. New York, 1981).

159. *Scaligerana I*, pp. 142-3, s.v. RAMVS; *Scaligerana II*, p. 527, s.v. RAMVS.

160. On Ramist mathematics see e.g. the article on Ramus by M. S. Mahoney in
DSB; R. Hooykaas, *Humanisme, science et réforme. Pierre de la Ramée (1515–
1572)* (Leiden, 1958); J. J. Verdonk, *Petrus Ramus en de wiskunde* (Assen,
1966). Many years after the Manilius appeared, Scaliger opposed the introduction of Ramism into the University of Leiden, on the grounds that the
inevitable quarrels between Ramists and Aristotelians would destroy the institution; see *Epistolae*, pp. 130-1.

161. Pico, *Disputationes in Astrologiam*, XII.3, *Opera Omnia* (Basel, 1572), p. 721:
'Solent quicunque in aliquam disciplinam se totos ingurgitarunt, omnia ad
illam referre quam libentissime, non tam propter ambitionem, ut scire per
illam omnia videantur, quam quod ita illis videtur, quibus scilicet usu venit
quod per nives iter agentibus, nam caetera quoque illis alba videri solent, candoris hàbitu in oculos iam recepto, reliqua in se transformante . . . Qui Theologus est, nec aliud quam theologus, ad divinas causas omnia refert, Medicus ad
habitum corporis . . . hac ratione cum essent veteres Chaldaeorum in coelestium
motibus metiendis et stellarum cursibus observandis iugiter assidui, nec aliud
quicquam eorum magis ingenio detinerent, omnia illis erant stellae, hoc est,
ad stellas libenter omnia referebant, id quod de Aegyptiis dictum pariter intelligatur.' There is a modern edition of Pico's work with valuable notes, by
E. Garin (Florence, 1946). Pico's critique of the astrologers strikingly resembles
Aristotle's critique of the Pythagoreans in *Metaphysics* 985 b 23 ff.

162. Ibid., XII.3-XII.5, pp. 721-7.

163. Ibid., XII.5, pp. 726-7: '... talibus usi demonstrationibus, quasi filiae araneae rete praestigiosum contexuere, quod si procul aspicias fallat mentita filorum magnitudine et illecebra textus novitatisque lenocinio, si comminus intuere contemnas, si tangas manu disrumpas atque dissolvas.'

164. Ibid., XI.2, p. 714: 'Hipparcus et Ptolemaeus principes astronomiae, ubi pro dogmate statuendo veterum observationes afferunt, nullas afferunt ipsi vetustiores his quae sub rege Nabuchodonosor apud Aegyptios Babyloniosve fuere, post cuius regnum sexcentesimo fere anno floruit Hipparcus, a quo ad nostra haec usque tempora anni non plus mille sexcentis aut circiter fluxerunt. Mendaciter igitur et fabulose tot seculorum habere se iactant observationes, eas vero quas habent necessario esse falsas, ... facile demonstratur.'

165. Ibid., p. 715: 'Quod si tam insigniter in Lunari motu tam facili familiarique nobis errabant, quid de motibus siderum aliorum occultioribus tardioribusque sit putandum? Sed non est opus hic coniectura. Legatur Ptolemaei liber cui titulus Magna compositio, patebitque citra suspitionem veteres omnes in coelestium motibus, toto ut dicitur coelo, penitus aberrasse: de motu quem dicebamus sideris proximioris, nihil non modo verum, sed nec proximum vero deprehensum ab antiquis ibi cognosces. Hipparcus primus in Rhodo insula ducentesimo fere ante Christum anno Lunae cursum verius observavit, sed nec tamen ad liquidum, quare corrigitur a Ptolemaeo, qui proximius quidem Hipparco accessit ad veritatem, sed ita ut non attigerit. Ab Hispanis deinde astronomis emendatus. In Solis motu quo caeteros metiuntur adhuc quoque caecutiunt, nedum illum antiquitas sit consecuta.'

166. Ibid.: 'In ascensionibus, quas anaphoras Graeci vocant, signorum dinumerandis, quantum exciderent a veritate quicunque in Aegypto per sidera divinabant, et primo Apotelesmaton Ptolemaeus, et Apollinarius in commentariis * testatus est.'

167. Ibid., XII.7, p. 729 (on the transmission of astrology from the Near Eastern nations to the Greeks): 'Primus ... eam coluit [ed. Garin: consuluit] Ptolemaeus, sed parcius quam caeteri, ita ut non tam insaniae isti favere quam modum ponere voluisse videatur, utcumque authoritas unius hominis semper mathematici, raro philosophi, tot contra in mathematicis philosophiaque hominum clarissimorum obstantibus praeiudiciis, relabitur.'

168. Ibid., XII.6, p. 729: '... ista partitio decanorum, irrisaque et neglecta penitus a Ptolemaeo ...'.

169. See Scaliger, *Commentarius*, pp. 90-1 *ad* II.468; pp. 137-8 *ad* III.72; 142 *ad* III.170.

170. Pico, *Disputationes*, VI.3; *Opera*, p. 586: 'Quod si Mallium evolvamus, qui se veterum ait dogma aliquando imitatum, quoque nullus antiquior extitit apud Latinos rerum coelestium (vel ut verius dixerim fabularum) enarrator, invenimus de locis 12. rem ab omni quae nunc referatur opinione ita diversam, ut omnis praedicendi ratio penitus immutetur. Quod in occasu collocarit Martem, cui primam sub occasu sedem alii decreverunt. Quid alia illa tradita a Mallio coeli loca 12? Nonne ab omni quae nunc in manibus Astrologia diversa? Nonne rationem omnem variant praedicendi?'

171. Ibid., p. 588: 'Hactenus Mallius, cuius sententiam liquet quidem ab omni, quae nunc in usu, Astrologia discrepare. Sed tamen a nemine puto adhuc intellectam ex his qui se Mallii faciunt interpretes et sectatores.' The last sentence would seem to be directed against Bonincontri, whom Pico follows elsewhere.

172. Scaliger, *Commentarius*, p. 138 *ad* III.72: 'In qua tamen re pueriliter lapsus est Phoenix saeculi sui, illustris vir Picus Mirandulanus, deliciae Musarum atque alumnus Philosophiae. Is putat ea, quae Manilius mox expositurus est de themate actionum, ad thema geniturae referenda esse: neque aliud praeter

thema γενέσεως hic proponi a Manilio. Atqui longe differunt ista, ut dixi, quantum sane Horoscopus a Sorte Fortunae.'

173. *M. Manilii Astronomicωn libri quinque*, ed. 1579, sigs. ā ii^r-ā iii^v.

174. Of the many treatments of Pico's work, E. Cassirer, 'Giovanni Pico della Mirandola', *Journal of the History of Ideas*, iii (1942), repr. in *Renaissance Essays*, ed. Kristeller and Wiener, is especially helpful. See also the articles by P. O. Kristeller, P. Rossi, and others in *L'opera e il pensiero di Giovanni Pico della Mirandola* (Florence, 1965).

175. Scaliger, *Commentarius*, pp. 34–5 *ad* I.451: '*Et versas frontibus Arctos*] Quanvis, inquit, Arctos, quae in altero polo sunt, non videmus, tamen eas nostratibus similes esse ratio ponit, καὶ ἡ ἀναλογία. Quod tamen falsum est. Nam Septentriones nulli sunt in altero polo, nulla maior Vrsa, nulla minor. Neque ullas alias stellas lucidas habet is polus praeter quatuor primae magnitudinis in quadrum aequilatus dispositas: quae vicem plaustri nostri esse possint. Id nos docuit ex iis, quae in literas retulit, Americus Vesputius, vir immortalitate dignus. Supersunt et hodie, qui testari possint, qui αὐτόπται rei fuerunt.'

176. Scaliger, *Commentarius*, p. 23 *ad* I.312: '*Quae quia dissimilis*] Ab aere stellas temperari vult: quasi ab aere ipsae vires accipiant, et non potius aerem inficiant ipsae. Simile nescio quid argutatur Ptolemaeus de Luna, cum ait eam ideo humectare, quod terrae vaporibus vicinior sit. Nimirum hoc vult, Lunae humiditatem et frigiditatem a terra esse. Idem tinnit eius sententia, quae concludit Saturnum minus humectare, quia a terrae vaporibus remotissimus sit. Denique supra Lunam omnia cum Luna ipsa corruptioni obnoxia esse inde sequitur; siquidem terrae vaporibus Luna inficitur. Vt taceam, tantos vapores a terra excitari non posse, ut ad Lunam pervenire possint. Sed minus prudenter Cardanus, qui nobis persuadere conatur, Ptolemaei hanc mentem esse, ut intelligat, non Lunam infici vaporibus, sed potius trahere vapores illos. Quod alienissimum ab eius sententia. Disertim enim scribit, Lunam perinde humefacere, quia terrae vaporibus vicina est . . .'. Cf. *Tetrabiblos* I.4 and Cardano's commentary ad loc., *Opera Omnia*, ed. G. Naudé (Lyons, 1663), V, pp. 122–5.

177. Pico, *Disputationes*, III.4; *Opera*, p. 460: 'Ita patet in corporeo mundo nihil quidem fieri sine coelo, veruntamen quod hoc aut illud fiat, id a coelo non esse, sed secundis causis, cum quibus omnibus coelum talia facit, qualia ipsae facere natae sunt, sive illis [Garin: illae] ad speciem, sive ad individuum causae pertineant.' Cf. D. P. Walker, *Spiritual and Demonic Magic from Ficino to Campanella* (London, 1958), pp. 54–9.

178. Scaliger, *Commentarius*, p. 234 *ad* IV.585: 'Nam universalia apotelesmata validiora esse, quam sunt particularia, nemo dubitat.'

179. Scaliger, *Prolegomena de astrologia veterum Graecorum, in M. Manilii Astronomicon*, ed. 1599–1600, sigs. [β4^v] – γ^r; see Appendix to Ch. VII, below for the text.

180. *M. Manilii Astronomicωn libri quinque*, ed. 1579, sig. ā^{iiii}v:

> Quid praestare queat ludendo maximus heros
> SCALIGER, ingratus vel tacet Orbis adhuc:
> Testes Virgilius, Festus, Varro, Ausoniusque,
> Et tu cum sociis, docte Catulle, tuis.
> Vnius Manilii, quid possit seria tractans,
> Invidia possunt scripta fatente loqui.

181. De Thou's copy of the work, in the British Library, also contains the French version of this dedication; cf. Scaliger to Dupuy, 19.vii.1578, *Lettres françaises*, pp. 86–7: 'Au reste je vous supplie aussi de me mander vostre avis s'il sera bon de faire tailler les armoiries de France avecques la devise du Roi, pour les mettre à la seconde page, car la préface sera en la troisiesme, laquelle préface estant

en vers, et adressée au Roi, je ne sai s'il seroit bon, qu'elle fust aussi mise en vers françois, après le latin, seullement au livre que je présenterai au Roi, car aux aultres je ne vouldrois ainsi bigarrer mes livres.' The royal arms are in all copies.

182. Calderini de Marchi, *Corbinelli*, pp. 145–6.

183. I follow two notes in a copy of the 1600 edition of the Manilius given by G. Merula to J. C. Gevaerts and now in the Bodleian Library, shelf-mark Auct. S. 2. 23: 'Retulit mihi D. Heinsius, Jos. Scaligerum, cum Manilianis Commentariis recensendis occuparetur, et tum forte [several words heavily lined through] . . . prodiret ubi Notae Manilianae Scaligeri videntur, dixisse, *Nullum esse Jesuitam* [so I read the word, which is also lined through], *imo nec ullum alium eruditum modo vivere, qui hoc praestare potuisset in Manilio, quod ille praestitit, et praecipue in Sphaera Barbarica, seu lib. 5.* Idem mihi saepius narravit eundem Scaligerum dicere solitum, *Inter omnia opera sua, post opus De Emendatione Temporum, maxime sibi placere Commentaria Maniliana sua.* Et saepe de illis gloriatus est.'

184. Scaliger to Stadius, 31.vii.1579, *Epistolae*, p. 60: 'Cum hac integritate, atque, nisi serio dissimulare volunt, cum hac laude qui versatus sim, tamen doctissimorum virorum invidiam nunquam effugere potui. Atque ut ab Italis incipiam, cum primum in lucem exierunt notae meae in Varronis tres libros rerum Rusticarum, ab eo tempore maximi nominis atque plurimarum literarum vir, qui magna cum laude atque felicitate has literas tractavit, nunquam destitit me apud nostrates accusare: me unum in perniciem literarum natum: actum esse de literis, si porro vixero: me nimis ingenio confidere. Hoc, tanquam aliquod carmen legitimum, aut actionem, conceptis verbis ille gravissimus vir, id aetatis, ea veneranda canicie, nostratibus, qui Roma trans Alpes proficiscuntur, iterare solet.'

185. Ibid.: 'Sed non satis est hoc; Eas Notas excepit Sex. Pompeii editio; Dii boni. Plane me divinare et hariolari dixit quidam alius inter proceres rei literariae apud Italos primi nominis. Vide, amabo, quo genere excipere solent Transalpina ingenia Etrusci et Felsinenses Romuli, qui omnes extra Italiam positas gentes barbaras vocare solent. En modestiam! Hoc dicere solent ii, quibus libros meos ipse misi: quos ego quotidie laudavi.'

186. Ibid., p. 61: 'Nova trium Poetarum, quos nuper emisi, editio, Italorum atque nostratum animos quantum novitate rei percussit? Ipsam ἔρω Hesiodi in orbem terrarum misisse visus sum. Atque, ut illos Cisalpinos omittam, ita forum magistrorum Parisiensium excandefecimus, ut frequentes coirent, et de magna re publica deliberarent. Dicebantur sententiae graves. Parum abfuit, quin ad illud extremum decurreretur: Viderent Magistratus, ne quid detrimenti Republica accipiat. Annibal enim ad portas erat. Me nihil mentiri, testes sunt non solum gravissimi viri, amici mei, qui haec mihi non sine risu retulerunt: sed et boni adolescentes, qui quotidie similia declamantes magistros audire solent.'

187. Ibid., pp. 63–4: 'Nam ea in eo libello deteximus, quae isti boni medici ne in somnis quidem viderant, neque suspicati sunt.'

188. Ibid., p. 64: 'Cui rei omnis paedagogorum faex operas suas tradidit. Nemo enim fuit, qui sese putaret medicum (semper doctos excipio, ne forte quispiam me hic omnes putet comprehendere) qui dolorem suum ac invidiam dissimulare potuerit, quod ego ἀνιατρολόγητος Hippocratem et Celsum emendandum susceperim.'

189. Ibid., p. 66: 'Mitto enim ad te Manilium meum, quem quare liberalius quam alios libros meos excipiant, non video . . . Extabunt, qui solum Ptolemaeum et recentiores legerint, et videbunt me aliam a vulgari logisticen, aliam Astronomiam

sequi. Ilico totius Astronomiae imperitum me esse clamabunt. Hoc facient, puto, illi, qui quod pro viatico Ephemeridibus semper suffarcinati incedunt, eo solo nomine sese Astronomos putant: neque Astronomiam Manilii longe differre a Ptolemaica; neque, quod caput est, ipsum Ptolemaeum novam instituisse, aut potius veram restituisse, cogitabunt: non aliter ac fecit Aristoteles, qui non prius suam Physicen struit, quam Democriti, Pythagorae, et aliorum fundamenta diruerit.'

190. See esp. ibid., pp. 68–9: 'Ideo te huic rei defensorem paro. Totum enim humanitati, eruditioni, aequanimitati tuae me devoveo: praesertim ut mihi praesto sis, si quando doctissimorum magistrorum eiusmodi susurri aures tuas verberabunt. Quis enim hodie magis opportunus iniuriae vivit, quam ego? Quem vero magis idoneum defensorem, quam te ipsum, nancisci possum?'

191. J. Lipsius, *Satyra Menippaea. Somnium. Lusus in nostri aevi Criticos* (ed. Paris, 1585).

192. Ibid., p. 25: 'Ego ipse non Iosepho Scaligero civicam de me coronam dedi? Dedi, libens meritoque.'

193. Ibid., p. 15 (from Cicero's speech): 'Sed quis ex istis nos adit, nos legit, nisi urendi secandique caussa? Id enim vocant corrigere. "Hoc rectum est, hoc non rectum. Hoc non implet aures meas. Hoc non Latinum, etiamsi Cicero ita locutus sit. Stigmatias hic locus. Hic mutilus." Bene et in tempore acclamastis P.C. crucem illis.' The printed marginal note to the formulas in quotation marks reads: 'Verba Lambini'.

194. Ibid., sig. Aii^{r-v}; Scaliger thanked Lipsius for the dedication in a letter of 23.v. 1581, *Epistolae*, pp. 89–91.

195. See esp. Nolhac, 'Piero Vettori et Carlo Sigonio: Correspondance avec Fulvio Orsini', *Studi e documenti di storia e diritto*, x (1889), pp. 91–152; the long series of letters from Orsini to Vettori on editorial matters is most revealing.

196. F. Orsini, *De Festi fragmento*, in *Sex. Pompei Festi De verborum significatione fragmentum ex vetustissimo exemplari Bibliothecae Farnesianae descriptum* (Florence, 1582), sig. N 4^r (Misnumbered 0 4): ' ... curavimus paginas ipsas, eo quo Festus scripsit ordine, numero versuum in singulis pagellis, et litterarum in uno quoque versu, nec aucto, nec diminuto, ita ut sunt in exemplari, qua potuimus diligentia, describendas ... '.

197. Ibid.: 'Hoc amplius, partem paginarum mutilam, habita spatii, quod supplendum fuit, ratione, infinitis locis resarcivimus: multa ex eorum scriptis, quos supra nominavimus, mutuati, multis etiam de nostro additis.'

198. *Sexti Pompei Festi De verborum significatione quae supersunt cum Pauli Epitome*, ed. K. O. Mueller (Leipzig, 1839), p. xxxvii.

199. Scaliger to Dupuy, 21.vi.1582, *Lettres françaises*, p. 123.

200. Orsini, *De Festi fragmento*, sig. [N 3^v] 'Quam quidem editionem [scil. that of Agustín] doctissimi viri postea secuti, tam multa in ea restituerunt; ut ex iis, quae Lutetiae vulgarunt, intelligi facile possit, quid facturi fuissent, si emendatiorem codicem nacti essent.' Originally, Orsini had meant to be more conciliatory. On 26.ii.1580 he wrote to Vettori that 'Circa lo Scaligero, io non lo nominarò se non una volta nella prefatione, et all'hora con honore et laude, ... dicendo ... che il Scaligero havendo seguitato quella editione, così poco fidele, et nella quale era confuso l'ordine de Festo, et non era notato il spatio del mancamento, hà fatto miracoli à supplire così bene molti luoghi ... ' (*Studi e documenti di storia e diritto*, x, pp. 123–4). But Vettori evidently advised Orsini to delete his explicit reference to Scaliger, for on 3.iii.1581 Orsini wrote to him that 'Circa poi quello che V. S. desidera, per rispetto del Scaligero, cioè de non essere nominato, si farà; ne anco io voglio nominare quell'huomo se non in bene, che non ho mai fatto professione di dire male' (ibid., pp. 131–2).

201. Scaliger to Dupuy, 21.vi.1582, *Lettres françaises*, p. 123: 'Bref il se fait tres bien aider *d'i travaigli di Huguenoti, et Tramontani*, sans les nommer toutes-fois. Je suis bien aise que ce peu que je fais soit si bon, que nos adversaires mesmes s'en servent.' Scaliger was not always so charitable to Orsini; cf. *JWCI* xxxviii, p. 177.

202. *Callimachi Cyrenaei Hymni, epigrammata, et fragmenta, quae exstant*, ed. B. Vulcanius (Antwerp, 1584; hereafter '*Callimachus*, ed. Vulcanius') pp. 245-62.

203. *Callimachi Cyrenaei Hymni (cum suis scholiis Graecis) et Epigrammata. Eiusdem poematium de coma Berenices, a Catullo versum*, ed. H. Estienne (Geneva, 1577), pp. 53-9 (including Catullus 65 and Muret's notes on it).

204. *Callimachus*, ed. Vulcanius, pp. 227-8 ad loc.: 'ἢ μεγάλ' ἀντ' ὀλίγων ἐπράξαο] Politianus vertit, *Magna nimis parvis mutas*: quod mihi magis arridet, quam quod Hen. Stephanus dicit se malle, *Magna rei parvae merces*, quod contentione utriusque versionis inter se planum faciam. Nam cum Politianus vertit *Magna nimis*, exprimit illud ἢ Callimachi, quod magnam Emphasim, magnamque diversitatis in commutatione significationem habet. Deinde, ἀντ' ὀλίγων, quis non malit, ut numerus numero respondeat, *Paucis*, quam *Parvae rei* vertere? Praeterea *Mutas* melius respondet τῷ ἐπράξαο utpote verbo verbum, et quidem mercium commutationem figurate significans, quam *Merces*, quam absurdum fuerit deam ab homine capere. Adhaec in Pentametro, cur malis *Rapis*, quam *habeas*? An quia tuis auriculis disyllabo melius clauditur pentametrum, quam trisyllabo? Praeterea anne honestius de dea et convenientius verbo ἔχειν dicitur quod *Habeat* oculos alterius, quam quod *rapiat*? Cum ipsamet Pallas infra ver. 100 declaret alienum hoc a se ὄμματα παίδων ἁρπάξειν. Et nihil certe habet commune *Merces* cum *Rapina*. Imo vero potius ut Callimachi verbis utar, τόσσον ὅσον διὰ πλεῖστον ἔχουσιν.
   Ergo tuum frustra est, nisi vox sit Cimbrica, Malle.
   Malle etenim, sapere est, hac ratione, male.
   Atque haec quidem tuendi Angeli causa a me dicta, boni consule.' Elsewhere Vulcanius describes Poliziano's version as so good '. . . ut exiguum aut potius nullum novae laudi locum reliquerit' (ibid., p. 224).

205. *Callimachus*, ed. Vulcanius, p. 244: ' . . . non tantum Catulli vulnera, quae illi Sciolorum quorundam temeritas inflixerat, curavit, sed magnam etiam Callimacho lucem adfert. Vtinam vero magnus ille vir etiam Callimachi fragmentis, quae misere lacera collegi, medicam aliquando manum adhibeat.'

206. G. E. Diller, *Les Dames des Roches. Étude sur la vie littéraire à Poitiers dans la deuxième moitié du XVIᵉ siècle* (Paris, 1936), esp. pp. 11-14.

207. *Les Serées de Guillaume Bouchet*, ed. C. E. Roybet (Paris, 1873-82), ii, pp. 25-6. For this and other texts describing Scaliger's life in Poitou see J. Plattard, 'Le séjour de Joseph-Juste Scaliger en Poitou', *Bulletin philologique et historique*, 1926-7, pp. 107-18.

208. Scaliger, *Lettres françaises*, p. 93-8. By the end of the year Scaliger recovered to the point where he could finish off a set of notes on M. Guilandinus, *Papyrus* (Venice, 1572), which he had long before promised to Dupuy; see the article cited in n. 145, above.

Appendices

APPENDIX TO CHAPTER II

i. P. Vettori, *Variarum lectionum libri XXV* (Florence, 1553), X. 22, p. 153:

Latini poetae, cum saepe novis rationibus loquendi uterentur, inauditisque auribus Romanorum, in culpam non incidebant, qua non caruissent oratores, si ita locuti fuissent: neque enim venia eadem datur iis, qui soluta oratione utuntur, quae conceditur certis numeris, mensurisque, ipsam vincientibus. Praecipue autem hoc committebant, ut a consuetudine discederent, qui Graecos scriptores volutabant: versati enim diu in sermone illo, imitabantur etiam modos loquendi proprios eius nationis: verbaque aliter construebant, ac suae gentis homines vulgo facerent. Hoc qui accurate attendet, inveniet saepe fecisse Horatium, qui multis modis intelligitur valde delectatus fuisse illo sermone, Graecorumque disciplinas a Graecis scriptoribus hausisse. Vt alia autem nunc omittam, cum in epistola de studio poetarum inquit: Invitum qui servat idem facit occidenti [467], manifesto hoc facit; neque enim idem illi, cum idem quod ille significare volunt, Latini homines dicunt: sed Graeci ταυτὸν ἐκείνῳ passim aiunt, nec aliter loquuntur; exemplis enim in re clara uti minime oportet. Lucretius quoque eundem modum loquendi usurpavit, in Latinumque e Graeco transtulit, ubi de contemnenda morte copiose, eleganterque disserit. De Homero enim excellentissimo poeta loquens, qui quum dignus perpetua vita foret, nihil praecipui in hac re habuit ab aliis inertissimis hominibus, cecinit: quorum unus Homerus Sceptra potitus, eadem aliis sopitus quiete est [III. 1037-8].

ii. G. P. Valeriano, *Castigationes et varietates Virgilianae lectionis* (Rome, 1521), *Castigationes in Bucolica* (separately paginated), p. i:

Antea quam rem ipsam aggrediamur, nomina, quibus insigniores quosdam codices citamus, praedocere visum est. Ea sunt, Codex Romanus, ille quidem dubioprocul antiquissimus; eum vero ideo Romanum appellamus, quod eius characteres Romanis propiores sunt, iis quippe, quos in antiquis marmorum, aut ex aere tabularum inscriptionibus, et in nummis saeculis illis elegantioribus notatos ubique legimus. Custoditur is in interioribus Vaticanae Bibliothecae penetralibus magna diligentia, digitalibus pene litteris perscriptus. Alter, qui minoribus est litteris et ipse admodum vetus, a paginarum facie Oblongus nuncupabitur. . . . Est et Mediceus inter emendatos. Aliquot etiam aliunde perquisivimus; neque enim uni cuipiam exemplari tantum tribuendum fuit, ut siquid in aliis elucesceret boni, eos reiiceremus. Quamvis vero omnes, si diligentius inspicias, perversionibus, erroribusque ad unum scateant. Ex plurium tamen collatione consensuque, aut veriora, aut certe veris similiora deprehendimus. Verum age iam, quod ipsi codices tradant, videamus.

i. H. Estienne, 'Observationes in Anacreontis carmina', in *Anacreontis Teii Odae* (Paris, 1554), pp. 78-9:

Ex Pindaro quoque nonnulla mutuatus est Horatius, ut hoc odes initium, Quem virum aut heroa lyra vel acri Tibia sumis celebrare Clio? Sic enim Pindarus,

ʼΑναξιφόρμιγγες ὕμνοι Τίνα θεὸν, τίν' ἥρωα,
Τίνα δ'ἄνδρα κελαδήσομεν;

Denique Horatius multa ex iis quos nominavimus poetis aliisque aperte transfert: quae autem aliunde ita mutuatur, ut sua tamen velit videri, ea ita in varias formas commutat, ut vix ab eo cuius sunt, si adsit, agnosci possint. Et hoc est honeste furari. Nam non esse turpe ex antiquo scriptore furari, docuerunt nos suo exemplo ipsi Graeci, quorum furta memoriae prodita sunt quamplurima. Ipse enim Homerus ex Orpheo et Musaeo multa furatus est; ex Homero vicissim posteri fere omnes multo plura. Quid poetae tragici? Euripides multa non Homero tantum, sed et aliis compilavit qui Homeri aetatem secuti sunt. Sophocles rursus haud pauca Euripidi. Sed nec ipsi Comici alii ab aliorum scriptis manus abstinuerunt. Ita igitur furari turpe non est: sed furti convinci, hoc vero longe est turpissimum.

ii. H. Estienne, *Annotationes in suam hanc editionem alterius voluminis poetarum*, in *Poetae Graeci principes heroici carminis, et alii nonnulli* (Geneva, 1566), Pt. II, pp. xxxviii-xxxix:

Ἔστι γάρ] Quoties huius versus recordor, toties Ioannis Aurati recorder necesse est, qui cum in restituendis multis aliis poetarum locis sagacitatem suam ostendit, tum vero in hoc vel maximam. Nam quum antea passim legeretur ἔστι γὰρ εὔϋμνός τις, ἀν' οὔρεα Φοῖβον ἀείδει, et ita exponeretur, mutando pauca in Graecis, Est enim Phoebus facile laudabilis [vel laudibus abundans] : quis per montes Phoebum canit? Auratus aliud mendum sub hoc versu latens subolfecit, quum nullum vel in speciem aptum huic loco sensum elici posse videret, et ex ἀν' οὔρεα faciendum esse ἂν οὐ ῥέα affirmavit. Quam emendationem docti etiam viri ita amplexi sunt, ut eorum κορυφαῖον Adrianum Turnebum, quum ipse quoque antea in hoc loco publice interpretando et lectionem et ei consentaneam interpretationem vulgo receptam sequutus esset, postea se et male eum legisse et male interpretatum esse, seque pedibus in Ioannis Aurati sententiam ire, fateri publice itidem non puduerit. Quod ego tantum abest ut studio laedendae eius famae dixerim (cuius quam antiqua mihi cura sit, a me non multis abhinc mensibus scripta in eum epitaphia carmina testantur) ut potius admirabilis et pene incredibilis in tam docto homine candoris ac modestiae exemplum proponere voluerim. Sed quod ad hanc Aurati emendationem attinet, eam et ipse in contextum recepi, non iam tamen sola eius coniectura nitentem, sed veteris etiam codicis testimonio comprobatam. Interim vero exemplum etiam praebere poterit hic locus magnae depravationis quae alicubi reperitur, etiam manentibus iisdem literis.

iii. M.-A. Muret, *Variae lectiones*, IV. 14:
> *Theriacam olim bibi solitam, verum non videri.*
> *emendatus Varronis locus.*

Profecto quo quisque plus auctoritatis habet in litteris, eo solicitius ac circumspectius cavere debet, ne quid sibi, quod parum exploratum habeat, excidere patiatur. Nam leves ac contempti homines, cum tale aliquid designant, facilis jactura est. Non est verendum, ne quis eos sequatur duces. Horum ut maximo quisque in pretio est, ita maximo periculo peccat. Sed humanus animus novitatis studio ducitur. Ejus interdum specie illectus, neque satis id quod objectum est attendens, vana pro veris, pro solidis inania amplexatur. Equidem de Petro Victorio nihil a me, nisi ut de viro summa doctrina praedito, dictum velim. Neque aliter decet: qui non fateri tantum, sed prae me ferre etiam ac praedicare soleam, tantum me ex illius vigiliis cepisse fructus, quantum ex alii, qui hoc tempore vixerit, neminis. Sed cogor interdum, quod bona ipsius pace ac venia dictum sit, plusculum in eo diligentiae et accurationis desiderare. Nam quale tandem est, quod de Leda matre Helenes prodidit? eam, Euripidem facere, in leaenam esse conversam: cum in eadem illa tragoedia, unde ipse se mirificam illam metamorphosin eruere putavit, tam saepe legatur, Ledam laqueo sibi elisisse fauces, prae dolore quem e filiae dedecore perceperat. Sunt enim hi versus in ipsa embasi:

Ελέ. ἀπωλόμεσθα. Θεστίας δ' ἐστὶ κόρη;
Τεῦ. Λήδαν ἔλεξας; οἴχεται θανοῦσα δή.
Ελέ. Ουπω νω Ελένης αἰσχρὸν ὤλεσε κλέος;
Τεῦ. φασί, βρόχῳ γ' ἄψασαν εὐγενῆ δέρην.

Itaque Helena ipsa paulo post mala sua percensens, ita de matris morte loquitur:

Λήδα δ' ἐν ἀγχόναις
Θάνατον ἔλαβε αἰσχύ-
νας ἐμᾶς ὑπ' ἀλγέων.

Sic enim legendum puto. Et chorūs ἐπαιάζων:

Μάτηρ μὲν οἴχεται.

Locum autem illum, quem ipse de Leda accepit, de Callistone accipiendum esse, vel caeco appareat. Quid, quod in primo De Oratore, *actionibus*, sine ullo certo argumento, legi voluit? Vbi noster postea Duarenus, *cretionibus*, legendum esse demonstravit. Ac sunt sane in illis Variarum lectionum libris ejusmodi plura, quam vellem. Valde enim ejus viri gloriae faveo. Sed quod libro primo de theriaca prodidit, id, quia errorem objicere alicui potest, dissimulandum non videtur. Ait enim theriacam videri olim bibi solitam: quare necesse esse, ut tum liquidior fuerit: hoc enim tempore crassiorem ac duriorem conformari. Hoc elicit ex verbis M. Varronis, quae leguntur apud Nonium, e libro De liberis educandis. Sunt autem haec: *Vel maxime illic didici, et sitienti, theriacam, mulsum; esurienti, panem cibarium, siligineum: et exercitato somnum suavem.* Non, ita vivam, possum satis mirari, hoc Victorium, talem ac tantum virum, dixisse. Primum enim ubi tandem verbum unum de ista liquida theriaca legerat? Nam nostram quidem, quae, ut opinor, et veterum fuit, cujusmodi sit, omnes agyrtae ac pharmacopolae sciunt. Deinde cum constet, ibi Varronem vulgares, et plebeios cibos lautis et opiparis opponere: quaero, cui se hoc probare posse speraverit, tenues olim et egenos homines, ut panem cibarium esse, ita theriacam, amaram videlicet quandam et tristem potionem, bibere solitos? Quam quidem cuicuimodi fingas, oportebit, ut reor, pluris venire, quam mulsum, quasi vero aquam gratis sumere non praestiterit, quam emere quod torqueret. Nam si amarum aliquid e medicinis quaerebat, quod mulso opponeret; debuit sane eadem ratione siligineo pani opponere, non panem cibarium, sed agaricum, aut colocynthidas. Ego quod senseram de illo Varronis loco, antequam Victorius Variarum lectionum libros ederet, idem nunc quoque sentio: idque nunc aperiam, ut ex contentione, utra verior sententia sit, existimetur. Puto igitur ita legendum esse: *Vel maxime illic didici, sitienti videri acam mulsum, esurienti panem cibarium siligineum, et exercitato somnum suavem.* Nam e duabus vocibus, *sitienti videri,* suspicor factum ab imperitis librariis, *sitienti teri. Acam* autem pro *aquam,* antiqua scriptura est: ut *loci,* pro *loqui: coad,* pro *quoad: cotidie,* pro *quotidie.* Hoc igitur dicet Varro, se illic didicisse, sitienti videri aquam mulsum. Quae conjectura si cui displicet, ipse meliorem afferat. Quidvis certe potius, quam ut illam liquidam theriacam sorbeamus. Crediderim autem, Varronem, cum illa scriberet, respexisse ad hunc locum Xenophontis e primo παιδείας. εἰ δέ τις αὐτοὺς οἴεται ἢ ἐσθίειν ἀηδῶς, ὅταν κάρδαμον μόνον ἔχωσιν ἐπὶ τῷ σίτῳ, ἢ πίνειν ἀηδῶς, ὅταν ὕδωρ πίνωσιν, ἀναμνησθήτω, πῶς ἡδὺ μὲν μᾶζα, καὶ ἄρτος πεινῶντι φαγεῖν, πῶς δὲ ἡδὺ ὕδωρ διψῶντι πιεῖν. Eo magis, quod alium locum reperio ex eodem Varronis libro, qui ex eodem Xenophontis conversus est. Xenoph. αἰσχρὸν μὲν γὰρ ἔτι καὶ νῦν ἐστι Πέρσαις, καὶ τὸ ἀποπτύειν, καὶ τὸ ἀπομύττεσθαι, καὶ τὸ φύσης μεστοὺς φαίνεσθαι. Varro: *Persae propter exercitationes pueriles modicas, eam sunt consecuti corpore siccitatem, ut neque spuerent, neque emungerentur, sufflatoque corpore essent.*

APPENDIX TO CHAPTER IV

i. A. Duchesne, *Preuves de l'histoire de la maison des Chasteigners* (Paris, 1633), p. 124.

Monseigneur, ie vous remercie de la bonne souvenance qu'il vous a pleu avoir de vostre filieul accompagnée d'une liberalité si grande, que ie eusse heu honte de l'accepter, si le bon Hesiode, ou plus tost la necessité ne m'eust apprins que,

Αἰδὼς οὐκ ἀγαθὴ κεχρημένον ἄνδρα κομίζει.

Ie n'euseré point d'autre rhetorique *ad ornandum munus verbis*, sinon que bien qu'il soit grand de soy, la necessité ou ie me suis trouvé ces iours passez me l'a fait trouver μυρίον ὅσον plus grand. Ie ne sçay si Monsieur l'Escale vous l'a dict, car à luy seul comme *tutissimis auribus deponere ausus eram: ut ille non ignarus mali aliquando miseris succurrere disceret*. La cause de ma necessité ha esté, les procés, l'acquisition de ma maison et reparation d'icelle, et qui pis est la longue absence du Roy, qui est πολλῶν ταμίας, *in quibus etiam meus*, comme dict nostre Pindare, duquel ie achevois la première Ode des Pythies, où il presche fort de la liberalité des Seigneurs envers les lettres, quand vostre χρυσέα φόρμιγξ Ἀπόλλωνος καὶ ἰοπλοκάμων σύνδικον μοισᾶν κτέανον m'a esté apporté, *dulce in sudore levamen*, par vostre bon Marc. Et afin que la petite lettre ne soit ἀφιλολόγητος, ie vous prie de demander à vostre Phoenix, non seulement *quia te docet Achillea quadam indole praeditum, sed etiam quia unicus pene videtur esse de quo dicatur* οἷος γὰρ πέπνυται τοὶ δὲ σκιαὶ ἀΐσσουσι, si il trouvera bon que σύνδικον ne signifie à mon avis σύμφωνον, comme lit le Scholiaste et son interprete Henry, mais *communis iuris, id est possessionis, ut sit pignus commune cithara Musarum et Apollinis. Quod colligo ex alio loco, corrupto licet, Ode 5:* σφὸν ὄλβον υἱῷ τε κοινὰν χάριν ἔνδικον ἀρκεσίλα, *ubi lego* σύνδικον, ἐκ παρομοίου τοῦ κοινάν. *Sed hoc unum ex infinitis quae muto. Et quia Latinum aliquando Pindarum meditor iisdem numeris edere, et singulas Odas singulis amicis consecrare, tua iam esto, cuius* εὐτυχῶς *absolvendae auspicium mihi fecisti . . . Hodie nihil novi, quod sciam, nisi Ferdinandi Historiam ab amico Polono scriptam non tam ornate quam vere, in quem ego Elegiam scripsi rogatus. Vt inde colligat noster Scaliger; si hoc Auratus externo parvae notitiae caussa, quid mihi faciet si non patri, certe fratri charissimo in meo Varrone?*

ii. Scaliger, Daniel, Varro.
The undated letter from Scaliger to Daniel published by Hagen, *Zur Geschichte der Philologie*, pp. 30-2, ends as follows:

De Varrone autem nostro, non est quod pluribus eum tibi commendem. Satis enim confido, tibi curae fore. Est tamen, quod te moneam. In tertio libro Annotationum mearum, qui est sextus liber Varronis, ubi disputat ipse de Delphorum umbilico, velim haec verba reponas in annotatione, quae incipit: 'Ut tesauri specie', in fine, inquam, tu repones, 'quanquam simplicius fuerit, si dicamus foramen quoddam allatum esse Delphis, ut ibi esset quasi thesaurus quidam, quod Graeci vocarunt ὀμφαλὸν a similitudine humani umbilici.' Haec tu statim, ut acceperis literas meas, reponas velim, et me certiorem facias. Vale. IX. Cal. Apriles. Tuffoni.

A *terminus ante quem* is provided by the fact that this addition appears in the first edition of Scaliger's *Coniectanea*, placed, as he directed, at the end of the relevant note (Paris, 1565, p. 133). Scaliger's dedicatory letter is dated December 1564. The book itself, according to its colophon, appeared during August 1565 (p. 221: 'EXCVDEBAT ROBERTVS STEPHANVS TYPOGRAPHVS REGIVS, LVTETIAE PARISIORVM, X. CAL. SEPTEMB. ANNO M.D. LXV.')' As Daniel went to Paris before 8 September 1564, the letter could conceivably come either from 1564 or 1565. But given that Scaliger treats the work as completed and at — or soon to be at — press, and that Daniel was definitely in Paris in March 1565, it seems likeliest that the letter was written then, after the dedication was completed and before the book came out. (For Daniel's addresses see P. de Félice, *Lambert Daneau*, Paris, 1882, pp. 262, n. 1, 276.)

Scaliger's references to 'Varrone . . . nostro' and his 'Annotationes' seem at least to concern works that are separate, or not identical. Hence the hypothesis advanced in n. 89, above.

APPENDIX TO CHAPTER V

i. A. Agustín, *De M. Verrii Flacci, et Sex. Pompei Festi libris*, in *M. Verrii Flacci quae extant. Ex Sex. Pompei Festi De verborum significatione, lib. xx* (Venice, 1560), sigs. I ii^r–I iii^r:

Sex. Pompeius Festus his viginti libris, quos de verborum significatione sive priscorum verborum cum exemplis inscripsit, libros Verrii Flacci eiusdem argumenti in breviorem formam redegit. Abstulit enim verba nimis antiqua, intermortua iam, et sepulta, ut ipse Verrius dicebat; quaeque nullius erant usus et auctoritatis. Apertius quoque et brevius de eisdem verbis tradidit minori volumine librorum prisca verba referendo, exempla etiam in aliis libris reperta recensuit. Saepius autem Verrii errores notavit: et cur id faceret, non minus docte semper reddidit rationem. Accidit vero huic libro, ut multis modis ab antiquitate laederetur. Nam neque quis hic Festus fuerit, neque quo tempore haec scripserit, potuimus invenire. Vix etiam voluminis huius aliqua mentio reperitur in Charisii et Macrobii uno, atque altero libro. Cumque liber ipse totus extaret Caroli Regis tempore: Paulus nescioquis operaepretium fore ratus est, si epitomen quandam efficeret eorum, quae ipsi magis placuerunt. Is liber indoctis viris adeo placuit, ut pro Festo in omnibus bibliothecis substitueretur. Vnus adhuc liber extabat totius cladis superstes; sed qualis, victis commilitonibus et occisione occisis, miles truncis naribus, altero oculo effosso, mutilo altero bracchio, cruribus fractis repit alicunde. Eius libri, advecti ut ferunt ex Illyrico, habuit aliquas pagellas Pomponius Laetus, ut Pius, ut Politianus scripserunt; maiorem libri partem Manilius Rallus. Ab his Angelus Politianus librum accepit, agnovit, et exscripsit, et ex eo in centuria versum Catulli emendare temptavit. Ab eodem Politiani exemplo Petrus Victorius aliquot locis in variis lectionibus vulgares Festi libros emendare doctissime, ut solet, coepit. Pervenerunt ipsae reliquiae libelli ad Aldum Manutium, qui conatus est cum Pauli epitome eas coniungere, .et unum corpus ex duplicibus membris conficere. Sed tam multa omissa sunt, tam multa aliter edita, ut alios emendatores res desiderarit. Simili ratione ex utroque libro confectus alter liber extat apud Achillem Mafeum Bernardini Cardinalis fratrem, qui Aldino locupletior est. Ita tres eiusdem libri editiones, omnes autem imperfectae, exstiterunt. Vetus ille liber Festi dimidiatus, cuius ante M. literam nihil extat; ab ea vero littera ad finem vix dimidium est, quod superest, eius, quod antea fuerat. Alter liber est Pauli epitome, quae quam negligenter facta sit, ex collatione verborum Festi et Pauli, quod hac editione ostendimus, vel indoctissimus quisque agnoscere potest. Tertius est ex utroque confectus, quales sunt Aldi, Mafei, et noster.

ii. Scaliger, *Castigationes*, in *M. Verrii Flacci quae extant. Sex. Pompei Festi De verborum significatione libri XX* (n. p., 1575), pp. lxxxi–lxxxiii:

Marspedis] Corrige ex iudicio Adriani Turnebi, quo doctiorem nostra non tulit aetas, in precatione Solitaurilium. Quicquid dubitet Messalla, constat in formula solitaurilium ad lustrandum agrum ambarvali sacrificio, solum Martem nominari: MARSPITER TE PRECOR, etc., ut constat ex Catone Titulo CXLI. Pro quo suspicor Marspedis dictum a veteribus. At, quod putant doctissimi viri Marspedis esse Martis filium, hoc est, Martis παῖδα, plane est Horatianum, Humano capiti cervicem equinam. Quare merito explodendum. Sed illud notandum, Martem in Solitaurilibus aut aliis precationibus rusticorum non esse alium, quam Silvanum. Propterea coniunctim aliquando vocatur Mars Silvanus. Idem Cato: Votum pro bubus, ut valeant, sic facito: Marti Silvano in silva interdius, etc. De quo sic in libris de limitib. agrorum: Omnis possessio tres Silvanos habet. Vnus dicitur domesticus, possessioni consecratus. Alter dicitur agrestis, pastoribus consecratus. Tertius dicitur orientalis: cui est in confinio lucus positus: a quo inter duo, pluresve fines oriuntur. Ideo inter duo pluresve est lucus. De tertio intelligi apud Catonem necesse est. Primus vocatur etiam Silvanus larum, ut in illa inscriptione, quae extat Romae:

SILVANO
SANCTO
LARVM
PHILEMON
P. SCANTI
ELEVTERI

D. D. Alterius, hoc est Silvani agrestis, mentio est in altera inscriptione, quam ex fide doctissimi amici nostri Aldi Manutii huc exscripsimus:

SILVANO
AG. SACRVM
IN MEMORIAM
C. RVFI ANTHI
IIIIII VIRI
TALLVS. LIB.

D. D. Et de eodem intellexit Ovidius: — nec dum degrandinat, obsit Agresti fano supposuisse pecus. Mars pedis igitur et Mars pater apud Catonem intelligendus est Mars Silvanus orientalis agrestium, in interfinio duum aut plurium agrorum. Est autem ex iure veterum Atheniensium. Nam in sacramento cui dicebant ἔφηβοι, adiiciebatur: ἴστορες θεοὶ ἄγραυλοι. Deinde ponit eos, ἐννάλιος, ἄρης, ζεύς. Vbi ζεύς etiam est, quem dapalem Cato vocat.

APPENDIX TO CHAPTER VII

i. J. J. Scaliger, *Prolegomena de Astrologia veterum Graecorum*, in *M. Manilii Astronomicon a Iosepho Scaligero ex vetusto codice Gemblacensi infinitis mendis repurgatum* (Leiden, 1599-1600), sigs. $a2^r$–$a3^v$:

Quum multa sint in omni genere disciplinarum a Graecis prodita, omnes tamen Graeciam bonarum artium magistram potius, quam parentem agnoscunt; quod non sua, sed Chaldaeorum inventa excoluerit. Qui quum ita iudicant, videntur mihi aut Graecorum vetustatis obliti esse, aut eorum illustria in literas merita ignorare. Si enim rem ab ultima origine repetamus, deprehendemus artes non solum antiquitus a Graecis inventas et perfectas fuisse, sed etiam ab illis ad eas nationes derivatas, a quibus Graecos hausisse volunt isti. Quum enim magnarum rerum tardi sint progressus, et ad earum scrutationem una aetas non sufficiat, earum quaedam primo rudimenta sunt, neque cum perfectione sua ad nos transmittuntur: propterea accidit, ut ad maiorum inventa aliquid procudendo posteriores adiiciant, et posteritati denique semper aliquid relinquatur a superioribus, quod aut emendatore aut illustratore indigeat. Quod quum in omni disciplina a Graecis factum sit, qui multum studii in hoc collocarunt, ut maiorum inventa illustrarent, emendarent, elaborarent: quis neget artes, quas Graeci quotidie meliores fecerunt, nulli nationi acceptas referri debere, quam iis ipsis Graecis, qui eas gradatim et quasi ex alto eruerunt? Nam Chaldaei et Aegyptii, a quibus omnia Graecos didicisse volunt, quid, obsecro, habent hodie, quod non a Graecis acceperint? Imo quos libros paulo vetustiores bonarum artium, quos non ad verbum ex Graecorum in suam linguam transfuderint? Quorum alteri nihil antiquum retinent, praeter characteres, qui nihil aliud sunt, quam Phoenicum et Cananaeorum literae interpolatae. Aegyptii vero ne suas quidem literas habent, sed ab Arabibus emendicatas. At sero Graeci literas a Cadmo didicerunt, sine quibus nulla disciplinarum memoria conservari potest. Hoc quidem nemo negare potest. Neque tamen propterea concedimus ab iisdem Graecos necessario artes accipere debuisse, a quibus literas didicerunt: siquidem literae omni disciplina vetustiores sunt. Neque enim eos medicinam aut Philosophiam docuit ullus Phoenix, Chaldaeus, aut Aegyptius: quorum altera minimum aberat a perfectione sua tempore Hippocratis, scriptoris antiquissimi: alteram tot sectae Philosophorum tam inter se discrepantes arguunt non potuisse ab ullo Chaldaeo aut Aegyptio proficisci, quae adhuc inter Graecos quaereretur. Restant Mathematica, in quibus Barbari aliquod ius vindicare possunt: quod eatenus verum, ut figuras quidem Geometricas ab Aegyptiis accepisse Thaletem aut Pythagoram non negemus, Geometriam autem ab iis didicisse quo minus credamus, obstant praeclara Epichiremata Pythagorae, quae si ipse ab Aegyptiis didicisset, Hecatomben non immolasset. Accedit Eudemus priscus auctor, qui historiam Mathematicam contexuit, in qua quis Graecorum quid gradatim in Mathematicis invenerit ab incunabulis ipsius disciplinae, ad suum ipsius saeculum, diligenter annotaverat: arduum sane opus, et quod rei literariae intererat non periisse. In Astrologia vero Graecos Chaldaeo aut Aegyptio magistro usos, ita accipiendum, ut eam quidem sero excoluerint, invitati partim ab Eudoxo, quem Aegyptii docuerunt Planetas contra mundi motum niti, partim ab observationibus eclipticis Chaldaeorum, quae mediocrem tantum vetustatem praeferebant, ut quae a Nabonassari initio deducerentur, quod est posterius prima Olympiade. Sed Geometriam ab Aegyptiis eos didicisse, quod ab illis figuras acceperint, aut Astrologiam, quod Chaldaei observationes defectuum in annales suos relatas Graecis indicarint, perinde est, ac si quis se eloquentiam ab eo didicisse crederet, a quo rudimenta Grammatices; aut Philosophiam, a quo principia Logices edoctus fuisset. Quamobrem historiam defectuum barbari Graecos docuerunt. Caussas defectionum Graeci indagarunt, et sero tandem repererunt, primum Conone Samio, qui defectiones Solis ab Aegyptiis observatas collegit, deinde Hipparcho, viro, ut Plinius ait, naturae consiliario eis viam praeeunte, qui primus utriusque sideris deliquia a Chaldaeis annotata ad menses omnium Graeciae nationum accomodavit, ex quo divino opere omnem historiam defectuum Lunarium hausit Ptolemaeus, qui in suo illo magno opere multa veteribus accepta refert, nulli plura, quam Hipparcho. Quod si rem propius putemus, etiam antequam ulla defectuum observatio Chaldaica ad Graecos pervenisset, iam prius Thales Milesius sine ullo magistro barbaro deliquia utriusque sideris didicerat, et adeo in illis profecerat, ut defectus ipsos longe ante praediceret.

ii. Ibid., sigs. [$\beta 4^v$] –γ^r:

Neque vero nos sumus, qui stellas et illa luculenta caeli corpora otiosa esse existimemus. Sed effectus illos his iocularibus argutiis et arbitrariis sectionibus contineri, id vero pernegamus. Tanta vero mutatio a posterioribus artificibus in hac arte facta est, ut cum priorum methodis comparata non eadem ars videri possit, imo in permultis contraria. Et tamen illi priores vera praedixisse visi sunt, neque minus isti posteriores, qui contrariam viam insistant, veraces esse perhibentur. Sed haec omnia confutare multi temporis multorumque librorum opus est. Quod quum a Comite Pico Mirandula et ab aliis factum sit, sat erit strenue ab illis hanc arcem oppugnatam, et tepide ab artificibus defensam fuisse, qui pudentius tacuissent. Quaecunque igitur ea ars fuit, nunquam caruit amatoribus, ut nunquam desunt levia ingenia, quae novitate rerum et futilibus inventis permoventur. Inferiora saecula omitto. Vnum felicissimum Augusti occurrit, in quo flos ingeniorum fuit, et inter illustres artes haec quoque ausa est verticem attollere, multis magistris clara, praesertim M. Manilio, qui non propter artem nobis carus esse debet, sed quia in eo rudimenta illius priscae astrologiae manifesta extant, hactenus etiam a doctis ignorata: ...

Index